Widespread praise for *A Nation in Torment*, recipient of the 1970 Friends of American Writers Literary Award:

"Every reader born after the Depression will have a fair idea of what it was like. . . .[Ellis] deals with every facet of those years always in terms of people, of human beings who were there and suffered. He has left abstract principles and cold statistics to others."

—Thomas Lask, *The New York Times*

"This is a vivid and spirited narrative that satisfies the best demands of scholarship and narrative art."

—Allan Nevins

"There is a greater wealth of detail packed into these pages than in any other book on the subject I can recall. . . . Open it anywhere and you come across colorful nuggets of long-forgotten news that Ellis must have preserved in that journal of his. . . . [A] vivid narrative."

—John Barkham, *The New York Post*

"A masterful narrative evocation of [a] tormented period in American history. . . . The book bids for definitive status as history, and will attract many readers."

—*Publishers Weekly*

"A massive and marvelous book. . . . It captures in vivid prose the spirit of those desperate days and may become the definitive work on the Depression."

—*Fitchburg Sentinel*, Fitchburg, Massachusetts ·

"Ellis proves in *A Nation in Torment* that a nonacademic writer can be analytical as well as entertaining and moving. . . . Ellis writes real history. . . [and] really understands what history and people are all about."

—*The Kansas City Star*

A NATION IN TORMENT

Books by Edward Robb Ellis

A DIARY OF THE CENTURY:
Tales from America's Greatest Diarist (1995)

ECHOES OF DISTANT THUNDER:
Life in the United States, 1914–1918 (1975)

A NATION IN TORMENT:
The Great American Depression, 1929–1939 (1970)

THE EPIC OF NEW YORK CITY:
A Narrative History (1966)

THE TRAITOR WITHIN:
Our Suicide Problem
(with George N. Allen, 1961)

A NATION
IN TORMENT

The Great American Depression

1929–1939

EDWARD ROBB ELLIS
With a new Preface by the Author

KODANSHA INTERNATIONAL
New York • Tokyo • London

To the Memory of My Beloved Wife
RUTH KRAUS ELLIS

Kodansha America, Inc.
114 Fifth Avenue, New York, New York 10011, U.S.A.

Kodansha International Ltd.
17-14 Otowa 1-chome, Bunkyo-ku, Tokyo 112, Japan

Published in 1995 by Kodansha America, Inc., by arrangement with the author.

First published in 1970 by Coward-McCann.

This is a Kodansha Globe book.

Library of Congress Cataloging-in-Publication Data
Ellis, Edward Robb.
    A nation in torment : the Great American Depression, 1929–1939 / Edward
Robb Ellis ; with a new preface by the author.
      p.   cm. — (Kodansha globe)
    Originally published: Coward-McCann, 1970.
    Includes bibliographical references (p.   ) and index.
    ISBN 1-56836-113-0
    1. United States—History—1919–1933. 2. United States—History—
1933–1945. 3. —Depressions—1929—United States. 4. United States—Economic
conditions—1918–1945. I. Title. II. Series.
E801.E7   1995
330.973'091—dc20   95-33214

For permission to reprint copyrighted material, the author wishes to thank the following:
    E. P. Dutton & Co., Inc., for *Bound for Glory* by Woody Guthrie, copyright © 1943 by E. P. Dutton
& Co., Inc., reprinted by permission of the publishers; Harper & Row, Publishers, Inc., for excerpts
from pp. 279–280, 296, 381–383 ("From My Diary—Stockton, California, May 27, 1936") in *My
America* by Louis Adamic, copyright © 1938 by Louis Adamic, reprinted by permission of Harper &
Row, Publishers; Harper & Row Publishers, Inc., and William Heinemann, Ltd., for excerpts from
pp. 413–414 in *You Can't Go Home Again* by Thomas Wolfe (Harper & Row, 1940), reprinted by
permission of Harper & Row, Publishers, Inc., and William Heinemann, Ltd.; Alfred A. Knopf, Inc.,
for *Not So Wild a Dream* by Eric Sevareid, published by Alfred A. Knopf, Inc., copyright © 1946 by
Eric Sevareid; Little, Brown & Company for *Factories in the Field* by Carey McWilliams, published
by Little, Brown & Company, copyright © 1935, 1939 by Carey McWilliams; Stormking Music,
Inc., for *Harry Bridges* by Woody Guthrie, published by Stormking Music, Inc., copyright © 1966
by Stormking Music, Inc., all rights reserved, used by permission; The Viking Press, Inc., for *The
Grapes of Wrath* by John Steinbeck, published by The Viking Press, copyright © 1939 by John
Steinbeck.

Printed in the United States of America

95 96 97 98 99   RRD/H   10 9 8 7 6 5 4 3 2 1

"What is necessary for a new disaster is only for memories of the last one to fade, and no one knows how long that takes."

—John Kenneth Galbraith
Harper's, November, 1969

Contents

Preface to the 25th Anniversary Edition

HISTORY IS a seamless story, a continuum. Although we talk about ancient history, medieval history and modern history, this is just a way to get a fix on the flow of events. In reality, everything blends into everything else. Yesterday becomes today, which becomes tomorrow. However, without memory continuity disappears. This is true of individuals and nations alike.

Those of us old enough to have lived through the Depression dare not forget it, for fear that such a catastrophe could afflict us again. Those too young to have suffered through it may learn about its horrors from this book. By reading about the Depression of the 1930s, you may arm yourself to fight off another one. Though some have said that ignorance is bliss, this is a lie; it is no more useful than a hole in your head.

Since this book is being reissued in 1995, as a new century comes into view, I am thinking of future generations even more than I did when the book was first published twenty-five years ago. Someone once said statistics are human beings with the tears wiped off. In writing this narrative history of the Depression I tried to show the tears, the pain, the puzzlement of the people. In writing this preface now, I am thinking of those who suffer today.

Does history repeat itself? Some people think so. The Bible says: "Whatsoever a man soweth, that shall he also reap." Is this also true of a society? When I look around the world today and see many of the same ills that dominated the world of my youth—homelessness, hunger, poverty, greed, racism and an ever-widening gap between those who have much and those who have almost nothing—I see how the world remains much the same. Yet it spins into previously unknown dimensions, fueled by revolutions in technology, communications and transportation that I could never have imagined as a young man. Despite happenings of this magnitude, there has remained one constant—human nature. Now, as in the past, men and women just want water and food and shelter and sex and children and a belief in something greater than their own lives.

*   *   *

When I was a child my parents were divorced. Thereafter my father sent my mother money, which she saved for my education. On October 5, 1931, while at the University of Missouri, I heard from my mother in my home town of Kewanee, Illinois. Here is what I wrote in my journal:

This morning I got a letter from mother saying that the First National Bank of Kewanee has closed. That's the bank that has every cent I own. Mother also said that Grandpa Robb had all of his money there, too, and now he is worried to death. Many of the people in Kewanee stood in front of the closed doors of the bank, weeping and cursing. One of mother's women friends ran up and down our block, bewailing the fact that her family had lost everything. Now I must think twice before spending so much as a nickel. Here I am at age twenty—absolutely penniless!

Like millions of other kids in those cruel years, I began working my way through college. There is nothing ennobling about having to work one's way through college; it robs the student of the leisure he needs to make the best use of his books. And, for a while, there was even a danger that the university might have to close for lack of funds.

One summer vacation I got a job handing out Palmolive soap coupons to housewives in several towns in Illinois. My salary was $19.25 per week. In Peoria the other five men in our crew and I walked through slums so horrible that in my diary I wrote: "If I had to live the way these people do, I'd commit suicide."

In a Bloomington secondhand book store I paid only nine dollars for the sixty volumes of *World's Greatest Literature*, published in 1901 for $105. That's how low prices had sunk.

From home my sister Kay wrote me about the effects of the Depression upon our family, saying that our stepfather "cries all the time and can talk of nothing except financial troubles."

My college roommate was Nace Strickland, who lived in a suburb of St. Louis. On August 8, 1932, he telephoned me in my home town to invite me to drive to California with him. His uncle knew a rich man in Long Beach who had an Essex Super Six designed for him. He wanted Nace to drive it from St. Louis to the west coast; there we would be paid $10 each. From California we would hitchhike home.

I left Kewanee with $12.03 in my pockets, hitching rides to within fifty miles of St. Louis, taking a bus the rest of the way. That awful August we drove through the Ozarks, where we saw poor farmers trying to eke out a living, saw dispossessed tenants, helpless and hopeless.

On August 16, Nace and I arrived in Long Beach and got a hotel room for the two of us for five nights for $2.50. Six huge oranges cost five cents. Two pounds of pears cost ten cents, a dozen rolls five cents, a quart of milk seven cents. For the first time in my life I swam in the Pacific Ocean and rented a surfboard for ten cents.

Nace and I did not have to hitchhike all the way back because we met a woman professor who wanted someone to drive her home to Lubbock, Texas. From there, however, our troubles began. Few motorists would pick us up. In desperation, we hopped a freight train and rode in the empty gondola of a coal car, sharing this space with unemployed men. By the time we reached Kansas City our faces were black, our spirits low, our pockets empty. All we had left was five cents—and we still had to cross the entire state of Missouri. We were starving.

We were lucky enough to get a ride with a man from Kansas City to St. Louis, and then made our way to Nace's home in the suburb of Webster Groves. His folks were away, but we broke into the house and ran toward the refrigerator. That September 1, 1932, I wrote in my diary:

> I'd sometimes wondered what it feels like to be hungry, ravenously hungry, and now I know. It begins in the belly with a burning sensation the size of an apple. Hour after hour without food and the hot spot swells up to the size of a grapefruit. Next the belly feels like chamois skin dipped in hot water, then stretched taut. Finally the headache, the relentless headache! When Nace and I reached the refrigerator we stuffed food into our mouths the next twenty minutes—then almost vomited.

Back at the University of Missouri I worked in a drugstore jerking sodas for twenty-five cents an hour and by October 31, 1932, I had only $5.76 left with which to finish the semester. Returning to my home town for the holidays, I wrote in my journal:

> Kewanee, Illinois, Christmas, 1932. . . . This surely was a Depression Christmas. We had no Xmas tree because they cost 50 cents and my step-father said he couldn't afford one. I was unable to buy presents for my mother and three sisters. The family came here for dinner and Grandpa Robb gave the blessing. Poor soul. He got about halfway through and then stopped. I waited, head bent, then peeked and saw that Gramps was crying. Later we gathered around the radio to listen to Eddie Cantor. Now that we're in a depression, clowns are important.

I returned to the university and on February 16, 1933, my mother wrote to say that a third bank had failed in my home town. This left my stepfather with only thirty cents. He went to a fourth bank, the only one in town still open, to borrow $25 to buy groceries. Mother added:

> . . . the bank closing has caused a great deal more suffering in Kewanee. The Depression has caused so much worry that people are dying of heart trouble, and some are losing their minds. I understand that Mrs. J. B. is losing her mind over it. She asked me if I thought the Lord had brought this upon the people to make them suffer . . .

In those days many Depression victims believed or half-believed that their lives had been ravaged because of something they had done wrong. They felt vaguely responsible for their wretchedness.

In May of 1934, a friend drove me to St. Louis, where we saw a Depression hamlet called a Hooverville, after former President Herbert Hoover, who had failed to prevent the Depression. In this camp were 1,200 woebegone people; they perched on a levee in danger of being flooded by the rising Mississippi River.

After I received my bachelor of journalism degree on June 6, 1934, my first job as a reporter was with my hometown newspaper, the *Kewanee Star-Courier*. My beginning salary was exactly *nothing* per week. In August I received an offer from the chief of the New Orleans bureau of the Associated Press.

Moving to New Orleans I began working for the AP for $25 a week. Five months later my boss fired me, saying I was not the Associated Press type, although he thought I had talent; he got me another job with the *New Orleans Item*.

My salary on the *Item* was $18 a week. For a while I could afford one dollar a day for food. Somehow I managed to eat; I could get a heaping platter of red beans and rice for thirty-five cents. As a reporter, I watched cops break up an open air meeting of jobless men and women. I seethed in impotent fury as those New Orleans policemen violated the civil rights of impoverished people.

Throughout the South the *New Orleans Item* was known for its low-wage-scale and tightwad publisher, James McIlhany Thomson. My mother needed a cancer operation in the Mayo Clinic in Rochester, Minnesota, and I wanted to be with her but lacked the train fare. I borrowed $50 from the *Item*. The operation was a success; the loan was outrageous. My newspaper charged me 20 percent interest.

Back in New Orleans, where 8,000 people were starving, I saw kids eating out of garbage pails. One evening I was solicited by four black prostitutes; each offered herself to me for fifty cents. I shuddered.

One day in the French Quarter I saw a penniless family of five—father, mother, three children. The kids were begging. I walked past them but then felt so guilty that I turned around and called one of the boys to me. Into his hand I slipped a few coins. That night in an apartment on Bourbon Street I got drunk with friends and paced the floor raging about the Depression.

On May 6, 1935, President Franklin D. Roosevelt signed an executive order creating the Works Progress Administration, a federal agency for the relief of unemployment. In November of 1936, I moved from New Orleans to work on the *Oklahoma City Times* for $35 a week. On my daily newspaper run I visited state headquarters of the WPA. One morning when I entered the building a young man I knew gave me a candy bar. I was eating it when I was approached by a social worker, whom I also knew.

"We don't allow eating in here," she said to me.

Thinking she was joking, I uttered a wisecrack.

"We don't allow eating in here," she repeated sternly. "Some of these people haven't had any breakfast. We make it a rule among ourselves never to eat or drink Cokes in front of them."

Instantly ashamed, I mumbled something and slunk away. I wanted to throw away the candy bar but felt that that, too, would be a sin.

The owner of the *Oklahoma City Times* was one of the richest men in the state. We reporters knew times were hard when we learned that he sold some of his renowned herd of cattle. Then he fired more than a dozen of us. We agreed that it hurt him more to sell his cows and bulls than it did to put us out to pasture. By this time I was married and now I had no job.

For the next few weeks I was frantic with worry. The skin on my hands broke out in some kind of rash. Then I managed to get work on the *Peoria Journal-Transcript* in Peoria, Illinois, only fifty miles south of my home town. I began there at $32.50 a week. One chilling day my wife and I were horrified to realize that all the money we had in the world was $3.

In Peoria I found a heart-warming story. It concerned an eighty-five-year-old man named Charles M. Putnam, who was moderately wealthy. One day he saw a ragged young woman holding a baby in one arm and leading another child by the hand. She was weeping and walking toward the Illinois River. It looked as though she intended to drown her children and herself. Stopping her, he asked what was wrong. She said her husband had beaten her up, she had been locked out of her home, she had no food and no money to buy food for her kids. Handing her some cash, the old man decided then and there to help the poor of Peoria. A private citizen, acting alone, week after week he fed 425 persons representing 85 families. He was one of the greatest men I ever met.

As I say in the last chapter of this book, in the 1940s the United States became the arsenal of democracy. Factories expanded operations, new plants opened, men and women were hired, industrial production soared. It was World War II that restored American prosperity; by 1943 large-scale unemployment disappeared.

However, the Great Depression scarred me, just as it scarred everyone who managed to live through it. Whenever I think about prices and wages there is a part of my mind that remains stuck back there in those dour, dingy days. All of us lived with one word in our hearts and on our lips. The word was *HELP!* Nowadays, when people look toward Washington, D.C., what they see is gridlock and corruption and passing of the buck. The business of business is making a profit, to be sure, but the proper business of government is helping the people, because the people are the government.

And yet, anarchy is everywhere, it seems. Murders and rapes and drugs and racism and undernourished and undereducated children and AIDS and not enough money to rebuild our crumbling infrastructure. Under the New Deal of President Franklin D. Roosevelt a safety net was knitted to keep Americans from falling into total despair and destitution. Now this safety net is frayed and few in government see it as their responsibility to mend it. Some actually want to rip it apart. More and more Americans are becoming helpless, hopeless and cynical. Nowadays many people don't even bother to vote. With the loss of faith in government, with democracy itself being challenged, with galloping greed on Wall Street, with the gap between rich and poor becoming wider, these times are nearly as troubled as those of the Depression.

In troubled times most people prefer order to anarchy, but they may wind up with totalitarianism. No longer is communism our national enemy. Who or what *is* the enemy? The government? Wall Street? Immigrants? Cartoonist Walt Kelly's Pogo said: "We have met the enemy and he is us." In 1838, Abraham Lincoln said much the same thing: "If destruction be our lot, we must ourselves be its author and finisher. As a nation of freemen we must live through all time, or die by suicide."

My hope is that the republication of this book, twenty-five years after its first appearance, will contribute to the preservation of memory, and to the continuity that links generations one to another; I hope that *A Nation in Torment* will serve as an antidote to amnesia, and prevent us from running headlong into another national catastrophe like the one we suffered in the 1930s.

EDWARD ROBB ELLIS

New York City
April 1995

Preface

THIS BOOK is mostly about people—about men, women and children and what happened to them during the great American Depression of 1929–1939.

The story of this decade must include economics and politics, high finance and corporations, but behind such matters there were the people themselves, and I have focused on them as much as possible. How did they feel? What did they think? What did they do? What did they say? How did they survive?

This is a narrative history with certain episodes described at length and in depth in an attempt to evoke the moods of that troubled time. I am acutely aware of all that I have been forced to omit. To tell the full story of the Depression would require publication of a set of ten or twelve books.

I agree with Barbara W. Tuchman, who said of her role as a historian: "I am a seeker of the small facts, not the big Explanation; a narrator, not a philosopher." In researching and writing my book I collected tens of thousands of details and then watched them form patterns like pieces in a mosaic. For the most part, I reasoned from the particular to the general. This method caused me to change my mind about some preconceptions I had held.

Although a book of this size is bound to contain a few errors, I worked hard to make it as accurate as possible. Here and there I have reported that a certain individual *thought* thus-and-such a thing at a given moment; in each instance, I have documentary support for this private reflection, since the person later wrote down what he was thinking or told others about it. I have not invented a single scene or quotation. Wishing to keep the story flowing as smoothly as possible, I excluded footnotes and other scholarly apparatus. My bibliography lists only some of the books and periodicals I consulted.

I am a product of the Depression. Having enough money in the bank to go through college, I entered the University of Missouri in September, 1929—and a month later Wall Street crashed, and soon my hometown bank failed. Like thousands of my contemporaries, I then worked my way through school by jerking sodas, waiting tables, selling stationery and clerking in a bookstore. While still a college student, I stood a few inches from Franklin D. Roosevelt as he spoke in Jefferson City, Missouri, during his first Presidential campaign.

After being graduated with a bachelor of journalism degree, I got my first newspaper job. From then until the end of the Depression decade I worked as a reporter and feature writer for wire services and newspapers in various parts of the country.

In New Orleans I watched cops break up a hunger march and listened to Heywood Broun urge the formation of the American Newspaper Guild. In Oklahoma City I sat in a press section a few feet from President Roosevelt as he made a speech in that city. I tasted grit in my mouth as Oklahoma endured dust storms, covered the state's WPA headquarters on a daily basis, met and married a girl who was first violinist in the state's WPA symphony orchestra.

In later years, as a newspaperman in Peoria, Chicago and New York, I met and conversed with several New Dealers, together with some other persons mentioned in this book.

Among them were Herbert Hoover, Harry S. Truman, Dwight D. Eisenhower, Richard M. Nixon, Wendell Willkie, Adlai E. Stevenson, Norman Thomas, Eleanor Roosevelt, Elliott Roosevelt, James Roosevelt, Douglas MacArthur, Henry Ford, Bernard M. Baruch, James A. Farley, Harold L. Ickes, Henry Wallace, Raymond Moley, Felix Frankfurter, John L. Lewis, William Green, W. Averell Harriman, Patrick J. Hurley, Alben Barkley, Everett M. Dirksen, Sinclair Lewis, John Steinbeck, William Allen White, Dr. J. Robert Oppenheimer, Joe Martin and Billy Rose.

All these people are described in the diary I have kept since I was sixteen years old, and in writing this book I have drawn upon my personal observations of them.

I thank the New-York Historical Society, of which I am a member, for the use of its fine facilities while I was researching for this volume.

I owe a primary debt to Selma Seskin Pezaro for copy-typing uncounted pages of notes and for giving me constant encouragement. I also thank another dear friend, Lucy Wind, for her secretarial services and for keeping up my morale. To my Coward-McCann editor, Patricia Brehaut Soliman, I offer my gratitude for her brilliant editing, sensitive understanding and unflagging faith in me.

I am indebted to the St. Louis *Post-Dispatch* and the Philadelphia *Bulletin*. I thank my daughter, Sandra Ellis Emelio; my sister, Mrs. Kathryn Ellis Burton; my brother-in-law, Robert C. Burton; Jerry Moriarity, Walter Cowan, Charles L. Dufour, Lionel Heiden, Jack and Barbara Waugh, Anna Walinska and Concetta Scaravaglione.

EDWARD ROBB ELLIS

New York City
December 31, 1969

A NATION IN TORMENT

1

The End of the Old Waldorf-Astoria

THE WALDORF-ASTORIA WAS DYING.

This hotel, once the most famous in the world, was about to give up its gilded ghost. It was the end of an era as well as the end of a hotel, for the Waldorf was no mere hotel but an institution, a name connoting opulence like the name of Tiffany. Never again would New York City be quite the same.

And so, this evening of May 1, 1929, the mourners came, the mourners and the celebrants, 700 rich men and women seeking to share the sadness of loss, hoping to recapture for one final time the gaiety the Waldorf had given them in the past. Couple by bittersweet couple they walked into the Dutch Renaissance palace on Fifth Avenue at Thirty-fourth Street, aware that wreckers were ready to raze it to the ground to prepare a site for a new structure—the Empire State Building.

They came off Manhattan streets and onto the main floor, whose 70,000 square feet had more lounging space than any other hotel in existence, and they winced when they saw what was happening. Most of the carpets had been removed from the lobbies. At ten o'clock that morning the Waldorf's $2,500,000 worth of furnishings had been put up at auction, and before that first day's sale ended at six in the evening hundreds of valuable objects had been sold to sentimentalists and bargain hunters. One man bought a rug merely because Herbert Hoover, the current President of the United States, had walked across it. Others purchased the marble fireplace from the Presidential Suite where Woodrow Wilson had dreamed of universal peace, the Royal Suite's mirror that once reflected the image of the Prince of Wales straightening his tie, the red plush divan from the room occupied by Marshal Foch, the oil painting that Lillian Russell always admired.

The buyers' names could be seen on tags dangling from the displaced chairs and tables that impeded the progress of the 700 as they headed for the grand ballroom, one flight up. By early evening the hotel's top ten floors had been pretty well stripped of furniture and fixtures, but private parties were starting in suites and rooms on the first five floors. Seventy-five people, eager to participate in a historic event, had engaged rooms for this final night, while 149 of the Waldorf's resident guests were sticking it out until the following morning, when all service would be cut off.

They could have gone to the New Amsterdam Theater to see Eddie Cantor in *Whoopee* or to the Empire Theater to catch Katharine Cornell's performance in *The Age of Innocence*. To Waldorf patrons of a sentimental turn of mind, however, this was no night to be out on the town. Among those who elected to stay to the melancholy end was Edward H. Green, son of Hetty Green, the so-called Witch of Wall Street. Six feet four inches tall on his cork leg, Green was an eccentric and a womanizer who indulged in bizarre sexual adventures, who gave one lady friend a jeweled chastity belt, who spent $3 million a year for almost fifty years, but who nonetheless left a net estate of more than $42 million when he died seven years later.

As the Waldorf's 1,400 employees went about their duties for the last time, silent and efficient as ever, maintaining their reputation for the finest in service, the 700 guests took their seats in the grand ballroom. The gentlemen were officers and members of various organizations that had held their annual banquets in the Waldorf for decades, which meant that most were along in years. Some recalled that night, ten years previously, when the hotel's famous four-sided bar in the men's club had been closed with the advent of Prohibition. The lucky ones bragged that they had obtained slivers of the bar as souvenirs. Demolition of the bar had been bad enough, but now—this! Why? Well, said the knowing ones, now that the Waldorf was not permitted to sell liquor and since taxes had risen, it cost management $1.25 in taxes alone for each hotel room, occupied or not. Damned outrage, that's what it was!

Their gray-haired wives, brought up in an era when gentlemen withdrew from the ladies to enjoy cigars and brandy in brief isolation, were content this memorable evening to sit apart in the ballroom's balconies, balconies all gilt and rococo and almost hidden by friezes of arbutus and magnolia blossoms. As they looked down upon the luminaries sitting on a dais before a mauve silk backdrop, whispers passed from woman to woman like a breeze stroking a field of tulips: There sat Herbert L. Satterlee, the son-in-law of J. Pierpont Morgan. Time was when Mr. Morgan dropped into the Waldorf almost every day when he was in town, but now—poor dear!—he was gone. Of course his son, J. P. Morgan, was carrying on in the fine old family tradition. Look! That wide-browed gentleman with the strong nose—yes, the one who looked a little like George Washington—that would have to be Adolph S. Ochs, the owner of the New York *Times*. And the big-boned man, so fleshy and jowly—why, he must be John F. Hylan— no gentleman, of course, but at least a former mayor of New York City.

But where was Jimmy Walker, the present mayor?

George T. Wilson, former vice-president of the Equitable Life Assurance Society, was toastmaster for the evening. Wilson startled and delighted the audience with his very first words: "This is a historic gathering. We had hoped that Mayor Walker could be present to lend his presence on this occasion, but he was too busy. He was too busy, in fact, even to answer the committee's invitation."

"*Booooo-o-ooo!*"

The banqueteers vented their indignation at the absence of the city's playboy mayor. Shocked by their outburst and unsure of himself, as always, Hylan stiffened in his chair at the boos, took off his glasses, polished them industriously, put them back on his fleshy nose and gazed about the room with the wide-eyed bewilderment of an alien in a foreign land.

No open comment was made about the absence of Franklin D. Roosevelt, the governor of New York State, for it was known that he was vacationing in Warm Springs, Georgia. However, Roosevelt's thoughts may have turned to the demise of the Waldorf, since he knew it well. In fact, the hotel had played a part in a youthful episode of his life. A few years after the turn of the century, while studying law at Columbia University, Roosevelt had speculated in the stock market. His favorite brokerage house employed a young man who had attended Groton with Roosevelt. This youthful broker also speculated, speculated unwisely and soon found himself owing his own firm $2,000. One day after the market closed, Roosevelt, the broker and another friend had gone to a bar to do some drinking. The anxious young broker became drunk and tearful, vowing that if only he could make enough money to pay his debt, he would head west and start life all over again.

After the three young men left the bar, they entered a nearby gambling joint which was so posh that one had to obtain an introduction before being admitted. The drunken broker begged his friends to stake him to $25 apiece so that he might try his luck at the roulette table, and they obliged him. At first he lost, but then he began to win and kept on winning until he had nearly $2,000 worth of chips in front of him. Since this sum was almost enough for him to clear up his debt, Roosevelt and the third man pleaded with the broker to leave. He refused.

The third man ordered a whiskey, which he then spiked on the sly and handed to the drunken gambler, who gulped it down. Roosevelt got a second spiked drink, which the broker tossed down, his knees wobbling. Before he passed out, he ran his winnings up to $2,250. Roosevelt and the third man dragged their unconscious friend out of the gambling house, hauled him into a horse-drawn cab and took him to the Waldorf. After getting him a room and putting him to bed, Roosevelt and the third man gave a hotel official a sealed envelope containing the $2,250 in cash with instructions that it was not to be opened except in the presence of the broker, when he had sobered up, and one of the other two.

*   *   *

Former Mayor Hylan, who knew nothing of that long-ago escapade, tried to mask his uneasiness by pretending to take one long last look at the Waldorf's grand ballroom. Actually, having banqueted there many times, he took for granted such marvels as the softly radiant ceiling painting, an allegorical representation of Music and Dance daubed onto the world's largest single canvas, 45 by 66 feet. He was accustomed to the Waldorf's magnificent tapestries and frescoes, its handsome wood carvings, its marble and onyx mosaics, its rich furniture and costly tableware. To Hylan, as to thousands of other eminent New Yorkers, the Waldorf-Astoria was a home away from home.

Most were aware that this exalted hotel with the hyphenated name had been erected in two stages. The Waldorf half, fronting on Thirty-third Street, was opened in 1893. The Astoria, facing Thirty-fourth Street, made its bow in 1897. Operated as a single unit by one management team, the Waldorf-Astoria quickly won acceptance as the world's largest, costliest and most imposing hotel.

The best artists and artisans, using the finest materials, had been given all the time they needed to fabricate a pleasure palace rivaling Versailles in splendor, if not in magnitude. It was the first Manhattan hotel to cover an entire city block, the first with a roof garden, the first with a branch office on each floor, the first to offer real vintage wines. Peacock Alley, an interior promenade and refreshment oasis, stretched more than 300 feet along the Thirty-fourth Street side of the hotel, and every day one could hear conversations held in almost every language of the civilized world.

The Waldorf was not just a local marvel but an international institution. Every American President, beginning with William McKinley, had spent the night under its sharp-pitched and turreted roof. Kings and queens, premiers and dictators, ambassadors and special envoys, Cabinet members and governors, Senators and Representatives, military heroes and social arbiters, robber barons and merchant princes—all knew and loved the old Waldorf-Astoria. Within its walls million-dollar deals had been consummated, and the United States Steel Corporation, the first billion-dollar corporation in history, had had its genesis in talks held there. This same May Day in 1929 United States Steel had reported that monthly and quarterly earnings for the final year of World War I had now been equaled for the first time since the return of peace and that the company was producing at 100 percent capacity. All seemed well in the world. All seemed well but not quite the same, now that the old Waldorf was about to be torn down. New York's elite mourned and messages of regret were cabled from France by Marshal Joffre and from England by Sir Thomas Lipton.

To many thousands of New Yorkers, however, this symbolic death of an era meant little if anything. After all, this was May Day, a day traditionally devoted to demonstrations by workers who existed outside the Establishment. That noon, responding to a call by leaders of the American Communist Party, 5,000 men and women had gathered in Union Square. They wore red ribbons, red hatbands, and red neckties and carried red banners emblazoned with the hammer and sickle of Soviet Russia. They shouted their admiration of that new nation and screamed denunciations of Mussolini, Italy's Fascist dictator.

The American Socialist Party had scheduled a mass meeting in Madison Square Garden, and by 2:30 P.M. the arena was full and thousands of persons had been turned away. With standees jamming every aisle of the Garden, Norman Thomas arose to speak. This lanky man with the pale-blue eyes and skull-like face had been the Socialist Party's Presidential candidate in the last national election. Now, eloquent as ever, he told the massed thousands that the purpose of May Day was to give expression to "the cry of the workers against injustices and oppression," to demand "deliverance out of their house of bondage" and to voice sentiments of future triumph.

It is unlikely that many of the 700 gentlemen and ladies dining in the Waldorf had paid much attention to these demonstrations, these words. What, throughout the length and breadth of America, was there to complain about? This very day, in the New York Stock Exchange, 4,688,900 securities had been traded. A year ago on this same date there had been only 3,770,990 transactions, and the year before that 2,186,220. As plain as the nose on a man's face was the fact that business was getting bigger and better all the time, so why rock the boat?

In the privileged sanctuary of the Waldorf ballroom, toasts to a gaslight past were drunk in mineral water, and if a cork was heard popping here and there, no one thought of running to snitch to a Prohibition agent. Presiding at this final banquet was Charles C. Paulding, vice-president of the New York Central Railroad and president of the Yale Club, who took this occasion to attack Prohibition. "The most indefensible law ever written upon our statute books," he called it. He flatly blamed the dry law for the death of the Waldorf.

Between courses a bagpipe band skirled, while strolling troubadours sang "The Sidewalks of New York." Waiters diplomatically averted their faces whenever they saw a sentimental guest slip an engraved Waldorf spoon into his pocket. The venerable captain of waiters, white-thatched and stooping Joseph Hamburg, scuttled among the tables to retrieve a discarded souvenir booklet, thrust it protectively beneath one arm and started away. He was recognized, caught and introduced to the audience, which applauded him. Oscar Tschirky, known the world around as Oscar of the Waldorf—the broad-faced Swiss-born maître d'hôtel, greeter of dignitaries such as President Harding and Prime Minister Ramsay MacDonald—was introduced, cheered and presented with a silver loving cup engraved "For Auld Lang Syne."

One of the principal speakers was William T. Prendergast, chairman of the Public Service Commission, who put a bright face on the dim occasion by saying: "I came here with no feeling of sadness. I see another interpretation of tonight's function. I look upon this hotel as upon a person who has rendered a great public service and after many years is allowed to retire to a well-earned vacation. We are not here to observe a demise. We are here to honor a great institution which has been a great forum from which ideas of tremendous value in shaping the sentiments and events of this nation have come. Chauncey Depew, Bourke Cockran, William Jennings Bryan, Charles Evans Hughes and John W. Davis have spoken within these walls—walls which have echoed to the eloquence of Woodrow Wilson and the vigorous rhetoric of Theodore Roosevelt."

Another note was struck by an editorial writer for the New York *Herald Tribune*. "It is merely a coincidence, of course," he wrote, "that the Waldorf should close on May Day, that on this date devoted to radical exuberance and the festive celebration of spring there should occur the demise of a world famous institution, last and most conspicuous relic of a social era that is gone. But, coincidence or not, it heightens the drama of the occasion and seems singularly appropriate to the history of the gay old hostelry. The resemblance may be a little far-fetched, but one is reminded of those aristocrats of the *ancien régime* who, with heads up and faint smiles of derision, rode through the howling mobs of the French Terror to the guillotine. . . ."

*   *   *

On May 6, 1929, five days after the closing of the Waldorf, a small group of leaders of the American Communist Party gathered in the Kremlin in Moscow to hear a talk by Stalin, who was consolidating his powers as the dictator of Soviet Russia and all Communist parties everywhere.

Stalin said: "I think that the moment is not far off when a revolutionary crisis will develop in America. And when a revolutionary crisis develops in America, that will be the beginning of the end of world capitalism as a whole. It is essential that the American Communist party should be capable of meeting that historical moment, fully prepared, and of [*sic*] assuming the leadership of the impending class struggle in America. . . ."

2

Prosperity and Speculation

JOSEPH P. KENNEDY strode down Wall Street.

Six feet tall and built like an athlete, horn-rimmed glasses straddling his nose, freckles peppering his cheeks, Kennedy wore a dark suit and Homburg. To casual observers he may have looked like many of the other successful men in New York's financial district, but the father of a future President of the United States was in fact a maverick. The son of a Boston saloonkeeper, Joe Kennedy had become the youngest bank president in the nation by the age of twenty-five. From banking he had branched out into shipbuilding, movie financing and then stock market speculation. Now only forty years old and already a multimillionaire, Kennedy had decided to make an unaccustomed visit to Wall Street. He seldom appeared there, since he operated through others, but the way things were going he wanted a firsthand look.

Wall Street neither impressed nor daunted him. "Big businessmen are the most over-rated men in the country," he liked to tell his sons. "Here I am, a boy from East Boston, and I took'em—so don't be impressed."

This summer day in 1929 out-of-town visitors were impressed by their first sight of Wall Street, then the most influential spot on earth. Its reputation awed them. Its smallness surprised them. Gently sloping downhill from the Trinity churchyard on the west to the East River, Wall Street ran for only eight short blocks in length—little more than one-third of a mile. Canyoned by tall buildings, the street was so narrow that in some spots the sun shone on the pavement fewer than twenty hours a *year*. Many of the granite and limestone skyscrapers had ornamented façades—fluted walls, stone gargoyles, Corinthian columns, brick bas-reliefs and towering statues. Behind these imposing walls thousands of bankers and brokers, traders and attorneys kept their fingers on the financial pulse of the world. Wall Street was a gigantic heart pumping money across the land and around the globe.

23

Joe Kennedy emerged from the shade of Wall Street, blinked as he stepped into the artificial light of a brokerage office and began shouldering his way to the front. The room was jammed with men staring hypnotically at stock market quotations spewing out on ticker tapes and chalked across blackboards. As Kennedy knew, this tableau was common to brokers' offices and customers' rooms not only in Wall Street but across the entire country, for America was speculating feverishly. Everyone expected to become rich by playing the market. All dreamed of instant opulence. Well—almost everyone. Kennedy, who already had earned his ulcer, took one last glance, turned, pushed his way outside again. He could sort out his impressions while getting his shoes shined.

He found a brash young bootblack who fished for big tips by rattling off predictions of the way the market would end that day. Kennedy listened in amusement. But later that afternoon, after the 3 P.M. closing of trading on the New York Stock Exchange, Kennedy was surprised to discover that the shoeshine boy had called the turn with amazing accuracy. If a mere boy could predict the movement of the market, Kennedy concluded, then it certainly was no place for a man with plenty of money to lose. Then and there he decided to sell his securities. Telling this story in time to come, Kennedy gave the bootblack credit for getting him out of the market and saving his fortune, but it would be closer to the truth to say that this incident merely confirmed an unconscious decision already made.

Bernard Baruch had a similar experience about that same time. One of the shrewdest operators of his age, Baruch candidly called himself a speculator—but chose to define the word for himself. "A speculator," he said, "is one who thinks and plans for a future event—and acts before it occurs." Baruch was stopped outside his office by an old beggar, who shrilled: "I got a good tip for you!" Nothing in this encounter influenced Baruch, but he also got out of the market for reasons of his own. His practice was to sell when he had made a big profit instead of waiting until his stocks reached their peak.

Baruch gave sound advice to his friend Will Rogers, the comedian cowboy and columnist. Rogers later wrote that "just before the crash, I sorter half way decided to get a little dab of some kind of stock. Everybody all around me was just rolling so in profits, that it made my little joke-telling stipend seem mighty little. I had never, or haven't yet, got a dollar that I didn't tell a joke for, either on stage or paper, so I knowing Barney mighty well, and having a mighty high regard for him personally and as well being the last word in business, so in my little talk with him I asked him to invest in his own way a little dab that I thought I could spare.

"Well I had to naturally tell him something of my affairs, so I told him what I owed, mostly on unimproved Real Estate. Well he liked to have thrown me out of his Wall Street Office.'You owe that much, and you want to take some of your money and buy stocks? Say you go home and pay your debts. Lord knows how long it will take you to do em. But pay what you can on em. You won't like this advice, no man does. He dont want to pay his debts as long as he thinks he can make an easy dollar in something else. I wouldent invest a dollar for you anyhow, things are too high, they dont look good. Now go start paying on your debts.'

"Thats the nearest I ever come to owning stock. (I mean outside of a few Horses, and cattle.) Less than a month from the day I was in his office the Bust come. . . ."

*   *   *

Other Americans—more greedy, less cunning or ill informed—stayed in the stock market and lost all they had.

In the 1920's the United States of America seemed to be prosperous, exceedingly prosperous. The nation had come out of World War I with a magnificent industrial plant. Our wartime allies owed us huge sums of money. The war had transformed the United States into a creditor nation second only to Great Britain. In the Twenties our productivity per person increased more than 30 percent. Factories, like horns of plenty, gushed forth millions of automobiles and radios, vacuum cleaners and refrigerators —all the things people wanted and needed. On the average, real wages were the highest ever paid in the history of the nation. Employment was high and on the rise. Unions declined in membership and militancy. Radicals were few and impotent. The workweek was shortened. There were fewer and fewer strikes.

The United States produced 25 percent of all the world's goods and 40 percent of its manufactured items. Corporations made huge profits. Individual incomes grew much faster than population. The national income grew from year to year. The federal budget kept showing a surplus. The national debt fell throughout most of the decade. The gross national product rose. There were booms in construction and real estate, the production of radios and pleasure cars. It was obvious to Americans and foreigners alike that the American standard of living far exceeded that of any other country in the world.

Republicans had controlled the federal government ever since the inauguration of Warren G. Harding as President in 1921, and Republicans were rapturous over the glorious *status quo*. They believed that whatever helped business helped the government and all the nation. Harding, the most inept President in our history, echoed the United States Chamber of Commerce and the National Association of Manufacturers by calling for "less government in business and more business in government." His faith in big business, together with his policy of government by crony, resulted in a series of scandals that saddened him and may have contributed to his death in 1923.

Harding was succeeded as President by another Republican, Calvin

Coolidge. Before Coolidge had been in the White House five months, he publicly declared that "the business of America is business." Like Harding, Coolidge regarded business and businessmen with an almost religious fervor. "The man who builds a factory," he wrote, "builds a temple . . . the man who works there worships there." Coolidge also liked to characterize George Washington as the best businessman of his day—ignoring the fact that Washington lost money speculating in land. Coolidge never mentioned another historic fact: Abraham Lincoln once ran a grocery store that failed.

Nation's Business, the organ of the United States Chamber of Commerce, once quoted President Coolidge as saying that "the attitude of the Chamber of Commerce very accurately reflects that of public opinion generally." Irving Stone, the writer, sadly agreed, declaring that Coolidge had transferred "the seat of power from the White House across Pennsylvania Avenue to the United States Chamber of Commerce." For its part, *Nation's Business* gloated: "Never before, here or anywhere else, has a government been so completely fused with business."

Most big businessmen proudly believed that financial success is a true test of a man's worth, and Coolidge agreed with them. The President liked rich men, surrounded himself with them, took their advice, echoed their attitudes. When a reporter asked Coolidge why he invited only businessmen to the White House—ignoring painters and musicians, actors and poets—the President drawled: "I knew a poet once when I was in Amherst—class poet—name of Smith. Never heard of him since."

Coolidge venerated J. P. Morgan, the bankers' banker, who got preferential treatment from the Bureau of Internal Revenue. Specifically, a tax return was approved by a federal revenue agent in New York with this comment: "Returned without examination for the reason that the return was prepared in the office of J. P. Morgan and Company and it has been our experience that any schedule made by that office is correct."

If Coolidge was the high priest of the cult of big business, millions of other Americans were its acolytes, for they knew it to be all-powerful. Business, like religion, endowed true believers with rewards—and if these happened to be material rewards, so much the better. Business boomed, so it must be right. Whatever worked was okay. Success justified everything. Only nonbelievers dared to point out that the business of business is making a profit. Only the unwashed were impudent enough to declare that budget balancing and bookkeeping, however honest, are not necessarily equated with the welfare of the people.

In the Twenties big businessmen were petted and praised and honored and deified until they began to regard themselves as the lords of creation. Few of them winced even at flattery as outrageous as this estimate by Professor Charles Dice of Ohio State University: "The common folks believe in their leaders. We no longer look upon the captains of industry as magnified crooks. Have we not heard their voices over the radio? Are we not familiar with their thoughts, ambitions and ideals as they have expressed them to us almost as a man talks to a friend?"

While Coolidge praised Washington as the best businessman of his day, a modern businessman was presenting Jesus Christ as "a startling example of executive success." This judgment was offered by Bruce Barton, a New York advertising executive and later a Republican Congressman, in a book he wrote about Christ called *The Man Nobody Knows*. In his curious version of the New Testament, Barton declared that Jesus "picked up twelve men from the bottom ranks of business and forged them into an organization that conquered the world." Barton's book was a best seller for two years.

Profits, power, bigness, riches, optimism, success—such was the gospel of the Twenties. Get ahead! Make the most of your life! Ride the gravy train! Bet on the future of America! In frontier days careful people had tucked their savings into mattresses against a rainy day, but now the frontier was closed and the nation was industrialized. During World War I Americans had been urged in the name of patriotism to buy Liberty Bonds. Now, in the Twenties, it also seemed patriotic to turn a profit and share in the greatness of the nation by investing in corporations that owned factories that produced the goods so much in demand.

*   *   *

In 1924 individuals with savings and corporations with surpluses began buying common stocks. They did not rush headlong into the market but nibbled at its edges. There was nothing artificial about this early phase of the stock market boom since it reflected genuine industrial expansion. During the year 1925 there was an increase in both the prices of stocks and the numbers of shares traded. However, both slipped a little in 1926.

That year, E. H. H. Simmons, president of the New York Stock Exchange, declared: "We are seeing today a democratization of American industry and finance alike in this steady tendency of the employees and consuming public at large to become capitalists in their own right. . . . It must be apparent to us all that today we are merely entering a new era in which the benefits of the capitalistic system are becoming practically universal, and when the system itself is by force of this fact becoming animated by a spirit of broad and genuine democracy. . . ."

Soon, though, sound investment developed into rash speculation.

An investor is more concerned with a steady income and the safety of his principal than with fat returns at the risk of his capital. A speculator, on the other hand, seeks quick and lush returns and is willing to risk his principal to get them.

Quite early in this dangerous game of speculation a sense of uneasiness grew in Herbert Hoover, who then was secretary of commerce in President Coolidge's Cabinet. On January 1, 1926, Hoover said: "There are some phases of the situation which require caution . . . real estate and stock speculation and its possible extension into commodities with inevitable inflation. . . . This fever of speculation . . . can only land us on the shores of over-depression. . . ."

But the public paid scant attention to Hoover. In 1927 the speculative boom began in earnest, with the bulls far outnumbering the bears. According to the Wall Street jargon, there are two kinds of investors—the bulls and the bears. A *bull* is an optimist who bets that stocks will go up. A *bear* is a pessimist who bets that stocks will go down. Just as the ancient Israelites worshiped the golden calf, so now thousands upon thousands of Americans worshiped the golden bull of easy wealth.

Was stock market speculation just one form of gambling? Opinions differed.

Simmons of the Stock Exchange said: "Speculation in securities is not at all a bad thing in itself. . . . It is, however, necessary to recognize that we may have too much or too little security speculation." According to Methodist Episcopal Bishop James Cannon, Jr.: "Gambling in the stock market is not different from gambling in other business transactions. The purchase and quick resale of shares is not any more gambling than the purchase and quick resale of lots. . . . A man can buy stock for a small cash payment . . . and there is no reason to call him a gambler because he sells the stock shortly thereafter at a profit."

The bishop, who was himself deep in the market, may have had in mind the Florida real estate boom. Promoters had bought vast tracts of vacant land in that Southern state, laid out new cities on paper, used William Jennings Bryan and others to ballyhoo the area's rosy future, then sold thousands of acres at ridiculously high prices. The Florida boom reached its peak in 1925 and collapsed the following year. Although untold numbers of people lost fortunes, other Americans failed to learn from this disaster. Now stocks, not land, was the speculative rage.

Was this gambling? The idea was rejected by some who observed that a gambler wins only because someone else loses. In a poker game, one man wins the pot. In a horse race, one horse usually comes in first. But in stock market speculation, it seemed, everybody won and nobody lost. Stock prices went up, up, up. A man bought General Motors stock at $100 and sold it to another for $150, who sold it to a third for $200. All three made money. No one got hurt. Of course, this kind of reasoning ignored the fact that inflated stock prices did not represent the true value of the company property or its earning power. Ordinarily, what pushes stock prices up is profits.

Both then and later there were some individuals who indeed regarded speculation as gambling. Roy Helton, an author and lecturer, said: "There is . . . evidence that a ten-cent pair of dice knows somewhat more about the future than the most expensive human prophet." Ferdinand Pecora, who later headed a U.S. Senate investigation, called the New York Stock Exchange a glorified gambling hell. Agreement came from Republican

Senator Smith W. Brookhart of Iowa, who declared that the exchange was a gambling hell that should be padlocked. And Will Rogers, poking his tongue into one cheek, wrote in his column: "Don't gamble. Take all your savings and buy some good stock, and hold it until it goes up—and then sell it. If it don't go up, don't buy it."

But the speculative mania was encouraged by Arthur Brisbane, who earned $200,000 a year by dishing out banalities on the editorial pages of Hearst newspapers. In a column entitled "Get Aboard," Brisbane pontificated: "The important thing is to know when to *get aboard*. In buying real estate or stocks, in joining others in any undertaking, make up your mind and then GET ABOARD. If you are in doubt, keep away. If you can't afford the undertaking in hand, let it alone. But if you are able, and think you ought to do it, GET ABOARD."

The get-rich-quick mood also won the approval of John J. Raskob, a General Motors executive and an intimate of the powerful Du Pont family. In a magazine article headlined "Everybody Ought to Be Rich," Raskob said: "If a man saves fifteen dollars a week and invests in good common stocks, and allows the dividends and rights to accumulate, at the end of twenty years he will have at least eighty thousand dollars and an income from investments of around four hundred dollars a month. He will be rich. And because income can do that, I am firm in my belief that anyone not only can be rich but ought to be rich."

Raskob knew Franklin D. Roosevelt, who had continued to speculate after leaving law school and being admitted to the bar. In 1908, while working as a clerk in the New York law firm of Carter, Ledyard and Milburn, Roosevelt casually predicted to fellow clerks that he would be elected President and even explained how he would manage the office. He began his political career by serving two years as a New York state senator, spent seven years in Washington, D.C., as assistant secretary of the Navy, was defeated as the Democratic Party's Vice Presidential candidate and returned to private life in 1920.

Roosevelt joined the law firm of Emmet, Marvin & Roosevelt, with offices at 52 Wall Street, but only dabbled in the practice of law. For the next eight years he earned an annual salary of $25,000 as vice-president of the Fidelity and Deposit Company of Baltimore, a surety bonding firm, running its New York office. This was the first big money he ever made in business. He and his wife had inherited a total of about $300,000—all of it in bonds that paid them an income of $17,500 a year. This moderate, steady return did not satisfy Roosevelt, who decided to speculate in ventures promising faster and fatter profits.

Some of his investments were fantastic. Roosevelt helped organize a firm that planned to carry freight between cities by dirigible. He invested in resort hotels, speculated in German marks, wildcatted in Wyoming oil, and lost $26,000 after buying control of a company that planned to freeze Maine lobsters and hold them for a rise in the market. He sank money in a firm that made automatic vending machines and another that tried to place advertising in taxicabs.

Roosevelt was once rebuked by the Society for Promoting Financial Knowledge for lending his name to doubtful enterprises. He countered that it was difficult for a man who had been in public life to prevent his name from being used without authorization but promised to be more vigilant in the future. During the summer of 1928 he hoped to become president of a proposed multimillion-dollar Wall Street bank. Nothing came of it.

Everyone, it seemed, was trying to get rich quick. By word and example, the nation's leaders encouraged ordinary people to play the stock market and make their pile, since prosperity was here and now and eternal. Henry Ford, the automobile manufacturer, said it was wrong for people to save their money. Otto Kahn, the suave banker and patron of the arts, rhapsodized: "Democracy has found its way into finance. We have begun to be a nation of investors." A. Atwater Kent, who was making millions by manufacturing radios, once scolded his wife, saying: "Mabel, you just aren't spending enough money!"

In 1927 there were 290 millionaires in the entire United States; but by 1928 there were 496, and by 1929 there were 511.

Year in, year out during the Twenties, stock market speculation was big news. Big afternoon papers played up stock market news on their front pages. Closing quotations often competed with baseball scores for headline space in the final editions. Before World War I the Associated Press transmitted only about 500 words a day about news of the New York Stock Exchange and the other exchanges across the country. By 1929 the AP seldom devoted fewer than 5,000 words to stock transactions, with the total climbing to 10,000 words on heavy trading days. In the spring of 1929 the New York *Times* gave almost one-third of its news columns to financial events. Stock market tip sheets sprang into existence. One of these, costing 10 cents, was put out by Bernarr Macfadden, the health fanatic and sensational publisher. The tip sheets made it easy for speculators to understand the jargon of the securities market.

Alexander Woollcott got his tips from men he sneeringly called "big shots." The drama critic, book reviewer, radio personality and dedicated eccentric had saved $100,000 by the summer of 1929 and sank all of it in the market. Later he reflected ruefully: "No good ever accrued from these tips except the potential benefit which anyone can experience by merely losing all his money."

Woollcott's friend comedian Harpo Marx got his advice from different sources. Harpo later wrote: "I got my tips from Groucho, Groucho got his from his friend Max Gordon, the New York theatrical producer, and passed them on to me. While we were in Boston with *Animal Crackers,* Groucho lost touch, temporarily, with Max Gordon. So he settled for tips from an elevator operator in the Copley Plaza Hotel, which he duly and loyally passed on to me. We spent more time on the long-distance phone with our brokers than Chico did on the local phone with bookies."

Woollcott and Harpo belonged to the famous Algonquin Round Table, a loosely knit group of literary and theatrical celebrities who gathered in the Algonquin Hotel on Manhattan's West Forty-fourth Street for poker and wisecracks. These talented and playful people, like so many other Americans, were afflicted with market mania. Their late-afternoon poker games were forever being interrupted by arguments about market trends. One day columnist Heywood Broun announced that he had received a hot tip from editor Herbert Bayard Swope about the National Cash Register Company.

"He knows the president of it personally," said Broun.

Woollcott replied smugly: "I'm loyal to Radio." He meant the Radio Corporation of America, which had yet to pay a dividend, but whose stock was soaring ever higher.

The patois of finance colored their witticisms. When comedian Charles Chaplin said in passing that his blood pressure was down to 108, playwright George S. Kaufman drawled: "Common or preferred?"

Still another member of the Algonquin group was Franklin P. Adams, a New York newspaper columnist who wrote *The Diary of Our Own Samuel Pepys*. While visiting in Washington, D.C., Adams dined with David Sarnoff, president of the Radio Corporation of America; Michael Meehan, a noted Manhattan stockbroker; a cartoonist; and the Washington correspondent of a New York paper. From them Adams "heard talk about the stock market that involved such great figures and so many shares that I could not encompass it, and so found it wearying."

In those fateful Twenties almost every corner of the country buzzed with chatter about the stock market. Norman Thomas was astonished to hear an animated financial discussion between a ticket seller and another worker at a Chicago elevated station. The head of the Amalgamated Bank of New York said in equal surprise: "You ride in an elevated or streetcar and the conductor asks you: 'How is General Motors?' Bank stocks are just flying up and down, and everybody is speculating."

By word of mouth, by means of newspapers and radio, tip sheets and magazines, people heard of ordinary folks like themselves who cleaned up in the market. A nurse made $30,000 by betting on tips she got from grateful patients. A valet played the market and raked in a quarter-million dollars. A Wyoming rancher who lived 30 miles from the nearest railroad did all right for himself by trading 1,000 shares a day by telephone. In the tiny town of Galva, Illinois, a telegrapher sent wires to big-town brokers from local rich men, followed their tips, wound up a wealthy man himself. With their next-door neighbors making their pile, Americans told one another, why, so can all of us!

The mood of the dollar decade was expressed by the *Saturday Evening Post* in this jingle:

> Oh, hush thee, my babe, granny's bought some more shares,
> Daddy's gone out to play with the bulls and the bears,
> Mother's buying on tips, and she simply can't lose,
> And baby shall have some expensive new shoes!

Mother indeed was buying on tips, for American women were in the bull market as never before in history. In the 1870's Victoria Woodhull had established a brokerage business in New York with the aid of Cornelius Vanderbilt, and in the 1890's Hetty Green's stock market adventures had won her the nickname of the Witch of Wall Street, but other than these two, few women had actively traded in the market. In the Twenties, however, women grew from a mere 2 percent of all nonprofessional speculators to 35 percent. Spinsters and dowagers, wives and mistresses sat in customers' rooms across the land to listen to the chatter of ticker tapes. The *North American Review* reported that the modern housewife now "reads, for instance, that Wright Aero is going up . . . just as she does that fresh fish is now on the market."

Everything seemed to conspire to make it easy for everyone to speculate. Some bankers, abandoning their traditional roles as conservative men who gave sound advice to businessmen and widows and orphans, plunged into the speculative orgy. One leader of this new breed of bankers was Charles E. Mitchell, board chairman of the National City Bank, which was headquartered in Manhattan and had branches scattered across the country.

Chief executive officer of the richest bank in the nation, Mitchell behaved like a carnival barker. Whenever one of his salesmen complained that he was unable to find customers, Mitchell took him to the top of the Bankers' Club in New York, led him to a window, pointed down and cried: "Look down there! There are six million people with incomes that aggregate thousands of millions of dollars. They are just waiting for someone to come and tell them what to do with their savings. Take a good look, eat a good lunch, and then go down there and tell them!"

Many big banks set up investment affiliates. These affiliates, controlled by the parent banks, were corporations for the promotion and sale of securities. Bankers broke the law by speculating in their own stocks. They cheated their customers by using depositors' money to speculate. Bankers were supposed to give their customers disinterested advice; but let one come to them with the question of how best to use his savings, and the bankers referred the man to one of the bank's affiliates.

A whopping case in point was Mitchell's own bank—National City Bank. It created an affiliate named the National City Company, which grew into the largest investment firm selling securities to the public. By means of pep talks, prizes and other razzle-dazzle techniques, the affiliate whipped its salesmen into frenzied efforts to induce ordinary Americans to buy stocks and bonds. Mitchell was so successful at this that he boomed his own bank's stock to an all-time high of $585 a share. Ferdinand Pecora, who later probed Wall Street, said that under Mitchell's direction "the

National City grew to be not merely a bank in the old-fashioned sense, but essentially a factory for the manufacture of stocks and bonds, a wholesaler and retailer for their sale, and a stock speculator and gambler. . . ."

Free enterprise, running amok, victimized people left and right. Among these victims was Edgar D. Brown of Pottsville, Pennsylvania—an industrial city of about 20,000 inhabitants. In 1927 Brown was thirty-eight years old, tubercular, losing his hearing, the only support of his wife and children. However, Brown had $75,000 in cash and $25,000 more in United States government bonds. That year of 1927, as he considered making a trip to California for his health, Brown happened to see a national magazine containing this advertisement: "Are you thinking of a lengthy trip? If you are, it will pay you to get in touch with our institution, because you will be leaving the advice of your local banker and we will be able to keep you closely guided as regards your investments."

The ad was signed by the National City Bank. Brown wrote the bank and soon a representative of the National City *Company* called upon him. This agent was named Rummel. Brown, who thought he was dealing with the world's largest *bank,* put himself completely in Rummel's hands. However, Brown made one stipulation: He did not want to risk his wealth by speculating; instead, he wanted to play safe by purchasing only bonds paying fixed interest.

Rummel told Brown that United States government bonds were "all wrong." It would be wise, said the agent, to cash these federal bonds and then buy bonds of various private American corporations, together with bonds issued by the municipal and national governments of Vienna, Germany, Greece, Peru, Chile, Hungary, Ireland and the like. Brown unwisely took this advice, sinking his entire fortune of $100,000 in these foreign securities. Then, at Rummel's further suggestion, Brown borrowed more money to make more purchases until his "investments" came to a total of about $250,000.

But the foreign bonds declined in value. When Brown complained to Rummel, the National City Company salesman said: "Well, that is your fault for insisting upon bonds. Why don't you let me sell you some stock?"

Aware that the market was advancing, Brown replied: "Very well. Buy stock."

The National City Company bought thousands of shares of various stocks in Brown's name. He later said he never knew "whether the companies they represented made cake, candy or automobiles." The investment affiliate bought so many stocks and traded them so violently that at last even the naïve Brown protested to the main office in New York. By this time he was staying in Los Angeles. Officials in the main office listened to him sympathetically and once again changed his portfolio. Brown now found himself owning Anaconda Copper stock—*and* stock in the National City *Bank.*

Then these securities, like the foreign bonds, began to drop. Fed up with the whole situation, Brown walked into the Los Angeles office of the National City Bank early in October, 1929, to ask that all his stocks be sold. Instantly he was surrounded by salesmen who declared that he would be foolish to sell anything—but especially stock of the National City Bank. With all these self-styled experts pressuring him, Brown backed down again and let his stocks ride.

The Crash came a few weeks later. Edgar D. Brown, once worth a fortune on paper, was wiped out. By 1933 he was a broken man, clerking for the poor board in Pottsville, Pennsylvania.

Published at about this time was *The Sucker's Mother Goose,* which said in part:

> A flyer, a flicker,
> A twelve o'clock ticker,
> What wiped you out so soon?
> I should have sold at ten o'clock
> I stalled around till noon.

*   *   *

Others hung on as stock prices soared. Between 1923 and 1929 the prices of common stock rose 176 percent. During this same period the numbers of shares traded increased from 236 million to one and a quarter billion. College students flocked to classes teaching the sale of securities, brokerage houses opened ever new branches as though they were chain stores, and between 1925 and 1929 the number of persons employed in the field of finance rose by 400,000.

The first ocean liner to have its own brokerage office was the French Line's *Ile de France.* Besides its standard radio shack, it was outfitted with a special wireless station for the use of passengers playing the market. New York broker Michael Meehan soon had branch offices on three other transatlantic ships—the *Bremen, Berengaria* and *Leviathan.* He boasted that one of his oceangoing customers learned of the completion of a trade four minutes from the time he radioed his order.

Meehan drove himself so hard he nearly collapsed from nervous exhaustion. In 1928 and 1929 he made from $10,000 to $15,000 a *day* in brokerage fees. The latter year all American brokers earned a total of $277,000,000 in commissions. Wall Street's biggest operator, William C. Durant, who had founded four automobile manufacturing firms, supervised the investment of between $3 billion and $4 billion in the year 1928 alone. Whenever Durant visited Europe, he would place transatlantic phone calls to Wall Street a dozen times a day at a cost of as much as $25,000 a week.

The fantastic rise in stock prices was not due to any overall improvement in corporate enterprise but rather to greed, to fatuous optimism and to the lure of something for nothing. Competitive bidding became ferocious. As John K. Galbraith has observed, "Of all the mysteries of the stock exchange there is none so impenetrable as why there should be a buyer for everyone who seeks to sell." During the Twenties a favorite catchphrase was that "everybody is in the market," but this was not true.

In a nation of 120,000,000 people there were perhaps only 2,000,000 or 3,000,000 who bought and sold securities. Some were prudent investors, while others were rash speculators. Only about 1 American in every 100 was buying stocks on margin. However, the frenetic pace of their activity, the excitement they generated and the publicity they attracted made it appear that the entire nation was on a financial binge.

Most trading was done by men of substantial means—doctors and lawyers, manufacturers and processors, and the like. But dreams of opulence also possessed chorus girls, shoe clerks, schoolteachers, gangsters, housewives and cabdrivers. In the hope of doubling or tripling their money in a rising market, they gambled their life savings. Uninformed, gullible and lacking wise counsel, they snapped up anything offered them. One innocent thought that Cuba Cane, the largest sugar company in Cuba, sold walking sticks.

Obsessed by the chimera of clipping coupons and counting dividends, individuals and corporations became monomaniacal in their quest for wealth, often ignoring morals and sometimes even the law. The moral tone of the times was epitomized by New York City's playboy mayor, Jimmy Walker, in a single sentence that calls for a close second reading: "I don't think it is ethical," he said, "for anybody to do anything illegal." This certainly gave one a lot of latitude.

Those persons lucky enough to make it big in the market soon became conspicuous consumers. There was, for example, John Markle, a coal operator who made an enormous fortune. In 1928, with profits from his mines and investments, he moved into a Fifth Avenue apartment containing forty-one rooms and fifteen baths, together with a private telephone switchboard and a round-the-clock operator. When a reporter asked how he could use fifteen baths at once, Markle snapped: "It's nobody's goddamn business!"

This selfish materialism sickened some Americans. Playwright Eugene O'Neill attacked it in two plays, *Lazarus Laughed* (1927) and *Marco Millions* (1928). Democratic Senator William H. King of Utah characterized speculation as a "national disease." In a book called *Our Business Civilization,* businessman-historian James Truslow Adams wrote that in contemporary America wealth was the sole badge of success. And William Allen White, the perceptive Kansas editor, had his say: "What a sordid decade is passing! . . . The spirit of our democracy has turned away from the things of the spirit, got its share of its patrimony ruthlessly, and has gone out and lived riotously and ended up by feeding it to the swine. . . . We sit in our offices and do unimportant things and go home at night and think humdrum thoughts. . . ."

*   *   *

Labor unions speculated almost as wildly as banks. William Green, the president of the American Federation of Labor and a man usually known for his conservatism, advised workingmen to invest in stocks. At the 1929 convention of the AFL the head of the building trade unions, William J. McSorley, joined bankers in denouncing the Federal Reserve System because it had boosted discount rates on loans in a timid effort to pare down speculation.

American Communists still preached that the "internal contradictions" of capitalism would bring it down in ruins, but capitalism was riding high, while Communist Party membership was falling fast. Communist leaders William Z. Foster and Earl Browder railed at the "bourgeoisification of the working class." They had cause to worry.

H. V. Boswell, head of the Locomotive Engineers Bank of New York, echoed the sentiments of the workers when he said: "Who wants to be a Bolshevik when he can be a capitalist instead? We have shown how to mix oil and water—how to reconcile capital and labor. Instead of standing on a street corner soapbox, screaming with rage because the capitalists own real estate, bank accounts and automobiles, the engineer has turned in and become a capitalist himself."

To become a capitalist, to use money to make money, seemed tantalizingly easy. Americans learned that they could borrow money to speculate in stocks. This was possible by getting a "broker's loan" to "buy on margin"—two phrases that became commonplace. If a man got a tip on a certain stock and decided to buy $1,000 worth of it, he was able to do so with only $100 in cash. He gave the $100 to a broker. This sum was the margin—the customer's proportion of the total purchase price to be paid by the broker. In turn, the broker borrowed the other $900 from a bank— a broker's loan. The broker then bought $1,000 worth of the chosen stock and gave the bank the stock certificates to hold as collateral.

If the value of the stock rose to $1,100, the customer could order his broker to sell. By risking only $100 he had gained $100. Of course, he had to pay a broker's fee, interest on the loan and an income tax on his profit. Nonetheless, he had nearly doubled his money. Quickly. On the other hand, if the value of the stock fell to $900, the customer had to put up more cash—more margin—or lose his original $100.

Loans are classified in terms of their duration. A *time* loan is one citing a specific date on which it must be repaid. A *call* loan may be terminated at any time by either the borrower or lender. Brokers' loans were call loans, intended to remain in force only a few weeks or months. This was time enough, speculators felt, in which to make a killing.

Bankers made money by lending to brokers. Brokers made money by lending to customers. Actually, in many cases, brokers earned more money from margin accounts than from outright stock sales. The customers themselves were so sure of reaping huge profits that they did not mind paying any interest rate charged them. Even when a staggering interest rate of 20 percent was charged for brokers' loans, speculators refused to become discouraged. Why should they? On every hand they heard of fortunes made almost overnight.

An exhilarating case in point was the soaring stock issued by the Radio Corporation of America. Organized in 1919, this firm was largely controlled by the General Electric and Westinghouse companies. With the radio business booming in the Twenties, RCA stock vaulted from 94½ to 505 in only six or seven months—from March to September, 1929. In the spring of that year a speculator with only $1,000 in cash could have bought 100 shares of RCA by borrowing $8,450 from his broker. The following autumn, by selling at the peak, the speculator would have multiplied his investment more than forty-fold.

Aware that fantastic profits of this sort were being made, ever more people plunged into the market, many of them relying on brokers' loans. As a consequence, the American economy became top-heavy and honeycombed with credit. Industrialists, envying the role played by brokers and bankers, decided to muscle in on this golden game. Business conditions were so good that many corporations had excess cash above their requirements for current production or future expansion. Why not lend this spare cash to speculators? To make and market goods was more troublesome than to lend cash at up to 20 percent interest, as others were doing. So, one after another and then in a headlong rush, American corporations hired out their money to anyone wishing to play the market.

To cite just one example, Cities Service Company lent more than $285 million to plungers in the New York market in the year 1929. Of this sum, almost $42 million was lent by the firm *in a single day.*

Besides developing this new kind of business, corporations also ground out new issues of securities like so many cakes of soap. In the first ten months of 1929 alone, firms listed on the New York Stock Exchange floated a total of more than $3 billion in new securities. In addition, billions upon other billions were issued by companies listed on the Curb Exchange and also by swindlers not listed on *any* exchange. Money obtained from the sale of this stock was then put out on call.

Something different and dangerous had developed. Although few people seemed aware of it at the time, this reckless manufacture of unneeded securities reversed the traditional function of the stock market. Ordinarily, corporations issue stocks and bonds only when they need more capital— generally for expansion. They go to the stock market to find investors willing to put up the desired funds. Then the value of the new securities is determined by profits on increased production. In the past, business used the market to borrow money. Now business was using the market to lend money. This was a reversal in the role of the stock market. Now it fed upon itself.

Prices ceased to have any relation whatever to values. In their mad scramble for wealth, millions of Americans unwittingly became cynics, as

Oscar Wilde defined a cynic—"a man who knows the price of everything and the value of nothing." Banks used depositors' money to speculate in the banks' own stock—which was both illegal and unwise. Investment trusts, which sold their own stock to get money to invest in a variety of enterprises, invested in one another instead. Vicious circles within vicious circles. Herbert Hoover later called the system "rotten."

*   *   *

This judgment was not shared by Albert H. Wiggin, head of the Chase National Bank and known as the most popular banker in Wall Street. Wiggin described the market as "God-given." Richard Whitney, soon to become president of the New York Stock Exchange, called the exchange a "perfect institution." Both were wrong, of course. Both men were augmenting their fortunes by doing things that were either unethical or illegal, and Whitney wound up in jail. The truth is that in the late Twenties the New York Stock Exchange was an independent organization subject to no meaningful regulation by the United States or the state of New York. Run more or less as a private club, the exchange let its members take part in many questionable practices.

Among other things, the exchange did not ban pools. A pool is a secret agreement to raise or lower stock prices artificially. Bankers and businessmen, who pretended to believe that prices reflect the law of supply and demand, organized pools or took part in them. To identify just a few, pools were created to manipulate the stock prices of the National City Company, Chase Securities Corporation, Montgomery Ward, Radio Corporation of America, Standard Oil of California, American Tobacco, Union Carbide and National Cash Register.

A bull pool synthetically raised the price of a given stock. In this kind of operation the plotters began by organizing a small group of men sworn to secrecy and mutual trust. All were influential and rich. They decided how much each man would contribute to the pool. In advance, they also agreed about the division of the spoils. Then they picked one company whose stock they hoped to boost to spectacular and unrealistic heights. To direct this crafty campaign, they appointed one experienced manager.

Using the pooled resources of the ring members, this manager started buying stock of the chosen firm at the lowest possible price. As he bought more and more blocks of shares, there was, of course, a rise in the price of the stock. This attracted the attention of innocent speculators, who got the impression that the stock was a natural winner. These outsiders began buying, thus causing the price to soar ever higher.

Meanwhile, members of the pool traded shares of the given company among themselves, their buying and selling creating the illusion of general interest in this particular security. These transactions among the insiders were phony, for no money actually changed hands. Nothing was added to the true value of the stock. This pretense of a rapid exchange of shares was called wash sales.

Other tricks were used. The conspirators circulated rosy rumors about the firm in which they were interested, whispering about hidden assets, extra dividends or the likelihood that the stock would split. Allegedly, this dope came from "large banking interests" or "authoritative quarters" or "people on the inside." These glad tidings gradually appeared in newspapers, sometimes passed along by unsuspecting reporters, sometimes planted by corrupt reporters who sold their services.

Congressman Fiorello H. LaGuardia later proved that Wall Street pools had bribed financial writers on the New York *Times,* New York *Herald Tribune, Wall Street Journal,* New York *Evening Post,* New York *Evening Mail* and *Financial America.* A single press agent spent a total of $286,000 in bribing reporters.

The New York *Daily News* employed a financial columnist who called himself the Trader. He made $19,063 in ten months by playing this nefarious game. The columnist was friendly with John J. Levinson, a pool manager who earned more than $1 million a year. Whenever Levinson bought a certain stock with the intention of rigging its price, he told the columnist about it. The *News* writer then praised this stock in his column, hinting that it was about to perform miracles. Many of his readers innocently believed him, rushed to buy the stock and thus raised its price. Whenever Levinson launched a new pool, he would open an account with a broker in the name of the columnist, who thus took title to some shares of the escalating stock and profited handsomely.

Cunningly conceived and executed, a pool might sell as many as 100,000 shares of its patsy stock at 20 points above the price at which it had been bought by the insiders. To purchase the stock, engage in wash sales, spread rumors, bribe reporters, entice innocents to bite—all this could be done in weeks or a few months. At last, when the stock hit a fantastic peak, the pool manager quietly began unloading. After all the pool members had sold all their shares at whopping profits, the bottom dropped out of that particular stock. With this happening in pool after pool, the cumulative effect was the psychological demoralization of the market.

A bear pool worked in reverse: Stock prices were hammered down. In the Twenties a bear pool caused a sharp drop in the stock of the Yellow Cab Company, owned by John D. Hertz. He turned for help to Joseph P. Kennedy, who agreed to mastermind a counterattack. Kennedy's strategy was to buy and sell Yellow Cab so erratically that the raiders would become confused; then he would wrest control of the stock from them and stabilize Yellow Cab at the best possible price. Kennedy moved into the old Waldorf-Astoria, equipped his suite with a ticker tape machine and a battery of telephones, started calling brokers here and there across the land. He won his battle against the bears and saved Hertz.

In the year 1929 alone, more than 100 stock issues listed on the New York Stock Exchange were manipulated by means of pools and other devices. Few amateur speculators realized that they were being taken by the professionals, so many continued to buy. In 1928 a total of $2.9 billion in profits had been made by all speculators and during the first eight months of 1929 the plungers were throwing more than $17 million a *day* into the market.

*   *   *

In the Presidential election year of 1928 Calvin Coolidge declined to become a candidate for renomination, and his secretary of commerce, Herbert Hoover, won the GOP nomination.

The Republicans were puffed with pride. In their party platform they said: "No better guaranty of prosperity and contentment among all our people at home, no more reliable warranty of protection and promotion of American interests abroad can be given than the pledge to maintain and continue the Coolidge policies. . . ." In full-page newspaper advertisements they boasted: "The Republican Party isn't a 'Poor Man's Party'! Republican prosperity has erased that degrading phrase from our political vocabulary."

Making a campaign speech, Hoover said: "The poor-house is vanishing from among us. We have not yet reached the goal, but given a chance to go forward with the policies of the last eight years, we shall soon with the help of God be in sight of the day when poverty will be banished from this nation." Hoover won the election.

A few days before Coolidge left the White House he declared that stocks were "cheap at current prices" and that conditions were "absolutely sound." On the cold and rainy day of March 4, 1929, Hoover was sworn in as the thirty-first President of the United States, and in his inaugural address he said: "I have no fears for the future of our country. It is bright with hope."

Despite this public posture of confidence, Hoover worried in private about stock market speculation. To the White House he invited the publishers and editors of the nation's largest newspapers and magazines so that he might ask for their help in warning Americans against gambling in securities. Most of these men dutifully published strong editorials in the vein suggested by the President, but these had little, if any, effect.

Developing another line of attack, Hoover sent a personal emissary to Wall Street to talk to bankers and promoters. This agent was Henry M. Robinson, president of the First Security National Bank of Los Angeles. Authorized to speak for the President, Robinson warned the businessmen that the market was not sound, but they only scoffed at him.

Hoover then tried a third tactic. He sent for Richard Whitney, the vice-president of the New York Stock Exchange, and urged that the exchange itself curb the manipulation of stocks. Hoover told Whitney that although he preferred to let all American institutions and the forty-eight states govern themselves, something had to be done. Pointedly, Hoover remarked that of course the exchange had full power under its charter to control its own members and to prevent it from being used for manipulation contrary to the public interest. Whitney made profuse promises but did nothing. Hoover said he had no desire "to stretch the powers of the federal government" by legislation to regulate the Stock Exchange. That authority, Hoover felt, was vested only in the governor of New York.

Franklin D. Roosevelt, a Democrat, had been sworn in as New York's governor on January 1, 1929—two months before Hoover took office as President. In Roosevelt's own inaugural address he did not mention the speculative orgy, and in fact he was slow to comprehend its dangers.

Was there no person or institution which could have applied the brakes in time? Calvin Coolidge had been unconcerned. Andrew W. Mellon, whom Hoover kept on as secretary of the treasury, relished speculation because it was making him steadily wealthier. Hoover was sincerely concerned but ineffectual—largely because by his own admission he was reluctant to stretch the powers of the federal government—even in the face of a national crisis. And the Federal Reserve System acted too little and too late.

At a later date J. P. Morgan publicly criticized the Federal Reserve Board for encouraging what Morgan called the "speculative frenzy" of 1929.

In 1913 President Woodrow Wilson had signed the Federal Reserve Act creating the Federal Reserve System. This system was supposed to foster a flow of money and credit so as to promote orderly economic growth, a stable dollar and long-run balance in our international payments. The quasi-public system consisted of twelve regional banks which were coordinated by a board of governors headquartered in Washington, D.C.

In 1927 the Federal Reserve did indeed encourage speculation by lowering discount rates from 4 to 3½ percent. The discount rate is the interest that Federal Reserve Banks charge their member banks to borrow money. This made it easier for people to hire the money to play the market.

Early in 1928 some uneasiness was felt by members of the Federal Reserve Board in Washington, the so-called supreme court of finance. The board urged the twelve Federal Reserve Banks to boost their discount rates, and in three separate steps taken during this year of 1928 most of these banks did so. The discount rate rose to 4 percent, 4½ percent, finally 5 percent. Even this failed to dismay plungers, who paid the higher interest rates passed down to them and threw still more money into the market.

Roy Young was governor of the Federal Reserve Board with his office in the Treasury Building in the nation's capital. One day he leaned back in his chair—laughing, laughing, laughing. When a friend asked what was so funny, Young replied: "What I am laughing at is that I am sitting here trying to keep a hundred and twenty million people from doing what they want to do!"

Of the twelve regional Federal Reserve Banks, the richest and most powerful by far was the Federal Reserve Bank of New York. One financial writer described it as "the tail that wagged the dog in the Federal Reserve System." This bank urged that the discount rate be raised even higher—to 6 percent—thereby making credit so dear that speculation would have become unprofitable. Or so bank officials argued.

The Federal Reserve Board in Washington was reluctant to do this for fear that it might hurt all business. Board members were still sensitive to charges that in 1921 they had ruined farmers by pricking the bubble of inflated commodity prices. Now, in 1929, the board members could have acted boldly by pushing the discount rate ever higher, but they were paralyzed by timidity. They could have also asked Congress for power to stop trading on margin—as happened in 1934.

Instead, in a feeble compromise, in February, 1929, the Federal Reserve Board merely issued a warning to the effect that a member bank had no right to borrow from any of the twelve Federal Reserve Banks for the purpose of making speculative loans. The board also told its agents at the various reserve banks to scold individual bankers about overextension of stock market loans. By February the board was holding anxious meetings almost daily.

On February 14 columnist Franklin P. Adams walked into a New York restaurant and joined four famous artists at a table. One was Robert Ripley, the creator of "Believe-It-or-Not." Instead of esthetics, however, Adams was surprised to hear the four were discussing the Federal Reserve System. One of them darted away from the table to find a phone, returning a few minutes later with the news that the discount rate was the same as the previous day. This delighted his fellow artists but disgusted Adams, who had little interest in the market.

On January 1, 1929, the day Roosevelt became governor, Charles E. Mitchell became a director of the Federal Reserve Bank of New York. A few days later Roosevelt wrote a friend: "The business community is not much interested in good government and it wants the present Republican control to continue just so long as the stock market soars and the new combinations of capital are left undisturbed." In March the market broke, wiping out many small investors and sending the rate for call money up to 20 percent. Now, in his other capacity as board chairman of the National City Bank, Mitchell acted. At a moment when there was scant money available to the market, Mitchell borrowed $25 million from the Federal Reserve Bank to which he belonged and made it available in credit to traders. With a flourish, he announced that he was taking up the slack in Federal Reserve loans.

This outraged Senator Carter Glass of Virginia, commonly known as the Father of the Federal Reserve System. In a speech made from the floor of the Senate, Glass bitterly attacked Mitchell for "slapping the Reserve Board in the face and treating their policies with contempt and contumely. . . . He avows his superior obligation to a frantic stock market over against the obligation of his oath as a director of the New York Federal Reserve Bank . . . the bank should ask for his immediate resignation." Other Senators joined Glass in criticizing Mitchell, but Mitchell was not asked to resign.

It was obvious that control of credit had passed from Washington to Wall Street. This troubled Paul M. Warburg. A banker of enormous experience and prestige, Warburg had helped Senator Glass create the Federal Reserve System and had himself been a member of the original Federal Reserve Board. Now, in March, 1929, he was chairman of the International Acceptance Bank of New York. Warburg issued a public statement calling for a stronger Federal Reserve policy. If the orgy of "unrestricted speculation" were not stopped immediately, Warburg warned, there would be a stock market collapse. And such a crash, he added, would not hurt speculators alone but would "bring about a general depression involving the entire country."

Warburg was applauded by international bankers in Paris, Rome and Berlin, but in this country he was accused of "sandbagging American prosperity."

William Allen White of Kansas agreed with Warburg, writing to a friend: "I don't think the dawn of a better day has come. We have got to sink lower before we rise higher."

Will Rogers commented: "Give this country four more years of Unparalleled Prosperity and the people will get so tired of having everything they want that it'll be a pleasure to get poor again."

Another who worried was Charles E. Merrill, whose brokerage firm of Merrill & Lynch was located at 40 Wall Street. He was an aggressive salesman who had prospered during the great bull market of the Twenties, but by the spring of 1929 runaway speculation had thoroughly frightened him. Merrill went to a psychiatrist, and after a few sessions of therapy he began selling his holdings. So did his doctor.

Helena Rubinstein, often called the First Lady of Beauty Science, unloaded her cosmetic empire for $7.5 million, escaped the consequences of the Crash and a year later bought back her business for only $1 million.

Joseph P. Kennedy pulled out of the market, and when a friend expressed surprise, Kennedy told him: "Only a fool holds out for the top dollar."

Fools abounded in 1929. They bought more and more and more stock, sent brokers' loans soaring above $8.5 billion. They listened not to Paul M. Warburg but to Edward Henry Harriman Simmons, president of the New York Stock Exchange. He advanced the silly theory that if business in general had all the money currently in brokers' loans, it would swell up and burst. He said there was more capital around the country than the country knew what to do with. He declared that the safest place for all this capital was in the stock market. These remarks, made in a major speech by the head of the biggest exchange in the nation, amounted to a call for continued speculation, and within two days he received 40,000 requests for copies of his speech.

Speculation and prosperity hit a peak on Tuesday, September 3, 1929—a watershed date in the history of the United States.

The previous day had been Labor Day, and homeward-bound motorists had been delayed by massive traffic jams here and there throughout the nation. The weather was hot, the temperature in New York City reaching 94 degrees on September 3. With the Waldorf-Astoria Hotel vacated, demolition experts were getting ready to move in and begin their work. Herbert Hoover had been President of the United States for six months, and Franklin D. Roosevelt had been governor of New York State for nine months. The last American veteran of the Mexican War was dying, Thomas Edison was recovering from pneumonia, Al Capone was in a Philadelphia jail for carrying a pistol, Shirley Temple was four months old, and Samuel Insull of Chicago stood at the pinnacle of his career as a utilities czar.

The price of common stocks had risen from 115 to 225 points between June, 1927, and September, 1929. Congressman Adolph J. Sabath, a Democrat from Illinois, was preparing to present the House of Representatives with a bill recommending that the stock market be closed until legislation could be prepared for the protection of investors "and the country as a whole." Despite the fact that Bernard Baruch had sold his own stocks and urged friends to do the same, he told reporters that a further rise in stock prices was not only possible but probable. Gold flowed into New York from abroad.

Few people, that fateful September 3, 1929, realized that the stock market had topped out. On that day 4,438,910 shares were traded at the New York Stock Exchange. The New York *Times* industrial average touched an astronomical 452 points. The market was strong; according to financial writers, it also had a good undertone. Although the Radio Corporation of America had never paid a dividend, on this day its stock was quoted at a fantastic 505 points. General Electric reached 396, and American Telephone and Telegraph 304. In the previous week brokers' loans had increased by $137 million and New York banks had borrowed $64 million more.

No flags flew in joyous celebration of the peak of the great bull market, but a couple of days later a storm warning was hoisted by Roger W. Babson. This fifty-four-year-old economist and statistician dared to speak the truth as he saw it. In 1919, near Wellesley Hill, Massachusetts, he had founded the Babson Institute to train young men for careers in business and finance. Eight years later he had endowed his institute with $1.2 million. Every now and then, from his Massachusetts headquarters, he issued reports to investors and predicted the behavior of the stock market.

On September 5, 1929, Babson arose before an audience at his institute and said: "I repeat what I said at this time last year and the year before, that sooner or later a crash is coming which will take in the leading stocks and cause a decline of from sixty to eighty points in the Dow-Jones barometer. More people are borrowing and speculating today than ever before in our history. Sooner or later a crash is coming, and it may be terrific . . . factories will be shut down . . . men will be thrown out of work . . . the vicious circle will get in full swing and the result will be a serious business depression. . . ."

3

The Rise and Fall of Samuel Insull

CHICAGO'S NEW OPERA HOUSE opened for the first time on Monday evening, November 4, 1929.

Samuel Insull stood at the head of the receiving line in the foyer, basking in admiration under the mellow glow of chandeliers dangling from the lofty ceiling. Resplendent in white tie and tails, Insull triumphantly regarded the glittering assembly from behind his pince-nez. This very day, for the second time in his life, *Time* magazine had published his picture on its cover, together with a long article about his career.

Insull was a handsome old man. Stocky, standing five feet eight inches tall, he had white hair, a full white mustache and pink cheeks. As he bent over the diamond-studded fingers of matrons from Chicago's Gold Coast, his smiling lips lifted his mustache like the wings of a dove. His pince-nez were attached to his right ear by a thin black ribbon that trembled whenever he gave vigorous handshakes to the men who dominated the city's business and social life. He greeted everyone in a crisp English accent.

Six days earlier the stock market had crashed, but Insull securities generally held firm. In seven more days Insull would celebrate his seventieth birthday. He stood at the peak of his power and knew it and gloried in it. Apart from Al Capone, still directing the Chicago underworld from his Philadelphia jail cell, Insull was the city's uncrowned king, almost as much of a local landmark as the Gold Coast itself. One visiting writer had dubbed the city "Insullopolis."

He controlled a light and power empire worth almost $3 billion. He had a personal fortune of $150 million. In 1929 his income from salaries alone came to nearly $500,000. One million people had invested in his hundreds of corporations. In the fifty days ending the previous August 23 Insull securities had appreciated at a round-the-clock rate of $7,000 a *minute* for a total rise of more than half a billion dollars. Although the Depression had begun, Insull felt it would last no longer than panics he had weathered in the past.

Active in Chicago's opera life for years, Insull finally became the prime mover in the conception, financing and construction of the new forty-two-story Civic Opera Building on the east bank of the Chicago River at 20 West Wacker Drive, a few blocks west of the Loop. Mary Garden, the famous diva, said he had located it in the wrong part of Chicago, but she never cared for Insull and had sung for him for only one season. Miss Garden sniffed that Insull was unable to understand modern opera, and doubtless he agreed with her. He liked old things, traditional things. For this opening night he had chosen the Polish soprano, Rosa Raisa, to sing the title role in *Aida*. After all, this opera was so thoroughly traditional that it "disarmed criticism," according to one shoulder-shrugging music critic.

In a sense, this new $20 million opera house was Samuel Insull's monument to Samuel Insull. Viewed at a distance from the west, it resembled a gigantic chair made for a colossus, and already it was being called Insull's Throne. On its top floor Insull had installed himself in a penthouse the size of a small city block.

The premiere was a success, as almost everything in Insull's life was a success, although that very night in the world outside the opera house a shadow was creeping over the affairs of lesser men. Most stock prices continued to fall, the Chicago Federal Reserve Bank planned to lower its discount rate, and Harvard was laying off some of its scrubwomen.

*   *   *

Seventeen days after the opening of his stone throne, Samuel Insull walked into the White House in Washington to confer with President Hoover. Insull often visited there because various American Presidents considered his advice valuable. This time he was one of several captains of finance and industry called in by Hoover to discuss the worsening Depression. They maintained that the fall in stock prices was only a temporary market condition. Hoover then urged them to go home and conduct their businesses as usual, proceeding with their expansion plans as though nothing had happened. They promised to do as he asked. In fact, so optimistic was Insull that in the following year his companies spent $197 million on capital investment.

In his seventy years of life, Samuel Insull had come a very long way. He was born in a scrubby part of London on November 11, 1859, the fifth of eight children born to Samuel and Emma Insull. His father ran a small dairy and served as a lay preacher in the dissenting Congregational Church. His mother supplemented the family's meager income by presiding over Insull's Temperance Hotel. Young Sammy never drank a drop of liquor. As a boy, he was bright and ambitious, cocky and diligent, bursting with energy. Despite the family's low social status, he spent eight years in a good private school under the tutorship of Oxford students.

When Sammy was fourteen, he became a junior clerk for an auctioneering firm and used his spare time to teach himself typing and shorthand. When his boss fired him to hire the son of a customer, Sammy answered an advertisement in the London *Times* and was taken on as secretary to Colonel George E. Gouraud, an English representative of America's electrical wizard, Thomas Edison.

Insull worked in the battery room of the Edison Telephone Company in London, and for a brief time his assistant was a skinny redheaded lad named George Bernard Shaw. Insull's ability and zest impressed Americans visiting the London plant, so one day the young man got a cable announcing that the great Edison wanted him to be his private secretary. In 1881, only twenty-one years old, Insull arrived in New York.

He soon made himself indispensable to Edison, sharing the inventor's erratic hours, buying his clothes, answering his letters and—being given the power of attorney—even signing his checks. Edison called him Sammy and sometimes chided him for "always thinking of the dollar angle." Even so, Edison appreciated Insull's devotion and drive, proclaiming him "tireless as the tides." By slaving at the right hand of the genius who was creating the electrical industry almost overnight, Insull learned almost all there was to know of its technology, its financing. At the end of Insull's first year of employment, Edison gave him stock worth $15,000. The harder Insull worked, the more responsibility he was given and the higher he rose within the Edison organization. He represented the inventor in the founding and management of three companies, built and ran the Edison Machine Works at Schenectady, New York, and finally accepted the presidency of the Chicago Edison Company. That was in 1892.

Back in the days of crude utility service, long before Insull took up residence in Chicago, the people of that city kept candles at hand to light up whenever the electric current failed. After Insull took charge, he improved their service. First, however, he lumped his savings with $250,000 borrowed from merchant prince Marshall Field I, bought stock in the firm he now headed and thus laid the foundation of his personal fortune.

Insull was as much a key figure in the development of the economics of electric supply as Edison was in its technology. With his wide and intimate knowledge of utilities, Insull was also a genius at organization. Brilliant and creative, able to synthesize mountains of facts, capable of memorizing infinite details, given to daring innovation, he devised new ways to operate central power plants.

He pioneered modern cost accounting. He conceived the idea of the open-end mortgage, which a firm could use to refinance its debts indefinitely. He realized the advantages of mass production. He felt that competition was economically wrong and regarded the utilities industry as a natural monopoly. However, despite his knowledge of sound fiscal practices, Insull was driven by such a lust for power that he sometimes indulged in financial follies that left his growing empire structurally weak.

When he took over the Chicago Edison Company, it was only a $883,000 firm serving a small area embracing part of the present-day Loop. At the beginning he told his board of directors: "We have got to be the main producers of electrical energy in our community, or else the other fellow has got to own us." Insull started gobbling up one after another of the small inefficient plants in Chicago, wiping out all his competitors. And in his eagerness to own and run everything, he paid outlandish prices for poor properties.

By 1907 Insull's annual salary was $50,000, and he controlled all of Chicago's electric industry, his kilowatt production exceeding that of Manhattan, Brooklyn and Boston combined. Ten years later he was selling power to several states via a network of transmission lines. In 1919 he became president of the People's Gas Company of Chicago and introduced electric utility principles to gas operations. In 1926 he declined an offer from Prime Minister Stanley Baldwin of England to become chairman of a royal commission to direct the development of electric power in Great Britain. And by 1929, when he opened his opera house, he was one of the most powerful men on earth.

*   *   *

On top of his operating companies he had piled stock-selling companies and holding companies and super-holding companies. He was president of 11 companies, was board chairman of 65 companies and sat on the boards of 85 companies. He controlled 6,000 power plants in thirty-nine states. He manufactured more than 10 percent of this nation's power and sold it to 20,000,000 customers. He employed more than 150,000 workers.

His corporations had annual revenues of $400 million. He supplied the power that ran Chicago's streetcars. He controlled that city's elevated transportation system and its three electric railroads. Here and there across the United States he owned paper mills, a shoe factory, textile mills, a tire-fabric firm, mines, oil wells, a hotel company, an automobile-manufacturing plant, dairies, an asbestos company, groves of citrus fruit, and so on. He held honorary degrees from three colleges and decorations from several foreign governments.

So potent was his touch that one Chicago reporter observed it was "worth a million dollars to any man to be seen talking to Sam Insull in front of the Continental bank." He seemed so much larger than life that one of his vice-presidents made a speech calling for "Super Humans for Super Institutions." Mary McCormic, a singer and protégée of Mary Garden, heard a rumor that Insull was to become head of a great international utilities trust that would encircle the globe. Impressed, she exclaimed to him: "Why, this would make you the most powerful man in the world—another Napoleon!"

Insull murmured: "Napoleon was only a soldier."

He had married Margaret Bird, a young actress whose stage name was Gladys Wallis, but so neglected her for work that they drifted apart. Fond of books, she developed an especial interest in the life of Napoleon, and one day she urged her husband to study the emperor's career, saying: "Sam, you should learn about that man and what happened to him. If you don't, that's what's going to happen to you."

But Insull was too busy with other things. For thirty-five years he was perhaps the most powerful political manipulator of all American business leaders. During every election in Chicago, just to play it safe, he gave money to both political parties, and in 1926 alone he casually passed out $238,000. English-born American-naturalized Insull never seemed to mind supporting "Big Bill" Thompson, Chicago's longtime Republican mayor, who always ran for office with the ridiculous promise to "bust King George on the snoot!" Insull also slipped money to the chairman of the Illinois commission responsible for that state's supervision of utility rates.

When Insull also tried to elect United States Senators, Nebraska Senator George Norris observed: "It is quite apparent that his interest in the Senate is a financial one. He is interested in what he can get out of it. He is interested in making money, and nothing else."

Insull believed that the best way to win friends for the utilities was to get his own workers and customers to invest in his properties. He turned his employees into part-time stock salesmen, who offered to sell Insull securities on the installment plan—$10 down and $10 a month. Ordinary people were eager to buy, since year after year Insull securities paid dividends of 8 percent.

Whenever Insull needed big sums of money fast, he borrowed from Chicago or London banks, bypassing Wall Street bankers whom he disliked. His profits were so large and his enterprises seemed so sound that a few bankers almost pleaded with him to accept their money. Insull's bookkeeper, Phil McEnroe, once said: "The bankers would call us up the way the grocer used to call my mamma, and try to push their money at us. 'We have some nice lettuce today, Mrs. McEnroe; we have some nice fresh green money today, Mr. Insull. Isn't there something you could use maybe ten million dollars for?'"

One night at a party the president of the Continental Bank of Chicago sashayed up to Insull's only son, Samuel Insull, Jr., and purred: "Say, I just want you to know that if you fellows ever want to borrow more than the legal limit, all you have to do is to organize a new corporation, as we'd be happy to lend you another twenty-one million dollars."

All was not gold and glory, however. Insull was fought at every turn by two Chicago reformers, who later became important figures in the New Deal. They were Donald R. Richberg, special counsel for the city of Chicago in gas litigation, and his law partner, Harold L. Ickes, who took particular interest in the public ownership of utilities. During one hassle over Chicago gas rates, Insull personally offered Ickes a retainer. Interpreting this as a bribe, Ickes snapped: "I am Richberg's partner!" Lamely, Insull said: "Ah, yes . . . I had forgotten."

In the midst of one assault on the Insull interests, Insull convened some of his executives, declared their public relations stank and ordered them to remedy the situation. They soon put together an Insull propaganda machine called the Illinois Committee on Public Utility Information under the direction of Bernard Mullaney, who had been a top political reporter for the Chicago *Times-Herald*. A lackey of the vested interests, Mullaney once said within earshot of Ickes that Theodore Roosevelt was a madman. Teddy Roosevelt, of course, had opposed monopoly.

Buckling down to his new job, Mullaney said: "We are trying to develop the idea rapidly among newspapers that public utilities offer a very fertile field for developing regular, prompt-paying customers of their advertising columns. When that idea penetrates the United States—unless human nature has changed—we will have less trouble with newspapers than we have had in the past." Honest editors and reporters correctly translated this remark as follows: *Fellas, treat the utilities gently in your news columns, and we'll spend one helluva lot of dough in advertising.*

The Illinois Committee on Public Utility Information grew into a geyser spewing out facts, propaganda disguised as facts, half-truths, quarter-truths and outright lies. It tried to persuade people that utility rates were fair, that competition was bad, that monopoly was good and that this nation's future would be safe in the hands of enlightened power executives—especially those of Samuel Insull. It distributed millions of pieces of literature. It mailed free news bulletins to 900 Illinois newspapers. It sent thousands of pamphlets to schools throughout the state. It dispatched speakers to service club luncheons to proclaim that electricity was "the thing," that America was entering a power age.

Insull wanted the public to get the "facts" only as he saw them. A multimillionaire, a disciple of laissez-faire, he resented anything and everything which he felt threatened his empire and his way of life. One utilities spokesman reflected Insull's attitude when he said: "Through co-operation with educational institutions we have been able to substitute sound economic theories for biased, and in some cases socialistic or communistic doctrines, that are taught in our public schools."

At a meeting of power executives in 1929, Insull denounced radicals and agitators, declaring there should be some way to silence all critics of big business. Among those present was a thirty-seven-year-old lawyer and utilities official, Wendell Willkie, who later became a Republican candidate for President. Someone asked Willkie for his opinion. Undaunted by the great Insull, Willkie said he believed in the right of the opposition to be heard. If a given idea were valid, society would benefit; if invalid, it would fall on barren soil and hurt no one. When Willkie finished speaking, an awkward silence fell. Then, turning toward Willkie, Insull sneered: "Young man, when you are older you will know more!"

Insull's own propaganda machine was so efficient that the National Electric Light Association used it as a model in the creation of a nation-wide public relations section. This was done at the behest of Insull's younger brother and associate Martin Insull, when he headed the national group. Now, the length and breadth of the land, all Americans were doused with the bilge water of utilities propaganda. The Federal Trade Commission has said that this campaign was perhaps the most powerful ever launched in the United States with the possible exception of official federal propaganda during war.

The power trust sought to inflate the value of utilities securities, persuade ever more persons to invest in them, cast doubt on the efficacy of public-owned power plants, distort public information for its own selfish purposes. Matthew S. Sloan, head of the Brooklyn Edison Company of New York, lamented that it was "perhaps impossible to make our public relations work stretch from the cradle to the grave," but it did not fall far short of this grandiose ambition. Kindergarten children were given copies of a thirty-two-page utility booklet called *The Ohm Queen*. An ohm is a unit of electrical resistance. Two Insull men actually induced changes in a high school civics text by deleting mention of Insull's donations to *both* major political parties in the Illinois campaign of 1926.

While all this was happening, Samuel Insull said sanctimoniously: "I am engaged in the public utility business for profit, but it affords me great satisfaction that in making a profit I can render a real service to the state. . . . The money-making side of it is merely incidental . . . the great public utility business of the country, as a whole, are [sic] not over-capitalized. . . ."

Martin Insull naturally agreed: "We have made no profits in the sense in which profit is known. When you come right down to it, the work that we are doing, over and above the fair wage that we can get for the energy that we put into the arduous business, is the work that we do for the public itself." His fatuous theme was set to music by a Wisconsin utility group, which sang it to the tune of "Yes, We Have No Bananas":

> Yes, we've NO excess profits,
> No overgrown surplus today.
> We've interest increasing,
> And taxes increasing,
> And all of the help to pay.
> We have an old-fashioned Commission
> That holds rates down with precision,
> But yes, we've NO excess profits,
> No overgrown surplus today!

For a dozen years the power trust bombarded the nation with ballyhoo —not all of it quite this insipid. Struggling young writers were subsidized, so-called educational movies were produced, foundations were financed, university chairs were endowed and semantics was used as a cunning tool. *Public* ownership of utilities was slyly attacked as *political* ownership. Insull tried to substitute the term "investment company" for "holding company." The power industry even tried to identify itself with the state, one executive declaring that "an attack upon the principles for which we stand is an attack upon our very Government itself."

Besides Insull's army of workers who doubled as salesmen, he used the investment firm of Halsey, Stuart & Company to sell his stocks and bonds. This Chicago concern alone sold more than $2 billion worth of Insull securities. Its experts wrote radio scripts extolling the virtues of Insull properties, and these scripts were read over the air by a honey-voiced man called the Old Counsellor, who posed as an impartial adviser on all investments. In reality, the Old Counsellor was an English professor from the University of Chicago who was paid a piddling $50 a week to peddle propaganda prepared by the Insull machine.

All this dismayed Will Rogers, who wrote: "When you hop on the power trusts [*sic*], you are standing on the very arches of the Republican party. I had a joke about the power lobby in the papers and I got so many letters from power magnates saying 'there was no power lobby' that it almost made me lose faith in rich men."

Despite what Martin Insull said about the utility business reaping "no profit," Samuel Insull seemed to get along fairly well. Near the village of Libertyville, 38 miles northwest of Chicago, he bought and developed an estate of 4,445 acres, 101 of them elegantly landscaped. There he raised purebred Swiss cattle, together with the blooded Suffolk-Punch draft horses he had admired as a boy on London streets. This was just a hobby, of course, since he never made money on them.

He called his lordly manor Hawthorne Farm. It had sunken gardens, bird sanctuaries, a huge swimming pool, three lagoons graced with goldfish and swans and a greenhouse big enough to furnish flowers for a hundred funerals. Waited on by a staff of servants, Insull lived in a French Riviera mansion with gold-plated bathroom fixtures and rooms imported intact from European castles. One room had a roof that slid back on summer nights to reveal the stars. Hawthorne Farm had perhaps the only post office in the nation maintained on a private estate.

Wearing knickerbockers and playing lord of the manor, Insull happily roamed his green acres, where villagers "built homes on Insull real estate, sent to an Insull school children born in an Insull hospital, used Insull light, cooked with Insull gas, travelled on an Insull road, saved in an Insull bank, and played golf on an Insull golf course."

Away from his country place, Insull dressed faultlessly. He wore a starched collar, conservative ties, monogrammed shirts whose French cuffs were caught by priceless cuff links, a white handkerchief foaming from his breast pocket, striped trousers and spats. Although he shunned liquor, he doted on cigars.

He was arbitrary and ruthless, one banker describing him as "the most dominating man I ever knew." The welfare of others seldom concerned Insull. With the deepening of the Depression, his only response to growing unemployment was: "My experience is that the greatest aid to efficiency of labor is a long line of men waiting at the gate."

His empire was sound—or so it seemed on the surface. Certainly his properties weathered the early stages of the Depression better than those of most companies. Chicago bankers continued to lend him money while refusing to buy tax warrants issued by the city of Chicago. At one public hearing the witness stand was occupied by Silas Strawn, a Chicago lawyer and president of the United States Chamber of Commerce. An alderman asked: "Do you mean to tell me that the credit of the city of Chicago is not so good as that of Samuel Insull?" Strawn replied: "Exactly that."

Halsey, Stuart & Company went even further by suggesting that Insull securities were safer than United States Government bonds. One firm member urged a woman investor to buy shares in one of Insull's holding companies, Corporation Securities Company of Chicago, rather than federal bonds, because the market for such bonds was "artificially stimulated to a great extent."

One man who thought highly of the Insull empire was industrialist Cyrus S. Eaton. Born in Canada, once an assistant to John D. Rockefeller, Sr., Eaton was worth $2 million by the time he was thirty years old. Despite Eaton's association with Rockefeller and the magnitude of his own fortune, he was such a renegade that in years to come he would praise Soviet Russia and blame the cold war on the United States.

Eaton lived in Cleveland, where he headed the investment banking house of Otis and Company. He knew the stock market game better than Insull, and in 1928 he and his colleagues quietly began acquiring a large block of Insull securities. Eaton bought when the stock fell. Then, when the price rose, Eaton would throw back on the market just enough shares to test Insull's strength and intentions. Resolved never to let control slip from his grasp, Insull himself always bought back as much of his own stock as he could get. Nonetheless, over a period of time, Eaton and his associates obtained Insull stockholdings exceeding those of Samuel Insull. At last Eaton struck by offering to sell all his Insull stock to Insull—at Eaton's price.

At that time the market value of Eaton's holdings was around $52 million, but he wanted $63 million for them. He strongly hinted that if Insull did not want these securities, it would be easy to sell them to a syndicate of New York investment bankers. This frightened Insull, for he knew that the Morgan interests were moving into the utilities field.

*   *   *

The Federal Power Commission, created by Congress back in 1920, had been unable or unwilling to curb the malpractices that developed during the Twenties as the private utilities industry swelled into a $12 billion Goliath. By 1930 about 90 percent of all the power generated in the nation was being distributed across state lines, but states seemed as helpless as the federal government. Senator George Norris of Nebraska explained the reason for their impotence:

"The power trust is the greatest monopolistic corporation that has been organized for private greed. . . . It has bought and sold legislatures. It has interested itself in the election of public officials, from school directors to the President of the United States. It has succeeded in placing its friends in office unbeknown to the people. Its representatives have been carefully placed in seats of honor and trust. Its lobbyists have control of legislation in practically every state of the union. It has managed to infest farm organizations; it has not hesitated to enter the sacred walls of churches and religious organizations. It has influenced, wherever it could, the election of judges in the various state courts, and the appointment of judges to the federal bench."

President Hoover was well aware of the mounting anxiety about the influence of the power trust, but the only remedy he suggested was the federal regulation of interstate power "in *co-operation* with state authorities." (Italics added.) Norris knew that such a plan would not work for the simple reason that many state authorities were completely dominated by the utilities industry. Along with other liberals in Congress, Norris sought to attack the problem from another direction by trying to pass legislation that would have converted some Muscle Shoals plants into federally owned and operated facilities.

Issuing vetoes, Hoover flared: "I was very indignant at Senator Norris and other so-called Progressives whose opposition was born of desire to force the government into operation of power. Their theory was apparently to oppose adequate control of private operation in the hope that public resentment of unrestrained, greedy action would forward their cause. That in a nutshell was the American system of regulation running squarely against socialism."

*   *   *

On June 3, 1930, Samuel Insull agreed to accept Cyrus Eaton's high-handed offer, although Insull had no idea where he could lay his hands on so much money. Insull's own companies had nothing like $63 million in fluid capital, now that the Depression had begun to hurt his business, and tens of thousands of average people were no longer able to invest in the Insull empire. In addition to buying out Eaton, Insull realized that he had to reorganize at a cost of many millions more—but where was the money to be found?

By this time Chicago's overextended banks were more interested in saving their own skins than in helping Samuel Insull. Across the waters, London's banks had cracked down on credit. Well, how about Wall Street? Unfortunately, only a month before this date Insull had blasted the concentration of financial power in New York in the course of a public speech, and Wall Street men resented Insull's contempt for them. Charles Stuart, manager of the New York branch of Halsey, Stuart & Company, explained: "Mr. Insull wouldn't let bankers tell him how to run his business, and when it touched his affairs he told them how to run theirs. He pushed bankers around. He said the only way to deal with them was to get so you could call them on the phone and make them come to your office to do business. Maybe you could do that in Chicago, but you couldn't do it in New York. These New York fellows were jealous of their prerogatives, and if you wanted to get along you had to be deferential to them and keep your opinions to yourself. Mr. Insull wasn't, and that made bad blood between them. Real bad blood."

However, Insull now had to pocket his pride to save his pockets. For the first time in his life he made an overture to Wall Street. Eleven financial houses—most from New York, a few from Chicago—agreed to lend three Insull companies more than $87 million. Significantly, these were short-term loans. In trying to avoid the heavy thumb of Cyrus Eaton, Insull placed himself under the fist of Wall Street.

Insull then began a frantic reorganization of his failing firms, but all too late. Down through the years, in his zest to expand, he had struck bad bargains by paying inflated prices for inferior properties. He had issued too much stock against these assets—in the face of his declaration that the utility business was not overcapitalized. He had paid unduly high interest rates on his debts. He had siphoned profits from his operating companies into his holding companies. His financing methods were as loose as fishing nets while his bookkeeping had become surrealistic. He had taken losses in the stock market. His credit was gone.

His operating companies, topped by stock-selling companies, topped by holding companies, topped by super-holding companies, now soared into the sky and trembled like a pyramid of Jello.

In the past he had controlled this mélange through his minority stock-holdings. In theory, a corporation belongs to the people who own its securities. In reality, a corporation can be controlled by smart men who own a small minority of the stock. Machiavellis of the minority-control game, Insull and his relatives and friends invested $100 million and wound up controlling more than $2.5 billion. In other words, for every $1 put up by the Insull group, they won control of $2,500 of the public's money. Insull called all the shots while owning only 1/2500 of the assets.

The key to Insull's power lay in the holding company. There are several varieties, but in the main a holding company is a corporation owning stock in other companies. During the days of Insull's grandeur, *operating* companies were subject to state regulation. *Holding* companies, on the other hand, were immune from regulation, many were formed to thwart antitrust laws, and they were relatively free to water their stock by assigning unrealistic values to their assets. A Chicago financial editor wrote that "a holding company can do almost anything short of murder and keep within the law." Will Rogers said it better: "A Holding Company is a thing where you hand an accomplice the goods while the policeman searches you."

Insull's wheeling and dealing had become so complex and intricate, so ponderous and deranged, that they baffled all comprehension. The human mind grows faint when one tries to follow a single strand of this cobwebbed pattern: His two top holding companies, Insull Utilities Investments and the Corporation Securities Company, controlled, among others, the Middle West Utilities Company, which controlled the National Electric Power Company, which controlled the National Public Service Company, which controlled the Seaboard Public Service Company, which controlled the company that actually generated the power—the Georgia Light and Power Company. Owen D. Young, the eminent corporation lawyer, declared that Insull himself could not understand all he was trying to do. Robert E. Healy, chief counsel for the Federal Trade Commission, said: "I do not believe that the human being ever lived that could know enough to run the whole Insull outfit."

With the continuing fall of stock prices, including those of Insull outfits, all banks clamored for more collateral. When the National City Bank of New York insisted that Insull reduce his loan, he managed to borrow $1 million from the General Electric Company. But day after day, the market value and liquidating value of Insull's collateral kept declining. He could float no more loans, find no more profits to draw on.

At last the eleven financial houses decided—the New York bankers positively, the Chicago bankers hesitantly—that to protect their loans to Insull, they had to take over his empire. They summoned the old man to Manhattan.

*   *   *

On Friday afternoon, April 8, 1932, Samuel Insull arrived at 120 Broadway and walked into the office of Owen D. Young, chairman of the General Electric Company and of the New York Federal Reserve Bank. Young had agreed to serve as mediator between Insull and the eleven financial houses that had lent him more than $87 million on a short-term basis. Before the discussion began, Insull noted in surprise and apprehension that five men from Morgan banks filed into the office. Insull himself was asked to wait in a small adjoining room.

He waited for an hour. He waited, and he fretted. He was realistic enough to expect the loss of his two super-holding companies but felt sure he could save that capstone of his empire—Middle West Utilities Company. A $10 million note against Middle West was due on June 1.

At last Insull was asked to join his creditors in Young's office, and

instantly he took the offensive, rattling off the numbers of shares they held
in three of his operating firms, arguing the soundness of this collateral,
insisting—

He stopped. In the eyes of the men who sat staring at him he saw
something frightening. Owen D. Young, who sat next to Insull, now turned
to the old man to say it had been decided that no one would put up any
more money for Middle West.

Insull asked breathlessly: "Does this mean receivership?"

"I'm very much afraid it does. I'm sorry, Mr. Insull."

Insull's face twitched, and it looked as though he might collapse. Then
he murmured: "I wish my day on earth had come!"

This was the beginning of the end, and Insull knew it. He had created a
paper Frankenstein which now was about to devour him.

That terrible day the Insull creditors decided that four top Insull companies should be placed in receivership until bankruptcy petitions could be
filed. Receivers were to be selected within the week. Former President
Calvin Coolidge was invited to become a receiver for Middle West Utilities
but declined.

The action shifted back to Chicago. On April 10, 1932, a meeting was
held in that city to draw up a slate of receivers. One of the first men chosen
was Edward Eagle Brown, vice-president of the First National Bank of
Chicago. Insull himself was offered the chance to become one of the
receivers of Middle West, but having caught his breath, having turned
stubborn again, he refused. He abhorred the thought of sharing his authority with anyone else.

Brown, confronting the old man head on, said firmly: "Mr. Insull,
you've either got to be a receiver with the *other* receivers, or be left out of
the picture altogether." Insull gave in and agreed to become one of the
receivers.

Across the land raced the word that the Insull empire was falling apart.
This interested Franklin D. Roosevelt, now actively seeking the Democratic nomination for President of the United States. Near midnight of
April 16, 1932, Roosevelt placed a long-distance phone call from Albany
to Cleveland and routed his chief speech writer, Raymond Moley, out of
bed. The governor told his aide that the news about Insull necessitated
some last-minute additions to the speech that Roosevelt planned to deliver
in St. Paul on April 18.

Roosevelt felt that it was the duty of state and federal governments alike
to see that electric power was produced and distributed to consumers at the
lowest possible cost. After Moley touched up his speech, Roosevelt said in
St. Paul: ". . . It is an unfortunate fact—which is not denied by the
leading bankers or the leading utility men themselves—that largely through
the building up of a series of great mergers and a series of great holding
companies, the capital structure, especially in the case of the electric util-

ities, has been allowed to expand to an extent far beyond the actual wise and necessary cash investment."

Meantime, receivers of defunct Insull properties had hired accountants to examine company books so they could report the true condition of the properties to the court. These CPA's discovered that there had been cross-loaning of collateral among the Insull firms. Millions of dollars had been taken from assets to pay questionable brokerage fees. Payrolls had been padded and loaded with Insull's relatives and friends. Some 1,600 favored persons got preferential treatment and huge profits denied average investors. Certain irregularities were traced to Martin Insull. Among other things, he had used more than $500,000 of company funds to cover the margin on his personal brokerage account. He had done this, too, with the knowledge, approval and help of his brother, Samuel.

These revelations caused Insull creditors and receivers to decide that Samuel Insull should be shorn of *all* his titles. It was agreed that this edict would be conveyed to the old man by his longtime friend, Stanley Field, who had stood beside Insull the night the opera house opened. Field, a banker and utilities executive, was a nephew of Marshall Field I, whose $250,000 loan had helped Insull along the road to success. On June 4, 1932, Field went to Insull's office and said: "Mr. Insull, we want your resignations, and we want them now."

"The hell you do!"

"Yes, we do—and we're going to have them!"

For a few moments the two men dueled with their eyes.

Finally, Insull growled: "All right! I'll resign from everything—but I won't do it through the back door on a Saturday afternoon! I'll do it properly. You call special meetings of all the boards for Monday, and you can have my resignations then."

Early on Monday morning, June 6, 1932, Samuel Insull entered the Commonwealth Edison Building at 72 West Adams Street, Chicago, walked into a paneled office, and sat down at the head of a long board of directors' table. Worse things than the abdication of a business emperor were happening here and there in the Depression-ridden country. In Chicago itself fifty men had just fought savagely over garbage outside the back door of a restaurant. Four days earlier Chicago's bankers and industrialists and civic leaders had begged President Hoover for federal relief. This very day Franklin D. Roosevelt was writing a letter criticizing "Hoover's inept leadership, or rather complete lack of leadership." Down in Texas a boy named Robert B. Anderson, who later became the nation's secretary of the treasury, was trying to raise $12 to buy a new suit for graduation ceremonies at the University of Texas. And Bernard Baruch was telling some visitors to his New York office that "business must go through the wringer and start over again."

Samuel Insull was going through the wringer as his son sat beside him, watching and struggling against tears. All day long secretaries staggered in and out of the boardroom, carrying heavy ledgers for all the many Insull corporations. All day long Insull dictated and signed papers, and all day long a procession of Insull directors walked into the room and then out again, some with moist eyes, all aware that they were witnessing the fall of a titan. They had been Insull's lackeys, they had jumped whenever he cracked the whip, but they had a grudging admiration for the old boy, so now they drew up resolutions praising his long and meritorious services and ordered that engraved copies be bound and sent to Samuel Insull. He drafted and signed resignations from chairmanships and presidencies and receiverships of eighty-five companies.

When the last document had been signed, Insull turned to his executive secretary and softly said: "Please get my wife on the phone—but don't disturb her if she is resting." The call was put through. Over the wire the old man said to Mrs. Insull: "Well, it is all over. . . . It was a very tiring day. . . . After dinner we will take a drive. . . . Good-bye."

As he hung up, an aide blurted: "You'll be back in six months, Mr. Insull! Your stockholders will demand it!"

"No. I will not come back. I am through."

He walked out of the boardroom and just outside the door, found himself surrounded by newspaper reporters. To these men, whom he always had considered his natural enemies, Insull said: "Well, here I go, gentlemen—after fifty years, a man without a job. I have ceased to be newspaper copy and I am out of public life and no longer a public figure, so I ought to be entitled to privacy."

*   *   *

Hardly.

Insull was bigger news than ever. The fall of his utilities empire was the biggest business failure in the entire history of the United States. When he crashed, American capitalism trembled, for Insull and his colleagues in the industry had gathered into their enterprises much of the nation's savings. A Chicago banker said: "The collapse of these companies has hurt our city more than did the great fire." This was not mere rhetoric. In the Chicago fire of 1871 only about $200 million had been lost. Insull's investors lost nearly three-quarters of a billion dollars. Soon Insull stock certificates were being used to paper the wall of a dining room in Chicago's Union League Club, a stronghold of Republican financiers.

Schoolteachers and clerks, stenographers and elevator operators, janitors and other ordinary Americans suffered—and so did extraordinary people like the artists once connected with the Chicago Civic Opera. Soprano Rosa Raisa, who had invested hundreds of thousands of dollars in the Insull empire, lost her entire investment. Conductors Giorgio Polacco, Emil Cooper, Egon Pollack and Roberto Moranzoni lost huge sums. So did baritone Cesare Formichi and stage manager Otto Erhardt. Contralto Augusta Lenska tried to kill herself by throwing herself in front of a streetcar.

On October 4, 1932, Franklin P. Adams, in a column for the New York *Herald Tribune,* wrote: "This day I read how Mr. Samuel Insull had done this and that in the matter of stocks and how he and his brother had been indicted for theft, which will be cold comfort to my sister, who invested her savings in Insull stocks, and I wondered whether Mr. Insull thought to himself of the money he had given to many Chicago projects and institutions and felt mighty sorry for himself. For I never knew a man, be he engaged in crime or philanthropy, especially in something combining the worst features of both, who did not justify himself to himself or have a violent attack of self-pity."

It was indeed on October 4 that a Cook County grand jury indicted Samuel and Martin Insull on charges of embezzlement and larceny. By this time, however, Martin had fled to Canada; two days after the indictments were handed up, Martin surrendered in Barrie, Ontario, was placed under arrest and then released on bail.

*   *   *

Samuel Insull read about these indictments while sitting in self-imposed exile in Paris. After hastily selling his $9 million Hawthorne Farm for a mere $780,000, he had slipped out of Chicago the previous June 14, made his way to Quebec and sailed from there for the continent.

Besides reading about the indictments in a newspaper, Insull also received a cablegram from John Swanson, state's attorney for Cook County, asking him to return to Chicago. Insull ignored this request, rumbling that no one was going to make political capital out of his misfortunes during an election year.

While Insull tarried on the Seine, Roosevelt won the Democratic nomination for the Presidency and then launched his campaign. One of Roosevelt's targets was Insull and his breed of profiteers. In one speech the candidate said: "Judge me by the enemies I have made. Judge me by the selfish purpose of these utility leaders who have talked of radicalism while they were selling watered stock to the people and using our schools to deceive the coming generation."

Insull left Paris for Turin, Italy. President Hoover asked Premier Mussolini to seize Insull, but by this time the old man had faded from Italy and taken refuge in Athens. He was acting on the advice of his attorney, who had cabled him the critical information that Greece had no extradition treaty with the United States. Insull now sought help from his old friend Sir Basil Zaharoff, the supersalesman of munitions and one of the world's richest men. In another gambit, Insull entered into an understanding with General Condylis, a would-be dictator of Greece. If Condylis had won power, Insull would have become a naturalized Greek citizen and then taken his place in a new cabinet as minister of electric power for that nation. But the general lost.

Although Insull was playing footsie with a would-be Greek dictator, he could not understand why public opinion in America had turned against him. Rhetorically, he asked: "Why am I not more popular in the United States? What have I done that every banker and business magnate has not done in the course of business?" What indeed?

Samuel Insull, Jr., who had remained in Chicago, shared his father's concern over the old man's public image. The son turned for help to Albert Lasker, board chairman of the Chicago advertising agency of Lord & Thomas and Logan, with whom his father had done business in the past. Lasker felt that advertising itself could do little, but perhaps a public relations campaign might brighten the Insull reputation. Insull junior was urged to consult with Lasker's specialist in publicity, an up-and-coming press agent named Steve Hannagan.

Hannagan agreed to take on the job if all his conditions were met. Hannagan himself must remain absolutely in the background. He wanted no personal contact with Samuel Insull, Sr. The old man had to agree to follow Hannagan's every suggestion, suggestions that would have to be transmitted to the distant tycoon via Samuel Insull, Jr. At this point Samuel Insull, Sr., was unaware of the source of the tactical advice that now began flowing to him in coded cablegrams. Insull was living comfortably enough in Athens. On the day he resigned his many titles, directors of three of his companies had voted him a pension of $50,000 a year. After the Cook County indictments were handed up against him, however, this pension ended, and Insull had to depend upon the charity of a few rich American and English friends.

Every top American correspondent longed to find Insull and interview him. Cornelius Vanderbilt, Jr., of *Liberty* magazine got a tip about Insull's location, sped to Athens, hopped into a cab and gave the driver an address. This, to Vanderbilt's astonishment, turned out to be a maternity home. Confused but determined, Vanderbilt gave his card to the receptionist and asked to speak to Samuel Insull. The receptionist handed the card to an orderly and asked him to wait. Then Vanderbilt was ushered into a courtyard. There he saw an elderly man with white hair and a white mustache, wearing a black cutaway coat and reading the afternoon edition of an English paper published in Rome. Affecting a bravado he did not feel, the reporter sauntered up and said: "Mr. Insull, my name is Cornelius Vanderbilt, Junior. I'm with *Liberty* magazine. I wonder if you would like to tell the American people your story and what you are doing here in Athens?"

Insull put down the paper, took off his pince-nez, looked up and asked: "Do you people intend to pay me, or am I to give you my story free?" Then, words tumbling from his lips, Insull babbled about losing everything in his unfortunate Chicago deals, declaring that he had been robbed blind and had left America broke. . . . How about the money for the interview?

Vanderbilt said he would have to ask his editor whether the magazine would pay for an interview. Then he asked Insull: "Do you mean a thousand dollars?"

"Hell, no! I mean a hundred thousand!"

With an uneasy laugh, Vanderbilt said: "Well, I know *Liberty* will never pay that much for anybody's memoirs—not even those of Samuel Insull." The reporter went on to say, though, that if Insull were interested in a reasonable sum such as $15,000 or $20,000—

Insull interrupted: "I'll tell you what I'll do: I'll think about this thing for a week. Where can I reach you? Can you come back and see me later?"

Vanderbilt said he was heading for Cairo, and Insull promised to write him there. When the correspondent asked for his autograph, the old man said he would send along a photograph with his name inscribed on it. Vanderbilt left, and that was the last he ever saw of Insull. Even this superficial encounter with the famous refugee had news value, however, so Vanderbilt wirelessed a story to *Liberty,* which printed the piece and then sold it to newspapers all over the United States, in Canada, South America, Europe, Africa and Asia.

In November, 1932, the U.S. Senate ratified a long-pending extradition treaty with Greece, and the Insull extradition battle began. At the request of the American minister to Greece, the Greek government arrested Insull. He was tried before Greek judges, who ruled there was not enough evidence to justify turning him over to American authorities. By February, 1933, Insull had been indicted in Chicago again, this time for using the mails to defraud, but since this was no offense under Greek law, the court again refused to expel him. Nonetheless, the notorious old man was becoming a nuisance to Greek officials eager to stay in the good graces of the American government. Various pressures were applied to the Greek hierarchy, and on December 5, 1933, the Greek foreign minister ordered Insull to leave on or before the following January 1. By pleading that Insull was sick, his attorney won an extension of this expulsion order until March 15, 1934.

The day this deadline arrived, Greek police were told to put Insull aboard a ship—but they could not find him. Not in Athens nor anywhere in Greece. Much annoyed, Greek officials radioed all ships that recently had sailed from Greek ports, ordering them to report the names of all their passengers. A prompt reply came from the captain of a tramp steamer named the *Maiotis.* Insull was aboard. He had chartered the *Maiotis* to sail to Egypt, his papers were in order, and he had left Greece on March 10 without notifying the authorities—simply to avoid publicity. The ship was summoned back to Piraeus, the chief seaport of Greece, and she complied. Insull's papers and the ship's papers were found to be valid, and after six hours' detention the vessel was allowed to resume her voyage.

Where was Insull heading now? Having received all this publicity, surely he would not proceed to Egypt, his original destination. The international press speculated about the ship's true port of call, and rumors, rising like startled pigeons, fluttered through the pages of papers all over the world. Insull was negotiating with French Somaliland to take up residence there. No—it was Ethiopia. Or was it Yugoslavia? Albania? Rumania? Turkey?

This guessing game ended on March 28, 1934, when the *Maiotis*, in need of provisions, put into the harbor at Istanbul, Turkey. By this time the American Congress had rushed through a bill authorizing President Hoover to nab Insull in any country with which the United States had extraterritorial rights. Earlier, the United States had adopted an extradition treaty with Turkey, but the Turkish government had not yet ratified it. Even so, at the request of the American government, Turkish officials took Insull off the ship.

Held in Istanbul's house of detention, he passed the time writing letters, reading novels and being tended by a valet whom he paid twelve cents a day. Then, in a twenty-minute session, a Turkish court ruled against Insull's plea for asylum in Turkey. He was taken to Smyrna and turned over to Burton Y. Berry, third secretary of the American legation in Istanbul. The prisoner was led aboard the American Export liner SS *Exilona,* which immediately weighed anchor for New York. During the voyage back to his homeland, Samuel Insull sank into such depression that he twice considered suicide.

Nosing through a morning fog, the *Exilona* docked in New York on May 8, 1934, and Insull's son climbed from a cutter onto the larger vessel. Trembling with excitement, making a curious slip of the tongue, the old man turned to fellow passengers and cried: "Gentlemen, my brother—I mean, my son!" As father and son embraced, Samuel junior slipped a paper into his father's hand. Reporters and photographers crowded close, shouting questions and barking orders. Taking off his gray hat, Insull snapped: "Keep quiet! There is plenty of time for taking pictures, but this is my mug and I have a proprietary interest in it. . . . I have a statement for the gentlemen of the press." Then, lifting the crumpled paper given him by his son, Insull read aloud a statement he never had seen until that moment:

"I have erred, but my greatest error was in underestimating the effect of the financial panic on American securities and particularly on the companies I was working so hard to build. I worked with all my energy to save those companies. I made mistakes, but they were honest mistakes. They were errors in judgment but not dishonest manipulations. . . . You know only the charges of the prosecution. Not one word has been uttered in even feeble defense of me, and it must be obvious that there is also my side of the story. When it is told in court, my judgment may be discredited, but certainly my honesty will be vindicated."

Later, beneath his breath, Insull asked his son: "Where the hell did that statement come from?"

"A very bright fellow named Steve Hannagan. He's handling our publicity. . . . You've got to do what he says."

"Hmph! . . . All right."

To thwart any legal maneuvers on behalf of Insull in New York, federal agents whisked him by car to New Jersey, put him on a train, and twenty hours later he was back in Chicago. While being booked at the Cook County jail, he learned that bail had been set at $200,000. This sum could have been raised easily by Insull's friends, but Hannagan wanted him to go to jail awhile. The press agent's gambit was to elicit public sympathy for this forlorn, white-headed old man, confined behind bars. So Insull let himself be led into jail as photographers snapped picture after picture. Reporters then filed inside to see the deposed power czar in his cell, clad in a Chinese dragon dressing gown. In a short statement, he told them: "I still think I did the right thing by leaving Chicago when I did, and I would do the same thing under similar circumstances."

After Insull had spent a couple of days behind bars, after Hannagan decided that the last drop of benign publicity had been wrung from this situation, bail was raised and Insull was released. Two days later, on May 14, 1934, Insull became the subject of a cover story in *Time* magazine for the third and final time.

Samuel Insull, Jr., and his family lived on Lake Shore Drive in a cooperative Gold Coast apartment bought in more prosperous days, but Hannagan advised Insull against moving in. The press agent persuaded him to maintain his new image of a broken old man by taking up quarters, instead, in the modest Seneca Hotel. The tycoon who once lorded it over a $9 million estate now paid $4 a day for his room. He attended a neighborhood movie house where, accidentally on purpose, he was discovered giving up his seat to a little old lady. He rode streetcars and buses. He was photographed smelling a rose held by his little grandson.

To some, presumably people who had lost money in Insull enterprises, there was something that smelled about this sweet-as-a-rose routine. Hostile strangers tried to force their way into the old man's hotel room, and he and his son got hundreds of anonymous letters threatening to shoot them, stab, bomb, burn or hang them. Taking fright, the Insulls hired thirty-six bodyguards, who were armed, paid $1 an hour and worked eight-hour shifts with twelve men per shift. Forsaking buses and trolleys, Samuel Insull now went out only in an armor-plated bulletproof limousine, as Al Capone had done.

Hannagan convinced Insull's lawyer that it would be wise to ask the court to try the old man by himself, rather than with his sixteen co-defendants. An application was made—and rejected. But the press agent got the kinds of headlines he wanted, for newspapers told how Insull sought to accept full responsibility for everything done by his subordinates. This made it difficult for anyone to argue that Insull hoped to pass the buck.

Samuel Insull stood trial three times in Chicago.

The first began on October 2, 1934, when federal Judge James H. Wilkerson opened the case of the *United States of America* v. *Samuel Insull, et al.,* for using the United States mail to defraud in the sale of stock of the Corporation Securities Company of Chicago, one of Insull's super-holding companies. A fifty-page twenty-five-count indictment was read by Dwight H. Green, United States attorney for the Northern District of Illinois. The jury consisted of five salesmen, two retail grain dealers, a grocer, a farmer, a garage owner, a bookkeeper and a heating engineer. Two were unemployed.

Insull's lawyer was Floyd Thompson, a former judge. He and Insull's son took Hannagan's advice and persuaded the old man to tell the story of his whole life in his own words when he took the witness stand. On November 1 Insull led off for the defense, and before the judge or prosecution quite realized what was happening, he began weaving a spell with his rags-to-riches story. He told of his bleak childhood in London, how he met Thomas Edison, how the great inventor fondly called him Sammy, how Mrs. Edison pressed his pants for him—and so on. It was a tearjerker, and when the prosecution objected to this monologue, the judge overruled the objection because he had become absorbed in the tale. Insull's attorney made certain that the old man ended on a dramatic note each afternoon, providing favorable headlines for the home editions of Chicago newspapers.

Day after day, Insull talked on, and when at last he finished his recital, the defense could have rested its case. However, Samuel Insull, Jr., also testified. Then Samuel Insull's lawyer summed up for the defense: "Gentlemen, you saw this old man on the stand. You saw this young man on the stand. You have heard their testimony telling you the story of this tragic period in their lives and in the lives of other people in this country. You have had a description here of an age in American history which we hope will never be repeated. I say that we are trying that age. . . ."

Insull's attorney admitted that money had been lost. Who got it? The attorney answered: "Old Man Depression."

The jury retired at 2:30 P.M. on November 24, 1934. On that very day the New York *Times* published a story about a New York City man who refused aid from the city's welfare department and collapsed from starvation. Some of the Insull jurors had been convinced of Insull's innocence even before he took the stand, and five minutes after being locked in a room together, all twelve men decided on acquittal. But, as one of them pointed out, the trial was so significant and its publicity so widespread that if they returned their verdict within a mere five minutes, they might be suspected of bribery. One juror's birthday fell on that date, so the gentlemen of the jury ordered cake and coffee and held a small birthday party, managing to kill two hours that way. At 4:30 P.M. they returned to the

THE RISE AND FALL OF SAMUEL INSULL 67

courtroom to announce their verdict: Samuel Insull and his sixteen co-defendants were innocent of all charges.

The Chicago *Times* interpreted the verdict to mean: "Insull and his fellow defendants—not guilty; the old order—guilty. That was the Insull defense, and the jury agreed with it."

Franklin P. Adams commented: "The public is a masochist at heart, and not only likes to be cheated, but has admiration for those who deceive and defraud it."

Nation magazine said the acquittal "illustrates once more the difficulty of sending a rich man to jail, no matter how flagrant his crime."

Samuel Insull stood trial a second time, along with his brother Martin, beginning on March 12, 1935, in the Criminal Court of Cook County on charges that they had embezzled $66,000 from Middle West Utilities Company. A second jury declared both men not guilty.

Samuel Insull stood trial a third time, along with his son and Harold L. Stuart, beginning on June 11, 1935, in the Federal District Court of Chicago. It was alleged that when the Corporation Securities Company of Chicago faced bankruptcy, they illegally transferred its property to save selected creditors, thereby flouting the Bankruptcy Act. The judge instructed the jury to return a verdict of not guilty, and it did.

This was the last of Insull's troubles in criminal courts, although civil suits continued to plague him. After all, his investors had lost more than three-quarters of a billion dollars. No longer Chicago's first citizen, eager to flee the scene of his three trials and many tribulations, Insull again left the United States to live in Paris. And on July 16, 1938, a gendarme wrote this report: "An unidentified man was found in a state of collapse on the platform of the Tuileries subway station near the Place de la Concorde. He was neatly dressed in a gray suit with red stripes, wore a brown felt hat and had 7 francs, 7 centimes [about 85 cents] in his pocket. He was of medium size with white hair. He had no identification papers but the initials 'S.I.' were on his handkerchiefs and underclothing. . . . Agent 2023."

Samuel Insull had died of a heart attack at the age of seventy-nine. All his life he had carried large sums of money on his person, and at the time of his death he was worth at least $10,000, so presumably he had plenty of cash in francs in his wallet when he left his apartment that morning. Presumably, too, some thief got to his body before the gendarme.

One of Insull's old antagonists, Harold L. Ickes, was at this time secretary of the interior in the Roosevelt Cabinet. Upon reading about Insull's death, Ickes wrote in his diary: "So passed a great and colorful figure from the American stage. After I came to know Insull I always had a sneaking liking for him, as I have found myself having for so many people of whom I have not been able to approve as citizens. He was a strong man even if he was dangerous to our economic well-being and a threat to our American institutions. . . ."

4

Wall Street Crashes

RICHARD WHITNEY, the vice-president of the New York Stock Exchange, was hailed as a hero one day in October, 1929.
This was long before it became known that he was a gigantic swindler, long before he was convicted of grand larceny, long before Fiorello LaGuardia scathingly compared him to Al Capone, long before court-appointed accountants entered his Manhattan home to list his assets. That grim day of reckoning Whitney led the accountants down into his wine cellar and watched as they began counting his champagne bottles, jotting down on paper two quarts here, six quarts there. Whitney shuddered and interrupted. "Gentlemen," he said haughtily, "they're not two-quart and six-quart bottles. They're *magnums* and *jeroboams!*"

Proper form meant much to this banker's son from a cultured New England family. Born in 1888 in Massachusetts, Richard Whitney was not directly related to the eminent Whitney clan of New York. Six years younger than Franklin D. Roosevelt, Richard attended the Groton prep school and Harvard, as Roosevelt had done. He was a natural leader, who captained both the football and the baseball teams at Groton and later pulled an oar on Harvard's sculling crew. Completing the four-year course in three years, Whitney was graduated from Harvard in 1911, and later that same year, at the age of twenty-three, he bought a seat for himself on the New York Stock Exchange. Within seven years he had his own brokerage firm of Richard Whitney & Company.

In bloodline, looks and connections, Whitney was the very prototype of the Establishment man, radiating pride in himself and his social class. He was tall and portly, handsome in a massive way, had a big nose and prominent eyebrows, parted his hair in the middle and slicked it back flat against his head. He wore a derby, a stiff collar à la Hoover, and a vest festooned with a gold watch chain. He was listed in the *Social Register*. He

68

married a widow of impeccable background—Gertrude Sheldon Sands, whose husband had been a son of Mrs. William K. Vanderbilt, while her father, George Sheldon, was a Morgan associate, treasurer of the Republican National Committee and president of the archreactionary Union League Club.

Despite Richard Whitney's blue-ribbon standing in society and finance, he had poor business judgment—a deficiency that somehow escaped the notice of J. P. Morgan. Whitney became known as the Morgan broker because, at a profit of $50,000 a year in commissions, he handled about 30 percent of all bond orders placed by Morgan's private bank. This failed to impress Harold L. Ickes, who described Whitney as "an errand boy for Morgan and Co." Besides his work for Morgan, Whitney handled perhaps 10 percent of all bond transactions at the New York Stock Exchange. His fifteen-room office was located at 15 Broad Street, and his inner sanctum overlooked the exchange itself. In 1928, at the age of forty, Whitney was elected vice-president of that institution.

It is not likely that he would have been elevated to this position had it been known that he had already become a thief. Beginning in 1926, Whitney misappropriated securities belonging to his wife and some of his customers, and with the development of the great bull market he used clients' funds to speculate. He stole from his customers; he stole from his father-in-law; he stole from his yacht club. He also borrowed heavily from his wife and brother.

George Whitney, three years older than Richard, became a Morgan partner in 1920 and led an honest life. But Richard Whitney kept on stealing, enjoying his $200,000 town house on Manhattan's East Seventy-third Street, raising prize pigs and chickens on his New Jersey estate, riding to the hounds, taking the air in one or another of his eight limousines and quaffing champagne.

Roger W. Babson's warning of September 5, 1929, annoyed Whitney, for both privately and publicly he favored speculation. "I claim that this country has been built by speculation," he once told a Senate committee. However, thousands of other Americans took Babson seriously, and immediately after Babson spoke, there was a sharp drop in stock prices. Throughout the rest of that September prices fell ever lower, rallied a couple of days, then resumed their decline.

On October 1 the president of the American Bankers' Association expressed grave concern at the pace of credit expansion. Two days later stocks took their deepest plunge so far in the year 1929. Babson's prediction and falling prices sent a chill down the backs of some speculators, and many of the smaller ones now began unloading their holdings. Nothing, though, could daunt Arthur Brisbane, the Hearst editorial writer, who cheerfully commented that "prosperity, real prosperity, has just begun." Brisbane also told his 25,000,000 readers that "stock gamblers may be worried, but the people at large feel cheerful."

On October 5 stocks did make a healthy recovery, sharp rises being scored by, among others, American Telephone & Telegraph, United States Steel, General Electric and American Tobacco. A week later the *Wall Street Journal* observed: ". . . bulls have had much the best of it over the last week or so, and this, perhaps, is the main reason why the market has been able to score such a quick comeback. A week ago you heard all over the Street pessimistic forecasts as to the future of the market."

On October 15 Charles E. Mitchell of the National City Bank sailed for home at the end of a visit in England, telling London shipboard reporters that the market generally was healthy and that values had a sound basis in the general prosperity of the United States. That same evening Professor Irving Fisher uttered a public statement that was to haunt him the rest of his life. Fisher was a brilliant monetary theorist who taught political economics at Yale and had made $3 million when his personal index card file system was merchandised by Remington Rand, Inc. Fisher now pontificated: "Stock prices have reached what looks like a permanently high plateau."

The next day it was made plain by members of a committee of the Investment Bankers Association that they did not share Fisher's optimism. They declared that speculation had reached a dangerous point, and they warned that many stocks were selling far above their intrinsic value. The latter part of this statement was ambiguous. "Intrinsic" or "real" value of stocks and bonds are mythical terms. All market values are relative and governed by opinion. The value of any security at any time is precisely what you can get for it. Of course, there should be a realistic relationship between the price of a given stock and the physical plant and volume of production of the company that issued the stock. In this sense, and for a long time, stock prices had become ridiculous. In some cases there was a 25 to 1 gap between stock prices and stock earnings.

On October 17 stocks rallied moderately, only to fall again the following day. As the market continued to weaken, Wall Streeters told one another reassuringly that a panic like the panics of 1873, 1893, and 1907 simply could not happen again. Ruling out another crash, they argued, was the nation's sound economic position, strong leadership on the Street and enlightened Federal Reserve policies. In their opinion, the trouble was being caused by several big bear pools, which were driving down selected issues.

In those days the New York Stock Exchange held short trading sessions on Saturdays, and on Saturday, October 19, the market broke from 5 to 20 points. Many brokers now phoned and wired their customers to ask for more margin—more cash. By this time certain stocks had fallen so low in value that banks, which held the certificates as collateral, were insisting they had to have more cash to maintain the collateral. For the first time the squeeze was felt by those speculators who had elected to stay in the market.

On Sunday, October 20, newspapers proclaimed that the worst was over and predicted that the next day the market would start getting organized support. This phrase "organized support" implied that big bankers would rush to the rescue, and people turned to the phrase like worshipers hypnotized by an icon. However, that Sunday morning, many American ministers preached about the nation's moral decline. Dr. Harry Emerson Fosdick called this a "money-mad generation." One pastor noted that in his daily paper he had found five of eight columns on the front page devoted to stories of fraud or other dishonest business practices.

On Monday, October 21, the morning edition of the *Wall Street Journal* said that the professionals in Wall Street were as "bearish" as they had been at any time thus far in this year. At 10 A.M. trading began with such a rush that only ten minutes later the stock ticker fell behind transactions. In those days the ticker, a telegraphic instrument that prints stock quotations, could tap out a mere 285 symbols per minute. Prices fell 2 to 10 points for active stocks and as much as 145 for inactive stocks. The 6,091,870 shares traded this day constituted the third greatest daily volume in exchange history. The New York *Times* said that the drop in stock prices was due to the readjustment of prices to a level more commensurate with earnings, unanswered margin calls, foreign liquidation, hammering by bears and terror among shareholders.

In the past, as prices rose in the bull market, the ticker had fallen behind several times, and speculators often had had to wait until long after the close of the market to learn just how much money they had made. Now it was a different story. This was the first time since the previous March that the machine had lagged behind falling values. Now the plungers discovered to their dismay that hours would pass before they learned how much poorer they had become. Not until 4:40 P.M., 100 minutes after the end of the day's trading, did the ticker record the last transaction.

At the beginning of this disastrous day, brokers' loans had stood at an all-time high of $6.8 billion. And throughout the day, as the market sagged, the harried brokers had called for more margin. This appeal antagonized some Chicago gangsters who had been speculating; they dynamited the home of the manager of a brokerage credit department and threw stink bombs into three brokerage offices. A Chicago police official said: "A new kind of wolf has invaded La Salle Street—the racketeer who replies with a bomb when called on for more margin."

On Tuesday, October 22, Professor Irving Fisher spoke up again: "Even in the present high market the prices of stock have not caught up with their real values. Yesterday's break was a shaking out of the lunatic fringe that attempts to speculate on margin." In his column Arthur Brisbane sneered: "Many earnest little lambs, when the ticker stopped, might have been mistaken for hairless Mexican dogs, shaved off." Roger Babson, predicting even further lows, urged people to sell their stocks and buy gold. And Charles E. Mitchell, landing in New York, told reporters that the decline had gone too far, but he was sure the market was fundamentally sound and would correct itself. On the exchange this Tuesday stocks rose 1 to 16 points but ran off at the close of trading.

The *Wall Street Journal* commented: "The stock market has had a very bad break, the most severe in a number of years. There may be some stocks that are still selling too high on the basis of selling price times earnings, but on the other hand there are numbers of stocks that are now selling at attractive prices. . . . There is a vast amount of money awaiting investment. Thousands of traders and investors have been waiting for an opportunity to buy stocks on just such a break as had occurred over the last several weeks, and this buying, in time, will change the trend of the market."

On Wednesday, October 23, investors living in the nation's interior were cut off from their Manhattan brokers when an ice- and windstorm felled telephone and telegraph lines in the Midwest. Over the radio, however, they heard the bad news: The industrial average had fallen 31 points, and stock prices had crashed 5 to 96 points. This 96-point drop was suffered by Adams Express, an investment trust that had been acquired in April by the Chase National Bank of New York.

Except for the storm-silenced plungers, frantic speculators in other parts of the nation ordered their brokers to sell. Prosperity began falling apart as the volume of liquidation mounted hour by hour. Federal Reserve officials in Washington expressed surprise, nervously studied the reports, talked of lowering the discount rate to halt the decline, did nothing. In the final hour of trading a phenomenal 2,600,000 shares of stocks changed hands on rapidly declining prices, and total sales for the day came to 6,374,960 shares. This time the ticker lagged 104 minutes in its efforts to make instant records of all transactions on the floor of the exchange. A total of $4 billion was lost on the New York Stock Exchange, while the nationwide loss came to $6 billion.

If $1 billion in $10 bills were laid end to end across the United States, they would form an endless line stretching from New York to San Francisco, back and forth, more than three times.

That Wednesday afternoon Huey Long, the governor of Louisiana, was lounging in the lobby of the Roosevelt Hotel in New Orleans. A New Orleans bank president rushed up to him and cried: "Governor! Hell's broken loose! The biggest crash of everything you've ever seen! It's going to be sixty days before this country will get back to normal."

Long, who stood on the threshold of national fame, turned to the banker and replied: "I've been expecting this crash for three years. It is here for many, many years. It can't end until there is a redistribution of wealth. Make your plans on that basis."

That night, in New York, brokers and bankers met in hotels and speakeasies to discuss the day's events and swap rumors. Some felt that the government would step in and take a hand. Others thought that the exchange might shut down until fear vanished. Still others, their optimism shaken, now predicted that the United States faced the worst financial crisis in its history.

*   *   *

In a figurative sense the country had become a vast theater holding an audience of millions of Americans about to witness a tragedy played out to its bitter end. Stage center was the main building of the New York Stock Exchange, located on the south side of Wall Street between New and Broad Streets. Fronting on Broad Street, completed in 1903 at a cost of $3 million, this ten-story structure was made of white Georgia marble. Its imposing façade resembled a Greek temple. On the exterior, six Corinthian columns rose five stories high, topped by a pediment, where eleven white marble figures loomed, symbolizing American commerce and industry. The central statue, a robed woman with outstretched hands, represented Integrity.

Many green speculators did not really understand the nature and function of the New York Stock Exchange. In point of fact, the exchange is a privately owned institution that simply provides a marketplace, or auction house, for people wishing to trade stocks and bonds. It owns no stocks, buys no stocks, sells no stocks. It just brings buyers and sellers together. It sets no prices. Its sole purpose is to provide a common meeting place for those who wish to buy and those who wish to sell. They set their own prices through competitive bidding. When most people buy, the market rises; when most sell, the market falls. At any given moment the price of a given stock or the prices of all stocks represent the combined judgment of everyone in the market.

In 1929 membership in the exchange was limited to individual brokers or brokerage firms that were partnerships; only later were corporations allowed to become member firms. A broker, of course, is an agent for buyers and sellers of securities. (After the Crash, Alexander Woollcott quipped that a broker is a man who takes your fortune and runs it into a shoestring.) Soon after seats first went on sale in 1868, they were priced as low as $500. In 1922 the cost of a seat, which gives a member the right to trade securities on the exchange floor, varied from $86,000 to $100,000. An all-time record price of $625,000 was paid for one seat on the exchange in February, 1929.

Exchange members occupied physical seats in the past, but by 1929 these resting places had long since been discarded. Nonetheless, by tradition a membership continued to be known as a seat. Total membership was limited to 1,375 men—men, not women, for in the Twenties no woman was allowed to trade on the floor. Not this many men actually held seats at the same time, however; on active trading days perhaps 900 brokers were on the floor. This trading floor, felt-padded in those days, had walls 86 feet high and was one of the largest rooms in the world—140 feet long and 115 feet wide—about two-thirds the size of a football field. The only real seats on the floor were clerks' stools.

The clerks sat inside twelve trading posts shaped like horseshoes. Along the center of the trading floor three pairs of these posts stood with their open ends almost touching, so that they resembled bronze stockades. The other six counters, or posts, were lined up along the two long sides of an annex, commonly called the garage, which had been opened in 1922. About seventy-five different stocks were bought and sold at each post, which displayed signs identifying them. Brokers stood along the rims of the posts, signaling bids and acceptances to one another and scribbling figures on slips of paper. Groups of unenclosed telephone booths, ten phones to a booth, stood along the edges of the huge floor. Brokers wore business suits with white badges identifying them, while their employees and Stock Exchange reporters wore regulation jackets and different badges.

The room was poorly lighted. Its east and west sides had windows 50 feet high and 96 feet wide. However, an eighteen-story building across the street to the west shut out much of the daylight, while a massive gold curtain across the eastern windows dulled light from that source. Electrical fixtures were old and inadequate. The north and south walls had big annunciator boards—electrical-mechanical devices for paging members wanted off the floor. Each member had been assigned a call number. If a broker's office wanted to get in touch with him, a card bearing his number was slapped loudly and repeatedly against one or the other of the two huge boards. An American flag hung over the north entrance to the room, along with the blue banner of the state of New York. A visitors' gallery stretched across the full length of the east wall, overlooking the entire scene.

*   *   *

On Thursday, October 24, 1929, the New York *Times* reported the previous day's trading in a front-page two-column headline that said:

PRICES OF STOCKS CRASH
IN HEAVY LIQUIDATION;
TOTAL DROP OF BILLIONS

The *Times* and other morning papers published Washington dispatches quoting treasury officials as saying that the market break had been due to speculation and did not represent any basic weakness in American business.

It was a cloudy day with the temperature in the low 50's and a light wind blowing from the northwest, so brokers and bankers wore topcoats to work. At 9:45 A.M. on the dot, as he did each business day, Otto Kahn stepped out of a limousine in front of his office at 52 William Street, one block east of the exchange. Kahn was senior partner of the renowned banking firm of Kuhn, Loeb & Company. Some said he had the slowest gait and the quickest mind in New York. Still a dandy at the age of sixty-two,

Kahn was a handsome man with white hair, a gray waxed mustache and intense dark eyes. He wore an English-tailored suit, stiff collar, gray spats, a carefully folded handkerchief peeping from his breast pocket, and a fresh boutonniere in his lapel. The faint calm smile on his face was somehow comforting to sallow red-eyed brokers who had slept little and now dreaded the day ahead.

When the clock on the west wall of the trading room struck ten, Superintendent William B. Crawford hit the gong to signal the opening of trading. Brokers rushed toward the posts clutching handfuls of customers' orders. Orders to sell. After holding firm for a few minutes, most stocks began declining. The securities were not sold in small lots but in huge blocks; they were being dumped into the market. Six thousand shares of Montgomery Ward sold at 83 points; earlier in the year this stock went for 156. Twenty thousand shares of Kennecott Copper were sold. So enormous was the volume of trading that by 10:30 A.M. the ticker was fifteen minutes behind. This lag was confusing, for spreads of up to 30 points developed between prices quoted on the floor and those recorded on the tardy tape.

By 11 A.M. all was panic. Prices were plunging 5, 10, even 15 points a minute. It seemed that everyone was scrambling to sell at whatever price he could get. On this spectacular day 1,100 brokers and 1,000 assistants thronged the trading floor and clustered about the trading posts, shouting and signaling. They were doing their best to handle the thousands upon thousands of selling orders that poured into Wall Street. Brokers feverishly made long-distance calls the length and breadth of America to demand margin, more margin, from their customers.

By this date the Marx Brothers had taken their show *Animal Crackers* to Baltimore, and during the morning a telephone call awakened Groucho Marx in his Baltimore hotel room. It was his broker.

"Sorry to disturb you," said the broker, "but there's been a little slump in the market and I'll have to ask you for more margin."

Groucho, who thought he was worth $240,000 in securities, asked in disbelief: "Margin? What kind of a slump *is* it? I thought I had everything covered so nothing could touch it."

"Well-ll-l," the broker replied, "it's sort of a . . . a crisis. . . . I don't know how much longer I can hold out."

The same bad news was radioed to the Cunard liner *Berengaria,* a day's run east of New York on a return voyage from England. She carried 1,414 passengers, many of whom had been playing the stock market. They now jammed the brokerage office set up on shipboard by Michael J. Meehan, and those unable to edge inside stood dejectedly just outside the door. The ones inside and up front watched the flying fingers of the board boy as he chalked the latest quotation on a blackboard. One trembling woman lost $160,000 in the first few hours of trading; later she recovered all but $40,000 of this sum. These shipboard passengers, so far from the center of action, traded almost 20,000 shares of stocks—with most of them losing.

City editors of New York newspapers pulled reporters and feature writers off routine assignments and sent them running toward Wall Street. One, a reporter for the United Press, was a thin-faced young man who had just moved to the big city, had only $10 to his name and knew nothing at all about financial news. He was told to go to an office at 111 Broadway, interview an important banker named Frank Vanderlip and find out what the whole thing meant. The reporter's name was H. Allen Smith, and in years to come he won fame as a humorist; but on this October 24, 1929, he saw nothing funny about his responsibility in reporting a crisis. Vanderlip, who took pity on Smith's ignorance, told him: "The fact of the matter is that I don't know what it means, either, my friends don't know what it means, and probably nobody knows what it means."

With bedlam developing inside the exchange and crowds gathering on the streets outside, Police Commissioner Grover Whalen decided to send police reinforcements to the scene. In the previous few days 60 detectives and 50 uniformed cops had been stationed in and around Wall Street. Whalen now dispatched an extra 100 detectives, 400 patrolmen and a detail of mounted men.

As newsreelmen set up their cameras at strategic points near the exchange, throngs before its doors swapped wild rumors. Word was passed that the Chicago and Buffalo exchanges had closed—which was untrue. Eleven big speculators were supposed to have killed themselves. When a repairman appeared on the high roof of a nearby building, people on the pavement murmured that he had lost a fortune and was about to jump. Ambulances were reported en route to other buildings where men allegedly had shot themselves. Sight-seeing buses abandoned their scheduled routes and detoured to Wall Street to see the excitement.

By 11:30 A.M., with the ticker forty-eight minutes behind, hysteria gripped the traders on the exchange floor, and panic rolled in waves from New York to California. The crisis was beyond belief. Twenty thousand shares of Du Pont stock were dumped on the market, but there was no bid. Minute after tingling minute not a single sale was made. Nobody wanted to buy. Everybody wanted to sell, sell, sell. Only after certain stocks fell to ridiculously low prices did some daring men purchase them.

At 12 noon reporters saw three prominent bankers enter J. P. Morgan's private bank at 23 Wall Street, just across the street from the exchange. They were Charles E. Mitchell, chairman of the National City Bank; Albert H. Wiggin, chairman of the Chase National Bank; and William Potter, president of the Guaranty Trust Company. Sidewalk gawkers did not recognize these men, but reporters shouted their names and titles to one another.

Morgan's bank was a squat, five-story gray building worth nearly $6 million—double the cost of the main building of the New York Stock

Exchange. With the great Morgan himself vacationing in Great Britain, the other bankers had been summoned by the senior Morgan partner, Thomas Lamont. Already present inside the bank was Seward Prosser, chairman of the Morgan firm, and the group was later joined by George F. Baker, Jr., chairman of the First National Bank of New York. Bernard Baruch had been invited to attend this meeting, but he stayed away because he thought he smelled a rat.

The emergency meeting of these influential bankers was called to order by Lamont in his small private office on the second floor of the Morgan bank. One of the most powerful men in the United States, Thomas W. Lamont at the age of fifty-nine was a renowned international banker, spokesman for the Morgan firm, diplomat, writer, editor, publisher, politician and statesman who was often consulted by Presidents, prime ministers and governors of European central banks. He was short and slender, slightly stooped, with gray hair. He did not always mask his emotions, as did many bankers, but had a highly expressive face. At all times he was charming and courteous.

Lamont now sat at the antique Italian table that served as his desk. The walls of his office were paneled in dark oak, and the north wall, overlooking Wall Street, was pierced by two windows containing small transparencies of the glass in Chartres Cathedral. Above the fireplace hung an oil painting of the 1813 engagement between the *Chesapeake* and the *Shannon;* only a little while before this critical day Lamont had paid $400,000 for another precious painting.

After he greeted his fellow bankers, who took their places in highbacked, carved and uncomfortable chairs, the first thing Lamont did was to telephone the White House and ask President Hoover to issue a reassuring statement. This was an ironic reversal of roles. Earlier in the year, when Hoover sent a personal emissary to Wall Street to ask the bankers to admit that the market was unsound, Lamont had rejected the President's appeal. Hoover later wrote in his memoirs that "Thomas Lamont of Morgan's wrote me a long memorandum which makes curious reading today."

Aware of the sickening crisis on the floor of the exchange, the six bankers decided to form a coalition to pump new life into the dying market. This they did by forming a pool, with each pledging $40 million for a total of $240 million. An additional $100 million was supplied by other financial firms, including the Guggenheim Brothers and James Speyer and Company. It was by far the largest concentration of pool buying power ever directed at the stock market. The bankers did not seek to establish any particular price level in the market. What they wanted to do was to indulge in a bold psychological gesture to end the panic—and protect themselves.

This strategy was agreed on in a mere twenty minutes. The bankers understood that to make a success of this pool, unlike other pools, they needed all the publicity they could get. As the other grim-faced financiers hurried back to their own offices, Lamont walked down one flight to the lobby of the Morgan bank, where he faced reporters. His expression serious, but his voice calm, Lamont announced to the press that "there has been a little distress selling on the Stock Exchange." This understatement has since become a Wall Street classic. Distress selling means a feverish wish to sell at any price. However, Lamont continued, this selling was "due to a technical condition of the market," rather than to any fundamental trouble. He was sure that things were "susceptible to betterment."

During the morning the frenetic action on the floor of the exchange drew 722 sightseers to the visitors' gallery, where their excited cries added to the deafening noise in the big room. At 12:30 P.M. these people were ushered out, and the gallery was closed. Among those who had been watching was a visiting Englishman, Winston Churchill, who recently had resigned as Great Britain's chancellor of the exchequer.

By 1 P.M., with the ticker now ninety-two minutes behind, stock values had shrunk a total of about $11 billion, and the newly formed bankers' pool was about to swing into action. E. H. H. Simmons, the president of the New York Stock Exchange, was far away in Hawaii on his honeymoon. In his absence, Lamont and the other bankers had chosen the vice-president, Richard Whitney, to make their move. Whitney was about to have his hour of glory.

At 1:15 P.M. he sauntered out onto the floor. Because Whitney was seldom seen there, because word of the bankers' emergency meeting had seeped into the exchange and because everyone could guess his mission, brokers gasped when they saw him. Debonair, almost jaunty, Whitney shouldered his way through the masses of men and up to trading post No. 2, where United States Steel was sold. When trading had begun in the morning, Steel had started at 205½, a point or two above the previous day's closing. During the day it sank to a low of 193½, and minutes before Whitney's appearance it had been hovering around 195.

In a loud and confident voice, Whitney now offered to buy 25,000 shares of Steel at 205—or 10 points *above* the asking price. This *beau geste,* this expression of confidence in the market, was so heartening to brokers that they burst into cheers. Order clerks shouted the electrifying news through direct-wire telephones to every brokerage house in New York, and within seconds it was relayed to every corner of the nation. The big bankers had made their move. They were protecting the market. The longed-for organized support had come to the rescue in the nick of time.

Then and there, Whitney bought 200 shares of United States Steel, leaving the balance of his order with a specialist—an exchange member who executes orders given him by other brokers. With all eyes following him, Whitney then moved on to other trading posts, purchasing other stocks in blocks of 10,000 and 20,000 shares. Inside half an hour he bought 200,000 shares of various securities at a cost to the bankers' pool of more than $20 million.

By 2 P.M. the market had taken a vigorous upward turn. Although some selling continued, Whitney's grandstand play seemed to have stemmed the panic. Stock prices rallied. General Electric, for example, bounced back 25 points. At the end of the day's trading, United States Steel closed at 206.

At 3 P.M., with the ringing of the gong, trading ended. Brokers leaned wearily against trading posts, their collars torn, their faces wet with sweat. A record-breaking total of 12,894,650 shares had been traded, and the industrial average was down a little more than 12 points. The ticker had fallen so far behind transactions that it did not stop chattering until 7:08½ P.M., more than four hours after the exchange closed for the day.

Only then could the magnitude of the disaster be calculated. All day long the exchange's telephone system had been clogged with calls from speculators eager to learn where they stood. Thousands of small investors now heard that they had been wiped out. In one small community in upper New York State 108 of 150 families had been playing the market on margin; now only 6 of these families had any securities left. Thousands of brokerage and bank accounts, prosperous a mere week earlier, had been wrecked.

Elliott V. Bell, a young financial writer for the New York *Times,* dropped in to see a vice-president of one of the larger banks in New York. The financier was walking back and forth in his office. Looking up, he said: "Well, Elliott, I thought I was a millionaire a few days ago. Now I find I'm looking through the wrong end of the telescope." Laughing bitterly, he added: "We'll get those bastards that did this yet!" The reporter never did find out what "bastards" he meant but later learned that the vice-president was not merely broke but hopelessly in debt.

In Washington a furious Senator Carter Glass snarled: "The present trouble is due largely to Charles E. Mitchell's activities! That man—more than forty others—is responsible for the present situation. Had the Federal Reserve acted and dismissed him, the trouble might be less. The crash has shown that stock gambling has reached its limit."

In New York, Mitchell himself commented: "This reaction has badly outrun itself."

In London, British economist John Maynard Keynes declared that the market break would benefit the world because it would liquidate unsound speculation. Keynes argued that credit which had been absorbed by the market now would be freed for the use of industry, and commodity prices would recover.

But this was theory. Reality, crushing reality, had broken over the heads of thousands upon thousands of Americans, who stared at tickers in their brokers' offices until the end of the business day, then slumped in chairs, their faces gray, too stunned and exhausted to get to their feet to stagger home. On Wall Street itself, lights blazed in windows of tall office buildings as overworked clerks and bookkeepers pawed their way through mountains of papers in an effort to catch up with the day's transactions. Hundreds of thousands of shares of stock also had to be earmarked for sale the next day. The workers fainted at their desks. Runners fell exhausted on the marble floors of banks and slept. Others, like fellow passengers on a sinking ship, indulged in a kind of frenetic gaiety of despair. Some messengers and boardroom boys, high on excitement they understood only dimly, frolicked along the sidewalks until cops were called to quiet them. The boys were given short and stern lectures: This was no Roman holiday but a national disaster! Hadn't they heard the news from Seattle about the secretary of a finance company who had shot himself to death?

*   *   *

On Friday, October 25, the New York *Times* published a front-page story under this four-column headline:

WORST STOCK CRASH STEMMED BY BANKS;
12,894,650-SHARE DAY SWAMPS MARKET;
LEADERS CONFER, FIND CONDITIONS SOUND

The New York *World* published an eight-column streamer that said:

NATION'S FINANCIERS DECLARE SECURITY PANIC HAS NO ECONOMIC BASIS

President Hoover, as requested, had issued a statement saying in part: "The fundamental business of the country—that is, the production and distribution of goods and services—is on a sound and prosperous basis." Years later, in his memoirs, Hoover explained his reasoning: "Obviously, as President, I had no business to make things worse in the middle of a crash. Loath to speak of the stock market, I offered as encouragement a short statement on our progress in the productive system and the long-view strength of the country."

Secretary of the Treasury Andrew W. Mellon declined comment.

During the night various newspapers had obtained from financial and industrial leaders a series of statements—all of them reassuring. Arthur W. Loasby, president of the Equitable Trust Company, said emphatically: "There will be no repetition of the break yesterday. I have no fear of another comparable decline." Walter C. Teagle, president of the Standard Oil Company of New Jersey, said: "There has been no fundamental change in the petroleum industry." Arthur Reynolds, chairman of the Continental Illinois Bank of Chicago, said: "This crash is not going to have much effect on business."

A somewhat different note was struck by Governor Franklin D. Roosevelt in a talk before members of a churchmen's club in Poughkeepsie, New York. In what may have been his first public expression of concern over speculation, Roosevelt said: "It is not good for anyone to go too far on the theory of getting something for nothing. . . . Much of the activity of the stock market is legitimate and proper, but in some cases improper schemes and questionable methods have been used in stock promotion, and many investors have lost sight of the real purpose of the exchange in a fever of old-fashioned speculation." Then, using words he probably later wished to eat, Roosevelt declared that business morality was improving.

Will Rogers, writing his syndicated column from Waynoka, Oklahoma, said: "What does the sensational collapse of Wall Street mean? Nothing. Why, if the cows of this country failed to come up and get milked one night it would be more of a panic than if Morgan and Lamont had never held a meeting. Why, an old sow and litter of pigs make more people a living than all the steel and General Motors stock combined. Why, the whole 120,000,000 of us are more dependent on the cackling of a hen than if the Stock Exchange was turned into a night club."

Arthur Brisbane, in his own syndicated column, correctly predicted that the big bankers would be praised. M. C. Brush, president of the American International Corporation, said publicly: "I think we are all indebted to the four gentlemen who met on the corner yesterday and through their action steadied the whole situation." Brokers and newspapers spoke gratefully of "the Big Six" as "the Saviors of the Market."

Time magazine called this a "financially historic moment for Hero Richard Whitney." Seven months later, when Whitney was elevated to president of the Stock Exchange, worshipful brokers gave him a souvenir— Trading Post No. 2, the Steel post where he had begun rallying the market. He had it installed in the lobby of his Broad Street office, where it became a Wall Street landmark.

In point of fact, the bankers' pool failed to save the market but did save the big boys themselves. They did not use all their $340 million to place a floor under falling prices. They did give temporary support to such market leaders as United States Steel, then quietly fed back into the market nearly all the shares they had bought—at a fair profit to themselves.

All day long on that Friday, October 25, the market was orderly and temperate, with a total of 5,923,220 shares being traded. Some foolhardy speculators bought wildly in the hope of getting stocks at bargain prices, touching off a mild upswing that continued throughout the day, with only a few declines. For the most part, however, trading proceeded at an even pace. Thirty-five of the largest brokerage houses on the exchange, which did 70 percent of all trading there, had wired clients all over the country predicting that the market would recover quickly.

On Saturday, October 26, eighty-five newspapers across the land published paid advertisements prepared by the house of Hornblower and Weeks recommending the purchase of "sound securities." Alfred P. Sloan, Jr., president of General Motors, called the decline in stock prices beneficial to the market. Arthur Brisbane said: "No buildings were burned down, no industries have died, no mines, railroads, fields have vanished. Paper profits have been reduced to scraps of ticker tape. That's all!" He had a point. Although October 24, 1929, had been the eleventh day of overt panic on the stock market since Black Friday of 1869, it was the first one that had occurred without major business failures. However, on this Saturday, the market weakened again.

On Sunday, October 27, ministers across the land preached sermons suggesting that greedy people had suffered divine retribution for their sins. Too many Americans had lost sight of spiritual values in their lust for wordly goods. The Right Reverend Frank Theodore Woods, Bishop of Winchester, England, made a guest appearance in a New York church and declared from its pulpit that "the gambling craze practically means an attempt to get something for nothing—to secure a far higher reward for an investment than it really deserves." A different sentiment came from some worshipers who bowed their heads in churches to offer prayers of thanks for the bankers who had saved the market.

*   *   *

Monday, October 28, opened with rumors about a gigantic backlog of buying orders that had piled up over the weekend. The morning papers carried still more advertisements by brokers advising smart people to pick up stock bargains while they could. All these heartening words meant nothing, though, for the moment the Stock Exchange opened at 10 A.M. utter panic erupted.

Not buying orders but selling orders had accumulated. Country bankers had decided to liquidate their holdings, and individual speculators simply refused to believe the reassuring statements. Brokers soon learned that once again thousands of their customers wanted to sell at any price, however low, just to get out of the market. Margin accounts became exhausted as commission men sent out other frantic calls for more cash.

By this time the Marx Brothers had taken their show to Pittsburgh. That Monday morning Harpo Marx's 35,000 shares of stock were worth an average of $72 per share—or so he thought. Harpo's broker wired from New York to Pittsburgh: FORCED TO SELL ALL HOLDINGS UNLESS RECEIVE CHECK FOR $15,000 TO COVER MARGINS. Harpo scraped together $15,000, sent it to his broker and prayed that he had survived the crisis.

Franklin P. Adams went to his office in the New York *World* and found "great turmoil over the descending prices of stock, the turmoil being so great that one journalist did ask for my opinon, which made me laugh albeit my heart was breaking. So Alison Smith comes [*sic*] to my office, and hearing somebody say something about the stock of A.T. & T., said that she thought she could make a fortune in American Kiss & Tell, which I thought to nominate for the Wheeze-of-the-month."

AT&T sank 34 points, General Electric 48, and Westinghouse 34. Alfred P. Sloan, Jr., changed his mind about the benefit of stock declines as General Motors lost nearly $2 billion in paper values. United States Steel dropped 18 points, but on this fearsome Monday Richard Whitney did not step forward to bolster Steel and other key stocks as he had done the previous Thursday.

At 1:10 P.M., however, Whitney was seen entering the Morgan bank, and seconds later this supposedly good news was flashed over the stock market ticker. On the strength of this information alone, Steel bounced back 4 points, only to drop again when Whitney failed to appear on the trading floor. The anticipated help was not forthcoming. Anxiety spread. Had the big bankers abandoned the market to its fate?

The ticker lagged farther behind as prices kept falling. Arthur Curtiss James, chairman of the Western Pacific Railroad Company, was losing millions, but he sat in his estate in the posh resort town of Newport, Rhode Island, playing Mah-Jongg and manifesting no concern whatsoever. Trading on the exchange ended at 3 P.M. as usual, but the ticker was so far behind that only 167 minutes later was the last quotation printed, revealing the magnitude of the disaster. The total volume of 9,212,000 shares traded was less than on the previous Thursday, but prices had dropped lower. Sixteen leading issues were down $2.8 billion, while the total loss in stock values was estimated at between $10 billion and $14 billion.

At 4:30 P.M. that same Monday afternoon the big bankers who had been hailed as the saviors of the market gathered again in the Morgan bank and conferred for two hours. They had been joined by Owen D. Young, an influential corporation lawyer, and C. A. Austin, president of the Equitable Trust Company of New York. After these financiers finished talking, Thomas Lamont released a press statement declaring that the situation "retained hopeful features"—but without indicating what they were. The handout went on to say that the bankers had never intended to maintain any particular price level or protect anyone's profits. They had hoped to stabilize prices by creating an orderly market—one in which offers would be met by bids at some price or other.

This statement was weak tea for faltering men. Were these bankers the brave lions they had seemed to be at first, or were they skulking jackals waiting for the kill? Now, for the first time, their reputations started to decline, and so, by extension, did the reputations of all bankers, once so lordly. That evening the financial world crawled with ugly rumor.

Governor Roosevelt was in Springfield, Massachusetts, attending a banquet given in his honor by the Western Massachusetts Democratic Club. A telegram arrived, addressed to Roosevelt and signed by Alfred E. Smith, his friend, fellow Democrat and former governor of New York. It was read aloud: WILL THEY BLAME THE STOCK MARKET ON THE DEM-

OCRATS? Roosevelt was puzzled, for this did not sound like the sort of thing Al Smith would say. The telegram was a hoax.

*   *   *

Then came Tuesday, October 29, 1929.

The weather was on the chilly side, the sky partly cloudy and the temperature averaging 44 degrees. New Yorkers read in their morning papers that the great George M. Cohan could be seen at the Fulton Theater in his new play called *Gambling*. William Randolph Hearst's friend Marion Davies was appearing on the screen of the Capitol Theater in *Marianne,* billed as "M-G-M's greatest of all talking, musical pictures." Up in the Bronx movie star John Gilbert's latest film, *His Glorious Night,* was being shown at Loew's Paradise.

At 10 A.M., when trading opened on the New York Stock Exchange, it was hit by a tidal wave of selling. Never had the nation seen such a fury of liquidation. Obviously, the big speculators were now scrambling to get out of the market, for at first most of the trading consisted of huge blocks of 5,000 and even 50,000 shares. Regardless of price, these were unloaded like so many bales of hay.

By 10:20 A.M. the ticker was six minutes late. Corporations and out-of-town bankers wanted to convert their securities into cash amounting to billions of dollars. Housewives who had speculated with the grocery money wanted to liquidate before their husbands discovered what they had done. Bookkeepers who had embezzled company funds to play the market were frantic lest they lose all, be discovered, go to jail.

By 10:30 A.M. a total of 3,259,800 shares had been traded. This alone was almost a full day's work for the exchange. As the figure appeared on the ticker tape uncurling from inverted glass bowls in brokerage houses and newspaper offices, men involuntarily whistled in amazement. Bending over a ticker in the city room of the New York *World,* Franklin P. Adams reflected that it is more fascinating to be an observer of the news when things are going badly than when they are going well. Samuel Cahan, a staff artist for the *World,* grabbed pencils and pens and sped to the floor of the exchange to sketch the historic scene. Claude A. Jagger, filling in as financial editor of the New York *Times,* sent squads of reporters galloping to Wall Street.

It would be misleading to imply that *all* Americans were concerned with the crisis on Wall Street, for they were not. One eighteen-year-old college freshman, a self-proclaimed sheik in the parlance of that era, wrote that day in his diary: "I took Clyda to Workshop to see three plays presented, two of which had Kappa Sigs in the leading roles. It was drizzling a trifle when we got out, but we walked a few minutes and then took to our favorite bench. Here I grasped her to me to kiss her repeatedly. . . ." Twenty-five-year-old J. Robert Oppenheimer, a brilliant physicist, was so intent on his own theories that he read no newspapers, had no telephone and did not learn about the Crash until the spring of 1930.

Here and there across the nation ordinary folks, as well as unusual people, lived their daily lives as ever, unaware that prosperity was coming apart at the seams. The bull market was dying. A nation was trying to sell out. The country's financial structure was tumbling down. From the swamps of Louisiana to the timberland of Oregon, from New England hamlets to Miami Beach hotels, big and little speculators rushed to telephones and to Western Union offices to order their brokers to sell, sell, sell—sell at any price, however low! The New York Telephone Company recorded 11,000 more calls than on a normal Tuesday. Western Union reported that telegraphic traffic between the Far West and New York was up almost 300 percent. Transatlantic telephone messages more than doubled, as Americans vacationing in Europe and financiers living in Asian capitals tried to get out of the market before it was too late.

On the floor of the New York Stock Exchange frenzied brokers milled about, fought their way to trading posts, sought bids. There were almost no buyers. The visitors' gallery was still closed, empty. The volume of trading was immensely greater than on the previous Black Thursday. At noon a few clerks, sneaking out for a quick bite, yelled to people on the street that in the first two hours of business more than 8,000,000 shares had been exchanged. Police Commissioner Whalen had sent still more policemen to the financial district, where a few political speakers were now haranguing the crowds.

Although brokers had solicited business from women, they considered women poor losers. Elderly ladies now jammed uptown brokerage offices, and when they learned of the developing debacle, they turned on their brokers, blaming them for everything. One old woman wearing four rings on one hand and smoking gold-tipped cigarettes taken from a jewel-studded gold case stalked about announcing in a brassy voice that she had lost $10,000. She seemed almost proud of the fact.

Four other women left in a chauffeur-driven limousine to visit one commission house after another on upper Broadway, making a social occasion of a national disaster. At each office they would enter regally and parade to positions from which they could see the latest quotations and stare about haughtily. All wore the rimless helmet-shaped hats then in fashion. One of the proud ladies let it be known that she had dropped $15,000, raked the room with disdainful eyes and remarked: "This place is depressing." The quartet then departed to descend upon another office.

A businessman took to the radio to warn Congress against making any "ill-advised" moves against the nation's various stock exchanges. Members of the Federal Reserve Board sat in continuous session in Washington, not even breaking for lunch. Treasury Secretary Mellon, an ex officio member of the board, attended the early part of the meeting and then left for the White House to attend a Cabinet meeting. Washington correspondents were unable to learn whether the market situation was discussed by President Hoover and the Cabinet members.

On Wall Street one of the vital questions was whether to shut the Stock Exchange. This action had been considered and then rejected on Friday, October 25. Some brokers felt that the present day's frenzy was due to the fact that word had leaked out about closing the exchange. By now, however, hysteria was sweeping the country, the market had gone out of control, and order was dissolving into chaos. A decision to close the exchange could be made only by that institution's governing committee of about forty members.

Beginning at noon, committee members slipped away from the trading floor in twos and threes, hoping their absence would not be noted in the excitement. They did not go to their usual conference room, gathering instead in the office of the president of the Stock Clearing Corporation, directly below the big room. This office was too small to accommodate all of them easily, so some sat or stood on tables. They lit cigarettes with shaking hands, took a drag or two, ground them out, lit up again. Every few minutes they heard that certain stocks had dropped to new lows. Even so, they decided that to close the exchange would only aggravate an already critical situation.

Another noon meeting of grave importance was in progress elsewhere. Once again members of the bankers' coalition met in the House of Morgan. All were agitated by the fact that the exchange floor was rife with rumors that they were selling, rather than buying. Aware that these reports were being believed, the bankers feared for their reputations. They admitted to one another that their pool was falling apart. Very well, then, since they were unable to continue to prop up the prices of selected stocks, at least they could try to maintain some semblance of order, beat an orderly retreat. On into the day the bankers debated how to do this.

By 1:30 P.M. of this October 29 a total of 12,652,000 shares had been traded on the disintegrating exchange, and early editions of New York's afternoon papers reported the growing calamity. On the Bowery, a few blocks north of the financial district, some ragged bums got the idea that stocks were selling at a nickel a share, so they panhandled some money, pooled their coins as the bankers had pooled their millions, and descended upon Wall Street with the intention of investing in the future of America. This ragged individualism was thwarted by hard-faced cops, who turned them away.

The panhandlers were not too far off in their evaluation of the crisis. White Sewing Machine stock, which had hit a high of 48 in the previous months, had closed at 11 the night before and now sank to almost nothing. Nobody bid for White stock, except a bright messenger boy who worked for the exchange. He offered to pay $1 a share and immediately was given a chance to purchase 10,000 shares.

Various attempts were made to restore confidence. Jimmy Walker, the city's playboy mayor who always spent more than he earned, showed up in the Hotel Astor at a meeting of film exhibitors and begged them to "show pictures which will reinstate courage and hope in the hearts of people." John J. Raskob of General Motors declared that now was the time to buy stock at bargain prices. State Superintendent of Insurance Albert Conway urged firms under his jurisdiction to buy common stocks. United States Steel and the American Can Company declared extra dividends of $1 per share. But all these gestures were as futile as King Canute's command to the tide to stay away from his royal feet.

The floor of the Stock Exchange had become a bubbling caldron of confusion. Brokers frantically wigwagged hand signals to one another, sweat staining the armpits of their jackets. Afraid of losing collateral, they mauled one another to close in on the few buyers who appeared. They tore at one another's hair and coat lapels. They lost shoes and glasses and false teeth. They thronged the trading posts like college boys storming the goalposts at the end of a football game. They gathered in agitated knots, made frenzied deals, broke apart. They scurried to and from conferences. Whenever another key stock sank to a new low, here and there a trader collapsed and fell to the floor. All was bedlam. The uproar sounded different to different people. Some said it reminded them of the roar of lions, others the yowling of tigers, still others the yelping of hyenas. One witness to the day's insanity was a seventeen-year-old coupon clerk named Art Linkletter, who later became a famous television personality. Another was a twenty-year-old assistant in a brokerage house, Everett Sloane, who developed into a distinguished movie and television character actor.

By 2:10 P.M., with 13,838,000 shares already traded, prices were plummeting so fast that even brokers on the floor could not keep track of the situation. Mistakes multiplied as everyone reached the breaking point. One customer was sold out twice. Orders to sell were stacked up so high in brokers' offices that clerks fell two hours behind in the mere task of telephoning them to the floor. Under this avalanche of selling, accounting systems failed and communications systems ruptured. Many commission houses hired boys just to untangle telephone cords on trading tables. One firm thought it had gone bankrupt, only to learn later than an exhausted clerk had made a mathematical error. Women workers fainted and were sent home. One male employee passed out but was revived and put back to work again. After the close of trading one broker found a big wastebasket of orders he had forgotten to process in the excitement.

In commission houses in other big cities across America, people with wet hands stood pale and trembling, hovering over ticker tape machines like relatives at the bedside of a rich uncle. Widows—who had speculated with the insurance money left them by their dead husbands. Chorus girls—who had skimped on hosiery to play the market. Furniture salesmen—who had thrown their life savings at the feet of the golden bull. Now, because the ticker was so tardy, they could not be sure just how much they had lost.

Every new quotation they saw could be one or two hours late; maybe more. All realized, though, that they were being wiped out, and each reacted in terms of his own temperament. Some were stunned, speechless. Others babbled hysterically. A few, struck by the absurdity of a world gone mad, laughed dry and mirthless laughs.

In Providence, Rhode Island, a coal dealer dropped dead of a heart attack while watching the ticker in his broker's office. In Kansas City an insurance man, eyeing the quotations in the Kansas City Club, shouted, "Tell the boys I can't pay them what I owe them!"—and fired two shots into his chest. Down in the Antarctic a member of Admiral Richard Byrd's expedition announced cheerfully that he had been wiped out but could not think of a better place to be without a cent to his name.

At 2:30 P.M., in New York City, Richard Whitney tried to become a hero a second time. His hat tilted at a jaunty angle on his head, he entered the trading room of the exchange once again to saunter conspicuously across the floor, a Mona Lisa smile on his lips. If Whitney thought his smooth appearance was oil on troubled waters, he was quite wrong, for by now a distrust of big financiers choked the throats of many drowning men. It is true that in the final fifteen minutes of trading some stocks made a 4- to 14-point rally, but this was due to rich bargain hunters picking up the pieces rather than to Whitney's reassuring smile.

At 3 P.M. the ringing of the bell ended the most disastrous day in the history of the New York Stock Exchange. For a split second, brokers froze on the floor like ballet dancers completing a frenzied whirl. Then, in slow motion, they lowered their heads and arms to trudge with weary steps through torn slips of paper carpeting the floor like dry autumn leaves.

*   *   *

The ticker, more than two and one-half hours late, finally caught up with quotations at 5:32 P.M. Only then did everyone learn the official figure of the volume of trading on the biggest exchange in the land: A record-breaking 16,410,030 shares had traded hands. This figure was not to be exceeded for thirty-nine years, not until the year 1968. More than 16,000,000 sales? Why, this was more than triple the volume once considered a fabulously big day in the market.

And what of prices? The industrial average had fallen 70¾ points during the day, then recovered 40⅞ during the last-minute surge of buying. Westinghouse had opened at 131, dropped to 100, rallied to 126. American Can had started at 130, sunk to 110, risen to 120. United States Steel, for which Richard Whitney had bid 205 the previous Thursday, fell to 167 in the course of the day but closed at 174. Prices for the day were down a general average of 24⅝. A majority of stocks had become thoroughly demoralized.

In late afternoon Federal Reserve Board members announced from Washington that margins would be reduced to 25 percent for stock loans, but other than this, they felt no action was necessary. At 6:45 P.M. members of the bankers' coalition concluded their conference, and once again Thomas Lamont met with reporters. Already sensitive to criticism, he ended by declaring: "The group has continued and will continue in a cooperative way to support the market and has not been a seller of stocks." Not on this day, perhaps, but in time to come, as has been said, the bankers emerged from their salvage operation with a profit which Lamont described as "slight."

Throughout this anxious day Englishmen holding American securities rushed to sell in London, and the London *Daily Mail*'s financial editor wrote: "We are watching the complete disorganization of a complex market by an assault upon it of a leaderless and panic-stricken mob." Many Americans who had been living abroad on paper profits now hastily reexamined their leases and began packing their bags. On this sour day the Dow-Jones industrial average fell more than 48 points, while the New York *Times* industrial average dropped 43 points. For the first time since the beginning of the bull market, brokerage houses suffered, three of them failing.

What did all this mean? It meant that the great golden bull was dead and buried. It meant the end of prosperity. It meant that the rainbow ride was over—with no pot of gold at the end. In the words of Edwin P. Hoyt, the *important* capital which had been wiped out "was not the big money of the business community. The disastrous losses were the cash reserves of small companies and the thousands and tens of thousands of dollars of middle-class savings which had been diverted from banks, bonds, insurance, and actual ownership of homes and automobiles while the public bought goods on the installment plan and sank savings into the speculative market." Thus far, this was a financial debacle, not a business crisis; that would come later.

How much money was lost? No one knows for sure, not even to this day. The very question is pointless, for it was not just money that was lost but arbitrary values with no roots in reality. Additionally, mistakes were made in bookkeeping, some sales were not recorded and other trading took place outside the walls of organized exchanges.

After the catastrophe of October 29 stock prices continued to sink, although fewer shares were traded. Prices finally plunged to their lowest point on November 13, 1929.

However, men who stood in the eye of the hurricane of October 29 and historians since then have guessed that the losses ranged from $26 billion to $74 billion. If the latter figure is valid, this means that stockholders lost three times as many dollars as the United States spent in fighting World War I. In paper values, it must be remembered. William C. Durant, who bought and sold more stocks than perhaps any other single man during the bull market, believed that the total loss was $50 billion. Impressed by this figure, he got out pencil and paper and made a quick calculation. If 50 billion silver dollars were piled on top of one another, they would soar into the sky to a height of 100,000 miles.

*   *   *

In its issue of October 30, 1929, *Variety* printed this immortal headline:

WALL ST. LAYS AN EGG

*   *   *

A stricken America lay back exhausted.

5

Who Lost What?

AUTUMN IN MASSACHUSETTS is a many-splendored scene. Even the bleak soul of Calvin Coolidge expanded a little as he gazed upon trees flashing in gold and flaring in scarlet, spilling color on hills and meadows. Then, October 30, 1929, the former President opened his copy of the Northampton *Gazette* and read about the death of "Coolidge prosperity." All beauty vanished from his life. Until then Coolidge had enjoyed the willows and maples and beeches in and around the small town of Northampton, to which he had retired seven months previously after leaving the White House. At the very moment he first read about the Crash he was negotiating the purchase of a sixteen-room mansion set on nine beech-shaded acres. That first word about the tragedy on Wall Street was bad enough for Coolidge, but the very next day he also read that Senator Joseph T. Robinson, Democratic minority leader of the Senate, was blaming the Crash on the former President's optimistic statements about the condition of the stock market.

The little man with the thin nose, thin lips, thin body and thin personality must have realized that this was the end of the way of life he had symbolized. Did he now recall how, in the previous June, he had been criticized by Senator Carter Glass for aiding speculation during his administration? Did he remember the month of July and his purchase of some securities from J. P. Morgan at a bargain price? Morgan had offered a group of insiders a new stock issue of Standard Brands, Inc., at 32—which was 8 points below the price on the open market. Later, in public testimony, Morgan said: "The shares were only offered to clients and friends who could afford to take the risk . . . regarded as too speculative for the general public." Was this not the same Morgan who had accused the Federal Reserve Board of encouraging the "speculative frenzy"? Coolidge, a private citizen again in the summer of 1929, had bought 3,000 bargain shares from Morgan.

Coolidge had benefited from "Coolidge prosperity." In 1928, while still President, his investments were worth at least $200,000. Between the day of his departure from the White House and the Crash he had earned $100,000 more by writing magazine articles. Now, in addition to his Massachusetts properties, he owned land and buildings in his native state of Vermont. Since most of his investments were so sound that he did not lose much money during the ensuing Depression, he did not suffer physically, but he suffered terrible spiritual torments.

Coolidge, who had told Will Rogers that he kept fit for the Presidency "by avoiding the big problems," now may have begun to wonder whether he had given that exalted office all the attention it deserved. He was a Puritan, with a rigid conscience and a limitless capacity for guilt. There in Northampton his wife and friends and neighbors saw him sicken steadily. Always a man of few words, he now spoke less than ever. He brooded. Gazing out a window of his new home or riding in the big car he had bought secondhand from the White House garage, Coolidge stared unseeingly at everything and nothing, worry lines snaking across his broad forehead. He endured regret, bewilderment, heartbreak. A shallow man of hand-me-down opinions, the former President had no idea about how to cope with the Depression. About all he could do was to mumble: "We need more faith in ourselves. Largely because of some decline in trade we have set about finding fault with nearly everybody and everything." In speaking about *fault,* Calvin Coolidge spoke from the heart.

He said nothing of comfort to those who had lost in the Crash.

*   *   *

Clarence Darrow, the famous criminal lawyer, was left almost penniless at the age of seventy-three. Otto Kahn, the respected banker, suffered grave losses and paid no income taxes for the next three years. Robert Clairmont, the millionaire poet and playboy of Greenwich Village, lost everything and gladly accepted the candy and cigarettes sent him by newspaper readers. Flo Ziegfeld, impresario of the *Ziegfeld Follies,* dropped $2 million. Theodore Dreiser, the eminent writer, was taken for about $75,-000, although he liked to boast that "I lost $300,000 in a few days."

Willard Huntington Wright, who wrote mystery novels under the pen name of S. S. Van Dine, was another heavy loser. Composer Jerome Kern, who had sold his rare autographs and books in 1928, lost these profits and just about everything else in the Crash. Rex Stout, who had lived on dividends while writing psychological novels, now needed quick money, so he dreamed up a superdetective named Nero Wolfe and began cranking out thrillers. A fortune was lost by Hugh S. Johnson, a manufacturer of farm plows who later became an important figure in the New Deal.

A young man named Cesar Romero had to start looking for another job, while still dreaming of becoming a movie star. Comedian Eddie Cantor lost $2 million and then described his experience in a humorous book called *Caught Short!* According to some Wall Street men, Chicago stockbroker Arthur W. Cutten lost a whopping $40 million. Arthur Curtiss James, head of the Western Pacific Railroad Company, found himself $9 million poorer.

Broadway producer Al Woods was abroad when the stock market started tumbling; in New York a family friend persuaded his wife to use the cash in his safe-deposit box to buy falling stocks on margin; when Woods got home, he found he was broke. Joseph E. Higgins, a Curb Exchange broker and pool operator, lost $14 million. Herbert Bayard Swope, former executive editor of the New York *World,* had ignored the advice of his friend Bernard Baruch to sell his stockholdings; in September, 1929, Swope had been worth nearly $14 million, on paper; two days after the Crash he owed $2,345,000. Max Gordon, another Broadway producer, took such heavy losses in the market that he suffered a nervous breakdown.

Edwin S. Porter, who had helped Edison invent the movie camera and had produced a pioneer film called *The Great Train Robbery,* was completely wiped out and spent his old age as a minor employee of an appliance firm. Charles M. Schwab, the powerful steel magnate, lost many millions of dollars as the Depression deepened. The Vanderbilt family, in the shrinkage of railway stocks alone, lost $40 million. And in the depths of the Depression the Rockefeller family fortune shrank to one-fifth its size before the Crash.

A few days after the Crash, comedian Harpo Marx got a collect call from his friend Alexander Woollcott. By this time the Marx Brothers were appearing in Cleveland. Woollcott was phoning from New York. In his autobiography entitled *Harpo Speaks,* Harpo describes the call:

> His voice sounded strangely tired and sad. I thought: *Somebody in the mob has died.* But it was nothing like that. "I'm home alone with a terrible case of the cringes," Aleck said. "I'm calling you to make a confession."
> I asked him what happened. "Harpo" he wailed. "Dear, dumb Harpo! Remember last spring when we took up a collection at the Thanatopsis to buy a present for the Hacketts' baby boy?" Sure, I remembered. "Remember, you all entrusted me to select the present and deliver it?" Yes, that too. "Do you know what I bought? Harpo, do you know what I gave the innocent little Hackett?" No, that I didn't know.
> "I gave him a share of United States Steel," said Aleck. "I can never forgive myself."
> That was when I knew it was all over.

Woollcott, who had been earning $30,000 a year writing for magazines, lost more than $200,000 of his own money in the Crash. Word that he was wiped out was phoned by his broker to Woollcott on a day when he was playing croquet on a Long Island estate. Mrs. George S. Kaufman, the wife

of the playwright, was present on that occasion and later reported that
when the fat little man got off the wire, he returned to the lawn and finished
his game without batting an eye. By December, 1929, Woollcott was
$7,000 in debt. However, he upped the price of his magazine articles and
became perhaps the best-paid book reviewer in American history.

Woollcott cherished one memory of the Crash and told the story again
and again. It concerned a rich man living on a vast estate at East Hampton,
Long Island. One day the man came home, visibly pale and nervous. He
told his neighbors that he had lost $4 million in the market and was
finished. Deciding to cut down on expenses, he fired his three gardeners,
five stablemen, the first and second butlers, the assistant chauffeur, his beagle trainer, the pastry cook and various other employees. A week or so later
the man summoned up enough courage to double-check his stock portfolio—and discovered he still had more than $3 million in sound invest-
ments. He celebrated by rehiring his beagle trainer.

One of Woollcott's friends was Margaret Case Harriman, who wrote
The Vicious Circle, a story of the Algonquin Round Table. Harpo Marx
lost $250,000 in the Crash. Miss Harriman tells what happened to his
brother Groucho, who had invested $240,000 and lost all of it. As soon as
Groucho got back to New York from Cleveland, he hastened to see his
attorney, Morris Ernst. This was while stock prices were still dropping.
Groucho showed Ernst his investment list, and the attorney, running his
finger down the page, began asking questions. Pointing at one stock, Ernst
asked: "Where did you get this recommendation?"

"From Bernard Baruch," Groucho said truthfully.

"And this one?"

"Holy mackerel! From Gerard Swope himself!"

At last Ernst came to a certain stock that had fallen only a single
point.

"For God's sake! Where'd you get *that* tip?"

Groucho peered over Ernst's shoulder at the item.

"Oh, *that!* I got that one from a wardrobe woman in the Shubert
Theater in Chicago."

*   *   *

A few days after the crash a New York *World-Telegram* reporter visited
the Manhattan home of Fanny Brice, the famous singer and comedienne.
She had lost about $500,000. The reporter asked Miss Brice why she had
begun playing the market and why she thought she had lost so heavily. In a
voice familiar to millions of Americans because of the way she sang "My
Man," she answered: "I was on the inside of the inside. My cousin's
husband was a customer's man. I started with Kayser Silk. That was something close to me. I could understand it. Everybody has got to have silk
underwear. It's a necessity. So gradually I worked outward. . . . Do you
know, for four years nobody spoke to me above a whisper: 'Buy this, buy

that!' The lower they whispered, the more authority it had. . . . I like to talk a long time on the telephone, so I bought American T. and T. Then I met a big man. 'Listen,' he said to me. 'I lost five fortunes already, so I ought to know something about this game.'

"After that, I didn't even know the names of the stocks. I had thirty or forty different kinds. Anaconda I can't forget—it's a beautiful name. I remember I went into my broker's office with Jay Brennan and a big fellow, one of the real insiders, with a low mumble, said to me, 'Miss Brice, you must have some Anaconda.' So I said, 'Un-uh! I prefer American Consolidated Foreign Investment Corporation,' or something like that. I don't remember exactly. But he said, 'Give Miss Brice five hundred shares of Anaconda.' Just like that. 'What a nice man he is,' Jay said to me. 'He gives you that stock.' It cost me 158. The next day it went down to 154, so I said to this insider, 'What does that mean?' He said, 'It means you should buy five hundred shares more.' Finally I sold the one thousand shares for 12."

Miss Brice's biographer, Norman Katkov, has told what happened to her a few days after this interview. She had been married only a little while to Billy Rose, who had made his first fortune by writing more than 300 songs. The Crash took Rose for $50,000 and left him penniless. He told his wife of his plight as they sat in the kitchen of their town house. When she pointed out that he would continue to get royalties from his songs, Billy Rose retorted that the loss of his money did not gall him so much as the realization that he had taken a beating. Although Miss Brice had lost half a million dollars, she still had $50,000 left. Her husband asked her to lend it to him. She asked why.

"This afternoon," said Billy Rose, "I studied the stock market charts for years back. After a big break, the market usually snaps back about one-third. If I had fifty thousand dollars, I'd load up when the market opens tomorrow. With any kind of luck, I figure to have all my money back by one o'clock in the afternoon."

Miss Brice asked what would happen to her money if his plan didn't work. Rose said in that case if this occurred, he would sign over to her all his subsequent song royalties. The next morning the two of them went to her bank where she withdrew the $50,000 from her savings account and gave him a cashier's check in that amount. Rose hurried to his broker and bought $50,000 worth of stock on a 10-point margin. By 2 P.M. that same day some of his new holdings had risen almost 20 points, and before the market closed, he made a fat profit. Billy Rose sold out and gave his wife the $50,000 she had lent him. This fast transaction also left him enough money to make a new start.

*   *   *

Polly Adler, who ran the best-known whorehouse in New York, was vacationing in Montreal that last week in October, and when she heard the news from Wall Street, she forgot about sight-seeing, hurrying instead to a brokerage office, where she sat and anxiously scanned the ticker tape. Every cent she owned was tied up in stocks. With the reports bad and getting worse, Miss Adler broke off her Canadian trip and raced back to her Manhattan home, finding it snowed under with telegrams from her broker calling for margin. She had been wiped out. Stunned, suddenly weary, too confused to take off her coat and hat, she slumped for hours in her travel clothes in the empty apartment, trying to decide what to do next.

The nation's most notorious madame thought her business would fall off, but instead it boomed. Her once-wealthy clients still came around, but now they were more interested in liquor than sex. Seeking alcoholic escape from financial worries, they heedlessly paid $30 a bottle for champagne and $1 for a glass of beer and drank themselves into frenzies or stupors. One man kept muttering that he used to control Wall Street but now was unable to pay his next month's rent. Another said he returned night after night because a whorehouse was the only place where he could weep without being ashamed. A certain client, always a gentleman in the past, now asked for a particular girl and then mistreated her sadistically. The next morning the man went to his office and shot himself.

*   *   *

Suicide became a favorite topic of conversation.

A Rochester man who had risen from office boy for Thomas Edison to prominence in public utilities circles killed himself in his home because of his market losses. In Milwaukee a man committed suicide and left a note willing his body to science, his soul to Treasury Secretary Andrew Mellon and his sympathy to his creditors. In New York a commission merchant used the Hudson River to drown himself, his pockets crammed with margin calls and $9.40 in change. The president of a cigar company crawled out onto the ledge of a Manhattan hotel, was grabbed by a waiter, struggled free and fell to his death. Comedian Eddie Cantor evoked guffaws from audiences when he impersonated a hotel clerk asking a broker whether he wanted a room for sleeping or jumping. Another popular joke concerned two men who jumped hand in hand from a high window of the Ritz because they had a joint account.

One of the most celebrated suicides was that of James J. Riordan, founder and president of the New York County Trust Company and intimate friend of former Governor Alfred E. Smith, Mayor Jimmy Walker and the wealthy broker Michael J. Meehan. In 1928, when Smith opposed Hoover for the Presidency, Riordan decided to help Smith by lending the Democratic National Committee $1 million in funds from his bank. The law said no corporation could make a political contribution, so it was necessary for some of Smith's friends to endorse this note. Riordan assured them they would never have to repay this money, for after Al Smith had been elected President, many men would be happy to make up the deficit. But Hoover defeated Smith. During the spectacular bull market Riordan also gave hot market tips to several members of Smith's family. These relatives, who speculated without Smith's knowledge, were wiped out in the Crash.

Riordan also lost heavily. On Friday, November 8, 1929, the forty-eight-year-old financier shot himself to death in his home on West Twelfth Street in Manhattan. Minutes later Smith was told of this tragedy, and he wept. Besides being good friends, both Smith and Riordan were Catholics, and Catholics regard suicide with especial horror. Smith, a member of the board of directors of Riordan's bank, feared that the news might start a run on it by uneasy depositors. Smith raced to Riordan's home to intercept the medical examiner, pointing out that if the full story were told at once, the bank's depositors might bring it tumbling to earth. Because of the prestige and personality of the former governor, the city official agreed to delay his announcement. Then, in the words of John Kenneth Galbraith, there was "a long wake through which the distinguished mourners kept one eye on the corpse and the other on the clock."

News of Riordan's suicide was not made public until Saturday after-noon—after his bank had closed. Auditors quickly checked its condition, found all its funds intact and learned that its resources came to more than $30 million. New York City officials then announced they were leaving municipal deposits in the bank—a fact much publicized over the weekend.

Like other suicides, Riordan did not take his life because of a single thing but rather because of many. Apparently he was depressed over the loss of his own money, ashamed of the part he played in losing money for Al Smith's relatives, and perhaps he worried about the $1 million he had lent the Democrats. Catholic officials ruled that he was temporarily insane when he killed himself and thus was eligible for burial in holy ground. Smith headed the list of honorary pallbearers, all of them eminent men. Michael Meehan was so shaken by the tragedy that he had a nervous breakdown.

The stock market crash did not launch a huge suicide wave. However, the national suicide rate began climbing in the latter part of 1929 and continued to rise until the Depression hit bottom in 1932.

6

What Caused the Crash?

P EOPLE LAUGHED when they read in their newspapers of November 7,
1929, about a New York cop who found an escaped parrot shuffling
along Fifth Avenue at Eighty-first Street. The parrot was squawking:
"More margin! More margin!"

But people did not laugh very long. They wanted an answer to one
overriding question: What caused the Crash on Wall Street?

At the time of the Crash, soon thereafter and even down to the present
day a variety of explanations were offered to the public. There is nothing
surprising about this diversity of opinions. Economics is not an exact
science. Stock market operations cannot be reduced to one simple mathematical formula. Whenever J. Pierpont Morgan had been asked what he
thought the market would do, he always replied: "It will fluctuate." This
was no wisecrack. Morgan never indulged in wisecracks. He simply described the market's essential trait: It goes up and it goes down. Now, in
1929, it had gone down so fast and far that everyone was bewildered.
When they were able to collect their thoughts, when they tried to comprehend this complex and massive event, each saw it through the prism of his
own personality and experience.

Calvin Coolidge may have suffered personal remorse but he was not
willing to accept public blame. In an article written for the *Saturday Evening Post* the former President listed a variety of factors, then said: ". . .
It will be observed that all these causes of depression, with the exception of
the early speculation, had their origin outside of the United States, where
they were entirely beyond the control of our Government."

President Herbert Hoover offered several explanations of the Crash and
the following Depression.

He declared that "our immediate weak spot was the orgy of stock speculation which began to slump in October, 1929." As for speculators them-

selves, Hoover added that "there are crimes far worse than murder for which men should be reviled and punished." But a second cause, according to the President, was World War I and its aftereffects. Hoover's war hypothesis was publicly attacked by Senator Carter Glass, who growled that the Depression was no more caused by World War I than it was by the "war of the Phoenicians or the conquest of Gaul by Caesar." It was also criticized in private by Harlan F. Stone, then an Associate Justice of the United States Supreme Court and later its Chief Justice.

Hoover then fell back on Coolidge's argument that the chief causes of the Crash and Depression lay outside the United States. This did not square, however, with findings of the impartial Brookings Institution of Washington, D.C., after its experts had studied conditions in twenty-seven nations, including the United States. According to their report, before prosperity ended in the United States, it had been terminated in eight other nations—Canada, Argentina, Brazil, Germany, Finland, Poland, Australia and the Netherlands Indies. The United States entered the Depression at just about the same time as three other nations—Belgium, Italy and Egypt. However, the United States plunged into the Depression *earlier* than fifteen other nations—Great Britain, Switzerland, Holland, Austria, Czechoslovakia, France, Denmark, Norway, Ireland, Yugoslavia, Japan, India, British Malaya, New Zealand and South Africa.

*　　*　　*

Democrats were quick to blame the Depression on the Republicans. Democratic Congressman John Nance Garner of Texas, fated to become the next Vice President of the United States, said of the Republicans: "Their failure to balance the budget of a family of 120,000,000 people is at the very bottom of the economic troubles from which we are suffering."

Governor Franklin D. Roosevelt's mother lost heavily in the Crash, but he was slow to understand what had happened. As belatedly as December 1, 1929, in a private letter, Roosevelt referred to the debacle as "the recent little flurry downtown." Ten weeks after the collapse on Wall Street the governor issued a rosy report about New York State finances. In October, 1930, Roosevelt spoke of the need for renewed confidence and private investment. Like many others, he did not think the Depression would last very long. Not until months after the Crash did Roosevelt begin to study it in depth. In another private letter he said: "It would be misunderstood if I were to tell the public that I regard the present business slump as a great blessing, for while a nation goes speculation crazy and everybody is employed, the average citizen simply declines to think of fundamental principles."

Much later, when Roosevelt was the Democratic candidate for President, he attacked Hoover in these words: "So I sum up the history of the present administration in four sentences: First, it encouraged speculation and overproduction, through its false economic policies. Second, it attempted to minimize the crash and misled the people as to its gravity. Third, it erroneously charged the cause to other nations of the world. And finally, it refused to recognize and correct the evils at home which it had brought forth; it delayed reform; it forgot reform."

The Democratic Party's official explanation, as spelled out in its next national platform, was that "the chief causes of this condition were the disastrous policies pursued by our government since the World War, of economic isolation, fostering the merger of competitive businesses into monopolies and encouraging the indefensible expansion and contraction of credit for private profit at the expense of the public."

For obvious reasons, the Republicans disagreed, but the next GOP platform did allude to "the orgy of gambling on the stock exchanges, bank failures and consequent loss of confidence."

Socialist leader Norman Thomas said it was unfair to blame the Crash and Depression on President Hoover since no one man was big enough to cause them. According to Thomas, the cause of the crisis lay within the system itself. The Socialist Party platform elaborated on this, saying in part: ". . . We are facing a breakdown of the capitalistic system. This situation the Socialist Party has long predicted. . . . The capitalistic system is now creaking and breaking in every joint. . . . Capitalism is outworn, obsolete, ready for the museum of social history."

Was this radical talk? Perhaps. However, much the same ideas were being entertained and articulated by men and institutions long in the good graces of the captains of finance and industry. "The capitalistic system is on trial." Who said this? Charles G. Ross, chief Washington correspondent for the eminently respectable St. Louis *Post-Dispatch,* who won a Pulitzer Prize in journalism for his long analysis of the Depression. Ross went on to say: "Men who are not afraid to question the wisdom of unrestricted capitalism—which is practically what we have today—are the real conservators of our institutions. The real threat to them comes not from the handful of Communists in our midst but from the conservative extremists who are not willing to yield an inch. There is vastly more danger to the established order from the economic reactionaries in Congress than there is from the so-called radicals."

One freethinking Republican spokesman, Kansas editor and author William Allen White, wrote a biography of Calvin Coolidge that included this comment: "Speculation alone did not create our economic structure in the Coolidge years. The whole business of blame, credit, responsibility or careless impunity in the journey down the rapids to the economic holocaust lies not in any man, not in any group or institution. Given the American ideals of 1921–29, indeed for two or three previous generations, and the resultant development of those ideals in the American mind alone—with or without Calvin Coolidge or the Federal Reserve System or Andrew Mellon —and the New York bankers would have sped inevitably, sooner or later, to the abysm [sic] of catastrophe. For we had what all Christendom had—a Chamber of Commerce complex."

The International Chamber of Commerce blamed the crisis on: (1) overproduction; (2) decline in commodity prices; (3) world agricultural crisis; (4) industrial unemployment; (5) political unrest; (6) partial closing of several world markets, notably China and India; (7) varied bases for monetary circulation; (8) disequilibrium between short- and long-term credits; (9) fall in silver prices; (10) dumping of goods by Soviet Russia; (11) unprecedented taxation to meet international indebtedness; (12) excessive state participation in private enterprises.

The National Association of Manufacturers said that the main factor in the Depression was the misuse of credit, although misdirected government action was also responsible. The reactionary NAM went on to argue that the Federal Reserve System failed to apply credit brakes and that the government encouraged risky foreign loans. Restrictions were continued on the international movement of goods, although we had shifted from a debtor to a creditor nation. However, the NAM concluded, public opinion supported the inflationary policies pursued by business and government.

William Cardinal O'Connell of Boston was himself a conservative, but he declared that the Depression was due to a "ghastly failure of industrial leadership." Treasury Secretary Mellon singled out overproduction as the principal cause of all the trouble. The *Commercial and Financial Chronicle* blamed everything on the Federal Reserve's policy. Congressman Fiorello H. LaGuardia of New York blamed the bankers, crying: "The bastards broke the people's back with their usury!" John L. Lewis, president of the United Mine Workers, agreed with LaGuardia, declaring: "A horde of small-time leaders in industry and finance looted the purse of the population."

Professor Irving Fisher said the disaster was due to "mob psychology" and then added—à la Morgan—that "the market went down because it went down." Bertrand H. Snell, soon to become the Republican minority leader in the House of Representatives, called the Depression "the ghost of the World War stalking over the earth." William Randolph Hearst, the prince of publishers, said the Depression was caused by enormous over-capitalization which had stolen billions from small investors; he also said that "if profits had been distributed in wages, prosperity would have been maintained and increased."

Governor Roosevelt agreed with Hearst. "Our basic trouble," said Roosevelt, "was not an insufficiency of capital. It was an insufficient distribution of buying power coupled with an over-sufficient speculation in production. While wages rose in many of our industries, they did not rise proportionately to the reward to capital, and at the same time the purchasing power of other great groups of our population was permitted to shrink."

Agreement came from Senator James Couzens of Michigan, a Republi-

can and a multimillionaire. Couzens said: "Notwithstanding the general
assumption that wages were high, all available statistics show that during
the years preceding the depression the increase in productivity per man was
greater than the increase in wages. In other words, although the worker got
more money, he produced still more goods. Somebody got the difference,
and we all know who it was."

Capitalists were paid too much. Workers were paid too little. Charles G.
Ross said in his prizewinning article: "The wealth created by the machine
has gone, in appalling disproportion, to the owners of the machine." Other
sources pointed out that 12 executives in the tobacco industry received
salaries equivalent to the gross income of 30,000 tobacco farmers and their
families. Republican Senator William E. Borah of Idaho said that Bethlehem Steel gained 160 percent in earnings the first six months of 1929,
that the Republic Iron and Steel Company showed profits of 208 percent,
and the Youngstown Sheet and Tube Company's profits rose 145 percent.
Borah might have added that between 1924 and 1929 the steel industry did
not grant a single wage increase.

This cynical indifference to the welfare of workers played right into the
hands of the Communists. Karl Marx had declared that in the end
capitalism would provide "its own grave digger." He claimed to have
discerned several trends in capitalism which would inevitably cause its
collapse: an incessant urge to accumulate more and more capital; an increasing concentration of the means of production in the hands of fewer
and fewer monopolists, accompanied by the ruination of most businessmen; a steady fall in the rate of profit in relation to capital investment; and
an increase in the misery of the working class. On the basis of these trends,
Marx developed a theory of the business cycle in which each depression
would be more disastrous than the last, until finally the last crisis would
bring about the collapse of capitalism.

The Roman Catholic Church, which vigorously opposed Communism,
nonetheless took a position somewhat similar to that of the Marxists. On
May 15, 1931, Pope Pius XI issued an encyclical bearing the title "On
Reconstructing the Social Order." In part, the Pope said:

> . . . it is obvious that not only is wealth concentrated in our times but
> an immense power and despotic economic dictatorship is consolidated in
> the hands of a few, who often are not owners but only the trustees and man-
> aging directors of invested funds which they administer according to their
> own arbitrary will and pleasure.
> This dictatorship is being most forcibly exercised by those who, since
> they hold the money and completely control it, control credit also and rule
> the lending of money. Hence, they regulate the flow, so to speak, of the life-
> blood whereby the entire economic system lives, and have so firmly in their
> grasp the soul, as it were, of economic life, that no one can breathe against
> their will. . . .

Governor Huey Long of Louisiana said much the same thing in plain words: "The wealth of the land was being tied up in the hands of a very few men. The people were not buying because they had nothing with which to buy. The big business interests were not selling, because there was nobody they could sell to. One percent of the people could not eat any more than any other one percent; they could not wear much more than any other one percent; they could not live in any more houses than any other one percent. So, in 1929, when the fortune-holders of America grew powerful enough that one percent of the people owned nearly everything, ninety-nine percent of the people owned practically nothing, not even enough to pay their debts, a collapse was at hand."

*   *   *

What caused the Crash?

Greedy people wanted more than they needed. Foolish people thought they could get something for nothing. Impulsive people bought now in the hope of paying later. Income and wealth were distributed unfairly and dangerously. The rich regarded themselves as an all-knowing elite. The masses were not paid enough money to consume all the goods they produced. The economy was unsound. The corporate structure was sick. The banking system was weak. Foreign trade was out of balance. Business data were inadequate and often faulty.

This constellation of conditions left the economy a flawed and loaded gun, and when the stock market crashed, the gun did not merely fire—it exploded in everyone's face.

7

And Banks Came Tumbling Down

FRANCESCO M. FERRARI had a bellyache. When he woke up on the morning of January 30, 1929, the pain was so acute in the lower right-hand side of his abdomen that he phoned the main office of his company to say he was sick and could not get to work. Ferrari was the founder and president of the City Trust Company of New York with headquarters in Manhattan. His condition worsened, he was rushed to the Fifth Avenue Hospital, he was operated on for appendicitis, but he died early in the evening of February 1.

When news of his death reached other officers of his bank, they quickly huddled and decided to say nothing about it publicly for a day or two lest there be a run on the bank. They were careful, however, to break the news immediately to Frank H. Warder, New York's superintendent of banks, for he and Ferrari had been close. Very close.

Born in Italy, Ferrari had acted like a lawyer in that country, although he was not a member of the bar, and he was charged with larceny before he emigrated to New York in 1912. Here in the New World he clerked in a shipping office, was employed by a private banker, finally became a private banker himself. In 1923 Congressman Fiorello H. LaGuardia asked the New York State banking department to approve Ferrari's plan to organize the Harlem Bank of Commerce. Ferrari later became president of the Atlantic State Bank of Brooklyn, and in 1928 these two banks merged to become the City Trust Company.

Now a leader in New York's Italian community, Ferrari blossomed. Ambitious and restless, handsome and genial, he wore his fedora at a rakish angle and never protested when people exclaimed that he looked like an actor. Robert Moses later said: "He was shrewd, vain, pompous and boastful, with a large element of showmanship in everything he did."

His City Trust Company, however, was weakly structured, engaged in poor banking practices and even committed illegal acts. Among other things, Ferrari bribed Warder, the very state official who should have forced him to live up to his responsibilities. The bank's other officers had cause to worry, and as soon as Ferrari's death became public knowledge, there was a rash of rumors about that institution's improper use of funds. Ten days after the death of Ferrari the bank closed, terrorizing its 16,936 depositors.

The state banking department took over the bank, and in the following three months Banking Superintendent Warder tried to sell it. Since most of its depositors were Italian-Americans, an appeal was made to A. P. Giannini, himself of Italian ancestry, to try to save the defunct institution. A native of California and a resident of San Francisco, Giannini owned the Bank of America and was a banker of towering reputation. He now ordered his auditors to check the Ferrari bank, but they found its records so untrustworthy that Giannini refused to have any part of the mess.

This left Warder in charge of a very dead, very large and very white elephant. Panic-stricken, he remembered the bribes—the chickens, eggs, bottles of fine liquor and huge sums of money given to him by the late Ferrari. Because of his fear, he withheld any public comment about the bank's failure. But New York newspaper editors would not let it go at that; they were curious, they pressed for an explanation, and finally they demanded that the state banking department launch a formal investigation.

Warder had had no financial experience at all before he had joined the department in 1920. Six years later, however, Governor Al Smith had made him superintendent of banks. It was customary for the top officials of state departments to resign whenever a governor ended his term of office. Al Smith ceased to be governor in 1928, but for some unexplained reason Warder's term was allowed to run to July, 1929. Now, with depositors clamoring for the $6,500,000 they had put into the City Trust Company, a sweating Warder wished he had quit sooner. On April 22, 1929, he suddenly resigned. Reporters quickly learned that he had obtained a passport and planned to flee to Europe.

When this news broke, Governor Roosevelt was relaxing in Georgia and Lieutenant Governor Herbert Lehman was serving as acting governor. Lehman wanted to act before Warder could get away. Without bothering to call Roosevelt long distance, Lehman invoked the Moreland Act, which gave the governor or his representative the power to probe any branch of state government. He named Robert Moses a Moreland Act commissioner and ordered him to investigate the relationship between the state banking department and the City Trust Company. The day after the Moses appointment Warder abandoned his plan to head for Europe and agreed to cooperate with the new commissioner.

Moses was an extremely able man, brilliant and scholarly, articulate and honest. Al Smith, a Democrat, had chosen Moses, a nominal Republican, as his secretary of state. That had been some time in the past, but now,

when Roosevelt learned that Lehman had appointed Moses, the governor
was angry. Moses was the one man against whom FDR held a lasting
grudge. When Smith had been governor, he had made Roosevelt a member
of the Taconic Park Commission, and subsequently Roosevelt had made a
request of Moses, who had jurisdiction over state parks. FDR wanted the
job of secretary of the commission to go to Louis Howe, Roosevelt's
political mentor and intimate friend. This post paid $5,000 a year. Moses
refused to appoint Howe, telling associates he did not believe that Howe
was interested in parks but would use the salary while continuing to "advance Roosevelt's interests, as he always has done."

Armed with the power to subpoena witnesses, records and other books,
Moses deeply probed the operations of the City Trust Company and reported his findings to Governor Roosevelt on July 10, 1929—more than
three months before the Wall Street Crash and three years before the bank
panic of 1933. Moses blamed the failure of the bank on Francesco Ferrari,
Ferrari's immediate assistants and Warder. Of the former state superintendent of banks, Moses said: "The evidence shows that Frank H.
Warder is a faithless public official who accepted gifts and gratuities including money and securities; that he knew of the dishonest management
and bad conditions of the Ferrari banks and deliberately prevented exposure and proper official action; that he authorized the expansion of these
enterprises and placed the seal of the State's approval on Ferrari's methods.

"He prostituted his department and the banking law for unworthy friends
and illegal personal gain, and this offense is the more heinous and con-
temptible because it threatened the small savings of the poor, the ignorant
and the defenseless, and undermined the confidence of all foreign groups in
the financial system and the very government of the State."

Warder was tried, found guilty of accepting a $10,000 bribe, and sen-
tenced to a term of five to ten years in Sing Sing.

The Moses report was a masterpiece of legal reasoning and literary
excellence; Walter Lippmann called it the finest document of its kind he
ever had read. More important than the censure of Ferrari and Warder,
however, was Moses' series of recommendations for improving the state
banking department and for revising the state banking law. Moses urged
that the demoralized state banking department be reorganized, with higher
salaries being paid for better-qualified personnel. He suggested that all
department officials be prohibited by law from holding, owning or speculating in stocks or bonds under their jurisdiction. Declaring that all banks
should be supervised by either the state or the federal government, Moses
said: "At present, the strongest and the weakest escape; among the former
are the great banking houses in Wall Street, among the latter institutions
like Clarke Brothers which recently failed."

He proposed that existing private banks be brought under state jurisdiction and that the creation of new private banks be prohibited. Moses said:
"There should be no more private banks. . . . There is no good reason

for them." He also was for regulating the issuance of securities "down to the last detail, whether they are those of a bank or a utility company." He said it should be mandatory for the chairman of the board of directors to see to it that all loans were officially approved at regular meetings of the board. He denounced the practice of creating bank affiliates, mostly on paper, which then were financed with depositors' funds and used mainly to promote gambling in securities and real estate for the profit of the bank's officers. These were just a few of the many sound suggestions in the Moses report, which ran to some forty pages of fine print.

But the Moses report was virtually ignored by Franklin D. Roosevelt, the Democratic governor, and by the Republican-dominated legislature.

Perhaps Roosevelt's behavior can be explained by his personal dislike of Moses. Perhaps Roosevelt was reacting with the conditioned reflexes of the son of a banker, the nephew of bankers, and as a man who himself once hoped to become president of a Wall Street bank. FDR had not yet begun to distrust bankers; he was about to learn the hard way. He merely referred the Moses report to the Joint Legislative Committee on Banking and Investment Trusts.

Despite the existence of this committee, the governor appointed his own Commission on Revision of the Banking Law. Now New York State had both a *committee* and a *commission* allegedly concerned with banking practices. In an obvious snub, Roosevelt did not name Moses to this new commission but stacked it with bankers and businessmen. One of them was Henry Pollock, a director and vice-president of the Bank of the United States—another institution soon to explode into newspaper headlines.

The governor asked his commissioners to suggest banking reforms before the state legislature met in its next regular session in January, 1930. And Roosevelt added weakly: "I hope that the banking commission will tighten up a bit on the functioning of directors and officers of banks." This was akin to asking the foxes not to eat the hens.

The longer-established committee said: "The report of Moreland Commissioner Robert Moses in relation to the City Trust Company closes with certain recommendations for changes in the banking law. . . . Yet no one of the many leaders of the banking profession, officials of the banking department or other recognized authorities with whom this committee has consulted, has been of the opinion that there is *any necessity for sweeping changes* in the law in this regard." (Italics added.)

Moses, who had the fastest tongue in the East, snapped that the committee's words "will come back to haunt the gentlemen who wrote them."

The governor's own commission studied the testimony gathered by the committee but took no testimony of its own and held no public hearings. On January 1, 1930, in his annual message to the legislature, Roosevelt said: "The meshes of our banking laws have been woven so loosely as to permit the escape of those meanest of all criminals who squander the funds of hundreds of small depositors in reckless speculation for private gain. The entire banking law is in need of revision and the banking department needs immediately far more adequate inspection facilities."

But Roosevelt still failed to recommend any specific remedial legislation.

At the end of January his commission reported to him. As might have been expected, its report was conservative and in some ways even negative. Although it agreed with some of Moses' minor recommendations, it rejected his major ones. It opposed his call for stricter regulation of banks and bankers. It held that good banking was a moral problem, not a legal one, since good men ran good banks and good men could not be created by laws. It disagreed with Moses' wish to abolish private banks, suggesting instead that they be controlled by the state banking department. The commission did, however, recommend higher salaries in the banking department, more bank examiners and the appointment of an assistant superintendent for the department.

Roosevelt, who had shunned Moses' stern recommendations, readily accepted the lax ones offered by his own commission. Its conclusions, plus those of the legislative committee, were embodied in four bills, which the governor signed on April 22, 1930. These measures were supposed to protect depositors. Roosevelt called them "some of the most necessary, important and constructive banking legislation proposed in recent years." Norman Thomas disagreed, pointing out that both the commission and committee "almost completely disregarded the Moses report and solemnly concluded that everything would be all right if everybody would put his money in a sound bank."

After Warder's resignation as banking superintendent, Roosevelt had replaced him with Joseph A. Broderick. Unlike Warder, Broderick came to the job with wide experience in banking. He had been state bank examiner, chief examiner of the Federal Reserve System and vice-president of the National Bank of Commerce. However, as events were to prove— particularly his handling of the Bank of the United States—Broderick sometimes moved slowly and his judgment was questionable.

*   *   *

The Bank of the United States had been founded in 1913 on Manhattan's Lower East Side by a Jewish garment manufacturer. By 1930 its main office was located at 320 Fifth Avenue, and its president was Bernard K. Marcus, the son of the founder. Despite its name, the Bank of the United States was not chartered by the federal government and had no connection with it. Instead, it was a state-chartered bank, wholly subject to state inspection and regulation—or supposedly so. The lobby of the main office displayed an oil painting of the Capitol Building in Washington, a large gold American eagle and gold-lettered signs saying FEDERAL RESERVE SYSTEM and DEPOSITORIES OF CITY AND STATE FUNDS. The bank's name and decorations misled some ignorant people into believing that it was owned by the federal government—and Marcus did not go out of his way to correct this impression. Since most of the bank's officers and main stockholders were Jewish, a few New Yorkers snidely called it the Pants Pressers' Bank.

Saul Singer was second-in-command with the title of vice-president. He and Marcus vigorously ballyhooed the bank. It grew fast through a series of mergers, absorbing other banks by exchanging its stock for theirs at high prices. People who had owned huge blocks of stock in the other banks now found themselves holding stock in the Bank of the United States. When they saw the bank's enticingly high price on the market, they sold at a fat profit. This distressed Marcus and Singer, who decided that instead of a few stockholders who owned huge blocks of their bank stock, they would prefer thousands of small investors, who would not be likely to dump their securities on the market.

They opened fifty-seven branch banks, and by 1930 they had more than 500,000 depositors—most of them Jewish and people of modest means. This was an impressive figure even in a city with a population of almost 7,000,000. Marcus and Singer also created a series of affiliates which they used to circumvent the law by engaging in speculation with money on deposit in the parent bank. They also organized a syndicate which launched a pool operation intended to boost the price of the bank's stock. When this pool failed to attract outside money, the syndicate spent more and more of the bank's money to buy more and more stock to support the price of the bank's stock. In other words, the syndicate borrowed the depositors' money in the parent bank to play this crazy game. Nor was this all; Marcus and Singer also used forty dummy corporations to invest millions in real estate.

Marcus, now far removed from his boyhood days on the Lower East Side, always insisted on a special van to carry his thirty-odd pieces of luggage every time he went to Europe in the most luxurious suite of the most luxurious ship. He wooed respectability by donating money to Columbia University to support a course in anthropology. Singer, who likewise courted prestige, was guest of honor at a dinner given by the Beth Israel Hospital Alumni Association.

On July 1, 1929, Joseph A. Broderick took office as the new banking superintendent. State law required each state bank to be examined twice a year. On July 13 more than 100 examiners from the state banking department and the Federal Reserve Bank of New York studied the books of the Bank of the United States. Horrified by what they found, the examiners told Broderick that the bank's policies and condition were highly questionable. They were extremely critical of Marcus and Singer, declaring that the two men were not qualified to run the affairs of such a huge bank.

Broderick met with the pair, who boldly asked him to write a letter congratulating them upon the operation of their bank. Instead, he recommended that they make sweeping changes in policy and personnel. They later told him that they had drawn up some new plans; but they never carried out their plans, and Broderick seemed to forget all about them. Despite the alarming report from the examiners and despite the law calling for semiannual examinations of state banks, Broderick failed to order another inquiry into the Bank of the United States until July, 1930.

Now it was discovered that the bank's surplus and undivided profits had been completely dissipated; therefore, its capital was badly impaired. Even so, Broderick still failed to act decisively, while Marcus and Singer continued to issue glowing financial statements to depositors, stockholders and the public.

On December 2, 1930, President Hoover delivered his annual message to the Congress, saying, among other things: "The fundamental strength of the nation's economy is unimpaired."

He was not believed by some depositors of the Bank of the United States, who had begun to hear ominous whispers about its true financial condition. On December 10 a Bronx merchant tried to resell his stock in the Bank of the United States to the manager of one of its Bronx branches. The manager refused to buy back the stock. A garbled version of this incident led to a rumor that the bank had declined to let the merchant withdraw his deposit, and a run began on most of the Bronx branches of the bank. By the end of the business day 2,500 Bronx depositors had withdrawn $2 million, and throughout the rest of New York City people were telling one another that the Bank of the United States was failing.

This news frightened a sixty-one-year-old janitor, George Gelies, who lived in the basement of an apartment house in the Bronx. After working for forty years, he had saved $1,000, which he now had on deposit in a Bronx branch of the Bank of the United States. He hurried to the bank, took his place in line with other worried depositors, waited fifteen hours but did not even get up to a teller's window. At 1 A.M. the following day the janitor got in line a second time, standing in the rain without a bite to eat until long after normal banking hours, when he finally reached a pay window and managed to borrow $200 against his $1,000 deposit.

Soon after getting home with this cash, the janitor took to his bed, for he had come down with a heavy cold. His condition worsened, a fever set in, and Gelies began raving about a chicken farm he had wanted all his life. He refused to let his wife call a doctor, since they could not afford one. His wife took over his chores, tending the furnace in their building and in others in the neighborhood. While she was gone, he hanged himself from a steam pipe after writing this note: "Let my wife have all the money—if she gets any—Good-bye George, be a good boy."

Their son George was a sailor aboard the USS *Nevada*.

After the janitor's wife found his body, she sobbed: "The two hundred dollars my husband got from the bank will just about pay for the funeral! Now I have no money and no husband!"

*   *   *

Albert J. Kobler, publisher of the New York *Mirror*, owned thousands of shares of the bank's stock, which he had used as collateral in borrowing money. If the bank failed and he had to cover this equity, he would have to come up with almost $900,000. He told his managing editor, Emile Gauvreau, that he was afraid he would lose control of the *Mirror*. On the midnight following the first run on the bank's Bronx branches, the top bank officers met in its main office to discuss what to do. Kobler took Gauvreau to this midnight conference. One bank official, aware that Gauvreau was an accomplished writer, asked him to compose advertisements saying that the bank had $300 million in assets which were slightly frozen at the moment but would soon thaw out. The idea was to publish these ads in the morning newspapers. Gauvreau declined; he did not relish the prospect of a cell in Sing Sing.

That tense night of December 10–11, 1930, another conference was being held—this one in the New York Federal Reserve Bank in the Wall Street area. A group of prominent financiers were trying to find some way to save the Bank of the United States. Among those present was Martin Eagan of the House of Morgan. Early in the morning Eagan telephoned the home of Elliott V. Bell of the financial staff of the New York *Times*. Eagan told Bell: "It's all over. They can't agree on any plan. There is only one chance in a thousand that the bank will open tomorrow morning."

Bell called his office and was ordered to come in and write the story. He had just begun to grind out his copy when the night desk told him to stop. *Times* publisher Adolph Ochs had been informed of the situation. Ochs had decided that if there remained even a 1,000 to 1 chance that the bank might survive, publication of Bell's story might intensify the panic. The December 11 issue of the New York *Times* carried an article on page five about the run on the Bronx branches but said nothing about the indecision of the big financiers.

That same December 11 runs resumed in the Bronx and also—for the first time—at the main office of the Bank of the United States. This was just around the corner from the Communist Party's national headquarters at 50 East Thirteenth Street. As soon as passing Communists saw the growing line of anxious and angry depositors, they raced into the headquarters to report to their leaders. This crisis was exactly the kind the Red leaders wanted. Now they decided to do their damnedest to make a bad situation worse.

All party members lounging around the headquarters were called together and told what to do. A few of them really had money of their own on deposit in the bank. Others were instructed to pose as depositors. All were to rush to the bank, get into the waiting line and then try to arouse the crowd to fury. They were to spread rumors about the imminent collapse of other banks as well. These tactics, according to the Communist leaders, might heighten the panic and trigger runs on all banks in the financial heart of America.

The police were called to control the bona fide depositors, who would have set up a howl even if no Communists had existed on the face of the earth. At first the cops tried persuasion, telling the people that their money was perfectly safe. Here and there a bluecoat could be heard saying: "I only wish I had money in that bank!" Although the Red provocateurs were unable to start a riot, the crowd became increasingly impatient and indignant as hour followed hour, and at last the lines were threatened by mounted policemen.

Finally, that same day of December 11, 1930—and at long last—Banking Superintendent Broderick stepped in and closed the Bank of the United States. Like the shock of an earthquake, a tremor ran through New York and across the country. This was the first New York City bank to fail since the Crash, the largest bank failure so far in the nation's history and an ominous hint of things to come. There was an immediate drop in the prices of other bank stocks.

Although the bank's small depositors outnumbered its large ones, many big institutions were hit. For example, the New York City government had $1.5 million on deposit, the state government $1 million, and the New York *Times* $17,000. Some of the large depositors banded together to try to get their money out of the closed bank. They called themselves the Bank of the United States Depositors' and Stockholders' Association and hired as attorney Max Steuer, a noted criminal lawyer with intimate Tammany connections.

Communist leaders did much the same thing by organizing many small depositors, to demand that the frozen funds of the big depositors be seized to pay off all small depositors, dollar for dollar. The group insisted that Marcus and Singer be arrested and convicted of criminal responsibility for the bank's failure. It urged immediate nationalization of all banks in the nation.

Norman Thomas pointed out that the Bank of the United States had been chartered by the state of New York, charged that the state banking department was under suspicion and declared that Governor Roosevelt had done nothing to avert the fall of the bank despite warnings that it was weak.

W. Kingsland Macy, soon to become chairman of the New York State Republican Committee, called for Broderick's removal, accusing him of breaking the law and behaving much like his predecessor in the City Trust affair. Macy cried that stockholders and depositors would have been protected and this tragedy avoided if only the superintendent had done his duty back in 1929 when "four of his examiners . . . separately signed reports severely criticizing the administration of the bank."

The bank did not have $300 million in assets, as one of its officers had told Gauvreau; Broderick soon announced that its net deposits came to only $161 million. Marcus, the bank's president, said he was unable to explain this shrinkage of assets, except for depreciation of the bank's securities. To relieve the hardships endured by small depositors, the state banking department ruled that they might borrow half their deposits at 5 percent interest. This fee, it was explained to the bank's outraged customers, was meant to keep them from feeling that they were receiving charity.

A Communist-led committee of small depositors made arrangements to meet with Mayor Jimmy Walker in City Hall. On the appointed day the committeemen arrived on time, but after waiting half an hour, they were told that the mayor would not be back until 4:30 P.M. However, if they wished, they would be received immediately by the mayor's assistant, Charles F. Kerrigan, a man whom Heywood Broun once compared to a cuttlefish. The delegation was shown into a large Colonial room.

Another wait; then in walked Kerrigan. Tall, pasty-faced, he had begun to imitate some of the mannerisms of his boss. Flipping his eyebrows up and down, cocking his head to one side, Kerrigan turned mocking eyes on the committee's spokesman, M. D. Littman, who began reading a statement. The delegation demanded that all small depositors be paid first and in full; that stockholders be taxed the face value of their shares if there were not enough bank funds to pay the small depositors; that all the property of the stockholders and bank directors be attached immediately. The young and determined Littman went on to demand that more bank branches be opened for depositors, who had been waiting in line from six to eleven hours a day to get the loan of half their deposits. Littman told Kerrigan that his own wife had caught cold while standing in the rain outside a branch office and was now in bed with pneumonia. He said that when he himself reached a teller's window, the teller would not lend him any money on his deposit because he did not have his sick wife's signature. Littman also complained about the city police. He said some cops took bribes to place people near the head of waiting lines. When some angry depositors announced their intention of getting out of the rain and into the bank to protest to bank officials, according to Littman, the cops beat them up. One man was clubbed unconscious. Six persons, one a sixty-year-old woman, had been arrested.

"I ask you!" cried Littman to the mayor's assistant. "Here's a run on a bank where not a single disorderly act is committed, not a window is broken, and while stockholders and big depositors get Max Steuer—who is so good at defending criminals, to protect their interests—us poor buggers get beaten up by the police and called foreigners and Reds!"

When Littman finished speaking, Kerrigan said: "I know that the mayor has been very seriously concerned about this—we've got one and a half millions in the bank ourselves. Of course, the difference is that we're not being evicted from our houses and we're not in a position where we can't afford to pay our bills, but it's just as much to our interest as yours to see that this is straightened out. As for the police beating people up—this is the first complaint of that kind we've had. That'll be stopped." Then Kerrigan added: "We've heard of the police taking people *out* of the line where they *didn't* belong and putting them back where they did—and they did that because it was—was the right thing to do—but we've never heard of this—other thing."

Kerrigan peered at the statement Littman had handed him. "We can't do anything about these first requests," he said. "The whole thing is up to the state. . . ."

Although city officials did nothing to help small depositors, the city itself began legal action to recover the $1.5 million it had on deposit in the bank. The New York *Times* published a letter calling the Bank of the United States a misleading name, and a minister preached a sermon on this same subject. District Attorney Thomas C. T. Crain, a bumbling old Tammany wheelhorse, launched a grand jury investigation of the bank's affairs. In a letter to Crain, Governor Roosevelt urged vigorous prosecution of bank officials.

Legal proceedings were complex and so protracted that they stretched into the year 1932. It was proved that the bank had been warned of its precarious condition, that bank officials had concealed this fact, books had been falsified, a truckload of records had been destroyed, minutes of board meetings had disappeared, bank officers had received huge loans without the knowledge of the board and so on.

Marcus, Singer and six other bank officials were indicted on the felonious charge of misappropriating funds. Among these other half-dozen defendants was the very Henry Pollock whom Roosevelt had appointed to his Commission on Revision of the Banking Law. Marcus admitted from the witness stand that he had not told his own board of directors about the criticism made by the state banking department. In a trial lasting almost thirteen weeks Marcus and Singer were found guilty of misappropriation of funds and sent to Sing Sing for three to six years. The jury disagreed about Pollock's guilt, so he was set free. After a very long wait the depositors of the Bank of the United States got back more than 90 percent of their money.

Various people continued to demand that Broderick be removed as state banking superintendent, and finally he was indicted on charges of neglect of duty and conspiracy. He loudly proclaimed his innocence. Governor Roosevelt not only promised to back Broderick to the end but took the stand in his behalf and even tried to share his blame for tardiness in closing the Bank of the United States. At the end of an eight-week trial Broderick was acquitted.

The Bank of the United States was just one of 1,326 banks that failed throughout the nation in 1930, but it was by far the most important failure.

It evoked panic, protests and arrests. It proved that some bankers were crooks and others were incompetent. As the New York *Times* pointed out, it shook the faith of many Americans in bankers and the banking system. It helped Communism, for many people wondered how all Communists could be all wrong when injustice was so obvious.

And as for Franklin D. Roosevelt, perhaps for the first time in his life, he began to eye bankers with cold suspicion.

8

Scrubwomen and Stockholders

O N NOVEMBER 1, 1929, Harvard University fired Mrs. Emma Trafton, who had scrubbed floors there for thirteen years. Despite her long years of service, she was discharged out of hand. Then, the day before Christmas, another scrubwoman, Mrs. Katherine Donahue, who had worked for Harvard for thirty-three years, was told that her services were no longer required. More and more women were laid off, until a total of twenty Harvard scrubwomen found themselves unemployed and penniless.

One of the worried women was a member of a Methodist church in East Cambridge, Massachusetts, and turned to her minister for help. The Reverend Doctor William M. Duvall listened to her story in growing astonishment, and when she had finished, he wrote to Dr. A. Lawrence Lowell, the president of Harvard, asking why that great institution was discharging its scrubwomen.

Lowell replied that the Massachusetts Minimum Wage Board had been complaining about Harvard's scrubwomen. At that time Massachusetts had no minimum wage law covering men, but it did have one for women. Under this statute, women in certain industries had to be paid 37 cents an hour. Harvard was paying its cleaning women 35 cents an hour. Although Lowell did not say so, the state was complaining about Harvard, not about its employees. What Lowell told the minister was that in order to comply with this law, and also to save money, Harvard was laying off its scrubwomen and replacing them with men.

The nation's press landed on this story with both feet. Harvard was breaking the law? Rather than pay its scrubwomen 2 cents more an hour, Harvard was firing them left and right? Incredible! Ridiculous! Criminal! Why, in the past year Harvard had received more than $11 million in bequests. Heywood Broun, who had attended Harvard, pointed out in his column that even if the university were to pay its cleaning women a legal

116

minimum wage, the extra cost would amount to only about $6,000 more a year—less than the cost of equipment for the scrub football team for one season. Broun added that "unless Harvard takes immediate steps to fix a pension system for its veteran employees it will forfeit any right to stand as a leader in enlightenment."

On the campus itself student members of Socialist and liberal clubs criticized the dismissals and handed out pamphlets attacking Harvard's "capitalistic attitude." The *Harvard Crimson* ridiculed the Ivy League school in a parody of "Frankie and Johnny." Fifty-two alumni signed their names to a letter asking Harvard to make amends to the scrubwomen, but administration officials did nothing to rectify this injustice. After many months, a group of Harvard graduates, students and teachers raised $3,880, which they distributed among the twenty unemployed cleaning women.

*   *   *

That same November 1, in Minneapolis, the W. B. Foshay Company, together with its allied firms, went into receivership with liabilities of $20 million.

Foshay had built a public utilities empire by gluing together odds and ends of power companies in thirteen states, Alaska, Canada and Central America and shaping them into a flimsy pyramid of companies within companies. His stock promotion circulars bore this slogan: "All your money—All the time—On time." This was supposed to mean that investors would receive an endless stream of monthly dividends—and for a while they did. However, as federal investigators later learned, these dividends came not from earnings but from new capital poured into Foshay's enterprises by gullible speculators. Genuine profits had been small.

This gigantic business failure kept staring directly into the faces of the people of Minneapolis, since only three months prior to his fall Foshay had opened a skyscraper in their city. Named the Foshay Tower, this building was thirty-two stories tall and resembled the Washington Monument. The Foshay Tower went on auction—time and time and time again—and at the *seventeenth* auction a contemptuous bid of 15 cents was made for the 447-foot-high structure.

Foshay said he had failed because of his inability to keep up his volume of stock sales and maintain his bank credit, but he was convicted of mail fraud in connection with the sale of securities.

*   *   *

The youthful radio industry had been one of the gleaming facets of the golden bull market during the Twenties; in 1929 alone millions of Americans spent a total of $850 million to buy radio sets. One radio manufacturing firm was the Kolster Radio Corporation, whose chairman and chief stockholder was Rudolph Spreckels, a resident of San Francisco and a member of a rich family that controlled sugar plantations in Hawaii.

In 1928, for some puzzling reason, Spreckels discovered that Kolster profits had dropped to almost nothing. He sought help from George F. Breen of New York, known in financial circles as the "Doctor of Sick Markets" and "Hero of a Hundred Pools" because of his ability to rig stock prices. Breen had learned how to read a stock ticker before he was seven years old. Spreckels wanted to sell his 250,000 shares of Kolster at the best possible price. Breen agreed to form a pool and boost the stock. Hiring a press agent for $40,000, Breen began his undercover work. Soon financial writers were prattling about "highly favorable developments" in the Kolster operation, while brokers working for Breen started buying and selling huge blocks of Kolster stock. All this attracted the attention of unsuspecting speculators, who rapidly acquired Kolster securities for themselves, pushing the price up, up, up.

When Breen decided that he had boosted Kolster as high as it could go, he and his fellow conspirators unloaded. This pool worked so well that one insider who had spent only $1,500 for Kolster stock made a profit of $3 million. Spreckels came out of the game almost $13 million richer, and Breen earned more than $1.3 million for his trickery.

But what of the suckers who had bought Kolster stock as a result of the pool operation and calculated publicity? They lost millions upon millions of dollars. From an artificial high of 78¾, the price of Kolster stock dropped to a low of 5⅛ by December, 1929, and a month later the company went into receivership. The hurt and angry stockholders banded together into a committee, sought to retrieve their losses, hurled charges of stock rigging. Breen denied this charge, saying he merely had tried to stabilize the stock. The matter was heard before a special master of chancery, who ruled there had been no rigging. Spreckles and his colleagues were absolved.

*   *   *

If misery loves company, these Kolster stockholders were far from lonely. After a tentative pause following the Crash, the American economy began to sag. Declines were registered by almost every business index— industrial production, building construction, exports, imports, the volume of stock transactions, call money, automobile output, farm production, railway freight loadings and the like. During the first quarter of 1930 sixty major firms earned from 15 to 20 percent less than they had in the first three months of 1929, the heaviest losses being taken by automobile companies and auto accessory firms.

On the other hand, higher profits were made by the entertainment, advertising and tobacco businesses. As the general gloom deepened, people sought distraction in show business, bought newspaper ads to try to prove they were not downhearted and nervously smoked pack after pack.

In 1930 the American Tobacco Company turned a profit of $43 million, or nearly 16 percent more than in the previous year. Its president, George Washington Hill, earned just under $2.5 million in salary, bonus, stock allotment and special cash credits. While many of his fellow Americans worried about how they could eat and where they could sleep, Hill kept up his membership in clubs such as the Metropolitan, Williams, Congressional, Ardsley, Westchester Country, Greenwich, Knollwood Country, Blind Brook, Sleepy Hollow Country and Seaview Golf Club.

Soon his American Tobacco Company would pay its workers as little as $15.86 a week.

People who had lost money and jobs now bought fewer goods and services, resulting in less production and more unemployment. All this led to a demand for relief.

Of crucial importance during this early stage of the Depression was President Hoover's concept of relief. He was crystal clear about it, saying in his memoirs: ". . . I insisted that the first obligation of direct relief rested on local communities, and that they should not call upon the state and Federal governments until the load overtaxed their capacities. . . . I added emphatically that direct relief to individuals from the Federal government would bring an inevitable train of corruption and waste such as our nation had never witnessed."

So much for *direct* relief. On the other hand, Hoover favored *indirect* relief, which he defined as "Federal and state public works, together with stimulation of private construction, 'spreading the work,' restriction of immigration, governmental financial measures to support private employment, and action in the foreign field."

In the middle of November, 1929, in separate White House sessions, the President met with three different groups of men—the heads of twelve of the nation's leading railroads, the nation's outstanding labor leaders and the nation's biggest industrialists. At the beginning of the conference with the industrialists, some of them revealed that they were not impressed with the gravity of the situation. They sobered up quickly enough, however, when Hoover said he considered the crisis more than a mere stock market crash, announced there already were 2,000,000 to 3,000,000 unemployed citizens and declared that it was his duty to alleviate their distress.

Among those present at the meeting was Henry Ford, the auto manufacturer. When it broke up, Ford stepped outside the White House and there, on its steps, made a sensational announcement. Ford began with the declaration that the stock slump was not the cause of the business decline, but its effect. "American production," he said, "has come to equal and even surpass, not our people's power to consume, but their power to purchase." Ford then announced that he intended to do his part by raising his workers' wages $1 a day—from $6 to $7. He also promised to give proportionate salary increases to Ford employees already earning more than this daily minimum.

Ford's words made the front page of every big paper in the country, enhancing his reputation for boldness and generosity. On December 4 his son, Edsel, who had just paid $400,000 for a new yacht, elaborated on his father's plan. Edsel said that the two of them hoped to contribute "to a continuance of normal business conditions by putting a bit more of buying power into the pockets of workmen." With prices and profits slumping, this announcement did not sit well with the other industrialists who had met with President Hoover. Besides, they felt secretly that Henry Ford was grandstanding—and he was.

Although Ford's new basic wage of $7 a day remained in force at his plants for the next two years, it cloaked a scheme for cutting his payroll through ruthless efficiency. Despite his promise to his better-paid employees, he pared their salaries. He fired workers in one department and rehired them in another department at lower pay. He intensified his notorious speedup system. One of his foremen told workers: "Go like hell, boys! If you're gonna get that raise you gotta increase production." While on the job, Ford workers were forbidden to talk, whistle, sing or smoke, and they got only fifteen minutes for lunch. Company spies watched men suspected of loafing.

By farming out most of his production to the sweatshops of the auto industry, Ford hammered down supplier prices until these parts makers had to slash their own payrolls. In 1930–31 Ford laid off 45,000 men, and two years later the number of Ford unemployed had doubled.

*   *   *

From the start of the Depression and on through the decade, one of the most controversial questions was just how many Americans were unemployed. This prime problem was first brought out into the open by Miss Frances Perkins, whom Governor Roosevelt had named industrial commissioner of the state of New York. Born a Boston Brahmin, educated at Mount Holyoke College, witty and gay, brainy and talkative, Miss Perkins usually wore a triangular hat and had a nose as blunt as her character. Like some other state employees, she had an office in New York City, and on the morning of January 22, 1930, while riding to work, she opened the New York *Times* and read a Washington dispatch quoting President Hoover as saying that employment had risen and things were getting better. Miss Perkins was horrified. She knew that employment was falling in New York State and she suspected that it also was falling in other parts of the nation. Her boss, Governor Roosevelt, had not mentioned the state's rising tide of joblessness in his January 1 message to the state legislature, and at that time Miss Perkins had kept silent. Now, however, she decided to take it on herself to correct the President.

From the Bureau of Labor Statistics in Washington she obtained figures on unemployment in other states, and then, aided by a statistician, she related them to New York data. The next day Miss Perkins called reporters to her office and announced that the President was wrong. Employment everywhere was down, unemployment was up, and things were getting worse, not better. Miss Perkins felt that if Americans were told that everything was rosy, but still could not land a job, they might wind up cynical and despairing. Her blast at Hoover made headlines across the country.

Before issuing her statement, Miss Perkins had not even thought of consulting Governor Roosevelt, so when he phoned her the following morning, her heart sank. Just as she started to apologize, she heard his cheery voice boom: "Bully for you! That was a fine statement and I'm glad you made it." Despite this, she begged his pardon for her failure to consult him in advance, but Roosevelt said: "Well, I think it was better you didn't. If you had asked me, I would probably have told you not to do it, and I think it is much more wholesome to have it right out in the open."

Never in the history of the United States had the federal government taken a regular census of unemployment. Instead, from time to time the Labor Department had asked for unemployment data from 35,000 business firms whose total work force was fewer than 5,000,000 employees. This was too small a sampling. Furthermore, if a man worked only one day out of six, he was reported as having a full-time job. Using inadequate figures and drawing wrong conclusions, the Labor Department then made projections of unemployment across the nation.

In April, 1930, perhaps stung by Miss Perkins' criticism, President Hoover ordered the first house-to-house census of the jobless ever taken. Before the end of the month the Commerce Department reported that 45,000,000 citizens were gainfully employed, 2,429,000 were looking for work, and 755,000 had been laid off the job. Thus, the unemployed totaled 3,184,000. Hoover said publicly that "unemployment amounting to distress is concentrated in twelve states"—but he did not name the states. Secretary of Labor James J. Davis admitted there was "distressing unemployment."

* * *

Of course, mere figures could not adequately describe the magnitude and character of this suffering. Louis Adamic, an author who was interested in people as human beings, collected case histories about the unemployed. In his book *My America,* Adamic told of a man whose first name was Jim. A steady worker, Jim had driven a truck for a trucking firm for five years, earning $45 a week. In April, 1930, this company went bankrupt, and Jim lost his job. For the next five months he was without any kind of work. In September he got two weeks' work driving for another trucking concern— at a mere $23 a week. After that he was unable to find any kind of employment. In December he lost his life savings—$350—when his bank failed.

Jim was thirty-six years old, happily married and the father of four children. When two of his children fell ill, he and his wife had to pawn some of their belongings and then borrow money to pay the doctor and druggist. By September, 1931, they were three months behind in their rent. When their landlord threatened to evict them, Jim "got out of his mind," as his wife later described it.

Living in their apartment building were two other men—also husbands, also fathers, also unemployed. Jim teamed up with them to commit a robbery that yielded only $33 and resulted in their arrest. Although Jim's problems were explained to the district attorney, and despite testimony by his friends about his fine character before the Depression, he was sentenced to five years in Sing Sing. His wife felt disgraced. She and the children moved into a one-room flat, and for the first time in her life she asked for charity. Given a few dollars every now and then, she managed to somehow keep them alive. Charity paid for a railway ticket to the penitentiary so she could visit her husband, and when she saw him, her face went gray. Jim's forehead was waffled with blue scars, for whenever his anguish became too great to bear, he banged his head against the walls of his cell.

Back home again, one dull day following another, Jim's wife watched helplessly as her children reacted painfully to the absence of their father. All five slept in the same room, except for the oldest boy, who slept in the tub in the windowless bathroom. The others huddled in bed to try to keep warm in the unheated flat. Lacking proper food, the children lost weight; lacking heat, they came down with colds. They bawled. Their mother wept. When Adamic visited her, she wailed: "We'd be better off dead!"

*   *   *

Meantime, *True Story* magazine made its own curious contribution to the national crisis by paying many newspapers to publish full-page advertisements that urged Americans to buy luxuries on credit. Not necessities. *Luxuries!*

*   *   *

Franklin D. Roosevelt watched a sad drama unfolding before his eyes. He owned an estate at Hyde Park, New York, and he knew a man who owned a sweater mill in a small village nearby. Before the Depression this man manufactured a good-quality ladies' knitted sweater that retailed for $9 or $10. His 150 employees were paid wages high enough so they could live comfortably in their community. The work was reasonably steady since the millowner had developed a regular market with a few excellent wholesale houses. After the Depression began, though, these wholesalers gave him fewer orders because they got fewer orders from retailers. In the past, retailers had bought a dozen sweaters at a time; now they wanted only one or two of them.

At first the millowner closed down for longer periods of time between big orders, but finally he had to lay off about half his workers. The wholesalers asked if he could make a cheaper sweater. He tried. He got small orders for the cheaper sweater, but they did not bring him enough work.

He was a local man, and his employees were his friends. When their savings became exhausted, they begged him for something to do, since there was no other work in the vicinity.

Finally the millowner went down to New York City to canvass the streets where the wholesalers and jobbers were located. They were as frantic as he. They had to sell something or they, too, would have to go out of business, leaving their own workers unemployed. At last the millowner found a jobber who said: "We just got an order for five thousand sweaters to sell at two dollars apiece. Can you fill it?"

"How could I? You know that doesn't touch the cost."

"I know. I hate to suggest it to you, but if you reduce wages way down, stretch out the hours and use shoddy yarn, you can do it."

Thinking of his workers, the millowner agreed to try, adding: "There will be nothing in this for me."

"Perhaps not. There won't be much for me, either, but see what you can do."

The millowner went home, called his workers together and put the proposition up to them. He said he would forgo his profit. The order would give them a few weeks' work at wages he hated to mention. He asked them to figure out what wages they thought he could pay them on a sweater selling at $2. In their desperation, his employees finally told him to take the order if they could get as much as $5 a week. The boss did so, getting no return at all on his capital.

Governor Roosevelt visited the mill and saw firsthand the workers' plight. Miss Perkins, who tells this story in her biography of Roosevelt, went on to say: "He realized how desperate people can become. This experience helped him to understand the economic phrase 'the descending spiral.' "

*   *   *

On March 29, 1930, Governor Roosevelt spoke up about the problem of unemployment: "After the crash of 1929, and indeed for some time before that, the state of New York faced the problem of a growing number of unemployed. The federal government had adopted the policy of doing very little for the relief of distress among the unemployed, either by providing food and shelter, or by furnishing work. Accordingly, the state was compelled to attempt to do the task with such assistance as it could obtain from local government which was already overburdened by taxes and debt."

Then, after a tardy start, Governor Roosevelt swung into vigorous action. He appointed a State Committee on Stabilization of Industry to develop a long-range program for the prevention of unemployment. He advocated an unemployment insurance system. He offered the use of state armories to mayors throughout New York to shelter people lacking a roof over their heads.

One of Roosevelt's sons, twenty-year-old Elliott, asked his father what he thought of using National Guard air squadrons to fly surplus farm products from upper New York State down to New York City for distribution to the jobless. Elliott argued that this would focus attention on the problems of both the farmers and the unemployed. The governor told his son that the plan would not work "because of the great weight of things like apples or other fruits or vegetables." Even 1,000 pounds of any raw foodstuffs, Roosevelt said, "would be a mere drop in the bucket in the food supply of New York City, and the cost of getting it there would be approximately five hundred times as much as if it came in a freight car or even in a motor truck."

A tough kid out of New York's Hell's Kitchen successfully pulled off the stunt that Elliott Roosevelt had suggested—with a twist. Young Roosevelt and his father had been concerned with the welfare of the people, as well as the logistics of this problem, but the young man was concerned solely with profits. Reared in a Catholic orphanage, shunted from foster home to foster home, a high school dropout at the age of fifteen in the year 1931, a layoff man for a gambling syndicate and then an inventory clerk in a chain store, he took flying lessons and bought a secondhand single-engine plane.

This was in the middle of the Depression. People in New York were hungry, while down in Virginia and the Carolinas whole fields of unsold corn rotted on the ground. Time after time, this young man flew south of the Mason-Dixon Line, bought up field after field of produce, flew back to New York and sold the foodstuffs to stores at cut-rate prices. He claimed that by the time he was twenty he had earned $1.5 million.

Later he became a novelist and wrote an honest and simple story of poverty during Depression years which he entitled *A Stone for Danny Fisher*. Then he turned to sensational themes in books such as *The Adventurers* and *The Carpetbaggers*. In 1968 *Life* magazine was to call him "the world's best-paid writer." His name was Harold Robbins.

9

Apple Peddlers and Breadlines

A DROUGHT that began in 1930 crippled the production of apples and other produce. In certain hard-hit states ripe apples were smaller than in the past, while the harvest was only about half what it had been between 1924 and 1928. However, in Oregon and Washington, where plenty of rain had fallen, production was as much as 19 percent higher than usual. These two states, long noted for the excellence of their fruit, now had an abundance of apples, and this very abundance raised the question of how to market them.

Back in 1929, at a farm dinner in Syracuse, New York, Governor Roosevelt had said: "We all know the story of the Oregon apple. We must take off our hats to the energy and salesmanship of our friends in Oregon and Washington who have created a demand in New York State's cities for apples which have to be transported three thousand miles. The story of the success of the western apple is well known in every eastern city in spite of the knowledge that we can, if we want to, raise equally fine and perhaps better tasting apples in our own orchards. One trouble is, of course, that too many thousands of farmers in the east continue to flood the local markets with inferior, under-sized, badly packed apples, with the result that the average retail merchant prefers to handle the product from the Pacific Coast, because the buying public wants something that looks good as well as tastes good."

The Pacific growers were even shrewder than Roosevelt realized.

In the fall of 1930 they discussed ways of selling their apple surplus. When an official of the International Apple Shippers' Association urged the use of the unemployed to sell apples on street corners, his colleagues were so delighted that they gave him an award. Developing this idea, the association decided that growers would give apples on credit to jobless men, who in turn would retail them at 5 cents apiece. Their press agent

125

coined the slogan: "Buy an apple a day and eat the Depression away!" The growers counted on prospective buyers sympathizing with forlorn men standing on sidewalks with nothing to sell but apples.

And the public did—at first. Millions of apples were shipped from the Northwest to the Eastern Seaboard and elsewhere, and apple vendors soon became stereotyped figures on the American scene. It was in October, 1930, that apple salesmen first appeared on the sidewalks of New York. Kindhearted and high-spirited members of the New York Curb Exchange celebrated Halloween by auctioning off all the stock of all the apple merchants in their neighborhood. By November the city of New York had 6,000 apple peddlers, while Chicago and St. Louis and other big cities were reporting their appearance.

In New York the wholesalers had their main apple warehouse on West Street at Harrison Street, down on the Lower West Side of Manhattan. Above its door a large red sign announced: HELPING UNEMPLOYED. About six o'clock in the morning, in the cold and dark, ragged men started lining up outside this door in such numbers that soon they formed a queue a block or more in length. Many had breakfasted on nothing more than evil-smelling mush and so-called coffee at a nearby city dormitory. Each man was given a box containing seventy-two apples, together with a printed sign saying: UNEMPLOYED . . . BUY APPLES . . . 5¢ EACH. Hoisting the crates onto their shoulders, the men then set off for various parts of the city.

At the depot each man had paid $1.75 for his crate of apples. If he sold all of them at 5 cents apiece, he would gross $3.60 and make a net profit of $1.85 for a day's work. Theoretically. Of course, some apples were sure to spoil, and there was no guarantee that the peddler could sell all his day's stock. In November the wholesalers raised the price from $1.75 to $2.25 per box.

As competition became keener, some of the desperate men began cutting their retail price to two apples for a nickel. Before long peddlers were complaining that they were losing 25 cents a crate. Their gripes were investigated by Charles Yale Harrison, a thirty-two-year-old reporter for the New York *American*. Posing as an unemployed man and dressing the part, Harrison lived for a week in a dank city flophouse and lined up each morning at the apple warehouse on West Street. He observed that starving men knew no color barriers, for the waiting vendors included white men, black men and yellow men. Some wore two shirts made of burlap as protection against the bitter winds whistling through lower Manhattan. There was even a one-legged man who left with his apple crate in a little wagon.

"Nobody cared what you were, who you were," Harrison wrote. "We were all starving together." The undercover reporter paid for a bundle of paper bags, paid for subway fares, found some of his apples so damaged they could not be sold, and at the end of a twelve-hour working day he found he had made a total profit of 95 cents. He could understand a man he overheard muttering: "Damn! I'm never going to forget this year! Nineteen-Thirty! I can spit on it!"

Gene Fowler, another noted Manhattan reporter, wrote: "Apple sellers crouched at the street corners like half-remembered sins sitting upon the conscience of the town."

People pitied the poor apple peddlers, and a few sad poems were scribbled in their honor. Soon, though, sentiment changed.

The song's sarcasm reflected growing disenchantment with the apple vendors. Some prissy citizens complained that discarded apple cores endangered life and limb, merchants paying rentals in stores frowned on alfresco competition, and cops in several cities chased the apple salesmen away from certain areas. President Hoover made one of the most astonishing remarks of his life when he wrote: "Many persons left their jobs for the more profitable one of selling apples." One wonders where the President got the information on which he based this remarkable judgment. Perhaps it came from the Bureau of the Census, which classified apple peddlers as employed persons.

Lack of profits, public disfavor and official harassment soon caused apple vendors to vanish. To the people who lived through that dismal decade, however, they remained the lasting symbol of the Great Depression.

*   *   *

One gusty March day in 1930 a huge and untidy man got out of a cab near the Little Church Around the Corner in mid-Manhattan. He was forty-one-year-old Heywood Broun, a syndicated Scripps-Howard columnist and a fellow so careless of his appearance that a friend said he looked like an unmade bed. Clearheaded but sentimental, Broun always sympathized with the underdog. He had arrived for a look at the first breadline opened by the church since the Panic of 1907.

Hungry men stood in a triple line with their backs to the wind like cattle facing away from a storm. At first this breadline had been single file, but this made it so long that it coiled out of Twenty-ninth Street and far north up Fifth Avenue—a distressing sight to the residents of that celebrated thoroughfare. As Broun expressed it, they did not want to see "a worm that walks like a man." Two thousand had flocked to this Episcopal church upon learning that it would give them a bite to eat, and regrettably, 500 of them would have to be turned away empty-stomached.

Broun shambled along the line like a friendly bear, handing out cigarettes here, asking questions there. He had come to this sad scene not only as a journalist in search of a story but as an American whose conscience was tormented by his countrymen's anguish. Gently conversing in turn with this man and that, Broun found one with a skill he thought might be used by a particular industry, then another with a different specialty. He suggested places where they might apply for work.

Two young women were passing out Communist literature to the men in the breadline, and Broun took a leaflet. It said: "The whole capitalist government is filled with fury at the refusal of the unemployed to starve in silence." And it called for unemployment demonstrations.

After handing out the last of his cigarettes, Broun hailed another taxi, grunted his way inside it and started uptown, stopping to pick up late editions of the morning newspapers. President Hoover was exuding more confidence. Broun sighed. If the President were to see a breadline with his own eyes, perhaps he might become more realistic. But until Hoover acted decisively, what could the average Joe do to help things? Suddenly the columnist had an idea. Upon arriving in his penthouse at 120 West Fifty-eighth Street, Broun gave his dog an absent-minded pat on the head and then sat down at his typewriter. Cranking in a sheet of paper, he started writing:

> Give a job till June.
> There can be no question that unemployment is acute and that millions are in want. Something should be done, and it should be done now. President Hoover's remedy seems to be a set of promises. Mr. [William Z.] Foster, the revolutionary, has offered the hungry a series of parades. Thus there has been little consolation from the right or from the left.
> It is up to us of the middle class to stir ourselves. And so I say, "Give a job till June." This column will start immediately to act as a clearing house for unemployment. Naturally, its scope is small, but when so much cries out for the doing even a scratch upon the surface may not be wasted.
> Specifically, then, I will start the movement by giving one job, and I hope to enlist support from some readers in this give a job till June campaign.

Dale Kramer, in his biography of Broun, says that one of Broun's helpers was "a tall, big-eared youth from the Pennsylvania coal fields named John O'Hara, who had written short stories and wanted to be a novelist." Kramer quotes O'Hara about this episode in his life:

> When Heywood Broun was running the "Give-a-Job-Till-June" Campaign in his column. I was out of work myself, so I wrote and asked him if there was anything I could do to help. Right away he called me up and said he had a lot of chores I could help out with, such as handling his mail and contributions from his daily WMCA broadcasts and some interviewing, etc.
> I ate lunch at his penthouse every day the first week I was with him, and incidentally it was usually the big meal of the day for me. At the end of the week I was genuinely surprised to receive a pay check for $35, which he gave me all the time I worked for him. And I know it came out of his own pocket, because I knew, through my job with him, quite a lot about his current financial situation, his checking accounts, etc. Until I got a regular

newspaper job he kept me on his personal payroll (I may say there was plenty of work to be done) and also he used to take me out at night, always, of course, picking up the tab wherever we went.

*   *   *

Apple peddlers disappeared. Breadlines remained. Regardless of what they were called—breadlines, soup kitchens, emergency kitchens—they became a familiar and disturbing sight in big cities and small towns, nagging the consciences of Americans who had enough to eat.

Between the fall of 1930 and the early part of the following winter one new breadline was started almost every day in New York City. By January, 1931, the metropolis had eighty-two breadlines serving an average of 85,000 meals a day. A New Yorker could not walk more than a half-dozen blocks or so without coming upon a line of hungry men, caps tugged low over their foreheads, waiting for a handout. Most of these breadlines served scanty meals: bread, soup and coffee . . . or stew and bread . . . or cheese or meat sandwiches and coffee . . . or beans, bread and coffee . . . or oatmeal, bread and coffee. Since this kind of fare was hardly filling, some men spent all day going from one breadline to another, eating as many as ten or twelve meager meals a day. At some places nickels or dimes were given to the luckless men.

The Salvation Army had a dozen breadlines of its own. Others were organized by churches and hospitals, rescue missions and veterans' groups, fraternal societies and the YMCA, religious orders and convents, racketeers and Tammany Hall, private individuals and newspapers.

William Randolph Hearst, always quick to set up public "benefactions" if there was enough publicity in it for himself and his newspapers, now established two Manhattan breadlines, one at Times Square and the other at Columbus Circle. This placed them at each end of the Great White Way, and Broadway managers howled in protest since they felt that the dismal spectacle of starving men would depress theatergoers and cut into Broadway business.

Louis Adamic wrote a description of one Hearst breadline:

> I often watched the bread line at Times Square. The wretched men, many without overcoats or decent shoes, usually began to line up soon after six o'clock—in good weather or bad, rain or snow. The big truck, accompanied by a screeching motor-cycle police escort which made all Broadway pause and look, usually came on the spot long before eight o'clock. There were huge signs on the truck informing the public that the food was provided by the munificence of this newspaper.
>
> As a rule the men in charge did not begin to distribute the sandwiches till half past eight, and sometimes later. They worked very slowly; to all seeming, deliberately stretching out the serving and keeping the men in the cold rain or snow or wind, their wretchedness exposed to the gaze of the theater crowds. Thus they advertised the high-mindedness and generosity of one paper directly in front of the building which houses the main offices

of another. [Note: the New York *Times*.] They fed on an average of only 960 men an evening; and part, if not most, of the expenses—about $600 a day—were contributed by the readers of the newspaper. [Note: Hearst's New York *American*.] In fairness to Hearst, it must be added that these two breadlines were not his idea, but that of one of his executives.

This nightly ritual, this constant parade of scarecrow figures along the Great White Way, continued to agitate the theater owners. Hearst, who realized that show business men advertised their plays in the *American*, finally gave in and shunted his private breadlines off Broadway and onto side streets.

At a time when Mayor Jimmy Walker increased his own salary from $25,000 to $40,000 a year, a municipal lodging house was serving 12,000 free meals a day, the city government was giving away tons of food in 50-pound bags, a Good Samaritan opened a free cafeteria for women, and New Yorkers were horrified to discover that even children were standing in breadlines. Robert F. Wagner, a Democratic Senator from New York, showed a picture of one breadline to his colleagues at a hearing held in Washington by the Senate Commerce Committee.

Pittsburgh began feeding 2,500 people daily and soon had other thousands begging for food. In Philadelphia 12 women fainted from hunger while standing in a breadline. Soup kitchens opened in Milwaukee. Al Capone, the overlord of vice in America, made a grand gesture of opening his own private breadline in Chicago. In Oklahoma a Tulsa school ran a soup kitchen for the children of the unemployed. Hungry folks were fed from the local jail in Berryville, a small town in the harvest-lush Shenandoah Valley of Virginia. A Newark man told police he had stolen $4 and wanted to be sent to jail for life, since at least he could eat in jail. In Pittsburgh a father stole a loaf of bread for his children and then hanged himself in shame.

And in Washington, D.C., something happened that shocked and angered Senator George W. Norris.

In December, 1930—at a time when banks were failing, farm prices were falling, railroad stocks were rising, wages were declining, less milk was being drunk and women were fainting from hunger—an ostentatious debutante party was held in the national capital. The party was arranged by Mr. and Mrs. Henry L. Doherty for Helen Lee Eames, daughter of Mrs. Doherty by a former marriage. Doherty was the chief organizer and first president of the Cities Service Company, a holding company that controlled almost 200 public utilities and oil enterprises worth more than $1 billion. Doherty felt that nothing was too good for his stepdaughter. Guests were whisked from New York to Washington in a special chartered train paid for by Doherty and then quartered in the Mayflower Hotel, a fashionable center of Washington life. He took over the hotel's public entertaining rooms and rented several floors for the vast entourage of guests, servants and entertainers.

On the eve of her debut Miss Eames gave a dinner for a dozen intimate friends, presenting each of them with a new Ford especially decorated with hunting pictures painted on the sides. She also bestowed an extra Ford on someone she called her "absent friend"—Alfonso XIII, King of Spain. Then came the lavish debutante party itself, with the finest cuisine being served in abundance. Newspapers estimated that the entire affair cost Doherty $250,000. As the carefree, wealthy people feasted in the Mayflower, on another part of that same block and at that very hour a breadline was creeping along—ragged and gray-faced men shivering in the cold, waiting for a morsel of food to keep them alive.

The next day Norris took the floor of the Senate chamber, recited unemployment figures, denounced the flagrant waste of so much money and food while millions of others Americans suffered, and then said of the partygoers: "I don't know how they had the heart to do it."

10

The Threat from Left and Right

ACROSS THE LAND the mood of the people began to change.

In 1930 the crisis of the Depression was as grave as war, according to Arthur Woods, who was organizing the President's Committee for Unemployment Relief.

O. Max Gardner, the governor of North Carolina, wrote a friend: "I am facing the gravest situation that has confronted North Carolina since the Civil War. Many of our people . . . have accepted the psychology of defeat."

If some Americans felt defeated, others felt rebellious. There were threats to blow up the Senate wing of the Capitol Building in Washington, causing District cops and Justice Department agents to tighten security measures. In Chicago, New York City, Cleveland and Philadelphia, mobs of unemployed men demonstrated in front of city halls and even attacked them.

*   *   *

Russian newspapers and magazines exaggerated the American Depression. One Moscow paper published pictures of holes dug in Broadway by repairmen, saying in lying captions that these pits had been caused by "bombings" and "riots." Top Soviet leaders did not necessarily believe all their propaganda, but there was rejoicing on the part of Joseph Stalin and members of the Comintern.

The Comintern, or Communist International, had been established in 1919 by Lenin in the hope of fomenting revolution throughout the world. The Bolsheviks felt that the proletariat everywhere was in a revolutionary mood. They also believed that their young Soviet state could not survive unless successful revolutions in other parts of the world brought them aid. Comintern members were tools in the hands of the Communist Party leadership. They adopted a platform aimed at the destruction of the bourgeois capitalist order by "methods of mass action leading logically to direct clashes with the bourgeois state machine in open struggle."

After Lenin's death in 1924 a power struggle broke out among the Soviet elite, and soon this developed into a political duel between Stalin and his archrival, Leon Trotsky. One of their major points of difference was the nature of the Communist revolution. Trotsky advocated permanent and worldwide revolution. Stalin countered with the slogan of "building socialism in one country." Their dispute has wrongly been interpreted to mean that Trotsky urged immediate world revolution while Stalin opposed it. In reality, the issue was theoretical hairsplitting on whether the security of the Soviet regime in Russia depended on the spread of revolution abroad.

Stalin won the duel and the power. Trotsky was expelled from the party in 1927, exiled to Central Asia in 1928 and kicked out of Russia in 1929. With Trotsky out of the way, Stalin could forget his own talk about "building socialism in one country." He did not settle back to develop Russia alone; far from it.

According to Trotsky, Stalin's master plan was based on the idea that "Russia was marching toward unprecedented prosperity, while in the rest of the world the entire social structure was rapidly disintegrating and ripening for Communist revolution; hence the duty of Communists to mobilize the masses and train them for the impending insurrections in all countries except, of course, the Soviet Union. The policy had many stupid and ludicrous and some very tragic consequences. . . ."

In the early part of 1929, besides consolidating his dictatorial powers within Russia itself, Stalin also won control of the American Communist Party by intervening personally in its affairs. The American party had been split between an anti-Stalinist faction led by Jay Lovestone, its secretary-general, and a pro-Stalinist faction led by William Z. Foster, the so-called grand old man of American Communism.

Stalin summoned the top American Communist leaders to Moscow. In meetings held in the Kremlin, Stalin accused Lovestone of "exceptionalism"—the doctrine that special circumstances in the United States made it impossible for the American Communist Party to fight capitalism along traditional Marxist-Leninist lines. Lovestone pointed out that certain features in the economic, social and political life of America sharply distinguished it from the general trends in other capitalist nations.

Foster, on the other hand, was so cravenly loyal to Stalin and the Comintern that he said: "I am for the Comintern from start to finish . . . and if the Comintern finds itself criss-cross with my opinions, there is only one thing to do and that is to change my opinions to fit the policy of the Comintern." Stalin ordered the American Communists to choose between Lovestone and Foster. The short, stocky dictator rumbled: "If the comrades of the American delegation accept our terms—good and well. If they don't—so much the worse for them!" His threat worked: Lovestone was deposed as secretary-general, and Foster took his place.

It was during this showdown in the Kremlin that Stalin had said: "I think the moment is not far off when a revolutionary crisis will develop in America. . . ."

After the American Communist leaders got home, they continued to wrangle internally, but despite this, they obeyed Stalin's decisions and all orders issuing from the Comintern. Growing unemployment, anxiety and bewilderment in the United States gave them the greatest opportunity they had had in their decade of existence. By making the most of this discontent, they hoped to increase party membership, win control of the unemployed, provoke the police, foment civil strife, trigger a nationwide revolution, overthrow the United States government and kill capitalism.

*　　　*　　　*

As early as January 11, 1930, the American Communists issued a manifesto calling on the unemployed to organize, defy the industrial speedup, fight job losses and protest against wage cuts. This document was headlined: WORKERS, DON'T STARVE! FIGHT!

On January 14 the Reds in this nation got word from the Comintern to set up unemployment councils under the auspicies of the Trade Union Unity League, which was headed by Foster. The next day the Comintern ordered every Communist Party in nations around the world to launch unemployment demonstrations. Tactics were carefully spelled out: "These demonstrations should not make for the traditional meeting place but for such places as government buildings, parliaments, town halls, barracks. . . . The appearance of the demonstrations is very important. They must have a revolutionary and proletarian aspect. . . ."

The demonstrators were told to carry placards with slogans reading: DEFEND THE SOVIET UNION . . . WE DEMAND JOBS . . . THERE IS NO HUNGER IN SOVIET RUSSIA. Some of these slogans were Red herrings, for life was far from pleasant in Russia. In 1929 Stalin began a drive to win control of all of Russia's farm production and distribution, breaking up independent peasant holdings and amalgamating them into collective farms. This program was stoutly resisted by peasants, and armed uprisings took place. Attributing the opposition to richer peasants, or *kulaks,* Stalin cracked down ruthlessly on them, deporting some to "corrective labor camps." More than 5,000,000 peasant households disappeared. Heedless of all consequences except the growth of his own power, Stalin collectivized Russian agriculture so fast and ferociously that crops failed and an artificial famine resulted. Many years later, at the Yalta Conference, an American diplomat named W. Averell Harriman heard Stalin remark without a flicker of emotion that he had purposely starved millions of kulaks just to get control of the peasants.

Besides this great loss of human life, the collectivization of agriculture

debased the standard of living of the masses. *No hunger in Soviet Russia?*
It had starving people and breadlines and ration cards. Unemployed
Russians were forced to take any job offered them, regardless of their skills
or lack of skills—or forfeit their ration cards. Under this harsh system,
Russia had only 1,235,000 unemployed in the spring of 1930, while in the
United States unemployment was edging up toward the 4,000,000 mark.
Although American Communists did not mention the fact, the Soviet
government refused to let any foreign relief agency ship food to famine
areas within Russia. One Russian, referring to Prohibition in the United
States, told a friend: "Hoover has taught the Americans not to drink." His
friend replied: "Stalin has taught Russians not to eat."

Socialist leader Norman Thomas, much reviled by the Communists, was
alert to conditions in Russia, as well as to the tactics of the American
Reds. He knew that their demands for unemployment relief in the United
States were meant to "politicalize" the workers and prepare them for
revolution. Spurning this trick, Thomas said: "No men—still less children—can live on the bread of Utopia. They hunger now. Cold and hungry
children make for no constructive social revolution. They add to the
needless weight of the world's woes."

Socialists in New York State wrote and wired Governor Roosevelt,
urging him to end unemployment immediately. The women's section of the
Socialist Party opened a soup kitchen. The Socialists also sent 585 delegates to an emergency conference on unemployment. They called for
speedy signing of public works contracts, the replacement of slums with
public housing, adequate employment offices, the prompt distribution of
food, clothing and rent checks.

The Socialists, who disagreed with President Hoover's preference for
local relief over federal relief, scorned his February 12 speech in which he
said: "Victory over this depression and over our other difficulties will be
won by the resolution of our people to fight their own battles in their own
communities." Sometimes Hoover forgot himself and used the word "depression," rather than the word "recession," which he preferred.

In 1930, after nearly a decade of internecine warfare, the American
Communist Party had only 7,000 avowed members. Nonetheless, they
pretended to believe that with the help of concealed party members, fellow
travelers, opportunists and dupes, they could bring an American nation of
124,000,000 citizens to its knees. William Z. Foster said flatly: "Today
our party is small and the parties of the capitalists are large and strong, but
the day will surely come when the Communist party will be the only party
in the United States."

The Comintern set March 6, 1930, as the date for unemployment
demonstrations in most of the big cities of the world. Within the United
States they hoped to make the biggest impression in New York City, which
had by far the greatest number of Communists. By this time, in addition to
the breadlines, there were 200 percent more New York families on relief

than before the Crash. The city's police commissioner, dapper Grover Whalen, a former floorwalker in the Wanamaker department store, was openly anti-Communist. In a public attack on party members, Whalen declared that "these enemies of society are to be driven out of New York *regardless* of their constitutional rights." (Italics added.)

By means of articles in the Communist paper, the *Daily Worker,* and the mailing of 100,000 postcards, the party urged all discontented people to take part in an unemployment demonstration on March 6 in Manhattan's Union Square—sometimes called Red Square because Communist orators harangued crowds there. The three men in charge of the scheduled mass meeting were Foster, Robert Minor, editor of the *Daily Worker,* and Israel Amter, a local Communist organizer. Whalen asked them to come to police headquarters to confer. When they arrived, he said that a city ordinance required them to get a permit three days in advance of the outdoor meeting. They refused to apply for a permit, snarling that they did not respect the laws of the United States, the state of New York or the city of New York. Turning on their heels, they strode out of Whalen's office.

Thursday, March 6, 1930, was a clear and windless day in New York City. By 10 A.M. a crowd began to gather in Union Square. Hard-core party members were reinforced by thousands of sympathizers and curiosity seekers. Commissioner Whalen, wearing a dark overcoat and light homburg, set up emergency police headquarters in a summerhouse inside the square. He did not interfere with newspaper photographers and silent movie cameramen who took up positions on and near a wall, three feet high, surrounding the park. However, he forbade any picture taking by photographers for the new talking pictures, later explaining: "I saw no reason for perpetuating treasonable utterances, and I don't mean to engage in censorship, but why glorify these people?"

More and more men and women thronged the square. Whalen estimated that more than 100,000 people had congregated, but New York *Times* reporters guessed that the figure was closer to 35,000. Five speakers' platforms had been erected in the center of the square, and diehard Communists pressed close to them. These party members jiggled placards declaring that they wanted no charity, protesting evictions of the jobless and insisting that public buildings be used to house the homeless.

Subway exits near the square became so congested that Whalen ordered all underground trains on the East Side of Manhattan to skip all stations between Brooklyn Bridge and Grand Central. Just before the rally started, the police commissioner had Foster, Minor and Amter brought to his field office. Accompanying them was a black sailor and a white soldier. The five men said they constituted a committee of workers, soldiers and sailors. Whalen pointed out that their rally was illegal, since they had failed to obtain a permit, but said he would allow it to proceed if it ended promptly at 1 P.M. Again the Communist leaders stamped out of his presence.

Just then a Soviet flag began rising on a flagpole and topped the American flag on the mast. Blue-coated cops bellowed to the Red leaders that none of them would be allowed to speak until the flags were rearranged. When this had been done, the five radical orators climbed onto their portable stands and started denouncing "Whalen's Cossacks" and their "brutality." Whalen, who stood on the porch of the garden house, could hear himself being abused. One speaker proposed that when the rally ended, everyone should march south to City Hall to demand that Mayor Jimmy Walker remove Whalen as police commissioner.

Whalen was not afraid of losing his job, but this was a turn of events he had failed to anticipate. Quickly making up his mind, he called for reinforcements to prevent a march on the seat of city government. Soon more than 300 patrolmen, detectives, mounted cops and motorcycle policemen were gathered in and around Union Square. Also summoned to the scene were firemen under orders to turn hoses on the demonstrators if they got out of hand.

At 12:50 P.M. cops stood fingering nightsticks. Whalen told some of his staff officers to bring the five Red leaders back to his temporary headquarters. There Whalen worked to control his Irish temper. He ordered the quintet to break up the meeting in precisely ten minutes and then disperse without trying to advance on City Hall.

In a curious blend of courtesy and commercialism, Whalen said: "If we allow you to pass down Broadway it will cost the innocent merchants along that thoroughfare thousands of dollars. You will never accomplish anything by force of numbers. I will give you a police car and will myself accompany you to City Hall, and I will tell the mayor that you are a committee representing fifty thousand or more individuals."

Foster and his colleagues spurned this compromise, turned their backs on the police commissioner and again plunged into the middle of the crowd. Jumping onto a stand, Foster shouted: "They won't let us march! Will you stand for that?"

Anger swept over the multitude. Men shouted. Women shrilled. Placards waved ever more furiously. Resentment and frustration, resolution and doubt showed in the faces of the people, and as these emotions fermented, Foster and his lieutenants faded from the scene, found a taxicab and drove down to City Hall.

Then 2,000 disciplined Communists moved in a solid body west out of Union Square and turned south on Broadway. A squad of mounted cops maneuvered their horses into the path of the marchers. A police emergency truck lunged into Broadway, braked hard, stopped in the middle of the street to serve as a metal restraining wall. Hundreds of patrolmen and detectives, faces flushed, arms raised, rushed into the advancing columns. They struck out with billy clubs and blackjacks and bare fists, hitting anyone within reach. Down went a man here . . . there. . . . Some

Communists fled into side streets. Others fought back and, according to the *Times,* "this only served to spur the police, whose attack carried behind it the force of an avalanche."

A detective in a sheepskin coat ran back and forth clubbing person after person. Other detectives, thinly disguised as reporters by press cards in their hatbands, yelled and charged and attacked everyone indiscriminately. A *World* reporter saw a policeman pin a girl's hands behind her back to let another cop smash in her face with a blackjack. Francis Rufus Bellamy, editor of the sedate magazine *Outlook,* stood at an office window to watch in horror as a dozen cops beat and kicked two men until they almost fainted. Seven and eight cops at a time would gang up on mere boys to pound them unmercifully. An old man was dragged into a doorway, knocked down, hauled to his feet, knocked down, hammered with clubs and fists. There were shouts and screams and curses and thuds and running feet and sagging bodies and blood blossoming from noses.

In fifteen minutes the riot was over. It left the sidewalks and pavements littered with more than a score of badly injured persons, together with a hundred others suffering assorted cuts and cruises.

"Cossacks!" screamed a woman. "Murderous Cossacks!"

That bloody afternoon a seventeen-year-old boy named Victor Riesel staggered away from Union Square, his body unharmed but his mind wounded by the violence he had seen. Almost sleepwalking, he made his way to the office of a union to which his father belonged, a small embroidery union with a tiny and shabby office. There, for the first time in his life, the boy saw a grown man weeping. The man had no job, no money and nothing to feed his family. Then and there, Victor Riesel decided to devote his life to the welfare of the workers, and eventually he became a noted labor columnist.

In the aftermath of the riot one New York newspaper editorialized: ". . . the mob of troublemakers that raised all the fuss in Union Square was made up of Communist loafers who wouldn't work if a job was handed to them on a silver platter. . . . Sure, times are tough . . . but any real, honest American workingman who wants a job can find one. . . . This is the U.S.A., not Red Russia! Nobody goes idle here and nobody starves unless he's too lazy to work. . . ."

Most newspapers, however, denounced Whalen and criticized his cops for attacking the marchers. Although photographers had snapped pictures that clearly showed people being clubbed, Whalen blandly said he had seen nothing of this sort. Norman Thomas demanded that the police commissioner be removed from office.

Among the thirteen persons arrested were Foster, Minor and Amter. These three were found guilty of unlawful assembly and sent to jail for six months. Herbert Benjamin, secretary of the local Communist Party, called the riot "a great success." He described the demonstrations in Union

Square and elsewhere in the world as the prelude to the "overthrow of capitalism and the establishment of a revolutionary workers' and farmers' government."

* * *

In San Francisco, that March 6, Police Chief William J. Quinn not only let the local Communists parade but gave them a police escort and, grinning broadly, marched at the head of the procession. When the demonstrators reached the civic center, a Communist named William Simon delivered a speech. He was followed by San Francisco's mayor, James "Sunny Jim" Rolph, Jr., who pointed at the American flag flying over City Hall and declared that Communists were as safe under it as any other Americans. The mayor then extended his courteous best wishes to the unemployed and everyone else. As a result, San Francisco saw no riot and no arrests.

In the nation's capital, that same day, President Hoover was writing at his desk in the White House as a small crowd of demonstrators gathered just outside the gate to the grounds of the executive mansion. They started waving banners, making speeches and singing the "Internationale." Hoover ordered guards and police not to interfere with them unless they got out of hand. But when a man tried to climb over the fence to get to the White House, police pulled him back, charged the crowd, threw tear gas grenades, lashed out with blackjacks, started a panic among the spectators and arrested eleven men and two girls.

In Chicago and Detroit, Pittsburgh and Milwaukee, Cleveland and Los Angeles, Denver and Seattle—in dozens of cities across the land, unemployed people, some of them Communists, some not, finally made themselves heard, finally voiced their resolve not to remain mute and passive in the throes of a Depression not of their making. What was happening to this country? Why should Americans starve to death? Why should they suffer in silence? Were the Communists completely wrong?

The Reds *were* completely wrong, in the opinion of Boston's mayor, James M. Curley. Born in the slums of Roxbury, reared in a tenement, Curley developed into a Democratic politician and demagogue, winning the nickname of the Irish Mussolini. That tense March, 1930, the Communists of Boston asked for permission to use a bandstand and the facilities of the Boston Common for a demonstration. Mayor Curley publicly announced that he would receive a three-man delegation in his office to discuss the matter.

Into his office marched an Irishman, a Jew and a Negro. As Curley tells the story in his autobiography: ". . . I blasted them, informing them that I would under no circumstances permit them to desecrate the Common or sully the reputation of the Cradle of Liberty by parading their heresies." That evening a reporter for the Boston *Post* caught the mayor paying off the Irishman, the Jew and the Negro, hired by him to enact the role of Communist leaders.

Boston had its unemployment riot.

*   *   *

Fear of Communism, indifference to the fate of others and insulation from the realities of a worsening situation left many affluent people deaf to all cries for help. Growing unemployment made almost no impression on the substantial citizens who belonged to the National Economic League. Responding to a poll that asked what they considered the prime problems the nation faced in 1930, the gentlemen of the league listed unemployment in *eighteenth* place.

They paid as little attention to Theodore Dreiser, the author. In the spring of 1930 Dreiser said: "We call this country a democracy. It's really an oligarchy. The seat of government is Wall Street, not Washington. . . . Why, democracy is a joke. Everything about it is a joke. Voting? Here's what it amounts to: That people who go to the polls are merely going through the motions of voting. . . . For a long while the country has been moving unconsciously toward communism. Whether or not it will come to that I don't know. But some change must come."

While Dreiser seemingly welcomed this threat from the left, Governor Roosevelt was becoming apprehensive about it. However, FDR was equally sensitive to the dog-in-the-manger attitude of the extreme right, saying: "There is no question that there will be a gain throughout our country of communistic thought unless we can keep democracy up to its old ideals and its original purposes. We face in this country not only the danger of communism but the equal danger of the concentration of all power, economic and political, in the hands of what the ancient Greeks would have called an oligarchy."

William Allen White, a Republican, shared the balanced opinion of Franklin D. Roosevelt, a Democrat. In a personal letter, White said: ". . . I suppose I have two or three strong political convictions: first, a thorough distrust of the proletariat when it is organized on its own exclusive basis; second, a thorough distrust of the plutocracy when it is organized or when it tries to influence the political activities of the middle class. I distrust the proletariat because it is ignorant and selfish, and the plutocracy because it is cunning and greedy. . . ."

Although Roosevelt and White used different words to describe the threat from the right, they meant much the same thing. An *oligarchy* is government by a few. A *plutocracy* is government by the wealthy.

In the late summer of 1930 the members of this small clique were identified by James W. Gerard, who was himself a rich man. Gerard was a corporation lawyer, former American ambassador to Germany, treasurer of the Democratic National Committee, and had a mansion on Manhattan's Fifth Avenue. Recuperating from one operation and facing another,

Gerard was relaxing at the Newport estate of Cornelius Vanderbilt. To while away the time and also to formalize his thoughts, Gerard drew up a list of what he called the fifty-nine men who ruled the United States. Later he expanded this list to a total of sixty-four names. "They themselves are too busy to hold political office," Gerard said, "but they determine who shall hold such offices." They controlled the nation's purse strings. They dictated national policy.

Here were "America's rulers":

John D. Rockefeller, Jr.—oil
Andrew W. Mellon—banking, aluminum
J. P. Morgan—banking
George F. Baker—banking
John D. Ryan—copper
Walter C. Teagle—oil
Henry Ford—automobiles
Frederick E. Weyerhaeuser—lumber
Myron C. Taylor—finance
James A. Farrell—steel
Arthur V. Davis—aluminum
P. M. Gossler—utilities
R. C. Holmes—oil
John J. Raskob—finance
Seven Du Ponts—chemicals, etc.
Edward J. Berwind—finance
Albert W. Wiggin—banking
Charles E. Mitchell—banking
Samuel Insull—utilities
Seven Fisher brothers—automobiles
Robert R. McCormick—publishing
Joseph M. Patterson—publishing
Julius S. Rosenwald—merchandising
A. P. Giannini—banking
William Green—labor
Matthew Woll—labor

Charles M. Schwab—steel
Eugene G. Grace—steel
Harry M. Warner—movies
Adolph Zukor—movies
William H. Crocker—banking
O. P. and M. J. Van Sweringen—railroads
W. W. Atterbury—railroads
Arthur Curtiss James—railroads
Charles Hayden—finance
Daniel O. Jackling—copper
Daniel Willard—railroads
Sosthenes Behn—utilities
Walter S. Gifford—utilities
Owen D. Young—utilities
Gerard Swope—utilities
Thomas W. Lamont—banking
Daniel Guggenheim—mining
William Loeb—mining
George Washington Hill—tobacco
Adolph S. Ochs—publishing
William Randolph Hearst—publishing
Cyrus H. Curtis—publishing
Roy W. Howard—publishing
Sidney Z. Mitchell—utilities
Walter Edwin Frew—banking

Publication of Gerard's list caused a sensation. The Washington *Post* said that if a crisis should come, the real rulers of the United States—the people—would soon put every individual in his place. This was nonsense, in the opinion of Franklin P. Adams. The New York *World* columnist wrote: "I think it is just this kind of flattery, often journalistic, that makes it easily possible to recruit great armies of 'the people,' who are told that they are the real rulers, and that one man is as important as another, and, if he is unimportant, a whole lot more important than another."

Franklin D. Roosevelt reacted to the Gerard list with the comment that he was tired of a handful of men controlling the destinies of 120,000,000 people. He added that the only way to curb their control was to do away with holding companies.

Another kind of note was struck by some of the nation's intellectuals with the deepening of the Depression. One of their spokesmen was the critic and editor, Edmund Wilson, who wrote: ". . . a darkness seemed to descend. Yet, to the writers and artists of my generation who had grown up in the Big Business era and had always resented its barbarism, its crowding-out of everything they cared about, these years were not depressing but stimulating. One couldn't help being exhilarated at the sudden collapse of that stupid gigantic fraud. It gave us a new sense of freedom."

11

Food Riots and Hoovervilles

THE LEVEL of the Mississippi River fell in the summer of 1930 and
continued to fall. People living along its cliffs and delta stared at the
muddy water as it sank lower and lower and lower, exposing slimy
root-gnarled flanks never before seen. The largest river in the country, the
mighty "Father of Waters," seemed to be drying up. Although they knew
the Mississippi would never vanish and leave an arid riverbed, they did
worry about this strange change. Only two years previously Congress had
passed a flood-control bill to tame the unruly river.

Everyone realized that the Mississippi was falling because none of its
headstreams, none of its tributaries, was getting enough rain. Up and down
the Mississippi Valley and elsewhere in the land the absence of rainfall was
causing concern. The federal Weather Bureau reported that in all the time
it had been keeping records there had never been such scant precipitation.
The days of drought had begun.

Widespread droughts had afflicted the nation in the past—in 1881,
1894, 1901, 1911, 1916 and 1924—but none had been so severe as the
drought that started in the year 1930. Now, over most of America, the sun
stared like an evil eye at the earth, beating the soil into powder, scorching
grass, drying up ponds and creeks, dooming huge trees.

Farmers worried. Meteorologists studied charts. Federal officials held
hurried conferences. The Hopi Indians of Arizona, who believed in the rain-
evoking power of snake dances, intensified their timeless ritual. A Protestant minister went on a coast-to-coast radio hookup to pray for rain. In
Port Chester, New York, members of a Negro congregation chanted
appeals for rain and congratulated one another when a teasing shower fell.
But still the sun stood in a steel-blue sky.

This natural calamity doubled the woes of the man-made Depression.
More than 300 counties in thirty states were affected, and this vast area

held 1,000,000 farm families and 20,000,000 farm animals. Life had been hard for farmers even during the prosperous Twenties. It was true that farm prices had risen by one-third, but farmers had to pay prices one-half higher, so their net purchasing power was far less than before. They sank deeper into debt, lost their farms, began moving into town, despaired.

Now the drought brought warnings that the corn crop would be the smallest in a long time. Secretary of Agriculture Arthur M. Hyde said he saw no danger of a food shortage, but frightened housewives began hoarding. Grocers begged them to leave a little for others to buy. President Hoover had planned a vacation trip to California, but as the crisis mounted, he canceled it and appealed to all Americans to stop food profiteering.

The drought of 1930 developed into the worst in the entire history of the nation; more were to come later. The people of the Mississippi Valley endured their greatest economic losses since the Civil War. Farmers who owned their own land were hurt badly enough, but tenant farmers and sharecroppers suffered even more. They had no money and almost nothing to barter. Farm animals began dying for lack of fodder. Thousands of farms were owned by rural banks and now these banks started failing.

In Arkansas some farmers shot at Negroes brought in from an adjoining county to work on roads; the farmers felt they should get these jobs. Here and there across the countryside infants wailed for lack of nourishment, while older children went chalk-faced with hunger. Maryland police watched lest someone divert public water and use it illegally. There was fear of a milk famine in New Jersey. In the New Jersey community of Pitman an umbrella mender was considered such a public affront that he was jailed as a vagrant. The danger of forest fires increased. Ohio fire engines pumped water onto fruit trees in an attempt to save them. Drinking water was sold in West Virginia.

Herbert Hoover's background included enormous experience in administering food and relief programs abroad, so the present American drought was a crisis he felt he could handle. According to his newspaper friend Mark Sullivan: "To overcoming the drought President Hoover turned with something like a sense of relief, almost pleasure."

It was vitally necessary to get water and forage to livestock in parched areas of the country, but few farmers could pay for long railway hauls. Hoover asked the railroads to apply to the Interstate Commerce Commission for cut rates for moving these commodities. The carriers made this request, and the ICC granted reductions amounting to one-half the standard freight rates in the Eastern and Southern parts of the nation, and one-third those in the West. Under this emergency system, more than 60,000 freight cars delivered livestock necessities to farmers. This helped allay a fodder shortage estimated at 400,000 bushels of grain.

Then the President convened a meeting of drought-state governors in Washington on August 14, 1930. These governors, working with federal officials, set up state and county relief committees to coordinate federal services, the Red Cross and private credit agencies. Hoover directed the Federal Land Bank and the Farm Board to expand their credit facilities. He secured an initial grant of $5 million from the Red Cross. He expanded federal highway construction to provide some jobs for farmers in stricken areas.

More water was diverted from Lake Michigan to help Illinois farmers. Artillery ranges in Virginia were converted into pastures. Montana cattle were permitted to graze in other states. The federal Department of Agriculture allotted $600,000 for seed loans. Work was speeded up on federal waterways and flood-control projects to provide further employment for farmers.

All this was not enough. It became obvious to many people that federal funds were needed to aid farmers in drought regions, but they disagreed about the size and nature of this governmental relief. In Washington, D.C., two opposing fronts were formed. Lined up on one side were Democratic Senators and Representatives. The other side consisted of the Republican President and Republican Senators and Representatives.

William Gibbs McAdoo, a Democratic Senator from California, urged that the Farm Board donate its wheat to feed hungry people, but the head of this agency said that the law prohibited it from giving anything away. McAdoo retorted that it was time to start feeding people, as well as animals. President Hoover proposed that federal aid take the businesslike form of secured loans to enable farmers to buy fodder. Outraged Democrats taunted the President, saying that while he thought it was all right to feed starving cattle, he was against feeding starving men, women and children.

The Senate appropriated $60 million for loans to farmers, but before the House could consider the measure, the President called this sum excessive. He demanded that relief be limited to $25 million. Hoover was afraid of anything that smacked of a dole or constituted what he considered a raid on the treasury.

John N. Garner, a Democratic Congressman from Texas, suggested that the Senate bill now before the House be amended to permit the purchase of food for human beings. Republican Congressmen balked, reporting the bill under a rule barring amendments. Garner took the floor to berate the GOP leadership for acting under a gag rule when human welfare was at stake. The future Vice President of the United States also took this occasion to voice his opinion on relief: "Speaking for myself alone, if it ever comes to a point that starving people must be taken care of, I will help take care of them, if and when absolutely necessary, out of the treasury of the United States. It is unconscionable to think that you may picture a situation where a large percentage of the people of this country are starving and that we, as members of Congress, cannot find a sound economic policy that will help them, out of the treasury of the United States."

Senate and House conferees agreed on a compromise appropriation of $45 million, and both houses of Congress then passed the bill on December 19. By this time the Red Cross was using its entire relief fund of $5 million to aid those suffering from the drought.

*   *   *

England, Arkansas, was a farming community of 2,000 citizens that lay within the sprawling alluvial plain of the Mississippi River, 22 miles southeast of the capital of Little Rock. On January 3, 1931, this hamlet burst into headlines.

The combination of Depression and drought had resulted in the worst disaster in the history of the entire state of Arkansas—worse even than the 1927 flood that had left one-fifth of it underwater. In the summer of 1930 the temperature had stood at or above 100 degrees for forty-two days while the rainfall was not enough to wet a man's shirt. During the last six months of the year a total of 143 banks had failed in Arkansas. Farm prices continued to drop. It took 16 bushels of wheat, or more than the average yield of 1 acre, for a farmer to buy a pair of $4 shoes for one of his children.

At the beginning of 1931 there were 200,000 destitute people in Arkansas, and a state representative wept as he described the tragic conditions in his district. One family of eight had nothing to eat but turnips and turnip greens for an entire week. Another family got just one meal a day—bread, molasses and occasionally beans or "white lightning," which was salt pork.

Across the nation, by the end of 1930, the Red Cross had given food, clothing and other relief to almost 50,000 families at a cost of more than $500,000, but relief funds averaging $10 per family hardly put a dent in the desperate situation. As the year 1931 dawned, the Red Cross was helping seventy-three of the seventy-five counties in Arkansas—on a tiny scale. A single person got 75 cents for food every two weeks; a couple with no children got $2; and a family of twelve got $9. Franklin W. Fort, a Republican Congressman from New Jersey, made a radio appeal for more help for Arkansas, recalling how the people of that state had denied themselves sugar and flour to feed the American Expeditionary Force in World War I.

Back in August, 1930, when the Red Cross first began helping drought victims in Arkansas, it had insisted on delivering relief directly to white and black tenant families. This angered plantation owners, who demanded that they be allowed to hand out Red Cross staples—"obviously," as President Hoover pointed out, "to keep these dependents under their control." Hoover, who was president of the Red Cross, rejected this demand. Tenant farmers and sharecroppers clearly understood what their bosses were trying to do. It made no difference that the state motto was "The People Rule."

On Saturday, January 3, 1931, 500 farmers and their wives invaded England, Arkansas.

About half the men were armed with shotguns, rifles and pistols. Most of the men were white, but a few blacks were among them. All were hungry— so hungry that their guts rumbled. The city marshal watched them anxiously as they headed straight for the county Red Cross chairman. Quietly, they asked him for more food. Nervously, he said he had run out of the forms that every relief client had to sign.

The crowd began to mutter. A local plantation owner named George E. Morris tried to make a speech but was interrupted time after time. Here and there cries arose: "We're not going to let our children starve! . . . We want food and we want it now! . . . We're not beggars! . . . We're willing to work for fifty cents a day, but we're not going to starve and we're not going to let our families starve!"

Turning their backs on the plantation owner and spectators, the people headed for the local stores. Although some of the men in the crowd held revolvers, they did not point these weapons at the storeowners. However, they asked for food and threatened to take it by force if it was not given to them. Some of the merchants themselves were broke, but the pressure on them by the angry crowd was so great that they handed out a total of $1,500 worth of flour and lard. Only then did the crowd move away and disperse, its members returning to their shacks.

Not a shot was fired. No one was manhandled. No violence whatsoever took place, although there had been menacing actions and words. However, across the nation news spread that an armed mob had invaded a peaceful little town in Arkansas.

Morris, the local plantation owner who had tried to make a speech, warned of a second invasion, crying: "The merchants of England either must move their goods or mount machine guns on their stores!"

Will Rogers said in his syndicated column:

> We got powerful Government, brainy men, great organizations, many commissions, but it took a little band of five Hundred simple country people (who had no idea they were doing anything historical) to come to a country town store and demand food for their wives and children. They hit the heart of the American people more than all your senatorial pleas and government investigations. Paul Revere just woke up Concord, these birds woke up America. I don't want to discourage Mr. Mellon and his carefully balanced budget, but you let this country get hungry and they are going to eat, no matter what happens to Budgets, Income Taxes or Wall Street values. Washington mustn't forget who rules when it comes to a showdown.

Much was made of this event by Whittaker Chambers, a Communist who later triggered the trials of Alger Hiss. Chambers did not see this Arkansas invasion, since he lived in New York. Daring to pass private judgment on the official party line, he felt that the Communists were trying "to turn the economic psychosis into premature and irresponsible violence." Chambers thought he might try to influence events by writing stories that everyone would want to read, stories "in which the correct conduct of the Communists would be shown in action."

Upon reading about what had happened in the town of England, Chambers decided he had found exactly the plot he needed. Writing all one night, he produced a short story about a farmers' uprising in the West and the part played in it by an intelligent Communist. There was no evidence that any Communist had anything to do with the affair in Arkansas, but this did not bother Chambers. In describing the locale of his story, he drew on memories of the village where he had been raised, and to depict the Communist, he borrowed from his recollections of Louis Katterfeld, a Kansas wheat farmer and former secretary of the party.

Chambers took his story to Walt Carmon, editor of the *New Masses,* the Communist-controlled literary magazine. Carmon liked it, entitled it "Can You Hear Their Voices," and published it in the March, 1931, issue. The piece evoked instant and widespread attention. The New York *World-Telegram* wrote an article about it. Lincoln Steffens and others hailed it as a classic of revolutionary literature. International Publishers, the official Communist publishing house, issued it as a pamphlet. Hallie Flanagan, who headed Vassar's Experimental Theater, turned it into a play. Within a few months the story was translated into many languages, including Chinese and Japanese, and was produced in workers' theaters all over the world.

*   *   *

There was no second invasion of England, Arkansas, although conditions worsened in the state. From the floor of Congress it was charged that the Red Cross was starving the people of Arkansas and that the federal government itself was not doing enough to help them. One Representative declared that while the government gave 29-cent meals to federal convicts, it hesitated to provide 3-cent meals for starving farmers. Such an outcry arose about "rioting" in Arkansas that the President sent his military aide, Lieutenant Colonel Campbell B. Hodges, to investigate; Hodges reported that no riot had occurred. Debate continued to rage over the issue of the federal government giving food to the human victims of the drought, as the Red Cross was doing.

Joseph T. Robinson, a Democratic Senator from Arkansas, felt that even the Red Cross was not doing enough in his home state. When the Red Cross chairman, John Barton Payne, said that his funds were sufficient to meet relief needs through the winter, trigger-tempered Robinson exploded. He accused Payne of ignorance about the extent of misery in Arkansas, where people were burning their furniture to keep warm. Payne was jealous of the honor of his organization, but in the face of mounting criticism from

Robinson and others, he now reversed himself and requested that Hoover ask the public for $10 million more to aid Red Cross relief work. The President did as asked.

This still did not settle the issue of direct federal food relief for the needy, and Robinson threatened a filibuster unless the government came through. President Hoover and some fellow Republicans balked at the idea, and tempers flared. A New Jersey Congressman suggested that the United States replace its 2-cent postal stamp with a special 3-cent drought relief stamp, but nothing came of it. At just this time another frightening confrontation occurred. On January 19, 1931, a crowd of men and women gathered in front of City Hall in Oklahoma City. There were about 500 of them, as there had been in England, Arkansas. They shouted that they were hungry and jobless. The state of Oklahoma, which was selling cheap ice made by convict labor, was not doing much for its poor and unemployed. Francis Owens, who headed the Oklahoma City Unemployed Council, led a delegation inside City Hall to confer with City Manager E. M. Fry and demand immediate relief. Fry responded by asking for the names and addresses of members of the Unemployed Council. Owens rejected this demand. Realizing they would get no satisfaction from city officials, Owens and his delegation walked out of City Hall and urged the waiting crowd to march on a nearby grocery store.

They did so. They attacked the store, insisting that they needed food to live and were going to get some. When the store manager tried to stop them, one of the hungry men shouted: "It's too late to bargain with us!" They ransacked the grocery, falling upon one shelf after another, stripping them of canned goods and cartons, wrecking the place. In a few minutes the cops arrived and threw tear gas bombs into the midst of the marauders. In trying to flee, some of the looters leaped through windows, breaking the glass and cutting themselves. Twenty-six men and five women were trapped inside. The police released the women but arrested the men. One of the men was charged with inciting to riot.

Hunger riots? In America? Thoughtful citizens stirred uneasily.

By this time the average Red Cross food grant was 10 cents a day. Ten cents a day? What human being could live on this? During this month of January, 1931, the number of Red Cross relief clients jumped by 225,000 to a total of 750,411. At 10 cents per person per day, this meant that the Red Cross needed more than $7 million for its drought relief work, but its new campaign for funds had brought in only a little more than $5 million. Even so, Red Cross Chairman Payne still refused to accept any relief money from the federal government, relying instead on private voluntary contributions. President Hoover himself gave $7,500 to the Red Cross. A group of Tennessee convicts donated $51.

At wearisome last, after disputes and deadlocks and name-calling, Congress agreed upon a new $20 million relief fund for farmers in drought areas, and under a clause entitled "farm rehabilitation" some of this money could be used for food. "Rehabilitation" avoided the bugaboo word "dole." The Red Cross finally reached and surpassed its campaign goal of $10 million, and by March 17, 1931, the Red Cross and the federal government were giving drought relief to 2,000,000 Americans.

During the Congressional wrangle President Hoover had been criticized so viciously that his feelings were deeply hurt. Finally he spoke out in self-defense, saying in part: "This is not an issue as to whether people shall go hungry or cold in the United States. It is solely a question of the best method by which hunger and cold shall be prevented. . . . No one is going hungry and no one need go hungry or cold. . . . I do not feel that I should be charged with a lack of human sympathy for those who suffer. . . . I would no more see starvation amongst our countrymen than would any Senator or Congressman. . . ."

*   *   *

And Hoover was fated to suffer more mental anguish. A compassionate man, he was so shy that he revealed his winning personality only when in the company of a few intimate friends. He had been orphaned as a child, knew poverty as a teen-ager, worked his way through college and by the time he was in his thirties he had developed into one of the world's leading mining engineers. He knew more about things than he did about people. He knew that 2 and 2 make 4 and that 12 inches equal 1 foot, but he did not understand that politics is the art of compromise. A prisoner of his personal past, he clung to the frontier philosophy of rugged individualism after the frontier was closed, after society had become complex and highly industrialized. Rigid in character, he tried to apply old solutions to new problems. As President of the United States, he was the wrong man at the wrong time.

Millions of suffering Americans cared little about the personality and character of their President. What they did know—and in painful detail—was the intensity of their own tragedies. And, as always happens in troubled times, they sought a scapegoat to blame. They blamed businessmen and bankers, true, but with the possible exception of J. P. Morgan they could not visualize one physical man, were unable to sharpen a montage of newspaper faces into a single target for their rage—except for President Hoover. Now, in their frustration, they turned on the man in the White House, the fat man with the pudgy hands and high stiff collar. Hoover's name was applied in derision to many things. "Hoover flags" were empty pockets turned inside out. "Hoover hogs" were the jackrabbits shot by hungry farmers for food. "Hoovercrats" were people who defended the President. And "Hoovervilles" were villages of squatters dwelling in huts and shacks.

As more and more men lost their jobs and savings, they were unable to pay their rent, so tens of thousands of them were turned out of their homes by landlords, who had their own problems. Where could they live? In city after city there soon was a shortage of space in municipal shelters and lodging houses, so homeless people had to shift for themselves. Using boxes and crates and abandoned cars, they built squalid colonies of the dispossessed, made pathetic displays of the American flag and in some places even elected their own so-called mayors. The *New Republic* said that Hoovervilles constituted a separate nation, with separate codes, although the men living in them were still subject to "a sort of imperialist intervention."

*   *   *

By the spring of 1931 New York City had about 15,000 homeless men and perhaps 200 homeless women. Some of them slept in subway trains, subway stations, telephone booths, in empty lots and parks, under bridges. Those with a few cents left could spend the night in a flophouse by paying a quarter or buy one drink in a speakeasy for the privilege of making a bed on the sawdust floor. The city government had a six-story Municipal Lodging House on East Twenty-fifth Street, and in the past nonresidents were entitled to sleep there free one night each month while residents could stay five nights a month. Now, with misery having become so massive, these restrictions had been lifted. By April, 1931, a total of 3,300 persons bunked nightly in the city shelter, and of this number about 100 were women.

In New York's Chinatown, down on the Lower East Side of Manhattan, a former convict named Tom Noonan kept his famous Rescue Society Mission. This Doyer Street mission became crowded as never before. Noonan had taken over an old Chinese theater, and on the ground floor, in a room where Chinese actors had staged their interminable plays, food was served to broken and hapless men. Down in the basement, with its bricked-in arches, beds were stacked one atop another.

Volunteer census takers were trying to learn just how many men on the East Side were without work. One of these volunteers was a young girl. The moment she stepped into Noonan's mission her eyes widened in surprise at the number of jobless men. Trying to mask her embarrassment she nonetheless had to ask embarrassing questions—name, age, place of birth, trade and so on. There on the first floor the men shuffled past the girl, averting their eyes, answering in subdued voices.

Although few of them were under thirty, one of the exceptions was twenty-nine-year-old John Bentley. He had been born in Kansas, and his trade was house painting. When building construction fell off in his native state, he had heard of a job in the East and had come to New York, where he worked only briefly before being laid off. Now—this. The young man had a clear-cut profile and a long upper lip. His shoulders sagged; his shoes were cracked. Defeat had dulled his eyes, and he answered all questions tonelessly.

At last the girl shut her notebook and walked down to the basement.

With her first look she gasped: "My God! They're sleeping on the floor!" Indeed some men were sleeping on the stone floor of the underground vault, since there were not enough bunks to go around. Suddenly a group of about twenty well-dressed people appeared on the stairs. They were led by a guide, who chanted: "Ladies and gentlemen, this was one of the underground resorts of old Chinatown. This used to be the place where Chinatown came to hit the pipe. You would find white people and Chinese together—sodden in opium dreams. Behind these bricked-in arches was where the plutocrats and the society people used to come to smoke their pipes in privacy."

"My Lord," cried the young census taker, *"tourists!"*

*   *   *

One December day a reporter named Joseph Mitchell spent a tense half hour in the anteroom of a magistrate's court talking with a gaunt woman who had stabbed her husband to death. He had taken the $1.85 she had saved for Christmas presents for their children and spent it in a gin mill. "I sure fixed his wagon," she said. Then she began to moan. That same afternoon Mitchell was sent to Hoover Village, one of the largest squatters' colonies in New York.

It had arisen on the east bank of the Hudson River at Seventy-fourth Street and Riverside Drive—a drive often called the most beautiful thoroughfare in the world. Thin-faced men, many of them veterans, had used discarded boards, sheets of corrugated tin, strips of tar paper and wire to put together a cluster of shanties for themselves and their families. They cooked scraps of food over open fires within sight of passengers on the double-decked buses that rolled up and down the drive.

Joe Mitchell's boss had ordered him to ask these squatters what plans they were making for Christmas. The sensitive reporter later wrote: "The gaunt squatters stood and looked at me with a look I probably never will get over; if they had turned on me and pitched me into the river I wouldn't have blamed them."

A stone's throw away from these miserable huts there loomed one of the most magnificent mansions in America, the home of Charles M. Schwab, the steel executive. Schwab had a fortune of about $200 million and his income for the year 1932 alone came to $250,000. His riverside estate embraced an entire square block between Seventy-third and Seventy-fourth Streets. Merely by lifting their eyes, the residents of Hoover Village could see the iron picket fence enclosing the spacious grassy lawn and the granite château with twin minarets 100 feet high. Schwab's home and its furnishings were worth an estimated $8 million. It had seventy-five rooms, forty baths, a basement and two subbasements. Deep underground was a vault that could hold 20 tons of beef—enough to feed a family of five for eighty years. This pleasure palace also contained a $50,000 organ, a marble swimming pool, a gymnasium, a billiard room with ten tables, bowling alleys, a mahogany wine closet, three elevators and a private chapel with a marble altar weighing 10 tons.

In the spring of 1934 the seventy-two-year-old Schwab returned from a European trip and was surprised to learn that the squatters across the street from him had been ordered to break up camp and move along. To a reporter he said: "We visited back and forth. They had been up to my house and very kindly assisted us around the grounds in getting rid of the heavy snows last winter. Mrs. Schwab frequently drove down to visit them in their homes. And I also called on them many times. When we had a surplus of produce from our farm at Loretto, Pennsylvania, we were happy to share it with them. They had looked forward to staying there, I know, until business improved. We shall miss them. They were not bad neighbors at all."

*   *   *

New York City officials tried to take care of the growing numbers of homeless men by opening annexes to the Municipal Lodging House, by letting them use vacant warehouses and lofts, by converting a ferry terminal into a shelter and by making dormitories of two rebuilt piers. One of these docks was Pier 5 on the East River at the foot of East Twenty-fifth Street. A man who slept there just once always remembered it as the most terrifying night of his life. Years later, he said: "I had been in the trenches in World War I, but the cold dock was worse. It was damp and bitterly cold. There was one thin blanket to a man on a rough spring. Outside, you could hear the tugs. Inside, you could hear the guys coughing their lungs out. In those days a lot of the unemployed were fellows who had a touch of gas and who could only live by selling apples. About midnight I couldn't stand it. I got out of bed to find half the place was up, sitting around wrapped in their blankets like Indians. I'll never forget the man who sat next to me. He gave me a drag from his butt. Later he told me he was a graduate of Wisconsin."

A college education was no guarantee of either employment or shelter. One young man with a Doctor of Philosophy degree camped for eight months in Manhattan's Morningside Park near Columbia University; because of the care taken of trees in the city parks, it was said that "ten-cent men sleep under thousand-dollar trees." Another youth sneaked into the bowels of the famous Roxy Theater to huddle within its warmth for three days and nights, his ears assaulted each afternoon and evening by the blaring of the pipe organ.

In February, 1931, a *New Yorker* article said: "Anyone who wants actually to see civilization creaking will do well to visit the corner of West and Spring Streets. . . . There is a whole village of shacks and huts there, made of packing boxes, barrel staves, pieces of corrugated iron, and whatever else the junkman doesn't want, and the people who live there do so because the New York Central [Railroad] hasn't got around to driving them off."

A group of Portuguese Negroes and Latin Americans took over an empty Armour packing plant on Manhattan's West Thirtieth Street, climbing to the top floor each night by means of a rope ladder; after a year of occupancy this penthouse jungle was broken up by the police. Only a few blocks away, on West Thirty-eighth Street between Tenth and Eleventh Avenues, another jungle was cleared so a garage could be built on the site; the cops found one man dead of exposure and another near death.

In St. Louis the residents of a Hooverville built and dedicated a church made of orange crates. Near New Orleans jobless men lived in old houseboats. In Connellsville, Pennsylvania, unemployed steelworkers kept warm inside the huge ovens they had once stoked. In Jersey City the police evicted 300 homeless men from a Hooverville and then burned their shacks. In Oakland, California, some desperate men lived in sewer pipes the manufacturer was unable to sell. In Los Angeles a local street railway company donated fifty ancient trolley cars to workless men to use as homes.

In June, 1932, an unemployment commission in California issued a report about one of that state's jungles, this one a camp containing 185 single men and 86 families with 150 children. "Sanitation," said the report, "is bad; grounds filthy; no garbage collection; open improvised toilets, inadequate in number. Only one water faucet within half a mile of camping site. . . ." Many residents of this Hooverville were infected with venereal disease.

In California's Sacramento Valley, near the small town of Marysville, about fifty farmworkers bought small plots of worthless land on the installment plan. This community was described by a rural relief agent named Laurence Hewes, who later became an assistant to Rexford Tugwell. In a book called *Boxcar in the Sand,* Hewes wrote:

> Each had built for his family a rickety shelter of salvage lumber, boxes, cardboard, and tin cans. Each small holding was pitifully cultivated in a hopeless diversity of crops. Some had strawberry beds, others spindly orchards; here and there tobacco and cotton stalks evidenced either imagination or a cotton-belt origin.
>
> The entire settlement was a dreary, sodden mess; stagnant rain water stood three to six inches deep; outdoor privies had overflowed shallow wells; sickness was rampant. I stared at the dismal scene in a steady autumnal downpour. Lank men in patched denim pants puttered lethargically; a few in groups whittled and spat; half-clad urchins peered through windows or skittered through slop. There wasn't a dollar in the whole settlement; summer cannery and fruit-picking wages were long since spent and there would be no new cash until the next season began.

John Dos Passos went to Detroit to see how things were going and then he wrote a *New Republic* piece sardonically called "Detroit: City of Leisure." One of the idle buildings of the Fisher Body plant had been turned into a giant emergency flophouse, but by the time Dos Passos got to the motor city, this shelter had been closed. It was closed, went the official explanation, for lack of money. Dos Passos said the real reason was that some of Detroit's worthy citizens thought the place was turning into a "nest of Reds."

When the Fisher flophouse was shut down, it threw several thousand jobless men out into the streets and parks of Detroit. Dos Passos saw them everywhere—in shacks and shelters along the waterfront, in the back rooms of unoccupied houses. "In one back lot they have burrowed out rooms in a huge abandoned sandpile. Their smokestacks stick out at the top. All along the wharves and in the ends of alleys that abut on the waterfront you can see them toasting themselves in the sun, or else patiently fishing. . . ."

*   *   *

Manhattan's famous Central Park became a favorite haven for homeless people. An unemployed carpenter, James Hollinan, lived with his wife for nearly a year in a cave in the park. A single man pushed a big baby buggy into the park and used it as a dwelling place; each night he let down the dashboard, lowered the back of the seat, crawled in, covered himself with a rubber sheet and pulled the buggy's hood down over his head. Robert Nathan wrote a novel about derelicts who lived in Central Park, calling his book *One More Spring;* Hollywood turned the novel into a film that depicted actor Warner Baxter as a penniless producer roasting a partridge in his makeshift home in the park.

The Great Lawn is a flat meadowland, studded here and there with outcroppings of rocks, near the center of Central Park and just behind the Metropolitan Museum of Art. In this area a group of vagrants built a shantytown and named it Hoover Valley—a name officially recognized by the city park department. By the end of December, 1931, there were six shacks in this temporary village. Police arrested seven of the squatters but soon released them and let them go back to their shantytown. Hoover Valley kept on growing, and by the following autumn it had a total of twenty-nine huts. Seventeen of them were semipermanent structures, all furnished with chairs and beds, some even boasting carpets on their floors. The most impressive single place was constructed by jobless bricklayers—a brick house 20 feet high with a roof made of inlaid tile. The bricklayers called it Rockside Inn, since it stood in front of a boulder, but other squatters referred to it as Custer's Last Stand. Another shack, put together from egg crates and fruit crates, flew a tattered American flag over its door and bore the name "Radio City," since it contained the only radio in this urban jungle; all residents of Hoover Valley were welcome to step inside and listen to the news.

Behind these seventeen rather substantial dwellings there arose a dozen lesser shacks set out in a row called "Depression Street." Each morning the rising sun cast long shadows of sumptuous Fifth Avenue mansions across Hoover Valley, and each afternoon the shabby colony was overlaid with shadows of impressive buildings along Central Park West. Upon arising the squatters walked to comfort stations to shave and keep themselves as neat as possible and then tended to their housework, sweeping and tidying up their little homes.

Police and park officials said they believed that almost all the men of Hoover Valley were New Yorkers and none was a genuine hobo. However, city health authorities worried about sanitary conditions, so at last the police were ordered to oust the squatters. The night of September 21, 1932—with the current issue of *Fortune* magazine reporting that 34,000,-000 American men, women and children were suffering from the Depression—Acting Captain George Burnell of the arsenal station led a squad of apologetic cops into Hoover Valley. Both the cops and the squatters behaved politely toward one another, but twenty-five residents of the camp were arrested for vagrancy. All got suspended sentences.

*   *   *

At about eight o'clock in the morning of July 8, 1932, a Brooklyn cop named Richard Palmay walked to the Atlantic Theater at Flatbush Avenue and Dean Street. He had orders to clear up a fire hazard discovered a few days previously by a fire department inspector. Mounting an outside fire escape, the policeman climbed to the top landing, where the fire hazard existed—an improvised shelter made out of cardboard. Strung above it was a clothesline with socks and a spotless shirt trembling in the breeze. What drew the cop's attention, though, was one wall of the cardboard box which had a sign written in neat old-fashioned penmanship. It said:

NOTICE

Please be kind enough not to destroy or take anything from this resting place. I have no money and I can't find a job, so please leave me alone. I'll appreciate your kind consideration and

THANK YOU

The cop winced. Then, peeping over the unroofed side of the shelter, he looked down on a sleeping man, an old man, a thin and white-haired man with skinny arms. Palmay could not bring himself to disturb the slumbering figure and left quietly. An hour later the cop returned, for after all, orders are orders. He arrived just in time to see the frail old fellow pick his way down the fire escape, walk to a rain barrel and start washing his face. The policeman, his fists clenched in embarrassment, walked up. Hating the sound of his own voice, he said: "You'll have to move, old man."

As the vagrant lifted his face, water trickled down his pinched cheeks.

He cried: "I can't stay? I'm not bothering anyone. They don't use this theater in the summertime and I keep everything clean and I—"

"They gave me orders . . . It's against the fire laws."

The man nodded vacantly. In a dreamlike way he said his name was Louis Bringmann and that he had lost his job as head chef of a big Manhattan hotel—he would not say which one. Now he was sixty years old, jobless, penniless, friendless. Wearily, he climbed back to the top landing of the fire escape, took down his wash, carefully dressed, rolled up his blankets and hefted a little sea chest under one bony arm. There was nothing of value in this chest, he said. Only a collection of faded menus. He picked his way back to the ground and began trudging away. The cop thrust a 50-cent piece into the old man's free hand and quickly walked away.

The unwanted chef, immaculate in a blue jacket and worn brown pants, plodded toward the waterfront, down through Brooklyn's Red Hook section. Louis Bringmann had not wanted to end up in the jungle he now approached. This was one of the most infamous shantytowns in all New York, a four-acre camp of makeshift dugouts and tin huts and hulks of automobiles. Fords were called Tin Lizzies, and there were so many abandoned cars on this site that it was called Tin Mountain City. It festered at the foot of Henry Street.

This was home to many of the 6,000 to 8,000 men who wore out shoe leather daily as they sought jobs along the Brooklyn waterfront. There were husky Irish longshoremen, brawny Scandinavian seamen—all types of men. In Tin Mountain City they had improvised their own crude schools and banks and department stores. From time to time the squatters would send delegations to Brooklyn Borough Hall to demand sewers and medical care for their people.

By late afternoon the old chef was sitting on his upended sea chest, trying to adjust to his new environment, wondering whether and where and how he could make himself another home. The sympathetic cop who had run him away from the theater had got in touch with a reporter, who now listened to Louis Bringmann.

"The past," said the old man, "is a turned-over page. When I read it, I read it alone. They tell me now that I'm even too old for dish-washing— that's the whole story. I have no friends and my money is gone."

And then he sat and stared.

12

The Bonus Army Invades Washington

WALTER W. WATERS was too young and too stubborn to take defeat without putting up a good fight. By early May, 1932, he was one of 12,000,000 unemployed people in the United States. Waters lived in Portland, Oregon, and had worked as foreman in a canning factory until he lost his job through no fault of his own. That had been a year and a half ago, and he had been unable to find any other work since. Now his home and car had been repossessed, his money had run out, and he ached as he saw his wife and two small daughters suffer. His wife was a tiny blonde weighing only 93 pounds.

Waters was a thirty-four-year-old veteran, tall and handsome, restless and dynamic, his thick blond hair pushed back from his forehead. Never in his Army experience had he been an officer, but he liked to wear smart officer's boots and breeches, and he carried a cane. As a private he had skirmished along the Mexican border with Pershing, and as a sergeant attached to the 146th Field Artillery he had fought several battles in France. Glory lay behind him. Now, about the only thing he could call his own was a piece of paper known as an adjusted service credit certificate—a soldier's bonus. Flipping this back and forth in his strong fingers, Waters decided that he wanted action and he wanted it now!

During World War I the American doughboys had been paid $30 a month while in uniform, and when they were discharged, each got $60 in cash and a ticket home. But while they were saving democracy at about $1 a day, shipyard workers and munitions makers on the prosperous home front were earning $90 a week and strutted around in silk shirts. Furthermore, when the federal government took over the nation's railroads during the war, it had adjusted the pay of railway employees.

In 1919 the American Legion had broached the idea that since the soldiers had been paid so poorly, they, too, should get adjusted compensation. Subsequently, both houses of Congress passed a compensation bill, but it was vetoed by President Harding. The measure was revived, passed again by the House and Senate, but again it was vetoed—this time by President Coolidge. However, in 1924 both branches of the Congress passed the bill over Coolidge's veto, and it became the law.

On January 1, 1925, about 3,500,000 veterans received adjusted compensation certificates. Not money—just pieces of paper. These certificates were like paid-up twenty-year endowment insurance policies paying 4 percent interest compounded annually. Each veteran was credited with $1 a day for each day's service within the United States and $1.25 for each day served abroad. A man entitled to, say, $400 would get about $1,000—in the year 1945.

By 1931, though, with Depression blighting the land, members of the American Legion pressured its executive committee so hard that the Legion finally asked for immediate payment of the certificates. With other demands being made on it the federal government finally decided on a compromise measure. While veterans still could not cash their certificates in full, the government agreed to lend them half the face value of their bonuses at 4½ percent interest. Even this failed to satisfy the veterans. As more and more of them lost their jobs and homes, they demanded the full and immediate payment of all certificates.

Representative Wright Patman, a Democrat from Texas who had been a machine gunner during the war, urged the House of Representatives to pass a bill calling for the immediate payment of all certificates by issuing $2.4 billion in fiat money. Fiat money is paper currency that is declared legal tender by law. It does not represent specie, such as gold or silver. It is not based on specie. It contains no promise of redemption.

Patman's opponents screamed that this would result in inflation. Denying this charge, Patman replied: "We don't expect to start out on any wild program like Germany did. We are willing to tie to a 40 percent gold basis." He went on to say that there was still $4 billion in gold in the Treasury, that this was enough to support the $10 billion in currency, but even so there was only $5.5 billion in paper money circulating throughout the country. To print another $2.4 billion, Patman declared, would leave the nation safely below the danger mark.

President Hoover disagreed. Banks were failing; cash was being hoarded; stock prices were plummeting. Besides the cry for the soldiers' bonus, the President was beset by a variety of proposals to induce inflation and provide unemployment benefits. He declared that "the urgent question today is the prompt balancing of the budget. When that is accomplished, I propose to support adequate measures for relief of distress and unemployment."

Governor Roosevelt also disagreed with Patman, saying: "I do not see how, as a matter of practical sense, a government running behind two billion dollars annually can consider the anticipation of bonus payment until it has balanced the budget."

Walter W. Waters of Portland knew little and cared less about budget balancing and national finances. He knew he was suffering needlessly and he wanted something done about it. He liked what Patman said about the Reconstruction Finance Corporation: "The millions released to the R.F.C. went to the big boys by way of New York. The millions involved in the full-payment bonus bill will go to the little fellow, into every nook and corner of the nation. It will take money not now in circulation and put it into circulation. It will mean increased revenue to the government."

Waters was struck by a remark made by President Hoover about "the locust swarm of lobbyists who haunt the halls of Congress." Lobbyists? Waters grinned to himself and slapped his cane against his boots. He told other Portland veterans that it might be a good idea to get some of the boys together and go to Washington to lobby for passage of the Patman bill, which was bottled up in the House Ways and Means Committee. Why not? It was worth a try. Anything was better than a guy sitting around on his can waiting for total disaster. The vets had their rights. Why not agitate for them?

His listeners nodded and passed along the word, and soon Waters was addressing ever larger groups, speaking forcefully like the born leader he was. March on Washington! March on Washington! Jobless men pinched their chins in thought, scratched their stubbled cheeks, mulled over the idea, then beat calloused hands together in applause. On May 10, 1932, the day that Patman began collecting signatures on a petition to get his bill out of committee, the Oregon veterans organized themselves into a quasi-military outfit.

They dubbed themselves the Bonus Expeditionary Force. They donned faded uniforms or parts of uniforms—high-collared tunics, canvas leggings, khaki caps. They promised not to drink any booze, forswore panhandling and proclaimed themselves true Americans—not radicals. There were 300 of them, and when they turned their collective pockets inside out, they found they had less than $30 in cash among them. The nation's capital lay more than 3,000 miles to the east. How were they to get there?

By riding the rails, they decided. So they hopped freight trains out of Portland and rode into one sunrise after another. At first they went unnoticed by the national press, much concerned at this time by the discovery of the Lindbergh baby's body, but after the BEF reached East St. Louis, Illinois, it burst into headlines. That was on May 21. When the Oregon travelers swarmed aboard a Baltimore & Ohio freight, railway officials ordered the engineer not to start the train. Cursing, the veterans piled off, slipped out of town, waited until the train was in slow motion, fell upon it, uncoupled cars, cut air lines and soaped the tracks so the engine wheels would slip. Illinois National Guard units were called out to restore order, and this "Battle of the B. & O." focused the attention of the American people on the Bonus Expeditionary Force. The veterans forgot their resolve not to accept charity when East St. Louis townspeople—some sympathetic, some fearful—gave them 200 pounds of sausages and lent them enough trucks to carry them out of town and all the way across Illinois.

Governor Paul V. McNutt of Indiana was so apprehensive about the invasion of his state by this shabby little army that he also gave them trucks to whisk them through, asking only that they promise not to move en masse through Indiana on their way back home. And so, that May, 1932, while Mayor Jimmy Walker of New York City fought for his political life in a witness chair, while Nazis chased Communists around Berlin, while 224 New York families were homesteaded on farms to grow their own food, the Oregon veterans accepted handouts and free rides, moving steadily on trucks across Ohio, West Virginia, Pennsylvania and Maryland. The evening of May 28 they bedded down on the floor of a skating rink in Cumberland, Maryland, only one day away from the capital. By this time Walter W. Waters had won the title of regimental commander of the BEF, the University of Chicago's department of economics had declared that the bonus would not restore prosperity, and federal officials were worrying about the imminent invasion.

At last, on Sunday, May 29, 1932, the Oregonians rolled into Washington, D.C., riding in sixteen trucks, shouting jubilantly, waving American flags and a banner that said: GIVE US A BONUS OR GIVE US A JOB. Chills ran up the spines of Washingtonians when Waters announced that he and his men were ready to stay there until 1945, if necessary, to get cash payment for their certificates. To the surprise of the West Coast veterans, they found that about 1,000 other veterans had preceded them to the national capital. Publicity about the BEF, plus legislative pressure to pass the Patman bill, had attracted other ex-servicemen there, and still more were on their way.

Who were they? They were former soldiers and sailors. They were the unemployed. They were white and black. They were blue-collar workers and white-collar workers. In the recent past they had slumped in barbershops and on front porches, in Legion posts and in grocery stores, staring at their hands, their idle hands, and they had mumbled and muttered and then lifted their voices and their faces and decided to go to Washington. It ain't good for a fella to sit around with no work to do. Man's gotta right to what's his, that's fer dang sure! This here Congressman from Texas— what's his name? Patman—maybe Patman got the right idea. Let's drop in at Washington and sort of help him along a little.

They were the jobless truck driver from Philadelphia, once with the Fifteenth Engineers, his wife holding the only job in the family and supporting the kids. They were the coal miner from Morgantown, West Virginia, proud of his record in the Rainbow Division, out of work the past eighteen months, a grown man getting pocket money from his paw and maw. They were the Pole from Chicago, a veteran of the Thirty-ninth Division, unemployed for three years, his wife dead, their kids with his mother, a man who had moaned while sleeping in flophouses. They were the idle steel-metal worker from Columbus, Georgia, once an infantryman with the First Division, now three years behind in his debts.

As warriors they had known violence, as Depression victims they now knew despair, and Walter W. Waters of Portland, Oregon, tall in his boots with more than 3,000 miles under his dusty belt, looked out over them and said in a voice of brass: *"We are going to stay here until the veterans' bill is passed!"*

Washington trembled.

*   *   *

Within the previous six months the capital had endured two smaller unemployment marches, the first led by Communists, the second by a Catholic priest from Pittsburgh. People with long memories recalled that back in 1894, on the heels of an earlier depression, a rich businessman named Jacob Coxey had herded 1,200 ragged and jobless men from Ohio to Washington to clamor for road-building projects and public works to relieve unemployment. In none of these cases had there been any rioting but now, as thousands of more veterans spilled into the capital, apprehension grew.

District of Columbia affairs were run by a three-man board of commissioners appointed by the President. Laws were enforced by Major General Herbert B. Crosby, the district commissioner in charge of police matters, through Pelham D. Glassford, superintendent of the metropolitan police department, and his 660 cops. Glassford, who had taken office the previous November, totally lacked police experience. When a reporter asked about his qualifications as chief of police, Glassford grinned and replied: "Well, I've been arrested—once for driving through a red light and once for speeding on a motorcycle." His flippancy was deceptive. A man of high intelligence, Glassford had buckled down to a cram course in criminology and abnormal psychology.

The son of an Army officer, he was born in New Mexico, met Douglas MacArthur when both were West Point cadets, served as a soldier in the Philippines and Hawaii and along the Mexican border, fought in France during World War I, and at the age of thirty-four became the youngest brigadier general in the AEF. After the war he worked as a San Francisco reporter, as a circus sign painter, as pinch hitter for a barker, and then took up residence in Washington to study art. Zestful and fearless, fair-minded and friendly, Glassford was known to all his many friends as "Happy."

The day that Waters arrived in Washington he met Glassford and was so impressed that he wrote: "Here was certainly no hard-boiled disciple of the old police school. In him the human element was above the law." Glassford, who kept a diary, noted "Waters' blue eyes in which there sometimes burned an almost fanatical gleam." The two men sat on the grass together, the police chief letting the veterans' leader do most of the talking. Glassford later said: "I agreed, of course, with their determination to be law-abiding and orderly. . . . As I listened to this first group, I suddenly realized that what was ahead of me was not a mere local police job. It was national. From all over the United States ex-soldiers were heading for Washington and what would be the result? I didn't know. Nobody knew. . . . I told the commissioners that the few hundred men already in Washington were only the advance guard of what might turn out to be a huge army and I wanted to be told how they wanted it handled. Imagine my surprise when it was suggested to me that I treat these men as indigents, pass them along to the Salvation Army or any other charity organization that would feed them, and then make them move on as rapidly as possible."

Through Washington there spread a rumor that 1,000,000 veterans would descend on the capital. Those already present banded together and adopted the name first used by the Oregon contingent—the Bonus Expeditionary Force—and elected Waters their commander in chief. Glassford had greeted the bonus marchers so pleasantly that the grateful men named him their secretary-treasurer. This position enabled the police chief to keep in constant touch with the veterans and to kid and cajole them into keeping the peace.

Despite the fears of district residents, Washington's crime rate actually dropped while the bonus army was in town. Newspaperman Mark Sullivan wrote: "To go out among them was to recognize instantly their complete harmlessness. A child or a lost pocketbook would be safer among them than among any average cross-section of a city population." Correspondent Floyd Gibbons described the veterans as "at all times law-abiding and orderly." Will Rogers wrote: "They hold the record for being the best behaved of any fifteen thousand hungry men assembled anywhere in the world. Just think what fifteen thousand clubwomen would have done to Washington even if they wasn't hungry. The senate would have resigned and the President committed suicide."

Exactly how many veterans finally gathered in Washington? No one will ever know for sure. BEF leaders claimed 80,000, but this figure is far too high. Glassford probably was closer to the mark when he estimated the peak number at 22,000. Even so, this was but a tiny fraction of the 3,500,000 veterans living in the United States. Glassford also believed that there were never more than 300 Communists among the bonus marchers. When a reporter asked him whether he considered all the bonus marchers dangerous, he replied: "Dangerous? No—except the danger of gradual rust and rot which attacks those with no occupation and no incentive. These are just middle-aged men out of a job."

And so they were, for the most part, but Secret Service agents were already infiltrating their ranks, for Communists were trying to take over the movement.

*   *   *

About a year earlier American Communists had demanded immediate payment of the bonus. Then, in December, 1931, the Reds had led a hunger march to Washington to agitate for jobs, a minimum wage and national unemployment insurance. For two days 10,000 jobless persons paraded through the streets, picketed the White House and chanted slogans such as: "The Hoover program—a crust of bread on a bayonet!" They tried to provoke incidents, but Glassford's policy of gentle firmness kept the situation from getting out of hand.

The failure of the December demonstration frustrated Red leaders in New York and Moscow, but now, with the coming of spring, peaceful and patriotic Americans had stolen their thunder by staging a middle-class march on Washington. The Communists had been caught off guard, and this worried Earl Browder, who had succeeded William Z. Foster as head of the American Communist Party. A Comintern representative now hastened from Moscow to the United States with an urgent directive. Browder and other Red leaders were ordered to: (1) take the bonus army leadership away from Waters and his commanders; (2) establish the National Provisional Bonus March Committee of the Workers' Ex-Servicemen's League: (3) trick the veterans into hating the federal government; (4) provoke riots that might result in a massacre of the veterans; (5) use the consequent resentment to increase membership in the Communist Party; (6) above all, try to touch off a revolution.

While a Communist secret board of strategy remained at the Red headquarters in New York, a party front organization was opened in Washington at 905 I Street, NW. Presiding over this National Provisional Bonus March Committee was Emanuel Levin, a former Marine, a Communist candidate for the California Assembly in 1928 and now editor of the *Daily Worker*. The task of trying to take the bonus army away from Waters was given to John Pace of Detroit. Also a former Marine, Pace had joined the Communist Party in 1931 after losing his contracting business.

As this Communist plot slowly uncoiled, unsuspecting veterans kept streaming into Washington from every corner of the nation. Besides being jobless and penniless, they were almost aimless. Walter W. Waters himself said that "not one man in twenty really expected to get the bonus." The *New Yorker* magazine observed that the BEF "was something more than a lobby; it was the expression of men's desire to huddle together when their courage is gone." In his book *The Lean Years*, Irving Bernstein wrote: "This bonus march might well be described as a flight from reality—a flight from hunger, from the cries of the starving children, from the humiliation of accepting money from worn, querulous women, from the harsh rebuffs of prospective employers." A welfare worker said: "Their real demand was for security, and in their bewilderment and confusion they seem to have reverted to the old army ways and to the earlier institutional situation where shelter and food are provided."

President Hoover tried to ignore the presence of the veterans, refusing time and again to receive any of their leaders. Governor Roosevelt announced that he would arrange to get the fare for any New York bonus marcher who cared to come home. No official of the federal government or the District of Columbia cared to assume responsibility for either sheltering the veterans or evicting them. The sole exception was Police Chief Glassford, but he lacked orders, funds or food. In his opinion, the crisis boiled down to the alternative of feeding them or fighting them—and he had no stomach for fighting men with whom he had soldiered.

His chief's cap on his head, his gold badge pinned to his white shirt, wearing dun-colored breeches and puttees, Glassford mounted his blue motorcycle to chug here and there on errands of mercy. Breezily he begged funds from the rich and comfortable, besides spending $733 of his own money on the men he called his friends. He cajoled his cops into staging a boxing match and donating the net receipts of $2,500 to the veterans. He pried a donation out of Jimmy Lake, proprietor of the Gayety burlesque house. From the National Guard he obtained the use of secondhand pup tents.

One of the richest women in Washington—and in all the world, for that matter—was Mrs. Evalyn Walsh McLean. She owned the fabled $2 million Hope diamond, was heiress to a mining fortune, reigned as Washington's society queen and lived in a vast $1 million estate called Friendship on the northwest edge of the district. Her husband, Edward B. McLean, was proprietor of the Washington *Post* and the Cincinnati *Enquirer*.

Seldom seen without her jewels, she wore huge horn-rimmed spectacles that made her look half-astonished, half-inquisitive. Feverishly devoted to the pursuit of pleasure, Mrs. McLean confessed that for a time she had been a morphine addict. During one of her wild parties at Friendship the scene was surveyed by Senator William E. Borah, who then commented bitterly: "This sort of thing is what brings on a revolution."

Mrs. McLean watched as the families of the bonus marchers joined them in the national capital, and her first reaction was one of anger "because I felt that crowd of men, women and children never should have been permitted to swarm across the continent."

Later, though, after reading in the newspapers that they were starving, she decided in the middle of one night to help them. She also felt that her son Jock should see this chapter in American history. Taking him along, she drove to a camp and got out of her car to talk to the veterans.

"Have you eaten?" she asked one man.

He shook his head from side to side.

Just then Mrs. McLean was approached by Police Chief Glassford, whom she knew. Glassford said: "I'm going to get some coffee for them."

Mrs. McLean cried: "All right! I'm going to Child's."

It was 2 A.M. when she and her son walked into the restaurant. When a waiter came to take their order, she asked: "Do you serve sandwiches? I want a thousand. Oh! And a thousand packages of cigarettes."

"But, lady—"

"I want them right away! I haven't got a nickel with me, but you can trust me. I am Mrs. McLean."

After feeding some veterans that night, Mrs. McLean went the following day to see John Barton Payne, head of the Red Cross, whom she also knew. Despite her barrage of words, she was unable to persuade him that the bonus army was part of a national crisis with which the Red Cross was morally obligated to deal. Barton did promise her a little flour, which she accepted. Next, she visited local headquarters of the Salvation Army, finding girls hard at work doing all they could to help the veterans. Their harried officer told Mrs. McLean that what the men most needed was a big tent to serve as headquarters for registering newcomers, so she ordered one delivered from Baltimore. Time and again she went out among the bonus marchers, giving them clothing, books and radios.

At last Mrs. McLean succeeded in getting Walter W. Waters to visit her at her estate. He showed up with his wife, who had just reached Washington dressed as a man, her tiny feet encased in shiny boots. She was tired and dirty after her long bus trip from Oregon. Mrs. McLean led the exhausted woman upstairs and into the guest bedroom her father had designed for use by King Leopold of Belgium, urged her to lie down and ordered a maid to draw a bath.

"You get undressed," the hostess suggested, "and while you sleep I'll have all your things cleaned and pressed."

"Oh, no! Not me! I'm not giving these clothes up. I might never see them again!"

However, she did agree to rest awhile. Mrs. McLean then joined Waters, who said: "I'm desperate! Unless these men are fed, I can't say what won't happen to this town!"

That evening, with Waters standing by her chair, Mrs. McLean phoned her friend Charles Curtis, the Vice President of the United States. Urgently she said: "These men are in a desperate situation, and unless something is done for them, unless they are fed, there is bound to be a lot of trouble."

Vice President Curtis told Mrs. McLean that he would call a secret meeting of Senators, but nothing came of it.

* * *

Glassford turned for help to his old friend Douglas MacArthur, the Army chief of staff, and MacArthur lent the bonus marchers some of the Army's rolling kitchens. These made it possible to feed the men for only seven cents a day, but this infuriated one Congressman, who took the floor of the House to warn: "If they come to Washington, sit down and have three meals furnished them free every day, then God knows what will happen to us! . . . If the government can feed those that are here, then we can expect an influx that will startle the whole country." The rolling kitchens rolled away.

Some veterans took over empty buildings within the federal triangle just northwest of the Capitol, while others grouped together in camps in and around the city. Ultimately, there were twenty-two BEF billets. The largest was Camp Anacostia, located on swampland south of the Capitol near the confluence of the Potomac and Anacostia rivers, on the southern bank of the Anacostia, stretching from the Anacostia Bridge south to Bolling Field. From this site the ragged campers could see the Capitol dome with its bronze statue called "Freedom."

The men were free to exist as best they could. Many used cardboard to patch their shoes; some had no shoes at all. They wore old army caps, tattered trousers, wash-faded denim shirts and other odd garments. They scrounged through city dumps to collect old newspapers, cardboard boxes, tin cans, tar-paper roofing, egg crates, packing cases, hunks of tin and the carcasses of abandoned cars. Sweating in the humid heat of Washington, they made huts out of this junk.

The veterans picked weeds from the edge of the river and wove them through chicken wire and old bedsprings to improvise beds. One man slept in a coffin set on trestles; another in a barrel filled with grass; a third in a piano box. They gagged at sewage flowing just a few feet away, swatted at flies and mosquitoes. The surgeon general of the United States warned of the danger of an epidemic, so the bonus marchers appointed their own sanitary officer. In the soft marshy ground they dug latrines which they called Hoover villas.

And when they had finished putting up their miserable shanties and torn tents, they stuck American flags here and there, muttering in disgust because they had been disowned by both the American Legion and the Veterans of Foreign Wars. Feverish men lay in one tent with a cynical sign saying: THE LAME, SICK AND LAZY. Breezes shook a poster promising: "Don't cry, little girl, I will come back home." Sick and hungry, dirty and deprived, falling back on half-remembered habits to ward off chaos, these middle-aged men fell asleep and came awake to the sound of a bugle, sucked in bellies to drill before visitors, asked for passes to leave camp.

And waited.

The Communists announced that the veterans would hold a "monster demonstration" in the streets of Washington, but when only 160 men showed up at the staging area, the demonstration was called off. Glassford heard from a Washington reporter that the Communists, despite all their efforts, were making almost no impression upon the bonus marchers. On June 10 John Pace arrived at the head of a small unit of Detroit Communists. This was so heartening to the Reds already present that on that same evening 200 of them attacked Camp Anacostia. The radicals got the worst of it, however, the Washington *Herald* reporting: "Husky buddies from the Texas plains vied with lanky New Englanders for the privilege of 'going to work' on the Communists." When Glassford got to the scene, he found the Reds cowering in a corner of the camp, trying to use their arms to ward off blows. He and his cops pulled the angry veterans off the Communists, led them off the grounds and marched them to the relative safety of a vacant lot some distance away.

Washington, a city of 486,000 population, had 19,000 of its own residents who were without work. The need for jobs for local people, the lack of proper facilities to care for them and now the presence of a growing army of veterans—all this created a strain too great to be handled. Glassford wired all forty-eight state governors, urging them to try to keep more veterans from converging upon the capital. He also begged Congressional leaders to end the crisis by bringing the bonus bill to a vote.

The Patman bill was discharged from committee and debated in the House, which was mostly Democratic. All the Representatives knew that every bonus seeker and everyone influenced by a bonus seeker would vote against the Congressman who voted against the bonus. Congressman Edward E. Eslick, a sixty-year-old Democrat from Tennessee, died of a heart attack while arguing in favor of paying the compensation. The next day, June 15, the House passed the Patman bill, 209 to 176. Most Democrats favored it, while most Republicans opposed it.

By this time delegates to the Republican National Convention had gathered in Chicago to nominate a Presidential candidate, and some Chicago veterans noisily invaded convention rooms. Despite this disorder, Herbert Hoover was renominated. Some wishful-thinking veterans felt that Hoover would not dare veto the bill if it reached his desk in this election year of 1932. The measure was sent to the Senate Finance Committee, which reported against it. Now the entire Senate met to consider the issue. If Senators rejected the bill, what would the veterans do? Some members of the administration were so frightened that they wanted to mount machine guns on the roof of the Capitol, but this horrified Glassford so it was not done. On June 17 the Senate opened debate.

With the fate of the BEF trembling in the balance, agitators raced through various camps shouting: "On to the Capitol! On to the Capitol! Over the bridges, comrades! The Senate is going to defeat the bonus bill! Everybody to Washington!" A local newspaper called this "the tensest day in the capital since the war."

Groups of ragged, menacing men pushed their way into the Capitol Building and stretched out on the marble floors of corridors. Guards eyed them uneasily and uncertainly, afraid to touch them for fear of sparking a riot. Most of the bonus marchers—perhaps 10,000 strong—assembled in the plaza fronting on the Senate chamber, squatted on stone steps, sprawled on green grass, muttered and sang and dozed and stirred restlessly all afternoon long and into the evening. Within the Senate the debate dragged on. Every now and then a Senator would tiptoe to a window, peek down on the multitude, anxiously shake his head, creep back into the chamber.

The legislators' apprehension was openly voiced by Republican Senator Hiram Johnson of California, an old man in a baggy blue serge suit with white piping on his vest. Johnson prophesied: "This marks a new era in the life of our nation. The time may come when this folderol—these trappings of government—will disappear, when fat old men like you and me stop making speeches to sleepy galleries and be lined up against a stone wall."

Outside the fear-soaked chamber, out in the plaza, the tall and lean and sunburned Walter W. Waters stood waiting, flicking his cane against his boots. A reporter asked him: "What's going to happen when these men learn of the defeat of the bill? It's going to be swamped, you know." To the reporter's surprise, Waters replied: "Nothing will happen."

But who could be sure?

Darkness fell. Out of a door of the Capitol came an elderly man with a sharp nose, pale and shrewd eyes—Senator Elmer Thomas, an Oklahoma Democrat who favored the Patman bill. An acre of eyes locked on this slim figure and followed it as Thomas stepped up to Waters and whispered into his ear. Waters' jaw muscles tightened. Then, when the Senator had finished whispering, Waters climbed onto a pedestal at the edge of the Capitol steps and spread out his arms.

"Comrades!"

His voice was low and tired. The veterans scrambled to their feet, babbling and shouting. Waters waggled his outstretched arms and at last got silence—silence as menacing as a razor's edge.

"Comrades! . . . I have bad news for you. Prepare yourselves for a disappointment, men! . . . The bonus has been defeated . . . sixty-two to eighteen. . . ." (Another sixteen Senators had abstained from voting.)

"Booooooooo-oooo-oooo!"

The sound, like an artillery barrage, rose and rolled and rumbled throughout the plaza. Then the men stood in stunned silence. They did not seem to breathe. Fists clenched. Muscles were rigid against ragged sleeves. For a split second Waters looked uncertain, fearful. Near him stood Elsie Robinson, a middle-aged newspaper columnist with a furrowed face. She whispered to Waters: "Tell them to sing 'America'!"

Waters shouted: "Let's sing 'America,' men—and then go back to your billets!"

Snatching caps off their heads, the dazed and disappointed veterans sang as ordered. At the end of the song there came cries: "North Carolina—fall in here! . . . New Mexico—over here!" Soon the shapeless crowd fell into patterns as the men formed platoons and began tramp-tramp-tramping out of the plaza and back to their encampments. Half an hour later silence swathed the plaza. Senators wiped their brows and went home.

Some disgusted veterans—the police said 1,000, the BEF said 200—now started drifting away from Washington. Fifteen thousand or more remained, however, and these diehards tried to cheer up one another by chanting: "Stay until 1945!" Actually, those who stayed were not really sure what to do next. Some resented the seemingly casual way in which their leader had accepted the Senate's decision. John Pace, the Communist agitator from Detroit, tried to use this dissension to wrest power from Waters. The veterans wrangled among themselves so ferociously that the BEF almost fell apart. In three days two new leaders were elected, but then Waters staged a coup, regained his title of commander in chief and won dictatorial authority.

Waters now began talking about organizing a paramilitary force like the Nazi storm troopers and the Italian Blackshirts, naming it the Khaki Shirts of America and demanding "reform" of the American government. He demanded rigid obedience and took to saluting his men with the stiff-arm gesture of Mussolini. When some veterans objected, Waters bellowed: "I'll do what I want to do whether you like it or not, and those that don't can get the hell out of the BEF! I'm going to be hard-boiled!"

"Hot Waters," as some now called him, believed that what this country needed was a hard core of 100 percent Americans to serve as a shield against Communism. As Waters heated and hardened, Glassford watched in dismay, scribbling in his diary that the BEF leader "saw 'Red' a little too strenuously." But Waters kept on roaring that he would do things his own way "if I have to detail five hundred MP's!"

He already had his own self-proclaimed "military police," a band of more than 300 men under the immediate command of a colorful character named W. D. Atwell. When the police chief accused Atwell of throwing seven Communists into the river, Atwell snarled: "Sure, I did! They needed a bath!" Under orders from Waters and Atwell, kangaroo courts sentenced Red leaders to fifteen lashes across the back with belts, destroyed their leaflets and booted them out of camp.

The bonus marchers had their own five-cent newspaper, *The B.E.F. News,* which now flailed radicals and the rich alike. It warned that wealthy people were "making it easier for the Reds to add to their ranks." It shrilled: "Eyes front—not left!"

With the widening of the split between Red activists and other veterans, Earl Browder proclaimed from New York: "The Bonus revolutionary force in Washington is the significant beginning of the mass struggle against the deepening consequence of the crisis." The Communists' secret board of strategy, together with the representative of the Comintern, distributed a quarter-million copies of a manifesto. In bold type it screamed: ONLY MASS ACTION WILL WIN BONUS FICHT!

John Pace, stepping up his activities, led radicals and others into the center of Washington, to a spot three blocks from the Capitol Building, to an area bounded by Third and Fourth Streets, NW, and Missouri and

Pennsylvania Avenues. There they took over four abandoned buildings that already housed some veterans. These red-brick half-demolished structures, owned by the Treasury Department, were scheduled to be torn down completely to make space for a new project. District Commissioner Crosby now accused Glassford of dereliction of duty by failing to enforce an ordinance banning the use of buildings that lacked sewers. Crosby told Glassford to evict the squatters. Glassford told him that this would result in a riot, and then the Army or National Guard would have to be called out. A crisis of this kind, Glassford told all three commissioners, would threaten the safety of everyone in the city. He pleaded with the commissioners to confer with the disgruntled veterans, but they refused.

As the situation worsened in Washington, the Democratic National Convention opened in Chicago. Governor Roosevelt was so sure he would win the Presidential nomination that he began drafting his acceptance speech, sitting in his Albany office in shirtsleeves, smoking one cigarette after another. A fellow Democrat, Senator Huey Long of Louisiana, called him long distance and coaxed him to come out for immediate payment of the bonus. Roosevelt said he did not favor the bonus. Huey Long rasped: "Well, then, you're a gone goose!" But the Senator was wrong. Roosevelt won the nomination on July 1.

In Washington the bonus marchers were so low on food that Waters flew to New York City, where he managed to get a donation of one ton of supplies. On the Fourth of July the veterans paraded through the streets of the capital, but instead of the 20,000 BEF members claimed by Waters, a mere 5,000 or less trudged forlornly behind two buglers and a single drummer. This turnout was so disappointing that at last even Waters confessed that perhaps the bonus army might as well dissolve and its members leave for home.

Taking shape at this time were plans to make it easy for them to get out of town. Glassford had been negotiating with railroads for cheap fares, and both the Pennsylvania and Baltimore & Ohio lines had offered the veterans a one-cent-per-mile rate for a ride home. President Hoover had asked Congressional leaders to introduce a joint resolution authorizing the Veterans Bureau to spend $100,000 for this kind of transportation. Some veterans said they might take this money if it were offered to them, but others shouted that they wanted meal tickets, not train tickets.

BEF morale was low when 700 California veterans arrived in Washington under the leadership of Roy W. Robertson of Los Angeles. While serving in the Navy, Robertson had broken his back in a fall from a bunk, and he still wore a back brace and a clamp on his head. A bluff and arrogant man, he scorned both the Communists and the men loyal to Waters. During his only conference with Waters, he snapped: "We came to Washington to petition Congress, not to picnic!" The night the Californians arrived they slept on the lawn of the Capitol, and the next morning they boldly walked into the House Office Building to shave and wash.

This was the beginning of an ominous demonstration. The militant West Coast veterans, joined by others, started marching in single file back and forth in the Capitol plaza. They called their demonstration a Death March because of the imminent adjournment of Congress. Back and forth, day and night, in sunshine and in rainfall, occasionally booing President Hoover, the men marched, marched, marched, until they unnerved Vice President Curtis.

Charles Curtis was a political hack; one cynic said that Curtis thought the Trinity consisted of the Republican Party, the high tariff and the Grand Army of the Republic. As a Senator from Kansas he had accepted money to endorse Lucky Strike cigarettes, and upon assuming the Vice Presidency, he had become the target of ridicule by insisting on preferred protocol for his half sister, Dolly Curtis Gann. President Hoover did not think highly of Curtis.

Eager to quash the demonstration in front of the Capitol, Curtis called out the Marines. They arrived from the navy yard in something less than military style, for they rode trolleys and taxicabs. Police Chief Glassford took one look at them and exploded. Getting in touch with Curtis, he roared that he alone was responsible for law and order in the District of Columbia—with the sole exception of the President of the United States. He shouted that he was fed up with "hysterical meddlers." After slamming down the phone, Glassford found a Senator who was willing to call the White House and ask the President whether he would take responsibility for summoning the Marines. Hoover replied that he would not. The Marines were withdrawn.

But on July 14 some blustering veterans invaded the Vice President's office, and another tremor of fear rolled across Washington.

The next day the hazardous situation was discussed at a conference held in the office of General Douglas MacArthur. Among those present were ranking Army officers and Glassford. According to the police chief, MacArthur said flatly that the Army would not be used against the bonus marchers "unless directed by the President." Vice President Curtis sent word to the conferees that he wanted the Capitol grounds completely cleared of demonstrators. Glassford argued that this would aggravate matters. After further discussion, Glassford agreed to a compromise—only the plaza in front of the Capitol would be cleared. His cops managed to herd back the veterans without any trouble, but the Death March continued at a greater distance from the Capitol Building.

That same day, Hoover cut his Presidential salary by 20 percent. Independently wealthy, Hoover never used any of his public salaries for personal purposes, giving them instead to charity. His Cabinet members also reduced their salaries by 15 percent so there could be no complaint by federal employees, whose wages had been slashed by 8¼ percent.

That same day, too, acceding to the President's request, Congress appropriated $100,000 to get the BEF out of town. Now the Veterans

Bureau could advance each veteran the price of a railway ticket home, plus 75 cents a day for food during the trip. The sum given each man represented a loan without interest; if it were not repaid, it would be deducted from his bonus—if and when he got it. Glassford hopped onto his motorcycle and chugged through the camps and shantytowns, handing out copies of a letter in which he urged the men to accept the government's offer. Many of them balked. Why go back home when no homes or jobs awaited them? Why not stick close to the seat of power and fight to the finish? Besides, the veterans groused, Hoover's offer of a lift out of town was his first official acknowledgment that they even existed.

Agreement on this last point came from Walter Lippmann, who wrote in his column: "Mr. Hoover does not shrink from holding conferences and issuing statements. How can he justify the fact that he never took the trouble to confer with the bonus marchers?" Historian Arthur M. Schlesinger, Jr., has pointed out: "The President himself had ample time in these weeks to receive Jim Londos, the heavyweight wrestling champion, delegations from Eta Upsilon Gamma Sorority and from the Baraca Philathea Union, adolescent winners of essay contests and other dignitaries; but audiences were denied to the leaders of the B.E.F."

Only a few hundred veterans took the tickets and departed for home, leaving behind thousands of resentful men. Tension tightened. *The B.E.F. News* whipped up emotions: "A dog in the gutter will fight to feed its pups," but for three years "you have cringed and fawned and begged for crumbs. . . . Why stand you thus, when all is within your power? Are you truly curs and cowards? Or are you men?"

On July 16, the day Congress was due to adjourn, the bonus army took up vigil at opposite ends of Pennsylvania Avenue. About 17,000 men gathered near the Capitol Building. A small group approached the White House, clamoring to get inside to talk to the President, but they were turned away. Numbering only about 50 men, they stayed as close to the White House grounds as possible. They knew it was customary for the President to go to the Capitol on the final day of each session to sign bills and watch the closing ceremonies. Hoover had announced he would make this short trip, and for two hours a limousine waited at the White House door.

Outside the Capitol, "Hot Waters" climbed onto a portico and shouted to his massed men: "You've got to keep a lane open for the white-collar birds so they won't rub into us lousy rats! We're going to stay here until I see Hoover!"

Hours passed, night came, and still the President failed to leave the White House. Commissioner Crosby was so worried about Hoover's safety that he ordered Glassford to tighten security at the White House and in the surrounding area. No gathering of large groups. No demonstrations. Cops to be responsible for Pennsylvania Avenue and all approaches, except from the south. Park police to patrol the East and West Executive Avenues and the southern approach. White House gates shut and chained. And Crosby told Glassford: "In the event of a call for federal troops, responsibility shall pass to the commander thereof."

Three hundred armed soldiers had been assembled inside the nearby Munitions Building, although few persons knew it at the time. Now the police went into action, driving veterans away from the vicinity of the White House and jailing three of them. All pedestrians and cars were chased off Pennsylvania Avenue and adjacent streets. If these thorough-fares had not been cleared instantly, reporters were told, the President would have called out the Army.

But veterans and spectators backed away from the White House, Hoover sat tight, Waters and his legion waited in vain, Congress adjourned, and at last the bonus army drifted disgustedly away from the Capitol. This crisis had been weathered—but what next?

The administration decided to step up its pressure against the veterans. During the previous weeks the Treasury Department had made no overt objection to the fact that veterans had occupied its four vacant buildings within the federal triangle. Now, however, an assistant secretary of the treasury ordered Glassford to oust the squatters so that wrecking crews might finish demolition of the buildings. The police chief recognized this as a ruse, for he also was told that the BEF would be chased out of all its camps. The worried Glassford consulted with the district commissioners, but they seconded what he called "this sudden and drastic change of policy." Glassford went to Waters and begged him to tell his men to take the railway tickets and go home; Waters refused.

On July 26 an emergency conference was held by administration leaders, Red Cross officials and BEF representatives. Commander in chief "Hot Waters" had his chief of staff and attorney at his side as he faced the others—the first confrontation they had been given with any federal official other than Glassford. The meeting lasted five hours.

One of the participants was Secretary of War Patrick J. Hurley, a picturesque and fearless loudmouth. One day during the bonus troubles he had attended a barbecue held by Washington correspondents, had shown off a toy that roared like a bull, had slapped reporters on their backs and cried: "I like my beef raw!" After this emergency meeting, Waters quoted Hurley as saying: "You and your bonus army have no business in Washington! We are not in sympathy with your being here. We will not co-operate in any way with your remaining here. We are interested only in getting you out of the district. At the first sign of disorder or bloodshed in the B.E.F., you will all get out—and we have plenty of troops to get you out!"

Another man who took part in the conference was Chief of Staff Douglas MacArthur—handsome and brilliant, rigid and imperious. Harold L. Ickes once said: "MacArthur is the type of man who thinks when he gets to heaven, God will step down from the great white throne and bow him into His vacated seat." Mistakenly believing that the Communists had seized leadership of the BEF, MacArthur had referred to the veterans as "traitors," "the enemy" and "the mob."

The general paced the floor most of the time during the long conference. As it broke up, Waters turned to him and asked: "If the troops should be called out against us, will the B.E.F. be given the opportunity to form in columns, salvage their belongings, and retreat in orderly fashion?" According to Waters, MacArthur replied: "Yes, my friend. Of course!"

Waters now realized that the government meant business. The next day he called together his 182 group commanders and warned them that one false step would bring out the Army. If an attempt was made to evict any of the veterans, Waters said, they were to offer "absolutely no resistance." He suggested that the men occupying the federal buildings withdraw to Camp Bartlett on Alabama Avenue, SE. At Glassford's request, this 32-acre estate had been lent to the BEF by its owner, John H. Bartlett, a former governor of New Hampshire and former assistant postmaster general. About 1,000 veterans were already billeted in Camp Bartlett, which Waters now called the last resort of the BEF.

While Waters was talking to his men, Hoover was talking to his own assistants, Hurley and MacArthur among them. Hoover said that order could be restored in Washington only if "disturbing factions" were driven from the center of town. He specified, however, that he did not want them chased out of the entire district. As the President later explained: "I did not wish them driven from their camps, as I proposed that the next day we would surround the camps and determine more accurately the number of Communists and ex-convicts among the marchers."

The afternoon of that July 27 Glassford summoned Waters to the office of the district commissioners. Although Waters had been in the capital eight weeks, he had not met the commissioners—and he did not meet them now. They sat in an inner office, Waters sat in an anteroom, and Glassford acted as an envoy, shuttling back and forth between them and him. Waters chuckled: "It isn't every ex-sergeant that can have an ex-general for messenger boy." At issue was the question of when Waters had to pull his men out of the four old government buildings. After much bickering by proxy, he was told the deadline was Monday, July 31. Three days of grace.

At 4:57 A.M. the following day, Thursday, July 28, 1932, the sun rose in a cloudless sky over the city, and a soft breeze blew from the southwest. By 9 A.M. the mercury had risen to 81 degrees, foretelling another of those sultry summer days for which the capital is noted. Shortly after 9 A.M. a bugle blast called veterans to a meeting in an improvised theater in the middle of the 300 block of Pennsylvania Avenue, a block containing the four disputed buildings. Waters took the rostrum and pleaded with the men to leave the area and take up new quarters in Camp Bartlett. Just then Glassford's secretary walked onto the stage and handed Waters a paper.

This was a Treasury Department order demanding the evacuation of the armory—one of the four buildings—by ten o'clock that morning. Not three days of grace. Minutes. Waters read the order aloud, then roared: "You've been double-crossed!" Despite his own anger and chagrin, though, he redoubled his arguments about the advantages of Camp Bartlett. They could settle down there for a long siege. The sullen veterans heckled their leader.

When he could make himself heard, Waters asked: "Will you move or won't you?"

"No! No! No!"

This chant broke up the meeting and the men straggled out into the sunshine, grumbling.

At 10 A.M. Glassford arrived at the head of a force of 100 policemen in white shirts. The cops swiftly strung a rope around the armory and then took up positions at eight-foot intervals inside this thin barrier. Waters kept on begging his men to leave peacefully. Glassford ordered them out. They refused to evacuate the place. Six treasury agents walked up, each protected by a pair of cops. These agents, the policemen and Glassford himself entered the ground floor of the armory.

The first-floor veterans put up no fight and were led outside, one after another. One woman, smiling broadly, emerged on the arm of a treasury agent. Cheers arose from the 1,500 bonus marchers who waited outside, some of them sitting on a pile of rocks.

Now, with the ground floor cleared, agents and cops climbed to the second floor. There they met their first resistance. A black veteran lay on the floor. Agents asked him to get up. He refused. Three patrolmen grabbed him, and although he tried to fight back, they half dragged, half carried him downstairs and out to a patrol car. On that second floor the cops found a big basket filled with bricks, which they thoughtfully removed. Then they cleared the floor of all veterans, who walked out of the building carrying their belongings in boxes, bundles and pails.

A hundred Texas veterans held the third floor, and they yelled that they would have to be carried out. So far, except for the scuffle with the black veteran, the eviction had been a fairly good-natured affair. But now, with the arrival of 3,000 angry veterans from Camp Marks, the mood soured. Men in overalls and dirty shirts started throwing rocks and bricks at the cops. Stolidly, the authorities charged the third-floor Texans, drove them down the stairs, pushed them into the open, shoved them into paddy wagons.

By 11:50 A.M. the last man had been ousted from the armory.

Three minutes later Attorney General William D. Mitchell ordered the immediate evacuation of all veterans from all federal property in the District of Columbia. As the temperature rose, so did tempers. At 12:17 P.M. the police learned that thousands of veterans from billets throughout the district were approaching lower Pennsylvania Avenue. In the avenue's 300 block wrathful veterans continued to mill around the roped-off armory. About thirty-five of them tried to push past the rope and police line to get back into the building. They were brought up short at the barrier. Another hail of bricks and stones fell on the cops, who retaliated by clubbing anyone within arm's length. The police chief's badge was torn off his shirt. A cop who tried to protect Glassford was knocked down and kicked unconscious.

Glassford roared: "Be peaceful, men! Be peaceful! You may have killed one of our best officers!"

"Hell! A lot of us were killed in France!"

Glassford yelled: "Come on, boys! Let's call an armistice for lunch!"

Laughs. Cheers. In five minutes the battle was over.

Glassford raced back to the office of the district commissioners to report that the first building had been repossessed by the Treasury Department. He warned his superiors, though, that the veterans were becoming so ugly that it would be unwise to attempt any more evacuations that day. Ignoring his advice, misrepresenting his attitude, the commissioners sent the President a message asking that the Army be called out. Glassford felt then, as well as later, that it was a mistake to summon the Army. But he had been shorn of much of his authority. Governmental wheels began to turn. Hoover told War Secretary Hurley to send the Army into action. Hurley conveyed this order to Chief of Staff MacArthur.

As he sped back to the federal triangle, Glassford did not know about this order. In the 91-degree heat, thousands of veterans and hundreds of cops shifted from foot to foot and eyed one another uneasily. Some veterans argued among themselves about what to do next.

At 1:25 P.M. two veterans began scrapping on the second floor of a squatter-occupied building at Pennsylvania Avenue and Third Street. Glassford told four of his cops to break up the fight. As they got near the second floor, they were attacked. One officer was knocked down the steps. Another had his head bashed in with a garbage can. A third was about to be slugged with a brick when the fourth cop drew his gun and fired.

Glassford's head jerked up when he heard the shot. "Don't shoot!" he screamed up the staircase.

Too late. In the melee above Glassford's head a penniless Chicago veteran named William J. Haska was drilled through the heart, while mortal wounds were inflicted upon Eric Carlson of Oakland, California. The veterans outside the building had heard the gunfire, and as the police left, they had to run a gauntlet of missiles. Four cops were injured and had to be rushed to a hospital.

This second disturbance of the day was also brief, if bloodier. Walter W. Waters blamed the trouble on John Pace and his Communist followers. Moments after peace was restored Glassford learned from a reporter that troops were on their way.

To the press War Secretary Hurley had given copies of his reply to the district commissioners: "In response to your information that the police of the district were overwhelmed by an organized attack of several thousand men, and were unable to maintain law and order, I complied with your request for aid from the army to the police."

This was not at all what Glassford had told the commissioners.

Hurley's statement was published in early editions of afternoon papers, so now every veteran in the district knew that the Army had been called out. Hordes of excited men swarmed out of their camps and headed for the federal triangle, where the next action seemed most likely to occur.

It had been 2:55 P.M. when Hurley told MacArthur that Hoover wanted to use troops. The general asked the secretary to put this order in writing, and Hurley did. The order did not require MacArthur to take personal command of the operation, but he never shirked his duty—as he saw it. A few days earlier MacArthur had said to a fellow officer: "If the President gives me orders to act, I would not give this distasteful and disagreeable job to any other officer of the United States Army. If anything should go wrong, it will [*sic*] be the kiss of death for that officer's future."

The fifty-two-year-old general had a forty-one-year-old aide named Dwight D. Eisenhower. When Major Eisenhower heard that MacArthur planned to take active command in the field, he had the audacity to object. If the affair turned into a riot, Eisenhower argued, it would be highly inappropriate for the chief of staff to get involved. MacArthur curtly disagreed. Declaring that the issue was maintenance of federal authority in the district, the general barked that there was "incipient revolution in the air!"

In 1932 military officers wore civilian clothes in Washington because the Hoover administration did not want too many uniforms visible in the streets. MacArthur was wearing a white linen suit when he got the word to act. Now, ordering Eisenhower into uniform, he said he was going to his own quarters to change. As MacArthur strode out of his office, Joseph Baird of the United Press fell into step with him. The reporter asked if he might accompany the general. MacArthur said: "Sure—but you'll have to ride home with me first." Baird rode in MacArthur's big black army car out to Fort Myer, where the general lived with his elderly mother. There MacArthur changed into riding boots and spurs, flared whipcord breeches and a jacket ornamented with eight rows of ribbons and medals.

When he got back to his office, he found Eisenhower uniformed and wearing a Sam Browne belt. A colonel told MacArthur that the President forbade any troops to cross any bridge spanning the Anacostia River; Hoover did not want the veterans followed into any of their camps far from the center of the city. MacArthur paid no attention to the colonel's words. Noticing this, another general repeated the Presidential order. Eisenhower later recalled: "In neither instance did General MacArthur hear these instructions. He said he was too busy and did not want either himself or his staff bothered by people coming down and pretending to bring orders."

MacArthur called out a total of almost 1,000 soldiers. They constituted the second squadron of the Third Cavalry from Fort Myer; the third battalion of the Twelfth Infantry from Fort Howard; and six tanks from the first tank platoon from Fort Meade. About 4:30 P.M. this force rendezvoused just south of the White House.

Several historic firsts were in the making: It was the first display of armed force by the United States Army since the American expedition to Siberia had been withdrawn in 1920. It was the first time in American history that federal troops had been summoned by a President to attack American citizens in their national capital. It was the first time soldiers used gas masks in warfare in their own country. It was the first use of new-style tanks.

With the deepening of this fateful afternoon, throngs of curious veterans, file clerks, secretaries, Congressmen, women shoppers and out-of-town sightseers gathered in and near the federal triangle. They sat and they dozed; they chatted and they strolled in the sun; they bought popcorn and lemonade from sidewalk vendors. They mopped their brows and fanned themselves, for the temperature still stood at 91 degrees. At 4:45 P.M. their heads whipped toward the southeast as they heard the clanking and rumbling of an approaching military force.

It came from around a corner of the White House and advanced on the pavement of Pennsylvania Avenue. Four cavalry troops, each horseman holding a drawn saber that glinted in the sunshine. Six tanks bristling with machine guns. Behind the tanks, trotting on the double, foot soldiers wearing steel helmets, tear-gas grenades jiggling from belts, fixed bayonets at the ready.

From the three disputed buildings still held by the veterans, the men gazed down upon this show of military might—and hooted. Other veterans stood on the ground in front of their ramshackle huts along the block and jeered the boyish-looking soldiers: "Yellow! Yellow!" A prankster tied a white handkerchief to a wire and poked it through a slit in one of the tanks. Onlookers laughed.

The cavalrymen, their faces blank, deployed along the north side of the avenue and halted. A black veteran pranced back and forth in front of them, waving a big American flag. Two troopers raised curved swords in salute. The others were impassive as they sat their horses. Then a command rang out. The troopers waved their sabers and charged the crowd. Men, women and children screamed and fled. Some ran along the pavement. Others cut through vacant lots, tripping over debris. Swords flashed. Horses reared, pawing the air. People who had fallen to the ground twisted desperately to roll out of the way of the hooves.

Most soldiers acted with restraint, but a few—through fear or inexperience or self-importance—were violent. A man in civilian clothes bellowed his resentment at this attack by Americans on Americans. A cavalryman cried: "We hate this worse than they do—but they brought it on themselves!" A spectator shouted: "The American flag means nothing to me after this! The American flag means nothing to me after this!" General MacArthur started toward him and barked: "Put that man under arrest if he opens his mouth again!"

One mounted man was about to ride down a flag-carrying veteran when an officer threw up his hand, screaming: "No, no, no!" However, other cavalrymen used the flats of their swords to whack fleeing veterans across their shoulders. A few frenzied horse soldiers cut off the ear of one veteran, stabbed another in the hip and slashed a teen-age boy across the arm. For no rational reason, one trooper threw a tear-gas bomb into a telephone booth where a reporter was on the line with his city room.

This cavalry charge drove most of the people back a distance of several blocks.

Meanwhile, the infantrymen wheeled and advanced across an empty lot toward the three veteran-held buildings and the crowd still massed in front of them. They executed this maneuver so fast that the people had no time to break and run. As the soldiers closed in, the people in front shrank back. Those in the rear, trying to relieve the pressure on them, pushed forward. As a result, the whole group was immobilized in the face of the advancing soldiers.

An officer snapped an order. The uniformed men halted, stepped back a pace, jerked gas masks from their packs, tugged the masks onto their faces, snatched grenades from their belts and lobbed them into the middle of the crowd. Everyone panicked. The tear-gas bombs exploded softly: *Pfuttt-pfuttt-pfuttt!* Here and there a veteran snatched up a hot can and threw it back at the soldiers. Some bombs accidentally fell into front yards jammed with Negro women and children. One bounced onto the porch of a home, and two little girls keeled over, choking and screaming.

The southwest breeze blew the sickly-sweet gas into the faces of thousands of sightseers and federal employees, soldiers and veterans, reporters and photographers. Glassford and MacArthur were among those gassed. Except for the soldiers wearing gas masks, everyone else choked, coughed, vomited, wept and wobbled away.

The infantrymen drove the hacking veterans from all three buildings and chased them out of the 300 block of Pennsylvania Avenue. Then, joined by cops, they moved methodically through the flimsy billets along the avenue, tearing down American flags, using torches to set fire to huts and shacks and tents. One woman begged for permission to run into her shanty to get a suitcase, but a soldier growled: "Get out of here, lady, before you get hurt!" And put the torch to her miserable home. Horsemen formed lines along the block to keep outraged veterans from interfering with this official arson. It was finished by 6:05 P.M.

Congressman Fiorello H. LaGuardia had been following these events by means of a teletype machine in his office in the House Office Building. The more he read, the angrier he grew. At last, his face flushed, he ran out of his office and slapped a paper onto the desk of an assistant, Ernest Cuneo. "What do you think of *that?*" LaGuardia shrilled.

Cuneo saw at a glance that it was a draft of a telegram to the White House. It said: BEANS IS BETTER THAN BULLETS AND SOUP IS BETTER THAN GAS . . . F. LAGUARDIA. Cuneo, a graduate of Columbia University, automatically replied: "You've got to say 'Beans *are* better than bullets' or 'A bean *is* better than a bullet.' " LaGuardia screamed at his aide: "The capital in flames and *you* talk *grammar!* Wise guy!" But the New York Congressman corrected his wire before sending it to President Hoover.

That evening the soldiers herded veterans down one street after another, past shantytown after shantytown, down toward the southeast. They kept bombarding the bonus marchers with tear-gas bombs, and the tattered and tired men retaliated by hurling bricks and stones at the uniformed youths. Men on both sides were hurt. Hospitals began receiving dozens of people suffering minor injuries.

By 7:15 P.M. every bivouac in the city had been evacuated and burned. An hour later 200 harried veterans fled from the District of Columbia and sought shelter in the open fields of Virginia. Nervous officials of that state announced they had been promised military aid in the event of trouble.

Now, disobeying President Hoover's order, MacArthur commanded his troops to pursue the raggle-taggle bonus seekers across the Anacostia Bridge. His belief that the veterans were Communist-dominated had been augmented by word that some veterans in outlying camps had armed themselves with weapons. MacArthur snapped: "I will not permit my men to bivouac under the guns of traitors!"

Eisenhower, who disagreed with his superior's judgment, later wrote of the veterans: ". . . most of them, after their arrival on Pennsylvania Avenue, however misled they may have been by a few agitators, were quiet and orderly. They insisted upon enough discipline within their ranks to guard against lawlessness or collapse into mob anarchy."

Colonel Edmund W. Starling, chief of the Secret Service, also disagreed with MacArthur and sided with Eisenhower, saying: "Our agents were among them, keeping us informed of the number of radicals in every group, and checking on the influence they had with the men. Generally speaking there were few Communists, and they had little effect on the men's thinking."

Many years later, after quitting the Communist Party, John Pace testified that there were no more than 100 Communists in the BEF. Pace added that "the active party group—party faction, that we knew were reliable party members—would number no more than twenty-five."

But MacArthur had made up his mind, and on that dreadful day of July 28, 1932, he told Glassford: "We are going to break the back of the B.E.F.!"

*   *   *

MacArthur's intentions were so clear that veterans ran to their camps on the south side of the Anacostia River to lead their women and children to safety. Seeing a woman at Camp Anacostia, one veteran shouted to her husband: "For God's sake—get her out of here! There'll be shooting in a few minutes!" The wife wailed: "I won't go! If he's going to be killed, I'm going to stay here and be killed with him!" Most women and youngsters, however, straggled out of the cantonment and up nearby Good Hope Hill, where they waited and watched and wept.

Since Anacostia was the largest of all the BEF camps, they expected it to be attacked by the main body of troops. So, from various parts of the city, with mingled motives, veterans streamed into Anacostia. Those without hope collected their few belongings and departed toward the south. Others, spurred by anger, began building a barricade of old autos and trucks around a part of the campsite. A few hotheads strode about carrying rifles, and others boasted of weapons buried in the ground nearby. Reporters were told to get the hell out of the place unless they wanted to be lynched.

As MacArthur's troopers clattered toward the illuminated Anacostia Bridge, district citizens by the thousands gathered on the span and near it, eager to see what might happen. The advancing military force was led by policemen, who pushed spectators to the southeast end of the bridge to clear a path for the soldiers. The people fell back as ordered, but it was obvious from their muttered comments that they sympathized with the veterans, the unseen veterans who huddled and waited in the darkness below the bridge, in the flatland of the camp.

MacArthur had decided on his battle plan: His tanks would crash through the car-and-truck barrier along the north side of Camp Anacostia. This done, he would send in trucks equipped with floodlights to light the battleground, attack with bayonet-brandishing foot soldiers, back them up with cavalrymen and with lorries mounting machine guns. Because of the soft breeze still wafting from the southwest, his men would have to don gas masks again when they threw grenades at the veterans. A reserve force of 3,000 soldiers was heading for the city to be thrown into combat if necessary.

"Hot Waters" rushed to the camp and raced here and there, begging the veterans to forget about resistance, pleading with them to leave peacefully while there still was time. "I don't want any more bloodshed!" Waters cried. Glassford also showed up, his white shirt wet with sweat, and rode his motorcycle around the site, yelling to the men to get out before they got massacred.

MacArthur sent word that he wanted to parley with the camp commander, W. D. Atwell. Waving a white shirt as a flag of truce, Atwell walked alone onto the broad parade ground to confer with the general, who had been given safe-conduct inside the camp. The general said he had orders to evacuate Camp Anacostia and would give the veterans one hour to leave. Earlier in the evening Atwell had urged his men to dig up their guns and fight. At the end of his brief conference with MacArthur, however, Atwell cried: "Give way, boys, give way! They've got the tanks and you haven't got a chance in hell!"

At 10 P.M. the troops attacked. Leaving the high ground at the southeast end of the bridge, they descended into the dark flatlands below. First the black hulks of tanks, their grinding gears blanking out the chirps of crickets. Then the trucks laden with floodlights, thudding and crunching over the rough terrain. Next the foot soldiers, sweating in their jackets and puttees, heavy shoes squishing in marshland, slogging forward anxiously, bayonet-tipped carbines held in slippery wet hands, moving single file along the dim riverbank. Behind them they heard the comforting purr of lorries and the metallic jangle of harnesses as horses picked their way down the steep embankment and into the camp.

All went as planned. The tanks broke through the flimsy barricade, opening a path for the trucks. *Click-click-click!* The huge floodlights punched blue-gray hazy holes through the black night. In this instant glare stood row upon row of tents and lean-tos. The lights pinned long shadows to the feet of all the angrily dancing veterans who dared to stay and fight. Then tear-gas bombs were thrown at these men, who cursed and shook their fists and retreated. They gave ground, weeping their fury, as they went down, disorganized and outnumbered, under a military force the like of which they had seen on the battlefields of Europe.

When the veterans broke and ran, the soldiers lit torches, long flaming brands, ran from hut to hut and tent to tent, peered in to make sure no one was left inside, then set fire to each dwelling. *Whoosh!* A pillar of flame arose from the camp platform that had been used for speechmaking and boxing matches. *Whoosh!* A second column of fire snaked into the night sky as the torch was put to the big gospel tent.

In their sullen retreat the veterans felt they might as well bring down the whole damned place in ruins, so they themselves began setting fires. One man dashed about begging for matches and ran to an edge of the billet to burn everything he could find.

The breeze had died down, so the smoke rose straight toward the heavens as flames snapped and stuttered, eating their way through Camp Anacostia. Over the national capital the sky seemed to hemorrhage. The bloody stain could be seen through the windows of the Lincoln Study in the White House, where President Hoover sat conversing with Seth Richardson, an assistant attorney general, and with Henry M. Robinson, a California banker and lawyer. Near the President stood his chief bodyguard, Colonel Starling, who stared at the crimson horizon and thought that the sight was shameful.

High and higher still licked the lemon-tipped flames until their glow could be seen from many miles away. In that twitching light, faces seemed to appear, vanish, reappear in the erratic sequence of an old-time movie.

The fleeing veterans had been careful not to burn the National Guard pup tents that Glassford had got for them, but the soldiers put the torch to everything—the tents and huts and shanties and crates and beds—until the crazy-quilt camp sagged into ashes and hot metal, until the only things silhouetted against the glare were iron bedsteads looking like muted harps.

By midnight all was over. After two months, the Bonus Expeditionary Force had been driven from the national capital—but at what cost?

The police had killed two veterans. The Army had not fired a single bullet, but swords and gas had taken their toll. An eleven-week-old baby was gassed so severely that he later died. An eight-year-old boy was left partially blinded by gas fumes. More than 1,000 people felt the effects of the gas grenades. Sixty-three persons were injured. A total of 135 persons were arrested. And the Hoover administration suffered a fatal loss of prestige, one historian declaring that the BEF "goaded President Hoover into committing political suicide."

Chief of Police Glassford declared he had not reported that the situation was beyond the control of the police and that he had not asked for troops. Major Eisenhower felt sorry for the dispersed veterans. Governor Roosevelt shuddered and shook his head in sorrow. Mrs. Eleanor Roosevelt recoiled from the news in horror. Newscaster Lowell Thomas called the affair a "tragic spectacle." Senator Hugo L. Black of Alabama denounced the Army attack as "unnecessary and ill-timed." Norman Thomas said that Hoover's decision to use the troops was due to "a bad case of nervous irritation mixed with fear." Senator William E. Borah of Idaho was too embittered to say anything.

About 11 A.M. on the day after the "Battle of Camp Anacostia," General MacArthur went to the White House to make a personal report to President Hoover and War Secretary Hurley. The two of them, according to MacArthur, "expressed gratification at what had been accomplished." There seems to be no evidence that the President rebuked his chief of staff for exceeding his authority, for disobeying a Presidential order, by stampeding the veterans out of the District of Columbia. Instead, Hoover gave the press this comment: "A challenge to the authority of the United States government has been met, swiftly and firmly. After months of patient indulgence, the government met overt lawlessness as it always must be met if the cherished processes of self-government are to be preserved. We cannot tolerate the abuse of Constitutional rights by those who would destroy all government, no matter who they might be. Government cannot be coerced by mob rule. . . ."

The B.E.F. News managed to publish an edition on July 30, and half the front page was taken up with a cartoon of Hoover wearing the Capitol on his head like a Prussian helmet, while his face was painted with a spiked mustache that made him resemble Kaiser Wilhelm of Germany. But the newspaper, like the veterans themselves, faded from the scene.

By early August some 9,000 confused bonus marchers milled aimlessly about Johnstown, Pennsylvania, whose mayor had given them a refuge despite the protests of some citizens. A woman offered to give them 25 acres of land in Maryland for use as a permanent colony, but Walter W. Waters realized that the game was up. When he urged the veterans to disband and go home, they did so—having irrevocably changed the nation. The nature of this change was summarized by Thomas L. Stokes, a United Press reporter who had witnessed the smashing of the BEF in Washington. Stokes wrote:

"This, I said to myself, may be the end of this country as we know it. The United States Army turned on to American citizens—just fellows like myself, down on their luck, dispirited, hopeless. My mood was one of despair. It was an experience that stands apart from all others in my life. So all the misery and suffering had finally come to this—soldiers marching with their guns against American citizens."

13

The Reconstruction Finance Corporation

B ABE RUTH, a glutton who almost killed himself by overeating on one occasion, was offered $70,000 a year by the New York Yankees early in the Depression, but he held out for $80,000. When a friend told Ruth that this was more than the salary paid the President, the Sultan of Swat snorted: "So what? I had a better season than he did."

Unfortunately, this was the truth. Although President Hoover swung time and time again at the evils of the Depression, his batting average remained low, and as he fanned the air, he heard a mounting chorus of *booooos* from the national grandstand. Hoover worked killing hours, his face grayed with fatigue, his eyes saddened, and it hurt him to realize that many Americans regarded him as a Jonah on a sinking ship. Nonetheless, Hoover clung to his fixed ideas. He did not even brighten, at first, when a new concept was presented to him by his friend and confidant Eugene Meyer. After making a fortune as an investment banker, Meyer had been appointed the head of the War Finance Corporation during World War I. This federal agency had been created in 1918 to give financial support to industries and banking institutions that were helping in the war effort. Some people called it America's wartime Socialism.

In the early winter of 1931 Meyer was visited by Louis B. Wehle, who had served under him as general counsel to the War Finance Corporation. Wehle felt that the Depression might be overcome by creating another corporation patterned after the wartime agency. A new agency of this kind might save the national economy by lending money to banks, railroads and other businesses in danger of bankruptcy. Meyer, known as an astute financier, liked Wehle's proposal. He asked Walter Wyatt, general counsel of the Federal Reserve Board, to draft a tentative bill calling for the establishment of a Reconstruction Finance Corporation.

Meyer then went to the President and urged him to use his influence to get the measure passed by the Congress. Hoover hesitated. If the federal government lent money to private business, wouldn't this put the government in business? Hadn't it been the credo of the Republican Party that what was needed was less government in business and more business in government? There also was another consideration: The Democrats had a majority in the House and virtually controlled the Senate. How would they react to this innovation? Meyer, an autocratic multimillionaire, cared very little what Congressmen thought.

With the American economy in a vicious downward spiral, business was bad and getting worse. The national income had fallen from $80 billion to $40 billion. Dividends had dropped more than 56 percent, salaries were down 40 percent, and wages had plunged 60 percent. At least 10,000,000 Americans were unemployed. With too many goods chasing too little money, the nation was suffering from acute deflation—consumer spending curtailed, bank loans contracting and the amount of money in circulation reduced. Credit, both private and national, was faltering. United States government bonds were selling at only about 83 cents on the dollar. Total reserves of Federal Reserve Banks had fallen to within $50 million of the lowest level allowed by law. As credit became harder to get, the money market tightened and private enterprise wobbled. Selling waves pushed stock and bond prices to such low depths that banks, insurance firms and other financial institutions came apart at the seams.

The American banking system was so archaic that President Hoover called it "rotten." Bank deposits were dropping. In the year 1931 a total of 2,294 banks failed. Bankers were calling in loans and refusing to make new ones. Americans, together with foreign investors in American securities, were losing faith in the value of the American dollar. Panic-stricken foreigners threw their American holdings onto the market and then withdrew their dollar balances from this country.

In September, 1931, Great Britain abandoned the gold standard, and other European nations soon did the same. European banks were breaking down. Frightened American capitalists, anxiously searching for some safe depository for their funds, shipped hundreds of millions of dollars in gold to this or that institution in France, Holland or Switzerland. Others, equally afraid that the United States would go off the gold standard but doubtful about European banks, loaded their safe-deposit boxes with gold. People of lesser means stuffed gold certificates into mattresses and hidden tin cans. By the autumn of 1931 about $1 billion in currency was being hoarded in secret places in this country.

These were the problems that Hoover and Meyer discussed. A month or so before their talk the President had called on bankers and insurance executives to meet the emergency by forming a private credit association. In early October these business leaders responded by creating the National Credit Association, capitalized at $500 million and offering to lend money to banks in sums up to 2 percent of their total deposits. Although this new association made loans to more than 750 banks, 522 other banks failed that very October. Now, with the National Credit Association reaching the end of its resources, it was obvious that it had failed to realize its aim of propping up business.

What Meyer was suggesting was a *public* corporation to lend *public* money to failing *private* institutions. This was what disturbed Hoover. He did not want to push the federal government into the national economy. And, as he admitted, he had "no taste for any such emergency powers in government." An intelligent and compassionate man, Hoover lacked the instincts of a politician and failed to exert the full powers of the Presidency. More than a year earlier, when the governors of all the states had petitioned him for a $1 billion emergency relief appropriation from the federal government, he had turned them down. More than once he said that it was not the function of the federal government to relieve individual men of their responsibilities to their neighbors, to relieve private institutions of of their responsibilities to the public, or of local government to the states, or of state governments to the federal government.

But Meyer persisted in his appeal, and at last the President acquiesced. Although Hoover had no way of knowing it at the time, the Reconstruction Finance Corporation was to become his greatest contribution to the solution of the nation's problems. Even as he agreed, however, he clung to two modifying concepts: He hoped it would not be necessary to use the RFC very extensively, and he regarded it as only an emergency measure which might be discarded at the end of two years.

Now, having made up his mind, Hoover sought immediate action. On December 8, 1931, in his annual message to the Congress, he urged the legislators to pass a bill establishing the corporation. Its very existence, said the President, would "strengthen confidence." However, his proposal ran into opposition from some Democrats and even some Republicans. Republican Senator John J. Blaine of Wisconsin, for one, tried to block Senate consideration of the bill on the grounds that while it would help banks, it would not help the unemployed.

Other Senators, who favored the proposal, prophesied that if the RFC lent money to banks and railroads and insurance companies, business in general would revive, smoke would pour from factory chimneys, and ultimately workers and farmers would also benefit. This argument was rejected by two Democratic Senators, Burton K. Wheeler of Montana and J. Hamilton Lewis of Illinois. Wheeler took the Senate floor to declare that "when you pass this bill everybody will be down here in Washington wanting money out of the treasury." Lewis, a conservative Senator noted for his pink whiskers and elegant attire, sidled up to Wheeler's desk and whispered: "Boy, you're right! Give'em hell!"

Wheeler whispered back: "Do you want to speak against this bill?"

In a low and intense voice Lewis replied: "No, I can't, because I represent a damn bunch of thieves—*thieves,* I tell you!—who want to reach their hands into the public coffers and purloin the money. My God, if I were a free man, I'd tear this thing from limb to limb!"

But the Senate, after modifying the original bill, passed it on January 11, 1932. The liberal vote was split. Among the liberals voting for the RFC was Robert M. La Follette, a Progressive Republican from Wisconsin. Wheeler asked why he supported the measure. La Follette said he was afraid that the national economy might crash. Wheeler snorted: "Yes! And the sooner it's over, the better! This will only prolong the depression."

Debate in the House of Representatives lasted longer. Congressman Fiorello H. LaGuardia, a Progressive Republican from New York, predicted that the RFC would become "a millionaires' *dole*"—an early use of a word soon to become a commonplace. The President chafed as Congressmen wrangled, but the House approved the bill on January 15. Hoover complained that in view of the national emergency both houses might have acted six weeks earlier.

Control of the new RFC was to be vested in a board of seven directors appointed by the President with the advice and consent of the Senate. Because of Democratic strength in the Congress and because Hoover wanted the RFC to be nonpartisan in nature, he told House Speaker John N. Garner and Senate Democratic Leader Joseph T. Robinson that each might pick one director. Garner, who happened to be a director of two Texas banks, proposed the name of a fellow Texan, Jesse H. Jones of Houston. Strangely, although Garner and Jones were perhaps the two Texans best known to the nation at that time, they were only slightly acquainted with each other. Senator Robinson, who came from Arkansas, submitted the name of another Arkansan, Harvey C. Couch, a utilities executive.

Three days before Hoover signed the RFC bill, he announced the names of the seven men he had chosen to head the new agency: Eugene Meyer was made chairman. Charles G. Dawes was chosen as president. Ogden L. Mills, undersecretary of the treasury, was named a director. The others chosen were Jones and Couch, Gardner Cowles and Wilson McCarthy. Certain Democratic leaders disapproved of what they felt was premature selection of the directors.

On January 22, 1932, at 6:06 P.M., one minute after it reached his desk, President Hoover signed the bill creating the Reconstruction Finance Corporation. Then he made a statement to the press. "It brings into being," he declared, "a powerful organization with adequate resources, able to strengthen weaknesses that may develop in our credit, banking and railway structure, in order to permit business and industry to carry on normal activities free from the fear of unexpected shocks and retarding influences. . . .

"Its purpose is to stop deflation in agriculture and industry and thus to increase employment by the restoration of men to their normal jobs. It is not created for the aid of big industries or big institutions. Such institutions are amply able to take care of themselves. It is created for the support of the smaller banks and financial institutions, and through rendering their resources liquid to give renewed support to business, industry and agriculture. It should give opportunity to mobilize the gigantic strength of our country for recovery. . . ."

Not for big institutions? Hoover soon had cause to wish to eat some of his words.

*   *   *

Jesse Jones was a handsome man standing six feet two inches tall. He had cold blue eyes, silvery hair, dark eyebrows, fat cheeks and a small slit of a mouth. One of the richest men in Texas, he owned or came to own most of downtown Houston—hotels, a bank, a newspaper plant, a skyscraper and other property. He spoke the rough-grained language of the Texas cow country and detested Eastern bankers. He played a mean game of poker and almost never read books. Shrewd and hard, energetic and ambitious, he began his long working days at 6:30 A.M. Selected for his conservatism by the conservative Garner, Jones had no deep interest in reform.

Charles Dawes, who had been Vice President of the United States under Coolidge, was a colorful figure with a flair for publicity. A banker by occupation, he had made his fortune by the time he was forty-five years old. Posing as a hard-boiled guy, he frowned most of the time, wore a high stiff collar with sharp points, kept an underslung pipe between his clenched teeth. Despite his forbidding appearance, he delighted in such practical jokes as slipping a piece of ice down a lady's back at a party. He played the piano and flute and composed a number that was performed on the violin by Fritz Kreisler. During the anti-Red hysteria after World War I, superpatriot Dawes organized the Minute Men of America, which waged war on organized labor. When the Depression hit the land, he agreed with Hoover's rejection of public relief in favor of private charity.

As soon as Jones learned he had been named to the RFC board, he telephoned his wife in Houston and said: "Pack your trunk and come on up. I'm stuck with a 365-day-a-year job." Jones then got in touch with Dawes, and the two of them began hunting for office space. Dawes said: "Maybe Uncle Andy Mellon will lend us a room."

Dawes had just resigned as the United States ambassador to Great Britain, and Andrew Mellon, who had served as secretary of the treasury under three Presidents, was preparing to go to London to succeed him. Before Jones and Dawes got to Mellon's office, Dawes changed his mind, suggesting that they drop in, instead, at the office of the comptroller of the currency; between 1898 and 1901 Dawes himself had been comptroller. The present comptroller was not in his office but out in California keeping an eye on a proxy fight between A. P. Giannini and Elisha Walker for control of the huge Bank of America. To the reception-room secretary

Dawes suggested that he and Jones occupy the comptroller's private office until other arrangements could be made. She, of course, agreed.

Jones said to Dawes: "I think whoever wins that Bank of America proxy fight will be our first customer."

Dawes agreed.

Jones, Dawes and the other RFC directors soon took over two floors of the old Department of Commerce Building at Pennsylvania Avenue and Nineteenth Street, and before long they occupied the entire building. They established thirty-two regional offices throughout the country. To process the expected avalanche of applications for loans, they assembled an expert staff, recruiting many from regional Federal Reserve Banks. Various citizens howled in outrage when it became known that 180 RFC employees were being paid more than $400 a month each. The directors received annual salaries of $10,000.

They met for the first time on February 2, 1932, and eleven days later made their very first loan—to the Bank of America, as Dawes and Jones had anticipated.

This was not just a bank but a financial empire. It had been founded in San Francisco by A. P. Giannini, the California-born son of Italian immigrant parents. At first it was called the Bank of Italy. Giannini, who thought the only safe banks were big banks, bought up small ones and converted them into branches of his Bank of Italy. In 1928, a rich and powerful man, he organized Transamerica Corporation as a holding company for all his banking, insurance and industrial enterprises. In 1930 the Bank of Italy became (its full name) the Bank of America National Trust and Savings Association. In California it lent money to fruit growers and movie producers and then, opening branches in the East, financed showmen like Flo Ziegfeld.

Also in 1930, Giannini decided to "retire," chose New York banker Elisha Walker as his successor and sailed for Europe. While abroad, he learned that Walker had sold the New York branches of his bank, was about to dispose of other branches in Southern California and had fired "Giannini men" from Transamerica. Speeding back to his home state, Giannini launched a proxy fight to regain control of his holding company. After stumping California to collect stockholders' proxies, he wound up with 63 percent interest in the firm, ousted the Eastern managers and was reinstated as board chairman of the holding company.

Although Giannini had seized power again, the battle had cost him so much money that he was left in a shaky financial condition. The last act of the proxy war had taken place in Wilmington, Delaware—a state known for its generous tax laws in regard to capitalization. Giannini went directly from Wilmington to Washington, where he conferred informally with Dawes, who admired him, and with RFC Chairman Meyer. The California capitalist told the two how he planned to restore the magnitude of his bank and impressed them so favorably that Dawes offered to lend him up to $100 million.

The bill creating the RFC had provided the new agency with a cash capital of $500 million and had authorized it to issue debentures in the amount of $1.5 billion more. When Dawes said he would lend Giannini $100 million, he was thus offering one-fifth of the RFC's initial capitalization—to a single private institution. That same month of February, 1932, wooden money was being issued in Tenino, Washington, railway wages had been cut by 10 percent, families were being evicted from their apartments in the Bronx, 305 cities were asking the federal government for direct relief.

On February 13 the RFC directors gathered around a big table in the old Commerce Department Building to take up formal consideration of the request for aid from the Bank of America. Waiting just outside the hearing room was the sixty-one-year-old Giannini, white-haired and square-faced, a burly man standing six feet two inches tall and weighing 240 pounds. Among the others waiting in the cold and drafty corridor were a couple of shy and quiet men, two important railway executives—the brothers Oris and Mantis Van Sweringen. LaGuardia's prediction had come true: The millionaires were standing in line waiting for a handout.

Giannini was ushered in. He made his formal presentation to the directors, declaring that he would need a lot of money to meet withdrawals from his bank. On that day the RFC approved an initial loan of $15 million to Giannini, and by the following July 15 he had received a total of $64.4 million from the new agency. Although this was not so much as Dawes had been willing to lend him, this infusion of public money into the private bank did save Giannini's holding company, which subsequently developed into the largest private bank in the world. American taxpayers may or may not be proud of this record.

After Giannini walked out of the RFC boardroom, in walked the Van Sweringen brothers. They were an odd couple, unmarried brothers who chose to live quietly in their country home with their two maiden sisters. Except for horseback riding, they had no interest in life other than their railroad empire. That winter day in 1932 they controlled a $3 billion network of railway lines with a total of 28,031 miles of tracks—the greatest mileage of any railway system in the United States.

However, they were in deep trouble. Part of their plight was due to the fact that only twelve days previously the House of Morgan had lent them $1.5 million for one of their subsidiaries, the Missouri Pacific, to help meet a bond maturity. J. P. Morgan & Company had stipulated that it would make this loan "only on the basis of the expectation that the RFC will lend you the sum necessary to repay such loan on February 15, 1932." This was only a fraction of what the Van Sweringens owed Morgan. Now they asked the RFC to lend them $14.7 million. One-half of this amount would be used to repay Morgan, while the other half would be used to meet other pressing needs.

Ogden Mills made a strong argument to his fellow directors for granting this sum to the brothers, but Jesse Jones objected. Jones knew all about the Morgan deal. At a later date, Jones explained his objection this way: "I didn't think the government should bail out private banking houses that for years had been profiting from railroad financing." Although this comment might indicate that Jones was a liberal, it is more likely that he objected because of his Texan dislike for Eastern bankers.

Jones' outburst surprised the other board members. Dawes then suggested that the Van Sweringen loan be authorized, with Jones recorded as voting no. Jones balked again. He asked that the directors defer action on the railroad loan until the following day. He did not want the RFC to start making loans on a divided basis. Jones told his peers that if on the following day he could not win them to his point of view, then he would not vote against the Van Sweringen loan. He failed to convince them, and the brothers got their millions.

Jones denied that he was "afflicted with any 'anti-banker' complex." He went on to say that he "felt in this particular situation and others of a similar nature that the bankers had no right to unload their bad or slow debts on the government. The bankers did not need the relief. I could see ahead of the R.F.C. a long and ugly road along which we should need the confidence of the Congress if we were to revive the depressed state of our entire economy."

*   *   *

A swarm of capitalists, their attorneys and hired lobbyists had descended on Washington even before the President had signed the RFC into being. Democratic Senator Robert F. Wagner of New York was annoyed with this fat-bellied well-groomed breadline. He marched onto the floor of the Senate, and his colleagues, looking up from their desks, saw that his usual good humor had vanished. Speaking vigorously, his Phi Beta Kappa key jiggling from his watch chain, Wagner delivered a sarcastic tirade in which he contrasted Hoover's pet philosophy of rugged individualism with the well-heeled locusts now clustered in the capital. In Wagner's Tammany East Side diction the word "work" came out as *woik*. He said: "When adverse circumstances compelled the railroad presidents to come to Washington, we listened attentively to their story. . . . We replied that we would lend them the aid of the federal government, that we would lend them money out of the United States treasury. . . . We did not preach to them rugged individualism. We did not sanctimoniously roll out sentences rich with synonyms of self-reliance. We were not carried away with apprehension over what would happen to their independence if we extended them a helping hand. We followed the same procedure in an effort to strengthen the banking situation. . . .

"But when millions of Americans, foot-weary and heart-sick, cry out in despair, 'Give us woik!', we suddenly are overwhelmed with devotion for the preservation of self-reliance. We plug our ears to the cry of the multitude while the prophets burn incense upon the altar of rugged inividualism, and the fanatics would sacrifice the nation to preserve its empty slogans! . . ."

Wagner's speech, as it turned out, was as much a prediction as a protest. Now that the RFC had begun to function and now that the one-sided nature of its acts became public knowledge, there developed the very criticism that Jesse Jones had feared. The President of the United States had said that the RFC was "not created for the aid of big industries or big institutions." Was the Bank of America small potatoes? Was the Van Sweringen railway empire vending peanuts? Was the House of Morgan a shoeshine stand?

Obviously, Hoover's concept of relief was the percolation theory—the belief that if funds were poured in at the top, some of it might seep down to the bottom of society. This was fine, of course, with the American Bankers' Association, with most of the nation's capitalistic press and with William Allen White, who said that the RFC was "the greatest fiscal measure ever adopted by any government in all times."

But it hardly pleased millions of other Americans. Congressman La-Guardia said publicly that J. P. Morgan was dictating RFC policies. One irreverent wit spoke of the theory of feeding the sparrows by feeding the horse. Rexford Tugwell observed that the RFC was "putting fertilizer up in the branches of a tree" when what was needed was "to feed the roots."

Will Rogers wrote in his column:

> The Reconstruction Finance Corporation is made up of fine men, honest, and mean well [*sic*] and if it was water they were distributing it would help the people the plan was meant to help. For water goes down hill and moistens everything in its way, but gold or money goes uphill. The Reconstruction loaned the railroads money, medium and small banks money, and all they did with it was pay off what they owed to New York banks. So the money went uphill instead of down. You can drop a bag of gold in Death Valley, which is below sea level, and before Saturday it will be home to papa J.P.

Rogers had put his finger on a significant point: Banks and railroads used RFC loans to repay debts and maintain credit standing, rather than create employment. RFC money sustained high salaries for executives and high dividends for stockholders, but did not find its way into payoll envelopes. In some cases, help was given to institutions so grossly overcapitalized that it might have been better if they had been allowed to fail.

The rising chorus of criticism stung President Hoover. Twenty years later he still felt so hurt that he said: "Far from 'bailing out' the rich, as one orator says, 90 percent of the loans under the Republican administration went to saving building and loan associations, savings banks, insurance companies, small country banks and farmers' loan associations. These were not the institutions of the rich. They represented the small savings of the people."

At an even later date Harris Gaylord Warren, chairman of the history department of Miami University in Oxford, Ohio, rebutted Hoover's argument:

> There is considerable truth in this description of how the R.F.C. operated, but it is far from being the whole truth. There is a vast difference between 90 per cent of the loans and 90 per cent of the money loaned. . . . Of the first $61 million loaned to 255 banks, $41 million went to three banks and $15 million of that went to the Bank of America; and shortly thereafter $90 million was loaned to one bank. Of the first $264 million loaned to railroads, $156 million went to the Van Sweringen, Morgan and Pennsylvania groups. . . . Most of the loans went to small institutions but most of the money went to the big institutions.

One citizen suggested that the government lend $25 to each of the 124,822,000 people living in the continental United States in 1932, but this proposal was ignored by the RFC. Under this plan more than $3 billion would have been lent to the entire populace. Even so, this would have been less than one-third of the $10 billion disbursed by the RFC by the end of 1939. And, after all, one of the agency's main purposes was to get more money into circulation.

Hoarding, which had begun in the spring of 1931, worried President Hoover. He appealed to Will Rogers, who wrote in a column: "Hoover is worried about this money hoarding and asked me 'Write a joke against these hoarders. Humor might show'em how foolish they are. Now go do that.' So after all my kidding about Hoover commissions I am finally on one, 'the Hoover anti-hoarding joke commission.' So anybody knowing any anti-hoarding jokes send'em to me. I want to be one commission to make good."

People were afraid to deposit money in shaky banks, afraid to invest in faltering enterprises. The continued withdrawal of foreign deposits resulted in the calling of loans by domestic banks, which further resulted in stifling industry and affecting prices. By the autumn of 1931 about $1 billion in gold and currency had been squirreled away by anxious Americans. On November 28 the *American Banker,* a daily financial newspaper, printed a headline declaring that GOD'S DECREE FIXES GOLD AS PERMANENT SYMBOL OF MONEY. Besides being impious and nonsensical, this was like whistling in the dark to keep up one's courage, for bankers were not at all sure that the United States would not follow Great Britain and continental nations off the gold standard.

More than $750,000 in currency was discovered in a New York hotel room occupied by a rich recluse, Mrs. Ida E. Wood, widow of Benjamin Wood, who had owned the old New York *Daily News.* One New York businessman kept $380,000 in gold and gold certificates in his safe-deposit box. Other hoarders, equally concerned about the future of the paper dollar, converted their bank deposits into cash and then cash into gold.

Soviet Russia had its own hoarding problems. Eight persons, including two priests, were shot to death after the Soviet secret police charged that they had hoarded silver and gold coins and engaged in anti-Communist propaganda. Of course, this kind of direct action was unthinkable in a democratic society. Instead, President Hoover asked representatives of various civic and patriotic groups to confer with him about the evils of hoarding, and after a White House meeting on February 6, 1932, he issued a statement saying: "There is now a patriotic opportunity for our citizens unitedly to join in this campaign against the depression. . . . That service is to secure the return of hoarded money back into the channels of industry. During the past year, and with an accelerated rate during the last few months, a total of over a billion three hundred millions of money has been hoarded. That sum is still outstanding . . . citizens hoarding money do not realize its serious effect. . . . Every dollar hoarded means a destruction of from five to ten dollars of credit. . . ."

Then the President announced that a national antihoarding society had been formed under the name of the Citizens' Reconstruction Organization. For its chairman he picked Frank Knox, publisher of the Chicago *Daily News.* Its members soon began making public statements, A. D. Noyes calling hoarding "lunacy" and J. B. Clark declaring that in the end hoarding would paralyze the nation's monetary system. Knox himself announced that $100 million had been returned to circulation in the first three weeks of February, but in March there was a decrease of $39 million in the money exchanging hands.

On March 11 Hoover declared that the antihoarding drive had already produced "positive and useful results," and twenty days later the Republican National Committee called it an instant success. This was not quite true. The following autumn the *Saturday Evening Post* published an article by Garet Garrett, who flatly called the campaign a failure. Garrett said that "only a small part of the enormous aggregate of money estimated to have gone into hiding has been returned to the banks," and his judgment was corroborated by other observers.

Jesse Jones, who said that bankers were among the hoarders, liked to tell a story revealing the extent of the hoarding. A South Dakota bank foreclosed on a big farm and put it up for sale at $12,000. A man and his wife went to the bank and asked to be taken out to see the property. They saw it, liked it, agreed to buy it at the asking price and said they would settle the deal in a few days. Soon thereafter they returned to the bank, carrying a big tin can filled with money. They handed the can to the banker, who counted the bills, looked up in surprise, and said: "Why, there's only ten thousand dollars here!"

The man looked at his wife in puzzlement and said: "Mamma, that can't be right. You count it."

She did.

"That's right," she said in surprise. "There's only ten thousand here."

A disgusted look spreading over his face, the man drawled: "Well, Mamma, I guess you brought the wrong can."

*   *   *

The problems of unemployment, lack of housing and food were placing such a strain on private agencies, cities and states that many people were afraid society would break down altogether unless the federal government rushed to the help of everyone—not just banks and private corporations. It was obvious that the RFC was not doing enough for enough people. Senate Leader Robinson pushed a plan drawn up by a group of influential and conservative Democrats, who insisted on direct federal relief. Hoover, who could not afford to ignore Robinson, called him to the White House to confer.

After they met, the President issued a statement saying: "The policy steadfastly adhered to up to the present time has been that responsibility for relief to distress belongs to private organizations, local communities and the states. That fundamental policy is not to be changed. . . ." Despite Hoover's standpat remark, however, that policy did change. Under pressure, the President agreed for the first time to grant federal relief to faltering cities and states.

Congress set to work to draft bills extending the powers of the RFC and giving it more money. The Senate Democrats organized a legislative drafting committee headed by Senator Wagner, who had been critical of handouts to big business. Members of the Wagner committee agreed on a bill providing $300 million in relief loans, $1.5 billion for self-liquidating projects, and $500 million for public works. Hoover, still balky, appeared in person before the Senate to denounce the public works feature of the Wagner bill—in the name of a balanced budget. However, the President did endorse the $300 million RFC authorization for loans to states for unemployment relief.

The Senate Banking and Currency Committee held hearings, and their principal witness was Ogden Mills, now secretary of the treasury and an ex officio member of the RFC. Mills had become annoyed with his wife when she reduced their staff of servants because of the Depression. "Dorothy," he had said, "there are only ten servants in the house! Never before in my life have we had fewer than fifteen." Now, appearing in his official capacities before the committee, Mills made it clear that the Hoover administration had embraced federal relief with something less than rapture. He warned that the federal government must fix rigid tests to determine whether a state's resources were exhausted, rather than rely on the word of the governor. His main objection to extension of the RFC powers, he said, was that it unbalanced the budget.

The Senate passed the Wagner bill despite the further objection from President Hoover that it allocated relief to states on the basis of population rather than need.

House Speaker Garner presented the House with a bill of his own—one that went further than the Wagner measure. The Garner bill proposed: (1) a $1.2 billion bond issue for construction of public buildings, highways, waterways and flood-control projects; (2) a $1 billion increase in the capitalization of the RFC so that it could lend money to states, cities and towns for public works; (3) a grant of $100 million to the President to make loans to any person or firm serving the general ends of agriculture, commerce, industry or the reduction of unemployment.

Hoover angrily attacked the Garner bill as pork-barrel legislation—the appropriation of public funds on local projects not critically needed. But worse than this, in the President's opinion, was a provision in the Garner bill that called on the RFC to disclose the names of every institution that received an RFC loan, together with the size of each loan.

For the first five months of its existence the RFC had operated in secrecy. The act establishing the agency *did* order its directors to make quarterly reports to the President and Congress about the *aggregate* amount of money lent to each *class* of borrower—such as banks, railroads and insurance firms. It did *not,* however, require any disclosure of precisely who got exactly how much. RFC Chairman Meyer tried to run the organization high-handedly, keeping reporters away from its headquarters and, along with his Republican colleagues, antagonizing the directors who were Democrats. Jesse Jones said tartly that the Republican members had not yet "learned the desirability of taking us three country-boy Democratic members into their confidence and counsel. Apparently they expected us blindly to do their bidding."

There had been leaks about the huge loans to the Bank of America and the Van Sweringens, and reaction in some quarters had been bitter, but such revelations were not a part of official policy. This secrecy angered certain Congressmen and interested citizens. After all, the RFC's capital came from the national treasury, which meant from taxes, which meant from taxpayers. The American people surely had a right to know who was getting their money and how it was being spent.

Garner said: "I have contended consistently that there has been too much secrecy about what has been going on. . . . If the truth scares the people, let it come. Let the people know all about everything the government does."

Hoover, who rather liked Garner, was taken by surprise. Garner was so rich and so conservative it seemed unlikely that he was acting on principle or out of any sense of moral outrage. His motive remains something of a mystery. Rexford Tugwell later theorized that Garner fell back on "the safest gambit in political strategy. He spoke up for the little fellow." That spring of 1932, when Garner demanded full publicity, William Randolph Hearst was promoting him as a possible Democratic candidate for the Presidency. Garner also had made a dramatic appeal to balance the budget by passing a sales tax, and although this would not have helped the little fellow, it certainly would have helped Hearst by lightening his own income-tax load. Whatever his motive, Garner touched off a political fight.

Sixty-two years old, a member of Congress since 1903, Garner had seen generations of Congressmen come and go. He was picturesque in looks and habits. With his short-cropped white hair, shaggy eyebrows, tiny nose, fat face and tight mouth, he resembled an owl. Once a cowpuncher and still fond of hunting, he played poker, puffed on stogies and belted down bourbon with branch water. Ignoring Washington society, declining invitations to the customary round of dinners and parties, he went to bed early and arose with the sun. There was about this Texan a kind of rawhide dignity which kept others at a distance; even his wife and close friends addressed him as "Mr. Garner." In and around his hometown of Uvalde he owned banks and stores, farms and ranches, beehives and pecan orchards, herds of cattle and sheep and goats. Worth perhaps $2 million, Garner was no enemy of big business, although he did hate utilities firms.

After brief and bitter debate the House passed the Garner bill. Next, a group of Congressmen and Senators met to try to blend the Garner and Wagner bills into a single measure. Despite appeals to Garner, he refused to back down on his insistence that the RFC lend money "to any person" and that it give full publicity to all loans. These provisions were retained in the joint Garner-Wagner bill, which was soon passed by both houses of Congress. Hoover vetoed the measure, saying: "This proposal violates every sound principle of public finance and of government. Never before has so dangerous a suggestion been seriously made to our country. Never before has so much power for evil been placed at the unlimited discretion of seven individuals. . . ."

Anticipating a Presidential veto, Senator Wagner had begun drafting a substitute bill even before the Senate acted on the joint measure. He brushed aside a proposal by Senator Henry Ashurst of Arizona that the RFC lend money to Indians living on reservations and accept their hand-made blankets as collateral. Senator James Couzens pressed for an inquiry into RFC loans already granted, but he too was sidetracked. Wagner told Senate and House conferees that if they hoped to get *any* relief bill past the President, they had better make a couple of compromises. Furthermore, with the bonus army filling the capital with alarm, lawmakers planning to vote against the bonus bill realized they had better pass some legislation to take the heat off themselves. They agreed to the slight modifications that Wagner wrote into a new bill.

On July 14—the same day the angry veterans invaded the office of Vice President Curtis—the House passed the Wagner Bill. Two days later—as the buzzing bonus army stood vigil outside the Capitol to watch Congress adjourn—the Senate also approved the measure. In normal times a new law of such great significance might have been signed by the President with ritual dignity, but Washington was so tense that Hoover indulged in no ceremony when he put his signature to the act on July 21, 1932.

This historic Emergency Relief and Construction Act: (1) boosted the RFC's resources to $3.5 billion; (2) let the RFC make big loans for productive works and for unemployment; (3) created Agricultural Credit Banks; (4) permitted the RFC to lend money to states and cities. However, the bill did *not:* (1) let the RFC lend money "to any person," as Garner had wished; (2) order full disclosure of all details about all loans, as Garner had demanded.

Thus, for the first time—however indirectly—the federal government had committed itself to a positive role in helping the unemployed and had launched a public works program far greater than any in the previous history of the nation. Although Senator Wagner was not completely satisfied with the bill, he said it "wrote into law the position which I have continuously maintained—that modern unemployment is a consequence of national developments which must be dealt with, not as a purely local concern, but as a national problem."

Hoover, for reasons of his own, was also less than pleased with the measure. It earmarked $300 million in RFC funds for loans to needy states at 3 percent interest, with no more than 15 percent of this total sum going to any one state. Just before signing the bill, the President said anxiously: "I do not expect any state to resort to it except as a last extremity."

He should have known what would happen, considering the distress in all the forty-eight states. Immediately the RFC was flooded with requests from the states for relief funds. In fact, before the end of July the agency got applications totaling $171 million from thirteen states, while other state officials scrambled to fill in the proper forms. Some governors complained because the RFC directors were slow to process the loan applications. Social workers, who saw misery at close range, became especially critical of the RFC. By the end of 1932 the agency had lent only $30 million for relief.

Although Garner's position on publicity had been watered down, the RFC's operations now became public knowledge through a fluke. Under the modified Wagner bill, the agency had been directed to give Congress confidential reports about the names of the borrowers, the size of the loans they received and the amount of interest they paid. But this confused the clerk of the House, who somehow thought that all information should be released to the press, and soon everyone knew who was getting what.

These disclosures angered Hoover, who had considered Garner's original idea "dangerous." They bothered Henry I. Harriman, president of the United States Chamber of Commerce. They annoyed Arthur A. Ballantine, undersecretary of the treasury. They irked the New York *Herald Tribune,* a staunch Republican paper. These men and institutions were afraid that if depositors heard that a bank containing their savings was about to get an RFC loan, they would quickly withdraw their money. James Byrnes, a conservative Senator from South Carolina, warned: "If publicity results in immediate withdrawals, it defeats the very purpose of the loan."

While it is true that some banks hesitated to ask for an RFC loan after the publicity broke, this did not bother Jesse Jones. Years later he wrote: "Some bankers whose banks failed in 1932 and 1933 felt they could have weathered the storm if it had not been made public that they were getting help from the RFC. It is doubtful whether any of them were right."

Jones' viewpoint was supported by Walter Lippmann, who said in one of his columns: "The publication of the RFC loans merely made the general public realize what the better informed depositors already knew; namely, that the poorer banks were freezing their remaining assets in order to pay off their smarter depositors, and that the other depositors were holding the bag."

*   *   *

On June 6, 1932, the New York *Times* published this article:

Eugene Olsen, 16 years old, a senior at George Washington High School, standing high in his classes and especially interested in scientific studies, committed suicide by hanging himself with a dumbwaiter cord in the basement storeroom that was his home. His father, a carpenter, had been out of work for several months. Unable to pay the rent, the family had been evicted and were occupying a basement storeroom rent-free. The father said the only reason he could give for the boy's suicide was worry over their financial condition.

That same June 6, in Washington, D.C., Charles Dawes scurried into the RFC boardroom and astonished his colleagues by announcing that he was resigning as chairman of the agency. Immediately. He was heading home, he explained, to try to save his own bank. Dawes then turned on his heels, ran out of the room and ten minutes later was aboard a train leaving for Chicago.

Jesse Jones was flabbergasted. He knew that soon after the turn of the century Dawes had organized the Central Republic Bank and Trust Company, but he also was aware that Dawes had not been active in its affairs the past seven years. It was news to Jones that the so-called Dawes bank was in trouble.

Cook County, the city of Chicago and the state of Illinois were also in trouble, bad trouble, and at a time when both the Republicans and Democrats were due to hold their national nominating conventions there.

The Democratic Party itself was bankrupt, and its leaders were hinting that it sure would be nice if Barney Baruch reached for his checkbook and pen. Within the previous few days twenty-five suburban banks had closed their doors, a chain of seven more failed to open a day or two later, and eight smaller banks in the Loop folded. Now it was questionable whether Chicago's five major banks, including the Dawes institution, could survive.

Samuel Insull's utilities empire had just crashed. Chicago had dismissed 832 municipal employees in an attempt to economize. The city had 700,000 unemployed people. By the shore of Lake Michigan hungry men were fighting over garbage. Chicago schoolchildren were listless because of malnutrition. The city owed its 14,000 schoolteachers $20,000,000 in back pay. More than 800 of these payless teachers, having exhausted their savings and insurance, were in hock to loan sharks who ruthlessly charged them 42 percent interest.

Chicago's industrialists, bankers and civic leaders were appealing to President Hoover for relief. Mayor Anton J. Cermak said the federal government had the choice of sending relief or troops. Less than a month earlier the governor of Illinois had sent 300 National Guardsmen to East St. Louis to restore order among the Oregon bonus marchers who were harassing a B. & O. train. The high command of the Illinois National Guard was issuing a manual called *Emergency Plans for Domestic Disturbances,* which contained the order: "Never fire over the heads of rioters."

As soon as Dawes reached Chicago, he announced that he would help rehabilitate the Insull system—but it was too late. A few days later he had himself elected chairman of the board of his Central Republic Bank and Trust Company. Representative LaGuardia charged that Dawes had resigned from the RFC because he wanted an RFC loan for his bank and did not wish to have to approve the loan himself. Dawes was worried because within the past year his bank's deposits had fallen from $240 million to half that amount and because a run had started on Chicago's remaining banks.

On Saturday, June 25, Jesse Jones arrived in Chicago as a delegate to the Democratic National Convention. After checking in at a hotel, he walked through the Loop, grimly watching the tail end of runs on the big downtown banks. Thousands of frantic depositors milled about the doors of every bank on La Salle, Clark and Dearborn streets. Bank lobbies swarmed with other nervous customers. Many of these people already had lost heavily in the collapse of neighborhood banks, while others had seen their savings vanish when the Insull empire disintegrated.

At 11 A.M. that Saturday Melvin A. Traylor, chief executive officer of the First National Bank, pushed through a crowd of anxious depositors in the savings department of his bank and climbed onto the pedestal of a marble pillar. After waving his arms until he got silence, he began making a speech. He told the people he did not blame them for worrying, considering all that had happened to the banking business in Cook County, but he assured them that if they would talk to the people who knew the facts, they would learn that the First National, which had been in business for seventy years, was sound and could pay all its depositors all their money.

That afternoon Traylor telephoned President Hoover. Because of the hot weather in Washington, the President was resting at his retreat on the Rapidan River in the Blue Ridge section of Virginia, 100 miles from the capital. Traylor told Hoover that while his own bank could survive for some time, the Dawes bank was in mortal danger. He said he could help Dawes but was unable to carry the full load and therefore wanted assistance from the RFC. Traylor ended the long-distance conversation with this grim warning: "If we do not get such support by Monday, every Chicago bank—ours among them, of course—will have to close its doors."

The especially strong run on the Dawes bank mystified Hoover at first, but later he became convinced that it was due to a Communist plot. There seems to be no proof that this was so.

The President spent the rest of that Saturday on the phone trying to locate his various financial advisers. Also because of the heat, not a single director of the RFC was in the capital or in New York City. Mills was relaxing on Long Island, Meyer in upstate New York. After much frantic work by the President's chief telephone operator, he managed to get in touch with all the directors. He also spoke to the federal bank examiner in Chicago and ordered him to look into the situation. He reached Jones in Chicago, along with Wilson McCarthy of the RFC, who had arrived in that city to attend the Democratic convention.

Sunday morning, while Chicago hotels teemed with Democratic politicians and reporters, Dawes met in his office with the executives of his bank and the heads of the other big Chicago institutions. He announced that his bank would be unable to open the following Monday morning. Traylor, who was among those present, darted out of the room and sped to the hotel where Jones was staying. The Chicagoan asked the Texan to accompany him to a meeting of bankers. He did not tell Jones the purpose of the meeting or where it was being held. Jones let Traylor lead him to the Central Republic Bank, the two of them arriving there shortly before Sunday noon.

Still assembled there were thirty to forty of Chicago's leading bankers, businessmen and industrialists. Dawes repeated to Jones what he had told the others about not opening his bank the next day. Then, speaking to everyone present, Dawes said he wanted to make it clear that he was not asking for their help. He just wanted to let his fellow bankers know in advance about his plans so they could take whatever steps they felt were necessary to protect themselves.

The men sent out for sandwiches, peeled off their coats, unloosened their collars and got down to the business of seeing what could be done. For sixteen hours they talked and argued and discussed figures. At one point,

Jones ducked out to phone the President and say he felt it was too hazardous, from the national standpoint, to let the Dawes bank go under; he was willing to accept responsibility for an RFC loan. Jones later explained: "I felt certain that if the bank closed, all Chicago banks would have to close, and that would soon mean a closing of all banks in the country."

Hoover said he would discuss the matter with Secretary Mills and others and then call back. One of those to whom the President spoke was Dawes himself. When Hoover again got on the wire with Jones, he told him to save the Dawes bank.

Just before daybreak in the morning of Monday, June 26, the last details were worked out for making an RFC loan of $90 million to the Dawes bank. It opened for business as usual. That Monday and the following day $40 million was put into the bank's vaults as a first installment on the RFC loan.

Naturally, there was a burst of anger over the news that $90 million had been lent by the RFC to the recently resigned RFC chairman at a time when veterans were being denied payment of their bonus, when Hoover was urging a moratorium on war debts owed by foreign nations to the United States, construction workers' wages were being cut by 25 percent, William Green was predicting that 13,000,000 Americans would be jobless by the following winter and the federal government was ending its fiscal year with a deficit of $2.8 billion.

President Hoover, forced onto the defensive, replied to this criticism in a speech at St. Louis the following November 4. He said the Dawes bank served 122,000 depositors and was associated with 755 other banks in fifteen states which served 6,500,000 depositors and that these banks in turn were associated with still other banks serving 20,000,000 people. As some critics were quick to note, if Hoover had extended his curious line of reasoning another step or two, he might have "proved" that in saving the Dawes bank, he had saved about half the population of the United States.

In time to come, both Hoover and Jones made much of the fact that Dawes paid back the $90 million in full—at about 2 percent interest.

Neither mentioned the additional fact that the state of Illinois got an initial RFC loan of only $3 million—which it repaid at 3 percent interest.

There is another interesting contrast: In 1932 the RFC lent $90 million to the Dawes bank and $30 million to various states for relief. In other words, one private bank got three times as much as the needy states.

*   *   *

Governor Roosevelt of New York was ambivalent about the Reconstruction Finance Corporation. As eager to save capitalism as Hoover was, he realized that the banking system needed help. On the other hand, Roosevelt was afraid that most RFC funds would go to the big boys. On April 7, 1932, the governor said publicly that the RFC started relief at the top. Six days later, in a private letter, he remarked: "I have an idea that I am still absolutely correct in saying that the great bulk of their loans will not reach down to the individuals at the bottom of the pyramid."

During the fall of 1932, when Roosevelt and Hoover were rival candidates for the Presidency, Roosevelt made some slighting comments about RFC operations. This pricked Hoover into making a testy answer: "Practically the only evidence of the Democratic candidate upon this program is the sneer that it has been designed to help banks and corporations, that it has not helped the common man. . . . Millions of men and women are employed today because there has been restored to their employer the ability to borrow the money to buy raw materials and pay labor and thus keep his job."

Was the RFC, under the Hoover administration, a success? Perhaps the best answer is a qualified yes. It did not cure the Depression, but briefly it acted as a brake against even more serious economic collapse. While it saved some banks, it did not save the entire banking system, which later fell into ruins. Although it prevented the bankruptcy of some railroads, one-third of all American railway mileage went into receivership before the Depression was over. The RFC was administered efficiently, its operating expenses being less than 1 percent of total loans. However, it propped up weak banks at too great a cost, since its loans were issued against increasingly shaky security. To a banking system in need of massive surgery, it offered a pep pill.

Of course, every businessman who sought and got aid from the RFC was confessing the emptiness of his belief in rugged individualism—although none liked to have this pointed out. Will Rogers was so amused by them that he wrote:

> In one of my little poems I said the bankers were the first to go on the "dole." The "wrath of the mighty" ascended [sic] on me. Even the *Wall Street Journal* . . . editorially said I should confine my jokes to some semblance of truth. Now I want to be fair, even with bankers, for they are pretty touchy now. I have had critics come out and say "As an actor old Bill is not so hot." Well, I just wanted to come out and call him a liar, but in my heart and conscience I knew he was right. So I know how you "boys" feel. Now if you will take this money and loan it out to a lot of the little fellows that need it you bankers got a chance to redeem yourselves. People are not "pointing with pride" to your record in this crisis up to now. Will be glad to reprint any alibis.

Neither the bankers nor Hoover dared face up to the fact that by plunging the government deep into business, by using public credit to support private enterprise, they had taken the longest step in American history toward state Socialism.

After Roosevelt defeated Hoover and became the new President, he changed his own tune about the RFC. Roosevelt said: ". . . The establishment of the R.F.C. in 1932 came about as the necessity became clear of giving government aid to the banking system. . . . The theory was, however, that if the federal government would support the nation's financial system, fear would be dissipated. But the aid given by the government through the R.F.C. up to March 4, 1933, was not enough to make the corporation one of the positive agencies for recovery rather than simply a means intended to avert an impending disaster. . . ."

After Roosevelt took office, he appointed Jesse Jones board chairman of the RFC despite the fact that the two men did not care very much for each other. Roosevelt, who considered the Texan imperious and self-righteous, called him "Jesus Jones" behind his back. Jones, for his part, despised FDR. But the new President, who knew that Jones was an able financier and an honest man, continued to put up with this man who once dared to say to the nation's chief executive: "Promise me that you will forget that there is a bank in the United States, and I will promise you there will be no more bank trouble."

Under Roosevelt's New Deal administration the Reconstruction Finance Corporation expanded into the most gigantic banking organization on the face of the earth.

14

How Can the Depression Be Cured?

ONE WAY to cure the Depression, according to a letter received by Senator Arthur Vandenberg of Michigan, would be to hire men to move the Rocky Mountains.

Another method, suggested by economist Stuart Chase in a whimsical mood, called for a group of millionaires to employ an army of workers to bail out Long Island Sound.

A Belgian professor named Paul Otlet urged the United States to use its credits in Europe for the construction of a gigantic, neutral world city on the Scheldt River, which rises in northern France, crosses Belgium and enters Holland; such a titanic project, according to the professor, would provide work for the 30,000,000 unemployed people in the world.

A horde of people, from screwballs to philosophers, advanced a variety of schemes for dealing with the Depression. They disagreed with Supreme Court Justice Oliver Wendell Holmes, who said he did not believe in panaceas. Many felt they had the magical formula that would set everything right again. Franklin D. Roosevelt, however, read fifteen articles by fifteen different economists and then commented bitingly: "Two things stand out: The first is that no two of them agree, and the other thing is that they are so foggy in what they say that it is almost impossible to figure out what they mean." Paul M. Mazur, a partner in Lehman Brothers, noted that there were as many suggested remedies "as there are people who give opinions."

A retired army officer, Major Edward L. Dyer, said that mercy killings "should be considered in cases of old age where the persons are of no use to themselves or anyone else." Bernarr Macfadden, the health cultist and publisher, had long been on record with the proposal that in hard times all unemployed people should be put in cold storage and then revived after the return of prosperity. Congressman Martin Dies of Texas was among the many people who believed that the way to cure the Depression was to deport all aliens. Fiorello H. LaGuardia got a letter containing this equation:

$$\frac{MT-MW \times D}{MT}$$

The nut who sent it to LaGuardia claimed that it was a foolproof formula for recovery but failed to explain what it meant.

*   *   *

Down through history, in periods of intense stress, many people have turned consciously or unconsciously to magic and religion for relief from tension, indulging in occult rituals and strange incantations. Man finds it difficult to live with uncertainty and impossible to exist without hope. It is not at all surprising that fortune-tellers did a thriving business during the Depression of the Thirties.

In one city in Virginia a thousand businessmen paraded through the streets carrying three effigies labeled DEPRESSION, PESSIMISM and MISFORTUNE, listened to an oration by the governor of the state, lynched the dummies, stuffed them into coffins and cast the coffins into the sea. When a new subway line opened in New York City, a padded figure wearing a sign proclaiming it OLD MAN DEPRESSION was hanged from the hook of a construction crane, while well-dressed men stood beneath it waving an American flag and yelling with joy. In Manhattan's famous dance hall the Roseland Ballroom, a New Year's Eve party featured still another dummy called OLD MAN DEPRESSION; amid fanfare and rowdiness, this figure was tried, found guilty of murdering PROSPERITY and was then sentenced to death. No doubt these same Americans would have scoffed at a voodoo witch doctor sticking pins into little wax dolls.

Roger W. Babson, the professional statistician and a religious fundamentalist, said that religious revivals would solve the unemployment problem. Patrick Cardinal Hayes, the Archbishop of New York, ordered every priest in his archdiocese to offer prayers for relief at all masses, while a committee in the township of Winslow in New Jersey set aside one week for prayer in the hope that this would help matters. More than 125,000 Mormons in Salt Lake City, in their first special fast of the past fifty years, ate but one meal a day for a while so that the financial equivalent of their other meals might go to needy brothers and sisters.

The bishops of the Protestant Episcopal Church issued a pastoral letter that called attention to "the contrast between individual want and collective plenty." This, the letter continued, "cannot be accepted as in accordance with the will of God." Our "acquisitive society," the bishops declared, stands bewildered in the presence of a crisis caused not by physical catastrophe, "but apparently by the competitive, profit-seeking principles upon which, it has hitherto been assumed, general prosperity is based."

The Federal Council of Churches denounced capitalism as a complete failure and called for a thorough reconstruction of the economic order. "The facts of the situation themselves," the council declared, "constitute a challenge to the churches to assume their rightful place of ethical leadership; to demand fundamental changes in present economic conditions; to protest against the selfish desire for wealth as the principal motive of industry; to insist upon the creation of an industrial society which shall have as its purpose economic security and freedom for the masses of mankind, 'even these least, my brethren,' to seek the development of a social order which shall be based upon Jesus' principles of love and brotherhood."

*   *   *

Many proposed cures were self-serving. Walter P. Chrysler, president of the Chrysler Corporation, said the Depression would end if enough people bought automobiles. The Association Against the Prohibition Amendment, together with the United States Brewers Association, vowed that more than 1,000,000 men could be put to work if beer were legalized. Billy Minsky, who ran a chain of burlesque houses, said that continuous burlesque was the answer for half the American population. "Give the people something else to think about," Minsky urged. "No man plots or even thinks when he attends my shows."

William "Big Bill" Thompson, the rambunctious mayor of Chicago, had a scheme which he said would double the city's retail trade. He wanted merchants to give away a coupon with each 25-cent purchase. Cash prizes totaling $975,000 would be awarded to 16,503 lucky holders of coupons. Thompson's press agent told reporters: "Nobody realizes the great mental ability of our mayor. None but a genius could have figured out, as he did, how to award a million dollars without breaking the law. Because nobody else can figure it out, all of his enemies jump to the conclusion that the scheme is a lottery." But Chicago merchants were not interested and the school superintendent ignored the mayor's plea to have teachers distribute circulars promoting the plan. It failed. Nonetheless, lotteries were tried elsewhere in the nation.

The New York *Times* published a letter suggesting that employed people give away their clothes and buy new ones to revive prosperity. Charles Edison, the son of the famous inventor and the owner of Thomas A. Edison, Inc., in West Orange, New Jersey, plastered his plant's white walls with signs exhorting his workers: "Buy something—buy anything, anywhere; paint your kitchen, send a telegram, give a party, get a car, pay a bill, rent a flat, fix your roof, get a haircut, see a show, build a house, take a trip, sing a song, get married. It does not matter what you do—but get going!"

President Hoover said to Rudy Vallee, the popular crooner: "If you can sing a song that would make people forget their troubles and the depression, I'll give you a medal." Hoover also invited essayist and novelist Christopher Morley to the White House and said to him: "What this country needs is a great poem. *John Brown's Body* was a step in the right direction. I've read it once and I'm reading it again—but it's too long to do what I mean. You can't thrill people in three hundred pages. Three hundred words is about the limit. Kipling's *Recessional* really did something to England when it was published. It helped them through a bad time. Let me know if you can find any great poems lying around."

Although Hoover wanted Americans to laugh at the Depression, many laughed at him instead. In one vaudeville routine the straight man said: "Business is improving." The comedian asked: "Is Hoover dead?"

Franklin D. Roosevelt also understood the therapeutic value of laughter. "I shall have no fear for the future of America," he said, "so long as we are able to laugh at ourselves as we learned to do with Mark Twain. He was the embodiment of that sense of humor without which the essential qualities of American human nature could not have been the same. Mark Twain did not bring humor to the American people—he brought it out. He enabled us to focus our minds upon our extravagances, our shortcomings and our idiosyncrasies."

* * *

Bruce Barton, the advertising man who had written a Rotarian-flavored biography of Christ, said the Depression could be cured by retiring everyone at the age of forty-five. In an article called "How to Fix Everything," published in *Vanity Fair,* he said that people forced into retirement could be paid half their former earnings. C. Stewart McCord, a Seattle dentist, came out with a proposal entitled "The Mercy Death for Surplus Labor"; this advocated the retirement of old people from the labor market with $50-a-month pensions to be paid for by means of a sales tax. The Utopian Society, headquartered in Los Angeles, not only urged that everybody retire at forty-five but also proposed making jobs available by keeping students in school until they were twenty-five years old.

J. Roy Ellison of Portland, Oregon, wanted to eliminate every tax except a tax on machines; he said this would reduce the use of machines and spread jobs among more workers. Stuart Chase and Representative Hatton W. Sumners of Texas called for a moratorium on inventions by refusing to grant new patents for the duration of the Depression. A New Orleans resident was all for drafting jobless men and sticking them in military barracks. From White Bear Lake, Minnesota, came this idea: "What I envisage is a sort of voluntary dictatorship." A Chattanooga man wrote: "It would be better for our peace if we abandoned the capitalistic system at once and forever." A New Mexico rancher wanted: "Abolition of money and the private ownership of productive property. Bingo! Mammon will be on his back, dying." John Dewey, the eminent philosopher and educator, spoke bitterly about the brutality of laissez-faire and said flatly: "Capitalism must be destroyed."

Bernard Baruch felt that the Depression would end when businessmen regained their confidence, but the people had lost faith in business leaders and some of them had lost faith in themselves. It was strange to hear Otto Kahn, the Wall Street banker, urging the government to intercede; he thought that government should start an upward cycle by reducing unemployment, leading the way to business expansion and ultimately restoring buying power. Agreement came from the president of the Amalgamated Clothing Workers of America, Sidney Hillman, who said: "This depression won't end until mass buying power is restored." Agreed. But how, exactly, was this to be done?

Dr. Nicholas Murray Butler, president of Columbia University and egghead-in-waiting to the Establishment, denounced the "easy diagnosis" and "smug prophecies" of those business leaders who said we would automatically come through the Depression. Butler felt that it was necessary to plan. "Gentlemen," he said ominously, "if we wait too long, somebody will come forward with a solution that we may not like."

The United States Chamber of Commerce, which represented small businessmen and retailers, endorsed what its own president called "the philosophy of a planned economy." This was an astonishing change, a radical change, in the thinking of conservative men, formerly such devout believers in laissez-faire and rugged individualism. The chamber's document said that freedom of individual action which might have been justified in the simple life of the past century "cannot be tolerated today," for the unwise action of a single individual might adversely affect the lives of thousands. "We have left the period of extreme individualism and are living in a period in which national economy must be recognized as the controlling factor."

This was a part of what Socialists and Communists had been saying a long time.

The free enterprise system was by no means so successful as capitalists had claimed. In his book *The Rich and the Super-Rich,* Ferdinand Lundberg says: "In business, under the American system, each year the failures exceed the new successes by a very, very, very wide margin. In business, under the American system, hundreds of thousands more have failed, generation after generation, than the few who have succeeded. If we are to judge by the preponderance of individual successes over failures or vice-versa, then the American system, businesswise, is a record of steady, almost unrelieved failure. It has failure literally built into it. . . ."

In the middle of the nineteenth century Henry Thoreau wrote in *Walden* that the rate of business failures in his day was 97 percent. In this era Kirby Page has said that the average life-span of a factory is seven years, while Professor Paul A. Samuelson has declared that the average life expectancy of any given American business is six years. It is an eye-opener to read tables of figures about the numbers of commercial failures and bank suspensions in this nation down through the decades. To cite just a few examples, in the year 1921 a total of 19,652 businesses failed and 501 banks closed, while in 1932 there were 31,822 commercial failures and 1,456 bank closings.

Praise of capitalism, free enterprise, laissez-faire, rugged individualism and the so-called American way of life sprang from the lips of an extremely small minority of men who had made it big—through an advantageous start in life, good luck, keen business acumen, hard work, a greater concern for profits than service, an elastic conscience, bending laws and sometimes shattering them. H. L. Mencken once said that the ability to make money is like the ability to play a banjo and should command no more respect. But many rich men, merely because they knew how to play the business game, felt they were superior to Americans whose talents and tastes ran to other things.

Walter Lippmann, who had helped organize a Socialist club while attending Harvard, had outgrown Socialism by 1928, when he praised the "unplanned activities of big business men." By this time "planning" was almost a dirty word in America—primarily because Soviet Russia had gone in for planning in a big way.

*   *   *

The father of the theory of planning a nation's economy was not Karl Marx but a German economist named Friedrich List, who committed suicide in 1846. Five years before his death he wrote: "It is the task of national economy to accomplish the economical development of the nation." Down through the subsequent decades most hardheaded capitalists had resisted the idea of a government formulating long-term plans about almost every aspect of the national economy. But despite their objection to government planning, they carefully planned the future of their own businesses and industries. They believed in capital expenditures—which means the spending by corporations of money to build new plants and equipment and to modernize and replace obsolete facilities. Naturally, capital spending had to take into account factors such as population growth, the migration of people from one region to another, the development of new products, increased consumer demands and the like. No man in his right mind would locate, finance and erect a huge steel plant without looking far into the future.

While it was all very well for capitalists to plan within their own framework of reference, they felt their liberties might be infringed if the government itself made long-range plans. In 1937 Lippmann said that general plans of social reconstruction "are the subjective beginnings of fanaticism and tyranny." He knew that Lenin's planning for Soviet Russia was based on precedents established in Germany by List and others. He also was familiar with the amorality of Lenin, who once wrote: "The Communists must be prepared to make every sacrifice, and, if necessary, even resort to all sorts of cunning, schemes, and stratagems, to employ illegal methods, to evade and conceal the truth. . . ."

The official Communist line is that under "Socialism" the aim of production is not profit but the satisfaction of man's needs. Furthermore, an essential condition for planning the national economy is public ownership of the means of production and all natural resources. Soviet Russia's first long-range plan, drawn up in 1920, called for electrification of the country. The Communists used two types of plans: (1) long-term, such as five-year plans, seven-year plans, or even longer; (2) current plans, such as annual, quarterly and monthly. The first Five-Year Plan was launched in 1928. Each long-term plan called for certain goals to be achieved within a specific time, allocated all national resources to these goals and prescribed the total national income and physical volume of production for all major commodities. Not every segment of the national economy was planned directly by the state. Collective farms, for example, formulated their own goals—under supervision from the top.

The Communists' long-term plans did not work out so well as their propagandists claimed they did. None of the plans ended as originally conceived, some goals being surpassed while others were never reached. Under the whip-and-carrot theory of human conditioning, some Russian workers made spectacular increases in their productivity, but the speedup was as bad if not worse than the frenzied pace at which Henry Ford's employees were driven. Nonetheless, Russia did become industrialized with surprising speed. In 1928 the Soviet Union produced 5½ percent of the world's industrial goods, by 1931 this proportion had increased to 11 percent, and by 1932 Russia stood second only to the United States as an industrial power.

Although many American capitalists said they hated and feared Soviet Russia, some of them helped that nation reach its objectives. There existed, for example, an American-Russian Chamber of Commerce. While President Hoover withheld American recognition from Soviet Russia large numbers of important American businessmen visited that country. American engineers designed and built dams in Russia. Communist engineers and technologists were welcomed to the United States to study our industrial methods firsthand. Some of these very American capitalists later said they had their doubts about one of Roosevelt's advisers, Rexford Tugwell, because Tugwell also was interested in Soviet planning. It was as easy for these capitalists to forget what they wanted to forget as it was for the Communists to try to rewrite history.

After 1930 Russia had no unemployment, according to Soviet leaders. Walter Duranty, a New York *Times* correspondent in Moscow, wrote that not only was work available for all, but there actually was a shortage of labor. Additionally, Duranty pointed out, there was a shortage of food. By means of starvation, forced labor and other kinds of coercion, Soviet Russia did reduce its rate of unemployment below that of the United States, although there continued to exist temporary joblessness, seasonal fluctuations in work and concealed unemployment among the rural population.

Will Rogers wrote: "Those Rascals in Russia along with their Cuckoo stuff have got some mighty good ideas. . . . Just think of everybody in a Country going to work."

Amtorg, a Russian abbreviation for "American trade," was a corporation founded in 1924 in New York to conduct trade with the United States. Its shareholders were Soviet import and export trade organizations, and its headquarters were in Moscow. One of Amtorg's functions was to try to recruit skilled workmen and technicians in foreign lands to help fulfill Russia's industrial goals.

In the autumn of 1931, with about 8,000,000 Americans unemployed, Amtorg let it be known the length and breadth of the United States that 6,000 jobs were available in Russia for qualified Americans. In one week alone Amtorg received 280 inquiries, and before long, more than 100,000 people in this country had applied for these positions. While industrialized states represented the largest number of applicants, all but ten states had some citizens and aliens who declared that they wanted to work in Russia. These people said they applied because of unemployment in the United States, because of their disgust with conditions in this country and because of their interest in the Soviet experiment.

*   *   *

Returning from a visit to Soviet Russia, Stuart Chase asked rhetorically: "Why should Russia have all the fun of making a new world?" Apart from his flippant suggestion that Long Island Sound be bailed out, this American economist said the Depression could be cured by instituting a series of reforms—high taxes on high incomes, lower tariffs, higher wages, shorter working hours, public housing and the electrification of farms.

During the Thirties in America, out of the welter of ideas about what might be done, there emerged three groups of social planners:

1. Those who wanted ownership and control of industry to remain in private hands, but subject to supervision by the government—a position taken by Franklin D. Roosevelt and liberals in general;

2. Those who wished to socialize industry as fast as possible, subject to public opinion and the organization of the workers, consumers and voters, with ever more segments of the economy covered by social ownership and social planning—a position taken by the Socialists;

3. Those who believed that effective social planning is possible only after the violent seizure of power and the establishment of a proletarian dictatorship—a position held by Communists and fellow travelers.

Many capitalists stubbornly refused to admit that any kind of national planning was needed. Their viewpoint was articulated by Dr. Benjamin Anderson, adviser to the Chase National Bank, who said: "In general it is not the function of government under the capitalist system to produce or perform economic services. The actual direction of industry, the decision whether more wheat shall be planted and less corn, or more shoes shall be produced and less hats, is not made by the state, or by collective society, but is left to the choice of independent producers. . . . The ability to understand the highly intricate economic life of today, the ability to see through it and to see the different parts in relation to one another, to coordinate wants and efforts, to distribute resources properly among conflicting claimants—this ability does not exist."

Therefore, Anderson concluded, any effort to use economic theory effectively "in the actual regulation of economic life," in the way of social planning and control, "is an impossibility." No doubt Anderson was unaware of the fact that, even as he tried to cut down the social planners, he was confessing that the capitalists themselves were unable to see the big picture and had failed to create a just and viable society.

Franklin D. Roosevelt, who did not pretend to be an economist, nonetheless was aware of the sad consequences of the lack of planning. While governor of New York State, he said: "What, for instance, is the economic use in the spectacle in [sic] huge dump scows being towed down New York harbor and out to sea for the purpose of throwing overboard dozens of carloads of cabbages which have come to the New York City market from the eastern and middle western states, and in many cases the far western states, all arriving the same day and in such quantities that they could only be consumed if the six million people in New York all decided to eat corned beef and cabbages three meals a day for a week . . . The fault lies not with the commission merchants, but with the lack of planning by the communities and the growers of the whole."

Charles A. Beard, the historian, said the Communists had no positive lessons for a free society since they ruled by "tyranny and terror, with secret police, espionage, and arbitrary executions." However, Beard added: "The cold truth is that the individualist creed of everybody for himself and the devil take the hindmost is principally responsible for the distress in which Western civilization finds itself." He advocated an American five-year plan consisting of a system of cartels in the basic industries and controlled by a National Economic Council representing business, labor and agriculture. In short, Beard had a vision of "the imperative necessity of planning."

Paul Blanshard, an author, attorney and municipal investigator, spelled out the Socialist position in these words: "Socialists propose to supplant the competitive planning of capitalism with a highly centralized planned economy . . . we Socialists would nationalize as many large industries as we could chew—and as speedily as such mastication could be accomplished. We would do it by peaceful democratic means unless Fascists and other reactionaries prevented peaceful change. Probably we would remodel industry into a series of great trusts, each trust to be ruled by tripartite functional industrial democracy. . . ."

Paul Douglas, a professor of economics and later a United States Senator from Illinois, felt that "a truly planned economy is almost impossible under capitalism and only practical under socialism." Having visited Russia, where he saw tyranny at close range, he said the problem in the United States was to get full employment while avoiding the "severe dictatorship and the denial of democracy which unfortunately is also a feature of the Russian program."

*   *   *

Simon Guggenheim, whose smelting and refining interests had made him very rich, declared: "As I see it, all one needs is sound common sense and a willingness to work." Simplistic thinking of this sort did not set well with Marriner Eccles, a banker and economist. Eccles said: "The theory of hard work and thrift as a means of pulling us out of the depression is unsound economically. True hard work means more production, but thrift and economy mean less consumption. Now reconcile those two forces, will you?"

"Inflation" was the single most popular remedy for the Depression. Inflation, recession and depression are such highly complex subjects that professional economists often disagree about their precise meanings. At the risk of sounding as simple as Guggenheim, this much may be said: Inflation is an excess of purchasing power or too many dollars bidding for too few goods, resulting in higher prices. Recession is lack of purchasing power or too many goods chasing too few dollars, resulting in lower prices. As the recession deepened and became Depression, many men felt that the American economy might be brought into balance if the prevailing deflation were offset by inflation.

Stuart Chase prescribed a "stiff dose of inflation," but few capitalists listened to him since they considered him a radical. However, they snapped to attention when J. P. Morgan declared: "The way out of the depression is to combat and overcome the deflationary forces." Professor Irving Fisher of Yale, also highly regarded by rich men, was another who advocated inflation.

The Reverend Charles E. Coughlin grandiosely asserted: "Silver is the key to world prosperity." This cure-all appealed to Senators from silver-mining states, who demanded that "free silver" be coined at a rate that would expand the currency base.

William Randolph Hearst urged the government to appropriate $5 billion to put men to work on public projects, and, as we have seen, this remedy appealed to John Nance Garner. But pump priming was offensive to Russell Leffingwell, a Morgan partner, who felt that large federal expenditures would retard recovery. Another who rejected this idea was Leonard Porter Ayres, an economist who had to live with the humiliation of his 1929 prediction that he did not think a serious depression would occur. Ayres favored an "orthodox" rather than a "planned" recovery. Time and again he said: "It is as futile for us to believe that we can spend ourselves rich as for us to suppose that a man can drink himself sober." Among those who disdained this analogy was the famous British economist John Maynard Keynes.

Businessmen and industrialists, worried about the growing demand for a planned economy, turned with interest to a proposal put forward by Gerard Swope, president of the General Electric Company. The kernel of the so-called Swope Plan grew in the brain of Owen D. Young, board chairman of the Radio Corporation of America, who had played a big role in the dissolution of the Insull empire. Swope brought this idea to maturity and presented it for the first time on September 16, 1931, at a meeting of the National Electrical Manufacturers Association in Manhattan's Commodore Hotel. He called his speech "The Stabilization of Industry."

The basic concept in the Swope Plan was that industry be allowed to work out its own problems through an organization of industrial or trade associations. This, of course, was comforting to industrialists. The eight-point plan was designed to stabilize industry, purify business management, provide more jobs and protect workers against unemployment. Swope, a more enlightened business leader than many of his peers, was truly concerned with the welfare of the workers. In his speech he gave more time and attention to his eighth point than to the other seven points combined, and this eighth point amounted to a call for a social security program for all industrial employees. Swope had hoped to fend off criticism from his colleagues by declaring "there is nothing new or original in what I am proposing," but this device failed to work.

Despite the eagerness with which capitalists welcomed the idea of more freedom in the management of their own affairs, they disagreed with Swope when he urged that every time a man changed his job, his insurance and pension accounts be transferred to the new company. Why mollycoddle the workers? One editorial writer said of the Swope Plan that "had it been prepared by a Wobbly ten years ago it would have landed him in jail." The plan also was denounced as reckless interference with the sacred operations of free enterprise, as pure Socialism and even as Fascism.

Swope's interest in the plight of the workers did not offset a genuine danger inherent in his plan. This danger was detected, although not revealed, by Herbert Hoover, of all persons. While the Swope Plan was being discussed across the land, the President was careful not to make any public comment on it, but twenty years later he revealed in his memoirs that he had sent a copy of the plan to his attorney general with a covering note. In this note Hoover pointed out the plan would have resulted in "the organization of gigantic trusts such as have never been dreamed of in the history of the world."

Although the Swope Plan was never placed in operation, it was analyzed in books and magazines, in colleges and universities. In fact, no single cure for the Depression attracted so much attention until the advent of Technocracy.

15

Technocracy

EUGENE O'NEILL sometimes interrupted his playwriting to pal around with his friend Howard Scott, an engineer who neglected his floor-wax business to spout odd theories in Greenwich Village joints.

In speakeasies and restaurants, in The Meeting Place and Lee Chumley's and Van's Place, patrons began to look forward to the arrival of Scott, a gaunt man who wore a leather coat, blue serge suit and red necktie. He perpetually predicted the death of capitalism. This prophecy was a commonplace in the early days of the Depression, but Scott attracted attention because of the reasons he gave for the demise of capitalism and because of the substitute he offered.

Born in Virginia, a rootless intellectual, once an economic adviser to the Industrial Workers of the World, Scott had drifted to New York after World War I, and there he met Thorstein Veblen, an iconoclastic economist and a social philosopher. One of Veblen's books, *The Engineers and the Price System,* bared the growing discrepancy between the *potential* and the *actual* productivity of mechanized industry under the profit system. Veblen believed that few capitalistic operations produced real wealth. He advocated economic revolution through the organization of a group of technicians who would take over and run the nation's plants in behalf of everyone. This idea impressed Howard Scott, who continued to ponder it after Veblen's death in 1929.

Scott also became familiar with the writings of William H. Smyth of Berkeley, California, a nationally known inventor and engineer. In 1919 Smyth had coined the name "Technocracy" by blending "technology" with "democracy." It meant rule by technologists. That same year Smyth explained Technocracy in three articles published in *Industrial Management.* He called it a theory of social organization and a system of national industrial management. He said that all social and economic systems had become obsolete owing to the technological advances of the previous century. If proper use were made of scientific discoveries and engineering skills, he felt, all mankind could bask in leisure and prosperity.

Howard Scott agreed with Veblen and Smyth. About a decade before the Crash, Scott and other engineers had organized the Technical Alliance of North America, a research group that began studying the energy resources of this continent. Nothing much came of it. However, never abandoning his faith in Technocracy, Scott continued to propagandize in its behalf. An engineer almost unknown to the engineering profession, a hand-me-down thinker, a poor writer whose prose resembled a tangled fishnet, Scott nonetheless talked well and had a flair for publicity. His nightly discourses in Greenwich Village began to attract a small band of disciples, including the debonair and sophisticated Max Eastman—poet, critic, teacher, essayist, editor and perennial radical—who traveled from his Croton-on-Hudson retreat to listen to Scott. At last Scott's influence spread beyond Manhattan's Bohemia.

In June, 1932, as the bonus army streamed into Washington, the New York *Times* published on page 40 an article about an engineer named Howard Scott who was predicting a new social system based on the control of natural resources and manpower. The following August all New York newspapers broke the story of an energy survey of North America being made by a group known as Technocrats, under Scott's direction and on the campus of Columbia University. This time the *Times* article appeared on page 13.

Scott had reassembled some of his colleagues from the defunct Technical Alliance of North America and also had recruited new members from the ranks of unemployed scientists and engineers, architects and economists, sociologists and biochemists. They were financed by the Architects' Emergency Relief Committee of New York. Walter Rautenstrauch, a professor of industrial engineering at Columbia and a new devotee of Technocracy, provided them with free offices in the university's industrial engineering department.

The official name of this new group was the Energy Survey of North America, and Scott's title was director. Unofficially, they were called Technocrats. They studied industrial and agricultural history and started preparing the first of 3,000 charts and graphs depicting this continent's energy potential.

The average American had trouble understanding Technocracy, mainly because the subject was strange and complex, because Scott tended to become secretive once Technocracy caught on and because few engineers can write plainly enough to explain their specialty to laymen. Scott himself wrote murkily: "Its methods are the result of a synthetic integration of the physical sciences that pertain to the determination of all functional sequences of social phenomena."

Even Theodore Dreiser was puzzled. The famous novelist, who had known Scott in Greenwich Village, sat down to have a long talk with him about Technocracy. Then Dreiser wrote to a friend, saying: "I see some things which I did not see anywhere near as clearly when I was in the midst of it last year, and one is the enormous significance of the machine in any equitable form of society, and the need of the technician as a part of the newer kind of state. The technician, the chemist, the physicist, the mathematician, the inventor and the economic student and expert are not quite the same as the factory hand or the farmer, but the introduction of the working formula with which to remedy their troubles is not quite clear. I am thinking about it. . . ."

In simple language, here were Technocracy's basic concepts:

Energy is the only source of life. Prior to the Industrial Revolution, only human energy produced the goods needed by society. Then man learned how to convert coal, oil and running water into steam and electricity. These new sources of energy turned machines that did the work of many men. As machines became more numerous and sophisticated, they replaced manpower. This resulted in technological unemployment.

Now, in 1932, with perhaps 12,000,000 Americans out of work, there was almost no need for human muscles to produce goods. Four modern turbine electric generators, each putting out 300,000 horsepower, could create as much energy as all adult workers in the nation. With technology making still further advances, by about April, 1943, there would be 20,000,000 unemployed Americans. As far into the future as anyone could see, unemployment was bound to worsen unless man mastered his machines and created a new kind of society.

The Technocrats offered frightening examples:

• One man working one minute could make almost 3,000 cigarettes, instead of the mere 500 he had produced in the recent past.

• One man working one hour could produce as much pig iron as was produced in 3,000 hours back in 1840.

• A mere 100 men in 5 plants could now make as many bricks as were produced by 2,370 plants running at full capacity as recently as 1929.

• A Milwaukee plant was so automated that 208 men could turn out 10,000 auto frames a day.

• Soon to be completed was a New Jersey rayon factory that could run twenty-four hours a day without a single worker in the shop; one company man, seated at a desk in New York City, could change the dyes in the New Jersey plant across the Hudson River simply by pressing a button.

If fewer and fewer human beings were needed to make more and more goods, society had to change. Orthodox economics and politics had become obsolete. The profit system must be junked. One Technocrat wrote that we behold "the spectacle of a gutted continent, its resources wasted and flung away in the crazy race for the profit that strangled the system."

Current economics was described as "the pathology of debt." Under capitalism, in the final analysis, wealth was merely symbols of debt—paper money and metal coins, mortgages and liens, stocks and bonds.

The only true wealth, the Technocrats insisted, is energy. It is energy alone that makes tangible things such as chairs and beds, radios and automobiles. Gold is no true measure of wealth since it fluctuates in value. Only energy is constant. And, unlike wealth, energy can be measured accurately—by means of ergs, horsepower, joules, calories, British thermal units, etc.

The Technocrats said that the price system, tied to gold, must be abolished. This was not necessarily a radical proposal. After all, capitalism was fairly new in human history, and the price system was not God-given. Goods should be produced for the benefit of all, not for the profit of the few.

The structure of society could be changed by means of the following steps: Study the natural resources of this continent to determine its energy potential. Find out what all Americans needed. Calculate the volume of goods that could be produced in a given time. Divide this total volume by the size of the population and distribute the goods on a pro rata basis. This could be done by substituting energy certificates for dollars. A central committee could decide who deserved what. The certificates could be issued at central distribution stations. Purchases could be made by punching a hole in each certificate or ticket. No one would be allowed to hoard these tickets or lend them at interest.

Few people would have to work. Adults between the ages of twenty-five and forty-five, laboring only four hours a day four days a week, could make enough goods for everyone. Each child, upon reaching the age of five, would begin to receive annual certificates worth $5,000 in goods. At the age of ten this would be increased to $10,000. Each year every adult would get $20,000 worth of tickets. All this would mean that the entire population of the United States could enjoy a standard of living ten times higher than the average income of 1929.

Of course, the entire system would have to be run by technologists.

Such was Technocracy's philosophy and program.

*   *   *

By means of articles in newspapers and magazines, lectures and debates, radio broadcasts and newsreels in movie houses, word about Technocracy spread until by December, 1932, it was the national rage. Whenever ship-news reporters boarded an incoming liner to interview a celebrity, their first question would be: "What do you think about Technocracy?" A majority of Greenwich Village Bohemians rejected the man who once had interested them, since many preferred Communism to Technocracy, but Howard Scott became the pet of some plutocrats and even won cautious attention on Wall Street. Although his comments now blossomed on page one of newspapers across the land, he generally played hard to get, refusing to pose for newspaper photographers and newsreelmen. Still, as a certified celebrity, he did consent to enact the role of Santa Claus at a Christmas party held by tenants of a big apartment house in New York.

Was he in fact a new kind of economic Santa Claus with a bagful of goodies for everyone? Among those who thought so were eminent scientists and businessmen, economists and engineers, editors and columnists, clergymen and Congressmen. But a dissenting group of equally distinguished persons regarded him not as a Santa Claus but as a Greek bearing gifts that needed close examination. According to this latter group, Technocracy was damned nonsense.

The average American did not know what to think about this subject, at once so complex and mystifying. Its very mystery appealed to a people hungering for a new messiah to lead them into the Promised Land. They had repudiated President Hoover at the polls; but President-elect Roosevelt had not yet assumed office, and all American life seemed to quiver in suspension. Republicans and bankers had lost their prestige. Orthodox economics seemed dead, and capitalism itself was suspect—otherwise, why were so many millions of Americans without work? Experimentation was in the air. The old order had failed, so why not try something new? If nothing else, Technocracy offered hope to the hopeless, promised permanent prosperity if all would share and share alike. Technocracy also evoked the gods of science and technology—something which could be understood, if only dimly, by a generation of American men who delighted in tinkering with their old flivvers on an idle Sunday afternoon.

The national mood was detected by Will Rogers, who wrote in his column of December 22, 1932:

> This Technocracy thing, we don't know if it's a disease or a theory. It may go out as fast as Esquimo pies, or miniature golf, but people right now are in a mood to grab at anything. They are sure of one thing and that is that the old orthodox political way of running everything has flopped. There is not a man in the whole world today that people feel like actually knows what's the matter. If there was he would be appointed dictatorship [sic] unanimously by the whole world. Our "big men" won't admit they don't know. They just keep on hoping they can "bull" their way through. The case has simply got too big for the doctors, but the doctors haven't got big enough to admit it.

That December—with Iowa farmers resisting the sale of mortgaged farms, with more than 100 self-help and barter groups operating in nearly thirty states, with the magazine *Common Sense* writing about starving kids, with hundreds of thousands of young people roaming the nation's highways—Technocracy had become a fad.

Mark Sullivan, a political writer of great reserve, made the wild statement that "no subject since Halley's Comet has stirred so much discussion." Dr. Virgil Jordan, president of the National Industrial Conference Board, avowed that the nation had gone "Technocrazy." Writing in the New York *World-Telegram,* Forrest Davis said that Technocracy's impact "jars the Park Ave. dinner table, the Hester Street delicatessen store, luncheon discussions in the Bankers' Club, New York, the Cosmos Club, Washington, whets curiosity in the Grange at Skaneatelles [*sic*], N.Y. and the Elks Club in Hamilton, O."

Printing presses poured out rivers of articles, pamphlets and books about Technocracy. There were Technocracy magazines, Technocracy plays, Technocracy movies, Technocracy sermons, Technocracy hymns, Technocracy debates and endless Technocracy jokes. Hoping to profit from this vogue, one man tried to copyright the word "Technocrats" so that he might collect five cents every time it was used in print. Columnist Franklin P. Adams amused himself and his readers by writing:

> So after dinner I fell to thinking that I would better hasten if I am to write a book about Technocracy, so did write down a few titles to submit to various publishers:
> *Technocracy on the Lower Mississippi.*
> *Technocracy's Chance; and How He Improved It.*
> *From Technocrat to President.*
> Yet I knew that none of these would be half so good as a book called *Sexnocracy: or What Makes the World Go Round, Grandpa?*

*   *   *

Who were Technocracy's advocates and critics, and what did they say?

Max Eastman wrote that "it swept the country because it is the scientific answer to the country's *one problem.*" (Eastman's italics.) He added that there was nothing in the physical world to stop us from riding straight into the Promised Land on these wonderful machines we had invented. Answering Will Rogers, Eastman said Technocracy "is obviously neither a disease or theory, but just a sound common sense volition to want to kick this price-system out of the way and get the machines running."

Stuart Chase quoted a man he described as "a distinguished engineer" as saying that all Americans could be fed from the fields of Kansas alone. All Americans could be clothed by making intensive use of fewer than half our textile plants, operated by a mere handful of workers. Chase declared that if the nation were to adopt Technocracy, a quarter of the gainfully employed could supply the entire population with adequate food, clothing, shelter and modest physical comforts.

One of the most ardent disciples of the new plan was Harold Loeb, a nephew of Simon Guggenheim and one of Ernest Hemingway's crowd of drifters. He worked closely with Howard Scott in the Technocrats' offices at Columbia University. Loeb said that food, clothing, housing—even luxuries such as automobiles, radios and entertainment—could be provided easily through the proper use of our knowledge, energy and natural resources. He pointed out that economic systems are not divine, but are man-made, and therefore can be changed at will. We are clinging, Loeb said, to an obsolete system benefiting no one. He urged Americans to junk the traditional price and distribution system. He pontificated that "poverty and destitution can be immediately eliminated."

Professor John Dewey gave guarded approval to Technocracy, as did Edward A. Filene, Boston's famous department store magnate. Filene wrote: "Technocracy is fundamentally correct, but too vague as to methods of procedure. Technocracy has been one of the delightful newspaper sensations of recent months having to do with the building of an altogether new Utopia, a Utopia of scientists and engineers—and they are going to throw out of human society everything that gets on the nerves of these scientists and engineers. I believe that they have already thrown out the price and credit system, and from what I understand of their Utopia, there will be no place in it for the business man. Well, I have no particular objections to this thing they call Technocracy, if it can be made to work."

Filene, an enlightened and progressive business leader, had put his finger on a prime weakness in the plan. It failed to take human nature into account. Few engineers and technicians are noted for their sensitivity to people's emotional needs. On the other hand, artists of all kinds throb to the invisible vibrations of personality and cut to the core of character. Heywood Broun, adducing this argument in one of his columns, said that if he understood the new messiahs, they held that we can be saved only by handing over our lives to the engineers. Broun also took a sideswipe at President Hoover, an engineer in private life, by declaring that "we have had enough of engineers, great or otherwise"—a sentiment soon echoed by Alfred E. Smith. Broun went on to say that the artist never has been a dictator, for he understands better than anyone else the variations in human personality. In a wry touch, Broun nonetheless mused that he was "not quite sure that I would argue that Edna St. Vincent Millay should upon the instant become the president of the Chase National Bank."

Other critics called attention to other faults in Technocracy. It was argued that Technocracy emphasized production at a time when distribution was the main problem. Were the Technocrats using sound scientific methods? After all, while they had promised to produce 3,000 individual studies, they had completed only 150 of them—a mere 5 percent sampling. Furthermore, they talked too much about the production of *goods* while employment was shifting to *services*. They spoke of "North America" as a unit, but Mexicans and Canadians might hold different views. They had failed to prove that machines would create permanent and widespread unemployment.

As for energy certificates—like gold and currency, these could be hoarded, could be used for speculation, could fluctuate in desirability and therefore in value, could be vulnerable to changes in mass psychology, could be counterfeited. Furthermore, if the engineers were to rule America,

how would they take power? Legally—through elections? Violently—by
means of a *coup d'état* or revolution? One Technocrat had already declared that the new system would be forced on the people.

But would democratic-minded Americans acquiesce in such a seizure of
power? What would the Technocrats do with those who refused to co-
operate? Establish a secret police and concentration camps? Since the
Technocrats called for complete ownership of all production facilities, were
they not camouflaged Communists or Fascists? In Soviet Russia, it was
pointed out, people were using the "bon," which was an unofficial currency. Was this not like the Technocrats' "erg," or energy certificate?

Howard Scott refused to link Technocracy with any political party or
system, professing to scorn Communists and Fascists alike. In his usual
muddy style, he wrote that Russian Communism "mistook the name tag of
one phase of the price system for that system's entirety." As for Fascism,
Scott called it "the last ditch of the price system."

Despite the distance he kept from these two ideologies, Scott threw a
scare into Communist leaders William Z. Foster and Earl Browder. Recog-
nizing Technocracy as a rival to their own dreams, they wrote a pamphlet
saying that Technocracy "represents only the dreams and illusions of a
baffled, unemployed mass of technicians who have been deprived of their
functions by the decay of capitalism."

Socialist leader Norman Thomas went on record as saying: "I don't
think much of Technocracy as a 'way out,' but it is performing a great
service by dramatically calling attention to the fact that we have the means
with which to wipe out poverty."

J. George Frederick, a publicist and economic adviser, claimed that "the
regime proposed by Technocracy is completely Fascist, and thus partakes
of autocratic control by a man or class. It is based on an utter denial of
democracy." Charles F. Abbott, executive director of the American Institute of Steel Construction, warned that Technocracy "would set up a rigid
dictatorship of engineers." Dr. Karl T. Compton, president of the Massachusetts Institute of Technology, said there was nothing new about an
energy survey and accused the Technocrats of faulty reasoning. However,
Compton added: "I agree that some of the types of chaos predicted by
Technocracy will happen unless we meet the situation with intelligent
planning and soon make effective a greater correlation of production and
consumption."

Senator William E. Borah of Idaho partially agreed with Compton when
he said: "We're not suffering from over-production, but from non-distribu-
tion and under-consumption. If the Technocrats would turn their engineering minds to devising schemes for improving distribution, instead of
prophesying chaos in eighteen months, it would interest me a great deal
more." Senator James Couzens of Michigan, for his part, temporarily
approved of Technocracy.

Dr. Virgil Jordan, president of the National Industrial Conference

Board, called Technocracy's doctrines "paralyzing superstitions." *L'Osservatore Romano,* the official Vatican newspaper, accused Technocracy of ignoring moral and social factors. Francis Delaisi, a French economist, argued that 800,000,000 people on earth were untouched by machines. Dr. Walter R. Ingalls, president of the American Institute of Weights and Measures, wrote: "Convalescing business has been hit below the belt by a pseudo-scientific fist, armed with the brass knuckles of an imposing but meaningless scientific jargon. Technocracy has presented a multitude of alarming conclusions, but has withheld supporting facts."

The Technocrats had said that they wanted to produce only one kind of everything, including just one style of automobile. The idea of total standardization was horrifying to women, who like variety when they go shopping. Mrs. Christine Frederick, a home economist, wrote an article called "The Psychology of Woman Under Technocracy," saying furiously:

> If anyone dares to suggest to me for America a waiting queue or punch-card system such as poor Russia offers its Job-like people today, I shall go plumb berserk. Of all the low, pitiful lots in life to which a proud human can descend, it is the permanent prospect of being limited to the material goods produced and allotted by a "central committee" and rationed off on a punch-card system, and "distributed" at "central distributing stations" to a waiting line of people.

When the Technocrats first arrived on Dr. Nicholas Murray Butler's campus at Columbia University, he had gazed on them with a benevolent eye and declared that their energy survey was "of large importance." However, sensitive to public opinion, he grew uneasy with the rising tide of criticism of Technocracy. He listened when the American Engineering Council, an influential national body of engineering societies, denied on January 14, 1933, that Technocracy represented professional engineering opinion. The next day Butler announced the formation of a commission of seventeen men to study the problems of the price system and the machine age—problems raised by Technocrats—but without mentioning Technocracy itself. On January 17 Butler said in a public statement that Columbia University had no academic connection with Technocracy or with Howard Scott. This brought to heel Professor Walter Rautenstrauch, who had given the innovators some office space.

When the professor bowed out as self-appointed patron to the Technocrats, they began quarreling among themselves, and on January 23, 1933, they split into two factions. Howard Scott was ousted as director and forced off the campus, but vain as ever, he muttered about direct action and armed seizure of power. The other faction accepted the leadership of Harold Loeb, who took the title of director of the Continental Committee on Technocracy and continued to propagandize in behalf of the central idea.

Thus, within six months—from August, 1932, to January, 1933—Technocracy rose and fell. Scott, who had enjoyed seeing his name on the front pages of newspapers, faded into obscurity, fell behind in his rent and was soon declared bankrupt.

*   *   *

Technocracy had won worldwide attention while it reigned, and after it was deposed, it left echoes. Yugoslavia's leading newspaper explained it to Serbian peasants. In Berlin the Technokratische Union announced that it was in general agreement with the idea of Technocracy. In England the president of the British Textile Association said that the future depended on the proper use of the machine and the suppression of its abuse. Russia's industrial growth, according to an American educator and writer named Harry Elmer Barnes, was due in part to the adoption of modified Technocracy. In Australia and New Zealand groups called Social Credit Reformers advocated something akin to Technocracy.

Long after Technocracy ceased to be a nationwide fad in America, it lingered as a regional movement. In California some people banded together into a Utopian Society, organized along Technocratic principles. They announced that every American family would receive $4,700 a year; they attracted 560,000 members; they emphasized mysticism and deplored the evils of capitalism. For a while Howard Scott was their high priest-in-residence. Up in the state of Washington a handful of Technocrats, along with members of the Unemployed Citizens' League, merged and reorganized as the Commonwealth Builders.

A few forthright devotees of Technocracy, such as Leon Henderson, and a few who saw some good in it, such as Adolf Berle, later became advisers and officials in the New Deal. In fact, Technocracy played a part in the public response to the New Deal by preparing the people for radical currency reform. It may even have laid the groundwork for subsequent discussions of the guaranteed income, or negative income tax. And the release of atomic energy gave fresh meaning to the predictions of the Technocrats.

16

What the Depression Did to People

THE DEPRESSION smashed into the nation with such fury that men groped for superlatives to express its impact and meaning.

Edmund Wilson compared it to an earthquake. It was "like the explosion of a bomb dropped in the midst of society," according to the Social Science Research Council Committee on Studies in Social Aspects of the Depression.

Alfred E. Smith said the Depression was equivalent to war, while Supreme Court Justice Louis D. Brandeis and Bernard Baruch declared that it was worse than war. Philip La Follette, the governor of Wisconsin, said: "We are in the midst of the greatest domestic crisis since the Civil War." Governor Roosevelt agreed in these words: "Not since the dark days of the Sixties have the people of this state and nation faced problems as grave, situations as difficult, suffering as severe." A jobless textile worker told Louis Adamic: "I wish there would be war again." In a war against a foreign enemy all Americans might at least have felt united by a common purpose, and production would have boomed.

Poor and rich alike felt anxious and helpless.

Steel magnate Charles M. Schwab, despite his millions and the security of his Manhattan palace, freely confessed: "I'm afraid. Every man is afraid." J. David Stern, a wealthy newspaper publisher, became so terrified that he later wrote in his autobiography: "I sat in my back office, trying to figure out what to do. To be explicit, I sat in my private bathroom. My bowels were loose from fear." Calvin Coolidge dolorously told a friend: "I can see nothing to give ground for hope."

Herbert C. Pell, a rich man with a country estate near Governor Roosevelt's, said the country was doomed unless it could free itself from the rich, who have "shown no realization that what you call free enterprise means anything but greed." Marriner Eccles, a banker and economist who had *not* lost his fortune, wrote that "I awoke to find myself at the bottom of a pit without any known means of scaling its sheer sides." According to Dwight W. Morrow, a Morgan associate, diplomat and Senator: "Most of my friends think the world is coming to an end—that is, the world as we know it." Reinhold Niebuhr, the learned and liberal clergyman, said that rich "men and women speculated in drawing-rooms on the best kind of poison as a means to oblivion from the horrors of revolution."

In Youngstown, Ohio, a friend of Mayor Joseph L. Heffernan stood beside the mayor's desk and said: "My wife is frantic. After working at the steel mill for twenty-five years I've lost my job and I'm too old to get other work. If you can't do something for me, I'm going to kill myself." Governor Gifford Pinchot of Pennsylvania got a letter from a jobless man who said: "I cannot stand it any longer." Gan Kolski, an unemployed Polish artist from Greenwich Village, leaped to his death from the George Washington Bridge, leaving this note: "To All: If you cannot hear the cry of starving millions, listen to the dead, brothers. Your economic system is dead."

An architect, Hugh Ferriss, stood on the parapet of a tall building in Manhattan and thought to himself that the nearby skyscrapers seemed like monuments to the rugged individualism of the past. Thomas Wolfe wrote: "I believe that we are lost here in America, but I believe we shall be found." Democratic Senator Thomas Gore of Oklahoma called the Depression an economic disease. Henry Ford, on the other hand, said the Depression was "a wholesome thing in general."

*   *   *

Obviously, the essence of a depression is widespread unemployment. In one of the most fatuous remarks on record, Calvin Coolidge said: "The final solution of unemployment is work." He might have added that water is wet. Senator Robert Wagner of New York called unemployment inexcusable.

A decade before the Crash the British statesman David Lloyd George had said: "Unemployment, with its injustice for the man who seeks and thirsts for employment, who begs for labour and cannot get it, and who is punished for failure he is not responsible for by the starvation of his children—that torture is something that private enterprise ought to remedy for its own sake." Winston Churchill now used the same key word, "torture," in a similar comment: "This problem of unemployment is the most torturing that can be presented to a civilized society."

Before Roosevelt became President and named Frances Perkins his secretary of labor, she was so pessimistic that she said publicly it might take a quarter century to solve the unemployment problem. A Pennsylvania commission studied 31,159 workless men and then reported that the typical unemployed man was thirty-six years old, native-born, physically fit and with a good previous work record. This finding contradicted Henry Ford's belief that the unemployed did not want to work.

However, the Pennsylvania study was *not* typical of the unemployed across the entire nation. Negroes and aliens were the last hired and the first fired. Young men and women were graduated from high schools and colleges into a world without jobs. Mississippi's demagogic governor and sometime Senator, Theodore G. Bilbo, vowed the unemployment problem could be solved by shipping 12,000,000 American blacks to Africa. The United Spanish War Veterans, for their part, urged the deportation of 10,000,000 aliens—or nearly 6,000,000 more than the actual number of aliens in the United States. Some noncitizens, unable to find work here, voluntarily returned to their homelands. With the deepening of the Depression, immigration dropped until something strange happened in the year 1932: More than three times as many persons left this country as entered it. No longer was America the Promised Land.

*   *   *

The Depression changed people's values and thus changed society.

The Chamber of Commerce syndrome of the Twenties became a mockery in the Thirties. Business leaders lost their prestige, for now it had become apparent to all Americans that these big shots did not know what they were talking about when they said again and again and again that everything would be all right if it were just left to them. Worship of big business was succeeded by greater concern for human values. The optimism of the speculative decade was replaced by the pessimism of the hungry decade, by anguished interest in the problem of having enough food on the table.

People eager to make a big killing in the stock market had paid scant attention to politics, but now they wondered about their elected representatives and the kind of political system that could permit such a catastrophe to happen. Indifference gave way to political and social consciousness. Dorothy Parker, the sophisticate and wit, cried: "There is no longer I. There is WE. The day of the individual is dead." Quentin N. Burdick, who became a Senator from North Dakota, said long after the Depression: "I guess I acquired a social conscience during those bad days, and ever since I've had the desire to work toward bettering the living conditions of the people." Sylvia Porter, who developed into a financial columnist, said that while at Hunter College she switched from English to economics because of "an overwhelming curiosity to know why everything was crashing around me and why people were losing their jobs."

People lost their houses and apartments.

Franklin D. Roosevelt said: "One of the major disasters of the continued depression was the loss of hundreds of thousands of homes each year from foreclosure. The annual average loss of urban homes by foreclosure in the United States in normal times was 78,000. By 1932 this had increased to 273,000. By the middle of 1933, foreclosures had advanced to more than 1,000 a day."

In New York City, which had more apartments than private houses, there were almost 200,000 evictions in the year 1931. During the first three weeks of the following year there were more than 60,000 other evictions. One judge handled, or tried to handle, 425 eviction cases in a single day! On February 2, 1932, the New York *Times* described the eviction of three families in the Bronx:

> Probably because of the cold, the crowd numbered only about 1,000, although in unruliness it equalled the throng of 4,000 that stormed the police in the first disorder of a similar nature on January 22. On Thursday a dozen more families are to be evicted unless they pay back rents.
>
> Inspector Joseph Leonary deployed a force of fifty detectives and mounted and foot patrolmen through the street as Marshal Louis Novick led ten furniture movers into the building. Their appearance was the signal for a great clamor. Women shrieked from the windows, the different sections of the crowd hissed and booed and shouted invectives. Fighting began simultaneously in the house and in the street. The marshal's men were rushed on the stairs and only got to work after the policemen had driven the tenants back into their apartments.

In that part of New York City known as Sunnyside, Queens, many homeowners were unable to meet mortgage payments and were soon ordered to vacate. Eviction notices were met with collective action, the residents barricading their doors with sandbags and barbed wire, flinging pepper and flour at sheriffs who tried to force their way inside. However, it was a losing battle; more than 60 percent of Sunnyside's householders lost their homes through foreclosure.

Harlem Negroes invented a new way to get enough money to pay their rent. This, as it came to be called, was the house-rent party. A family would announce that on Saturday night or Thursday night they would welcome anyone and everyone to their home for an evening of fun. Sometimes they would print and distribute cards such as this: "There'll be plenty of pig feet/And lots of gin;/Jus' ring the bell/An' come on in." Saturday night, of course, is the usual time for partying, while Thursday was chosen because this was the only free night for sleep-in black domestics who worked for white people. Admission to a house-rent party cost 15 cents, but more money could be spent inside. A festive mood was established by placing a red bulb in a light socket, by serving food consisting of chitterlings and pigs' feet and by setting out a jug of corn liquor. These parties often went on until daybreak, and the next day the landlord got his rent. The innovation spread to black ghettos in other big cities across the land, and some white people began imitating the Negroes.

In Chicago a crowd of Negroes gathered in front of the door of a tenement house to prevent the landlord's agent from evicting a neighborhood family, and they continued to stand there hour after hour, singing hymns. A Chicago municipal employee named James D. O'Reilly saw his home auctioned off because he had failed to pay $34 in city taxes at the very time the city owed him $850 in unpaid salary.

A social worker described one pathetic event: "Mrs. Green left her five small children alone one morning while she went to have her grocery order filled. While she was away the constable arrived and padlocked her house with the children inside. When she came back she heard the six-weeks-old baby crying. She did not dare to touch the padlock for fear of being arrested, but she found a window open and climbed in and nursed the baby and then climbed out and appealed to the police to let her children out."

In widespread areas of Philadelphia no rent was paid at all. In this City of Brotherly Love evictions were exceedingly common—as many as 1,300 a month. Children, who saw their parents' distress, made a game of evictions. In a day-care center they piled all the doll furniture in first one corner and then another. One tot explained to a teacher: "We ain't got no money for the rent, so we's moved into a new house. Then we got the constable on us, so we's movin' again."

In millions of apartments, tension mounted and tempers flared toward the end of each month, when the rent was due. Robert Bendiner, in his book *Just Around the Corner,* wrote about conditions in New York City:

> Evictions and frequent moves to take advantage of the apartment market were as common in middle-income Washington Heights as in the poor areas of town, and apartment hopping became rather a way of life. My own family moved six times in seven years. . . . Crises occurred monthly, and several times we were saved from eviction by pawning leftover valuables or by my mother's rich talent for cajoling landlords. On one more than routinely desperate occasion she resorted to the extreme device of having one of us enlarge a hole in the bathroom ceiling and then irately demanding repairs before another dollar of rent should be forthcoming.

In moving from one place to another, some families left their furniture behind because it had been bought on the installment plan and they were unable to meet further payments. Time-payment furniture firms owned warehouses that became crammed with tables and chairs and other items reclaimed from families without money. Whenever a marshal, sheriff or constable evicted a family from a house or apartment, the landlord would simply dump the furniture on the sidewalk. If the installment company failed to pick it up, each article would soon be carried away by needy neighbors.

What happened to people after they were dispossessed? Many doubled up with relatives—or even tripled up, until ten or twelve people were crammed into three or four rooms. Human beings are like porcupines: they like to huddle close enough to feel one another's warmth, but they dislike getting so close that the quills begin pricking. Now, in teeming proximity to one another, the quills pricked, and relatives quarreled bitterly.

*   *   *

The Depression strained the family structure and sometimes shattered it. Well-integrated families closed ranks in the face of this common danger and became ever more monolithic. Loosely knit families, on the other hand, fell apart when the pressures on them became too great.

After a man lost his job, he would trudge from factory to factory, office to office, seeking other employment, but after weeks of repeated rejections he would lose heart, mutely denounce himself as a poor provider, shed his self-respect and stay at home. Here he found himself unwelcome and underfoot, the target of puzzled glances from his children and hostile looks from his wife. In the early part of the Depression some women simply could not understand that jobs were unavailable; instead, they felt there was something wrong with their men. In Philadelphia one unemployed man begged a social worker: "Have you anybody you can send around to tell my wife you have no job to give me? She thinks I don't want to work."

The idle man found himself a displaced person in the household, which is woman's domain, and in nameless guilt he crept about uneasily, always finding himself in the way. He got on his wife's nerves and she on his, until tension broke in endless wrangles. If the man tried to help by washing dishes and making beds, he lost status in the eyes of the rest of the family.

The Depression castrated some men by dethroning them from their position as the breadwinner and the head of the family. Ashamed, confused and resentful, they became sexually impotent. In Western culture a man tends to think of himself in terms of the work he does, this self-identity being what Jung calls his persona. Man does. Woman is. To rob a man of his work was to rob him of his idea of himself, leaving him empty and without much reason for living. The displacement of the man as the head of the family and the way some women moved in to fill this vacuum were described sensitively by John Steinbeck in his novel *The Grapes of Wrath*. This great book tells the story of the flight of the Joad family from the dust bowl of Oklahoma to the green valleys of California:

> "We got nothin', now," Pa said. "Comin' a long time—no work, no crops. What we gonna do then? How we gonna git stuff to eat? . . . Git so I hate to think. Go diggin' back to a ol' time to keep from thinkin'. Seems like our life's over an' done."
>
> "No, it ain't," Ma smiled. "It ain't, Pa. An' that's one more thing a woman knows. I noticed that. Man, he lives in jerks—baby born an' a man dies, an' that's a jerk—gets a farm an' loses his farm, an' that's a jerk. Woman, it's all one flow, like a stream, little eddies, little waterfalls, but the river, it goes right on. Woman looks at it like that. We ain't gonna die out. People is goin' on—changin' a little maybe, but goin' right on."

Some adolescent girls felt their fathers' agony and tried to comfort them with lavish expressions of love, much to the embarrassment of the man and the uneasiness of his wife. This did emotional damage to father, mother and the young girl, whose fixation on her father retarded her normal interest in boys her own age.

Strife between parents, together with the realization that it cost money to marry and have babies, resulted in a decision by many young people to postpone their weddings. One young man joined the Communist Party and swore he never would marry or have children under "the present system." Unable to repress their human needs, however, young men and women made love secretly and guiltily, regarding pregnancy as a disaster. Despite an increase in the sale of contraceptives, the abortion rate rose, and so did venereal disease. The birthrate dropped.

It has been estimated that the Depression postponed 800,000 marriages that would have occurred sooner if it had not been for hard times. Margaret Mead, the noted anthropologist, argued that there was nothing wrong about letting girls support their lovers so they could marry sooner. Surprisingly, there even was a decline in marriages among members of the *Social Register*. Liberals and feminists pointed out that half of all births were in families on relief or with incomes of less than $1,000 a year; they strongly advocated birth control. Who could afford babies when a sixty-one-piece layette cost all of $7.70? Gasps of horror arose when it was reported in Illinois that a sixteenth child had been born to a family on relief.

Housewives suffered as acutely as their husbands. Many had to send their kids to live with relatives or friends. Others took part-time jobs, while a few wives actually became temporary whores to earn enough money to keep the family going. Lacking money for streetcars and buses, without the means to buy clothes to keep them looking attractive, they remained cooped up in their homes until their nerves screamed and they had nervous breakdowns.

All too often their men simply deserted them. A California woman said: "My husband went north about three months ago to try his luck. The first month he wrote pretty regularly. . . . For five weeks we have had no word from him. . . . Don't know where he is or what he is up to."

A young man who lived in the French Quarter of New Orleans was solicited by five prostitutes during a ten-block stroll, each woman asking only 50 cents. In Houston a relief worker, curious about how the people were getting along, was approached by one girl after another. For the benefit of an insistent streetwalker, the man turned his pockets inside out to prove that he had no money. Looking at him ruefully, she said: "It doesn't cost much—only a dime!"

The close relationship between poverty and morals shocked Franklin D. Roosevelt, who told reporters about an investigator who went to southeastern Kentucky: "She got into one of those mining towns," Roosevelt said, "and started to walk up the alley. There was a group of miners sitting in front of the shacks, and they pulled down their caps over their faces. As soon as she caught sight of that she walked up and said, 'What are you pulling your caps down for?' They said, 'Oh, it is all right.' 'Why pull your caps down?' They said, 'It is sort of a custom because so many of the women have not got enough clothes to cover them.' "

*   *   *

The Depression made changes in the country's physical appearance.

Fewer pedestrians were to be seen on the streets since many men did not go to work and women shopped less frequently; for lack of warm clothing and fuel, many people stayed in bed most of the day during winter. The air became cleaner over industrial cities, for there was less smoke from factory chimneys. The downtown business districts of most cities had long rows of empty shops and offices. Trains were shorter, and only rarely did one see a Pullman car. However, gas stations multiplied because millions of Americans drove their battered family cars here and there in endless quest of work. In conflicting attempts to solve their problems, farmers moved into town while city folks moved into the country to build their own houses and grow their own food. More and more blacks were seen in northern cities as desperate Negroes fled from the hopeless South. Telephones were taken out of homes, and mail deliveries were lighter. Houses and stores, parks and fences sagged and lapsed into unpainted, flaked ugliness for want of money to make repairs.

In his novel called *You Can't Go Home Again,* Thomas Wolfe described a comfort station in front of New York City Hall:

> . . . One descended to this place down a steep flight of stairs from the street, and on bitter nights he would find the place crowded with homeless men who had sought refuge there. Some were those shambling hulks that one sees everywhere, in Paris as well as in New York. . . . But most of them were just flotsam of the general ruin of the time—honest, decent, middle-aged men with faces seamed by toil and want, and young men, many of them mere boys in their teens, with thick, unkempt hair. These were the wanderers from town to town, the riders of freight trains, the thumbers of rides on highways, the uprooted, unwanted male population of America. They drifted across the land and gathered in the big cities when winter came, hungry, defeated, empty, hopeless, restless, driven by they knew not what, always on the move, looking everywhere for work, for the bare crumbs to support their miserable lives, and finding neither work nor crumbs. Here in New York, to this obscene meeting place, these derelicts came, drawn into a common stew of rest and warmth and a little surcease from their desperation.

Heywood Broun devoted a column to a description of a slum in San Antonio, Texas:

> . . . The Church of Guadalupe stands upon the fringe of what had been described to me as the most fearsome slum in all America. It covers four

square miles. At first I thought that the extreme description might have been dictated by local pride. It was my notion to protest and say, "Why, we in New York City know worse than that." But after we had gone up the third back alley I had to confess defeat gracefully.

You can see shacks as bad as these in several States, but I do not know of any place where they have been so ingeniously huddled together. This is flat, sprawling country, and there is much of it, and so it seems devilish that one crazy combination of old lumber and stray tin should be set as a flap upon the side of another equally discreditable. I did not quite comprehend the character of the alley until I discovered that what I took to be a toolhouse was a residence for a family of eleven people.

And these are not squatter dwellings. People pay rent for them, just as if a few rickety boards and a leaky roof constituted a house. They even have evictions and go through the solemn and obscene farce of removing a bed and a frying pan as indication that the landlord's two-dollars-and-a-half rent has not been forthcoming. . . .

Back at the Church of Guadalupe, the priest said, "I have other letters from those who fight federal housing because they like their rents." He tossed over an anonymous message, which read, "I could start a story that there is a priest who writes love letters to young girls and gives jewels to women of his congregation."

"Doesn't this worry you?" one of us asked.

"No," said the priest. "Last month we buried thirty-nine persons, mostly children, from this little church alone.

"I am worried," he said, "about people starving to death."

Louis Adamic and his wife were living with her mother in New York City in January, 1932. Born in Yugoslavia, now a naturalized American, he was a writer, a tall young man with a look of eager curiosity in his eyes. One cold morning at seven forty-five the doorbell rang, and Adamic, thinking it was the postman, opened the front door. In his book called *My America*, he told what happened next.

There stood a girl of ten and a boy of eight. They had schoolbooks in their arms, and their clothing was patched and clean, but hardly warm enough for winter weather. In a voice strangely old for her age, the girl said: "Excuse me, mister, but we have no eats in our house and my mother she said I should take my brother before we go to school and ring a doorbell in some house"—she swallowed heavily and took a deep breath—"and ask you to give us . . . something . . . to eat."

"Come in," Adamic said. A strange sensation swept over him. He had heard that kids were ringing doorbells and asking for food in the Bronx, in Harlem and in Brooklyn, but he had not really believed it.

His wife and her mother gave the children some food. The girl ate slowly. Her brother bolted his portion, quickly and greedily.

"He ate a banana yesterday afternoon," said his sister, "but it wasn't ripe enough or somethin', and it made him sick and he didn't eat anything since. He's always like this when he's hungry and we gotta ring doorbells."

"Do you often ring doorbells?"

"When we have no eats at home."

"What made you ring our bell?"

"I don't know," the girl answered. "I just did."

Her name was Mary, and her brother's name was Jimmie. They lived in a poor neighborhood five blocks away.

Mary said: "We used to live on the fourth floor upstairs and we had three rooms and a kitchen and bath, but now we have only one room downstairs. In back."

"Why did you move downstairs?"

The boy winced.

"My father," said the girl. "He lost his job when the panic came. That was two years ago. I was eight and Jimmie was six. My father he tried to get work, but he couldn't, the depression was so bad. But he called it the panic."

Adamic and the two women were astonished at her vocabulary: "panic" . . . "depression."

"What kind of work did your father do?"

"Painter and paperhanger. Before things got so bad, he always had jobs when his work was in season, and he was good to us—my mother says so, too. Then, after he couldn't get any more jobs, he got mean and he yelled at my mother. He couldn't sleep nights and he walked up and down and talked, and sometimes he hollered and we couldn't sleep, either."

"Was he a union man?"

"No, he didn't belong to no union."

"What did your father holler about?"

"He called my mother bad names."

At this point in the conversation, Adamic wrote, the little girl hesitated, and her brother winced again. Then she continued: "Uh . . . he was angry because my mother, before she married him, she was in love with another man and almost married him. But my mother says it wasn't my father's fault he acted mean like he did. He was mean because he had no job and we had no money."

"Where's your father now?"

"We don't know. He went away four months ago, right after Labor Day, and he never came back, so we had to move downstairs. The landlord didn't want to throw us out, so he told my mother to move in downstairs."

Between sips of milk the girl said her mother did household work whenever she could find a job, but earned very little money this way. A charity organization had been giving her $2.85 a week, but lately it had stopped. Mary did not know why. Her mother had applied for home relief, but had not yet received anything from that source.

The boy stopped eating, turned to his sister and muttered: "You talk too much! I told you not to talk!"

The girl fell silent.

Adamic said: "It's really our fault, Jimmie. We're asking too many questions."

The little boy glared and said: "Yeah!"

* * *

In Detroit someone gave another little girl a nickel, which seemed like such a fortune to her that she agonized three full days about how best to spend it.

In Erie, Pennsylvania, a seven-year-old boy named Tom received a tiny yellow chick as an Easter present. Using some old chicken wire, he built a coop for his pet beneath the back step to the house and fed and tended it carefully. His father was an unemployed molder, and the family often ate nothing but beans. Time passed. Now the little chick had grown into a full-sized chicken. One day Tom's father announced that the boy's pet would have to be killed and served for Sunday dinner, since everyone was hungry. Tom screamed in horrified protest but was unable to prevent his father from taking his chicken into the backyard and chopping off its head. Later that day the family sat around the table feasting on fowl, while the boy hunched in his chair, sobbing.

There was another boy who never forgot a scene from his childhood days during the Depression. He lived in a small town in Iowa. Every so often a train would stop there for a few minutes, and a man would get out carrying bags of buttons. He would distribute these buttons to waiting farmers and their wives, collect the cards to which they had sewn other buttons, pay them a meager sum for their labor, get back into the train and depart. This trivial piecework provided them with the only income they could get.

* * *

President Hoover was foolish enough to let himself be photographed on the White House lawn feeding his dog. This picture did not sit well with Americans who were hungry, suffering from malnutrition or even starving to death. Several times Hoover denied that there was widespread under nourishment in the nation, but he depended on unreliable statistics. Comedian Groucho Marx, who was closer to the people, said he knew things were bad when "the pigeons started feeding the people in Central Park." However, it was no laughing matter.

In Oklahoma City a newspaper reporter was assigned to cover state relief headquarters. Walking into the building one morning, he ran into a young man he had met through his landlady. This fellow offered the reporter some candy. The reporter did not want the candy but accepted it lest he hurt the other's feelings. As they stood and chewed, a social worker approached them.

"We don't allow any eating in here," she said.

The reporter, who thought she was jesting, made a wisecrack.

"We don't allow any eating in here," she repeated sternly. "Some of these applicants haven't had any breakfast. We make it a rule among ourselves never to eat or to drink Cokes in front of them."

Ashamed of himself, the reporter mumbled an apology and slunk behind a beaver-board wall. He wanted to throw away the morsel of candy remaining in his hand but felt that this would be even more sinful with hungry people so near.

Arthur Brisbane, the rich columnist and editor, walked into a Manhattan restaurant and ordered two lamb chops. When he had finished the first one, he looked longingly at the second but was too full to eat it, too. After much thought he summoned a waiter.

"What happens if I don't eat this chop?" Brisbane asked. "Will you take it back?"

"No, sir. We can't do that, sir."

"But what will you do with it? Will it be thrown away?"

"Not at all, sir. We give the leftovers to poor people."

Brisbane sighed in relief, nodded approvingly, paid his check and left.

In 1933 the Children's Bureau reported that one out of every five children in the nation was not getting enough of the right things to eat. A teacher in a coal-mining town asked a little girl in her classroom whether she was ill. The child said: "No. I'm all right. I'm just hungry." The teacher urged her to go home and eat something. The girl said: "I can't. This is my sister's day to eat." In the House of Representatives, during a debate about appropriations for Indians living on reservations, a Congressman said that eleven cents a day was enough to feed an Indian child. A Senate subcommittee learned that the president of a textile firm had told his workers they should be able to live on six cents a day.

AFL President William Green said: "I warn the people who are exploiting the workers that they can only drive them so far before they will turn on them and destroy them. They are taking no account of the history of nations in which governments have been overturned. Revolutions grow out of the depths of hunger."

Sidney Hillman, president of the Amalgamated Clothing Workers of America, appeared at a Senate hearing in 1932 and was told that it was not yet time to give federal relief. Angrily, he cried: "I would ask by what standards are we to gauge that time! Must we have hundreds of thousands of people actually dead and dying from starvation? Must we have bread riots? What is necessary to convince them that there is a need for federal and speedy relief?"

The Communists took up the slogan: "Starve or fight!"

At the University of Pennsylvania a prim audience was shocked to hear Daniel Willard, president of the B & O Railroad, say: "While I do not like to say so, I would be less than candid if I did not say that in such circumstances I would steal before I would starve."

Obviously, less fortunate Americans agreed. Petty thievery soared.

Children hung around grocery stores begging for food. Customers emerging from groceries had bundles snatched from their arms by hungry kids, who ran home with the food or ducked into alleys to gobble it as fast as they could. Small retail stores had their windows smashed and their display goods stolen. Grown men, in groups of two and three, walked into chain store markets, ordered all the food they could carry and then quietly walked out without paying for it. Chain store managers did not always report these incidents to the police for fear that publicity would encourage this sort of intimidation. For the same reason the newspapers engaged in a tacit conspiracy of silence.

However, newspapers did not mind reporting that in Manhattan a debutante supper for 600 guests at the Ritz-Carlton cost $4,750. On nearby Park Avenue, beggars were so numerous that a well-dressed man might be asked for money four or five times in a ten-block stroll. President Hoover not only denied that anyone was starving, but said: "The hoboes, for example, are better fed than they ever have been. One hobo in New York got ten meals in one day."

People of means thought up ways to protect themselves from panhandlers and from begging letters. Boston's mayor, James M. Curley, had a male secretary named Stan Wilcox, who was adept at brushing off approaches. Whenever a beggar asked if he had a quarter, Wilcox would reply: "Heavens, no! I wouldn't dream of taking a drink at this hour!" Alfred E. Smith received the following letter from Milwaukee: "This is unusual, but I am in need. Would you send me $2,500, as this is the amount I am in need of. I will give you as collateral my word of honor that I will repay you if possible. If not, let the good Lord repay you and he will also pay better interest."

Governor Gifford Pinchot of Pennsylvania flatly declared that starvation was widespread. Among the many pathetic letters he received was this one: "There are nine of us in the family. My father is out of work for a couple of months and we haven't got a thing eat [sic] in the house. Mother is getting $12 a month of the county. If mother don't get more help we will have to starve to death. I am a little girl 10 years old. I go to school every day. My other sister hain't got any shoes or clothes to wear to go to school. My mother goes in her bare feet and she crys every night that we don't have the help. I guess that is all, hoping to hear from you."

Bernard Baruch, who felt burdened by the thought of his wealth, got a desperate letter from his cousin, Fay Allen Des Portes, who lived in his home state of South Carolina. "The horrible part of the whole situation," she wrote to him, "is these poor starving people here in our midst. The banks can't let anyone have money, the merchants are all broke; the farmers can't let the poor Negroes on the farm have anything to eat. I don't know what is going to happen. I have about four hundred Negroes that are as absolutely dependent upon me as my two little boys, but I can't help them any more and God knows what is going to happen to them."

John L. Lewis, president of the United Mine Workers, once said to a group of mine operators: "Gentlemen, I speak to you for my people. I speak to you for the miners' families in the broad Ohio valley, the Pennsylvania mountains and the black West Virginia hills. There, the shanties lean over as if intoxicated by the smoke fumes of the mine dumps. But the more pretentious ones boast a porch, with the banisters broken here and there, presenting the aspect of a snaggle-toothed child. Some of the windows are wide open to flies, which can feast nearby on garbage and answer the family dinner call in double-quick time. But there is no dinner call. The little children are gathered around a bare table without anything to eat. Their mothers are saying, 'We want bread.' "

A writer named Jonathan Norton Leonard described the plight of Pennsylvania miners who had been put out of company villages after losing a strike: "Reporters from the more liberal metropolitan papers found thousands of them huddled on the mountainsides, crowded three or four families together in one-room shacks, living on dandelion and wild weed-roots. Half of them were sick, but no local doctor would care for the evicted strikers. All of them were hungry and many were dying of those providential diseases which enable welfare workers to claim that no one has starved."

In 1931 four New York City hospitals reported 95 deaths from starvation. Two years later the New York City Welfare Council said that 29 persons had died from starvation, more than 50 others had been treated for starvation, while an additional 110 individuals—most of them children—had perished of malnutrition. In one routine report the council gave this picture of the plight of one family in the Brownsville section of Brooklyn: "Family reported starving by neighbors. Investigator found five small children at home while mother was out looking for vegetables under pushcarts. Family had moved into one room. Father sleeping at Municipal Lodging House because he could get more to eat there than at home and frequently brought food home from there in pockets for children and wife. Only other food they had for weeks came from pushcarts."

A family of fourteen was on relief in Kewanee, Illinois, the hog-raising center of the Midwest. The family was given $3 worth of groceries a week, and of course this food soon ran out. After giving the last crumbs to the children, the adults would exist on nothing but hot water until they received their next grocery allotment.

In Chicago a committee investigated city garbage dumps and then reported: "Around the truck which was unloading garbage and other refuse were about 35 men, women and children. As soon as the truck pulled away from the pile all of them started digging with sticks, some with their hands, grabbing bits of food and vegetables."

Edmund Wilson described another Chicago scene: "A private incinerator at Thirty-fifth and La Salle Streets which disposes of garbage from restaurants and hotels, has been regularly visited by people, in groups of as many as twenty at a time, who pounce upon anything that looks edible before it is thrown into the furnace. The women complained to investigators that the men took unfair advantage by jumping on the truck before it was unloaded; but a code was eventually established which provided that different sets of people should come at different times every day, so that everybody would be given a chance."

A ballad called "Starvation Blues" was sung by some of the poor people of America during the Depression.

Prentice Murphy, director of the Children's Bureau of Philadelphia, told a Senate committee: "If the modern state is to rest upon a firm foundation, its citizens must not be allowed to starve. Some of them do. They do not die quickly. You can starve for a long time without dying."

Scientists agree that a person can starve a long time without dying, but this is what it is like to starve to death: After a few days without food the stomach cramps and bloats up. Later it shrinks in size. At first a starving child will cry and eat anything to ease hunger pains—stuffing his mouth with rags, clay, chalk, straw, twigs, berries and even poisonous weeds. Then, as the child weakens, his cries change to whimpers. He feels nauseated. All the fat is being burned from his body. This burning produces acidosis. The fruity odor of acetone can be smelled on the breath, and it also appears in the urine. When starvation reaches this point, nature becomes kinder. The child grows listless and sleepy. The bulging eyes are sad and dull. Now body proteins have been depleted, while the water and electrolyte balance has been destroyed. Degeneration of the vital organs, such as the liver and kidneys, proceeds in earnest. By this time the child lacks all resistance to diseases and may be killed by some infection.

*   *   *

John Steinbeck has told how he survived the early part of the Depression before he became a famous author. "I had two assets," he wrote. "My father owned a tiny three-room cottage in Pacific Grove in California, and he let me live in it without rent. That was the first safety. Pacific Grove is on the ocean. That was the second. People in inland cities or in the closed and shuttered industrial cemeteries had greater problems than I. Given the sea, a man must be very stupid to starve. That great reservoir is always available. I took a large part of my protein food from the ocean.

"Firewood to keep warm floated on the beach daily, needing only handsaw and ax. A small garden of black soil came with the cottage. In northern California you can raise vegetables of some kind all year long. I never peeled a potato without planting the skins. Kale, lettuce, chard, turnips, carrots and onions rotated in the little garden. In the tide pools of the bay, mussels were available and crabs and abalones and that shiny kelp called sea lettuce. With a line and pole, blue cod, rock cod, perch, sea trout, sculpin could be caught."

The sale of flower seeds shot up as Americans, tired of the ugliness of their lives, turned to the beauty of homegrown flowers. As might have been expected, there was widespread cultivation of vegetable gardens. Many did this on their own, while others received official encouragement. Big railroads rented garden plots for their workers. The United States Steel Corporation used social workers and faculty members of Indiana University to develop an extensive garden project for its workers in Gary, Indiana. In New York State, in the summer of 1933, jobless men and women were tending 65,000 gardens. The city of Detroit provided tools and seed for "thrift gardens" on empty lots, an idea which Mayor Frank Murphy said he had borrowed from Hazen S. Pingree. During the Panic of 1893 Pingree had been the mayor of Detroit, and confronted with a city of jobless men, he provided them with gardens to cultivate—"Pingree's Potato Patches" receiving national attention.

Now, in the present emergency, Henry Ford ordered all his workmen to dig in vegetable gardens or be fired. Out of his imperious command there developed what the Scripps-Howard Washington *News* called 50,000 "shotgun gardens." Rough-grained Harry Bennett, chief of Ford's private police, supervised this vast project and kept a filing system on all Ford employees. If a man had no garden in his own backyard or on some neighborhood lot, he was assigned a patch of earth somewhere on Ford's 4,000 acres of farmland around Dearborn, Michigan. Each workman had to pay fifty cents to have his strip plowed.

More than one-third of the men employed in Ford's Dearborn plant lived 10 to 20 miles away, and some protested that since they did not own a car they would have to spend an extra two hours daily just traveling to and from their allotted patches. A Bennett henchman would snarl: "Why don't-cha buy a car? You're makin' 'em, ain't-cha?" Bone-weary workmen who simply couldn't muster the energy to toil on their garden plots soon were brought into line by Bennett's personal deputy, Norman Selby, the former boxer "Kid McCoy."

*   *   *

In the spring of 1932 the Community Council of Philadelphia ran out of private funds for the relief of needy families. Eleven days elapsed before this relief work could be resumed with public funds, and many families received no help during this interim. A study was made to find out what had happened when food orders stopped.

One woman borrowed 50 cents from a friend and bought stale bread at 3½ cents per loaf. Except for one or two meals, this was all she could serve her family throughout those eleven days.

A pregnant mother and her three children could afford only two meals a day. At eleven o'clock in the morning she would serve breakfast, which consisted of cocoa, bread and butter. This left everyone so hungry that the mother began advancing the time of their evening meal, which was just one can of soup.

Another woman scoured the docks, picking up vegetables that fell from produce wagons. Fish vendors sometimes gave her a fish at the end of the day. On two separate occasions her family went without food for a day and a half.

On the day the food orders stopped, one family ate nothing all day. At nine o'clock that night the mother went to a friend's house and begged for a loaf of bread. Later she got two days' work at 75 cents a day. With this pittance she bought a little meat. Then, adding vegetables picked up off the street, she made a stew which she cooked over and over again each day to prevent spoilage.

One family ate nothing but potatoes, rice, bread and coffee, and for one and a half days they were totally without food.

*   *   *

Hunting jackrabbits to feed the family became a way of life among farmers and ranchers. This gave birth to a Depression joke reported by John Steinbeck in *The Grapes of Wrath*. One man said to another: "Depression is over. I seen a jackrabbit, an' they wasn't nobody after him." The second man said: "That ain't the reason. Can't afford to kill jackrabbits no more. Catch'em and milk'em and turn'em loose. One you seen prob'ly gone dry."

Audie Murphy was born on a Texas farm five years before the Crash, the son of very poor parents. Almost as soon as he could walk, he began hunting game for the family. Since shells were expensive, every shot had to count. Aware of this, Audie Murphy developed into an expert marksman— so expert that when he was a GI during World War II, he killed 240 Nazis and emerged as the most decorated American soldier of the war.

Wheat growers, bankrupted by drought, talked about heading for Alaska to kill moose to fill their growling bellies. In the timberlands of the great Northwest some desperate men set forest fires so that they would be hired to extinguish them, while in big cities other men prayed for heavy snowfalls to provide them with shoveling jobs. When some Pittsburgh steel mills reopened briefly, the steelworkers called back to their jobs were too weak from hunger to be able to work.

At the age of eleven Cesar Chavez, who later won renown as a Mexican-American labor leader, fished and cut mustard greens to help keep his family from starving.

Charles H. Percy, who wound up a multimillionaire and a United States Senator, never forgot what it was like to be a poor boy in Chicago during the Depression: "I remember a great feeling of shame when the welfare truck pulled up to our house. And you talk about cheating! Once they delivered us 100 pounds of sugar by mistake. My father wanted to return it, but my mother said, 'God willed us to have it,' and she wouldn't give it up." She swapped some of the sugar for flour and helped tide the family over by baking cookies that little Chuck Percy peddled door to door.

Americans under the stress of the Depression behaved with a dignity that varied in terms of their religious backgrounds, their mental images of themselves and their rigidity or flexibility. Brittle people snapped, while the pliant bent and survived.

In Georgia a blind Negro refused all relief, harnessed himself to a plow like a mule and tilled the fields, day after day. In Pittsburgh a father with starving children stole a loaf of bread from a neighbor, was caught, hanged himself in shame. In Youngstown, Ohio, a father, mother and their four sons preferred to starve rather than accept charity. Before they died, their condition was discovered by a neighbor who happened to be a newspaper reporter. They were existing on fried flour and water.

Charles Wayne also lived in Youngstown. He had been a hot mill worker for the Republic Iron and Steel Company until he was laid off. For the next two years he was unable to get any kind of work. Now a fifty-seven-year-old man, workless, hopeless, unable to feed his wife and ten children, he climbed onto a bridge one morning. He took off his coat, folded it neatly, then jumped into the swirling Mahoning River below. Instinct caused him to swim a few strokes, but then he gave up and let himself drown. Later his wife sobbed to reporters: "We were about to lose our home and the gas and electric companies had threatened to shut off the service."

An elderly man receiving $15-a-week relief money for his large family went out each day, without being asked, to sweep the streets of his village. "I want to do something," he said, "in return for what I get." A graduate of the Harvard Law School, now old and almost deaf, gladly took a $15-a-week job as assistant caretaker at a small park.

Rather than accept charity, a New York dentist and his wife killed themselves with gas. He left this note: "The entire blame for this tragedy rests with the City of New York or whoever it is that allows free dental work in the hospital. We want to get out of the way before we are forced to accept relief money. The City of New York is not to touch our bodies. We have a horror of charity burial. We have put the last of our money in the hands of a friend who will turn it over to my brother."

John Steinbeck wrote: "Only illness frightened us. You have to have money to be sick—or did then. And dentistry also was out of the question, with the result that my teeth went badly to pieces. Without dough you couldn't have a tooth filled."

Shoes were a problem. Upon reaching home, poor people took off their shoes to save wear and tear. Middle-class people bought do-it-yourself shoe-repair kits. Those unable to afford the kits would resole their shoes with strips of rubber cut from old tires. Some wore ordinary rubbers over shoes with holes in their bottoms. A miner's son, Jack Conroy, told what a hole in a shoe could mean to a man walking the streets looking for work: "Maybe it starts with a little hole in the sole; and then the slush of the pavements oozes in, gumming sox and balling between your toes. Concrete whets Woolworth sox like a file, and if you turn the heel on top and tear a pasteboard inner sole, it won't help much. There are the tacks, too. You get to avoiding high places and curbstones because that jabs the point right into the heel. Soon the tack has calloused a furrowed hole, and you don't notice it unless you strike something unusually high or solid, or forget and walk flat-footed. You pass a thousand shoe-shops where a tack might be bent down, but you can't pull off a shoe and ask to have *that* done—for nothing."

Keeping clean was also a problem, since soap cost money. Steinbeck washed his linen with soap made from pork fat, wood ashes and salt, but it took a lot of sunning to get the smell out of sheets. As the sale of soap declined across the nation, its production was reduced. Procter & Gamble did not lay off its workers, as it might have done under the circumstances, but put them to work cutting grass, painting fences and repairing factories until soap production began to rise again.

Steinbeck wrote a short story called "Daughter" about a sharecropper who shot and killed his own daughter because he had no food to give her. This could not be shrugged off as mere fiction, for in Carlisle, Pennsylvania, a starving man named Elmo Noakes actually suffocated his three small daughters rather than see them starve.

*   *   *

The Depression scarred many young men and women who later became celebrities or who already were well known. Jack Dempsey, former heavyweight boxing champion of the world, became so strapped for money that at the age of thirty-six he got himself sufficiently back into shape to fight fifty-six exhibition bouts. Babe Ruth, always a big spender, tried to supplement his income by opening a haberdashery on Broadway but lost his own shirt after five months.

Clifford Odets wrote his first play while living on ten cents a day. Lillian Hellman, who later became a renowned playwright, earned $50 a week as a script reader for Metro-Goldwyn-Mayer. William Inge, who also won fame as a playwright, acted in tent shows during the Depression, long afterward recalling: "We actors considered ourselves fortunate if we earned five dollars a week. Sometimes the farmers of Kansas would bring in flour and meat as barter for admission to Saturday matinees."

Songwriter Frank Loesser learned from his parents that they had lost all their money. He took any job he could get, including screwing the tops on bottles of an insecticide. He also worked as a spotter for a chain of restaurants, getting seventy-five cents a day plus the cost of each meal for reporting on the food and service. Later he reminisced: "I used to eat twelve times a day. When you're poor, you're always hungry from walking around so much."

Danny Thomas performed in saloons, but finally even this kind of work came to an end. The chance of getting another job seemed so slim that he considered giving up show business. In desperation, he prayed to St. Jude, the patron saint of the hopeless, and the next day he landed a job in Chicago that proved to be the turning point of his career.

Ralph Bellamy almost starved to death in the basement of a Greenwich Village apartment. Cary Grant was working in Hollywood as an extra. Dana Andrews worked four years as a gas station attendant in Van Nuys, California. Robert Young was employed as a soda jerk, grease monkey and truck driver. Ray Milland, living on credit in Hollywood, was about to go to work in a garage when he landed a part in a movie called *Bolero*. In Chireno, Texas, a twelve-year-old girl named Lucille Ann Collier began dancing professionally to help the family finances; later she grew into a long-legged beauty and won fame under the name of Ann Miller. In the Bronx a four-year-old girl named Anna Maria Italiano sang for WPA men working on a nearby project; today she is known as Anne Bancroft.

Victor Mature set out for Hollywood in 1935 at the age of seventeen, with $40 in cash and a car loaded with candy and chewing gum. He drove for five days and slept in his automobile each night, and by the time he reached the film capital he was almost broke. To his father in Louisville he wired: ARRIVED HERE WITH 11 CENTS. His father, an Austrian scissors grinder who had taken up refrigerator selling, wired back: FORTY-THREE YEARS AGO I ARRIVED IN NEW YORK WITH FIVE CENTS. I COULD NOT EVEN SPEAK ENGLISH. YOU ARE SIX CENTS UP ON ME.

The effect of the Depression on Hollywood extras was told by Grover Jones to an amused courtroom in a trial concerning Metro-Goldwyn-Mayer. Jones, once an extra and then a scriptwriter, gave this entertaining testimony: "They wanted eighty Indians, and I got the job only because I knew how to put on what they called bolamania—burnt umber and raw umber mixed. But they made me a chief. That meant I didn't have to go naked. I could wear a suit, you see. And at that time I was convinced I was fairly smart. So there were now eighty-one Indians. I had never seen a camera during all those months, because I was always in the background, waiting over in back of the hill for the call to come over the hill on the horses to rescue the child. And I had never been on horses. So we sat on these horses, each confiding in the other, and none of them had ever been on horses, except we were all hungry. Finally the man said, 'Now look, when you hear shooting I want you all to come over the hills, and I want some of you to fall off the horses.' Well, in those days they paid three dollars extra for a man who would fall off a horse, because it is quite a stunt. So we waited until finally we got the call to come over the hill, and somebody shot a gun off—and eighty-one Indians fell off their horses."

*   *   *

There was nothing surprising about the fact that men would risk injury or death by falling off a horse to earn an extra $3 a day. People felt that if they could just live through the Depression, they could endure anything else life had to offer. To *endure* was the main thing. Many took pay cuts without a murmur. A young man just out of college with a Bachelor of Journalism degree accepted a job on a newspaper at exactly *nothing* per week; a month later he was grateful to be put on the payroll at $15. Graduate engineers worked as office boys. College graduates of various kinds ran elevators in department stores. Unemployed architects turned out jigsaw puzzles. One jobless draftsman, Alfred Butts, used his spare time to invent the game of Scrabble.

Young men who might have grown into greatness chose, instead, to seek the security of civil service jobs, becoming policemen, firemen, garbage collectors. Fewer sailors deserted from the Navy. Enlistments rose in all branches of the nation's military establishment. When Congress voted a 10 percent pay cut for all federal employees, President Hoover secretly asked the Senate to make an exception for soldiers and sailors, because he did not wish to rely on disgruntled troops in case of internal trouble.

Women and children toiled for almost nothing in the sweatshops of New York City, welfare workers reporting these grim examples:

• A woman crocheted hats for 40 cents a dozen and was able to make only two dozen per week.

• An apron girl, paid 2½ cents per apron, earned 20 cents a day.

• A slipper liner was paid 21 cents for every seventy-two pairs of slippers she lined, and if she turned out one slipper every forty-five seconds she could earn $1.05 in a nine-hour day.

• A girl got half a cent for each pair of pants she threaded and sponged, making $2.78 a week.

Connecticut's state commissioner of labor said that some sweatshops in that state paid girls between 60 cents and $1.10 for a fifty-five-hour week. In Pennsylvania men working in sawmills were paid 5 cents an hour, men in tile and brick manufacturing got 6 cents per hour, while construction workers earned 7½ cents an hour. In Detroit the Briggs Manufacturing Company paid men 10 cents and women 4 cents an hour, causing auto workers to chant: "If poison doesn't work, try Briggs!" Also in Detroit, the Hudson Motor Car Company called back a small-parts assembler and then kept her waiting three days for a half hour of work, forcing her to spend 60 cents in carfare to earn 28 cents.

Two Maine fishermen put out to sea at four o'clock one morning and did not return to port until five o'clock that afternoon. During this long day of toil they caught 200 pounds of hake and 80 pounds of haddock. They burned up eight gallons of gas at 19 cents a gallon and used 100 pounds of bait costing two cents a pound. For their catch they were paid one cent a pound for the hake and four cents a pound for the haddock. Thus they earned less than two cents an hour for their day's work.

Meantime, Henry Ford was declaring: "Many families were not so badly off as they thought; they needed guidance in the management of their resources and opportunities." Ford needed no guidance. He managed to transfer 41½ percent of stock in the Ford Motor Company to his son, Edsel, without paying a cent in inheritance or estate taxes.

*   *   *

Ford, who liked to boast that he always had to work, declared in 1930 that "the very poor are recruited almost solely from the people who refuse to think and therefore refuse to work diligently." Roger W. Babson, the statistician, pontificated two years later: "Better business will come when the unemployed change their attitude toward life." Most rich men were quick to moralize.

The concept of hard work was central to capitalism and the Protestant ethic. Americans had been raised on a diet of aphorisms praising work and self-reliance. Benjamin Franklin said: "God helps them that help themselves." The Bible insisted: "In the sweat of thy face shalt thou eat bread." Thomas Carlyle said: "All work, even cotton-spinning, is noble; work alone is noble." Elizabeth Barrett Browning wrote: "Whoever fears God, fears to sit at ease." It was either Bishop Richard Cumberland or George Whitefield (no one is sure) who first said: "Better to wear out than to rust out." Most Americans agreed, but now in these Depression times men did sit at home and rust, through no fault of their own, losing the fine edge of their skills.

Idle, dispirited, hungry, defeated, withdrawn, brooding—people began to feel that somehow they were to blame for everything, that somehow, somewhere, they had failed. Maybe the Depression was punishment for their sins. After all, Protestant Episcopal Bishop John P. Tyler attributed it to the lack of religion. Perhaps Christians, if they wished to be good Christians, should bow to fate by accepting Christ's words that "to everyone that hath shall be given; and from him that hath not, even that which he hath shall be taken from him." But some found it difficult to find comfort in a sermon preached by the Reverend William S. Blackshear, an Episcopalian clergyman, in the bleak year of 1932. Blackshear said in part: "Christ was happy to be at the banquets of the rich. It was at such a place that the woman broke the vial of costly ointment and anointed His feet. There were those who cried out for the improvident and rebuked the woman, saying that this should have been converted into cash and given to the poor. It was then that Christ spoke on the economic plan, 'The poor ye have always with you.'"

This kind of sermon, representing conservative Protestantism, offended liberal clergymen. Forced by the Depression to rethink their values, they began searching for a new theology. Some began with the premise that if the church were to serve any purpose or perform realistically, it had to divorce itself from economic and political values. This developing viewpoint was expressed with crystal clarity by H. Richard Niebuhr, a pastor and a brother of Reinhold Niebuhr. He wrote:

> The church is in bondage to capitalism. Capitalism in its contemporary form is more than a system of ownership and distribution of economic goods. It is a faith and a way of life. It is faith in wealth as the source of all life's blessings and as the savior of man from his deepest misery. It is the doctrine that man's most important activity is the production of economic goods and that all other things are dependent upon this. On the basis of this initial idolatry it develops a morality in which economic worth becomes the standard by which to measure all other values and the economic virtues take precedence over courage, temperance, wisdom and justice, over charity, humility and fidelity. Hence nature, love, life, truth, beauty and justice are exploited or made the servants of the high economic good. Everything, including the lives of workers, is made a utility, is desecrated and ultimately destroyed. . . .

Other dissenters noted the supremacy of capitalism over every other value in the fact that church property was exempt from taxation. State constitutions and special statutes declared that no real estate taxes could be levied on church-owned properties, such as the church building itself, parochial schools, parsonages, the parish house and cemeteries. Why? A Missouri Supreme Court decision said that "no argument is necessary to show that church purposes are public purposes."

But was this really true? The United States of America was a Christian nation nominally, but not legally. No single religion, sect or church was recognized as the established church. Although the phrase "separation of church and state" does not appear in the Constitution of the United States or in that of any state but Utah, the idea for which it stands is found in the constitutional provisions against religious tests and in the words of the First Amendment: "Congress shall make no law respecting an establishment of religion. . . ."

During the Depression some liberal Christians, agnostics, atheists and others fretted about the special status given churches and church property. A few scholars recalled that President Ulysses S. Grant had said: "I would suggest the taxation of all property equally, whether church or corporation, exempting only the last resting place of the dead, and possibly, with proper restrictions, church edifices." Dissenters objected on principle to the exemption of church property, regarded this as an indirect subsidy by the state to religion and pointed out that personal taxes might be less if churches bore their share of the tax burden.

They got nowhere. At the core of capitalism was the belief that God looked with favor on the rich. This idea had been expressed as long ago as 1732 by one of J. P. Morgan's ancestors, the Reverend Joseph Morgan, who sermonized: "Each man coveting to make himself rich, carries on the Publick Good: Thus God in His Wisdom and Mercy turns our wickedness to Publick Benefit. . . . A rich Man is a great friend of the Publick, while he aims at nothing but serving himself. God will have us live by helping one another; and since Love will not do it, Covetousness shall."

* * *

J. P. Morgan himself flatly told a Senate committee: "If you destroy the leisure class you destroy civilization." When reporters pressed for a definition of the leisure class, Morgan said it included all who could afford a maid. In 1931, according to *Fortune* magazine, there still were 1,000,000 families with servants. One wealthy family announced that it had solved its Depression problem by discharging fifteen of its twenty servants—although the family members showed no curiosity or concern about the fate of the unemployed fifteen.

John Jacob Astor came of age in 1933 and thereupon inherited about $4 million. Nonetheless, he dabbled at a job in a downtown Manhattan brokerage house. Before long he quit with the explanation: "I didn't finish until five o'clock and by the time I got uptown it was six. And then I had to get up early the next morning." At a later date Astor was employed briefly by a shipping firm, and when he quit this second job, he commented: "I have discovered that work interferes with leisure." He was a representative of that leisure class which Morgan felt must be maintained to save civilization.

When Dwight Morrow was running for governor of New Jersey, he said: "There is something about too much prosperity that ruins the fiber of the people. The men and women that built this country, that founded it, were people that were reared in adversity." Morrow made this statement and died before Adolf Hitler declared: "It was poverty that made me strong." Joseph P. Kennedy, a busy member of the leisure class, felt that the rich had to make some sacrifices. Writing about the Depression, Kennedy said: "I am not ashamed to record that in those days I felt and said I would be willing to part with half of what I had if I could be sure of keeping, under law and order, the other half."

One member of the enormously wealthy Du Pont family seems to have been out of touch with reality. An advertising agency wanted his company to sponsor a Sunday afternoon radio program, but this Du Pont rejected the idea, saying: "At three o'clock on Sunday afternoons everybody is playing polo."

Everybody except the millions of Americans gobbling the last morsel of food from their plates in the fear that it might be their last meal—a habit that persisted in some people down through the next three decades. As Sinclair Lewis commented in his novel *It Can't Happen Here,* people were so confused, insecure and frustrated that they hardly could do anything more permanent than shaving or eating breakfast. They were tortured with feelings of inadequacy and guilt.

A young Alabama school teacher with eight years of tenure was fired after the Wall Street Crash. Eager to work, willing to take any job however low in the social scale, she became a maid in a private home. However, upon learning that she would be expected to work seven days a week, getting room and board but no wages, she quit. Then she took a job in a convalescent home which paid her room and board and $3 a week, but soon the home closed for lack of funds. The gentle schoolteacher completely lost faith in herself, confessing to a caseworker: "If, with all the advantages I've had, I can't make a living, then I'm just no good, I guess!"

Forty experienced secretaries found work after being unemployed a year, but the first few days on the job they were unable to take dictation from their bosses without weeping from sheer nervousness. After seeking employment for a long time, a man finally landed a job and became so overwrought with joy that he died of excitement. A corporation executive was given the nasty chore of firing several hundred men. A kind and compassionate person, he insisted on talking to each of them personally and asking what plans each had for the future. In a few months the executive's hair had turned gray.

*　　　*　　　*

The Depression began to erode freedom.

Some Americans, a little more secure than others, asked harsh questions. How about fingerprinting everyone on relief? Was it proper for a man on relief to own a car—even if he needed it to try to find work? Wasn't it wrong to sell liquor to the head of a family on relief? Did anyone owning a life insurance policy deserve relief? Should reliefers be allowed to vote? Did they deserve citizenship?

In New Orleans a federal judge denied citizenship to four qualified persons because they were on relief and therefore, in the judge's words, "unable financially to contribute to the support of the government." In California another judge withheld citizenship from Jacob Hullen; in response to the judge's questions Hullen had said he believed in municipal or federal ownership of public utilities.

In New York City, one cold and rainy day, the police arrested 38 men who had taken shelter in the Pennsylvania Railroad's ferry terminal on Cortlandt Street. All were marched to the nearest police station. Fifteen of them, able to prove that they had a few nickels and dimes in their pockets, were released. The other 23 men, who did not have a cent on them, were led before a magistrate, who sentenced them to jail for vagrancy. Newspaper stories about this obvious injustice raised such a hullabaloo, however, that the 23 prisoners soon were freed.

Robert Morss Lovett, a professor of English literature at the University of Chicago, wrote in his autobiography:

> An example of the injustice meted out to foreign-born workers involved a Yugoslav named Perkovitch. When conditions were at their worst in 1932–33 the unemployed on the West Side [of Chicago] were in the

habit of crossing the city to the South Side where food was sometimes available from bakeries, disposing of yesterday's bake, and where, at least, the garbage was more lavish.

One morning these itinerants were picked up by the police and held at the station house on the absurd pretext that a revolution was planned. Perkovitch told me that he and about one hundred others were kept in the basement all day without food. Once a lieutenant with a bodyguard of patrolmen raged through the room, striking and kicking the men in an ecstasy of sadism. At six the prisoners were released with no charges.

Paul D. Peacher, the town marshal of Jonesboro, Arkansas, arrested a group of Negro men without cause and forced them to work on his farm. A federal grand jury indicted him under Title 18 of the Anti-Slavery Act of 1866 for "causing Negroes to be held as slaves" on a cotton plantation. This was the first case ever tried under the slavery statute. A county grand jury absolved Peacher, but the federal Department of Justice would not drop the case. Now the marshal was forced to stand trial—this time before a *federal* jury. Taking the witness chair in his own behalf, he denied that he had done anything wrong. However, the jury disagreed with him and found him guilty. Peacher was sentenced to two years in prison and fined $3,500. He appealed, lost his appeal, paid the fine and accepted a two-year probationary sentence.

Someone asked Eugene Talmadge, the governor of Georgia, what he would do about the millions of unemployed Americans. Talmadge snarled: "Let'em starve!" It made him happy when the city fathers of Atlanta put unwanted nonresidents in chain gangs. When some textile workers went on strike in Georgia the governor had barbed-wire concentration camps built and threw pickets into them. Frank Hague, the mayor and ruthless boss of Jersey City, called for the erection in Alaska of a concentration camp for native "Reds."

Wise and temperate men worried about the growing loss of liberty in America, the land of the free and the home of the brave. George Boas, a professor of philosophy, sadly said: "It is taken for granted that democracy is bad and that it is dying." Will Durant, busy writing his many-volumed *Story of Civilization,* asked rhetorically: "Why is it that Democracy has fallen so rapidly from the high prestige which it had at the Armistice?"

17

March, 1933

O N MARCH 1, 1933, Franklin D. Roosevelt left his family estate at Hyde Park to travel to New York City and thence to Washington, D.C., to be sworn in as the thirty-second President of the United States. That day all the news was bad, for the nation was in the grip of a banking crisis.

With the worsening of business, there had been a flight from property into bank deposits, then a flight from bank deposits into currency, and finally a flight from currency into gold. Banks were failing all across the country. In large measure, their plight was due to the multiplication of state banks and the failure of state officials to supervise them properly. As we have seen, when Roosevelt was governor of New York, he had not done enough to strengthen the banks in his own state. The Reconstruction Finance Corporation, for its part, had been able to do little more than put a patch on the threadbare banking system. Watching the crash of one bank after another, depositors rushed to withdraw their savings.

In January, 1933, the money in this nation had consisted of $46 billion in bank deposits, $5.7 billion in currency and $4.5 billion in gold. Theoretically, every depositor had the right to turn his bank deposits into currency and his currency into gold, but practically it was impossible. Walter Lippmann pointed out in a column: "To have converted 46 billions into currency with each dollar backed by the 40 cents in gold specified by law would have required nearly twice as much gold as exists in the whole world. To have converted all the currency into pure gold would have required perhaps five times the amount of gold that mankind possesses."

Aware of this, dimly or sharply, depositors continued to make runs on banks. Nothing said or done by an anxious President Hoover or by frightened bankers could restore public confidence in banks—small or large. People chose to liquidate their wealth and hoard it, even at the risk of robbery, rather than risk losing everything if their particular bank should fail. Panic had begun about the middle of February, first in Detroit, and then had spread to other states. Now the crisis was reaching toward Wall Street, that bastion of capitalism.

The Depression was approaching its nadir. Every kind of index showed a decline in every kind of business. A Senate committee was told that 45,000,000 Americans were living in dire poverty. No one knew exactly how many people were unemployed, but the estimates ran from 12,000,000 to 17,000,000. More than 6,000,000 individuals were on state or municipal relief rolls. Uncertain of each tomorrow, let alone the future, worried people stocked their homes with cans of food and other necessities. Everyone was anxious and fearful, while many were angry.

Lippmann felt that the nation's citizens were "a congeries of disorderly panic-stricken mobs and factions." Herbert Hoover, now a lame-duck President because of his defeat at the hands of Roosevelt, was deploying troops near big cities, fearing the worst. Alfred M. Landon, the Republican governor of Kansas, openly confessed that he preferred "the iron hand of a national dictator" to total paralysis of the economy and social chaos. Over in Germany that nation's president, Paul von Hindenburg, had suspended all fundamental rights and placed the country in a state of siege. Soon he would be replaced by Adolf Hitler, who quickly forbade any criticism of himself.

Here in the United States the national income, which had been more than $80 billion in 1929, had halved. Industrial output, too, was only half what it had been. The Federal Reserve Board reported that a quarter billion dollars' worth of gold had poured out of the system in one week alone. Faith in the capitalistic system was so precarious that many Senators and Representatives—Charles Beard said perhaps a majority of them— wanted to abolish all stock exchanges and nationalize the banks.

The Reverend Charles E. Coughlin had just published an article entitled "The Suicide of Capitalism." The day Roosevelt left his estate Reinhold Niebuhr had come out with another article called "After Capitalism— What?" J. Frederick Essary, a Washington correspondent for the Baltimore *Sun*, described the crisis as "more ominous in all respects than any Washington news writer now living had ever dealt with." Henry Ford said: "Let the crash come. Everything will go down the chute, but I feel young. I can build up again."

Roosevelt, who usually radiated cheer, was understandably somber during his trip from Hyde Park to New York City. Newspapers on that March 1 reported that twelve more states had closed or constricted banks within their borders. One of the common sights of the day were neat typewritten notices on the doors of banks announcing that they had been closed by the governor of the state. The Cleveland Clearing House Association was planning to issue scrip—emergency "money."

Upon arriving in Manhattan, Roosevelt was driven to his town house at

49 East Sixty-fifth Street, where he went directly into conference with his advisers. Toward midnight, as was his habit, he went to bed and instantly fell asleep. As governor of New York he had had trouble getting to sleep only on nights when some criminal was about to be electrocuted in Sing Sing, but most of the time his temperament was so sunny, so free of guilt and anxiety, that he dropped off moments after his head touched the pillow.

The morning of March 2, Roosevelt awakened about eight-thirty, pulled an old sweater over his pajama top and breakfasted from a tray served him as he lay in bed. As he drank his fruit juice and coffee, ate his scrambled eggs and toast, he skimmed six or eight newspapers brought to his bedside. Then came a torrent of phone calls from around the nation, from governors and other high officials, pleading for help, offering suggestions. By now nearly half the forty-eight states were enacting or contemplating bank holidays. In addition to his work load and the even heavier burdens soon to fall on his broad shoulders, Roosevelt suffered a personal sorrow.

As attorney general in his Cabinet, Roosevelt had chosen seventy-three-year-old Thomas J. Walsh, Democratic Senator from Montana, a much-loved man of whom Roosevelt himself was very fond. Six days earlier Walsh had married Señora Mina Perez Chaumont in Havana, Cuba. One of the telephone calls that Roosevelt took informed him that Walsh had died of a heart attack on a train en route to the national capital that very morning. The bride had found her elderly husband dying on the floor of their stateroom as their train approached Wilson, North Carolina.

New York City was cold on that March 2, so after donning a business suit with the aid of a valet, Roosevelt put on a warm dark overcoat and a gray hat. Then he was helped into a limousine which glided behind screaming police sirens to a ferry landing in lower Manhattan, boarded a ferryboat to cross the iron-gray waters of the Hudson River. Upon reaching the New Jersey side of the river, he was assisted onto a special Baltimore & Ohio train waiting to carry him and his party to Washington. By this time it was late afternoon.

Under ordinary circumstances, Roosevelt enjoyed train rides, for he liked to look at the scenery. He was fond of such trips, however, only if the train ran at a moderate speed, since he was a cripple and could not brace himself as most people do. Now, as his special train nosed through mist and a cold rain, Roosevelt ignored the bleak industrial flats of New Jersey and the dripping trees of Maryland, for he had much to occupy his mind. With him he carried three valuable documents—his inaugural address and rough drafts of two Presidential proclamations. One called for a special session of Congress. The other declared a nationwide bank holiday. Federal Reserve Board members, devoid of any other suggestions, had urged President Hoover to announce a national bank holiday, but the Republican President would not consent to it. While the Roosevelt train was splashing closer to Washington, Hoover was making his formal farewells and telling friends he planned to rest for nine months.

On this March 2 state bank holidays were declared by the governors of Arizona, California, Louisiana, Mississippi, Oklahoma and Oregon. The city fathers of Atlantic City, New Jersey, already were issuing scrip to pay municipal bills. In Mount Kisco, New York, well-intentioned people were collecting leftovers from parties to feed the homeless housed in the local jail. In his syndicated column that day Will Rogers said in part: "The papers said the bank clerks had worked so hard lately that they should have a holiday, so as we are all on holiday, let's take it on the chin and grin. The Rogers having laid in no supplies against such an emergency will be living on horse meat as that's our sole product."

Among the men huddling near Roosevelt on the last car of his train was James A. Farley, the burly, brisk and canny New York politician who had served as Roosevelt's campaign manager during the election the previous fall. Farley shared credit with Louis Howe, Roosevelt's shadow and political mentor, for having elected him. The returns had been spectacular. Roosevelt, the Democratic candidate, had defeated incumbent President Hoover, the GOP candidate, by a popular vote of 22,821,857 to 15,761,841. In gratitude, Roosevelt had named Farley his postmaster general and invited him, his wife and three children to ride to Washington with him.

After finishing the business at hand with Farley, Howe and his other advisers, the President-elect asked Farley to stay for a private chat. By this time Roosevelt had recovered something of his usual buoyancy, but after exchanging a few words with Farley, he began to talk solemnly about religion. Farley sensed that Roosevelt, faced with overwhelming responsibilities, was trying to find solace in his faith.

Farley, a devout Catholic, knew that Roosevelt was an Episcopalian. Although Roosevelt had served awhile as senior warden of St. James' Church in Hyde Park, he cared little about the institutional side of religion. He had a kind of primitive faith. He believed in the fundamental goodness and decency of man and also in the efficacy of prayer. He sincerely felt that if he did the right things, the right results would inevitably follow. Other than the time when he served as a warden, Roosevelt did not attend church regularly. He found the pews too narrow to get in and out of easily. Besides, he disliked being watched as he said his prayers.

Roosevelt told Farley that in the present crisis the most important thing was the faith of the people. In the end, he said, the salvation of all mankind would depend on a proper attitude toward God. A good listener, Farley nodded his balding head from time to time and closely studied the fifty-one-year-old President-elect now approaching a test beyond measure.

*   *   *

Franklin Delano Roosevelt was a beautifully built man with the long muscles of an athlete, according to Walter Camp. The famous Yale coach made this observation before Roosevelt was stricken with infantile paralysis in 1921. After that, after long years of exercises to rebuild his body, Roosevelt was enormous from the waist up and puny from the waist down, his legs thin and shriveled. His big deep chest could expand to astonishing proportions. Roosevelt liked to jest: "Maybe my legs aren't so good, but look at those shoulders! Jack Dempsey would be green with envy!"

His head was huge. As a young man his face was long, narrow and almost cameolike in its delicacy. With suffering and maturity, his face became large and bull-like. He had a large mole on his left cheek and another above his left eyebrow. His straight nose, pince-nez and massively jutting jaw were the delight of caricaturists. Whenever he spoke to anyone, he cocked his head, squinting his blue eyes against the smoke coiling from a Camel cigarette in a long ivory holder clenched in his teeth and angled toward the ceiling. His long teeth sloped forward in his mouth, and his mouth usually was shaped like a V because of his constant grin. There was a gap between two of his lower front teeth; a single-tooth removable bridge had been made for it. Roosevelt disliked wearing this bridge and usually carried it in a tiny heart-shaped silver box. When this artificial tooth was not in place, he whistled slightly when pronouncing certain words.

Although infantile paralysis had reduced his stature, he was six feet one and one-half inches tall when he became President. His weight fluctuated on either side of 190 pounds. He had massive freckled fists, and his hands always trembled a little. This tremor did not result from his illness but was a family trait shared by his sons. Whenever he turned his head, his eyeglasses glittered like tinfoil in candlelight. His face, seldom in repose, was extraordinarily mobile, so much so that within a few minutes it could express a wide range of emotions—some of them mock emotions. Roosevelt was a superb actor and knew it. Every Christmas he read *A Christmas Carol* to his children, his expression and voice depicting the peculiarity of each character.

Most people—including some enemies—considered Roosevelt a charming man. After seeing him for the first time, Winston Churchill said: "Meeting him is like opening a bottle of champagne." Despite his paralysis, Roosevelt radiated animal magnetism. He wooed people because he liked people and wanted them to like him. Sensitive to the needs of others, he liked to hear them talk about whatever interested them—and picked their brains as he listened. At the same time, he was strangely slow to praise those who worked for him and sometimes hurt their feelings with his indifference to their fatigue and low spirits. He also could seldom resist the temptation to monopolize the conversation. Never bored himself, he never bored others—except close associates who heard him repeat the same anecdote over and over again.

Having brushed death while sick with infantile paralysis, Roosevelt lived intensely after his recovery. He simply felt grateful to be alive and welcomed every experience, opened his pores to every sensation. In this regard he was delightfully childlike. He laughed a lot, the laughter pouring out of him. Just to be near him made others feel good. His smile was radiant; his eyes were roguish. Obviously masculine, Roosevelt nonetheless also had a touch of the female in him. Seldom completely frank, often devious, he used his personality as a professionally beautiful woman uses her beauty.

Although born a patrician, Roosevelt had the common touch. Perhaps because of his own guile, he enjoyed the company of politicians. At first sight he called almost all men by their first names, although in his headlong wish to be liked, he sometimes got their nicknames wrong. Happily married, but deeply fond of most women, Roosevelt seldom addressed them by their nicknames, however. Of a teasing nature, he doted on flirting and every now and then would tell his wife in mock alarm that she had better not leave him alone with some particular female. But despite Roosevelt's appreciation of women, he never took any aboard when he went sailing.

He addressed his secretaries and some other women as Child. Like Ernest Hemingway, he often called himself Papa and wanted his intimates to do the same. Sometimes Roosevelt would refer to himself in the third person, asking: "Well, how did Papa do?" He always kissed his daughter and four sons upon meeting them or whenever they left. Grace Tully, his secretary, once expressed surprise at this habit, whereupon Roosevelt, surprised, replied seriously: "Why not? I'm a parent. I always kissed my father."

Roosevelt was the only child of a supremely happy marriage. His father, James Roosevelt, lost his first wife in death. His second wife, Franklin's mother, Sara Delano Roosevelt, was twenty-six years younger than her husband. James was fifty-four years old when Franklin was born, so his relationship with his father was more like that of grandson to grandfather than son to father. Franklin always admired his father's control of his mother, a strong woman, who in turn controlled him. In fact, she spoiled him. The only son of a doting mother and a kind and wealthy father, Franklin grew up with a sense of complete security and in abundant happiness. Perhaps it was this conditioning which caused an associate to say of Franklin D. Roosevelt: "He must have been psychoanalyzed by God."

He knew he was loved. As a child he never felt the need to rebel against his parents, but as an adult he flouted his mother's dislike of drinking. He suffered no guilt and was free of all fear—until he became a cripple. After that he was more afraid of fire than the average person because he was so helpless, but of course, this fear was practical, not neurotic.

Born on January 30, 1882, at Hyde Park, New York, within view of the majestic Hudson River, Roosevelt fell in love with water and trees and birds and continued to love them until he died. Once, in a rare moment of mysticism, he dreamily said that he felt the ocean was his true home. From childhood on, he was a strong swimmer and expert sailor, and much of his recovery from his later illness was due to the long swims he took, his thick arms pulling like oars, his thin legs trailing behind like weeds.

Rich and privileged from the start, Roosevelt casually and unthinkingly accepted his status as a kind of English squire to the manner born. Although the name Roosevelt means "Field of Roses" in Dutch, and although he liked to regard himself as a Dutchman, only about 3 percent of his blood was indeed Dutch, most of it being English. His early education came from governesses and tutors in classes held at home. He did not attend any school until he turned fourteen and was sent to Groton, an Episcopalian prep school in Massachusetts. There he slept in a tiny room 6 by 10 feet, took cold showers before breakfast and arrived for dinner wearing a stiff collar and patent-leather shoes. Roosevelt was no great success at Groton.

Harvard, which he entered in 1900, was more to his liking. Never a natural scholar, and certainly no bookworm, he nonetheless completed a four-year course in only three years, averaging about B. He majored in American political history and government, two subjects which always fascinated him. He hero-worshiped his fifth cousin, Theodore Roosevelt, who became President of the United States while Franklin was at Harvard; the young man called his distant cousin Uncle Ted.

Franklin's greatest pleasure at Harvard derived from his position as managing editor and then president of the student newspaper, the *Harvard Crimson*. All the rest of his life he considered himself something of an expert in journalism, once hoped to launch a national tabloid and for a while in the Twenties wrote a few book reviews. Wishing to write history as well, he produced a movie script about John Paul Jones and then another about the ship called "Old Ironsides." Nothing came of either venture.

Although he was not a prodigious reader, Roosevelt doted on books about American history, naval records and old diaries. He got a thrill out of buying books and sensual pleasure from scribbling his name in them. His favorite author was Mark Twain, whom he once met through his father. Roosevelt once said: "If people like my choice of words and my oratorical style, it is largely due to my constant study of Twain's works, which have influenced me more than any other writer." Roosevelt's style of writing never attained the grace and eloquence of, say, Adlai E. Stevenson's, but he knew the value of using short words and expressing himself simply.

Besides his "Uncle Ted," he hero-worshiped Benjamin Franklin, Thomas Jefferson and Woodrow Wilson. Although he did not sing very well, he became a member of the Groton choir and he also played the mandolin. He was an expert at bird calls. Next to swimming and sailing, he most liked horseback riding, golf, tennis and fishing—caring very little what kind of fish he caught.

Collecting things was an obsession with Roosevelt. He put together an impressive array of paintings and prints about ships and the sea, bought

9,872 books about maritime life, served as president of the Ship Model Society and collected stamps. He was eight years old when he started his stamp collection, and nearly every day the rest of his life he gave about a half hour to his stamps, working with the magnifying glass, tweezers and other paraphernalia of the philatelist. This hobby taught him geography, history and patience. He seldom paid more than $10 for a single stamp, specialized in issues from Central and South America, suggested ideas for new stamps and even helped design some. Stamp collecting also became occupational therapy after his illness.

He was felled by infantile paralysis in 1921 while vacationing at his summer home in Campobello, New Brunswick, Canada. Thirty-nine years old at the time, he was disgusted that he should be victimized by a disease of children. Nonetheless, he never complained. This critical illness was the most significant turning point in the life and career of Franklin D. Roosevelt. Roosevelt's ailment seems to have ennobled him. Purged by pain, he shed the shallowness of his youth, the superciliousness that had offended some people, and matured into a man of deep sensitivity and compassion. Forever afterward, he identified with others who were ill favored, ill fated, weak, wronged or unhappy.

With diamond-hard determination, he set about the task of bringing his body back into such shape as was possible. He exercised rigorously, swam as often as possible, overcame part of his weakness by laughing at himself. Free of false pride, he would crawl along the floor of his house or drag himself across a sandy beach, his helpless legs trailing behind. He let no one pity him, but never again in his life did he utter the word "golf."

He had to wear steel braces weighing 10 pounds. They strapped around his waist and clamped onto the heels of his shoes. The braces were jointed at the knees and had to be unsnapped before he could walk a few steps on crutches or with someone supporting him. If, as he sat in his wheelchair, he wanted to cross his lifeless legs, he would grab hold of a trouser leg at the knee and pull it up and over the other knee. Patches were sewn onto the sides of his pants at the knees where the braces cut the fabric. Especially made for him was a Ford with manual controls, and after being helped into it, Roosevelt would work the gears with his hands and drive off breezily. Because he was a cripple, he could never be left alone in safety, and although he was a gregarious person, this lack of occasional isolation saddened him.

Apart from his handicap, Roosevelt enjoyed superb health in the main, subject only to head colds. Doctors constantly treated him for sinus trouble, and this condition may explain his dislike of air conditioning. Chair-bound most of the time, Roosevelt did not waste energy as some men do by pacing the floor, and he boasted he never got tired. However, he needed eight hours of sleep nightly, usually retiring about midnight and awakening between 8 and 8:30 A.M. His habit of smoking two packs of cigarettes a day may have aggravated his sinus trouble. He was fond of exotic cheeses and of game served so raw that it dripped blood. Toward the end of each working day he looked forward to the cocktail hour, preferring martinis or old-fashioneds and generally limiting himself to a couple of drinks. He enjoyed mixing the drinks, although his brother-in-law, Hall Roosevelt, said that FDR did not know how to make a good martini. Tasting his first drink of the day, Roosevelt would smack his lips and cry: "Yummy! That's good!" Then he might ask a guest: "Will you have another smig?"

Annoyingly cute expressions of this kind were characteristic of Roosevelt. He seldom swore; one of his strongest terms of disgust was "Spinach!" Seldom given to introspection, to self-analysis, Roosevelt was heavy-handed in his humor and often laughed at feeble jokes—his own and others. He liked to tease his friends, his puns were terrible, and he doted on practical jokes. At the same time, he was a gifted raconteur.

Basically a gentleman, since he shrank from hurting others uninten-tionally, Roosevelt was a middle-brow sophisticate. Between the ages of seven and fifteen he was taken to Europe each summer by his parents. He spoke French fluently, felt that he knew Spanish and had a reading knowledge of German. As a young man in the company of a tutor, he bicycled through the Black Forest of Germany and was arrested four times in a single day—for knocking down a goose, picking cherries, parking his bicycle at a railway station and cycling after sunset. But with his charm and his mangled German, he was able to talk his way out of this trouble with the Kaiser's police.

No social climber, since he sat near the peak, Roosevelt loathed formal dinner parties and cared little about clothes. Like many rich people he was careful with money and always made out his own income-tax returns. Most of the time he wore shirts with soft collars; bow ties especially appealed to him. His business suits ran to various shades of gray and usually he relaxed in rough tweed jackets or an ancient wool sweater. He seldom carried any cash on his person, hated waste of any kind and never threw away any-thing. Contractors knew him for a sly bargainer whenever he had some building project in mind. Fond of attention, like many handicapped per-sons, he tended to be lofty at times and in his worst moods could become a prima donna.

Many men of the Depression era were much more brilliant than Roose-velt. This is not to say that he was not intelligent, though, for he was. The prime sign of intelligence is curiosity, and Roosevelt's curiosity was limit-less and aggressive. Instead of proceeding from one idea to another via a logical sequence of associations, his mind made vast leaps because of his high order of imagination. This, however, is another mark of a special kind of intelligence.

Owing to his rather grandiose temperament, Roosevelt had the capacity to think in global terms, expansively, hopping over the horizon. At the same time, stamp collector that he was, he liked details and gave them careful attention. Intuitive rather than logical, flexible rather than fixed, he welcomed new ideas and was willing to experiment. Unlike Herbert Hoover, he was not a prisoner of pat positions. He disliked debate but solicited the ideas of other men, neatly picking their brains like a mental pickpocket. Sometimes he even palmed off their concepts as his own. Harold Laski called him "a broker of ideas rather than an architect of systems."

Roosevelt, who had an astonishingly good memory, often astounded his friends with a recital of who did what, when and where and how. No specialist in any single field, he best knew American history, American politics and geography in general. He could compartmentalize his mind, shutting out extraneous data so that he might give full attention to the essence of any matter. While he was able to make quick decisions about important issues, he sometimes procrastinated so long that his aides and friends were left anxious and irritated. He had almost no interest in abstractions, shaping his ideas mainly in terms of people. This last quality—concern with human beings—was of cardinal value to a man about to assume power in the abyss of the Depression.

Roosevelt said: "Once I spent two years lying in bed, trying to move my big toe. That was the hardest job I ever had to do. After that, anything else seems easy."

Now a crippled man was about to teach a crippled nation how to walk again.

*   *   *

The evening of March 2, amid rain and sleet, Roosevelt's glistening train reached Washington and was backed into Union Station. Despite the bad weather, a crowd had gathered to welcome the President-elect, a crowd narrowly watched by blank-faced Secret Service men, who stood with their hands in their overcoat pockets. Cops in black raincoats cleared the area near the last car of the train, and soon Roosevelt stumped out onto the rear platform, his wife at his side. Under the dingy lights it was difficult to see him clearly. His twenty-five-year-old son James and his seventeen-year-old son John helped him down and into a waiting limousine. The moment Roosevelt sank back into its rear seat, he flashed a smile at the ring of photographers, waved and then drove off to the Mayflower Hotel.

Soon after he settled in his suite, he was visited by Congressional leaders, who had arrived, at his invitation, to discuss the mounting crisis. Many were pale and agitated. These Democrats, about to take power in the national capital, felt the edge of their elation blunted by the hard facts of the emergency. All looked to Roosevelt for guidance.

That same evening Federal Reserve Board members met in their headquarters on the second floor of the Treasury Building. A majority of them favored closing all the banks in the nation until Roosevelt was sworn in as President at noon on March 4; so did top officials in Hoover's Treasury

Department. They sent their recommendation to President Hoover in the White House. Hoover then let them know he would not act on their proposal until and unless he got the approval of the President-elect. The Reserve and Treasury heads passed Hoover's word to Roosevelt via his new secretary of the treasury, William H. Woodin.

Woodin and Roosevelt conferred in the Mayflower. Woodin then reported that the President-elect would not join the President in any such proclamation, would accept no responsibility without authority. Hoover would have to act alone, doing whatever he thought best. When Hoover heard Roosevelt's reply, he rejected the idea of closing all banks. Now he suggested a second and different proclamation, one merely controlling exchange and hoarding. What did Roosevelt think of this alternative? Once again Roosevelt refused to let himself be hobbled by tying himself to a mutual policy with the outgoing President.

The worried Hoover did not get to bed until two o'clock the following morning.

On Friday, March 3, the banking situation worsened. Bank holidays were declared by the governors of Georgia, Idaho, New Mexico, Texas, Utah, Washington and Wisconsin. The New York Federal Reserve Bank's gold reserve was depleted. The Chicago Federal Reserve Bank reported that its member banks were pulling gold out of it at an alarming rate. During the day the record-breaking sum of more than $116 million in gold was exported or earmarked for frightened foreign depositors in their New York accounts.

Howard Scott, the creator of Technocracy, officially was declared bankrupt. Ohio considered issuing scrip. In Wall Street and in Chicago's Loop, frenzied depositors stormed banks, waving bankbooks and demanding their savings, while police reserves struggled to keep order. In New York the Bowery Savings Bank, the largest private savings bank in the world, shut its doors in the face of a mob. Twenty-two states now had imposed banking restrictions.

Despite all this, Hoover felt that things had taken a turn for the better. He accepted the word of Treasury Secretary Ogden Mills that big city banks had taken steps that would prevent a general closing before the inauguration. After lunch his weak cheer turned to gloom when he heard that banks had closed in Minnesota and Kansas, while those in Virginia and North Carolina were about to go under. On this, his last full day as President, he accepted his final $500 paycheck from a Treasury Department messenger named Miss Catherine Shea. Cabinet members gave him a farewell gift of a desk set, and Hoover said good-bye to Washington correspondents.

In Fort Madison, Iowa, W. A. Sheaffer, president of the Sheaffer Pen Company, was writing a letter to Raymond Moley, one of Roosevelt's advisers. He said: "We have today our checks returned and refused from twenty-four states and it looks as though in a few days business would be at an actual standstill. Therefore, the most urgent emergency in the history of our nation is at hand. There must be adequate relief legislation immediately. It would seem that it could not wait for a week or ten days and with no money available for payrolls and salaries. It would seem to me that the country would be at a standstill. . . ."

The most urgent emergency in the history of our nation is at hand.
This was the way most Americans felt on Friday, March 3, 1933.

But even during a national crisis certain ceremonies must be observed to mark the transition of power from one party and one man to another party and another man. It was customary for the outgoing President to invite the incoming President to dinner at the White House. Considering the state of the nation, Hoover decided instead merely to ask Roosevelt to tea. FDR arrived with Mrs. Roosevelt and with their son James, rather than his usual bodyguard. They were escorted into the Red Room.

Roosevelt took a chair that carefully had been placed at some distance from the one to be occupied by Hoover. The careworn fifty-eight-year-old Hoover walked in and shook hands but did not look Roosevelt in the eye. The atmosphere, during this brief confrontation, was as brittle as that at a wake. Hoover made still another plea to Roosevelt to issue a joint proclamation to end the banking crisis, but once again Roosevelt declined to bind himself in any way to the discredited President. This rejection angered Hoover, whose face went red. Eleanor Roosevelt's cup of tea shook in her hands. Roosevelt knew that it was the custom for an outgoing President to return the call of the incoming executive, but he felt that Hoover would not care to endure this additional strain. Wishing to cut short the present meeting, Roosevelt said: "I realize, Mr. President, that you are extremely busy, so I will understand completely if you do not return the call."

Looking Roosevelt squarely in the eyes for the first time, Hoover said between clenched teeth: "Mr. Roosevelt, when you have been in Washington as long as I have, you will learn that the President of the United States calls on nobody!"

Roosevelt's blood began to boil, and his son felt like punching Hoover in the eye. Eleanor Roosevelt stood up diplomatically and said to Hoover: "It's been very pleasant, but we must go now."

Roosevelt, his wife and son were driven back to the Mayflower Hotel.

Exhausted bankers were holding around-the-clock meetings in Washington and in Federal Reserve Banks across the nation. Early that evening Thomas W. Lamont of the House of Morgan telephoned Roosevelt at his Washington suite to urge that no action of any kind be taken. Speaking from Manhattan, Lamont said that leading New York bankers agreed that the banks could pull through all right and reopen the following Monday if Roosevelt's inaugural speech pumped courage into the public. Although Roosevelt was cordial to Lamont, he had no intention of following advice from a Morgan man.

Contrary to Lamont's evaluation, Roosevelt and his advisers felt that if

New York and Chicago banks did open, they could not last two hours. Roosevelt felt that it was best to close all banks to gain enough time to examine them, one by one, in order to determine which were sound enough to open again with no loss of assets to depositors. Now was the time, he decided, to ask state governors to shut down the few remaining banks. Then, upon taking office as President, he would proclaim a national banking holiday. Legal precedence and authority for a nationwide holiday could be found, Roosevelt believed, in the Trading-with-the-Enemy Act of 1917, designed to prevent gold from reaching enemy nations.

Senator Carter Glass, who sat with Roosevelt, disagreed. He protested that no President possessed such authority. Roosevelt pointed out that the 1917 act had never been rescinded by Congress. Glass was gloomy when he left the hotel.

At 11:30 P.M. Hoover telephoned from the White House to the Mayflower and again asked Roosevelt to approve a Presidential order controlling withdrawals and exchanges. Once more Roosevelt declined, saying in effect that Hoover should do whatever he chose to do. At 1 A.M. Hoover called a second time. Helplessly, Hoover said that his treasury secretary and the Federal Reserve people still were undecided about what should be done. Roosevelt thanked him, pointed out that both men were fatigued and suggested that they turn in for the night.

Before turning out the light, a few hours before becoming the President of the United States, Roosevelt picked up a book from his bedside and read some thoughts written by Henry Thoreau.

*   *   *

On Inauguration Day, Saturday, March 4, 1933, the sun rose over Washington at 6:29 A.M., rose almost secretly, so it seemed, since the sky was cloudy, the day cheerless. A worn and haggard Hoover got up at 6 A.M. after about only four hours of sleep. Even so, he was strangely genial at first, aware that soon all the heavy burdens would be lifted from his shoulders. As he later wrote, he was leaving the White House with no regrets "except that the job of recovery and some needed reforms were incomplete." After nineteen years in public service, Hoover was about to become a private citizen again.

His mood changed when he heard what had happened as he lay sleeping. At 4:30 A.M. Governor Herbert Lehman of New York had proclaimed a two-day bank holiday for that state, and at almost the same moment Governor Henry Horner of Illinois had followed suit. Now the nation's two greatest financial centers had closed. Now almost every commercial bank in the country was shut. The American banking system was paralyzed and on the point of death. Capitalism itself seemed to be expiring. When Hoover heard the news, he muttered: "We are at the end of our string."

Lamont had been wrong when he said the New York banks could hold out. Actually, they had been undermined by withdrawals by foreign and domestic banks. Nine million dollars in gold was at that moment being loaded aboard the SS *Paris* in New York for shipment to Europe. Dollar trading was suspended in European capitals. The North Dakota legislature passed a bill authorizing the use of scrip and Detroit bankers were working on a similar plan.

Shortly before 10 A.M. came the staggering news that all security and commodity exchanges in this nation had been closed, except for the Chicago Livestock Exchange. In New York City policeman guarded banks and business houses against the theft of their cash. Here and there across the land rich people whispered about the machine guns stored in their country homes so they could be ready for "anything."

Rexford Tugwell, another Roosevelt adviser, later wrote: "I do not think it is too much to say that on March 4 we were confronted with a choice between an orderly revolution—a peaceful and rapid departure from past concepts—and a violent and disorderly overthrow of the whole capitalistic structure."

Already a crowd was gathering in front of the Capitol Building where Roosevelt was to be sworn in, and one spectator asked: "What are those things that look like little cages?" A woman giggled: "Machine guns." Up to the last moment of its authority, the Hoover administration was taking no chances. In front of the White House there had been erected a stand from which the new President could review the inaugural parade; Roosevelt wanted it open, but it had been enclosed in glass.

In New York and Chicago people lucky enough to have jobs worried about how they could get home at the end of the day if mobs barricaded highways and trains stopped running. Secretary of War Patrick Hurley admitted that troops had been bivouacked near big cities because of what "Reds and possible Communists" might do. Henry Wallace, soon to be sworn in as the new secretary of agriculture, heard from relatives that a secret clique of Army Reserve officers had been mobilized here and there across the country for use in case Roosevelt was unable to maintain order.

By train, by bus and private automobile, tens of thousands of Americans poured into Washington to see the inauguration until more than a quarter of a million people jammed the city. For the first time ever the federal government had not appropriated any money to cover the cost of the inauguration and parade. Roosevelt, wishing to economize, had suggested that the best seats be sold with first choice going to contributors to his campaign. This plan worked. Not only were all expenses covered, but a surplus of $60,000 was given to charity.

Among the spectators were a couple of crooks who had profited from the banking crisis. The previous morning a Brooklyn housewife had gone to three banks in which she had accounts, withdrawing $9,500 in currency and $80 in gold. As she entered a butcher shop, her money-laden handbag was snatched by two men who then jumped into a coupe and roared off. They drove to Atlantic City, lived it up that night, bought themselves new clothes. The morning of March 4 they drove to Washington where they mingled with dignitaries and attended one of the inaugural balls. By the time they were caught they had managed to spend less than $2,000 of their loot.

Shortly before ten o'clock the morning of his inauguration, Roosevelt attended a special religious service. A huge open White House limousine was sent to his hotel to get the President-elect, his wife, their children, some uncles, aunts and cousins. Eleanor Roosevelt looked smart in a blue suit. They were driven to St. John's Episcopal Church, a notable example of Federal architecture commonly called "the Church of the Presidents." Roosevelt had asked his Cabinet designees and members of their families to join him in worship. He also had requested that the service be conducted by his old Groton headmaster, the bald and aging Endicott Peabody, despite the fact that Peabody favored Hoover. In a squeaky voice the old man begged God to help "Thy servant, Franklin, about to become President of these United States."

After this service the Roosevelt family motored around Lafayette Square to the White House. The others got out while Roosevelt kept his seat in the car and waited beneath the north portico. Mrs. Roosevelt was ushered into another automobile. Within moments Herbert Hoover walked alone out the front door, looking oddly shrunken and old, and standing beside the tall white columns, he reached into the car and shook hands with Roosevelt, smiling wanly. Roosevelt greeted him warmly.

Hoover climbed in and sat down in the rear right-hand side of the seat. Both men wore tall silk hats, morning coats and fur-lined overcoats. However, Hoover wore his usual high stiff collar, while Roosevelt had on a more formal low-bent winged collar. The top of the car had been folded back so both men were exposed to the raw weather and also were highly visible to spectators as they started up Pennsylvania Avenue toward the Capitol.

Gutzon Borglum, the sculptor, once said that "if you put a rose in Hoover's hand it would wilt." Hoover, who could be charming and loquacious in small groups, tended to become remote before crowds, and now— on public display as the defeated candidate—he lacked almost all grace. Roosevelt, sensitive to Hoover's dejection, tried to engage him in small talk as they rode shoulder to shoulder past cheering crowds. Most of the cheers were for the incoming President, and Hoover knew it and Roosevelt knew it. Not wishing to embarrass Hoover or upstage him, though, Roosevelt did not respond at first to the outcries. Hoover sat like a stone statue, looking straight ahead, paying no attention to the people along the curbs.

At last Roosevelt thought: *Spinach! Protocol or no protocol, somebody has to do something. The two of us simply can't sit here on our hands, ignoring each other and everyone else.* He doffed his silk topper and acknowledged the cheers. Hoover kept his own hat firmly on his head. As Roosevelt kept on waving, he continued to try to draw Hoover into some dialogue, however trivial, but the only response from Hoover were a few

grunted monosyllables. Roosevelt, the master of the art of putting people at
their ease, became desperate. When the car passed a government building
still under construction, Roosevelt pointed and cried: "My, Mr. President!
Aren't those the nicest steel girders you ever saw?" The moment he heard
his own words he realized how inane they were.

It was noon when Roosevelt and Hoover arrived at the Capitol. The
second session of the Seventy-second Congress was expiring. With Hoover
walking beside him, Roosevelt was wheeled into the Senate wing and
thence into the small, ornate and gilded President's Room. Roosevelt
waited. Hoover sat down under a chandelier at an old oval marble-topped
walnut table to perform his last official duties as President. He signified
that he refused to sign a bill containing a $1 billion appropriation for the
Veterans Bureau and a bill intended to force up the price of cotton; these
were pocket vetoes.

Then the two men were escorted into the Senate chamber to watch the
retiring Vice President, Charles Curtis, administer the oath of office to his
successor, John Nance Garner of Texas. The florid-faced Texan was
unhappy about leaving his post as Speaker of the House to accept the Vice
Presidency, which he described as "a no-man's-land somewhere between
the legislative and executive branches." With Roosevelt and Hoover still
watching, new Senators took their oaths of office.

Hoover turned and left the Senate chamber, walking through a double
row of diplomats clad in full regalia, then halted a moment before emerging through a door and out onto a special stand erected at the east portico
of the Capitol. Of the 250,000 people in the city that day some 100,000
could be seen from the platform, standing in the chill beneath leafless trees,
blackening all of Capitol Park. Across the country 60,000,000 other
Americans crouched near radios, waiting expectantly.

Among those in the crowd near the Capitol were Adlai E. Stevenson, a
thirty-three-year-old Chicago attorney, and twenty-four-year-old Lyndon
B. Johnson, secretary to Representative Richard M. Kleberg of Texas.
Owing to the financial crisis Governor Gifford Pinchot of Pennsylvania
watched the ceremony with only 95 cents in his pocket. Many out-of-town
spectators were worrying about how they could pay their hotel bills and
find the fare to get home. In the lobbies of their hotels they had read
notices saying: "Members find it necessary that, due to unsettled banking
conditions throughout the country, checks on out-of-town banks cannot be
accepted.—THE WASHINGTON HOTEL ASSOCIATION." George Catlett Marshall, on the brink of fame as a general and diplomat, borrowed $5 from a
fellow officer and gave most of this to a bewildered old man and woman to
help pay for their tickets back to Oklahoma.

Roosevelt—who liked to tell how his great-great-grandfather Isaac
Roosevelt had led George Washington's horse in the nation's first inaugural
parade—waited in the office of the sergeant at arms of the Senate. He still
sat in his wheelchair. Asking an aide for the typed copy of his inaugural

address, Roosevelt scribbled a new first line: "This is a day of consecration." Members of the inaugural committee solemnly approached to announce that the time had come for him to appear. They turned and led the way as Roosevelt was wheeled behind them, across the floor of the vaulted rotunda, up to the east door. He was helped to his feet. Hatless and coatless, clutching the arm of his son James, stiffly he walked to the great bronze doors. A bugle sounded. The Marine band, in scarlet jackets and blue trousers, struck up "Hail to the Chief" as Roosevelt emerged. The crowd stirred. Then cheers and applause broke out.

Bernard Baruch leaped onto a bench and wildly swung his black silk hat. Mrs. Woodrow Wilson fluttered a handkerchief. Roosevelt's face was frozen with the physical effort he was making. Doggedly, slowly, carefully, he shuffled down a special ramp 35 yards to the center of the outdoor platform, which was high and white, decorated with Grecian columns strung with ivy and bedecked with flags. Hoover sat in a leather-upholstered chair to the left of the lectern. When Roosevelt reached the lectern, he turned right to face Chief Justice Charles Evans Hughes, a white skullcap on his head, his magnificent white whiskers flicked by the wind.

Eleanor Roosevelt, from her seat on the inaugural platform, looked out at a landscape of faces and thought they looked dazed and frightened. Not since Abraham Lincoln's first inauguration on March 4, 1861, had this nation been so close to total disaster. On that earlier date, six Southern states already had seceded from the Union, and others hung by an eyelash. In the lower half of the country state troops had seized forts and arsenals, barracks and vessels, and federal mints had been robbed. Jefferson Davis had been sworn in as president of the Confederate States of America while P. T. Beauregard had taken command of the Confederate Army. En route to Washington, and eager to keep the union intact, Lincoln said time and again that there was no crisis "excepting such a one as may be gotten up at any time by turbulent men aided by designing politicians." But this, as Lincoln knew, was not the whole truth. He was warned to sneak through Baltimore because of an alleged conspiracy to assassinate him there. An Army colonel, his voice quaking with fury, cried to Lincoln: "I'll get a squad of cavalry, sir, and *cut* our way to Washington, sir!" Lincoln dissuaded the officer but let himself be persuaded to don a disguise and bypass Baltimore, slipping into the national capital unheralded and almost unseen at six o'clock one morning.

Now, seventy-seven years and sixteen Presidents later, Franklin D. Roosevelt was about to take the oath of office under circumstances as grave as those Lincoln had faced. Between Roosevelt and Chief Justice Hughes there stood an aide holding open a huge Dutch Bible that had been in the Roosevelt family for three centuries. It had been opened to the First Epistle of Paul the Apostle to the Corinthians, Chapter 13, which ends: "And now abideth faith, hope, charity, these three; but the greatest of these is charity." Roosevelt placed his left hand on the Bible and raised his right hand as the oath of office was administered by the Chief Justice. He repeated the entire oath instead of merely saying at the end, "I do," as had been done by most previous Presidents. Then, awkwardly, he bent down and kissed the Bible. The time was 1:06 P.M.

Turning to his left and placing his huge hands on the sides of the lectern, the new President of the United States paused a moment, thrust out his great chin, and said: "President Hoover, Mr. Chief Justice, my friends, this is a day of national consecration. . . ." Roosevelt ad-libbed the word "national" in speaking the line he had just finished writing inside the Capitol. In his resonant voice, Roosevelt continued: "I am certain that my fellow Americans expect that on my induction into the Presidency I will address them with a candor and a decision which the present situation of our nation impels. This is preeminently the time to speak the truth, the whole truth, frankly and boldly. Nor need we shrink from honestly facing conditions in our country today. This great nation will endure as it has endured, will revive and will prosper. So, first of all, let me assert my firm belief that the only thing we have to fear is fear itself. . . ."

The massed thousands, for the most part uncertain and passive until now, jerked to alertness as though jolted by a bolt of electricity. People turned to look at one another, pleased. The only thing we have to fear is fear itself? That's right! Their applause sounded like an avalanche rolling down a mountain. When Roosevelt could make himself heard again, he said: "Plenty is at our doorstep, but a generous use of it languishes in the very sight of the supply. Primarily this is because rulers of the exchange of mankind's goods have failed through their own stubbornness and their own incompetence, have admitted their failure and have abdicated. . . . The money changers have fled from their high seats in the temple of our civilization. . . ."

The day's biggest demonstration came when Roosevelt hinted that he might need to assume powers usually given a President in wartime. "I shall ask the Congress," he said, "for the one remaining instrument to meet the crisis—broad executive power to wage a war against the emergency as great as the power that would be given to me if we were in fact invaded by a foreign foe." The people howled their approval.

In Chapel Hill, North Carolina, the inaugural speech was heard over the radio by Frank Graham, president of the University of North Carolina. The previous day his students had been addressed by Norman Thomas, the Socialist Party's candidate for President the previous fall. Now, listening to Roosevelt's speech, Graham turned to his wife and said: "Why, Roosevelt is repeating a great many of the things that Norman Thomas told us last night—about no half measures in dealing with the financial crisis, bank closures, unemployment, and the near collapse of our whole economic system!"

Roosevelt's first inaugural speech was truly great, one of those rare orations that actually change the course of history. Its tone surprised

Norman Thomas himself, who felt that it presaged great things for the country. Will Rogers wrote the next day of Roosevelt: "If he burned down the capitol we would cheer and say 'well, we at least got a fire started anyhow.' We have had years of 'Don't rock the boat,' go on and sink if you want to, we just as well be swimming as like we are."

In the next few days almost half a million Americans wrote letters to the White House, saying such things as: "Your human feeling for all of us in your address is just wonderful!" . . . "It was the finest thing this side of heaven!" . . . "It seemed to give the people, as well as myself, a new hold upon life." . . . "People are looking to you almost as they look to God."

*   *   *

Herbert Hoover, now a private citizen, drove directly from the Capitol to Union Station to board a train. "There came a great sense of relief," he later wrote in his memoirs. "It was emancipation from a sort of peonage— a revolution back to personal freedom. It was a release not alone from political pressures but from the routines of twelve to fourteen hours of work seven days a week. Even mealtime had to be given over to the discussion of the problems of the day; the nights were haunted by the things that went wrong; the so-called vacations were tied to the telephone and telegraph or to the visitor who knew that now was the time to discuss his problem."

Waiting at the station was a throng of Hoover's friends and admirers who wanted to see him off. Although the former President now lacked Secret Service protection, four handpicked railway agents closed in to guard him during his final moments in Washington. Harlan F. Stone, an Associate Justice of the Supreme Court, was among those who bade farewell to Hoover; the conservative justice felt so cool toward Roosevelt that he had left for the station without waiting to hear the inaugural address. One eyewitness said that as Hoover's train began to pull out of the terminal, the former President was weeping. Mrs. Stone merely said: "I shall never forget the expression on Mr. Hoover's face."

*   *   *

Moments after Roosevelt finished speaking, after trying to rally an entire nation, he faced a petty personal problem. As he turned from the lectern, he slipped his left arm beneath the arm of his son James, and someone placed his tall silk hat in his right hand. Unfortunately, the hat was handed to him the wrong way, so that when he was ready to put it on, it would sit backward on his head. With the fingers of his right hand, little by little, laboriously, he inched the brim of the hat around until it was in the proper position.

His wife drove with him from the Capitol down Pennsylvania Avenue to the White House. Every few feet the new President grinned and doffed his hat to the crowds along the street, while she smiled and waved. To Eleanor Roosevelt the scene was "very, very solemn and a little terrifying. The crowds were so tremendous and you felt they would do anything—if someone would tell them what to do." In those tense moments she may have forgotten that when Franklin was a boy and his mother rebuked him for ordering his playmates around, he had replied that if he did not tell them what to do, nothing would get done.

As soon as the Roosevelts entered their new home, the atmosphere in the White House changed from solemnity to gaiety, according to Ike Hoover, the chief usher. Herbert Hoover had been so grim that the servants were almost afraid of him. The chief usher had been surprised when Eleanor Roosevelt said she wanted hot dogs included on the menu for the inaugural day luncheon. An embarrassing moment occurred when the President, his relatives and guests reached the door of the dining room. Eleanor now was the First Lady of the land, but standing near Roosevelt was his seventy-eight-year-old mother, Sara, a *grande dame* who tried to preempt her son's affection. According to tradition, the President was supposed to take his lady's arm and lead the procession. He glanced helplessly at his wife. Then, masking his feelings, he took his mother's arm and, shuffling on his crippled legs, entered the dining room. Eleanor walked behind him.

When lunch was over, Roosevelt went out to watch the inaugural parade from in front of the White House. The temporary reviewing stand was a replica of Federal Hall on Wall Street, from whose balcony George Washington had taken the cheers of the crowd after he took office as the first President. Seated beside Roosevelt was his wife, smiling, her little round black hat tilted over one ear. Nearby, too, was Chief of Staff Douglas MacArthur, who had driven the bonus marchers out of Washington the previous summer. Despite the wet and chill, the parade lasted three hours with the biggest cheers, next to those for Roosevelt, going to Alfred E. Smith and to Tom Mix, the cowboy actor. In the wake of the parade a man found 20 cents and, showing the coins to everyone near him, shouted that this meant better times were ahead.

Inside the White House a new kind of service already was being given to the American people. Roosevelt had left instructions with his staff members, from top to bottom, that any needy person who telephoned the executive mansion should receive kind and interested attention. If a city homeowner was about to lose his house, if a farmer faced foreclosure on his farm, they were to be helped, if at all possible. In days to come, even Eleanor Roosevelt took some of these calls.

*   *   *

The morning of March 5 Franklin D. Roosevelt awakened earlier than usual, stared about the strange White House bedroom, sat up in bed and reached for the newspapers. They were not there. He complained because they were late, and when the newspapers did arrive, they were not to his liking. Because of the swirl of events, he may have forgotten that this was a Sunday. After breakfasting in bed, he was dressed with the help of his valet and then wheeled into the Oval Room on the second floor, the Presidential study. The valet parked the wheelchair behind the large brown desk and left.

The room's curving walls were bare, and Roosevelt detested bare walls. The top of the desk was also bare, except for two empty trays, a leather-cornered pad, a pen set and a lamp. Its drawers likewise were empty, which further annoyed Roosevelt. The pen did not work, and he was unable to find a pencil and pad to scribble a note. Suddenly the new President of the United States realized he was all alone. For a few frightening seconds his mind went blank. Because of the danger of fire, he had always had someone near him. Roosevelt searched the desk for some buzzers to push but could find none. Here was the one man in the nation on whom almost everything counted, and he sat helplessly in a bare room, seemingly cut off from all human communication. Rearing back in his chair, lifting his great chin, he gave a shout that brought secretaries tumbling into the room.

That same day, in New York City, 10,000 Communist-led demonstrators were demanding unemployment insurance and more relief. Herbert Hoover, now in Manhattan, was being guarded by New York's Finest. The New York Clearing House Association formally adopted the use of scrip, a Pasadena hotel was issuing scrip, and Philadelphia was preparing to put out some of this bogus money. In Germany the Nazis had won a majority in the Reichstag. From all over the United States haggard bankers were pouring into Washington, worried as never before in their lives but lacking any cogent plan of their own for what should be done. A few were so desperate that they urged Roosevelt to nationalize the banks—an idea favored by Socialists, whom the bankers despised.

In time to come the bankers were quick to forget their panic and their pleas for help, but Roosevelt never forgot. Two years later, in a public speech, he said: "In the spring of 1933 many of the great bankers of the United States flocked to Washington. They were there to get the help of the government in saving their banks from insolvency. To them I pointed out that the government would be compelled to go heavily into debt for a few years to come, in order to save banks and save insurance companies and mortgage companies, and railroads, and to take care of millions of people who were on the verge of starvation. Every one of these gentlemen expressed to me at that time the firm conviction that it was all well worth the price and that they heartily approved. . . . All begged that the government should intervene as much as possible."

These kings of finance and captains of industry had changed their tune from that time, not so long before, when they chanted that the government should stay out of business. As Victor Hugo once said: "Ah, danger, inevitable controverter, in his last hours the atheist invokes God, the royalist calls upon the republic!"

Now that Roosevelt was President he could: (1) do nothing—and watch banking and business go down the drain in thirty days; (2) nationalize the economic system—which would have meant Socialism; or (3) use federal facilities to help private enterprise resume its normal functions. He chose the third alternative.

If Roosevelt had been the radical his enemies claimed he was, he could have changed the nature and future of this nation at a single stroke, for businessmen had thrown themselves on his mercy and the new Congress was eager to do whatever he asked. He did not nationalize the banks. He did, however, take the United States off the gold standard—technically, if not yet formally—with a proclamation declaring an embargo on all gold exports and banning all dealings in foreign exchange. This country had been off the gold standard only twice since 1853.

That morning of March 5 Treasury Secretary Woodin conferred with bankers and federal officials. At 2:30 P.M. Woodin, other Cabinet members and Congressional leaders met with the President to discuss the banking emergency. They agreed it would be impossible to handle the situation on a state-by-state basis, since this would have meant forty-eight different ways of dealing with the crisis. It was decided, instead, that the President should declare a nationwide banking holiday, closing all the nation's 19,000 banks between 1 A.M., Monday, March 6, and Thursday, March 9. Of this total, 5,938 were national banks. Of course, to analyze the banks one by one to decide which were sound enough to be opened later was a problem of staggering complexity.

There was no precedent for such an action. Never in the nation's history had all its banks been closed so many days. But tradition and lack of precedent did not daunt Roosevelt, who knew that what Americans wanted most at this time was audacity.

The possibility of a national bank holiday had occurred to many businessmen—and disturbed them. A lawyer said: "My mind fails to function when I think of the extent of the catastrophe that will follow when the Chase National Bank closes its doors." This fear was not shared by Professor Edward S. Robinson of Yale, a psychologist with a knowledge of law and economics. To Thurman W. Arnold, he said: "Do you think that when the banks all close the people will climb trees and throw coconuts at each other? . . . Well, I will venture a prediction as to what exactly will happen. When the banks close, everyone will feel relieved. It will be sort of a national holiday. There will be general excitement and a feeling of great interest. Travel will not stop; hotels will not close; everyone will have a lot of fun, although they will not admit that it's fun at the time." The professor knew that adventure is discomfort remembered.

The evening of March 5 Roosevelt had an early dinner with his sons Franklin, Jr., and John, who had to hurry back to school. Their mother was worried because she was running short of cash, like everyone else, and the boys needed pocket money for their trip. She asked her husband what she should do. With a reassuring smile, he said he thought they would be able to manage. Mrs. Roosevelt gave the boys the last of her currency and then relaxed with the strange new feeling that living in the White House was different from living in a private home.

News of the bank holiday was announced at one o'clock the next morning, and Herbert Hoover went to bed in his New York hotel suite without hearing about it. When he and the 125,000,000 other Americans awakened, they found themselves in a Kafka-like situation, for not a single normal financial transaction could take place the length and breadth of the land. All banks were closed. Currency was hard to come by. All but one exchange had ceased to function. Even the Chicago Board of Trade, for the first time since 1848, had closed its doors.

At a Midwestern university an ill-informed and anxious freshman wrote in his diary: "Our newly installed President Roosevelt has pulled a fast one on us. Not two days in power, he issued a proclamation declaring a national banking holiday. This closed the doors of every bank in the U.S. Fortunately, I cashed a $5 check a day or two ago. Other than the change left from this, I have no cash, and even when the banks do reopen I'm in a bad fix. I have no more than $10 or $15 left me the rest of the semester. Unless something favorable happens—or, rather, until I cause it to happen —things look exceedingly ill for me. Chances are I'll have to leave the university and go home in a week or two unless I can float a loan or find a job. Christ! I'd hate to leave now!"

In New York columnist Franklin P. Adams had only $4 in cash to take care of his family and himself. William Randolph Hearst, the publisher, went to a Los Angeles bank to ask for a $600,000 loan with his fabulous San Simeon estate to be used for security, but of course, the bank could not accommodate him. One young woman decided to spend every cent she had rather than "wait for it to be swallowed up by others in some mysterious fashion."

As the Yale psychologist had predicted, although most Americans were puzzled and confused, they felt cheerful. Many even sighed with relief, for now that everything had hit bottom there was no place to go but up. Nonetheless, Will Rogers exaggerated when he described the nation as "united and happy, tickled with poverty." Common people were delighted to hear that millionaires were borrowing money from hotel bellboys. The prevalent feeling, one that takes hold during holidays and catastrophes, was that all were in the same boat.

*   *   *

Scrip is a means of exchange, a certificate of indebtedness issued as currency or in lieu of money. It was not new in American history. Scrip was used as far back as 1795 and perhaps even earlier. States, cities, the Confederacy and even colleges had issued scrip in the past. During the banking crisis of 1907 scrip had been issued with the blessing of J. Pierpont Morgan. Now, in March, 1933, many bankers demanded that the federal government issue scrip since there was not enough money in circulation and banks were closed. Roosevelt and his advisers considered the proposal and then rejected it.

However, plans for the manufacture, distribution and use of scrip went forward on state and municipal levels. New York State won federal approval for the creation of a state corporation to issue scrip. As the Newark Clearing House Association adopted scrip, the city fathers took steps to prevent speculation in this emergency money. At Princeton University the *Daily Princetonian* floated scrip to help students get through the banking holiday. Chicago, Seattle and other cities geared themselves for scrip. This instant demand for a new kind of paper money provided overtime work for employees of paper mills and engraving houses.

Trains did not stop running, but they carried fewer passengers. The major Hollywood studios closed, and attendance at movie houses dropped 45 percent. *King Kong* was playing in Manhattan's huge Radio City Music Hall, which announced that its box office would accept checks until scrip became available. Barberships closed for lack of business. Restaurants and stores accepted IOU's from old and trusted customers. Macy's department store, then on a cash basis, announced that it would honor charge accounts from other department stores.

The American Express Company said it would not cash any check for more than $50. People ducked into automats to get nickels and then left without buying a meal. Individuals lucky enough to possess regular paper money of any denomination soon found they were not lucky, after all, since they lacked the change necessary to buy cigarettes, ride buses or use pay phones. Churchgoers put paper currency in collection boxes and snatched up the coins.

Many strange forms of scrip and barter developed. Streetcar tickets, Mexican pesos, Canadian dollars, phone slugs and even stamps were used for currency. In Salt Lake City the Mormons designed their own paper money for local use. Detroit issued nearly $3,000,000 worth of scrip. Deacons in the First Baptist Church of El Paso accepted IOU's when they took up the Sunday collection. Hartford housewives rummaged through their cellars for empty soda bottles which they returned to grocery stores to get back the nickel deposit on each of them. A Broadway sports store accepted crates of vegetables in exchange for merchandise. Business and professional people of Greenwich Village agreed to deal in scrip issued by the Greenwich Village Barter Exchange, backed by notes of West Side merchants.

The Dow Chemical Company coined magnesium into something called Dowmetal Money. The Colonial department store of Detroit accepted herring in exchange for dresses, eggs and honey for other merchandise. Traveling salesmen, far from home and lacking cash for train fare, took to the highways to hitchhike rides. One clever salesman sold his shoe samples in the lobby of a Manhattan hotel to earn the money to take a train. Divorces fell off in Reno, for although women may have had enough money to pay court costs and legal fees, they did not have enough left to buy train tickets home.

In Manhattan the Commodore Hotel refused a room to a man with a $30,000 certified check because he had no cash. John D. Rockefeller found himself without a dime—his publicity-conscious tip—and had to give his golf caddie a whole buck. Taxi dancers in a New York dance hall accepted IOU's from any man who could show them a bankbook. On a Manhattan avenue a man with a $50 bill tried to buy $3.52 worth of shaving supplies but was told by a teasing clerk to grow a beard. Bootleggers were popular because they carried huge wads of bills at a time when everyone wanted currency.

*　　　*　　　*

On Monday, March 6, Nazi storm troopers took control of the streets in the chief cities of Germany, breaking into shops and homes, stealing and destroying private property, brutalizing and arresting thousands of Communists, Socialists and Jews. In the United States the crisis, so far, was financial, rather than physical. A small army of bank examiners worked at top speed trying to decide which banks were sound enough to reopen and which were so weak that they should be liquidated.

The month before his inauguration, Roosevelt had asked all state governors to meet with him in the White House to discuss state-federal cooperation in solving pressing problems. Now, this March 6, about twenty governors and representatives of twenty others gathered in the East Room and heard the new President speak for forty-five minutes about land use, taxation, unemployment relief and the like. Rooosevelt said: "The federal government does have to keep anybody from starving, but the federal government should not be called upon to exercise that duty until other agencies fail. The primary duty is that of the locality, the city, county, town. If they fail and cannot raise enough to meet the needs, the next responsibility is on the states. They have to do all they can. If it is proven that they cannot do any more, and the funds are still insufficient, it is the duty of the federal government to step in."

Ironically, these words echoed some of the sentiments of the departed Herbert Hoover. It also was becoming obvious early in the game that Roosevelt, despite his advocacy of the principle of planning, had not taken office with any carefully conceived master plan for ending the Depression. Of course, Oliver Wendell Holmes had been right when he said there was no panacea. But Roosevelt, unlike Hoover, was daring, imaginative and flexible in his approach to the crisis, willing to experiment, to wager, to improvise, content to scuttle any unworkable scheme and then try another.

The White House meeting of governors included Republicans as well as Democrats. To them there came a letter from a coalition of religious leaders, union officials, ranking industrialists and intellectuals requesting them to issue a proclamation declaring their confidence in the new President in the interest of national unity. They did as asked. Herbert Hoover, issuing a statement of his own from his New York hotel suite, also called for cooperation with Roosevelt.

By this time a multiple buzzer system had been installed on the President's desk, and late in the afternoon of March 6 all the buzzers in the executive wing of the White House sounded simultaneously. In alarm, five secretaries, two Secret Service men and a receptionist tumbled into the Oval Room. There sat Roosevelt like an organist, both hands on the keyboard of the buzzer system, a grin on his face. Suddenly he frowned and in bogus severity said: "Here's a President with nothing to do! Hasn't anyone got anything for me to do?"

At first everyone in the group was too surprised to say anything. Then the President's chief secretary, Marguerite LeHand, caught her breath and replied: "Yes, Mr. President. I have something for you to do: About two feet of mail. And you can start right now!"

All that Roosevelt really wanted was to relax a few minutes with his staff members, chat with them, ask how they were getting along. From that day forward a symphonic buzzing of all the buzzers meant that the President was convening what came to be known as the Children's Hour.

*   *   *

The spirit of free enterprise had not died in the United States. On this March 6, with banks closed and money scarce, a twenty-five-year-old man named Douglas Leigh launched a career that made him the top impresario of huge neon and electric advertising billboard spectaculars.

That grim morning he breakfasted as usual in a New York City automat, left the restaurant to buy a 50-cent camera and a roll of films, then rode a subway to the Fordham Road section of the Bronx. Previously he had scouted this neighborhood for its billboard possibilities. Leigh walked along Fordham Road until he came to a building offering a conspicuous space for a big sign, talked to the building owner, got an option on this space and took snapshots of it.

An unemployed artist friend, working on credit, enlarged one snapshot and then painted on it a sign singing the praises of the posh Hotel St. Moritz along Manhattan's Central Park South. Leigh called on the hotel manager and sold him the advertising space on the Bronx building. To get the money to erect this billboard, Leigh had to dispose of his secondhand Ford. The St. Moritz gave him $50 a month and a rent-free two-room suite for a year. Converting his bedroom into an office, using the hotel's stationery with his own name rubber-stamped on the top, Douglas Leigh then explored the advertising possibilities of Times Square and ultimately became famous.

*   *   *

On Tuesday, March 7, that staunchly Republican paper the Chicago *Tribune* praised Roosevelt's handling, so far, of the banking crisis—even though the *Tribune* had to meet its payroll that day partly in scrip. Harold L. Ickes, the new secretary of the interior, talked with a couple of other Cabinet members about a plan the President was considering. Roosevelt thought that the federal government might take over some vacant farm land in Florida, in cooperation with the state itself, and settle on it many unemployed people from other parts of the country. At the end of this meeting Ickes had to listen to a concert by a band of war-bonneted Sioux Indians who had not yet left Washington since taking part in the inaugural parade.

On this day many old bank notes started to come out of hiding. Commuters from Sault Sainte Marie, Michigan, to Sault Sainte Marie, Ontario, were scrutinized by United States border guards lest they try to smuggle gold into Canada. Although the issuance of scrip by the state of New York remained in doubt, Governor Lehman took no chances and named directors of a new Emergency Certificate Corporation. Rhode Island authorized scrip, and the Kentucky Highway Commission did the same thing to meet its payroll. That evening Treasury Secretary Woodin quietly but abruptly quashed the idea of having the federal government issue scrip on a nationwide basis.

The morning of Wednesday, March 8, newspaper readers turned to Will Rogers' column and smiled—faintly.

"It's surprising," Rogers wrote, "how little money we can get along on. Let the banks never open, let scrip never come. Just everybody keep on trusting everybody else. Why it's such a novelty to find that somebody will trust you that it's changed our whole feeling toward human nature. . . . For three years we have had nothing but 'America is fundamentally sound.' It should have been, 'America is fundamentally cuckoo.' The worse off we get the louder we laugh, which is a great thing. And every American international banker ought to have printed on his office door 'alive today by the grace of a nation that has a sense of humor.' "

One of Roosevelt's close friends was Felix Frankfurter, a Harvard law professor, who had difficulty in breaking himself of the habit of addressing Roosevelt as Frank after FDR became President. Frankfurter reminded him that March 8 marked the ninety-second birthday of retired Supreme Court Justice Oliver Wendell Holmes, one of the most brilliant men who ever sat on this exalted bench. Roosevelt, who could be Machiavellian, saw how he could achieve two things at once: He could pay homage to the great jurist, whom he truly admired, and by visiting Holmes' house, he could flout Hoover's terse comment that the President of the United States never calls on anyone.

Roosevelt was driven to Holmes' place on I Street. Gritting his teeth, step by painful step, he climbed the steep stairway to the second floor and shuffled into the old man's study. At lunch that day Holmes had celebrated by drinking three glasses of champagne and now sat reading Plato when the President entered his room. The jurist was a beautiful old man, tall and lean, with white hair and a sweeping white mustache. After wishing him a happy birthday, Roosevelt asked: "Why do you read Plato, Mr. Justice?"

"To improve my mind," replied the ninety-two-year-old man.

"You have lived through half of our country's history," said the President. "You have seen its great men. This is a dark hour. Justice Holmes, what is your advice to me?"

Holmes, who had seen action with the Union Army during the Civil War, peered at the President from beneath grizzled eyebrows and answered: "You are in a war, Mr. President. I was in a war, too. And in war there is only one rule: *Form your battalions and fight!*"

Holmes later said of Roosevelt: "A second-class intellect—but a first-class temperament!"

Guarding the President that day was Richard Jervis, chief of the Secret Service, who had served four years with Hoover. As Roosevelt emerged onto I Street, hundreds of waiting citizens applauded and cheered him. Jervis whispered to another agent: "Gosh, but it sounds good to hear that again!"

*   *   *

In an effort to end hoarding, to stop gold from leaving the country and to bring more currency into circulation, the Federal Reserve Board issued a thinly veiled threat: It ordered its member banks to report the names of all persons who had withdrawn gold since the previous February 1 and failed to return it by the following March 13—five days hence. Since no one cared to be branded publicly as lacking in patriotism by flouting the national interest, this threat brought immediate results. Gold and currency began flowing back into Federal Reserve Banks. All over the country some banks opened on a restricted basis—mainly to receive this flow. Food prices rose in some cities. The Treasury Department revoked its permission for New York State to issue scrip, and Governor Lehman obediently killed the new Emergency Certificate Corporation. By going to an incinerator, one man managed to recover the gold he had foolishly hidden on top of a trash can, which had been hauled away.

This Wednesday, March 8, Roosevelt held his first press conference since becoming President.

Although he had got along well with correspondents when he was governor of New York, now he was slightly nervous. Sunshine poured through the three tall windows of his office as 125 newspaper and radio reporters entered and took up positions around his desk. One of these reporters was Edgar G. Brown of the Chicago *Defender*—the first Negro newspaperman ever included in such a White House event.

By this time the walls of Roosevelt's office, which he had found distressingly bare, were hung with naval prints. His paper-strewn desk also held a vase of roses, a lamp, a telephone and a calendar. Wearing a double-breasted dark suit and light tie, the President sat in an upholstered chair, grinning, his long ivory cigarette holder cocked at its customary angle. One warm-up question was whether the President had enjoyed his first night in the White House.

"Off the record," he said, chuckling, "I haven't got much sleep since I've been here!"

Francis Stephenson of the Associated Press grinned back at Roosevelt and said: "On the record, I can say that we haven't, either."

Roosevelt laughed appreciatively. Then he announced he was going to end the practice of compelling reporters to submit written questions to him in advance of each press conference. "I am told that what I am about to do will become impossible," he said, "but I am going to try it."

Now the interrogation began. One after another, the President took up reporters' questions about his emergency legislative program, the gold standard, adequate but safe currency and the guarantee of bank deposits. Once he said: "As long as nobody asks me whether we are off the gold standard or gold basis, that is all right, because nobody knows what the gold basis or gold standard really is."

Roosevelt so obviously relished the give-and-take of the press conference and handled himself so well that at the end the correspondents broke into spontaneous applause.

*   *   *

By Thursday, March 9, thousands of hoarders were rushing to big-city banks to return the gold and gold certificates they had hidden in and near their homes. In Philadelphia, Richmond and Cleveland people carrying suitcases full of the heavy precious metal formed long lines outside the doors of banks, eager to surrender it before the government cracked down on them. This gold rush was most impressive in New York City; $30 million was deposited in various banks in just the one day, while the total of gold returned since the previous Monday came to $65 million. One man brought in $700,000. A single firm gave up $6 million in gold bullion.

Los Angeles and Seattle were getting ready to use scrip. Minnesota banks had been authorized to issue scrip. In Pittsburgh scrip was being printed under police guard. In the final analysis, money is anything which people agree to accept, and so scrip had become a currency worthy of the attention of crooks.

Members of the special session of the Seventy-third Congress met on March 9 to launch the famous Hundred Days of Roosevelt's first administration. By the time this Congress adjourned on June 16 it had rammed through the first phase of the New Deal by enacting a broad body of laws concerning banking, industry, agriculture, labor and unemployment relief. As freshmen Senators and Representatives milled about their respective chambers in search of their seats, they sensed that they stood on the brink of a historic session. Most were eager to do all that Roosevelt wanted done. To cite one example, an Iowa Congressman had written the President to say: "I will do anything you ask. You are my leader."

These pliant legislators were not disappointed in the high hopes they had set for Roosevelt. During the Hundred Days he acted boldly, swiftly and dexterously—guiding fifteen major laws through both houses, holding semiweekly press conferences and Cabinet meetings, delivering ten speeches, sponsoring an international monetary conference, conferring with heads of foreign states, never displaying fear and rarely losing his temper. This man, whom Walter Lippmann had considered a lightweight, proved to be astonishingly masterful. Oswald Garrison Villard, editor of the *Nation,* summed up the general reaction by saying: "There's been a miracle here."

Roosevelt began by asking for dictatorial power over transactions in credit, currency, foreign exchange, gold and silver. His request was embodied in an Emergency Banking Act, and accompanying it was a Presidential message in which he said: "I cannot too strongly urge upon the Congress the clear necessity for immediate action." The bill was designated House Resolution 1491.

Into the House chamber strode Henry B. Steagall, chairman of the House Banking and Currency Committee, waving over his head the only copy of the bill and shouting: "Here's the bill! Let's pass it!" Bertrand H. Snell, the Republican leader of the House, demurred that it was "entirely out of the ordinary to pass legislation in this House that, as far as I know, is not even in print at the time it is offered"—then ended on the lame note that after all, the Representatives should "give the President what he demands and says is necessary to meet the situation." Debate was limited to forty minutes but before this deadline some members cried: "Vote! Vote!" A few minutes after 4 P.M. the House unanimously passed a bill which few of its members had even seen.

The Senate also acted fast, but not so impetuously. Huey Long of Louisiana objected that the Emergency Banking Act failed to give sufficient protection to state banks, and he offered an amendment. Up rose Senator Glass of Virginia, the Senate's greatest fiscal expert, to do battle with Long, finally becoming white-faced with anger and accusing the Louisiana Senator of ignorance. Long's amendment was shouted down. Shortly before 7:30 P.M. the Senate approved the measure, 73 to 7.

An hour later newsreel cameramen stood behind their tripods in the Oval Room of the White House to record the historic moment in which Franklin D. Roosevelt signed the first bill of his first administration. Treasury Secretary Woodin dashed inside so fast that he evoked barks from Roosevelt's Scottie dog, Meggie.

Mrs. Roosevelt called: "Franklin, fix your hair!"

Impishly, the President grinned but did nothing about it.

His wife cried to Woodin: "Mr. Secretary, please help Franklin brush his hair down!"

The tiny Woodin gave the President's head a few playful pats.

Roosevelt accepted a $1.50 pen from a friend, cameras began grinding, and the President inked his name on his first law.

*   *   *

On Friday, March 10, he sent Congress a second message, this one asking for various economy measures. Roosevelt knew that many Americans were afraid the government might go bankrupt. Besides, the Democratic national platform of 1932 had a plank calling for a 25 percent reduction in the cost of running the government. Roosevelt began his message with a bow to Congress for its swift passage of his banking bill, then said ominously: "For three long years the federal government has been on the road to bankruptcy. . . ."

To balance the budget, Roosevelt now wanted: (1) reductions of up to 15 percent in the salaries of federal workers; (2) cuts in veterans' pensions—especially payments based on disabilities having nothing to do with service; (3) the reorganization of government agencies with a view to economy; (4) the reduction of salaries of Senators and Representatives from $10,000 to $8,500 a year.

Congress erupted. Legislators winced at the thought of cutting their own salaries, while the idea of antagonizing veterans paralyzed them with fear. The House Democratic majority went to pieces. Representative Joseph W. Byrns of Tennessee, the new floor leader, flatly refused to sponsor Roosevelt's bill. A caucus of Democratic chiefs wrangled heatedly and almost agreed to emasculate the bill, then adjourned.

Back on the floor of the House other leaders tried to restore discipline by using Roosevelt's name freely. One warned: "When the *Congressional Record* goes to President Roosevelt's desk in the morning, he will look over the roll call we are about to take, and I warn you new Democrats to be careful where your names are found!" Groans. Hisses. But the President rode out this first tempest. Although 92 Democrats, including 7 party leaders, voted against his second bill, 69 Republicans crossed the aisle to back him up.

The next day the House passed the measure 266 to 138, and four days later the Senate gave its approval, 62 to 13. Roosevelt had survived his first test of strength with Congress, but the legislators gingerly fingered letters and telegrams from outraged members of the American Legion.

The President had estimated that this act would save the nation a total of $500 million. Actually, the savings came to only about $232 million—and soon this was wiped out as the government assumed new functions, created new agencies and spent ever more money for relief.

*   *   *

The night of March 10–11 Roosevelt was awakened to be told that an earthquake had jolted southern California. A total of 120 persons were killed, and damage amounted to more than $40 million. Shocks continued at intervals for two days. The President made a few phone calls from his bed, and within fifteen minutes nearby resources of the military and the Red Cross were made available to the stricken coastal area. Herbert Hoover, still in New York, placed a long-distance call to his home in Palo Alto to make sure his wife was all right.

After Roosevelt got up and dressed for the day, he issued a statement assuring the nation that "technical difficulties which operated to delay the opening of the banks . . . have finally substantially been overcome by tireless work on the part of the officials of the treasury and the Federal Reserve System." Then he announced it would be possible to open the banks the following Monday through Wednesday.

On Saturday, March 12, Mrs. Eleanor Roosevelt donated $300 to unemployment relief. In New York, Chicago, Cleveland, Cincinnati and Pittsburgh, hoarders flocked to banks to turn in gold and gold certificates belatedly brought out of hiding. Irene Du Pont of the fabulously rich Du Pont family surrendered gold pieces she had been saving the past twenty years. Europe-bound travelers were not searched for contrabrand, but they were reminded of the embargo on gold. Vassar College was using scrip. By Saturday evening the various Federal Reserve Banks had recovered $300 million—enough to back $750 million in additional currency.

Roosevelt had decided to go on the radio to tell Americans why it had been necessary to close all banks and to reassure them that they would not lose their savings. A speech was prepared by treasury men and some of his aides, but he felt that it was far too technical. Stretched out on a couch, he dictated the speech himself—trying to visualize the workmen he had seen outside his window tearing down the inaugural reviewing stand, along with the farmers he knew back at Hyde Park. If he could make them understand what he meant, then he could get his thoughts across to all the people.

On Sunday, March 12, at 10:20 P.M. the President was wheeled into his White House study and placed behind a desk that held seven radio microphones. To his left stood a water carafe and two drinking glasses. Roosevelt, who was smoking as usual, glanced at his wristwatch. On folding chairs in front of him sat thirty relatives, friends and radio announcers. One of the announcers was Robert Trout of the Columbia Broadcasting System, who, noticing the white marble fireplace in the room, called this first Presidential broadcast a fireside chat. This term lived on for decades.

Roosevelt was scheduled to begin speaking at 10:30 P.M. The reading copy of his speech had been typed triple-spaced in pica type with a blue typewriter ribbon. In its margins he had scribbled notes to show where he should be at certain points in this 15-minute broadcast. Now the President quietly asked for this copy. No one had it. All his aides panicked, but not so Roosevelt. He simply picked up a single-spaced text that had been prepared for the press. The room quieted down. Silence. At that moment 60,000,000 Americans sat by 20,000,000 radios waiting to hear what their new President had to say. In the White House study radio announcers held up warning fingers. Roosevelt snubbed out his cigarette, took a sip of water. Ten thirty o'clock. The announcers, speaking softly, presented the President of the United States. Their fingers came down and pointed at him.

"My friends," Roosevelt began, "I want to talk for a few minutes with the people of the United States about banking. . . ." His voice was warm and firm, his manner informal and friendly. Although he never had been coached in radio technique, he was a natural at the microphone, completely relaxed, reading as though he were speaking, delivering about 100 words a minute.

In many homes across the country the most imposing piece of furniture in the living room was a console radio, and now, leaning close to it, were white-haired old ladies, farmers wearing suspenders, factory workers in windbreakers and nervous bankers. "Some of our bankers," Roosevelt said, "had shown themselves either incompetent or dishonest in their handling of the people's funds—" and, coast to coast, plain people looked at one another, their eyes narrowed, nodding in agreement. But the President did not criticize the bankers unduly and did not dwell on the past. Instead, he looked toward the future, especially the near future.

Roosevelt said that the next day, Monday, banks would reopen in the 12 cities with Federal Reserve Banks. On Tuesday, in 250 other cities with recognized clearinghouses, the doors would open to banks which federal examiners had found to be sound. Wednesday, subject to the government's physical ability to complete its evaluation of them, still other banks would resume business in smaller places throughout the nation.

"I do not promise you," said the President, "that every bank will be reopened or that individual losses will not be suffered, but there will be no losses that possibly could be avoided. . . . Together we cannot fail."

His first radio speech was a psychological masterpiece. Americans felt that at long last they had a leader who spoke the truth, one whom they could trust, a man who knew how to set the country on the right track leading out of the Depression. Will Rogers wisecracked that Roosevelt had explained banking in such simple terms that even bankers could understand it.

Within the next few days banks did reopen, more gold was returned to them, huge sums of cash were deposited, currency flowed back into Federal Reserve Banks, stock and commodity exchanges resumed business, prices rose—and the President was showered with praise. William Cardinal O'Connell called him a "God-sent man" while Newton D. Baker described him as a "providential person at a providential moment."

Throughout this crisis of March, 1933, one of the President's most trusted aides had been Raymond Moley, on leave from his position as a professor at Columbia University and the head of Roosevelt's Brain Trust. Although Moley later broke with Roosevelt and became one of his severest critics, he never reneged on his judgment that "capitalism had been saved in eight days."

18

Migrants and the Civilian Conservation Corps

L ONG BEFORE Roosevelt took office many Americans had become disturbed about a curious new social phenomenon—a migration of
despair.

Hordes of workless men, boys just out of school, entire families and
even single girls roamed across the country, hitchhiking on highways and
riding freight trains, sleeping in hobo jungles and in flophouses. No one
knew for sure, but by 1932 it was estimated that from 1,500,000 to
2,000,000 people were on the move. In general, they traveled from north
to south, from east to west. One hitchhiker got lifts across the entire
continent in five days simply by carrying a sign that said: "Give me a ride
or I'll vote for Hoover."

The wanderers were not hoboes, for hoboes shun work, while these
people wanted to work. There were unemployed husbands who could not
bear to go home again and tell their wives they had been unable to find
jobs. There were the elder sons of relief families who left home so more
food would be left for the younger children. There were younger boys, too,
recent graduates from grammar school or high school, who, in normal
times, would have taken jobs a few days after getting their diplomas. There
were girls who found their homes intolerable, what with their jobless
fathers moping around all day and their mothers endlessly complaining
about lack of money. They left hometowns where they *knew* there were no
job openings in the *hope* of finding employment in some distant place. And
of course, some youths hit the road because of their energy, romanticism
and curiosity about life beyond the horizon.

One of the main routes followed by this army of transients was federal
Highway 66, which unrolls like a gray ribbon between Chicago and Los

Angeles. In those days there was much talk about "the lonesome road," but one vagabond said: "Th' road ain't lonesome—it's th' people that's on it." Alan Lomax quotes this man as saying further: "Hitch-hikin' down the lonesome old road, been over that 66 enough to run it up to 6666. Thought maybe I could run onto a job of work. Heard some was openin' up in Utah. Hell, Utah ain't far! California ain't but a hop and a skip. Atlanta, Georgia—just a small blister in the shoe. Ain't far. I don't mind if I can go to work. Whew! You see a flock of big cars on th' road, don't you? Bunch of'em got plenty of room for me. I wouldn't jump on'em, er take their damn money. All I want's that job. Hell, if I was a outlaw or a robber like some folks think, I wouldn't rob a guy that treated me right. I ain't no heel. God! Never seen so many poodle dogs in my life! Women's got fur coats. Hell of a job to try to tell where one quits and the other begins."

Folk singer Woody Guthrie, who called himself "just a little one-cylinder guitar picker," wrote an introduction to a book entitled *Hard Hitting Songs for Hard-Hit People,* in which he said:

> . . . I've been a ramblin man, from Oklahoma to California and back three times by freight train, highway and thumb, and I've been stranded and disbanded, busted, disgusted with people of all sorts, sizes, shapes and calibres—folks that wandered around over the country looking for work, down and out, and hungry half the time. I've slept on and with them, with their feet in my face and my feet in theirs—in bed rolls with Canadian lumberjacks, in greasy rotten shacks and tents with the Okies and Arkies that are grazing today over the state of California and Arizona like a herd of lost buffalo with the hot hoof and empty mouth disease.
>
> Then to New York in the month of February, the thumb route, in the snow that blanketed from Big Springs, Texas, north to New York, and south again into even Florida. . . . Walking down the big road, no job, no home, no nothing. Nights I slept in jails, and the cells were piled high with young boys, strong men and old men; and they talked and they sung, and they told you the story of their life, how it used to be, how it got to be, how the home went to pieces, how the young wife died or left, how the mother died in the insane asylum, how Dad tried twice to kill himself and lay flat on his back for 18 months—and then the crops got to where they wouldn't bring nothing, work in the factories would kill a dog, work on the belt line killed your soul, work in the cement and limestone quarries withered your lungs, work in the cotton mills shot your feet and legs all to hell, work in the steel mills burned your system up like a gnat that lit in the melting pot, and—always, always had to fight and argue and cuss and swear, and shoot and slaughter and wade mud and sling blood—to try to get a nickel more out of the rich bosses.

As periodicals and Congressional witnesses gave proof of this growing legion of the homeless, fear was felt by Senators and others. There was, in fact, a frightening precedent to be found in recent Russian history. After the overthrow of the czar in 1917, and before the Bolsheviks brought iron order out of chaos, almost 3,000,000 Russian boys and girls, some only ten years old, organized into bands, robbing and killing and terrorizing whole villages and towns. These wild children of Russia were called the *bezprizorni*. Was the United States about to be torn apart by its own youths, its homeless and hungry and angry people?

In the halls of Congress men declared that the federal government should build camps for the wandering young people. While Hoover still was in office, Senator James Couzens urged that idle young be given shelter in Army camps, but his bill was rejected. Couzens angrily told the Senate that "the aristocracy of the army did not wish to be annoyed." The Child Welfare League of America asked that homeless migrants get individualized treatment. The National Education Association begged the government not to entrust the problem of homeless and jobless youths to the War Department, but to "recognized educational agencies." Missouri planned to buy 3,500 acres in the Ozarks for cultivation by boys. Henry Ford thought that the lads on the road were getting a good education. Rotary Club members expressed alarm at the increase in vagrancy among boys and young men.

Few of Russia's *bezprizorni* had been able to read or write; but most of America's vagrants were literate, and some were even professional men— unemployed doctors, lawyers, teachers and pharmacists. There were also tough boys from city slums and sad farmers, white people and black people. A few of the wanderers were a mere twelve years of age. Among the migrants were an estimated 25,000 families—including a weather-beaten elderly couple from New Mexico who had lost their small farm. Perhaps 100,000 were girls less than twenty-one years old, and some sold their bodies for 10 cents when they could find a man who had a dime.

Elliott Chapman was seventeen when he hit the road. He had tried to earn a living selling radios in Detroit, discovered that few factory workers had the money for such a luxury, went to Chicago, where he worked as a caddie, found these pickings too slim, finally set out in earnest. Like many other transients, he headed for a warmer climate, headed for New Orleans, but soon bumped into the hot stove of reality.

"They do not like you to stay there," Chapman later said, "especially in New Orleans and a few places where they arrive a couple of hundred a day. The Salvation Army places will feed you for a night—or, rather, let you sleep there. In the morning they will give you a bowl of beef broth or something. In the other places they give you coffee, soup and bread. But the soup, as one fellow puts it, is just some hot water with a little cabbage dipped in. . . . Most of the fellows—young fellows that start out—will not panhandle. They have a pride and are sort of scared to go up to a person. But you soon lose that, and there is a feeling when you are tired and hungry that you do not care much what happens to you."

Most cities and towns and counties, overburdened with the care of their own residents, were indeed inhospitable. Detroit drove its tramps out of town. Atlanta put unwanted nonresidents into chain gangs. In Miami the sheriff of Dade County would fill a truck with homeless men and drive them north to the next county, whose sheriff would load them into a second truck and dump them at the line of the next county, whose sheriff would transfer them into a third truck and deposit them at the border of still another county. At this point the men were ignored, neither fed nor housed nor chased elsewhere, so at last they would trickle back down the roads to Miami.

One day Woody Guthrie arrived in Tucson, Arizona. In early morning he started walking down a street in the business district, slowly becoming aware that he was being followed by a big policeman. Guthrie stopped and turned around. The cop smiled and said good morning.

"Good morning," Guthrie replied.

"Going to work?"

"Naw—just looking for work. Like to find a job and hang around this town for a while."

"No work around here this time of year."

Guthrie said carefully: "I'm generally pretty lucky at gittin' me a job. I'm a good clerk—grocery store, drug store. Paint signs, to boot."

"You'll starve to death around here—or make the can."

"Can?"

"That's what I said. Can!"

"You mean," Guthrie asked, "git in trouble?"

The cop nodded yes.

"What kinda trouble? I'm a good hand to keep outta trouble."

The cop said: "Listen, boy! When you're not working in this town, you're already in trouble. See?"

*   *   *

Yuma, Arizona, a more friendly place, fed 30,000 men and boys in soup kitchens in four and a half months. The transient poor became a political issue in Colorado. In one six-month period 45,000 migrants entered and left El Paso. Between 400 and 500 youths rode trains through Des Moines every single day in 1933, and it was believed that even more hitchhiked in and out of town. New York State opened its first transient camp in 1933, and the next year it was helping 20,000 drifters each month. Kansas City had 1,500 vagrants passing through it daily. In Washington, D.C., the Salvation Army served 7,512 transients in three months. The state of Florida and the city of Los Angeles were so inundated with nonresidents that at last they closed their borders to them.

Among these wanderers were a few men destined to become famous.

Robert Ryan, later a Hollywood star, collected bills for a loan shark in Chicago but felt so sorry for the poor whom he was dunning that he quit after two weeks and spent the next couple of years drifting across the country, digging sewers, herding horses and panning for gold in Montana.

Nelson Algren, who developed into a major American novelist, wandered through the South and Southwest. Burl Ives, a singer of ballads and then a movie star, crossed and recrossed the country, lugging a banjo on which he had painted "Burl Ives, the Vagabond Lover." John Toland, who became a journalistic historian, was hauled out of a boxcar in Indiana by cops who frisked him for weapons in the belief that he might be the notorious bank robber John Dillinger. Many poor people, eager to see any part of the Establishment get its comeuppance, applauded the criminal exploits of Dillinger and of "Pretty Boy" Floyd.

The campfires of the homeless could be seen along almost every railway line across the landscape. Their faces browned by the sun or blackened by coal dust after riding the rails, men and boys huddled in jungles—as their campsites near railroad yards were called. It was easy to pick out the ones who were new to this way of life, since their faces and clothing were cleaner. Some carried battered grips. Others clutched brown wrapping paper twisted around extra shirts. Most, however, had only the clothes on their backs, and the fabric soon fell apart from being rain-soaked, slept in, and from being boiled and fumigated at missions.

At night in these jungles the vagrants squatted near the pulsing flames of fires, their shadows writhing hunchbacks, and in the dark distance they heard the electronic concert of crickets. In dull voices they talked about jobs, or rumors of jobs, in some faraway city, how friendly or hostile that place might be, the time the next freight was scheduled to slow down nearby to take on water, the kinds of detectives employed by the railroad— but mostly they talked about food. Most of the time they were hungry, and malnutrition had taken its toll of them. Their ribs stuck out, their bellies were too flat, and even among the young the skin of their arms and legs was loose, flabby. They slouched. Their eyes were blank with fatigue, and they had nervous mannerisms. Too often their jungle-cooked meals consisted of potatoes burned to a cinder, coffee full of sand and ants and flies, sour chicken or evil-tasting boiled fish.

In cities with agencies that fed the wanderers there were two standard meals—stew and beans. In town after town after town it was stew and beans, beans and stew. Once in a while the fare included sandwiches— usually cheese or peanut butter—and perhaps once a week the vagrants got a boiled vegetable dinner or hash, along with stale bread that had been returned to the bakery. Whatever the free menu, though, the missions and soup kitchens refused to serve the same man more than about one day; after that he was expected to push on. At the end of a day or so without any food whatsoever, some transients were glad to root through garbage pails. Robbed of pride, their bellies burning, they begged for a morsel from grocers, restaurant owners and housewives. In his autobiography called *Bound for Glory,* Woody Guthrie tells what happened after he knocked at the door of a little brown wooden house in Texas:

. . . A lady opened the door. She said that she didn't have anything for me to do; she acted crabby and fussy, chewing the rag and talking sour to herself. She went back in the house again, still talking.

"Young men, old men, all kinds of men; walking, walking, all of the time walking, piling off of the freights, making a run across my tomato garden and knocking on my door; men out gallivantin' around over the country; be better off if you'd stayed at home; young boys taking all kinds of crazy chances, going hungry, thirsty, getting all dirty and ugly, ruining your clothes, maybe getting run over and killed by a truck or a train—who knows. Yes. Yes. Yes. Don't you dare run away, young nitwit! I'm a fixing you a plate of the best I got. Which is all I got. Blame fools! Ought to be at home with your family, that's where you'd ought to be. Here! Here, eat this! It'll at least stick to your ribs. You look like an old hungry hound dog. I'd be ashamed to ever let the world beat me down any such a way. Here! Eat every bite of it! I'll go and fix you a glass of good milk. Crazy world these days. Everybody's cutting loose and hitting the road!"

*　　　*　　　*

In 1932 the Southern Pacific Railroad ejected a total of 683,457 free riders from its trains. Few of these vagrants rode the rods, in the strict sense of the term, for by the time of the Depression newly designed freight cars lacked the underslung rods beneath them, once a favorite hobo roost. The new breed of wanderers rode inside boxcars and locomotive tenders, on top of refrigerator cars, between jolting and banging cars. Swinging onto a train as it began to pull away was a dangerous practice, for a man could slip and have his foot cut off. It also was necessary to beware of railroad detectives, known as deeks.

Official policy regarding this army of free riders varied from one railway line to another, and sometimes their detectives overlooked or exceeded company policy. The Santa Fe tried to exclude all vagrants. The Missouri Pacific ordered them off its trains and other property, but taking note of changed times, it did not hand them over to local police to be arrested, as in the past. On still other railroads the trainmen and detectives looked the other way when transients swung aboard an empty freight car. They knew it was pointless to threaten them with arrest, for the men would laugh and jeer and announce that that was just what they wanted, since jail would provide them with shelter and food. One brakeman said: "What chance would we have in bodily ejecting this army from the cars?" Sometimes a compassionate train crew would hook an empty and unneeded car to a freight train so the men and boys could ride in comfort.

Among those roaming the land was Eric Sevareid, who later became a noted television commentator. At that time he was so skinny that his companions of the road called him Slim. A sensitive observer, Sevareid was impressed by the scenic beauty of America, and in his book *Not So Wild a Dream* he says:

. . . I had forgotten that the clouds of summer were fat and laundered white and that small shadows moved over the surface of this inland ocean. I had forgotten the precision design of a furrowed field on a canvas so spacious that lines were long and clean and never crowded. I had forgotten how the rails were fixed to the earth, how they bent and fastened the world down at the far edge, where the curvature of the planet was apparent to the human eye. . . .

Riding a freight one day, Sevareid found that one of his companions was a fourteen-year-old boy named Freddie. Sevareid wrote:

Freddie was very nearly the cause of my death one night. We had re-assembled in the box car after a brief foray though a bleak Nevada hamlet, and now, as the train rumbled through the night, we squatted around a small fire in the middle of the car floor, exchanging tidbits. Freddie was missing; somebody thought he had caught the train at the other end, and when we heard a banging on the roof we knew he had, and that he had run over the tops, leaping in the darkness from car to car. Somebody slid the big door wide open, and we heard Freddie yell:
"Grab my legs I'm coming down."
We looked at one another. There was silence for a moment. A man said: "How about you, Slim? You got long arms."
I had no choice of action. I stood by the door, while a chain of three or four men fastened themselves to one of my legs. The wind blew in my face. The train was racketing along a narrow bridge over a dark canyon. Suddenly there were Freddie's dangling feet, then his legs, swinging in close, then away again as the box car tilted, then close again. I grabbed them, felt myself being torn out of the car, then was toppled over backwards, on top of the human chain, Freddie on top of me. Except for a moment, ten years later, when I found myself at the door of a plunging airplane, trying to jump, I have never known a greater terror. Freddie had stolen a bottle of cherry brandy. He was the hero of the evening, and we ate, drank, and sang to the accompaniment of a harmonica until long after midnight.

*   *   *

Another vagabond was a young man named Stanley Watson. The Depression had left him homeless, jobless, friendless. Packing his few belongings and taking what little money he had left, he turned tramp, as he put it, heading out of bitter winter weather toward the West, not knowing and not much caring just where he was going. By thumbing rides on the highways, he reached the Great Plains of middle America, where he ran into a snowstorm. At first he had been too proud to beg, but now he became so weakened by exposure that when he reached North Platte, Nebraska, he humbly asked for shelter and was grateful to get a cot in City Hall.

When he arose the next morning, the temperature stood at 38 degrees below zero. Refreshed, his pride would not let him ask for food after having been given shelter, so he marched out into the cold, haphazardly setting Cheyenne, Wyoming, as his goal. For a long time he had eaten nothing. The temperature sank lower and lower. Watson stumbled on, blindly, mindlessly—and then passed out. When he floated back to consciousness, he found himself in a hospital at Fort Warren, Wyoming. He had been picked up on a road outside Cheyenne, suffering from exposure and lack of food. The next two weeks he was kept in bed, and then he spent another week regaining his strength.

Upon resuming his lonely wandering, he rode a boxcar for the first time in his life. Now, forced to admit that he had been shorn of dignity, he began begging for food, and whenever he could get none, he stole from other vagrants, just as they stole from him. On and on he pushed, lacking hope as well as pride, traveling through all forty-eight states, seldom shaving, almost oblivious to the stench of his filthy flesh and clothes, sinking into apathy and laziness. "Why should I work," Watson later wrote, "when I could eat three times a day without the outlay of a single copper or an ounce of energy? I became a master of sob-stories."

After a year and a half of riding freights, begging and robbing for food, fighting pointlessly, committing various kinds of petty larceny, dodging cops, he arrived in the village of Woodbridge, New York, where he called on an aunt and uncle. They told him about something called the Civilian Conservation Corps, which would pay him $30 a month and give him room and board. Watson was amazed. He never had heard of it. At the insistence of his relatives, he promised to enlist. On July 23, 1934, Stanley Watson began what he happily called "a life of discipline and supervision."

*   *   *

Late in the afternoon of Friday, April 7, 1933, a gray taxi pulled up in front of an Army induction center in lower Manhattan, and four young men got out. In one last mild spree they had hailed the cab on the Lower East Side to make the short trip across town. Now, with the taxi meter registering 65 cents, they found they had only 50 cents among them. Just as the cabdriver started to give them a hard time, an obliging Army officer stepped forward to pay the balance.

Fiore Rizzo was the first of the quartet to walk into the granite building as reporters pressed close. This boy from the sidewalks of New York loudly announced that he was ready to go to work in the woods. He said he was one of a family of thirteen, was nineteen years old, unmarried, and had been unemployed for the past year. His father had been without work for three years. These facts had already been checked by the New York City Home Relief Bureau. An Army doctor listened to Rizzo's heart, thumped his chest, peered down his throat and declared him physically fit. Then the boy raised his right hand and took an oath.

When the ceremony ended, Rizzo danced an excited jig until a reporter commented that he probably would be sent to the Far Western part of the United States. Rizzo stopped jigging and began scratching his head. The reporter asked what was wrong. A typical New Yorker, the boy answered the question with a question. In all seriousness, he asked: "What the hell are we going to do about those Indians?"

That chilly spring day of 1933 Fiore Rizzo became the very first recruit in the new Civilian Conservation Corps.

*   *   *

The CCC, first of the many New Deal agencies to be created, grew out of Franklin D. Roosevelt's wish to save the nation's young people and its natural resources. To his way of thinking, the two went together. He once said: "The greatest single resource of this country is its youth." As a gentleman farmer and as the father of four sons, he knew much about both subjects.

As long ago as 1922 he had tried to form a syndicate to buy and operate a tract of land as a private venture. At his Hyde Park estate he could lie in bed and gaze out a window to the south overlooking a beautiful yellow poplar that soared 120 feet into the sky, a sight that always gave him joy. There were times when he planted from 20,000 to 50,000 trees on his estate annually, and he knew the unique qualities of the hemlock, Scotch pine, poplar and Norway pine. He said that forests "are the 'lungs' of our land, purifying our air and giving fresh strength to our people." As governor of New York he had put 10,000 unemployed youths to work in the state's forest preserves, and they had planted more trees than all the other states combined.

In accepting the Democratic nomination as a Presidential candidate, Roosevelt had planted the seeds of the Civilian Conservation Corps. He had spoken of a plan for "converting many millions of acres of marginal and unused land into timberland through reforestation. There are tens of millions of acres east of the Mississippi river alone in abandoned farms, in cut-over land, now growing up in worthless brush. Why, every European nation has a definite policy, and has had one for generations. We have none. Having none, we face a future of soil erosion and timber famine. It is clear that economic foresight and immediate employment march hand in hand in the call for the reforestation of these vast areas."

Soon after taking office as President, Roosevelt discussed his plan with Professor Nelson C. Brown of the New York State College of Forestry and had sent his assistant, Rexford Tugwell, to take up the matter with Major R. Y. Stuart, chief of the federal Forest Service. Then the President outlined his idea in a note to his new secretaries of war, labor, agriculture and the interior: "I propose to the Congress the creation of a Civilian Reclamation Corps, to be recruited from the ranks of the unemployed, ratable to the proportion of unemployment existing in the several states. The actual work to be undertaken covers a wide field, many of the projects being already a component of our national policy. They would cover roughly the fields of reforestation on national and state lands, prevention of soil erosion, flood control, power development, inland waterways, and inter-coastal communications."

Some of these Cabinet members felt it might be dangerous to lump thousands of sullen men in camps here and there across the country, but Roosevelt disagreed. They also warned him that his proposed corps might depress the wages of free labor, angering union leaders. The President insisted on going ahead with such projects as did not "interfere with normal employment."

On March 21, 1933, Roosevelt formally asked Congress to establish an agency that at first bore the name of the Civilian Corps Reforestation Youth Rehabilitation Movement. This awkward title was changed to the Civilian Conservation Corps and soon everyone was referring to it as the CCC. Before Congress could act—and as the Cabinet members had warned—organized labor denounced the plan. AFL President William Green touched all bases in his criticism, declaring that the idea smacked of "fascism, of Hitlerism, of a form of Sovietism." Although Congress did not let this criticism kill the project, it guarded its own flanks by authorizing the President to create the CCC by executive order and to define its program as he saw fit.

On April 5, 1933, the Civilian Conservation Corps came into legal existence. A call went out for 250,000 young men to be housed in 1,468 camps from coast to coast at a cost of $500 million a year for two years. Roosevelt sought to pacify organized labor by placing the project in the hands of a labor leader. As director of the CCC he chose fifty-seven-year-old Robert Fechner of Boston, vice-president of the machinists' union. During World War I Fechner had settled many labor disputes in plants that made war materials, and Roosevelt had come to know him when FDR had served as assistant secretary of the navy. Fechner took the CCC post at $10,000 a year, and labor, which liked and trusted him, soon ceased to complain.

What young people qualified for enrollment in the CCC? In the beginning, they had to be between the ages of seventeen and twenty-eight —although the maximum age later was reduced to twenty-four. They had to be out of school, out of work, American citizens, physically and mentally fit, single, of good character and members of a family on some relief roll—state or municipal. They also had to agree to let most of their wages be sent home. Each eligible youth would get $30 a month, but $23 to $25 of this would be mailed by the War Department to his family. This left each volunteer a mere $5 to $7 a month in pocket money, but the CCC took care of his basic needs. He got free transportation to his assigned camp, free medical attention, woolen trousers, flannel shirts, work pants, underclothes, socks, shoes, raincoat, jumpers, work hat, tie, belt, barracks bag, two blankets and a mess kit. Depending on the climate of the region to which he was sent, he was housed in a tent or in wooden barracks.

Thirty dollars a month was less than the going wage across the nation but as much as relief allotments. It exceeded the $21 monthly paid each private in the Army under the reduced military pay scale that had been instituted despite President Hoover; however, the soldiers could do as they wished with their money. CCC leaders were paid $45 a month and assistant leaders $36. Most important, the enrollment of 250,000 youths in the CCC meant that almost that many families throughout the nation were receiving monthly checks from the federal government.

Even so, with millions upon millions of people out of work, the CCC program helped only a fraction of the needy. As might be expected, there were something like six applicants for each boy taken into the corps. In an effort to spread the work and to assist as many families as possible, service within the CCC was limited to six to nine months; as some young men left to get jobs, having learned a skill and thus become more employable, others took their places. One of every ten or eleven CCC enrollees was a Negro, which was about the proportion of blacks to whites in the population, but more blacks than whites were jobless and disadvantaged.

In creating the CCC, Roosevelt had hoped, among other things, to bring boys from one region of the country into contact with those from another so that they might get to know one another better, to realize they shared a common heritage and to see areas of the nation about which they knew nothing. The results were mixed. Tough city boys, the sons of idle factory workers, found it difficult to understand country lads, the sons of bankrupt farmers. Some also had difficulty adjusting to a strange environment. A New York boy said: "I was sent to Utah. I'll never forget the ride up the mountains in this battered old truck. We had an old grizzled army sergeant in charge. When we got to the area, it was just thick woods.

" 'Where's the camp?' I asked.

"The sarge waved his hands around the trees.

" 'This is it. Break out the axes and chop like hell if you don't want to sleep on the ground.'

"We chopped and built cabins and even a mess hall. For the next three years I grew up, physically and mentally and spiritually, in that beautiful country. It was one of the most rewarding experiences of my life."

Although labor had been pacified by the appointment of Fechner as director of the CCC, it had no intention of letting the boys engage in any construction which it considered its prerogative. Union members built most CCC barracks, mess halls, libraries and the like.

Although most Americans looked with favor upon the CCC, a few strongly opposed it. Huey Long sneered that he would "eat every pine seedling they'll ever grow in Louisiana!" Governor Eugene Talmadge of Georgia accused the CCC of coddling loafers, but when he found himself unable to arouse fellow Georgians, he backed down a bit, denying he ever had called the CCC boys "bums and loafers." Herbert Benjamin, who sometimes wrote for the *Daily Worker,* charged that the CCC program would "establish and legalize a system of forced labor." At Roosevelt's seventh press conference he was asked whether the CCC camps were concentration camps. In alarm, he cried: "Do not use that word!" The Socialist Party called for the abolition of the CCC on the grounds that it threatened organized labor's wage and living standards.

Over in Germany, that spring of 1933, Hitler had decreed forced labor for every German male seventeen to twenty-five years of age for six months, regardless of education or social status. The Nazi dictator wanted to break down all class distinctions, besides cultivating swamps, moors, and the flats along the seacoast. Roosevelt, aware of Germany's program of compulsory labor and sensitive to its political implications, resisted pressure from American Army officers to institute military training in all CCC camps. If the President had been the dictator his enemies said he was, he easily could have converted the CCC into an arm of the military Establishment. But he did not do so. CCC enrollees entered the program voluntarily, not under duress. They did not drill. They saluted no one. They were not awakened each morning by bugles.

Every CCC camp was supervised by a captain or lieutenant from the Regular Army, one reserve officer and four enlisted men from the Regular Army. Acting on orders from the President, War Secretary George H. Dern said that the men in charge of the camps "had to learn to govern men by leadership, explanation and diplomacy, rather than discipline." This boiled down to discipline without discipline.

One rainy day a reporter and photographer from the Kansas City *Journal-Post* visited a CCC camp at Fort Leavenworth, Kansas. To their amusement they found that the trainees addressed the Army enlisted men as "Hey, you!" or "Listen, guys!" As the photographer lined up two captains and two sergeants to take their picture, about 100 CCC boys gathered behind him to mug at the regulars and razz them.

"Watch the birdie, boss, watch the birdie!"

"Hey, sarge! Look out or you'll smile!"

"Good-bye, camera!"

But when the photographic session ended and Captain John T. Zellars began speaking to the CCC youths, they became silent and respectful.

"Now listen, men," Zellars said, "you've worked hard today and you have done a good job. This rain isn't any fun, but we've got to make the best of it. Just as soon as you leave here, go to your tents and turn in your bedding for the laundry. Then get into some different clothing and dry your present stuff out. Don't play around about it, because we don't want any sick men turning up. And another thing: Tomorrow afternoon most of you will get passes to go to town and I want you to take care of yourselves. Remember, if you show up here Sunday night with a jag on, you won't get any sympathy. And don't get tangled up with any hot woman when you go to town. . . ."

Naturally, since the trainees were young and heedless and hot-blooded, there were incidents. In the American Northwest, one group tossed a major into a river, another stole a sheep and roasted it, another threw stones at the flag from the mess line, while still another traded some of their supplies with girls from a nearby town. In a CCC camp at Preston, New York, 6 Negroes were jailed and 34 were sent back to Harlem after rebelling against the camp authorities. In West Orange, New Jersey, 125 CCC boys demonstrated against the curfew.

Except in the case of a crime that called for punishment by civil authorities, camp leaders could impose no penalties except expulsion from the corps. This, of course, worked a hardship on the family dependent on its CCC allotment, and there were always plenty of other young men eager to step into the place vacated by an unruly trainee.

The assistant secretary of war was a brash man named Harry H. Woodring. He stirred up a tempest by writing that "whether or not it is true, as many hold, that the C.C.C. camps are the forerunners of the great civilian labor armies of the future, I believe that this activity should be expanded." Woodring went on to say that the Army was ready to organize the CCC, along with veterans and people on relief, into "economic storm troops." This was an unfortunate choice of words. Hitler's storm troopers, 2,000,000 strong, outnumbered Germany's army regulars 20 to 1. Americans shuddered at Woodring's remark.

Chief of Staff Douglas MacArthur also made waves when he testified before the House Military Affairs Committee: "I think there would be nothing finer than that the men in the C.C.C. camps should be used as a nucleus for an enlisted reserve. I think no method could be sounder than to take these C.C.C. men who have had six months in camp and give them perhaps two months more, in which they would receive military training."

Roosevelt, who had praised MacArthur for the fine work the Army was doing in establishing the CCC camps, still refused to let the trainees be subjected to military training. One day MacArthur went to the White House to see the President about another matter—a proposal to cut back the officer list. The general argued that this would weaken national defenses at a time when militarism was rife in Germany and Italy and as the Japanese marched into Manchuria and China. Roosevelt emphasized the need to balance the budget. MacArthur argued with him. Roosevelt held his ground. The chief of staff and the commander in chief exchanged sharp words. MacArthur arose and coldly told the President he might ask for his immediate relief as chief of staff and then take the issue straight to the American people. And the general stalked out, leaving behind a President red-faced with fury. MacArthur himself was so agitated that as he left the White House, he vomited on the lawn.

*   *   *

Because unemployment was massive and distress widespread, Roosevelt had urged speed in the creation of the CCC program—and speed he got. By June 30, 1933, a total of 275,000 youths had been enrolled and put to work in camps in every state of continental United States, in forests and parks and national monuments, on Indian reservations, in Alaska, Hawaii, Puerto Rico and the Virgin Islands. This figure was more than the 180,000 men mobilized in a comparable period in 1917 after the declaration of war. The CCC total also exceeded the number of American soldiers who served throughout the Spanish-American War. At its peak the CCC had about 500,000 young men on its rolls, while the turnover, as desired, gave others a chance.

A typical CCC camp had 150 to 200 trainees living and working and playing in tents or barracks, a mess hall, infirmary, recreation room, library, school, garage and workshop. Some camps were bleak, like many Army installations, while others were set in the midst of scenery so magnificent that it thrilled boys who once had run in street gangs.

They got up at 6 A.M., breakfasted at 6:30, policed their barracks and camp grounds, began working at 8, knocked off for the day at 4 P.M. After supper they were free to engage in sports, hike through the nearby countryside, listen to the radio, read books of their choice or study educational courses available to them. At 10 P.M. they went to bed. They followed this schedule Monday through Friday and were not compelled to work on Saturday or Sunday. The regularity of their lives, together with the wholesome food they ate, filled out their bodies—so gaunt when they joined the corps.

Most of the boys came from cities. Plucked from familiar surroundings and set down in distant places, some of which were exotic, they tasted adventures never before available to them. Young men from New York City, encamped in Mount Rainier National Park in the state of Washington, stared bug-eyed at live bears—and then were profoundly disappointed to discover that the bears were tame. Near Gettysburg, Pennsylvania, other boys dug up an unexploded shell from Civil War days; their leader declared it was too dangerous to be sent to a museum and called on an ordnance soldier to explode it, while the CCC boys danced in delight, calling this the last shot fired in the Civil War. Boston-bred boys were quartered near Pendleton, Oregon, which held an annual rodeo, and watched in fascination as cowboys roped steers. On the 16,000 acres of the Sipsey River game refuge in Alabama, CCC workers helped flush 400 deer from hiding. Not far from a CCC camp in Connecticut a deer was killed by lightning, cooked in the camp kitchen and served to boys who never before had tasted venison.

An ambitious Army officer named George C. Marshall, later to become secretary of state and secretary of defense, controlled twenty-seven CCC camps in the Northwest, unaware that in Montana one of the trainees was Walter Matthau, destined to become a famous actor. Another ditchdigging youth in the CCC program was Robert Mitchum, who wound up a Hollywood idol.

Marshall was so enthusiastic about the CCC that he hoped to be named its national director, but this never happened. It has been said that Marshall "ate, breathed and digested" CCC problems. In making the rounds of the camps under his command, it was his habit to descend on the site at dawn. At one camp he found the commander and another top officer asleep. Marshall awakened them with a few blue words, left them in a state of shock and then charged into the supply room where he discovered a lieutenant at work in his undershirt. Springing to attention, the young officer apologized for not being in uniform. Colonel Marshall broke into a rare smile and said: "You may not be in proper uniform, but you are the only officer I found working here!"

With CCC trainees beginning to outnumber the men in the Regular Army by more than two to one, thousands of reserve officers were called back to active duty to run the camps. This pleased the reserve officers because, like many other Americans, they were unemployed and desperate. According to Dwight D. Eisenhower, who was assistant to General MacArthur, this recall had political overtones. Years later he said that New Deal Democrats complained that all reserves summoned to duty were Republicans. "The charge," Eisenhower wrote, "was ridiculous; our records showed nothing about an officer's political affiliation. But it did indicate how seriously these questions concern a politician."

*   *   *

On May 9, 1933, just as the CCC was shifting into high gear, a new bonus army descended on Washington. More and more arrived until thirteen days later a total of almost 3,000 disgruntled veterans were gathered in and near the national capital, and once again apprehensive Americans held their breaths. Although this veterans' army was small, compared with the earlier one, it might consist of a nucleus that would attract greater numbers and grow into a huge and menacing monster.

Now one of the new sights were the tents flecking the greenery of Washington, while more sturdy quarters were provided the men at Fort Hunt just across the Potomac River. Roosevelt, far from being indifferent to the veterans as Hoover had been, not only let them use the fort but also provided them with three meals a day, all the coffee they wanted and a big convention tent where their leaders might confer. The new President conferred with these leaders, ordered the Navy band to play for the veterans, saw to it that Army doctors took care of their health and dentists pulled their teeth.

Roosevelt's closest political adviser and intimate friend was Louis Howe, a gnarled gnome of a man who suffered from ill health and ran on sheer nerves. Many years before, as Albany correspondent for the New York *Herald,* he had taken an instant liking to young Roosevelt and decided to make him President someday. Operating behind the scenes, it was Howe, a master strategist, who was mainly responsible, along with James Farley, for putting Roosevelt in the White House. And after Roosevelt became the nation's chief executive, Howe was one of the few persons who continued to call him Frank to his face. Whenever Howe spoke of the President to others, he always began by saying "Franklin and I—"

"Franklin and I," he once declared, "had that C.C.C. idea for years. We even had maps made and pins stuck in every place where we wanted camps placed."

Although Fechner was the titular head of the corps, whenever a big decision had to be made, he went to see Louis Howe. When the new bonus marchers began taking up quarters in Washington, the President said to Howe: "Go out and see the men in the camps. See that they have good food and shelter and—above all!—plenty of good hot coffee to drink. There's nothing that makes people feel as welcome as a steaming cup of coffee."

One rainy afternoon, with the ground a quagmire, Howe asked Mrs. Roosevelt to take an automobile ride with him out into the countryside. Because of the weather, she was puzzled. However, she did as Howe asked. As secretary to the President, he could use the official White House limousine complete with chauffeur, but on this day he dispensed with the chauffeur since he wanted Mrs. Roosevelt to drive. The tall and gracious First Lady got behind the wheel, Howe got into the front seat beside her, and they drove out of the District of Columbia, into Virginia. At a certain crossroad, Howe asked her to turn down a side road, which she did. A few hundred yards along he told her to draw up in front of some buildings where men were lounging about.

"Louis!" Mrs. Roosevelt cried. "What is this place and what are we going to do here?"

With a grin, he replied: "This is Fort Hunt and this is where the bonus army is quartered. You are going to go in there and talk to those men, get their gripes—if any—make a tour of the camp and tell them that Franklin sent you out to see about them. Don't forget that—be sure to tell them that Franklin sent you. Inspect their quarters and get the complete story."

"But, Louis—what are *you* going to do?"

"Me? I'm going to take a nap."

And with these words Howe curled up in a corner of the car.

Despite Mrs. Roosevelt's surprise, she knew how to handle this kind of situation because when her crippled husband had been the governor of New York, she had functioned as his legs and eyes. Now she stepped out of the car into the mud, and the waiting men stared at her curiously but courteously. The camp commander hurried up, recognized the First Lady, ordered that a cup of coffee be brought to her against the chill of the day. Then, wading through mud up to her ankles, she inspected the mess hall, the infirmary, the barracks and all the camp, chatted with her escorts about what France was like in 1919 and joined them in singing songs that had been popular during World War I.

When Eleanor Roosevelt got back to the car, she found Howe still curled up on the seat, fast asleep with his head resting on his hand. The two of them drove back into town and the moment they entered the White House she was surrounded by Secret Service men who demanded to know where she had been. She told them. Nervously, they said she had taken an unnecessary risk and should have had protection.

"Oh, it was all right!" she said brightly. "I did have protection."

The agents demanded to know who.

Nodding toward the grinning Howe, who did not mind being called "a medieval gnome," she said: "Why, that little man was with me all the time. He was so sure I'd be all right, in fact, that he stayed in the car while I was there and had himself a good nap."

The Secret Service men looked at Howe and shuddered.

Not long afterward a bonus marcher said: "Hoover sent the army. Roosevelt sent his wife."

*   *   *

The President's treatment of the veterans was motivated both by compassion and by politics. On the one hand, he truly felt sorry for them, while on the other, he realized that their presence in the District of Columbia posed a danger to peace in the capital. He offered them a chance to enroll in the CCC by waiving the age requirement, and although this meant hard physical labor in timberlands, on mountain sides and in swamps, more than 2,600 of the middle-aged veterans signed up. The 350 bonus marchers who felt unequal to such a strenuous life were given railway tickets home, and the menace to Washington evaporated.

Roosevelt was so enthusiastic about the CCC that he visited as many camps as possible. One day in August, 1933, he made an appearance at four of them. Starting from his home at Hyde Park, he traveled by train to Harrisonburg, Virginia, near the Shenandoah Mountain. At the station he was met by Harold Ickes, secretary of the interior, and Henry Wallace, secretary of agriculture, who climbed into an open car with him. Ickes noted that the townspeople lining the streets cheered the President, who grinned and waved at them.

They drove to a CCC camp in the Blue Ridge Mountains along the new Skyline Drive. The recruits, averaging nineteen years of age, looked healthy and happy; in fact, each had put on about 15 pounds. Farther along the Skyline Drive Roosevelt and his party stopped at another CCC site for lunch—steak, mashed potatoes, green beans, salad, iced tea and apple pie. According to the commanding officer, this was a typical meal, but his comment is open to question since steak was hardly a staple on CCC menus. In any event, the officer said it cost the government only thirty-five cents a day to feed the CCC boys.

Later that same day the President inspected two other camps, finding them clean and fairly comfortable. At one place the subject of education for all the trainees was raised, at which point a self-important officer talked on and on, repeating himself and boring everyone. However, Roosevelt had to hide a grin when the speaker declared: "There won't none of these boys leave these camps illiterates!"

Education, in fact, played a big part in the corps' program. About 2½ percent of the boys entering the CCC were illiterates, but even before they could be taught to read and write, they had to learn other basic facts of life. One camp commander, speaking only partly in jest, put it this way: "First I have to teach them to wear shoes." To the delight of some Americans, and the disgust of others, Negroes were among the advisers and specialists hired to educate the boys—using camp libraries and documentary films and supervising the publication of camp newspapers. After the illiterates learned to read and write, they were trained in various trades and skills. Many enrollees won high school diplomas, while more than 40,000 earned college degrees.

In the many camps across the country the boys worked on about 200 major types of projects. They cleared streams, cut firebreaks in forests, built truck roads into timberlands, marked trails, killed pests, preserved wildlife, prevented erosion, built miles of stone walls along highways, helped eradicate Dutch elm disease, constructed bird sanctuaries, threw up dams, fought forest fires, battled underground coal fires. They killed gypsy moths in the East, grasshoppers in the Midwest, and spruce sawflies and Mormon crickets in the Far West. They restored Revolutionary and Civil War battlefields. They stocked almost a billion fish, dug canals and diversion ditches, built more than 30,000 wildlife shelters and thinned 4,000-000 acres of trees. The CCC boys helped plant an incredible 190,000,000 trees on 210,000 acres of shelter belt. Of all the public and private forest planting in the nation's history, more than half was done by the CCC. All in all, the corps advanced national forestry programs by from five to fifteen years.

With this commendable record, the CCC became the most popular agency of the Roosevelt administration. In 1936, according to one poll, 82 percent of all American people favored it. Democrats were more enthusiastic about it than Republicans, for obvious reasons, but nearly two-thirds of all Republicans found something good to say about the corps. Two years later 78 percent of the people hoped that the CCC would become a permanent agency, as did Roosevelt himself.

Mayor LaGuardia of New York praised the CCC. War Secretary Dern told a Cabinet meeting that handling the corps had given the Army the most valuable experience it had ever received. Businessmen liked it; young men left the CCC with sound work habits, and industry had been stimulated by the huge purchases made by the government to keep the corps in operation. The United States Junior Chamber of Commerce was so delighted that it appointed itself a "godfather" to the boys in the camps,

George C. Marshall took ten CCC boys to a luncheon of the Portland (Oregon) Chamber of Commerce, where each talked about his training and his hopes for the future—making a big hit. The President bragged that the corps "has probably been the most successful of anything we have done." Many Americans felt that Roosevelt "sent the boys into the forests to get us out of the woods."

Nellie G. Toler and James R. Aswell of the Works Progress Administration interviewed a nineteen-year-old Negro boy about what his CCC experience meant to him. When Miss Toler asked whether he wanted to stay in the corps, Millard Ketchum replied: "Yes'm, as long as I kin, because I git plenty to eat here. I didn't always at home—not the same kind of stuff, anyhow. Guess we had plenty, such as it was, at home, but it jist wasn't good like this, nor enough of it for the kind it was. I git to go more, git to see more. I'm learnin', too. I watch the others, and then, I have more clothes and can keep cleaner, too.

"You see, where we is at home they don't go to school. None of them has gone any since they moved to Rivers county. They's three at home now to go to school, but they ain't went none and I guess they won't ever. I got higher'n any of'em. My littlest brother, he three year old now. I git thirty dollars a month and send twenty-two of it home to them. They need it. My papa he don't make enough to do for all, jist rentin' and farmin' like he does.

"You see, my pap drinks some. Not all the time, but he gits drunk at times, and that makes it hard on mama. I got drunk a few times. First time I jist all at once didn't know what was wrong. I jist couldn't walk, so I set down and went to sleep. I don't drink now. I quit since I got in the C's, which I've been in nineteen months now."

Although the CCC scarcely touched the key problem of unemployment, it saved thousands of young men from hopeless corrosion of their morale, improved their physical health, gave them a chance to see various parts of their country, made them proud to know that their salaries were helping their families, provided them with some education, taught them trades, reduced juvenile delinquency and helped preserve the beauty of the land.

Delaware never forgot the CCC. In the backwater areas of that state the mosquitoes were so thick that farm families huddled for protection near so-called smothers of smoldering green leaves, while their cows and horses bellowed in agony from stings of the attacking insects. That was before the CCC went into action. Working under the direction of the Delaware Mosquito Control Commission, the boys filled in more than 2,000 miles of ditches in about half the tidal marsh area, successfully eradicating the salt-marsh mosquitoes. The people were so grateful to have this plague brought under control that they suggested the erection of a monument to the corps. A ceremony was held one day in December, 1935, near Primehook Marsh. As smiling citizens watched benevolently, one CCC youth after another slapped a thick sod onto a rising conical mound—*plop, plop, plop!* This curious memorial took the name of Sod Monument. Every year after that the ceremony was repeated, a copy of the annual CCC work report for that region being inserted within a copper box inside the growing mound.

*   *   *

A total of 3,008,184 young men served in the Civilian Conservation Corps until it was suspended in 1942.

19

Little Pigs and Plowed-up Cotton

O NE DAY early in 1933 a hog buyer walked into a bank and met a
friend, Paul Angle, a young writer who had just written a book about
Abraham Lincoln. This was in Springfield, Illinois, in the heart of
the Lincoln country and also in the nation's Corn Belt. The hog buyer and
the author talked about how badly things were going for farmers. Suddenly
the hog buyer dug down into one of his pants' pockets, fished out a 50-cent
piece and tossed it onto the glass top of a nearby desk, where the coin
clattered and tinkled, faster and faster, then jiggled down flat and silent.
Pointing at the money, the man said: "Paul Angle, you're a sturdy fellow,
but you can't carry out of this bank all the corn that half-dollar will
buy!"

The writer made a quick mental calculation: *Corn was selling at only 10
cents a bushel . . . there are 56 pounds in a bushel of corn . . . 5 times
56 was—good Lord!—280! Fifty cents would buy a whopping 280 pounds
of corn, and no, he surely could not tote that much weight on his back.*

The hog buyer had dramatized the farmers' plight—or part of it, at least.
With prices so low, how in the world could a farmer make a decent living?
He couldn't. With both corn *and* hogs fetching such ridiculous prices it
was better to burn corn as fuel than feed it to pigs. Ten cents a bushel for
corn? This came to a mere $3.33 for a ton of corn!

Paul Angle's shock was matched at another time and place by an Oklahoma editor named Oscar Ameringer as he listened in growing dismay to
the story of a rancher who raised sheep in the Far West. The rancher found
himself in an economic bind. He owned 3,000 head of sheep. The top price
he could get for them was $1 per head—but it would cost him $1.10 each to
ship them to a packing center. He could not afford to feed the animals and
was too compassionate to let them starve to death, so one grim day he and

his ranch hands cut the throats of all 3,000 sheep and threw their carcasses into a canyon.

Such waste seemed downright sinful at a time when millions of Americans were unemployed, hungry and ragged. City dwellers found it difficult to understand the scope of the farmers' tragedy. The farmers' cash income was the smallest it had been for twenty-six years. A wagonload of oats would not pay for a pair of shoes. A truckload of hogs would not even pay the *interest* on a $1,000 loan. A farmer now had to sell two wagonloads of produce to get enough money to buy as much manufactured goods as one wagonload could purchase before World War I. Representative LaGuardia of New York said on the floor of the House that "the American farmer today is becoming a tenant peasant."

What had happened to the farm economy?

In the United States the traditional economy had been one of scarcity until the war. Then, to meet the needs of our armed forces and our fighting allies and our other friends, American farmers took 40,000,000 acres of idle grassland and placed them in cultivation. This converted our farm economy into one of not mere abundance but superabundance—and after the war the farmers went on producing as much as they could, even though there was less demand for their products.

Their standard of living slowly fell as the result of five major factors: (1) The market was glutted with farm surpluses; (2) farm prices slumped; (3) total farm income dropped; (4) there was no comparable decline in the prices of things that farmers had to buy; (5) their fixed charges, such as interest and taxes, remained high.

All this resulted in a farm crisis of gigantic proportions. As the farmers made less and less money, they took out loans on which they had to default, went steadily deeper into debt, began losing their property as mortgages were foreclosed. Some lost everything to a variety of creditors— banks, merchants, insurance firms and the federal government itself. Despite their traditional individualism, farmers began helping one another out of each sorry mess. In a revival of the frontier spirit, they gathered to prevent strangers from making successful bids for the property of a neighbor at a forced sale for debt or taxes. These tense affairs came to be called penny sales, for the sympathetic farmers would bid for the land and effects in pennies and then return them to their bankrupt owner. For example, at Mecosta, Michigan, a chattel mortgage sale was ordered to satisfy a debt of $150. The farmer's friends, scowling down greedy outsiders, bid 3 cents for a bean puller, 10 cents for a grain drill and 5 cents for a piano.

The fate of an Iowa tenant farmer named Johannes Schmidt (perhaps a pseudonym) was described in *Harper's Monthly* by Remley J. Glass, a country lawyer.

Schmidt was born to a farm family in Germany, arrived in the United States as a boy, became a citizen, soldiered abroad with the AEF during the war, returned to Iowa and married the daughter of a retired farmer.

Renting 120 acres from his father-in-law and 160 from the town banker, he began farming for himself. At first he flourished, but the 1931 drought killed most of his crops, and the next year he fell ever deeper into debt to pay for feed, back taxes and back rent. His 1932 harvest was bounteous—too late. By this time farm prices were so low he was unable to cover the cost of seed and labor, let alone taxes and rent.

After struggling and scheming as long as possible, Schmidt went to see lawyer Glass. After a discussion of the problem the farmer and attorney sadly agreed that Schmidt had only one resort—bankruptcy. The lawyer had to send a $30 bankruptcy filing fee to a nearby federal court, but the farmer did not have even this much cash; he had to borrow it from a brother-in-law. Came the day of the bankruptcy hearing, and the farmer and his family sat silently before the referee as the banker and landlord haggled over priorities of their liens and rights to Schmidt's crops and cattle. When all was over, the destitute farmer, his wife and children walked outside owning nothing in this world but a wagon, a team of old horses, a few sticks of furniture, five hogs, a couple of cows. Now they were homeless and with no place to go.

The deepening impoverishment of American farmers had worried Hoover when he was President. The nine-point program of farm relief he instituted failed to work; some critics called it a total failure. Among other things, Hoover created a Farm Board, and when this board urged that the American cotton crop be limited by plowing under part of it to reduce the surplus, Democrats had denounced the proposal as "economic blasphemy." During the 1932 Presidential contest between Hoover and Roosevelt, Roosevelt attacked Hoover's board for "the cruel joke of advising farmers to allow twenty per cent of their wheat lands to lie idle, to plow up every third row of cotton and to shoot every tenth dairy cow." Regardless of this attack, only a few days before Roosevelt was inaugurated, President Hoover told Congress that "it is essential temporarily to reduce farm production so as to remove the backbreaking surpluses of agricultural products and thus raise agricultural income."

This materialistic problem evoked a curious spiritual response. The Protestant Episcopal Church changed a prayer so as to ask God for better distribution rather than for huge harvests. But farmers kept on growing as much as they could. One Kansas farmer even installed underground wires in an effort to stimulate the growth of his cabbage and lettuce by electricity.

Among concerned and thoughtful Americans were some who felt that the problem was not overproduction but underconsumption. One of these was a Texas cotton farmer. In 1931, while Hoover was President, this Texan wrote to Agriculture Secretary Arthur Hyde. He suggested that the government convert 9,000,000 bales of surplus cotton into blankets and overalls and let the American Red Cross give them to the needy.

Secretary Hyde sat down to do some figuring. If 9,000,000 cotton bales were used this way, they would make 1.125 billion two-pound blankets and

2.250 billion pairs of one-pound overalls. This would be 9 blankets and 18 pairs of overalls for every man, woman and child in the nation. A family of five would get 45 blankets and 90 pairs of overalls. Hyde was unimpressed with this plan.

Actually, there was no simple solution to the web of problems ensnaring the farmers. It might seem that with vast surpluses on one hand and needy people on the other, all that was necessary was to get this food and fiber into the hands of the sufferers. This sounded good—but would it actually work? Producers, processors and distributors were bound together in a tangled skein of relationships, and each had his vested interest. As for the farmer, like everyone else under the capitalistic system, he had to make a profit. If he sowed and reaped for the entire nation and was left with nothing, he would have to go out of business. Then who would feed everyone?

The United States was not the only nation suffering from a farm crisis. On April 5, 1933, Chancellor Hitler of Germany declared that his government's paramount task was providing aid to German farmers.

Franklin D. Roosevelt's background made him especially sensitive to America's agricultural situation. He had been born on a farm in New York State and had lived there for a half century. Back in 1924 he had bought a 1,750-acre farm three miles south of Warm Springs, Georgia, and had raised cotton and cattle, but in the following eight years he had made no profit.

The Democratic Party's platform of 1932 had called for help to the farmers, and in Roosevelt's acceptance speech he had emphasized their plight. He pointed out that 50,000,000 Americans, or more than half the nation's population, depended on agriculture—directly or indirectly—for a livelihood. "If these 50,000,000 people," Roosevelt said, "have no money, no cash, to buy what is produced in the city, the city suffers to an equal or greater extent." Forgetting his attack on Hoover, Roosevelt said it was necessary to reduce farm surpluses. And he added: "I am sure that the farmers of this nation would agree ultimately to such planning of their production as would reduce the surpluses."

Beginning in the summer of 1932, before he became President, Roosevelt conferred repeatedly with farm leaders and important businessmen in an effort to help develop a national farm plan. Most agreed that one key to the solution of the farm problem was crop control.

This concept had many precedents.

The Bible urges men to let the land lie barren in the days of surplus. In ancient China the ever-normal granary was used to carry over the fat harvests. Dutch spice merchants burned crops to get higher prices. Colonial tobacco planters restricted production. In the 1890's American Populists advocated government control over surpluses. When Eugene Talmadge was Georgia's commissioner of agriculture (before he became governor), he called for reduction of the cotton crop—although he later changed his mind. In the 1920's Bernard Baruch wanted all the South to hold down its harvests—although he, too, had a change of heart. It was on August 12, 1931, that Hoover's Farm Board asked governors of fourteen cotton states to request growers to plow under every third row of the growing crop. In the summer of 1932 Governor Huey Long of Louisiana proposed that no cotton should be planted in the United States the following year. And a long list of other nations—Germany, England, France, Italy, Australia, Canada and Brazil—either cut current crop production or destroyed some existing surpluses.

In December, 1932, between the time of Roosevelt's election and his inauguration, an important farm conference was held in Washington. It brought together leaders of the three big national farm organizations, almost all the farm cooperatives, the farm press, other agricultural experts and some of Roosevelt's advisers. They agreed on a farm relief bill, which was presented to Congress in January. This plan was called unworkable by President Hoover, was opposed by Hoover's secretary of agriculture, and although it was passed by the House, the Senate took no final action on it by the time Congress adjourned.

Four days after Roosevelt took office, his new secretary of agriculture, Henry Wallace, at the bidding of the new President, convened another meeting of farm leaders in the nation's capital. Fifty agricultural spokesmen met on March 10, 1933, and approved a bill that became the Agricultural Adjustment Act. Roosevelt had urged great speed, for by now the 1933 spring crop was being planted—a crop that, when harvested, would pile up still more surpluses. Congress passed the AAA on May 10, and Roosevelt signed it two days later.

The Agricultural Adjustment Act was the most important farm legislation in the history of the United States. Not even in the midst of war had American lawmakers enacted such a significant farm bill. *Time* magazine commented: "For eight years the Republican party talked long and loud about farm relief but passed no major bill. Nine weeks in the White House, Franklin Roosevelt last week signed a monster farm measure. Most radical experiment so far in the New Deal, this bill not only bulged with dictatorial powers over the nation's food supply, from farmer's field to consumer's kitchen, but also was packed with the dynamite of currency inflation." (The AAA also authorized the President to devalue the gold dollar by not more than 50 percent.)

It was called the Agricultural *Adjustment* Act because it was intended to *adjust* farm production to national consumption. While it was being written, Baruch had warned Roosevelt that it was unconstitutional, poorly written and unworkable. Baruch, who owned a vast plantation in South Carolina, went on to predict that curtailment of cotton production would destroy the South. Roosevelt disagreed. For a long time he had felt that the South's one-crop policy was wrong.

The ultimate objective of the AAA was to produce a balance of farm products, not to promote scarcity as some critics charged. It was intended to raise the general level of farm prices until they became what they had been before the war. As a beginning, some crops would be reduced by working less land or by producing less per acre. Farmers would be asked to cooperate voluntarily. First to be affected were seven basic farm commodities—cotton, wheat, corn, hogs, rice, tobacco and milk. They were picked because the nation produced an exportable surplus of almost all of them and also because changes in their prices would strongly influence the prices of other products.

Cotton took first priority. By the time the AAA was signed in May, 1933, more than 40,000,000 acres had been planted in cotton—or 12 percent more acreage than in the previous year. If all this were harvested, it would yield a bumper crop and thus add to the huge surpluses already on hand. Southern warehouses already bulged with a three-year supply of cotton. The new cotton plants would boost this surplus by 17,000,000 bales, each weighing 500 pounds gross. Such an avalanche of cotton would mean that farmers would get only 5 cents per pound—and the South could not endure another winter of 5-cent cotton.

President Roosevelt wrote a public letter to Secretary Wallace, saying in part:

> . . . I myself am one of those who as a planter of cotton has suffered from the absurdly low prices of the past few years. What I am concerned about, and what every other cotton grower ought to think about, is the price of cotton next year if cotton acreage is not reduced.
>
> There are two reasons why every cotton grower should go along with the Government's national responsibility. The first is the patriotic duty of making the plan a success for the benefit of the whole country; and the second is the personal advantage to every cotton grower in helping as an individual to reduce oversupply of cotton and thereby obtaining a better price for what he grows. . . .

The farm leaders, Roosevelt, Wallace and others decided to try to cut cotton acreage by about one-fourth. This could be done if cotton planters would agree to destroy their growing cotton on 10,000,000 acres. If this happened, then they would harvest only about 13,000,000 bales instead of the anticipated 17,000,000 bales. Less cotton should fetch a higher price per bale.

Baruch told Wallace he thought George Peek would be the right man to administer the AAA, so Wallace appointed Peek. This proved to be an unfortunate choice—not because Peek was inept but because he did not agree with the heart of the AAA program. When Peek took office on April 5, 1933, he was sixty years old, tall and hardy and energetic. A former president of the Moline Plow Company, Peek had fought farmers' battles for a decade prior to Roosevelt's election. However, his pet remedy for the farm crisis was a system whereby exports would be subsidized at the expense of the American consumer. And although he was Wallace's subordinate, he fought the cotton control plan.

Peek had been born in Illinois, one of the states hardest hit in the subsequent Depression, and he had known Lewis Stevenson, another Illinoisan who had managed many farms in three Midwest states. While searching for young lawyers to help him, Peek remembered Lewis Stevenson's son, Adlai E. Stevenson, then thirty-three years old. In time to come, Adlai Stevenson would run for the Presidency twice on the Democratic ticket. Now young Stevenson was, as he later said, "all hot and bothered about the plight of the farmer." When Peek invited him to Washington to serve on the AAA staff, Stevenson accepted, taking a leave of absence from the Chicago law firm for which he worked.

"Those were frenzied days in Washington," Stevenson later recalled.

They were indeed. The Department of Agriculture Building was a beehive of activity, a babble of ringing telephones and excited conferences, the corridors crowded with farmers, farm leaders, processors, reporters and AAA press agents, all asking questions and mostly getting confusing answers. So much had to be done so fast. With the growing season so far advanced, it was, as Peek said, "a race with the sun."

The task was gigantic. There was a total of 1,800,000 cotton growers living in 956 counties of sixteen states in the Cotton Belt—which by this time stretched all the way west to California. Each farmer had to be seen so that the program could be explained to him, and then he would be offered a contract to rent part of his land to the secretary of agriculture. If the planter agreed to the contract terms, he then had two choices: (1) to plow under part of his growing cotton in exchange for a check; (2) to take a smaller sum of money, plus an option to buy at 6 cents a pound an amount of cotton equal to that which he destroyed.

Actually, the plan was much more complex than this, and delays were expected as farmers pondered it. Payments *without* the option would run from $7 to $20 per acre, depending on the yield per acre in previous years. Payments *with* the option would be about $6 to $12 per acre. No money would be paid for the destruction of cotton on land yielding less than 100 pounds to the acre. Where would the government find the money to fund this colossal program and pay such sums to so many farmers? From a processing tax. The AAA had a provision imposing a tax on the processing of cotton. At first this tax was set at 4.2 cents per pound of cotton. This brought squawks from processors who converted raw cotton into cloth and other finished products, and in the end they passed the tax along to consumers by raising the prices of their manufactured items.

Wallace set midnight of July 12, 1933, as the deadline by which cotton growers must sign up if they wished to take part in the crop reduction program. He and the President emphasized again and again that the plan was entirely voluntary. Long before this deadline, an army of 22,000 agents fanned throughout the Cotton Belt carrying leaflets that explained the plan, information sheets and blank contracts. Just to visit 1,800,000 cotton planters was an enormous physical problem.

The plow-up campaign was administered at the top by the AAA in Washington. Next came the extension directors of state agricultural colleges. Below them were the county agents, paid jointly by state governments and the federal Department of Agriculture. The county agent was the key man on the local scene. He appointed county committees consisting of leading farmers. The county committees appointed local committees, which had the job of "selling" the idea to the individual cotton growers. All in all, these 22,000 men did a surprisingly efficient job.

Many Americans expressed outrage at the thought of plowing under growing cotton, despite the fact that the production of oil and pig iron was being controlled. Roosevelt struck back at critics, saying: "Big manufacturers talk about control of production by the farmer as an indefensible 'economy of scarcity.' And yet these same manufacturers never hesitate to shut down their own huge plants, throw men out of work, and cut down the purchasing power of whole communities whenever they think they must adjust their production to the oversupply of the goods they make. When it is their baby who has the measles, they call it not 'an economy of scarcity' but 'sound business judgment.' "

But—cotton! Fiber to cover naked flesh. Americans who did not actually see the cotton being plowed up could visualize it, and a shudder ran through the country. Forgetting that the destruction had been suggested by responsible farm leaders and was carried on with their help, some people blamed Roosevelt, Wallace, Peek and the AAA in general. The *Daily Worker* sneered: "Roosevelt, himself a rich cotton planter . . . personally is interested in making money out of the destruction of cotton."

Many asked what seemed like a reasonable question: Why doesn't the government buy the cotton and give it to the needy? Well, the government tried to do this very thing by giving cotton to the unemployed so they could make their own mattresses—but objections were voiced by the mattress manufacturers. Even in an open and democratic society it is a fact of life that a given vested interest clashes with another vested interest, that a regional interest often is opposed by another regional interest. As regards agriculture, the framers of farm policy had to keep in mind the actual or potential conflicts between growers and processors of farm products—wheat as an alternate to corn for livestock feed; cottonseed meal or peanuts as an alternative to soybeans for high protein concentrates; butter as an alternative to margarine made from cottonseed oil, soybeans or animal fats; livestock feeds as against the poultry and dairy products into which they are converted.

The 22,000 AAA agents signed 1,026,514 cotton planters to federal contracts and the dramatic plow-up began in August, 1933.

* * *

One superstitious farmer agreed to destroy part of his crop when he saw a flash of lightning which he interpreted as a sign from heaven.

By the time the cotton planters began laying waste one-fourth of their growing crop some of the cotton bolls had opened and were flecking the soil like the shoreward fringe of surf. It was not easy to plow up the cotton plants. For one thing, some had grown high and tough. For another, there was no farm lore about the technique of destruction. Then, too, mules balked. Trained for years to walk *between* rows of growing cotton, Southern mules stubbornly fought the farmer when he tried to make them tread on the growing plants as they pulled the plow. Part of the cotton crop was left in the ground, of course, but the sight of bare earth between the untouched rows of cotton during the growing season—well, this was distressing to farmers. Some spent their own money for grass seed to cover the soil, and soon green stretches appeared amid the expanses of cotton.

Although Henry Wallace had found no good alternative to this plow-up, it nonetheless hurt him. Soon after he took office as secretary of agriculture, a reporter had asked: "Mr. Wallace, if you had to pick the quality which you thought most important for a man to have in plant-breeding, what would it be?"

Wallace replied: "Sympathy for the plant."

That August, 1933, he flew to the South and then out over the Mississippi Delta to watch from the air as the farmers tore out part of their crop, and when he landed, tears were seen in his eyes. Upon returning to Washington, Wallace said: "There are those, of course, who would say to let the weevil at this cotton and trust to luck. We have been trusting too long to luck. Insects have very small brains. They cannot be counted upon to get us out of troubles of our own making. Clumsily, to be sure, but with a new vigor and an eye to realities, we have started to take hold of this strange situation at both ends in an effort to bring sense and order to our use of the land."

Someone urged him to avoid public shock and anger by discouraging photographers from snapping pictures of the cotton plow-up. Wallace cried: "No! We must clear the wreckage before we can build. Rub their noses in the facts!" His response surprised people who regarded the gentle Wallace as a visionary, an impractical idealist. For his part, Roosevelt had said frankly in a message to Congress that the AAA was "a new and untrod path" and promised that if "it does not produce the hoped-for results I shall be the first to acknowledge it and advise you." Surprisingly, he had not cited the precedents for crop control.

The plow-up program was so far-flung and complex that certain mistakes and inequities were bound to occur. Among other things, some cotton growers cunningly overestimated their past yields by as much as 250 percent so as to boost their share of the cash benefits.

Former President Hoover said flatly: "Fascism came to agriculture by way of the Agricultural Adjustment Act of March 12, 1933, sent by the

President to Congress as a 'must' and passed with little real debate. This act and supplemental acts, in their consequences of control of products and markets, set up an uncanny Americanized parallel with the agricultural regime of Mussolini and Hitler. . . ."

Hoover had a friend who lived in Pennsylvania but served as an absentee executor for a big cotton ranch in California's San Joaquin Valley. During a trip to the West Coast Hoover visited the ranch and spoke to its local manager. The manager said he was growing cotton on 3,000 acres and that 800 of these acres were of poor growth. If he plowed under the 800 poor acres, the government would pay him more money than he could make by harvesting and selling the inferior cotton. On the other hand, if he destroyed his good cotton, he would make less this way. What should he do? Hoover replied that a good citizen would not take advantage of the government by picking his worst crop, no matter "how evil the government's practices." Just as Roosevelt had criticized Hoover's Farm Board for suggesting crop controls, only to agree to such controls later, so did Hoover forget his former approval of this plan and now denounce it as "evil."

A few months later Hoover saw the ranch manager again and asked what happened to his cotton. The manager replied: "I was sitting on the porch one afternoon when Secretary Wallace's county committee came up the front walk. The chairman called out to me: 'Here comes the Wall Street money! Have you any poor cotton?' I replied that I had 800 acres that were pretty poor. He said: 'Which quarter sections are they?' I told him. He filled out a written order to plow them under and directions how to get the money. We are about $12,000 better off than if we had grown it."

This transaction violated the rule that no payment would be made for the destruction of cotton on land producing less than 100 pounds per acre. This California cotton ranch was a large one, and unfortunately the AAA shored up some big plantations and farms that ran like factories—at the expense of small operators and tenant farmers. One big operator was paid $168,000 for plowing up part of his cotton.

In Washington, D.C., in a granite building of the Department of Agriculture, there was a vast room with an area equal to half a city block where 1,500 clerks worked twenty-four hours a day every day tending high-speed batteries of comptometers and checkwriting machines that ground out 80,000 crop curtailment checks daily. Hundreds of other departmental employees worked as fast as possible to mail these checks to the farmers. The sight of so much money flowing out of the national capital caused a Russian visitor to cry: "*This* is revolution!"

Hoover had erred in saying that the AAA began on March 12. Actually, as we have seen, Roosevelt signed the act on May 12, 1933. And on the following July 28 a Negro farmer from Georgia, a man named W. E. Morris, stood on the White House lawn to receive a medal from President Roosevelt for becoming the first person to plow under his quota of cotton.

That was the start of the program, and before it ended, the federal government paid a total of $112,600,000 to 1,032,000 cotton farmers. About 56 percent of the contracts between the farmers and the government called for cash benefits plus cotton options.

The plow-up plan managed to hold the cotton harvest down to 13,000,000 bales instead of the dreaded 17,000,000 bales. During the campaign the price of cotton nearly doubled, rising to a peak of about twelve cents a pound. However, it did not stick there, but fell seven and a half cents at the opening of the market season, when some cotton farmers began selling their curtailed crop. By late September the price rose to about nine cents.

Despite the program's partial success, it resulted in serious side effects. For one thing, sharecroppers were short-changed. Payments went to men who controlled the land, so planters received about 90 percent of the government checks. When the cotton contracts were being written, for example, a county agent in the Mississippi Delta conferred only with the landlords, who promised to treat their croppers "right." This AAA representative—who of course was a white man—later said: "You know, the government in Washington caused us quite a little trouble here. By mistake they mailed some of the checks made out to nigger croppers. They probably didn't know what they were doing when they did it. Imagine giving a check to a nigger cropper! Of course, I turned these checks over to the landlords anyhow. They'll have to get the croppers to endorse them before they take them to the bank, but that won't be hard."

Many landlords looked down upon their sharecroppers, regarding them more as peons than as tenant farmers. A cropper and his family would grow 10 to 20 acres of cotton and maybe plant a little corn and a small garden. The landowner supplied the land, mule, plow and other farm equipment. He kept the cropper alive during the growing season, before the harvest, by giving him meager rations. At harvesttime the crop was supposed to be divided equally between landlord and cropper. The theory was that the landlord's half was rent for the use of his land and gear, while the cropper's half was for his labor. In practice, though, when the crop was sold, all the profits went to the landlord. He simply took the cropper's half as repayment for the rations advanced during the growing season. Repayment—plus interest. And the landlord, of course, kept all the books. At the end of the year, no matter what the yield of cotton or its price, the cropper remained in debt to the landlord.

The rations were the traditional slave diet—molasses, meal and fatback (the top half of a side of pork that remains after the shoulder, ham, loin and belly have been removed). Food and lodgings supplied by the landlord to the cropper came to only about $50 or $60 a year some years. For a family of five, this amounted to roughly 3 cents per person per day. But most families consisted of some seven persons. The croppers, their wives and children wore rags stitched together and went barefoot, although some wore sandals made of burlap. Their dwelling was likely to be a wooden cabin consisting of one room and a kitchen, lacking paint and unchinked against winter frosts.

Amid such squalor, during the AAA program, the Cotton Belt's black earth was littered with tons of uprooted cotton, some of it ripe enough to use, but the ragged sharecroppers and their families dared not use it to clothe themselves properly.

The AAA had told local AAA committees to ask plantation owners not to discharge their croppers and tenants after reducing their cotton acreage. In point of fact, there was no massive eviction of workers by bosses. The cotton destruction came late in the growing season and after the landlord had advanced rations to his workers. Now he wanted them to work out in some way the money already spent on them, even if there was less cotton to pick.

But this general rule of no mass evictions was broken by dramatic and painful exceptions. Some heartless landlords plowed up all of a given patch of earth tended by an individual cropper and his family, closed the cropper's account book and sent him and his folks "down the road." This happened mostly in the Mississippi Delta, which had big plantations tilled by as many as fifty cropper families. The landowners said they could not afford to keep croppers on land that grew no cotton, and after all the government would not let other cash crops grow on reduced cotton acreage for fear of spoiling the prices of these other crops.

As more and more sharecroppers were turned out of their cabins and driven off the land, Socialist leader Norman Thomas became angry. He wrote a letter to Henry Wallace, whom he knew, protesting this treatment. Thomas was not satisfied with Wallace's reply that the croppers' "extremely low standard of living" was not due to the AAA. Thomas felt he might get some action if he went to Washington and confronted Wallace head on. But after arriving in the national capital, according to Thomas, he found himself foisted off on one of Wallace's assistants.

Thomas encouraged a professor of physiology at the University of Tennessee to study the effects of the AAA on sharecroppers. Dr. William R. Amberson began this project with the help of students and sharecroppers themselves. Perhaps the largest cotton producer in Tennessee was the Chapman and Dewey Lumber Company, which owned a 17,000-acre plantation, so the professor concentrated on it. He found that the contract between the government and this firm did not protect its sharecroppers; in fact, from 15 to 20 percent of them were left unemployed as a result of the cotton plow-up.

In Texas, although cotton was grown chiefly by tenants, a little higher in the economic scale than croppers, it was picked by field hands, who were even lower down the scale than the croppers. A good field hand could pick about 200 pounds of cotton a day. He was paid only 35 cents per 100 pounds, so after a full day of hard labor he made only 70 cents.

Uprooted like the cotton itself, croppers, tenants and field hands drifted from one small town to another, forever hurried along by nervous town fathers and relief officials. Alone or in family groups, they hitchhiked; they drove rattletrap cars; they even rode covered wagons throughout the Southwest in search of work, any kind of work. Conditions were worst of all among Negroes and Mexican-Americans, for whenever they found a crop that needed picking, they were told that this work was reserved for local white farmers. And since they were transients, they were not entitled to local relief. There was the further gritty fact that state relief organizations cut off all relief during the harvest period so that labor would not be "demoralized."

Norman Thomas was not the only important man who worried about this side effect of the AAA. Herbert Hoover charged that the cotton plow-up program "is producing hideous poverty in the sharecroppers of the South." Secretary Wallace was baited by reporters during one of his press conferences. Questioned about the displacement of cotton workers, Wallace said: "No, the tenants are not faring as well as the Southern land owners. We must seek out further ways, of greater justice." Wallace's assistant, Rexford Tugwell, was more specific, saying: "We must study and classify American soil, taking out of production not just one part of a field or farm, but whole farms, whole ridges, perhaps whole regions. . . . It has been estimated that when lands now unfit to till have been removed from cultivation, something around two million persons who now farm will have to be absorbed by other occupations."

After the summer of 1933 no more growing cotton was plowed under; instead, acreage was reduced before planting began. However, the AAA's program of boosting farm prices and decreasing surpluses by curtailing crops was applied to other farm products.

*   *   *

The afternoon of April 27, 1933, Judge Charles C. Bradley tugged a green eyeshade lower on his forehead, walked into his courtroom, sat down behind the bench and banged his gavel for order.

Through the windows of the Plymouth County Courthouse it could be seen that spring had come to Le Mars, a town of less than 5,000 population in the northwestern part of Iowa. Le Mars was a farm center where men in rough work clothes sold their produce and kidded the girls who worked in the local overalls factory. Recently there had been less kidding. As the fifty-four-year-old judge had noticed, all the farmers were restless, and some even muttered about "revolution."

The price of hogs, corn, butter and eggs was dropping lower and lower and lower. Farmers were sinking ever deeper into debt, and more and more farm mortgages were being foreclosed. One-third of a billion dollars in mortgages had been foreclosed in Iowa alone, some of the land being sold twice and even three times. Additionally, a billion-dollar mortgage debt hung over 45 percent of all Iowa farm property.

The discouraged farmers idly kicked at clods of earth and talked sullenly to one another. One of them growled: "I've put $25,000 and more into my farm and I don't intend to lose it to a mortgage holder!" The previous January 4, there in Le Mars, a mob with a rope threatened to hang an agent of the New York Life Insurance Company if he did not raise his bid so as to give full coverage of the $30,000 mortgage on John A. Johnson's farm at a scheduled foreclosure sale. He wired the company that his neck was at stake and sighed in relief when he was given permission to raise the bid.

That soft April afternoon Judge Bradley was about to sign another mortgage foreclosure paper in an unrelated legal action. The document lay on the bench before him. Lifting his eyes from it, he surveyed the crowd of perhaps 100 men filling his small courtroom. Some were farmers in ragged overalls. Others, who wore black shirts, looked like hoodlums from Sioux City, which lay 23 miles to the southwest. All the men had their hats on their heads, and most were smoking.

The judge snapped: "Take off your hats and stop smoking in my courtroom!"

That was when it happened.

Men lunged at him, arms outstretched, fingers clawing, and the next thing the judge knew he had been yanked from his seat and was being dragged out onto the greening lawn of the courtyard.

A man with a blue bandanna across his face yelled: "Will you swear you won't sign no more mortgage foreclosures?"

The judge answered quietly: "I can't promise any such thing."

He was struck in the mouth.

"Will you swear now?"

The blow had knocked him to his knees and loosened some of his teeth. Through the pain and the salty taste of blood the judge said: "No. I won't swear."

A man whipped out a dirty handkerchief and tied it across the judge's eyes. He heard a truck rattle up. Strong arms and hands boosted him into the truck. As it sped out of town, the judge must have remembered that sour January day when the insurance agent was threatened with hanging. After a brief ride the truck stopped. A lonely country crossroad. The chirp of a few birds. Otherwise, silence, except for mumbled words. The judge was dragged out of the back of the truck.

"Yuh promise yuh won't sign no more?"

"No."

He was slapped. He was knocked to the ground. He was kicked. He was jerked back to his feet.

A man brought out a rope. One end was fashioned into a noose. The loose end was thrown over a highway sign. The noose was put over the judge's head, down past his blindfold, down around his neck, where it was tightened.

"Now will you swear to sign no more damn' foreclosure orders?"

The judge was half-conscious. He choked: "N-no!"

One of the men ran to the truck and pried a hubcap from a wheel. The greasy hubcap was clapped onto the judge's head. Oil ran down his pale face. A youth yelped: "That's his crown!"

They threw dirt at the bound and sticky judge. The dirt stuck to the grease.

"Get down on your knees and pray!"

"I'll . . . gladly do . . . that."

They led him to the middle of the road. He knelt. The noose was around his neck.

"Oh, Lord," the judge prayed, "I pray Thee, do justice to all men—"

"Will you swear?"

"No!"

A man shoved the judge. He fell onto his back. They pulled off his pants and made lewd remarks as they smeared his trousers with grease, which they then peppered with dirt. They punched him. They slapped him a few more times. Next—nothing. No blows. In surprise, the judge heard the men scrambling back into the truck. Its motor snarled to life. A rasp of gears and the car roared off down the road.

Moments later a minister's son happened to drive up, saw a filthy man sprawled on the road and was appalled to recognize the judge. The boy drove the older man back into Le Mars. Judge Charles C. Bradley was not seriously hurt—but the nation was.

Wire services flashed the story from coast to coast. A judge had been hauled off the bench, had been assaulted, was nearly lynched? A *judge?* What was America coming to?

*   *   *

Chicago is located in about the center of the Corn Belt, which embraces most Midwest states, and the Chicago Board of Trade Building stands at the southern end of La Salle Street. This $22 million skyscraper structure towers up and ever upward in huge setback blocks and terminates in a 31-foot aluminum statue of Ceres, the Roman goddess of corn. The inside of the building is decorated with harvest scenes, and this is as it should be, for the Chicago Board of Trade is by far the largest grain exchange in the world.

In July, 1933, the grain market collapsed.

On the twenty-fourth of that month a group of grim-faced men met in Chicago's staid old Union League Club. They had gathered to discuss what might be done to raise farm prices. Five days earlier some corn and hog farmers from ten states had come together in Des Moines, Iowa. Among these earlier conferees were leaders of the nation's major farm organizations—the American Farm Bureau Federation, the Farmers' Union and the Grange—who temporarily put aside their traditional rivalries. There in Des Moines they had formed an emergency National Corn-Hog Committee of Twenty-Five. Earl C. Smith of the Farm Bureau was elected president of the committee, while an Iowa farmer, Ralph H. Moyer, was named its secretary. After completing the organization of their emergency committee, they had then agreed to meet again in Chicago on July 24.

To boost the price of corn, which they sought to do, they also would have to raise the price of hogs, since corn and hogs bear a natural relationship to each other. The control of one called for the control of the other. Like cotton, hogs were being produced in staggering surpluses. In 1919, for every fifty hogs marketed in the United States, thirteen were sold to Europe. By 1933, with the dwindling of foreign markets, only three of every fifty hogs were sold abroad. But American farmers went on raising as many hogs as they could. The results were tragic and ridiculous. In the Midwest a 400-pound sow sold for 90 cents per 100 pounds, or only $3.60. A curious farmer went to a meat market and asked the price of a 20-pound smoked ham; it cost $3.20. In outrage, the farmer realized that a 400-pound sow cost only 40 cents more than a 20-pound ham.

"I told them to go to hell!" he told a reporter. "I'd buy a whole hog and cut off a ham."

This was just one facet of the complex problem now engaging the attention of bitter farm leaders in their Chicago conference. Among those present was Claude R. Wickard, an Indiana farmer with a strong chin, plump cheeks, squarish nose, blue eyes and a ready grin. Seven years later he would become the nation's secretary of agriculture. Wickard listened carefully as the others talked. Very little corn was being made into breakfast cereal. Some was being burned for fuel. Most, perhaps, was fed to hogs and other livestock on the farm where it was grown. There had been a drastic cut in the export of lard, one of the chief products of swine. Hungry city folks could not afford sowbelly, let alone ham, which was ironic considering the abundance of hogs and the low prices they fetched. But in this summer of 1933 another massive hog crop had already been planted, so to speak. Millions of little pigs now snuffling in the fields would be harvested in the fall, but when they were slaughtered, there would be no market for them.

The Chicago conference was interrupted by an Ohio hog raiser named John Wilson. He said he knew as well as the next hog breeder that it would be difficult to solve the long-range corn-hog problem, but what about the new pig crop already fattening? Something had to be done right now. Wilson suggested that hogs, like cotton, should be "plowed under." In other words, to avoid an even worse surplus of hogs next fall, the little pigs should be slaughtered before they attained full growth; their meat could be distributed to the needy by the Red Cross.

The reaction to Wilson's proposal was described by Wickard: "At first I could tell that several people were startled by it. It seemed to be a little dramatic, I guess. It never occurred to me it was dramatic. The only thing that was in my mind was: *How effective is this in doing what we have been thinking about?* I didn't think about killing the pigs. They were going to be killed some time. You killed them at the most opportune time. Everybody did that. That's what you raised them for. It never occurred to me there was anything wrong about it or that anybody would get emotional about it."

In the Chicago Union League Club that fateful day no tears were shed for the little piggies that were to be cut down to push prices up. John Wilson's idea was adopted by the National Corn-Hog Committee of Twenty-Five. The premature slaughter of pigs would cut hog production by one-fourth, would remove 500,000,000 pounds of pork and pork products from the market, would boost hog prices. The farm leaders also decided to reduce corn acreage by one-fifth. Of course, there remained the problem of persuading the government to adopt this crop curtailment program. The conference ended, and the farmers went home.

Not long afterward Wickard was named assistant chief of the corn and hog section of the AAA and left his Indiana farm for Washington. His first day at work he was taken into Henry Wallace's office to be greeted by the secretary of agriculture. The tall and slender secretary with the rumpled hair and blue-gray eyes stood up behind his desk, held out his hand and asked: "Claude, do you think the Corn Belt farmers will be agreeable to reducing their production of corn and hogs?"

Unsure of where Wallace stood on this issue, Wickard stammered that if it were necessary, why, yes, he felt they would go along with it.

Henry Wallace thought long and hard about the plan presented to him by the National Corn-Hog Committee of Twenty-Five. Himself an Iowa farmer and an expert on hybrid corn, he shrank from the thought of killing any living thing unnecessarily or prematurely. However, the farmers' plight was a stark and pressing reality. Murmuring that "people are more important than pigs," Wallace made up his mind.

On August 18, 1933, in a speech at the Chicago World's Fair, Wallace announced that the government planned to buy 5,000,000 hogs by October 1. Most would weigh 100 pounds or less, and their early slaughter would lessen the hog tonnage due to reach the market in the fall. The meat thus acquired would be used mainly for relief purposes. Wallace estimated that this program would cost $55 million and would raise the price of hogs by 25 to 30 percent. The plan would be financed by imposing a processing tax on hogs weighing more than 235 pounds.

AAA Administrator George Peek shuddered at the thought of signing death warrants for baby pigs, but like Wallace, he reluctantly concluded that the emergency was so great he had to go along with the plan. This opinion was not shared by Treasury Secretary Henry Morgenthau, Jr., a gentleman farmer, who wrote in his diary: ". . . I think from the day we started killing pigs there has been a curse on this administration." Eleanor Roosevelt, for her part, was so upset that she ran to her husband. "With so many people hungry and in rags," she argued, "those surpluses should be given to the poor!"

The President, who knew that some of the meat was intended for the needy, tried to calm his wife. "Don't you realize," he said, "that what you want will upset Henry Wallace's program?"

Mrs. Roosevelt retorted: "But you have to think about those people, too!"

Later she telephoned Wallace and begged that he send some of the pigs to hungry miners in West Virginia. The sensitive secretary tried to explain all the ramifications of the master plan, but Eleanor Roosevelt was so concerned with the need for instant action, so touched by the sufferings of human beings, that she did not quite grasp all that Wallace said.

President Roosevelt was as humane as his wife, but he also was a pragmatist who took the long view. At a press conference he said: ". . . In the case of corn and hogs we are up against one of the most difficult problems that anybody could face because it is not just a case of a crop—it is a case of a crop plus a thing that the crop goes into. In other words, there are two factors, and we have laid down what might be called a two-headed program which calls for a reduction in the number of hogs that will be fed next year, for a processing tax which will pay for the reduction in hogs and, at the same time, for purchase by the government of just as many hogs as we can possibly use for relief purposes in order to cut down the tremendous surplus that exists in hogs at the present time.

"Now, of course, there is always the other added difficulty in the case of hogs. Hogs are perishable. Wheat and cotton are not. Hogs have to be taken care of within a certain definite number of months. Wheat and cotton you can carry from year to year. What we hope is that we shall be able to get the price of hogs up in the course of the winter—but that is not a guarantee that we can do it at once."

As soon as meat-packers heard of the plan to kill hogs and impose a processing tax to pay for this slaughter, they hastened to Washington to protest. They said they had no intention of absorbing all the tax but would deduct it from the prices they paid farmers or pass it along to consumers in the form of higher wholesale prices. George Peek warned the packers against using the processing tax as an excuse for raising their prices.

Among the spokesmen for the angry processors were Thomas Wilson of Wilson & Company and W. W. Woods of the American Institute of Meat Packers. Claude Wickard, finding himself in the middle of heated conferences, wrote his wife: "I must get to bed soon for I find that I have to keep my wits sharp at all times to keep up with this gang and then to battle against various interests such as the packers and their high priced attorneys."

Despite the packers, the government proceeded with the plan. Purchases of small pigs were to be made in Chicago and at five other Midwestern livestock terminals. On August 23, 1933, the United States made its first purchase at Chicago, procuring 30,000 hogs at double their market value. Six days later, amid cries of "topsy-turvy economics," the government bought 550,000 more swine.

Soon the President asked Peek: "How are you getting along with your wholesale murder of hogs, George?"

Hurt by this levity, Peek replied flatly: "I think we are progressing."

Roosevelt asked: "Wouldn't birth control be more effective in the long run?"

Peek felt that the subject simply did not lend itself to joking. "We think not," he said tersely.

The hog-reduction program ran into unexpected snags. Although Wickard worked day and night to arrange for slaughterhouses to handle the pigs bought by the government, the animals flowed into the abattoirs so swiftly and in such vast numbers that packers were swamped. Then it was discovered that little pigs could not be processed successfully by machinery designed for full-grown hogs; baby hams and baby shoulders would not fit. The government decided to salvage all it could by converting the pigs into grease and fertilizer—not clean white lard, but grease to be used as a base for soap. But storage facilities became exhausted, and there was not enough tankage left to store the grease and fertilizer.

Some packers, burdened with more pig meat than could be used or disposed of efficiently, dumped it into the Mississippi River at St. Louis. When the hog-choked waters became a health menace, the packers bought a farm where they dug huge pits and buried tons of sweet and tender meat at a time when West Virginia babies were chalk-eyed with hunger.

The Reverend Charles C. Coughlin sent Roosevelt a letter quivering with indignation about AAA officials "who have advocated the slaughter of six million pigs and have already defiled the countryside and the Mississippi River with their malodorous rottenness under the pretext that there was a superfluity of pork in this world while millions of Chinese, Indians and South Americans are starving. . . . My dear Mr. President, there is no superfluity of either cotton or wheat until every naked back has been clothed, until every empty stomach has been filled."

Indignation ran high among AAA officials themselves when they saw a Joplin, Missouri, newspaper containing this advertisement: "Dandy way to make money; buy this 13 acres for hog-raising. Sign up with the government not to raise, say, 500 hogs. It will pay you $1,000."

By the time the hog slaughter ended in early October, 1933, the government had bought not just the 5,000,000 animals suggested by Wallace, but 6,000,000. They were converted into grease, fertilizer and 100,000,000 pounds of pork. The pork was given to hungry people. Wallace said that the destruction of the pigs made it possible for more people to eat in 1934 than if they had not been killed. If these pigs had been fed and allowed to grow up, they would have consumed 75,000,000 bushels of corn. This would have caused distress in 1934 since a drought that year left the corn crop 1 billion bushels short.

In 1933 a *total* of 67,270,000 hogs was slaughtered in the United States. The 6,000,000 killed prematurely were regarded as a public scandal. The 61,270,000 others that met death at the hands of men evoked no tears, with the possible exception of vegetarians and other food faddists.

Henry Wallace said, somewhat defensively: "I suppose it is a marvelous tribute to the humanitarian instincts of the American people that they sympathize more with little pigs which are killed than with full-grown hogs. Some people may object to killing pigs at any age. Perhaps they think that farmers should run a sort of old-folks home for hogs and keep them around indefinitely as barnyard pets. This is a splendid attitude, but it happens that we have to think about farmers as well as hogs."

In the Department of Agriculture Building in Washington the gigantic checkwriting machines stirred and whirred again, and then postmen carried these checks to hog raisers throughout the Corn Belt. The hog reduction program benefited farmers by $31,000,000. Senator Arthur Vandenberg declared on the floor of the Senate that one hog grower was paid $219,825. Most farmers, of course, got much less.

What this money in the mailbox meant to individual farmers can be described in terms of a Dakota hog raiser named Lundborg. Having agreed to the hog-reduction plan, he knew that the government would send him $455—more than half of it immediately and the balance a year later. His neighbors got their checks before he did, but Lundborg was a stolid man who never worried about matters he was unable to control.

Nature had taught him patience. Walter Davenport, a magazine writer, said, "for more years than he cared to think about he had raised hogs and corn under a Dakota sky, which could blister Satan himself in the summer and be frozen granite from Thanksgiving to May Day." His land had been blasted by droughts and devoured by locusts. A black pestilence had killed some of his Poland China hogs. He owed money to a bank and was behind in his taxes. His twelve-year-old son Rolf had never owned a whole suit of clothes, and the boy's pants were hand-me-downs from older brothers. The farmer's elder daughter Anne had needed glasses for a year. The north side of the house was no longer winter-proof. The family had enough pork, beef, potatoes, apples, dried vegetables, applejack and homegrown flour— but they lacked money to buy sugar, coffee, salt and the like.

Lundborg's check came on a Wednesday. The first thing he did was to drive to the bank and convert it into cash—letting the bank wait awhile for the money he owed it. When he got home, he put out his big horny hand and gave the greenbacks to his wife. Then they called a family conference. Mrs. Lundborg held the bills in her left hand while with her trembling right hand she scrawled notes on paper: Let's see . . . Lumber for the house, staple groceries for the pantry, a payment to the grocer who had given them credit, store clothes for the kids, spectacles for Anne, a newspaper subscription, new parts for the car, something on that seed loan, two barrels of white paint and one of red—

The farmer raised his hand and stopped his wife. Enough figuring for now.

The following Saturday Mr. and Mrs. Lundborg drove alone to town, and after he let her off near the shops on West Main Street, he sauntered over to Steve's Southpaw Shave Shop. Six farmers were ahead of him; they had received their government checks a few days earlier. Lundborg studied Steve's price list: He could get a haircut and a shave, be singed and massaged and shampooed and all but drowned in bay rum for $1.75.

When the barber had an empty chair for him, Lundborg said: "I'm taking the works."

"The whole card? Why, Mr. Lundborg—"

"It's fifteen years," the farmer said doggedly, "since a barber shaved me!"

*   *   *

The 1933 hog-slaughter plan reduced the hog surplus slightly and slightly boosted the price of swine. However, it was attacked from many quarters. Norman Thomas cried: "No satirist ever penned such an indictment of a cruel and lunatic society as the A.A.A.'s author, who destroys foodstuffs while millions are still on breadlines!" Eugene Talmadge, now the governor of Georgia, snarled that he was hunting "for something to plant that doesn't have a processing tax on it!" Herbert Hoover described the tax as a "blow at the poor."

Joe Martin, a reactionary Congressman from Massachusetts, warned that the AAA would put us "on the road to Moscow." Martin may have alluded to the fact that the Russian famine of 1932–33 was created artificially by Stalin as a means of breaking the resistance of peasants to the collectivization of agriculture. But Russian officials, for their part, were as critical as Martin of the New Deal's farm control program.

A Russian textbook called *The Story of the Great Plan* was translated into English and published in the United States as *New Russia's Primer*. It was intended for Russian schoolchildren between the ages of twelve and fourteen. One page had this comment:

> We have a plan.
> In America they work without a plan.
> We have a seeding campaign.
> In America they destroy crops.

Few Americans knew or cared that Brazil burned millions of bags of coffee, that Holland destroyed tulips, that Denmark and Holland alike limited the numbers of pigs that could be raised for sale. Few Americans remembered that it was this nation's farm leaders, not Roosevelt or Wallace, who first suggested that little pigs be slaughtered. Even some farmers who benefited from the hog-curtailment plan forgot where the initiative came from. One farmer snapped: "The hell with Wallace, Peek, Tugwell and the rest of them down in Washington! What we farmers want is prices—60 cents for corn, a dollar for wheat, eight dollars a hundred pounds for hogs, 30 cents a pound for butter fat."

At Shenandoah, Iowa, a dummy labeled HENRY WALLACE was spanked by three farmers using barrel staves. A writer named John T. Flynn flayed the secretary of agriculture, speaking of "Henry Wallace, as mild-mannered a man and mystic as ever knelt on a prayer rug or slit a pig's throat or burned a field of corn. . . ." Some people called for abolishment of the AAA.

Hurt by this criticism, Wallace said again that some people seemed to feel that "every little pig has the right to attain before slaughter the full pigginess of his pigness. To hear them talk, you would think that pigs were raised for pets."

Pigs are not pets. As an Ellis Parker Butler character said: "Pigs is pigs."

*   *   *

American farm income rose from a little over $4 billion in 1932 to $6 billion in 1934.

20

The Blue Eagle

O NE SPRING DAY in Washington, as Japanese cherry trees unfolded pink petals along the Potomac River, Raymond Moley left the Capitol Building and headed for the Carlton Hotel for lunch. As he entered the lobby he happened to meet Hugh Johnson, whom he had not seen for more than a month. Johnson said he had just returned from South Carolina, where he had gone hunting with Bernard Baruch. And where was Baruch? Resting upstairs in his own apartment in the Carlton. Moley invited Johnson to eat with him, and the two men strolled into the hotel dining room.

This was on April 25, 1933, about seven weeks after Roosevelt had taken office as President. Moley, a former law professor at Columbia University, had been the key figure in that group of professors and lawyers known as the Brain Trust, which had guided FDR through the election and then been dissolved. Now he was assistant secretary of state, but this was a nominal title since the President constantly called on him for general advice and for writing speeches.

Moley was forty-six years old. A cool kind of man, complex and cultured, he had a high forehead and long nose, thin lips and close-set eyes. Fondling his pipe more than smoking it, as was his habit, he scrutinized his luncheon companion. Hugh Johnson was four years older than Moley. Johnson hero-worshiped Baruch, whom he served as an industrial researcher and assistant on economic matters. Thick-necked and red-faced, with fierce blue eyes set in a hard and furrowed face, smoking one Old Gold cigarette after another, talking in a gruff voice, Johnson was a self-styled tough guy. But he was also a sentimentalist who sometimes wept over operatic arias. He was widely read and wrote pungent prose. Johnson's ability to absorb, retain and articulate knowledge was so impressive that Moley regarded him as a near genius. Here, the professor decided, was the very man he needed.

Roosevelt had asked a host of men to draw up a tentative program to revive industry and increase employment, and now some 350 plans were floating around the national capital. Ideas came from both inside and outside government—from the President's advisers, new federal officials, big businessmen and labor leaders. Hugh Johnson had not been asked for his opinion, but going it alone, he had been drafting a code to control the cotton textile industry for more than two months. Less than a fortnight before Moley and Johnson lunched together, the President had hinted to reporters that he had some plan for securing "the regulation of production or, to put it better, the prevention of foolish over-production." In making this premature announcement, Roosevelt had succumbed to political pressures and tried to give a psychological lift to dispirited Americans. He knew very well that no single cogent plan existed.

There were two main groups of planners, one working under the direction of Senator Robert F. Wagner of New York and the other under Rexford Tugwell, a former member of the Brain Trust and quite the handsomest New Dealer of them all. Roosevelt, who had taken office without any clear-cut master plan for ending the Depression, was now so confused by these multiple and sometimes conflicting plans that he had asked Moley to collate them. After Moley had given Johnson this background, Johnson expressed surprise. He was unaware that anyone other than himself was at work on such a program.

Moley said Roosevelt wanted him to blend the best plans into a bill which the President could then present to Congress, but the former law professor was too overworked to take on such a colossal assignment.

"Nobody can do it better than you," Moley told Johnson. "You're familiar with the only comparable thing that's ever been done—the work of the War Industries Board."

Johnson, who had an ego the size of an elephant, agreed to accept this elephant-sized chore—provided he could get a leave of absence from his boss. As a matter of fact, said Moley, he would like Baruch's thinking on this matter, too. Johnson suggested that they go upstairs to Baruch's apartment and talk to him. Baruch warmly approved of the idea of having his assistant work on such a massive project.

A dynamo of energy and enthusiasm, Johnson did not even bother to go to his New York home to collect his clothes, but that very afternoon he went to Moley's office in the State Department Building near the White House. Sitting down at a desk, pulling out a couple of sheets of legal paper, he began scribbling an outline of a plan to place the entire industrial structure of the nation under federal control.

Such was the origin of the National Recovery Act.

* * *

That April, 1933, industry was stagnating and workers were worrying. The United States had gone off the gold standard, a new Fascist magazine called the *American Review* began publication, George Bernard Shaw lectured on the Depression before a New York audience, and Iowa farmers were becoming violent. Revolution might break out if conditions did not improve, according to Elbert D. Thomas, a Democratic Senator from Utah. Conversing with Harold L. Ickes, the new secretary of the interior, the Senator predicted that the CCC camps now under construction might turn into concentration camps. And if there were overt attacks on the federal government, Thomas added, these might be led by PhD's, since so many educated persons were without work.

Hugh Johnson, for his part, felt that World War I had been a less frightening reality to Americans than the present Depression. At a later date he wrote:

> One must consider the frightful results of depression on human labor that the great NRA goldfish bowl revealed—black men working in a steaming lumber swamp for seven and five cents an hour—ten and even twelve hours a day. Children toiling in factories for very little more—ten hours a day—55 hours a week—and sometimes on night-shifts. Women in sweat shops and garret slums bending night and day over garments and pieces of garments and not earning more than enough to buy food on a bare subsistence basis. From these right up to factories or stores on a ten to twelve hour day, six days a week, with wages equivalent to twenty cents an hour. . . .

And these were the ones lucky enough to have any kind of job. According to AFL President Green there were 12,540,000 people unemployed. Less than a year previously the American Federation of Labor had passed a resolution declaring: "So long as one workman is unemployed, the hours of labor are too long."

That same April, 1933, Senator Hugo Black of Alabama, who later became a Supreme Court Justice, presented the Senate with a bill to reduce the hours of labor. The Black bill prohibited the interstate shipment of goods produced by people working more than six hours a day or five days a week. Senator Black predicted that his measure would give work to 6,000,000 people since any employer who wanted to keep his production at current levels would have to hire 25 percent more workers to obey the law.

"Labor has been underpaid," Senator Black told his colleagues, "and capital over-paid. This is one of the chief contributing causes of the present depression. We need a return of purchasing power. You cannot starve men employed in industry and depend upon them to purchase."

On April 6 the Senate passed the Black bill, 53 to 30. William Green called it "the first constructive measure yet passed dealing with unemployment." But before the House began consideration of the rigid thirty-hour proposal, the administration swung into action against it. Raymond Moley thought that the Black bill was impractical. Roosevelt felt that it was not sufficiently flexible to permit adjustment to the complex structure of industry, which might become further paralyzed.

Frances Perkins, the new secretary of labor, got in touch with key Senators and asked them to amend the Black bill by insisting on minimum wages. She argued that such a provision was needed to prevent employers from cutting wages when they reduced the working day. She also felt that the government should be given the right to control production.

Her proposals angered big businessmen. They insisted that they alone were privileged to decide on wages and production. But something had to give somewhere if business were to be revived. President Roosevelt made a personal appearance at a convention of the United States Chamber of Commerce, appealing to business leaders to make concessions to labor in exchange for restriction of competition. Historically, big business always sought monopolies while small business and labor and consumers wanted truly free competition. During the Twenties, however, competition had become destructive, and since the Crash of 1929 wholesale prices had fallen an average of 45 percent.

In general, Roosevelt wanted recovery, reconstruction and reform—recovery from the evils of the Depression, reconstruction of the corporate structure and reform of social institutions. With the help of Moley he began working upon his second fireside chat to be delivered from the White House. This speech covered several subjects, and in the President's own draft there was a passage foreshadowing the NRA. Roosevelt called for "a partnership in planning" between government and business, with the government having the right to quash unfair business practices.

"You realize," Moley said, "that you're taking an enormous step away from the philosophy of equalitarianism and laissez-faire?"

Roosevelt fell silent. After several moments of deep thought, he finally said: "If that philosophy hadn't proved to be bankrupt, Herbert Hoover would be sitting here right now. I never felt surer of anything in my life than I do of the soundness of this passage."

The President believed that if wasteful competitive costs were eliminated by industry, it then could pay higher wages for shorter hours. He wanted a bill based on the principle of industrial self-regulation, operating under government supervision through a system of codes of fair competition.

Such was the goal toward which Hugh Johnson now was working. He had moved out of Moley's office and taken other quarters in the old Post Office Building, where he had the help of three assistants. From time to time he consulted with some of the other men busy with recovery plans—Senator Wagner; Harold Moulton, head of the Brookings Institution; Meyer Jacobstein, a Brookings economist; John Dickinson, assistant secretary of commerce; lawyer Jerome Frank of the Department of Agriculture;

Lewis Douglas, director of the budget; Donald Richberg, an attorney and author; Rexford Tugwell and others.

So many ideas from so many men began to confuse Johnson, as he told Moley. The professor then persuaded the President to summon these chief planners to the White House to resolve their differences and agree on a bill that Roosevelt could submit to Congress. They met and wrangled, with Roosevelt making an occasional comment and Moley remaining silent. At last the President ordered them to lock themselves in a room and stay there until they could come to some agreement. That was on May 10. The men holed up in Douglas' office, argued a few more days, finally emerged with a compromise measure which Roosevelt found acceptable.

This was the National Recovery Act, which historian Henry Steele Commager has said "was in some respects the most extraordinary law ever passed by an American Congress." A preamble declared that the purpose of the act was "to encourage national industrial recovery, to foster fair competition, and to provide for the construction of certain useful public works. . . ." It seemed to have something for everyone. It would help business by relaxing antitrust laws. It would help labor by giving workers the right to organize and bargain collectively through representatives of their own choice. The key to the act were the codes of fair competition. Under these codes, employers would promise to engage in fair marketing practices, establish minimum wages and maximum hours of labor, ban child labor, agree on prices and let labor bargain collectively.

Vice President John N. Garner had misgivings. "It is a moony adventure," he rumbled, "and I don't think it will work, but I am willing to see it tried. You probably can put the big industries under codes, but you can't manage the business of the whole country from Washington. If it is not administered right it can become a monopolistic, cartelizing scheme."

Garner was partially right. Broadus Mitchell, an economist and Socialist, said at a later date that each code "was something between a charter of a medieval guild and the agreement of a modern cartel." A cartel, of course, is a combination of rival firms regulating production and prices in a given field.

When the NRA bill was introduced in the House, its members dropped the Black bill and began debating the administration's measure, soon passing it by a vote of 323 to 76. The going was much rougher in the Senate, where the NRA bill was presented by Wagner at the request of the President. Senatorial opposition to the NRA was led by William E. Borah of Idaho, who believed that it represented a victory for big business and a defeat for small business and consumers. At one point in the debate Borah cried: "Shades of Stalin! Stabilization—what crimes are to be committed in thy name!"

Senator William H. King of Utah asked Wagner whether the bill was "drawn largely from the philosophy of Mussolini or the old Germany cartel system." Wagner denied it. However, Donald Richberg, who became general counsel to the NRA, admitted that it encouraged manufacturers to fix prices immune from prosecution, thus achieving the same ends as did European cartels. Herbert Hoover, following the Senate debate from a distance, flatly called the NRA "Fascistic." The former President found himself in strange company, for Communist leaders also attacked the NRA as "Fascistic." Historian James MacGregor Burns later wrote of Roosevelt that "it probably never occurred to him that the NRA . . . showed some likeness to the corporate state fashioned by Benito Mussolini." And after the NRA went into operation an Italian journalist enthusiastically told Norman Thomas that he would go back and tell Mussolini that he had seen *Il Duce*'s corporate state in full flower in the United States.

Much of the potential trouble lay in the fact that big business was so well organized and so powerful it had the upper hand in the writing of the codes, that labor was weak because union membership had sunk to a low level and that government was unable to control or discipline unethical individuals and corporations that violated the codes. The experience of the previous forty years had proved that antitrust laws could not be enforced—and now these laws were about to be suspended.

Trade associations were dangerous to the general welfare, as Herbert Hoover well knew. During his term as President five of the eight leading trade associations had been ordered dissolved by the Justice Department. But then, as Broadus Mitchell has said, the trade associations went underground. Prior to the birth of the NRA, Hugh Johnson said, trade associations were about as effective as an old ladies' knitting society, but "now I am talking to a cluster of formerly emasculated trade associations about a law which proposes for the first time to give them potency." Frances Perkins was disturbed by Johnson's fondness for Raffaello Viglione's book *The Corporate State,* which glowingly described the Italian system of dictatorship.

Senator Wagner, an ardent friend of labor, was grateful that Section 7-a of the proposed bill gave labor the right to bargain collectively, but he too worried about suspension of the antitrust laws. "The bill is frankly an experiment," he reminded fellow Senators, "designed to last not more than two years." It was true that President Roosevelt regarded the NRA as a temporary expedient. Johnson, however, felt that the law should become permanent.

"When this crisis is over and we have the recovery program started," Johnson told Perkins, "there won't be any need for a department of labor or a department of commerce, and perhaps some other departments. The NRA will embrace all these functions and carry them out effectively." Then, noting the dismay on the face of the secretary of labor, Johnson quickly added: "Oh, yes! The department of labor can be a research unit within NRA."

Worry about suspension of the antitrust laws was matched by concern about giving labor the right to bargain collectively. Section 7-a of the proposed bill was attacked by the United States Chamber of Commerce and the National Association of Manufacturers. Senator Bennett C. Clark of Missouri offered an amendment declaring that "nothing in this title shall be construed to compel a change in existing satisfactory relationships between the employees and employers of any particular plant, firm or corporation."

However much the measure seemed to offer something to everyone, it was offensive to many. Despite its imperfections, though, something had to be done and done fast, for, as Treasury Secretary Henry Morgenthau mused, the smell of revolution was in the air. After stormy debate the Senate passed the NRA bill on June 9 by a vote of 57 to 24.

*   *   *

Johnson had kept in touch with Roosevelt while overseeing the drafting of the NRA bill, and together they studied charts of the proposed organization to administer the program. One day the President glanced up from a chart and said: "Hugh, you've got to do this job." This offhand remark did not constitute a formal offer to appoint Johnson the head of the new agency. At some of these planning sessions there were Cabinet members present, and Johnson felt they were not very friendly toward him. He wanted to be named the NRA administrator. Working sixteen to eighteen hours a day, unsure of his status after the bill became law, he became drugged with fatigue and disgusted with the suspense.

One day an Associated Press reporter told Johnson he knew that Johnson had been selected to head the NRA. Johnson said he had heard nothing about it. But the next morning several newspapers published stories saying that Johnson was the man. Still lacking direct word from the President, Johnson spurned the congratulations proffered by friends. "It will be red fire at first," he cried, "and dead cats afterwards! This is just like mounting the guillotine on the infinitesimal gamble that the ax won't work."

During Johnson's period of uncertainty, Bernard Baruch made a social call one evening at the home of Frances Perkins. He said to her: "What's this I hear about Hugh Johnson being considered for administrator of the recovery program?"

Secretary Perkins said she thought it likely.

"He's been my number-three man for years," Baruch continued. "I think he's a good number-three man, maybe a number-two man—but he's not a number-one man. He's dangerous and unstable. He gets nervous and sometimes goes away for days without notice. I'm fond of him, but do tell the President to be careful. Hugh needs a firm hand."

What Baruch meant by calling Johnson "nervous" was that every so often he went on drunken sprees. Frances Perkins did not understand this point when she conveyed Baruch's advice to Roosevelt, and so the President knew nothing about Johnson's drinking habits. But Hugh was dangerous and unstable? Roosevelt began having second thoughts about appointing him.

June 16, 1933, marked the end of the special session of the Seventy-third Congress and also the end of Roosevelt's first 100 days as President—now known to history as the famous Hundred Days. That afternoon he convened a Cabinet meeting. Johnson was asked to wait outside the door. The President said he was glad that Congress had passed the NRA and announced that he planned to sign the bill in the presence of his official family of advisers. First, however, he wanted to discuss some features of the new measure. Title I dealt with industrial recovery. Title II was concerned with public works and construction projects. In approving the NRA, Congress had appropriated $3.3 billion to build roads and erect public buildings. Of his Cabinet members, Roosevelt asked: "What do you think about the administration of Title II? As the bill is written, it seems to be taken for granted that it will be administered by the administrator of Title I, but I suppose it could be separated. I have read the bill and I see no reason why I should not appoint, under the law, another administrator. What do you think of it as a matter of policy?"

Sensing that Roosevelt was inclined to name two different administrators, the Cabinet members agreed it would be wise to separate the two jobs. The administration of Title I was an enormous task in itself. To manage Title II, to make sure it would not become a pork barrel leading to corruption—that alone would be a massive chore. Interior Secretary Ickes knew that Johnson had already set up an organization to run the public works part, proceeding on the assumption that he would get both jobs. Some Cabinet members were happy to have the chance to cut a non-Cabinet man down to size. They agreed unanimously that Title II should have its own administrator.

"Well," asked Roosevelt, "who shall it be?"

Pause.

Frances Perkins glanced at her colleagues and then suggested: "Why not the secretary of the interior?"

"I am against creating so many independent agencies," said the President. "We ought not to create any more if we can help it. Is there any department or anybody better than the secretary of the interior?"

A long silence. Then Ickes said dryly: "This is so sudden, Mr. President, but I think I have at least the negative and austere qualities which the handling of so much public money requires."

When no one objected, Roosevelt grinned and appointed Ickes the administrator of the public works part of NRA.

The grin fading from his face, the President added: "It will be hard on Johnson. He won't like it, but I think it is the best thing to do."

Johnson was called into the Cabinet room. Glancing at the Cabinet members seated around the long mahogany desk, he felt that a couple of them "looked like the cat that has just swallowed the canary." Roosevelt beamed at Johnson, said he was about to sign the NRA bill and wanted to appoint him administrator. In his most charming fashion, the President went on to remark that he felt it would be asking too much of any man to expect him to administer both titles, so he had put Ickes in charge of Title II. Furthermore, Johnson would not report directly to the President but to a Cabinet board that would control the NRA.

Johnson's painted smile dimmed. His face reddened and then turned purple with rage. In an anguished voice he blurted: "I don't see why! I don't see why!"

Roosevelt pretended he had not heard Johnson. Dismissing the Cabinet, he beckoned to Frances Perkins, and as she bent over his chair, he whispered: "Stick with Hugh! Keep him sweet. Don't let him explode."

She walked toward Johnson, who seemed to be in a daze. Linking her arm in his, she led him to the door.

"He's ruined me!" Johnson muttered.

Secretary Perkins tried to cheer him up as they turned down a corridor, but Johnson paid no attention to her words.

"I've got to get out!" he mumbled again and again. "I've got to get out! I can't stay!"

In those first few minutes after his appointment as administrator of Title I—only—Johnson really wanted to resign. He felt that unless both parts of the NRA program moved abreast in perfect coordination, its entire economic basis would be endangered. Besides, his ego had been dealt a crushing blow.

Frances Perkins did not care to let any White House reporters see Johnson in his present condition, so she guided him out a side door and coaxed him into her waiting limousine. As it glided away, the chauffeur asked where she wished to go, and she told him to just keep driving— anywhere. They drove through park after city park, but the green gaiety of spring only deepened Johnson's depression.

"Don't blow up," Frances Perkins pleaded with Johnson. "Don't pull out!"

"It's terrible! It's terrible! It's terrible!"

Tactfully, she praised the great job Johnson had done in charting the NRA, and by the end of the afternoon he let her persuade him to accept the reality of the situation and take the job of administrator of Title I. The President signed the NRA into law after Johnson and the Cabinet members had left the White House. A day or so later Roosevelt summoned Johnson and gave him a pep talk, and before long the new head of the NRA was getting more publicity than the President himself.

*   *   *

Hugh Samuel Johnson was born on August 5, 1882, in Fort Scott, Kansas, the son of an unsuccessful and displaced country lawyer from Illinois. At that time Kansas was frontier land, and Johnson's first memory was of wolves howling. One bitter winter the Johnson family lived in a sod house on the prairie 16 miles from the nearest neighbor. When the boy was about four, his mother heard a ruckus outdoors and found him encircled by neighborhood bullies. Her son was screaming at them: "Everybody in the world is a rink-stink but Hughie Johnson, and he's all right!" As a grown man, Johnson confessed with a grin that both his mother and Bernard Baruch felt that this continued to be his outlook on life.

Mrs. Johnson encouraged Hugh to read good literature, and by the age of ten he had read all of Shakespeare and gone through *Huckleberry Finn* five consecutive times. As a boy of fifteen, he tried to run away to join the Rough Riders and fight in the Spanish-American War. He was caught on the station platform by his father, who mollified the lad with the promise of sending him to West Point. Dutifully, he attended the Oklahoma Northwestern Teachers College, and after graduation he traveled alone to the United States Military Academy on the west bank of the Hudson River. A country boy who knew nothing of the world, he bought a blue suit with red checks and had it cut into what he considered to be a dinner jacket.

Throughout his career at West Point he stood at the foot of his class in deportment, for he was chronically insubordinate. Johnson later admitted he was "a very bad cadet." He thought he was tough, he studied as little as possible, and he smoked cigarettes on the sly. Johnson graduated with the class of 1903, which included Douglas MacArthur, for whom he developed great hero worship. Emerging from the Point as a lieutenant of cavalry, Johnson remained in the Army until 1919.

During those sixteen years he saw duty in Texas, San Francisco and the Philippines. While stationed in those Pacific islands, he broke the jaw of a drunken private in a barroom brawl. Having read Blackstone under his father's guidance, he jumped at the chance when the Army offered to send him to the University of California, where he completed a three-year course in two years and won a degree as a Doctor of Jurisprudence. By this time he was writing short stories, juvenile books, magazine articles, nine of these potboilers being accepted by different periodicals in a single month. He accompanied General Pershing's so-called punitive expedition to Mexico, where one of his tentmates was George Patton, who became a famous general during World War II.

Johnson's job with Pershing was to review court-martial cases. "It was a peach of a job," he recalled. "It involved a comparative study of the whole body of constitutional, administrative, state and municipal law of both the United States and the republic of Mexico."

In World War I, much to his disappointment, he never heard a shot fired in anger. Instead of being sent abroad, he was headquartered in Washington, D.C., where he wrote most of the provisions of the Selective Service Act. In preparation for this assignment he spent two full days studying and absorbing the style of Woodrow Wilson. For weeks at a time he worked eighteen to twenty hours a day, grabbing naps on an office sofa. Promoted to brigadier general, he got a letter from President Wilson on May 14, 1918, naming him the War Department's representative to the War Industries Board. The next morning—a memorable day in Johnson's life—he met Bernard Baruch for the first time. Baruch was chairman of this board, and Johnson helped him whip it into an agency that controlled industrial mobilization.

"From that experience," Johnson wrote, "I went away with one outstanding lesson burned into my brain—governmental emergency operations are entirely different from routine governmental operations."

In 1919 Johnson left the Army to become a high-echelon officer of the Moline Plow Company in Illinois. He went to France and Russia in an attempt to sell harvester machinery, making few sales but seeing at close hand the French industrial methods and the workings of the Soviet regime. The farm slump in America forced the plow company to liquidate, and although eventually it was reorganized, Johnson left the firm to become an assistant to Baruch.

Commenting on the stock market speculation and the Crash, Johnson wrote:

> There was no excuse for what happened in 1926 to 1929. In retrospect it is as incredible as any of the phantasmagoria related by Mackay in his history of the world's popular illusions. But the very government was behind that mass madness and if anybody of substance had got up in the market and cried a warning, he would have been torn to pieces as a calamity-howling destroyer of "prosperity." It just had to run its course.
>
> When the collapse came, it came as Bernie had always said it would come —like a deluge. The story that it started in Europe is a myth on the face of every trend chart. We had been carrying Europe on our shoulders, and when we collapsed the world collapsed with us.

Eighteen months after the Crash, Baruch said to Johnson: "Let's just get out of everything, and begin studying the world and domestic fiscal and economic and political situation to see if there is any suggestion of a way out of this morass." For a long time the two men pored over mountains of data, charting and measuring and comparing the beginning, sequence and existing state of the Depression in this country.

In 1932, moments after Roosevelt was nominated for the Presidency, Baruch went to James Farley to offer his services, and those of Hugh Johnson, in the forthcoming campaign. This offer was accepted, and soon Raymond Moley and Rexford Tugwell visited Baruch's home in Manhattan to study the massive economic data assembled by Baruch and his assistant. It was in this way that Moley came to know Johnson.

*   *   *

Late that afternoon of June 16, 1933, while Frances Perkins attempted to soothe Hugh Johnson, the President signed the National Industrial

Recovery Act and then issued a statement saying: "History probably will record the National Industrial Recovery Act as the most important and far-reaching legislation ever enacted by the American Congress. . . . Its goal is the assurance of a reasonable profit to industry and living wages for labor. . . ."

Four days later Johnson announced the formation of the National Recovery Administration. The legislation was referred to by its initials, NIRA, soon shortened to NRA. The administration was also called the NRA. In the minds of most people the bill and the agency became known collectively as the NRA. General Johnson, hyped up on hope and enthusiasm, sprang onto this new horse and rode off in six directions at once. He was undaunted by what he described as the incredible job of trying to get all of American industry to agree to place itself under codes of fair competition as fast as possible and thus to revolutionize every employer-employee relationship in the nation.

Collecting aides like a sheriff deputizing citizens, Johnson set up headquarters in the new $17 million Commerce Department Building of which Herbert Hoover was so proud. The general, on the other hand, called it "the worst-planned and least efficient modern office building in the world"; its offices, he snarled, reminded him of the pay toilets in Washington's Union Station. He wanted Felix Frankfurter to serve as the NRA's general counsel, but Frankfurter declined and suggested the name of Donald Richberg, whom Johnson appointed.

In a memorandum to Richberg, Johnson said: "AAA thinks that government should run business. NRA thinks that business should run itself under government supervision." Johnson also told the National Association of Manufacturers: "NRA is exactly what industry, organized in trade associations, makes it." Naturally, this delighted big businessmen.

But the general's attitude worried Herbert Hoover, labor leaders, liberals, Socialists and Communists. Earl Browder, general secretary of the Communist Party, soon declared: "For the working class the Industrial Recovery Act is truly an Industrial Slavery Act. It is one of the steps towards the militarization of labor. It is a forerunner of American Fascism." In surprisingly similar language, Hoover told the president of the United States Chamber of Commerce that "this stuff was sheer Fascism, that it was merely a remaking of Mussolini's 'corporate state. . . .'" Hoover felt that the antitrust laws had emancipated and protected the American people; now that they were about to be relaxed, he felt anxious.

Every one of the NRA's proposed codes had to be approved by the President or by his representative. Once a code was approved it would become binding on the entire industry to which it applied and was to be enforceable in federal courts. Johnson hoped for quick approval of codes for the nation's ten biggest industries—textiles, coal, petroleum, steel, automobiles, garments, lumber, construction, wholesale trade and retail trade. They constituted the bulk of employment in America. Codes covering them would tend to set NRA policy by precedent. But it was not so easy to get the codes approved as Johnson wished. He tried to do too much too soon.

A megalomaniac who thought he could run everything, Johnson still could be humble in the presence of Baruch. Perhaps he was trying to prove to his hero that he was, after all, a great number one man. Among other people, however, Johnson swaggered like a dictator. To a man as distinguished as Clarence Darrow, the criminal lawyer, Johnson once cried: "I am the big cheese here!" Actually, Johnson was not a good administrator because his rule was much too personal, because he thought he could solve problems by issuing decrees, because he sometimes substituted publicity for sound governmental procedures and because he fell victim to his own optimism. President Roosevelt, himself an enthusiastic man, appreciated Johnson's enthusiasm and gave him his head at first, only to discover belatedly that he had lost control of the NRA to the general.

On July 9 the President approved the first NRA code. It covered the cotton textile industry. It established a forty-hour week with a limit of two shifts, minimum wages of $13 a week in the North and $12 in the South. Additionally—and perhaps nothing in Roosevelt's life gave him so much satisfaction—it abolished child labor. Proudly the President announced: "Child labor in this industry is hereby abolished. After years of fruitless effort and discussion, this ancient atrocity went out in a day, because this law permits employers to do by agreement that which none of them could do separately and live in competition."

But for the following six weeks the cotton code was the only major one that became law. That hot Washington summer of 1933 confused businessmen, baffled attorneys and wary labor leaders met in hotel ballrooms to talk and argue and shout, teetering dangerously on slim gilt chairs, sweat pouring down their faces, every now and then looking for guidance to some deputy NRA administrator, rushing out of hotels and into the Commerce Building to lay their problems in the lap of the rumpled and weary General Johnson.

Bargaining was primarily between organized industry and such organized labor as then existed. Small and scattered business units had almost no voice in drafting the codes, while consumers were almost forgotten. In the beginning it seemed that the federal government held the whip handle, but the know-how and unity and power of big business slowly began to be felt and finally overwhelmed most opposition, leaving the lords of creation with codes that kept them in the saddle. This was not understood by the average American, taken in by General Johnson's razzle-dazzle publicity.

He worked so hard and fast and thoughtlessly that he often signed official documents without even reading them. At this stage of the game the President, busy with other pressing problems, relied on Johnson to get the NRA going. One day the general darted into the White House—his coattails standing out behind him, as Roosevelt laughingly told Ickes—and slapped three codes on the President's desk for signing. Speaking fast in his gruff voice, Johnson told the chief executive that they had to be signed immediately so he could take them back and promulgate them. As Roosevelt scrawled his name on the third code, the general looked at his watch, bellowed that he had just five minutes to catch a plane, snatched up the papers and ran out. That was the last the President saw of him for the next several days.

From the beginning to the end of the NRA, codes were developed, as a matter of administration policy, from proposals initiated from within the industries themselves. Most were proposed and sponsored by some trade association. Many inactive trade associations came to life again, and many industries which did not have trade associations hastened to organize them.

Upon learning that this or that entire industry could not agree on a code, eager to get as many men back to work as soon as possible, Roosevelt announced what he called the President's Re-employment Agreement. Soon it was known as the PRA. This consisted of an agreement between the President and individual employers about wages and hours, prices and fair trade practices. This so-called blanket code was intended as a temporary expedient to be used pending the codification of all industries. Into operation went more than 2,300,000 of these individual agreements which covered about 16,300,000 workers. But the blanket code precipitated a deluge of other codes, making it ever more difficult to administer the NRA.

During a trip down the Potomac on the Presidential yacht, Johnson sold Roosevelt on the idea of creating the Blue Eagle. This became the NRA's official symbol, bestowed on those who were operating under approved codes or who had signed the President's Re-employment Agreement. Johnson, after chatting one day with Henry Wallace about thunderbirds, had drawn a rough sketch of this old Indian ideograph and then had a finished design prepared by Charles T. Colner of Philadelphia. It showed an eagle with outstretched wings, a toothed wheel clutched in the talons of its right claw, three lightning bolts held in its left claw. At the bottom of the design was the NRA slogan: WE DO OUR PART. Because the eagle was printed in blue ink, it came to be called the Blue Eagle.

There was nothing new about the idea itself. During World War I the War Industries Board had given retailers a card to display in their stores to prove that they were cooperating. Less than a month before the NRA became law, Baruch had said that "the insignia of government approval on doorways, letterheads and invoices will become a necessity in business." Roosevelt, in accepting Johnson's suggestion, said: "In war, in the gloom of night attack, soldiers wear a bright badge to be sure that comrades do not fire on comrades. On that principle, those who co-operate in this program must know each other at a glance."

Patriotic citizens were expected to patronize only those concerns displaying the Blue Eagle. Withdrawal of the right to display this insignia became an important moral influence to enforce compliance with the codes. Blue Eagles went up on a door of the White House, on the front of a small furniture factory Eleanor Roosevelt ran in New York State, over the doors of big industrial plants, in offices, in the windows of retail shops.

Most people regarded the Blue Eagle as a badge of honor—but not so William Randolph Hearst, who snarled that NRA meant "No Recovery Allowed." Arthur Brisbane wrote that "when Mr. Hearst looks at that Eagle, he has to postpone his dinner." Another publisher, Henry Luce, reproduced the Blue Eagle on the cover of *Time* magazine on August 21, 1933, and thereafter it appeared on the masthead. The *Daily Worker* printed a cartoon showing the Blue Eagle whirling into a swastika.

Tin Pan Alley came out with a song called "Nira," while Postmaster General Farley issued an NRA stamp. The President, in a lighthearted mood, dictated the following letter: "Dear Jim: Thank you for the NRA postage stamp and cover. The honest farmer, who looks like me; the honest business man, who looks like Grover T. Whalen; and the honest blacksmith, who looks like Lionel Barrymore, are magnificent. But Oh Heavens what a girl! She is wearing a No. 11 shoe, also a bustle, and if recovery is dependent on women like that I am agin recovery. . . ."

On Wednesday, September 13, 1933, New York City honored the NRA and the Blue Eagle with a parade that attracted more people than had gathered in any city anywhere in the nation since Armistice Day. Two million people watched a quarter of a million marchers. Collectively, this was more human beings than lived in Indianapolis, St. Louis and Birmingham combined.

The sun shone upon men, women and children as they gathered in and around Washington Square and then, at 1:30 P.M., stepped off for the long walk up Fifth Avenue. Among the marchers were dressmakers and brokers, hatters and florists, barbers and municipal employees, West Point cadets and oil workers, CCC boys and waitresses, metalworkers and soda jerks, bankers, newspaper editors and Chinese schoolchildren. A contingent of actors was led by Al Jolson and Ruby Keeler. Symphony conductor Walter Damrosch marched with radio performers. Cheers and whistles greeted the Rockettes, the shapely chorus girls from the Radio City Music Hall. Almost every trade, guild, calling and profession helped pay tribute to the Blue Eagle, which seemed to promise so much hope for all.

A pretty girl called "Miss NRA" rode a shell-shaped float the length of the three-mile route up the avenue, her smile hardening to marble before the day was done. Pictures of the Blue Eagle bobbed up and down in the line of march, groups carried banners proclaiming that they were 100 PERCENT ORGANIZED and 100 PERCENT NRA, bands blared "Happy Days Are Here Again," seventy-three airplanes droned overhead, and people watching from high windows unloosed a snowstorm of confetti, tickertape and torn telephone pages on the heads of the celebrants.

Three out of every ten New Yorkers saw the parade. They cheered. They yelled. Their clothes got mussed, so closely packed did they stand, and their feet hurt after hours of contact with the unyielding sidewalk. They guzzled soda pop and they fainted. At Fifty-eight Street a mass of spectators slowly began moving like the beginning of an avalanche, the pressure building and spreading until a plate-glass window was shattered. One man died of a heart attack that day, and forty-six others were injured. But most of the millions were delighted, and laughter was the rule of the day.

This was what most impressed Hugh Johnson. Posed on the reviewing stand, he remembered the Twenties, the slightly drunken hostesses in dance halls and their false, metallic laughter. This laughter seemed healthy and genuine, an expression of the belief that the NRA would lead America out of the Depression. Wearing a double-breasted suit, a handkerchief rimming his breast pocket, he waved at the marchers and enjoyed every minute of the parade—or almost every minute. Sharing the platform with him were other celebrities. There was sleek Grover Whalen, the city's perennial cheerleader. There was lanky W. Averell Harriman, New York State's NRA chairman, who was to become one of the most experienced diplomats in American history. There, too, stood Mayor John P. O'Brien, who had attended the last banquet held in the old Waldorf-Astoria, an ignorant man who had once referred to Einstein as "Albert Weinstein." Recently the mayor had proposed that new laws be imposed on Wall Street trading, and as stock exchange men marched past they booed him.

Newspaper photographers and newsreelmen had their cameras zeroed in on the reviewing stand. General Johnson, sensitive to criticism that the NRA was Fascistic, was careful not to raise his right hand higher than his shoulders lest someone say he was giving the Fascist salute. During the long parade all he did most of the time was to stick out his arm straight in front of him and wiggle his fingers as he greeted the marchers. Even so, *Time* reported that he gave the Mussolini salute and declared it had a picture to prove this. Johnson growled in rebuttal that the magazine had faked onto a photograph of his body the arm of Mayor O'Brien, who stood beside him.

On came the marchers, thousands upon thousands of them, laughing, cheering, chanting. Some spectators ducked into theaters to rest their feet, but when they emerged, they found the parade still going on. Hour after hour after hour, as confetti thickened on the pavement, the merrymakers surged in waves up Fifth Avenue, and when twilight softened the city, some marching brewers lit the red flares they were carrying. Streetlights lining the avenue had been equipped with amber bulbs for the festive occasion, bulbs that glowed goldenly against coming night. The parade lasted until a little after midnight, and as a light rain began falling, the city street cleaners hitched up their belts to start sweeping up after an event which the *Herald Tribune* described as "New York's greatest demonstration."

*　　　*　　　*

Wild excitement for the NRA had not infected coal-mine owners. Coal was the sickest of all industries, the value of soft coal production having fallen from $2.1 billion in 1920 to only $406 million in 1932. Among the many things wrong with this industry was the fact that the largest coal consumers—steel, railroad and utility corporations—pitted coal operators against one another. Since labor constituted two-thirds of all mining costs, the operators passed along their failing prices to the miners in the form of lower wages. And there was an enormous oversupply of labor.

Roosevelt mused: "It is a queer human fact that once a family goes into coal mining, they are never good for anything else. They would rather hang around the coal mining industry, in the hope of getting three or four weeks' work in a year, than to make an effort in another direction. Even if we started every coal mine in this country going on a basis of increased production, probably a third of the people would still be unemployed. It presents one of the most difficult problems we have in any industry."

In many a company-owned town a miner could buy what he needed only at a company-owned store, and its prices were usually higher than at other stores. It was customary for the miner to buy on credit until he got his next check, but when payday came, he was left with little, if any, cash. *Fortune* magazine reported that in Harlan County, Kentucky, "the company deducted an average of $11.80 monthly for rent, medical attention, powder and caps and insurance. To pay this deduction, a man had to mine forty-five tons of coal a month, which meant that he had to work nine days. Most of them worked a total of six days, and the result is a load of debt with no balance for food."

A Harlan miner wrote: "We are half fed because we can'nt feed ourselves and family's with what we make. And we can'nt go to a Cut rate Store and buy food because most all the company forbids such tradeing. If you got the cash. But now we have no cash. And the companies keeps their food stuffs at high prices at all time. So you can not clear enough to go anywhere. And if you do go some where and buy food you are subjects to being canned. . . .

"We have been eating wild green. . . . Such as Polk salad. Violet tops, wild onions. forget me not wild lettuce and such weeds as cows eat as a cow wont eat a poison weeds. . . . Our family are in bad shake childrens need milk women need nurishments food shoes and dresses. . . . But I can't clear a dollar per month that why I am here. that why hundreds are here."

Coal operators themselves felt that mining conditions were so bad the industry never could revive. During the first week of the Roosevelt administration a group of them called on the President in the White House. He was so busy with bank failures and a hundred other things that he shunted the delegation to Labor Secretary Perkins and Interior Secretary Ickes. Frances Perkins later described how she felt during the two days of hearings that followed: "Absolutely new in the government, Harold Ickes and I sat behind a table, looking solemn as owls and representing the Government of the United States. We were so new at being 'the Government' that it was really only the externals of representation."

She and Ickes listened as the operators told about whole communities practically shut down, local grocery stores unable to operate, school-teachers trying to exist without any pay, merchants and transportation systems almost bankrupt, everybody in debt to somebody. Unemployment in the mining fields was almost total. Then, as she remembered the scene: "The burden of recommendations from coal operator after coal operator was that the government must take over the mines. 'Will the government please take them?' they pleaded. 'The operators will sell the mines to the government at any price fixed by the government. Anything so we can get out of it.' "

This was a strange event in American history—capitalists begging the government to Socialize an entire industry.

Ickes whispered to Secretary Perkins: "What in the world would we do with the mines if we took them over? How could the government operate them? Nobody in this government knows how to run a coal mine. This isn't a nationalization program we have undertaken with Roosevelt."

Not every mineowner wanted the government to take over his property. The operators were as internally divided as they were united in their opposition to organized labor. Hugh Johnson said "there was almost as much hostility between different coal fields such as Southern and Northern Appalachian as there was between labor and management in certain fields."

Coal was one of the ten big industries that Johnson wanted to put under a code as soon as possible, but he knew he would have trouble about the NRA's Section 7-a, which provided for collective bargaining. And trouble he had. Thirty different proposed coal codes were drawn up.

The evening of September 6, 1933, coal operators and officials of the United Mine Workers of America met in the White House to try to agree on a code. Felix Frankfurter, who had nothing to do with this conference, had dropped by to see his friend the President before going to England to spend a year teaching at Oxford. A Presidential secretary told Frankfurter that Roosevelt wanted him to sit in on this meeting.

"Are you sure I shan't be in the way?"

"He says"—the secretary smiled—"that you are to come along."

Short and dark, brilliant and quick-moving, Frankfurter walked into the conference room. Already seated there were the President, Hugh Johnson, Donald Richberg and Harry Hopkins.

"Come along!" Roosevelt sang out. "How'd you like to act as secretary and sit in that corner?"

"If you're sure it's all right," Frankfurter replied. The Harvard law professor felt out of place. However, he took a pencil off Roosevelt's desk and headed for a corner of the room, saying: "I'm happy to take on the job."

Roosevelt cried: "Go to it!"

Minutes later the room began to fill up with mineowners and labor leaders. Frankfurter was still so queasy he hardly dared look up at them.

The President greeted the men cheerily: "Come along and sit ye down!"

Frankfurter got a quick look at a huge bushy-browed and black-maned man; he had to be John L. Lewis, head of the mineworkers' union. The thin rigid fellow, why that was John Morrow, president of the Pittsburgh Coal Company and also head of the powerful Northern Coal Control Association—organized by Mellon and Rockefeller interests.

Pleasantries were exchanged. Solemn small talk was made. Then Roosevelt got down to some brutal facts about mining and miners, finally saying: "I know of a case where a man has worked for two months and received nothing in cash. You can't explain that kind of thing away. I know that where a mine is short of cash there are difficulties and the mine will want to cut down the debts of its store department."

A mineowner said: "The trouble is, Mr. President, that employment is spread too thin in the coal mines. These deductions are against previous advances. It is unfortunate, but half a loaf is better than no bread."

"I realize how much there is to be said," Roosevelt commented diplomatically, "but I want you to see that in checking off, he gets something."

Another operator spoke up: "We know that there have been abuses and we hope that the code and the union will help to rectify these—but what has this to do with the contract? Wages will in some cases be increased fifty per cent."

There ensued a discussion of the overall problems of the coal industry. At last the President switched the conversation back to the main point. "Well," he asked, "can we write out something to suit everybody?"

Johnson handed Roosevelt a slip of paper and said: "This is it."

The proposed code was read aloud by the President. More discussion.

John L. Lewis said: "We'd waive our right to check off, if something were done about deductions. There are many extreme cases. I know of a man who has earned six hundred dollars in two years and in the last twenty-four months he's never seen a cent of it. . . ."

An operator wailed: "I don't know how we're going to get this price fixing done and set up the new machinery!"

Finally the President said firmly: "You get that contract written up tomorrow, and if you've anything else on your minds, just let me know. . . . Good night."

It was nearly midnight when the men filed out of the conference room.

Harry Hopkins strolled over to Frankfurter, flashed a grin and asked: "What's the betting? Fifty to one against?"

"No," Frankfurter said thoughtfully. "I don't see why they shouldn't come across. But you know them."

Over the next two weeks wrangling continued between mineowners and labor leaders, one man dropping dead of a heart attack and General Johnson snatching only about four hours' sleep each night on a sofa in his office. But at last, toward the middle of September, all agreed upon the terms of an NRA code covering coal.

John L. Lewis and John Morrow met again, formally, at a long shiny table in Room 800-B of Washington's new Shoreham Hotel to sign the pact. This fat document provided for unionization of all soft coal mines in Pennsylvania, Ohio, West Virginia, Virginia, Maryland, Tennessee and part of Kentucky. It prescribed working conditions for 314,000 miners. It gave the United Mine Workers their own checkweighmen and grievance committees, freed them from the necessity of living in company houses and trading at company stores, opened new jobs that had been held by 6,000 boys under the age of seventeen. Among the benefits obtained by the operators was a promise that there would not be another soft coal strike until at least April 1, 1934.

Morrow had sworn time and again that he never would sign another pact with the union. Now, sitting rigidly at the table in the hotel, he watched as Lewis scrawled his signature and then pushed the document toward him. The room was jammed with hard-boiled mineowners. They held their breath as Morrow picked up a pen. Despite all he had said in the past, he did sign. The men exhaled. Then Morrow and Lewis issued a joint statement: "Unquestionably this agreement is the greatest in magnitude and importance that has ever been negotiated in the history of collective bargaining in the United States. It marks the beginning of a new era."

Agreement came from a columnist and radio commentator, Jay Franklin, who used the pseudonym of the Unofficial Observer. He said the coal code was perhaps "the greatest single victory of organized labor in fifty years."

*   *   *

But steelworkers were unorganized, and steel was one of the ten biggest industries that Roosevelt and Johnson were eager to place under an NRA code. The steel barons, an autocratic breed of men, expressed general objections to the NRA and specific objections to the section that gave labor the right to bargain collectively. At last Roosevelt invited Charles M. Schwab to the White House.

The seventy-one-year-old Schwab was board chairman of the Bethlehem Steel Corporation at a salary of $250,000 a year, the once and future president of the American Iron and Steel Institute, the sybarite whose granite château overlooked the squatters' camp on Riverside Drive. The steel industry was paying its workers 63 percent less in weekly wages than it had in 1929. Nonetheless, since the Crash, a bonus of $1,623,000 had been paid to Eugene C. Grace, president of the Bethlehem Steel Corporation and second-in-command to Schwab.

Schwab told Roosevelt he could not accept the steel code because of his obligations to the Bethlehem stockholders. The President asked whether he had been looking after his stockholders when he paid those million-dollar bonuses to Eugene Grace and let his workers live in coke ovens. It was this sort of thing, Roosevelt added, which had discredited big business. At a Senate committee hearing this same year of 1933 Schwab confessed: "I was not engaged in making steel. I was making money!"

Frances Perkins was disturbed by the fact that the unorganized steel-workers had no one to represent them in bargaining over the proposed steel code. Going to the President, she said she had thought of speaking for them—but, of course, it was unorthodox for a government official to submit a case for a partisan position.

"It's no more unorthodox than the NRA itself," Roosevelt told her. "After all, we are trying to do something. It is like war. We are dealing with unusual factors. The codes have to be adopted. Otherwise we can't get recovery and purchasing power. Neither can we get the support of all the people unless they know that the real interests of labor have been con-sidered. I think the secretary of labor ought to be the secretary *for* labor. Go ahead! Do the best you can."

Secretary Perkins felt that steelworkers in remote communities might not understand the NRA, since they read local papers largely controlled by their bosses. Deciding to visit some steel-producing areas, she phoned the President to say she planned to go to Homestead, Pennsylvania. This, she pointed out, had had a bad labor history.

"That's a good idea," Roosevelt said. Then he chuckled and added: "But don't get yourself arrested."

Instead of starting out with an entourage of economic advisers, minor public officials, secretaries and press agents, Frances Perkins decided to take along only Father Francis Haas, a priest who was friendly to labor. Before leaving Washington, she phoned Myron C. Taylor, board chairman of United States Steel, and Eugene Grace. She said that above all, she wanted to talk privately with workers and hoped that the executives would give her their cooperation. Both promised. Instructions were passed down the line to plant managers of steelworks to give the secretary of labor all the help she wanted. She went to Pennsylvania, visited the plants, talked to workers on the job. In Pittsburgh she escorted reporters inside steel mills they had never been permitted to see before.

Then she continued to the borough of Homestead, located in south-western Pennsylvania on the Monongahela River seven miles southeast of Pittsburgh. This was a gigantic jackstraw of iron and steel factories. The borough's executive officer was known by the archaic name of the Burgess. He let Secretary Perkins and Father Haas hold a meeting on the second floor of the Hall of Burgesses.

Attending this meeting were the Burgess, other local officials, local newspapermen and workers from the mills. Although the steelworkers were not very articulate, they did air complaints and ask questions. As the meeting ended and Frances Perkins was bidding good-bye to the Burgess, she heard a disturbance downstairs. A reporter stepped up and whispered into her ear. The Burgess, he said, had forbidden many other workers to attend this meeting, and now they were gathered in the lower hall and on the sidewalk, protesting. She turned back to the Burgess and said she was sorry that these other men had been unable to attend. Might she have the upper hall for a few more minutes?

"No, no!" he cried, his face reddening. "You've had enough! These men are not any good. They're undesirable Reds. I know them well. They just want to make trouble!"

Secretary Perkins, who once had seized General Johnson by his coat lapels in a moment of irritation, was not easily thwarted. She began fantasizing about the public reaction if she ignored these other workers; newspapers might shrill: "Steelworkers have no voice, steel trust controls the code!" She also recalled Plato's remark that it is the duty of public officers to listen patiently to all citizens. Lifting her pointed chin, she bade a brisk farewell to the Burgess and walked downstairs.

On the street she found about 200 people. Many were furious. Cops had pushed them out of the building and onto the sidewalk and pavement. Her dark eyes flashing, Frances Perkins took up a position on the steps of the Hall of Burgesses and began making a little speech.

"My friends, I am so sorry that you were not able to get into the hall. It was very crowded, but perhaps we can hear what you have to say right here."

Out of the door burst the Burgess, crying: "You can't talk here! You are not permitted to make a speech here! There is a rule against making a speech here!"

A member of the Cabinet of the United States government was not permitted to make a speech in public? The burly steelworkers looked at the woman from Washington, wondering how she would handle this situation. Lifting her eyes, she saw a park across the way.

"All right," she said. "I am sorry. We will go over to the park."

But the Burgess and a couple of cops closed in on her.

"You can't do that!" he sputtered. "There is an ordinance against holding meetings in a public park!"

"This is just a hearing," she protested, "not a meeting. It won't take long. Only a few minutes."

"They're undesirable Reds!" the Burgess yelled. "They're undesirable Reds!"

She hesitated. Then she saw an American flag flying over a building at the opposite side of the square. That, she thought, must be the post office. As an official of the federal government she felt she had a right to speak on federal property.

"We will go to the post office," she told the crowd. "There is an American flag."

It was late afternoon, and the post office was about to close as Madame Perkins and the workers trooped inside; but after she explained the situation to the postmaster, he said, sure, she could use the building.

Nothing dramatic happened. She climbed onto a chair to talk briefly about the proposed steel code. Then she asked whether anybody cared to speak. Twenty or thirty men did. Some denounced the steel trust's tight control of the community. Others said they wished the government would free them. She was so impressed with one articulate speaker that she invited him to Washington to attend the forthcoming public hearing on the code. At last she got down off the chair, shook hands all around, and listened to expressions of rejoicing that the New Deal was not afraid of the steel trust.

A local reporter wrote a story about the attempt made by the Burgess to prevent the secretary of labor from speaking in public, wire services picked it up, and when she got back to the national capital, she found other newspapermen waiting to ask her what had happened. One of them wanted to know why the Burgess had behaved as he did.

Charitably, she replied: "Why, he seemed a little nervous."

President Roosevelt read about the nervous Burgess, got her on the phone, laughed at her description of the man and said she had done just the right thing.

"You know," he added, "the post office in every community ought to be the people's contact with the government. We ought to make more of it."

A few weeks later she convened a meeting in her Washington office to try to work out the final wording of a code to cover the steel industry. Because the steelworkers were unorganized and without representation, she asked AFL President Green to attend. He agreed. In fact, he was already seated in her office when the steel magnates entered. These were powerful men—Myron Taylor, Eugene Grace, Ernest Weir, Tom Girdler, William Irvin—along with officials of smaller steel companies. To her astonishment, they would not let themselves be introduced to the aging, phlegmatic Bill Green.

"They backed away into a corner," she later wrote, "like frightened boys. It was the most embarrassing social experience of my life. I had never met people who did not know how—with hypocrisy, perhaps, but with an outward surface of correct politeness—to say how-do-you-do even to the people they detested. . . . I was a little shocked, unable to believe that grown men could be so timid. But their faces were long, their eyes were solemn, and they were the picture of men with no self-assurance whatsoever."

William Irvin, president of United States Steel, was the only one among the steel executives who dared to walk over to Green, pull up a chair and begin chatting with him. For three-quarters of an hour Secretary Perkins tried to persuade the others to say something to the labor leader, but they refused. They whispered to her that if it became known that they had sat down in the same room with William Green, that they had talked to him, it would ruin their reputations.

Her three-cornered hat bobbing indignantly, she cried: "But Mr. Green doesn't represent the steelworkers! He is not a steelworker. I will tell you what he is going to say—" She handed them a copy of his prepared remarks praising the NRA and approving the proposed steel code.

Nothing worked. With the exception of Irvin, none of the steel tycoons would pass the time of day with Green, and finally the usually mild-mannered man left in a huff.

"As the great barons of steel filed out," she has written, "still looking solemn and sorrowful, I could not resist the temptation to tell them that their behavior had surprised me and that I felt as though I had entertained eleven-year-old boys at their first party, rather than men to whom the most important industry in the United States had been committed."

The NRA steel code was signed by President Roosevelt on August 19, 1933.

*   *   *

General Johnson called the NRA "a holy thing, the greatest social advance since the days of Jesus Christ." Driving himself like a madman, drugged with fatigue, he kept up a steady rat-a-tat-tat of publicity about the recovery program. Its alleged glories were heralded on highway billboards, by means of newsreels, in full-page advertisements in newspapers, by orators speaking in movie theaters, by ministers in their pulpits and by an endless geyser of radio talk. *Time* magazine called this "the biggest and loudest propaganda campaign" since World War I.

Late one night in the autumn of 1933 a twenty-five-year-old man named William Saroyan sat in his room in a cheap hotel on Times Square in Manhattan just across from the Paramount Building. He wanted to become a great writer. He had written one short story after another and mailed them to various magazines, but all had been rejected. A native of California, he then decided he might be able to advance his career by moving to New York, the center of the nation's publishing business. Saroyan traveled by bus from the West Coast to the East Coast, arriving with very little money and not a single friend in the big city. Now hope was fading. Sleepless with anxiety, he began prowling his lonely hotel room, turning on the radio for company. Then he became aware that he was listening to a radio commercial.

An announcer said the cold and sore throat season had come. The commercial ended with this profound proclamation: "Aspirin is a member of the NRA!"

Saroyan, who did develop into a distinguished author, later commented: "It made me laugh to hear that. But it is the truth. Aspirin *is* a member of the N.R.A. It *is* helping everyone to evade fundamentals, it *is* helping to keep people going to work. Aspirin *is* helping to bring back prosperity. It *is* doing its part. It *is* sending millions of half-dead people to their jobs. It *is* doing a great deal to keep the spirit of this nation from disintegrating. It *is* deadening pain everywhere. It *isn't* preventing anything, but it is deadening pain."

Across the Hudson River in Jersey City a small stooped tailor named Jacob Maged ran afoul of the NRA. He charged 35 cents for pressing a suit instead of the 40 cents required by the NRA's Tailoring Industry Code. For this infraction he was fined $100 and sentenced to thirty days in the Hudson County Jail. The case attracted widespread attention across the nation and abroad, as well, a London newspaper printing a headline that asked: WHAT IS AMERICA UP TO?

After serving only three days of his term, Maged was let out of jail. Scores of reporters and photographers were waiting as he walked into the sunlight. The Illinois Manufacturers Association, which was defying the Illinois branch of the NRA, was hailing the little tailor as a national hero, a rugged individualist. With members of the press trailing him, Maged walked back to his shop on Griffith Street, climbed onto his workbench, took the traditional cross-legged position of the tailor and held court.

"So the NRA threw me in jail for a nickel," he said, biting off a thread. "For a nickel I wasn't a gentleman. What do they know about tailoring, anyway? But I'm glad it's all over."

Getting off his bench he motioned to a reporter. "Come over here, reporter. I want to show you how to do business without the NRA."

Waving the newspaperman to the door of his shop, Maged said: "Now, you're coming in. You want to have a suit pressed. . . . Say it!"

Obligingly, the reporter said: "I want to have a suit pressed."

"The price is thirty-five cents," the tailor told him, "but for fifty cents I can do an extra special job. . . . How about it?"

Catching on, the reporter grinned and cried: "Sold!"

"You see? That's the way to do business. No NRA needed!"

Hugh Johnson was infuriated by the case of the defiant tailor, writing: ". . . Maged at once telegraphed me not to take his Blue Eagle away or disturb the code because it had been his salvation—and those newspapers knew that."

The general was also displeased when a St. Louis Negro bootblack signed a code, refused to work more than forty hours and then asked the NRA to pay him the balance of the $12 a week he had been earning.

When Johnson began his job as NRA administrator, he courted all the publicity he could get. At his first press conference he was asked whether code hearings would be open to the public. Johnson yipped: "We're gonna do this whole job in a goldfish bowl!" But with the advent of criticism about the NRA, after newsreel audiences booed film clips of NRA activities, the general started to blame the press and even barred a reporter from a subsequent press conference.

Time magazine began producing a weekly movie documentary called *The March of Time,* which became immensely popular during the Thirties. It dramatized news events in depth by taking cameras to the scene of action and having real-life characters repeat themselves in word and deed. The very first *March of Time* featured the case of Fred C. Perkins.

A resident of York, Pennsylvania, Perkins was a small-time manufacturer of storage batteries. Agreeing to let the *March of Time* people see what had happened to him, he allowed them to set up cameras in his shop as once again he called his workmen together to announce he could not afford to pay them more than 25 cents an hour. This was less than the wages decreed in the NRA code covering the electric storage and wet primary battery industry. No newsreel camera caught a subsequent scene in which a federal marshal entered the Perkins shop to say he was breaking the law. But cameras whirred again as Perkins reenacted that moment wherein he walked into the kitchen of his home to tell his wife that the NRA had cracked down on him. And, dutifully, she registered horror upon hearing that he had to post $5,000 bail or go to jail.

Unable to raise such a sum, Perkins went to jail, continuing to conduct his business from behind bars. After being imprisoned for eighteen days, he was released when bond was furnished by an outraged New Yorker. This case, like the one concerning the Jersey City tailor, provoked such massive indignation that several eminent lawyers volunteered their legal services to Perkins. One of these attorneys was John W. Davis, the Democratic Party's Presidential candidate in 1924 and now an anti-New Deal Wall Street lawyer. There were rumors that Hy Prather Fletcher, chairman of the Republican National Committee, also helped Perkins, but Fletcher denied them.

Perkins was tried in a federal court, found guilty and fined $1,500. *March of Time* cameras looked on as he and his attorneys planned an appeal to the United States Supreme Court. But before the nation's highest court got around to ruling on the Perkins case, it settled the fate of the NRA by deciding another one.

*   *   *

The NRA simply was not working out as had been hoped. It was being proved, as Vice President Garner had warned, that while the big industries could be put under codes, the whole business of the country could not be managed from Washington. Instead of confining the codes to huge segments of the economy, rules were being written to regulate the dog food industry, fishhooks, collar buttons, vaudeville, burlesque shows, burlap and so on.

At first many Americans had equated the NRA with the New Deal itself, but soon its defects became obvious. Codes were drawn up too hastily in some cases, were weighted in favor of big business and were difficult to enforce. Doubts about the NRA's constitutionality encouraged people to violate the codes. When farmers complained that the NRA raised the prices of things they bought faster than the rise in the prices of farm products, Hugh Johnson admitted that it had been designed primarily for urban workers. Suspension of the antitrust laws strengthened big business. The collective bargaining provision, upon which labor had counted, was flouted by some employers. There was a rising tide of criticism about cutthroat competition and unfair price fixing. Huey Long called the Blue Eagle a mangy buzzard.

Hearst condemned the NRA as "absolute state socialism." A millionaire who lined up with the NRA was called an anarchist. Dorothy Thompson wrote an article proving that the NRA was Fascistic. Frank H. Simonds wrote an article proving that it was Communistic. John Maynard Keynes wrote an article proving that it was neither Fascistic nor Communistic. Hugh Johnson, always in perpetual motion, sometimes disappearing for days to get drunk, fretted and fumed and listed the NRA's enemies as his own overly zealous friends, the Communists, extreme conservatives, employers who would not accept NRA's restrictions and code violators— whom he branded as chiselers.

Johnson angrily told how he had been used unwittingly by one swindler. This man had a client who had just signed a code, but now the code was about to be changed. The worried client told his representative he was afraid that this change, which he favored, might not be accepted. The con man said to the client: "Why, that's a cinch! Hugh and I are just like this!" Holding up a hand, he entwined two fingers. "I'll fix that for you this very morning. He'll be coming through this hotel lobby on his way to the office in a few minutes."

The man was waiting in the lobby when Johnson descended in an elevator with his two dogs on leashes, hailed him by his first name, and the genial general responded. The con man emerged from the hotel with the NRA administrator, and for a few moments the two men laughed and chatted about nothing whatsoever. That was all there was to it. In the ordinary course of events the proposed code change was made, whereupon the swindler collected a fee from his grateful and unsuspecting client.

The NRA was breaking down administratively. At one time its compliance division had 17,999 cases of wage and hour violations, together with 4,000 cases of unfair trade practices, awaiting action. Still other cases had been placed on the dockets of courts all over the land. Roosevelt, dissatisfied with the way Johnson was running things, ordered surveys and reorganizations, and several times the general threatened to resign. Despite his fanatical belief in the NRA he sometimes wondered about its constitutionality and shrank from an ultimate test in the United States Supreme Court.

*   *   *

Four brothers by the name of Schechter—Joseph, Alex, Martin and Aaron—lived in Brooklyn, where they ran a wholesale poultry slaughter business under two corporate names, the A.L.A. Schechter Poultry Corporation and the Schechter Live Poultry Market. The eldest brother, Joseph, was the head of both firms. They bought most of their fowl in Manhattan's famous produce center, the Washington Market, or at railway terminals serving New York City. Sometimes, though, they made purchases from commission men in Philadelphia.

Although the Schechter brothers had signed the NRA's Live Poultry Code, the federal government accused them of violating it. They were indicted on eighteen counts. They were accused of violating a provision calling for a forty-hour week and a minimum wage of fifty cents an hour for their employees. They were charged with undercutting competitors by selling chickens at four to eight cents a pound less than the market price set by the code. And they were accused of selling a chicken unfit for human consumption.

Such was the origin of the sick chicken case.

The Schechters hired Joseph and Jacob Heller, brothers and attorneys, to represent them. Their case was heard in the United States District Court in Brooklyn, and the jury convicted them on seventeen counts. The four brothers and their two firms were fined $7,425. Joseph was sentenced to jail for three months; Alex got two months; Martin and Aaron were given one month each behind bars.

They appealed to the United States Circuit Court of Appeals. Their lawyers argued that adoption of the poultry code was an unconstitutional delegation by Congress of legislative power, that it regulated intrastate business outside the authority of Congress and that certain code provisions were repugnant to the due process clause of the Fifth Amendment. But the Court of Appeals ruled that the code was valid, except for its regulation of wages and hours.

Except for wages and hours? Why, if these provisions were torn from the NRA, the entire program would collapse. Despite Johnson's fears, Attorney General Homer Cummings decided the time had come to test the constitutionality of the NRA. It had become obvious that there could be no enforcement of the NRA without a clear-cut ruling from the highest court in the land. On April 8, 1935, the Justice Department joined the Schechter brothers in asking the Supreme Court to review the matter.

Felix Frankfurter, a kind of mother hen to New Dealers, agreed on the need for an ultimate decision, but he doubted the wisdom of taking a stand on the sick chicken case. For that matter, Frankfurter felt that Cummings always gave the President bad advice. Frankfurter sent word to Roosevelt that he feared the Supreme Court would strike down all of the NRA if it sat on the Schechter case. Roosevelt wired Cummings to delay the appeal, but the message did not reach the attorney general in time. The NRA's

general counsel, Donald Richberg, optimistically felt that the high court
would find in favor of the government.

The afternoon of May 2, 1935, the Supreme Court opened its hearing
into the Schechter case. Since construction was not quite completed on the
new Supreme Court Building, the proceeding was held in the old courtroom
in the Senate wing of the Capitol. This semicircular room had a low half
ceiling and central skylights, and the black-robed justices sat in front of
dark red draperies. The importance of the case had attracted a crowd.

Joseph Schechter pushed his way past people and up to a door, where he
was stopped by a guard.

"Who are you?" the guard asked.

"Me? You don't know who I am?"

"No. Who are you?"

"*I* am Joe Schechter!"

The government's arguments were presented by Richberg, a bulky and
balding man, his normal energy depleted by overwork, by criticisms from
the press and by the guff he had to take from General Johnson. The NRA
counsel told the nine justices that the NRA code under question should be
viewed in the light of the grave national crisis, a crisis calling for broad and
intensive cooperation among those engaged in trade and industry. He declared that the NRA had brought great social progress, and he described
the collapse that surely would follow an unfavorable decision.

Joseph Heller then stepped in front of the justices to present the case for
the Brooklyn businessmen in a Brooklyn accent. In the indictment against
the Schechters ten counts were for violation of a provision calling for
"straight killing." There in the august chamber of the United States
Supreme Court he was asked to explain the straight killing of chickens.
Loudly, passionately and at great length, Heller described the art of
slaughtering fowl. The nine judges, usually so solemn, smiled and grinned
and chuckled and finally laughed aloud. Making no attempt to conceal
their amusement, they prodded the Brooklyn attorney with questions
seemingly meant to stir him to ever more colorful rhetoric.

Heller told how customers walked into the Schechters' place and tried to
take their pick of the chickens in the coops but, under the code, had to
accept the first bird that came out of the coop. At last one justice said, all
right, now he understood that "you have got to put your hand into the coop
and take out whichever chicken comes to you first. You then hand the
chicken to the rabbi, who slaughters it?" The Schechters ran a kosher
business.

Heller replied, yes, that was the way it was.

"And it was for this," asked James C. McReynolds, a conservative
justice, "that your client was convicted?"

"Yes—and fined five thousand dollars and given three months in jail."

Heller went on to say that if a customer wanted to buy half a crate of
chickens under the NRA code, he had to divide the crate itself. Justice

George Sutherland asked what would happen if all the chickens were huddled in one end of the crate. Everyone laughed. The attorney confessed that the question was a puzzler. Another burst of laughter.

Word of this hearing, so frivolous at times, spread throughout the country—and morale sank among the people employed by the NRA. Would the court kill the whole thing? Would the employees then lose their jobs? From the lowliest NRA stenographer to the attorney general himself there was a symbolic holding of breaths while the justices deliberated. Then came the day when they were to announce their decision.

High noon, Monday, May 27, 1935. Spring kissing the capital. Spectators seated in the old Supreme Court chamber with its mahogany furniture, classic columns and two great fireplaces. The court crier, Thomas Waggaman, steps into view and cries: "Oyez, oyez, oyez!" The audience rises. "The Honorable, the Chief Justice and the Associate Justices of the Supreme Court!" Nine black-gowned men file in and sit down in old leather swivel chairs. They look cheerful. Everyone sits down. The most powerful judicial body in the world is now in session.

Before announcing its decision in the NRA case, the court first disposes of two other matters. Justice Sutherland reads an opinion rebuking the President for removing William E. Humphrey, a federal trade commissioner, for trying to thwart administration policies. Decision unanimous. Then Justice Louis D. Brandeis delivers an opinion branding as unconstitutional the Frazier-Lemke Act for the relief of debt-burdened farmers. Decision unanimous. Momentary silence. Tension.

The white-whiskered Chief Justice, Charles Evans Hughes, who had sworn Roosevelt into office as President, announced that he himself would read the court's opinion in the Schechter case. Under ordinary circumstances, let alone on a day and in such a place so solemn as this, Hughes was a man of imposing dignity. In 1916 he had lost the Presidential election to Woodrow Wilson. Earlier, as the Republican governor of New York, he often received the support of a young anti-Tammany Democrat named Franklin D. Roosevelt. Now Hughes and Roosevelt had come to a dramatic confrontation. In the third year of the Depression the Chief Justice had said that "we cannot save ourselves unless we save society," but his legalistic mind was offended by some of the saving measures adopted by the New Deal. Now, as spokesman for the Supreme Court, he was about to pronounce a verdict on the entire American economy. Leaning forward in his chair, bracing his arms against the bench, stroking his beard from time to time, speaking forcefully in the silent chamber, he killed the National Recovery Act.

The decision he read was a long one that went into every detail of the case of *Schechter Poultry Corporation v. the United States,* 295 U.S. 495. Hughes discussed the question of the delegation of legislative power to code-making groups, and then the issue of the application of the provisions of the Live Poultry Code to intrastate commerce. At one point he said:

"Extraordinary conditions do not create or enlarge constitutional power." Donald Richberg turned pale and sank lower in his seat. Finally the Chief Justice came to the end of the opinion, declaring: "We are of the opinion that the attempt through the provisions of the code to fix the hours and wages of employees of defendants in their intrastate business was not a valid exercise of federal power. . . . We hold the code provisions here in question to be invalid and that the judgement of conviction must be reversed."

Decision unanimous.

As the courtroom erupted in a babble of voices, the nine justices got up and marched out. A page tapped the shoulder of Thomas G. Corcoran, a young lawyer who was assistant to the secretary of the treasury. Would Mr. Corcoran be good enough to come to the judges' robing room? "Tommy the Cork," as Roosevelt liked to call him, followed the page in perplexity. Justice Brandeis wanted to see him. When he entered the robing room, he saw the white-maned Brandeis standing with his arms held in the air as another page pulled off his robe, and for a split second he looked to Corcoran like a black-winged angel of destruction. Then, straightening his tie, Brandeis told "Tommy the Cork" triumphantly: "This is the end of this business of centralization, and I want you to go back and tell the President that we're not going to let this government centralize everything. It's come to an end. . . ."

Corcoran was shocked. He knew that Roosevelt liked Brandeis, often compared him with the prophet Isaiah, admired his crusading conscience.

Meantime, Richberg had hurried to a telephone to call the White House. When he told the President the bad news, FDR was surprised and hurt.

"Well," Roosevelt asked, "where was Ben Cardozo? How did he stand? And what about old Isaiah?"

Richberg told the President that the opinion had been unanimous, that Cardozo and Brandeis had gone along with the other justices. The fact that these two liberals voted with their conservative colleagues came as a jolt to Roosevelt. His face tightened.

That day, that Black Monday, that blackest of all days in the history of the New Deal, the four Schechter brothers awaited the verdict in Joseph's ten-room brick house on Brighton Beach Avenue in Brooklyn. Reporters and photographers filled the living room. The moment all heard the news from Washington they went wild. But moments later Joseph Schechter quieted down, for he was having second thoughts. To members of the press he said that he and his brothers had spent $20,000 on their legal battle.

"We're down to our last nickel," he said. "If I had known it would cost that much, we would have gone to jail."

* * *

AMERICA STUNNED! ROOSEVELT'S WORK KILLED IN TWENTY MINUTES. Such was the banner on the London *Express* the day of the NRA decision.

Here in this country a far different reaction came from the Hearst press, which declared that with the end of the NRA the role of Christ was restored. The New York *Herald Tribune* exulted over "a tyranny overthrown." Frank Kent, a conservative political writer, rejoiced that "the bottom has been knocked out of the New Deal." Huey Long, who was pious about nothing, said: "I raise my hand in reverence to the Supreme Court that saved this nation from fascism." Mark Sullivan declared that the court had invalidated "fully ten thousand ways in which a citizen might find himself haled into the criminal courts."

By executive order President Roosevelt suspended all of the NRA's 578 national codes and 200 supplementary codes that affected 22,000,000 workers. Then he approved the dismissal of 411 NRA legal suits brought by the government in an attempt to force individuals and firms to live up to the codes. He also worried about the future of the 4,200 NRA workers in Washington and the 1,200 others throughout the nation.

Most businessmen were initially delighted by the court's decision. The stock market rose on each of the four following days, and there was an upswing in business conditions across the nation those first two weeks afterward. Employers began cutting wages and lengthening the workweek. Within a few months the garment industry was paying only $7 a week for forty hours of labor, while wages in the retail jewelry trade dropped to $6 a week.

Then the businessmen began having second thoughts. No longer were they exempt from the nation's antitrust laws. While it was true that no longer could they be prosecuted as NRA "chiselers," once again they found themselves subject to prosecution as "monopolists." Their predicament was summarized by Walter Lippmann: "It is once more illegal for them to have an agreement to fix prices. It is once more illegal for them to make agreements to limit production. It is once more illegal for them to agree on quotas. It is once more illegal for them to eliminate new competition."

Some of the very industrialists who had jumped with joy when they heard the court's opinion now started appealing to the President to preserve part of NRA's achievements. Hugh Johnson said: "The principles of NRA will prevail and return in the end as sure as sunrise. That is true because they are both necessary and right." In a letter to William C. Bullitt, Roosevelt declared "the fact remains that the principles of NRA must be carried on in some way."

Attorney General Cummings was infuriated. Angrily striding up and down Roosevelt's office, pounding his fist into his hand, he vented his spleen against the nine justices, crying: "I tell you, Mr. President, they mean to destroy us!" The New York *Daily News* felt much the same way. "We are thrown, tied and branded by the Grand Lamas of legalism on the Supreme bench at Washington," it shrilled. "They are our real rulers. We have got to curb these men."

On May 31, four days after the court's historic decision, Roosevelt opened a press conference that was one of the most important in his entire career. His wife sat in his study knitting a blue sock. The President's desk was covered with yellow telegrams that had come to him from all around the country. He put a cigarette in his long ivory holder, lighted it, smiled and turned toward the reporters. The question uppermost in the mind of every correspondent present that day was put to the President by Francis M. Stephenson of the Associated Press: "Do you care to comment any on NRA?"

His smile widening into a grin, Roosevelt replied: "Well, Steve, if you insist. That's an awful thing to put to a fellow at this hour of the morning just out of bed. . . ."

Roosevelt spoke for the next hour and twenty-five minutes. His extemporaneous performance was an intellectual masterpiece. Calm and courteous, never referring to a note, smiling much of the time, his show of good humor masking his occasional irony, the President let the nation know for the first time how he felt about the court decision.

He said he had been impressed by the pathetic appeals that had been sent to him by concerned citizens begging that something be done. Gesturing toward the telegrams in front of him, he said that already he had received almost 3,000 wires and letters. An association of drugstore owners in Indiana had praised his efforts to protect the small businessman from ruthless and destructive trade practices. A printing company said that its business had been crippled by the decision. One man said he would hate to see Wall Street and the utilities ever win control again of the federal government. A New Yorker predicted that sweatshops would return.

Blandly denying that he resented the decision, Roosevelt nonetheless let his voice harden as he said: ". . . The country thought it was solving its problems gradually on a national basis, but now its attempted solutions are thrown back in the face of the American people, and the country is right back in the horse-and-buggy stage where it started."

The Associated Press reporter asked: "Can we use the direct quotation on that 'horse-and-buggy stage'?"

"I think so."

The Supreme Court of the United States had warned the President not to go to one extreme. Now he was warning the justices not to go to another. As had happened before in American history, the judicial and executive branches of the federal government were locked in combat. Over the next two years the court struck down one New Deal measure after another. In 1937 the President urged Congress to reorganize the federal judiciary. The key to Roosevelt's five-part plan lay in his suggestion that membership in the Supreme Court be increased from nine to possibly fifteen men.

Many Americans reacted immediately and furiously. They accused Roosevelt of trying to pack the court, of seeking to become a dictator. He lost the battle. Few people cared to realize that the size of the court had fluctuated during the republic's history. The Supreme Court was established with six members in 1789. It was reduced to five in 1801. It was increased to seven in 1807. It was increased to nine in 1837. It was increased to ten in 1863. It was reduced to seven in 1866. It was increased to nine in 1869.

*   *   *

A New Deal critic wrote Postmaster James A. Farley to say that since Farley was so prolific in issuing new stamps, he ought to design one commemorating the court's NRA decision. Farley, who knew Roosevelt's fondness for jokes, slipped this tart note between some other papers he had to show the President. When FDR found it, he chuckled, looked up at Farley and said: "All right! I'll draw you a picture of a sick chicken."

Roosevelt told Frances Perkins: "You know the whole thing is a mess. It has been an awful headache. Some of the things they have done in NRA are pretty wrong, though I think it is going better now. We have got the best out of it, anyhow. Industry got a shot in the arm. Everything has started up. I don't believe they will go back to their old wage levels. I think the forty-hour week will stick, except in a few instances. I think perhaps NRA has done all it can do. I don't want to impose a system on this country that will set aside the anti-trust laws on any permanent basis.

"I have been talking to other lawyers besides Homer Cummings, and they are pretty certain that the whole process is unconstitutional and that we have to restudy and revise our whole program. Perhaps we had better do it now. So let's give the NRA a certain amount of time to liquidate. Have a history of it written, and then it will be over."

Hugh Johnson resigned in a long and emotional speech. Congress voted to continue the NRA briefly as a skeleton organization. On January 1, 1936, the National Recovery Administration came to an official close. The following March 31 the last 600 NRA employees got their final paychecks.

During its brief life the NRA had covered 22,000,000 workers in about 500 different fields of business. According to Hugh Johnson, it had added $3 billion to the nation's purchasing power. However, he confessed, it did not solve the vexing question of wage differentials. It tended to reduce price competition. Prices, production figures, corporate profits and executive salaries rose, but wages lagged behind these advances. Workers who got jobs were paid more per hour but they were employed so few hours that their incomes remained small. Working conditions were improved. Labor unions, gulping the heady brew of collective bargaining, increased their membership rolls.

Senator Wagner felt that while the NRA had helped recovery, it had fallen far short of reform. Disagreement came at a later date from historian Arthur M. Schlesinger, Jr., who said that in the social field the NRA had accomplished "a fantastic series of reforms." Hugh Johnson, who turned into a critic of President Roosevelt, nonetheless is on record with this statement: "Franklin Roosevelt has taught our people that this country does belong to them!" The Blue Eagle had indeed restored hope and revived confidence. Frances Perkins said: "It was as though the community rose from the dead."

Walter Lippmann, who did not quite agree with her, pronounced this benediction: "Like Chanticleer, the rooster in Rostand's play, the Blue Eagle was a bird that thought the sun had risen because it crowed at dawn."

21

The San Francisco General Strike

A HAWK-NOSED MAN with hooded eyes rose to power on the San Francisco waterfront in 1934, shut down all shipping along the Pacific seaboard, sparked the second general strike in the history of this nation and became one of the most investigated men of his time. He was called "the bogeyman of the Pacific." His name was Harry Bridges.

Born in a comfortable suburb of Melbourne, Australia, he was christened Alfred Renton Bridges soon after his birth on July 28, 1901. His mother came from a family active in the struggle for Irish independence. His father was a prosperous real estate man once described as "a real British Tory." When young Bridges entered his teens, his father put him to work collecting rent from tenants living in the squalid houses and flats owned by the older man. The sensitive boy agonized over the sight of poor people painfully counting coins into his cupped hand; this door-to-door education in poverty scarred him for the rest of his life.

Refusing to work any longer for his father, the boy clerked in a stationery store, decided to go to sea after reading the adventure stories of Jack London, signed aboard one vessel after another and was twice shipwrecked. His father later said: "Alf went overboard with my mandolin and kept afloat on it until he was picked up." Arriving in San Francisco in 1920, young Bridges jumped ship, paid a head tax of $8, drifted to the Mexican oilfields, where he worked as a rigger. Bridges once told Theodore Dreiser that it was Mexico's strong laws protecting labor which "opened my eyes."

By 1922 Bridges was back in San Francisco, where he became a longshoreman and a first-class winch driver. His skill and experience won him a place on one of the so-called star gangs, where he would sweat and strain twenty-four to thirty-six hours at a stretch. During his free hours he lived a quiet life in a boardinghouse, paying his rent promptly and amusing himself evenings by plucking a mandolin. But he read books on labor, economics, sociology, and studied the problems of longshoremen and marine workers.

There was much to learn. Labor, before World War I, had been so strong in San Francisco that it elected its own mayor, only to have the townspeople turn against unions after the Preparedness Day bombing of 1916 and other violent incidents. In 1919 the city's industrial and financial interests broke a waterfront strike by organizing a Law and Order Committee, a group that soon developed into the Industrial Association and seized control of San Francisco.

A continuing issue in this seaport was the question of who should hire the men to load and unload ships. The International Longshoremen's Association wanted control of the hiring halls. However, during the abortive 1919 strike a company union called the Longshoremen's Association of San Francisco was formed as a splinter group within the ILA and promptly won recognition from the Waterfront Employers' Union—an odd name for a group of bosses. Before long the ILA lost power in most Pacific ports. Now the only men able to get stevedoring jobs were members of the company union—also known as the Blue Book Union.

Bad working conditions along the docks became even worse. By the very nature of the shipping industry the longshoremen's jobs depended on weather conditions, on irregular ship arrivals and departures. Now the bosses ran the hiring halls, which were located in saloons, poolrooms and cheap restaurants with gambling rooms attached to them. Now it was in such tawdry and tempting places that dockwallopers wanting work had to wait to be chosen.

The hiring foremen, loyal to shipowners, held dictatorial power. In picking a gang for a job, the foreman always selected Blue Book members and ignored those outside the fold. The laborers soon learned that their only chance of getting work was by bribing the foreman—and even Harry Bridges paid this kind of graft. Sometimes a bribe was as mild as a proffered cigar or an invitation to have a shot of booze, but many poor men, the fathers of large families, had to give the hiring boss a cut of their wages. Anyone willing to go along with this corrupt system could earn $40 or more a week. Bridges was so much in demand that he made about $60 a week.

However, three-quarters of the West Coast longshoremen averaged only $10 to $12 a week—some even less. In November, 1933, the federal Bureau of Labor Statistics said: "The balance [of longshoremen] is always on the brink of starvation and depends largely on outside support, chiefly charity. At the present time a very conservative estimate would probably place more than 50 per cent of all longshoremen on the relief rolls."

A few months later 16,000,000 Americans were receiving federal relief that averaged $24.53 per family per month. But even this, according to part of the business community, was too much.

Steamship lines and their officials endured no such privation, thanks to federal subsidies to shipping. Despite doubts about the constitutionality of such handouts, the government was generous in the subsidies it granted shipping interests. To cite just a few examples, the government paid $2,250,000 each for the construction of four cargo ships, which it then sold to the Dollar Line for only $300,000 apiece. Seven "President" type vessels costing the government $4,128,000 apiece to build were turned over to this same line for a mere $550,000 each.

Steamship executives' salaries, largely paid out of these subsidies, were fantastically high. To illustrate, between 1923 and 1932 four Dollar Line officials received a total of more than $14 million in salaries, dividends and bonuses. President Roosevelt preferred outright subsidies to the equivalent ocean mail contracts for shipping lines. In 1934 Commerce Secretary Daniel Roper pointed out that of the $145 million lent by the government under the 1928 ship construction loan bill, $126 million remained unpaid.

Harry Bridges was angrily aware of the help the shipowners were getting from the government. Help for the workers themselves was promised by the government on June 16, 1933, when Roosevelt signed the National Industrial Recovery Act—soon known as the NRA, which was discussed earlier. Like all workers across the nation, Bridges paid particular attention to the act's Section 7-a, which declared that employers must recognize the right of employees to organize and bargain collectively through representatives of their own choosing. George Creel, the NRA director for the Pacific coast, announced that this right was "something that does not permit of compromise or dispute."

Bridges reacted quickly. In July, 1933, he launched a drive to organize a new San Francisco local of the ILA, and from Fishermen's Wharf to China Basin he and other articulate dock workers urged idle and hungry longshoremen to desert the Blue Book Union and join them. By September about 90 percent of the city's longshoremen had rallied to the new local. That same month it won a charter from the International Longshoremen's Association, which was affiliated with the American Federation of Labor.

The following December George Creel acted as mediator in negotiations between waterfront bosses and the new local. As a result, wages were raised from 75 to 85 cents an hour, and agreement was reached for joint control of hiring halls. This satisfied Lee Holman, district president of the ILA, but it did not satisfy Bridges and other rank-and-file members. They argued that dual control of hiring halls would end with domination of workers by bosses, the continued blacklisting of active union members and the return of all the old abuses. Thus there developed a triangular fight between employers, conservative officials of the ILA and the militant rank and file.

In February, 1934, militants from up and down the Pacific coast held a convention from which they excluded all paid union officials. The delegates demanded recognition of the union by employers; union control of hiring

halls; a wage increase from 85 cents to $1 an hour, with $1.50 for overtime; and a thirty-hour week.

They wanted a shorter workweek because the bosses used such cruel
speedup methods. The faster a ship was loaded or unloaded, the greater the
profits to the employers. The best laborers were grouped into star gangs
and worked as long as a day and a half without sleep. This breakneck and
unbroken speed resulted in many deaths and accidents among the men.
Harry Bridges himself had been injured twice. The first time, improper gear
failed to hold a load, and three tons of steel crashed onto the dock beside
him, badly bruising his body. In the second accident, another load of cargo
fell and broke his foot.

Although ILA officials had been barred from the militants' convention,
they won control of an executive board supposed to reopen negotiations
with shipowners. However, their conservative power was neutralized by a
resolution declaring that any proposed settlement had to be approved by a
vote of rank-and-file members. After Lee Holman made certain bitter
remarks about the militants, he was deposed as district president.

On March 5, 1934, the longshoremen tried to renew negotiations with
the waterfront employers, but the bosses refused to recognize the new
union—let alone negotiate. George Creel warned President Roosevelt that
the shipowners wanted a showdown then and there. They were willing to
lose some money if they could kill off the new union. It so happened that
the very day the President heard from Creel he told a group of business
and industrial leaders in Washington that the recovery program, as represented by the NRA, was here to stay. Roosevelt urged a general 10 percent
wage boost linked to a 10 percent cut in working hours in order to give
jobs to 1,000,000 more people. The San Francisco dock workers wanted a
15 percent wage raise—which was hardly a revolutionary proposal.

On March 13 Henry Ford restored the $5-a-day minimum to 47,000 of
his 70,000 auto workers, saying: "No one loses anything by raising wages
as soon as he is able. It has always paid us. There is no economy in cheap
labor or cheap material."

San Francisco's ruling class, so eager to prevent the working class from
organizing, was itself well provided with organizations—the all-powerful
Industrial Association, the Waterfront Employers' Union and the Chamber
of Commerce, to name just three of them. With the backing of these
groups, the shippers declared they never would recognize the union. What
was sauce for the golden goose was bilge for the poor gander.

Faced with the shippers' ultimatum, which broke the NRA law, the San
Francisco Bay district of the ILA voted on March 17 to strike on March
23 unless a settlement could be reached. Up and down the Pacific seaboard
other ILA locals voted to join the walkout. However, the day before the
strike deadline President Roosevelt telegraphed William J. Lewis, president
of the West Coast district of the ILA, asking the longshoremen to stay on
the job until a fact-finding board could be appointed; this board would then

make a report on which the federal government might act. The workers called off the strike.

They waited six weeks, but when nothing constructive was done, they rescheduled their strike for May 7. Joseph P. Ryan, the international president of the ILA—and a man who shared the timid views of the parent AFL—wired an appeal to the dock workers to remain at work. Among other things, he feared that a strike could be broken by unemployed men to whom eighty-five cents an hour meant high wages. But nothing could dissuade the angry rank-and-file workers from walking off the job, and all along the West Coast other dockwallopers agreed to support their brethren in San Francisco.

These events, now set in uncontrollable motion, began to unfold within a lovely setting. The port of San Francisco is one of the world's most magnificent natural harbors. It has two huge bays varying in width from 3 to 12 miles, and it boasts about 50 miles of frontage together with 15 miles of wharfage. A port of entry since 1849, San Francisco built its prosperity on its maritime trade. In the city's downtown section one of the principal sights is the Embarcadero, a wide half-moon boulevard lined with piers and wharves for a distance of 3½ miles. The landward side is lined with stores and lodging houses used by longshoremen and sailors.

At 8 A.M. on May 9, 1934, there began the most complicated strike in the history of San Francisco, when local longshoremen refused to shape up and work the sixty ships then in port. And with the sole exception of Los Angeles, a rigidly open-shop town, every other Pacific port was shut down by a total of 12,000 longshoremen. A few strikebreakers, sorely in need or antiunion in sentiment, flouted the strike call by working a few of the vessels idling at San Francisco. To provide them with protection, police cars with screaming sirens raced up and down the Embarcadero to deposit cops here and there.

By May 11 shipping was at a standstill the length of the Pacific seaboard. That day San Francisco newspapers published this advertisement:

LONGSHOREMEN WANTED
Experience Desirable
But Not Necessary
Apply Navy Landing Pier, Foot of
Howard Street, San Francisco
85¢ an Hour Straight Time
$1.15 an Hour Overtime
Strike Conditions Prevail
Waterfront Employers' Union
By W. J. Peterson

The shippers hoped to recruit strikebreakers from the ranks of the unemployed, from among Negroes embittered by discrimination in other places and other jobs and from among college students. Bill Ingram, the football coach at the University of California, began rounding up athletes to act as scabs.

Hugo Winkenwerder, the president of the University of Washington up the coast, became so disturbed by rumors about strikebreaking students that he named a student committee to investigate. This committee reported: "The first place employers went to obtain strike-breakers was the University of Washington. All fraternity houses were contacted and students requested to cut their classes and participate in a labor difficulty of which they had absolutely no knowledge. Employers guaranteed them board and room and wages higher than those offered longshoremen. Students were provided free taxi service to work. More enterprising employers sent boats to the university docks to pick up student strike-breakers, but the dean of men prevented the boats from docking.

"Once on the waterfront, student strike-breakers were housed in boats tied to the docks. Excellent food, brand-new sheets and blankets and first-class Negro valet service convinced many that the life of the longshoremen was not so bad as they had believed."

Members of other maritime crafts, however, were not blind to the harsh reality of life along the waterfront. They were men, not callow college kids. As ship after ship ended its voyage at one place or another along the Pacific seaboard, entire crews deserted—seamen, firemen, oilers, cooks, water tenders and the like. Although they struck in sympathy with the longshoremen, they had their own complaints—low wages, long hours, poor food and forced membership in company unions.

Earlier dock strikes had been weakened by the scabbing of one craft against another. This time the longshoremen knew they needed the total support of members of other maritime crafts to maintain a united front. And as the bosses hired an increasing number of nonunion strikebreakers, the dock workers also had to devise a strategy to tighten their grip on the ports. With these two objectives in mind, rank-and-file longshoremen organized a joint strike committee of fifty and chose Harry Bridges as their chairman. This launched the thirty-two-year-old Australian winch driver on his spectacular career.

Woody Guthrie wrote a song about Bridges that begins this way:

> I'll sing you the tale of Harry Bridges,
> He left his family and his home,
> He sailed across that rolling ocean
> And into Frisco he did roam.
>
> Now Harry Bridges seen starvation
> A creepin' along that ocean shore
> "Gonna get good wages for the longshoremen,"
> That's what Harry Bridges swore. . . .

Boyish in appearance, Harry Bridges was short and lean and vibrant with energy. His black hair was slicked back into a flat pompadour on his long and narrow head. He was dark and razor-faced. Wrinkles chevroned his forehead, while sharp eyes glinted from beneath his sleepy lids. Every now and then his thin lips tightened in a sardonic smile. His humor was sly, his behavior often arrogant, his movements quick and furtive. Addressing union meetings in a Cockney twang, he strutted back and forth across the platform, giving an odd little hop at the end of each sentence. At all times he was calm under attack—and he continued to be attacked for more than a decade.

On May 12 six policemen and three strikers were hurt in a battle in San Francisco while in Seattle local longshoremen raided eleven ships and dragged nonunion workers ashore. That same day sympathetic longshoremen struck in New York City and in Galveston, Texas. The next day in San Pedro (part of the port of Los Angeles) pickets fired on stockades housing strikebreakers and for the first time in history not a freighter sailed from any Pacific port of the United States.

All along that coast, ships now lay idle, unable to discharge cargo or take any aboard. The teamsters, whose job it was to haul cargo from dock to warehouse to railway siding, joined the strike. With tons of goods immobilized, the shipping paralysis began affecting other industries: Oregon lumber mills shut down. A halt was called to construction of the Golden Gate Bridge and the San Francisco-Oakland Bridge because steel and stone could not be lightered to the unfinished structures. Nondelivery of medical supplies evoked an outcry from the city Board of Health in San Francisco, and residents shuddered when they read in newspapers that tons of perishable food had rotted.

By the end of May the shipping strike had cost San Francisco $300,000,000.

This emergency became the subject of discussion among Cabinet members in the White House, 3,000 miles away. Labor Secretary Perkins sent her assistant, Edward F. McGrady, to the West Coast to try to mediate, but McGrady was able to do almost nothing. He did summon Joseph P. Ryan, international president of the ILA, from his New York office to San Francisco. After flying to the coast, Ryan toured several Pacific ports and finally proposed a settlement. It was rejected by rank-and-file members. Deeper ran the rift between union officialdom and the militant dockwallopers.

On June 10 McGrady flew back to Washington with a new peace plan, which the employers rejected. As the deadlock hardened, a San Francisco painters' local and then a machinists' local urged that a general strike be called. A general strike is the ultimate weapon in labor's arsenal, for when all members of all unions walk off their jobs in unison, they can cause total paralysis of a city, a region or even an entire nation. So far in American history, the only general strike had occurred in Seattle in 1919 in support of striking shipyard workers.

President Roosevelt later said: "It appeared very clear to me just as soon as there was talk about a general strike, that there were probably two elements bringing about that general strike. One was the hot-blooded young leaders who had had no experience in organized labor whatsoever and said that the only thing to do was to have a general strike. On the other side was a combination of people out there on the coast who were praying for a general strike. In other words, there was the old conservative crowd just hoping that there would be a general strike, being clever enough to know that a general strike always fails."

The President told his secretary of labor to do all she could to avert a total walkout, and Miss Perkins immediately called upon both sides to accept federal arbitration. Bosses and workers sent separate appeals to Roosevelt, but because he was planning an extensive vacation, he referred them to Miss Perkins.

Besides the alarm felt in Washington, nerves tightened and twanged in California. James Rolph, Jr., the Republican governor, had died on June 2, and another Republican, Frank F. Merriam, had become acting governor. On June 23 Merriam declared he would not let the shipping strike continue all summer. "If the state cannot settle through negotiations," he said, "I shall take steps to force the issue and open up state property on the waterfront to the resumption of commerce."

That same day the Industrial Association announced that it would open the port—by force, if necessary. The Chamber of Commerce said $40 million worth of goods were piled up in the holds of ships and on the piers. San Francisco Police Chief W. J. Quinn conferred with the Industrial Association, the Chamber of Commerce, the State Harbor Board, and then said: "If necessary, every available police officer in San Francisco will be detailed to the waterfront to give necessary protection and prevent violence from either side."

On June 25 Roosevelt left Washington for Annapolis on the first leg of his long trip. Acting under his orders, Miss Perkins appointed a National Longshoremen's Board of Arbitration. For chairman she picked Archbishop Edward J. Hanna, head of the Roman Catholic see of San Francisco. Her two other choices were McGrady, the assistant secretary of labor, and Otto Cushing, a leading liberal citizen of San Francisco.

On June 27 Harry Bridges and other members of the Joint Strike Committee met in San Francisco's City Hall with Mayor Angelo J. Rossi, McGrady, and Andrew Furuseth, president of the International Seamen's Union. These three men begged the strikers to go back to work, but they refused. The strikers felt they would suffer total defeat unless they won the key issue of sole union control of hiring halls. Their obstinacy angered the Industrial Association's director, who declared that the port would be opened immediately. In alarm, the mayor persuaded the director to do nothing until at least July 3.

During this lull the police and shippers were making grim preparations. The local police department had ordered $14,000 worth of gas and gas equipment from a Pittsburgh firm called Federal Laboratories, Inc., and now its vice-president hurried to the scene of the impending battleground. The company manufactured a nausea gas which its promotional literature described as follows: "The liquid chemical is used for lachrymating [sic] purposes. It also causes nausea, severe headache, vomiting, etc. A severe dose will incapacitate a person for six to eight hours. While it is also considered a toxic gas in closed quarters, no reports of fatalities have ever been reported from its use in the field."

A company agent also rushed to the threatened city. The evening of July 2 he was invited by two cops to ride with them the next morning in the police headquarters car, bringing some of his gas equipment with him. They said they expected a riot and would appreciate it if the agent would give them the benefit of his knowledge of vomiting gas.

*   *   *

The morning of July 3, 1934, the sun shone on thousands of San Francisco citizens gathered on hills commanding a view of the Embarcadero, where the action was expected to start. The Industrial Association had organized the Atlas Trucking Company for the purpose of transporting cargo from Pier 38 to a warehouse near a terminal of the Southern Pacific Coast line. The pier's iron door was closed. Behind it a cavalcade of five trucks and eight police cars was forming. Except for a narrow slot just in front of the door, a long line of railroad freight cars had been shunted into a protective ring, like prairie wagons pulled together to ward off an Indian attack.

Behind the iron door and out of sight, nervous strikebreakers loaded cargo onto the waiting trucks while cops checked their revolvers and riot guns. Earlier that morning other police had pushed pickets away from Pier 38, back toward Front Street. The strikers were armed with clubs and bricks and railroad spikes. Now, waiting at a distance from the pier, they heard thumps and raspings from within—noises that only could mean that cargo was being shifted.

"Come out, you dirty scabs!" they cried. "Come out and get it!"

A rock thrown at the door zinged off at an angle. At that moment, from inside the pier, a whistle shrilled.

Slowly, like an evil grin, the door began opening. As it rose higher and higher, the pickets tightened their grip on their weapons. Now the door yawned fully open. Out burst a police car. On its running board crouched a police captain. He was flourishing a revolver. He shouted at the strikers: "The port is open!"

They roared their defiance. Behind the lead car came other police cars and then the trucks. The loaded trucks. The pickets surged forward like surf against rolling stones, screaming, cursing, lashing out with clubs, throwing stones and bricks. Cops, riding shotgun on the trucks, struck back with nightsticks and opened fire with pistols, riot guns and gas guns. The chemical company agent was riding with some cops. He shot a long-range projectile into the massed strikers. It hit a picket on the head and killed him instantly. The agent later said: "As he was a Communist, I have had no more feeling in the matter and I am sorry that I did not get more."

The action began at 1:27 P.M. and continued for almost four hours. Spectators gawked from the hills while two airplanes, filled with other curious people, buzzed the battlefield. Longshoremen, sailors and other strikers hopped onto the running boards of their own cars and chased the speeding trucks. Mounted policemen were dragged off their horses and beaten. Cops broke heads left and right. Cobblestones became slick with the blood of strikers and cops alike. Some policemen, who looked like creatures from another planet when they pulled gas masks over their faces, lobbed gas grenades on each side of the trucks running the gauntlet. The spreading gas enveloped the strikers. They vomited. They clutched their bellies, covered their eyes, slumped to the pavement, tried to crawl away.

By 5 P.M. the bosses had won by getting their cargo safely inside the warehouse at the railway terminal. The casualties were about even—twelve strikers and thirteen cops being injured. The first battle was over.

The next day, the Fourth of July, hardly seemed a proper time for Americans to fight Americans, so both sides agreed to a truce. But thrill-seeking citizens would not take a chance of missing a free show, and they flocked to hills again to take up commanding views of the Embarcadero just in case. Lunch-carrying mothers and chattering children crowded the windows of office buildings on lower Market Street, men with binoculars perched on rooftops, and here and there small boys shot one another with toy pistols and rolled over "dead."

The State Board of Harbor Commissioners had charge of the Belt Line Railway, which connected waterfront piers with terminals of transcontinental railroads. That July 4 the commissioners mustered fourteen freight cars to handle cargoes of the Matson Navigation Company. This maneuver was seen by watchful pickets, who swooped down upon the train and chased away its crew. The nervous commissioners called a conference. They told the strikers the train carried nothing but boxes containing infantile paralysis serum. Despite their skepticism that all this bulk consisted of medicine, the strikers reaffirmed their pledge not to fight on the holiday and withdrew.

But everyone asked: What will happen tomorrow? Will all hell break loose? Acting Governor Merriam summoned 2,000 National Guardsmen to the scene. Their commanding officer, Colonel H. H. Mittlestaedt, announced that if trouble broke out and any guardsman merely fired into the air, he would court-martial the soldier. The colonel wanted his orders clearly understood: If the strikers attacked again, first the guardsmen should use their rifle butts as clubs, then bayonet the attackers, finally shoot them. This was reported in the papers. Tension tightened.

Thursday, July 5, 1934, was even worse than expected.

The day was born in a caul of fog that dampened the streets and docks and buildings along the Embarcadero. Fading in and out of the murk, like microscopic objects magnified into focus and then lost to vision, the fuzzy figures of men appeared and disappeared, their breath blossoming white on white, their hands grasping heavy objects, ghosts floating through nothingness, the flannel pall muffling the sounds of their heels on the cobblestones. They were longshoremen in dungarees and work shirts, white-jacketed stewards, blue-uniformed cops and reporters carrying gas masks. And once again, in the dim distance, the townspeople bore witness from the sides of Rincon Hill overlooking the waterfront and the tracks of the Belt Line Railway.

By the time the rising sun had rinsed the city of fog, more than 1,000 strikers were waiting near the southern end of the Embarcadero, gripping clubs, hefting rocks in open palms, thrilling to the metallic feel of guns in calloused hands. Some pickets rode to and fro in cars, yelling through megaphones: "More of you fellows on the tracks there! . . . Go over to the pier! . . . Ten more men wanted at the King Street warehouse!"

Once again the focal point was Pier 38. Its iron door was closed, as before, but the pickets heard noises from within, and from time to time they saw faces peeping through dingy windows. The city's entire police force had been mustered on the waterfront. Masses of cops forced the growing horde of strikers back across the railway tracks, back into vacant lots some distance from the pier. Scores of high school boys and college students, inflamed by newspaper stories and itching for a fight just for the fun of it, had donned old clothes and slipped away from home without knowledge of their parents, and now they stood in knots along the docks, sourly eyeing the workers.

From behind the iron door the strikers heard the coughing of an auto engine racing in neutral gear. They braced themselves. Just then a police whistle drilled through the air like an ice pick. It was almost eight o'clock. Up slammed the door. Out lunged a car. Then another and another, police cars and trucks, a stampede of vehicles with cops holding on with one hand while brandishing weapons in their free hand. The driver of the first truck bent low over his steering wheel. A hail of rocks crashed against the hood and fenders. Again the strikers threw themselves on the roaring caravan, heedless of danger, trying to knock off the cops and disable the drivers. Again the cops laid down a gas barrage.

A foot patrolman chased a man to the tracks, knocked him down and held his head against a rail in order to beat him with a nightstick. Six workers swarmed over the officer, hammering him with clubs and fists. Other cops ran to the rescue of their fellow officer. At the corner of Federal and First Streets a blow ripped open the scalp of a red-headed worker. Men yelped in fury, bellowed in pain. Blinded by gas fumes, gasping in agony, strikers crossed their arms over their heads to ward off blows and then staggered away. Some collapsed like empty bags on paving stones and in vacant lots, lay unconscious until siren-shrilling ambulances roared up and loaded them aboard.

And amid all this confusion, through dust and gas and blood, truck after truck raced from the pier to the warehouse as the bosses made good their threat to open the port. At noon the rioting slackened, and both sides melted back to observe an unspoken truce. The walking wounded stumbled away to sit down and nurse bloody noses, battered skulls and blackened eyes. Newspapers with screaming headlines were passed from hand to trembling hand. Union leaders and agitators threaded their way through the broken ranks of strikers, shouting encouragement.

About 1 P.M., near the foot of Mission Street, a wild-haired woman shrilled: "The bloated scabherders aren't here! No! Why should they be? They've got their paid beat-up gangs, *their* police. And why do we pay taxes? I'll tell you why! So that we can have police to beat us, to choke us with tear gas. That's why!"

Early in the afternoon sullen pickets drifted back to the Embarcadero in groups of ten and twenty. Their new tactic was to avoid a massed confrontation. As one man explained: "Then the gas won't be no good." Ten more Atlas trucks lumbered between police lines from pier to warehouse. Once again the pickets threw themselves toward the fleeting vehicles. Cops beat them back. Fistfights broke out. Someone near a freight car yelled: "Fire! Fire!" A dozen men were seen fleeing from the tracks, leaving behind a flaming railway car. Up rolled fire engines and squad cars, and the blaze was put out, but another fire took hold of a second railway car.

The police shot off more gas guns, and 5,000 people took to their heels, some scrambling up Rincon Hill, where sightseers still watched. The smell of vomit, the sight of blood, the clouds of gas, the thud of billy clubs on skulls—these excited the strikers into making repeated attacks upon the police, who now began firing revolvers and riot guns.

"They're killing us now!" came screams. "Now they're using guns!"

This news was shouted up and down the two blocks from Market Street to the street in front of the Seaboard Hotel. A group of frenzied pickets moved toward a lone policeman. "Back!" he bawled. Mob members inched closer, brandishing sticks and threatening him with death. Again the cop shouted: "Back!"

But more strikers ran down Folsom and Howard Streets to the scene and advanced upon the white-faced cop. He retreated, still yelling warnings. In his quivering hands he held a riot gun. The crowd closed in. The officer shouted again. Then his gun barked. A man fell to the pavement. Dead. From nearby another gun sounded. Then another and another. There and elsewhere, that dismal day, men screamed, swore, vomited, bled, fell. The end came only as electric lights snapped on in downtown buildings and National Guardsmen arrived on the double. Then the shocked city counted its casualties. Two strikers and one sympathizer had been killed. Thirty-eight persons had been gassed. A total of 115 others—strikers, cops and bystanders—were wounded seriously enough to be hospitalized. The "Battle of Rincon Hill" was the bloodiest in the history of San Francisco.

On that day of agony President Roosevelt arrived in Haiti in the Caribbean, where he received a wire from the Joint Strike Committee that read: PICKETS ON SAN FRANCISCO WATERFRONT BEING ATTACKED BY POLICE. VOMITING GAS, REVOLVERS, PROJECTILES AND HAND GRENADES BEING USED FREELY. REIGN OF TERROR INAUGURATED AT THE REQUEST OF THE INDUSTRIAL ASSOCIATION, WHICH IS ATTEMPTING TO OPEN THE PORT. THE UNDERSIGNED COMMITTEE PROTESTS MOST VIGOROUSLY AGAINST THIS UNCALLED-FOR ACTION BY THE POLICE. AS AMERICAN CITIZENS WE URGE YOU TO TAKE NECESSARY ACTION TO ELIMINATE THIS TERRORISM AND BRING PRESSURE TO BEAR UPON SHIP OWNERS, WHO ARE ATTEMPTING TO CRUSH OUR UNIONS AND ARE FIGHTING US WITH MONEY BORROWED FROM THE GOVERNMENT.

That night Acting Governor Merriam announced that San Francisco was in a state of riot and declared martial law along the waterfront. Merriam, who was campaigning for governor in his own right, soon received a $30,000 campaign donation from the shipowners. That night, too, the city hummed with talk—in dingy union halls and private homes. Strikers and their sympathizers were appalled at the day's events. The bosses had used force to move cargoes. The police had shot and gassed workingmen. The National Guard had been summoned by the state's top official in the middle of a political campaign. Now, as the workers told one another, a regiment of Army regulars rested on their arms within the military reservation known as the Presidio, ready for instant action.

Harry Bridges said mournfully: "We cannot stand up against police, machine guns and National Guard bayonets."

Was there any effective action the union men might take? Some answered yes—the general strike.

Conservative union officials argued against a general strike, but militant workers retorted that nothing except this ultimate weapon would guarantee union recognition and prevent the bosses from reducing them all to peonage. Another appeal was sent to the President, now in Puerto Rico, asking him to intervene.

Communist leaders gleefully pounced on this opportunity to vex and harass capitalists. To the West Coast hastened Red leaders such as Earl Browder, Roy Hudson, William Dunne and Jack Stachel. When the presence of this handful of radicals became known, one San Francisco newspaper screamed that a "Red army" was marching on the city.

For some time now the Communist Party had published its own West Coast paper, the *Western Worker,* a weekly with a circulation of about 10,000. It was edited by George Morris, a former leader of the Young Communist League, whose real name was Morris Yussem. Naturally, the *Western Worker* endorsed a general strike. The longshoremen had their own newspaper, a mimeographed bulletin called the *Waterfront Worker.*

Anonymously edited by militant dockwallopers, it was hard to read because it was printed on paper so cheap that the ink blurred.

AFL President Green strongly opposed a general strike, and so did other conservative labor leaders. Deprived of their moral and financial support, Harry Bridges took help wherever he could get it. He did not hesitate to welcome aid from the Communists. When the major San Francisco dailies accused him of being a member of the Communist Party, he replied: "I neither affirm nor deny that I am a Communist."

The question of Bridges' supposed membership in the party was discussed for the next several years and was the cause for a series of legal actions. In 1939, testifying in his own defense in a deportation proceeding, he was asked by a federal attorney whether he ever told anyone he was a member of the party. Bridges replied that he had "kidded people at times because it got to be a joke on occasions, but soberly and officially I never have, or seriously I never have." In 1945 he became an American citizen.

The United States Supreme Court has also ruled: "The associations which Harry Bridges had with various Communist groups seem to indicate no more than cooperative measures to attain objectives which were wholly legitimate. The link by which it is sought to tie him to subversive activities is an exceedingly tenuous one, if it might be said to exist at all. . . . Harry Bridges was never a member of it [the American Communist Party]."

*   *   *

Ever since "Bloody Thursday" the bodies of the two slain strikers had rested in state in the ILA hall one block from the waterfront. One was a Communist—Nickolas Bordoise, a member of the cooks and waiters union. The other was Howard S. Sperry, a longshoreman and a veteran of World War I. The spot where they fell was decorated with flowers, and on the sidewalk someone had chalked "Police Murder. Two Shot in the Back." Police Chief Quinn forbade the workers from staging a public funeral for fear this might trigger another battle, but when he heard they intended to go through with it despite his ban, he wisely pulled all cops off the streets in that part of the city.

On July 9 there began the most dramatic and ominous funeral in the city's history. Longshoremen, their fellow union craftsmen and sympathizers gathered outside the ILA hall and filled the nearby streets a distance of five blocks. All were bareheaded, silent, grim. From loudspeakers above the door of the hall they heard this funeral oration: "You have been killed because of your activity in the labor movement. Your death will guide us to our final victory. Your killing has been inspired by the Industrial Association and the Chamber of Commerce. But organized labor will answer that deed manyfold throughout the land. . . ."

The two coffins were carried out of the hall into the street and placed on flower-laden trucks. In honor of Sperry, who had served overseas during the war, uniformed veterans marched at the head of the funeral procession, one carrying an American flag topped with black crepe. A union band struck up the slow cadence of Beethoven's funeral march, and the mourners stepped off in dignified and measured pace, swelling into an immense procession—40,000 men, women and children strong.

They walked solemnly, their faces hard, the men holding hats over their hearts, out onto Market Street. To the whump of muffled drums the people marched, marched, marched all afternoon long, marched past mute and uneasy spectators lining the streets, marched past streetcars whose motormen stopped the vehicles to place their regulation caps over their own hearts in sympathy, marched past businessmen with fear-frozen faces. Some well-dressed men failed to remove their hats. Sharp voices cried: "Take off your hats!" They did. Hastily and guiltily. The workers seemed to have taken over the city.

The day of the funeral the National Longshoremen's Board, appointed by Secretary Perkins, opened public hearings and begged both sides to submit to arbitration. Neither, however, would yield on the key question of control of the hiring halls. The Alameda Labor Council voted for a general strike. William Green sent wires forbidding it. Nonetheless, the teamsters' union reaffirmed its sympathy with the longshoremen, and on July 12 a total of 4,000 truck drivers walked off their jobs in San Francisco and Oakland. Taxis remained in garages. Gasoline deliveries were halted.

Motorists, fearful of a gas shortage, lined up at filling stations to get their tanks filled. Depositors fell upon banks, demanding their savings in cash. Housewives laid in supplies of canned food. Produce and other merchandise began moving by parcel post. The police ordered pawnshops and sports stores to remove firearms from their windows.

By July 13 there were 13 unions with 32,000 members on strike. The next day the Strike Strategy Committee held a mass meeting in the Labor Temple, bringing together the representatives of 115 unions with a total of 65,000 members. Harry Bridges made a motion that all labor unions in the Bay area support the striking longshoremen and marine workers by voting for a general strike to begin at 8 A.M., Monday, July 16, 1934. His motion was carried, 315 to 15.

It was agreed that the general strike would include the entire San Francisco Bay region, affecting the cities of Oakland, Berkeley, Richmond, Alameda, Palo Alto, Redwood City, San Mateo, Sausalito, San Rafael and other towns along the San Francisco and San Pedro bays. A General Strike Committee was chosen to supersede the Strike Strategy Committee, and with publication of the news that a general strike had been called, many city residents fled fearfully into the countryside.

William Randolph Hearst, who owned three newspapers in the Bay area, was at this time vacationing in London. Before leaving San Francisco he had become so disturbed by the growing labor crisis that he had conferred with his personal attorney and right-hand man, John Francis Neylan. Neylan was a native of San Francisco, became a crack reporter on Hearst's

San Francisco *Bulletin,* studied law and went into practice before signing on as Hearst's representative. Tall and gaunt, he reminded some people of Abraham Lincoln.

When Neylan heard that a general strike had been called, he got Hearst on the transatlantic phone, and Hearst volunteered to cable a story about the way that England's general strike of 1926 had been broken. Hearst also told Neylan to call a meeting of top officials of five major newspapers in the Bay area so they might present a united front to the strikers and plan strategy for putting them down.

The evening of July 14 Neylan sat down with his colleagues in the Palace Hotel. With him were the leading executives of the three Hearst papers—the San Francisco *Examiner,* San Francisco *Call-Bulletin* and the Oakland *Post-Enquirer.* Also present were the bosses of the San Francisco *Chronicle* and the Oakland *Tribune.* The only other big paper without representation at this conference was the Scripps-Howard San Francisco *News.* For the most part, the *News* was fair in its coverage of the strike, although it did omit from a late edition a Heywood Broun column criticizing shippers for using strikebreakers. In a speech Broun later made before the American Civil Liberties Union, he said that one San Francisco editor had told him that he considered news dispatches in the New York *Times* distinctly "Red" in their leanings.

Neyland and his cohorts saw "Red" wherever they looked. Agreeing that San Francisco was experiencing a Communist-led revolution, they vowed to do all in their power to avert the general strike or at least to blunt its effects if it did erupt. They would raise the cry of a "Red threat." They planned to try to split the ranks of the strikers by distinguishing between "good" and "bad" workers, conservative and radical leaders. They negotiated with conservative labor leaders and attacked militant members. In effect, these newspaper executives assumed the city's leadership which had been held, until then, by the Industrial Association. To make sure their strategy did not backfire, they gave pay raises to all the union men they employed—printers, delivery men and the like.

On Sunday, July 15, the newspapers opened their propaganda campaign. The *Chronicle* and *Examiner* published front-page editorials declaring that radicals had seized control of the city by intimidation and that the general strike was a revolution against constituted authority. That same day the Central Labor Council, representing sixty unions, voted for the general strike.

General Hugh Johnson, head of the National Recovery Administration, arrived in the area the next day. He came to the West Coast, so he said, to inspect the local NRA organization, not because of the all-out strike due to begin the following day. Johnson came in an Army plane too large to land at the Presidio in San Francisco, so it put down instead at Oakland. He expected to be driven by car into San Francisco. This proved to be impossible, for no gasoline was to be had, filling stations were closed, and transportation was paralyzed. Johnson transferred to a smaller plane that flew him to the Presidio, whose commanding general lent his personal car to the NRA administrator for the short ride into the heart of the city. During this trip, Johnson stared about in astonishment, observing that no streetcars ran and the entire city looked dead. He checked into the Palace Hotel, where a barber offered to give him a "bootleg" haircut, as Johnson expressed it.

One of the men who flocked to Johnson's side the moment he arrived was Hearst's man Neylan, whom Johnson mistakenly and repeatedly referred to as "Nyland." Johnson listened, frowning as he was told that the food supply was almost completely shut off, that it was feared all power, light and water would be closed down, that the city's economic life was being strangled. Harry Bridges was blamed for everything. Johnson nodded in agreement and soon began referring to Bridges as "an avowed Communist."

Johnson had been asked to address the students of the University of California on the Berkeley campus in a Greek theater donated to that institution by Hearst. Now he was told that university officials had canceled his speech when Berkeley police said they might not be able to protect him from Communist agitators. The general was furious. He telephoned the dean to insist on speaking, but the dean remained adamant. Neylan, standing beside Johnson in the Palace Hotel, took the phone from his hand and ordered the dean to let the NRA official appear as scheduled. The dean agreed. A Hearst underling had proven himself more powerful than a high official of the United States government.

* * *

The second general strike in the history of this nation began on Monday, July 16, 1934, in the San Francisco metropolitan area, which had a total population of 1,227,533.

There were 127,000 workers who stayed off their jobs. On hand at the beginning of this crisis were 1,800 policemen and 4,500 National Guardsmen. The citizen soldiers deployed to sensitive points in the city, where they set up machine guns and maneuvered tanks into place for quick thrusts at mobs. Mayor Rossi spoke on the radio, proclaiming a state of emergency, blaming the Communists, pleading for calm and calling the situation the worst the city had known since the earthquake of 1906.

The unions, for their part, warned the Communists not to try to use the strike for their own purposes. Factories, barbershops, theaters, laundries and streetcar service were shut down. Highways leading into the city were blockaded to prevent the delivery of fuel oil and food. However, there was some question of whether this really constituted a *general* strike, since the workers did not cut off the publication of newspapers, made no attempt to interrupt telephone service and let bread, milk and ice be delivered within the city.

The strike committee issued permits to a few truckers to carry food to hospitals, to hotels where visitors had been trapped by class warfare and to certain restaurants. The first day of the strike nineteen restaurants were allowed to remain open, and the next day this was extended to a total of fifty restaurants. Doctors were given gasoline for their cars to make house calls and get to hospitals.

But nothing could placate newspapers intent on frightening the people with talk about Reds and revolution. Farther down the coast the Los Angeles *Times* wrote:

> The situation in San Francisco is not correctly described by the phrase "general strike." What is actually in progress there is an insurrection, a Communist-inspired and led revolt against organized government. There is but one thing to be done—put down the revolt with any force necessary and protect the right of ordinary people to conduct their ordinary occupations in security. They move about on foot in peril of a rioting mob or stray bullet or brick. And for what? Not because there is any labor dispute, but in order that Red leaders of waterfront unions may dominate waterborne commerce of the Pacific coast and say who shall earn a living and not. These Red leaders will not arbitrate. They insist on rule or ruin.

Was it really revolution? Republican Senator Hiram Johnson of California thought so. The Senator, a political ally of Hearst's man Neylan, wired Interior Secretary Harold Ickes: HERE IS REVOLUTION NOT ONLY IN THE MAKING BUT WITH THE INITIAL ACTUALITY. Political columnist Walter Lippmann did *not* think it was revolution. He noted that the strikers were unwilling to starve the public, although they did cause inconvenience. Lippmann added that "there is no reason to think that organized labor in San Francisco is in control of revolutionaries."

Communist leader Earl Browder addressed himself to this same question, saying publicly: "Are the Communists proposing to make revolution now, beginning in San Francisco? No, that is absurd. The Communists do not propose to make a revolution until, by comradely discussion and conviction of the toiling masses, they have a majority securely behind the party. We have not yet got this support."

Men of reason were convinced by Browder's statement, since he did not deny the wish to launch a revolution but wanted to make sure it was well timed and fully supported. Furthermore, if the Communists had really been in control of the general strike, it is hardly likely that they would have been so permissive about restaurants and other public facilities. Men refusing to be panicked by wild talk in the newspapers believed repeated declarations by strike leaders that they were not revolutionaries. However, they did wonder about Harry Bridges, who continued to equivocate about the issue of his party membership.

The unions, by allowing certain vital services to continue to function, began the general strike with a built-in tactical weakness. Lippmann said:

"What we see is a revolutionary weapon being wielded by men who do not want revolution." What they wanted was control of hiring halls, better pay, fewer hours of work.

From across the country big newspapers rushed crack correspondents to San Francisco. William Green of the AFL was pessimistic about an early end to the strike. Mayor Rossi called on prominent citizens to set up a Committee of 500 to help get the wheels rolling again. The chief of police beefed up his force by 500 special cops and created an antiradical bureau within the department. Acting Governor Merriam went on the radio to blame alien radicals for the strike and to declare that their "actual purpose is revolution, violent, bloody and destructive."

Secretary of Labor Perkins publicly disagreed with him, but she found herself in a bind. The National Longshoremen's Board, which she had appointed, had the power to arbitrate the longshoremen's strike but not a general strike. By this time President Roosevelt was fishing in the Pacific. Was there any federal official or government agency that had the right and the power to step into this all-out strike? Neylan bluntly asked Hugh Johnson whether he was invested with any legitimate authority—intimating that someone had suggested Johnson had none.

Late in the evening of the first day of the general strike Johnson made a long-distance call from San Francisco to the White House and spoke to Marvin McIntyre, one of the President's press secretaries. According to Johnson, McIntyre authorized him to speak for the federal arbitration board, but Johnson was politically astute enough to know that no mere Presidential secretary had any right to confer such power on him. Ill at ease, Johnson placed another call to Secretary Perkins, with whom he was not now on the best of terms. He described the situation in San Francisco, and she said she was glad he was out there. Johnson happily noted that she did not express any objection to his wish to take command of events.

Hanging up, Johnson went into conference with Neylan and other members of the publishers' council in the Palace Hotel, talking and arguing with them until 3 A.M. Johnson urged that the shippers grant the longshoremen's demand to control hiring halls. Then arbitration could begin. The publishers reacted furiously. This, they shouted at Johnson, would be a compromise with revolution. Besides, what right did he have to meddle in this strike? Could he show them credentials authorizing him to act for the President? Well, no, but he had been on the phone with the White House. But actual credentials? No, he had none. Frustrated and angry, Johnson in turn began shouting at the publishers, only to be silenced by Neylan, who barked: "*I* do the shouting in this part of the country, General!" It was hinted that since Johnson lacked authority of any kind, the publishers might ask him to leave San Francisco.

At a later date, General Johnson said this was the first time he had "ever been up against a newspaper oligarchy."

On July 17, the second day of the general strike, the workers' General

Strike Committee offered to arbitrate, but the bosses turned them down. Pearl L. Bergoff, a notorious private detective and self-proclaimed king of professional strikebreakers, dispatched 100 goons from Chicago in the direction of San Francisco. Contrary to the wishes of the longshoremen and marine workers—now a minority group within the General Strike Committee—that body passed a resolution urging that West Coast governors and mayors appeal to President Roosevelt to intervene in the waterfront struggle.

The shape of things to come was seen in a speech made before the San Francisco Rotary Club by a vice-president of the McCormack Steamship Line, who predicted that raids were about to be made on all radicals. The Hearst press not only called on the police to take violent measures against the strikers, but also urged citizens to form vigilante groups to attack the "revolutionaries." Answering this mad call, mobs of hoodlums and misguided students, self-important in their role as self-appointed patriots, armed themselves with guns and clubs and launched one of the most chilling reigns of terror in the annals of this nation.

Led by brokers, commission merchants and various straw bosses, the vigilantes swarmed through certain areas of San Francisco, wrecking union halls, raiding clubs of the foreign-born, destroying the office of the *Western Worker,* tearing apart bookshops displaying "radical" literature, looting, pillaging, beating up strikers, nonstriking union members, real Communists, alleged Communists, Jews, liberals and intellectuals. The marauders knew all about intellectuals, since the Hearst press equated them with Communists. San Francisco was the home of a writer of popular mystery stories, a man who knew little about politics and cared less, but the self-righteous vigilantes invaded his house, beat him up and molested his wife.

In addition to these ugly scenes in San Francisco, other "patriotic" thugs terrorized the university campus at nearby Berkeley, attacking historians, sociologists, political scientists, economists, anthropologists, teachers of botany and mathematics. They broke into the homes of faculty members, beat the professors and slugged their wives, locked frightened children in clothes closets, splashed oil over books and household furnishings.

The police did nothing to prevent these lawless attacks by American storm troopers. In some cases, the cops even helped them. And of course, the Hearst press applauded those who took the law into their own rough hands. Some vigilantes had dressed in coarse clothes to look like workers, and at first the San Francisco papers pretended that the raids were made by "union labor." So transparent a lie could not be maintained for very long. The New York *Times* reported the general opinion that the vigilantes "were connected with the Committee of 500 organized by prominent citizens yesterday at the behest of Mayor Angelo J. Rossi." While the assaults were taking place the Industrial Association kept in close touch with the police and on at least two occasions got confidential reports about raids before they occurred.

The police mopped up behind the vigilantes by arresting more than 300 "radicals." Police Chief Quinn declared: "We want it clearly understood that none of these hangouts can be reopened." By "hangouts" he meant the ILA's soup kitchen, the Workers Ex-Servicemen's League, the Mission Workers' Neighborhood House, the Marine Workers' Industrial Union and Communist Party headquarters—all of which had been wrecked. Captain J. J. O'Meara, head of the police department's new radical squad, announced with a flourish: "The Communist party is through in San Francisco!"

Among those taken into custody were girls and young women, some of them high school pupils and college students, all of them imprisoned on trumped-up charges. The city's jails were jammed with these girls, with young boys and with militant adults—shoved into cells holding dope addicts, diseased prostitutes and hardened felons.

The New York *Times* declared that "constitutional rights were disregarded outright" by the mobs "or lightly brushed aside by the constituted authorities." The *Nation* magazine described San Francisco's reign of terror as "one of the most harrowing records of brutality to be found outside of Hitler's Third Reich."

The vigilantes had threatened to kill George Anderson merely because he was an attorney for the Communists, but he managed to escape with his life. Now he demanded jury trial for everyone arrested by the police. The fact that he insisted on their constitutional rights so infuriated Municipal Judge George Steiger that the judge threatened Anderson with contempt of court. Another municipal judge, Sylvian Lazarus, saw things differently. The next morning he released most of the prisoners with an apology. "I am disgusted," said this judge, "to think that this good old town should have acted like a pack of wolves. I don't know who is responsible, but it should be traced back to its source."

The evening of the vigilante raids General Hugh Johnson made his scheduled speech on the Berkeley campus. Of the longshoremen's strike, he said: "I think that labor is inherently entitled to bargain collectively through representatives of its own choosing. I think that the employer who denies or even obstructs that right is anti-social. . . . I will go a step further and say that in the American shipping industry, including the loading and unloading of ships, the right has not been justly accorded. . . ."

Of the general strike, Johnson said: ". . . But the *general* strike is quite another matter. It is a threat to the community. It is a menace to government. It is civil war. . . . Both sides are taking extreme positions. But insurrection against the common interest of the community is not a proper weapon and will not for one moment be tolerated by the American people."

That night and the next day there was a humming of telephone wires between San Francisco and Washington, D.C. With President Roosevelt cruising in the Pacific and heading toward Hawaii, the acting President of the United States was Secretary of State Cordell Hull. The morning of July 18 Hull asked Secretary Perkins to join him in his office. When she arrived, she found Hull and Attorney General Homer Cummings in conference, both visibly alarmed, the two of them surrounded by piles of books. In the *Encyclopaedia Britannica* they had found a definition of a "general strike." It had been written some thirty years earlier by P. Tecumseh Sherman, once commissioner of labor statistics for the state of New York. Instead of relying on a definition in some federal statute, Hull and Cummings had agreed with the encyclopedia's definition, had applied it to the situation in San Francisco, had decided that legally it was indeed a "general strike." Thus they felt that the federal government was empowered to take drastic steps to put an end to it.

Miss Perkins contradicted her fellow Cabinet members. She declared that a general strike was a strike by a large body of workers planned and coordinated in advance to force the government to take a position in the matter. Hull and Cummings shook their heads. No, they felt that the National Guard should be federalized and that the army should be called out to put down what they insisted was truly a general strike.

Miss Perkins disagreed again. She thought there was only a remote possibility that delivery and transportation services in San Francisco could be immobilized for very long. She said she felt it unwise to begin the Roosevelt administration by shooting it out with workers who were only exercising their rights to organize and demand collective bargaining. At any rate, Miss Perkins insisted, only the President himself had the right to make such a grave decision.

Hull and Cummings had to agree on this point. Miss Perkins wrote a radiogram and gave it to Louis Howe, the President's most trusted adviser, for transmission to the chief executive. To the Perkins message Howe appended his own note: "Only danger San Francisco is that mayor is badly frightened and his fear infected entire city."

Out in the Pacific, aboard the USS *Houston,* the President read their words and then radioed Secretary Perkins:

> Thanks your estimate of situation. If other means fail, you might offer complete arbitration of all employers and all unions involved on three conditions: First, work to be resumed; second, inter-union agreements to be mutually suspended; third, decision of arbitrators to bind all parties for a definite period as long as possible. If you think advisable, you can issue any statement or offer as coming from me or with my approval. It occurs to me that the country as a whole may not understand the history of the strike and that with any statement you may want to clarify the issues publicly.
>
> Confidential: Please consult with Hull and Cummings as to our authority to maintain food supply in affected areas, and with this concurrent maintenance of traffic and order.

I am inclined to think after Howe's radio today it is at present best for me not to consider change my itinerary. Keep Howe in touch. Wire me Monday.

ROOSEVELT

Obviously, the President refused to be stampeded into rash action. Musing on this matter at a later date, he told reporters: "In the San Francisco strike a lot of people completely lost their heads and telegraphed me, 'For God's sake, come back! Turn the ship around!' . . . Everybody demanded that I sail into San Francisco Bay, all flags flying and guns doubled shotted, and end the strike. They went completely off the handle."

On July 18, the third day of the general strike, the strikers voluntarily lifted the embargo on all foods, gasoline and fuel oil, permitted all restaurants to open again and let streetcars go back into operation. This marked the beginning of the end of the strike. Walter Lippmann wrote of the workers:

> They did not attempt to paralyze the city, to starve and terrorize the people, or to make the government helpless. Not being revolutionists, they recoiled from the logic of the general strike. They did not "mismanage" the general strike. They never intended to go through with it. Once the general strike committee showed they were not attempting to stop those vital services which would be the first and principal objects of attack in a genuine general strike, it was evident that they had blundered into certain failure. So they did not prostrate the city. They annoyed it. They did not paralyze government. They aroused it. They did not overwhelm the public. They provoked it.

On July 19 the General Strike Committee met in the Labor Temple to discuss ending the strike. This group included officials of all participating unions, some of them conservative AFL men. They were sensitive to the fact that AFL President Green had publicly censured San Francisco's Central Labor Council for endorsing the all-out strike.

Harry Bridges argued that the general strike should be continued until the bosses gave the longshoremen and marine workers everything they wanted, whereupon the meeting degenerated into a shouting match between diehard militants and uneasy conservatives. At last it was moved that a standing vote be taken on a resolution to end the strike. In a narrow decision, 191 members voted to end the strike, while 174 voted to continue it. Motion carried. Strike over.

Harry Bridges muttered that those wishing to end the strike had been able to win only because at the last minute they rushed in dozens of new and dubious "members."

The conclusion of the general strike still left unsettled, however, the strike by longshoremen and marine workers.

The night of July 19 Mayor Rossi went on a nationwide radio hookup to say: "I congratulate the real leaders of organized labor on their decision and the part they played in ending the general strike. San Francisco has stamped out, without bargain or compromise, an attempt to import into its life the very real danger of revolt." Then he added ominously: "We will deal effectively with the small group who opposed peace and plotted revolution."

The meaning behind his words became clear the next day. While the workers were returning to their jobs, vigilantes and police launched another series of attacks on those they considered radicals.

On July 21 the General Strike Committee agreed to let the National Longshoremen's Board conduct elections in all West Coast ports to determine whether the dock workers were willing to submit to arbitration. Harry Bridges favored this referendum.

The New York *Times,* which so recently had voiced concern about mob rule in San Francisco, now reversed itself in an editorial saying:

> This country may rightly take satisfaction at the way in which the general strike at San Francisco was met and conquered . . . the local authorities stood fast. . . . Best of all, perhaps, was the spirit displayed by the citizens near whom danger pressed. They were not thrown into panic. . . . Doubtless there must be some "mopping up" in other cities before troubles are over. But what has already been accomplished is sufficient demonstration that Americans will not harbor anarchists, nor tolerate revolutionists, and still are able, as Abraham Lincoln said, to "keep house."

Will Rogers arrived in San Francisco with his family to sail on a voyage around the world, and wrote in his syndicated column:

> In 1926 I was in England during their world-famous general strike. And brother it was general. Not a paper printed, not a train, not a bus, not a wheeled turned. Well, I never got through telling of the composure of those level headed people. Well, I went to San Francisco, and I tell you we are not quite so "nutty" under stress as you might think. It was as quiet as the British. The only thing went haywire was the headlines in the out of Frisco papers. I hope we never live to see the day when a thing is as bad as some of our newspapers make it.

* * *

On July 25, with fewer than two-thirds of all ILA members participating, the West Coast longshoremen voted 6,378 to 1,471 to submit their differences with their bosses to federal arbitration. The next day the last of the National Guardsmen withdrew from the Bay area. The Waterfront Employers' Union agreed to discharge all strikebreakers and promised not to discriminate against any worker for union affiliation or strike activity. On July 30 the marine workers also agreed to arbitration. On July 31, 1934, after nearly three months of labor turmoil along the Pacific seaboard, 12,000 longshoremen and 13,000 marine workers went back to work.

What had been won by the longshoremen—the first to strike? In October the federal board announced these gains: (1) a wage increase from 85 to 95 cents an hour, with from $1.25 to $1.40 for overtime; (2) replacement of the forty-eight hour week with a five-day thirty-hour workweek; (3) joint operation of hiring halls by the ILA and the bosses.

Harry Bridges called this a victory, although he knew it was only a partial one. He had been forced to compromise on the key issue of union control of the hiring halls. Nonetheless, the results were a triumph for rank-and-file workers. They had established the closed shop for longshoremen, flouted the conservatism of the AFL and killed off the company union.

The president of the Draymen's Association proclaimed that Harry Bridges was through as a union leader, but he was wrong. The strike raised Bridges to a position of great power, which he augmented and maintained for many years despite repeated efforts to have him deported as an alien or imprisoned for criminal syndicalism. And time after time after time, Harry Bridges swore that he was not a member of the Communist Party.

22

Huey Long

GOVERNOR FRANKLIN D. ROOSEVELT sat in the study of the executive mansion in Albany early in July, 1932, a few days after he had won nomination as the Democratic Party's Presidential candidate. He was discussing his campaign plans with Rexford Tugwell. A telephone rang. It was answered by a steward, who announced that Governor Long of Louisiana was calling.

Asking that the phone be brought to his table, Roosevelt beckoned Tugwell to inch closer so he might catch both ends of the conversation. Tugwell could easily hear the rasping voice of Huey P. Long.

Roosevelt began by addressing the Louisiana governor as Kingfish, since Huey liked this self-imposed title, but he had uttered only a few words when the Kingfish bellowed, "God damn it, Frank! Don't you know who nominated you? Why do you have Baruch and Young and all those Wall Street sons-of-bitches up there to see you? How do you think it looks to the country? How can I explain it to my people?"

For the next several minutes Huey Long continued to abuse Roosevelt. When Roosevelt was able to get in a word, he quipped that Bernard Baruch and Owen D. Young were people, too—and also old Democrats. The Kingfish brushed aside this remark, yelling that Baruch and Young were Al Smith men, who "would have scuttled your boom if they could!" Now that Roosevelt had been nominated, Huey complained, they seemed like the fair-haired boys, while no "real" Democrats had a chance.

Huey Long had really helped Roosevelt capture the nomination. Now, turning on the charm, Roosevelt tried to pacify the Louisiana governor, declaring he knew very well who his friends were, how much he owed the Kingfish. Huey himself should realize that the two of them stood for the same things. But after all, Roosevelt said silkily, he was just trying to heal the convention wounds and hold the party together. At last Roosevelt seemingly soothed Huey.

Tugwell, who tells this story in his biography of Roosevelt, reflected that Huey had some cause to feel irritated, for while Roosevelt was asking other party leaders to visit him in Albany, he had not extended an invitation to the Kingfish. After Roosevelt hung up the phone, he said to Tugwell: "It's all very well for us to laugh over Huey, but actually we have to remember all the time that he really is one of the two most dangerous men in the country."

"I suppose the other one is Father Coughlin?"

"Oh, no!" Roosevelt cried. "The other is Douglas MacArthur."

*   *   *

Huey Pierce Long was born on August 30, 1893, the seventh of nine children born to Huey Pierce and Caledonia Tison Long. Young Huey came into this world in a four-room log cabin set within his father's 320-acre farm near Winnfield, Winn Parish, Louisiana. The little town of Winnfield lies within the red clay hills of north-central Louisiana, a region of longleaf pine forests, dense canebrakes and fertile creek bottoms. In later years Huey described himself as a hillbilly, but this was an exaggeration since his father was not so poor as Huey pretended he was.

In Winn Parish the hill people earned only about $250 a year by sweating in sawmills or growing cotton on marginal land. Because of their poverty, the small farmers of that area were political radicals; in the 1890's the parish was a Populist stronghold, and in 1912 one-third of the voters cast their ballots for Eugene V. Debs, the Socialist candidate for President. Anglo-Saxons and Hard-Shell Baptists for the most part, they hated New Orleans, the sensual and sophisticated city lying 250 miles to the south.

Religion and politics were almost the sole topics of conversation around Huey as he grew up. His father was a Baptist and a radical, often growling about the need for a revolution to lift the blight of poverty and neglect from the region. Despite the elder Long's complaints about the indifference of the rich toward the poor, he and his family lived in fairly comfortable circumstances, and eventually the father became prosperous through the sale of land to a railway company. Six of the children were sent through college. As a small boy Huey went to church regularly, and as soon as he could read, he turned to the Bible, plowing through it from cover to cover and memorizing long passages. He hated farmwork, began smoking and chewing tobacco, tried to run away from home at the age of ten.

Always a fast talker, Huey excelled in debate at the Winnfield high school but was never graduated because of a disagreement with its principal. After working briefly in a printing shop, Huey hired a horse and buggy to jog through the countryside selling books. His debating skill won him a scholarship to Louisiana State University, despite his lack of a high school diploma, but he lacked the extra money necessary for textbooks and living expenses, so he resumed his career as a traveling salesman. Meandering through Louisiana, Arkansas, Oklahoma, Texas and Tennessee, and concentrating mostly on farmers, Huey peddled soap, furniture, patent medicines for "women's sickness" and a vegetable shortening product called Cottolene.

To promote its use as a substitute for lard, he held baking contests in various towns. In Shreveport, Louisiana, a young woman named Rose McConnell won the first prize offered by Huey Long and then won the man himself. They were married in 1913 and later had three children. Eager for a college education, Huey spent seven months studying at the University of Oklahoma Law School. Then, borrowing $450 from his brother Julius, he took his wife to New Orleans so that he might become a law student at Tulane University. That was in the fall of 1914. In a self-imposed crash program, Huey studied ferociously from sixteen to twenty hours a day, his weight falling to 112 pounds. Carried on the university records as a special student, he tried to cram a three-year course into a single year but did not complete all his courses. For lack of money he had to leave Tulane in May, 1915.

After studying in a private law office, he bearded the chief justice of the Louisiana Supreme Court, boasted about his Tulane record, announced that he was married and broke, declared he was unable to wait until the following June to take the bar examination and persuaded the judge to let the bar committee examine him immediately. The very next day the committee sat in special session to hear his oral arguments. He passed— easily. Thus, at the age of twenty-one, Huey P. Long was declared a full-fledged lawyer in the state of Louisiana.

Returning to his hometown of Winnfield, he rented a tiny space from a bank at $4 a month and hung out his shingle. For the next three years he and his wife lived a precarious existence. His first big break came when he defended State Senator S. J. Harper in a prosecution stemming from Harper's attacks on concentrated wealth. That was in 1918, and in that same year Huey wrote an open letter to the New Orleans *Item* about the maldistribution of wealth. No doubt Huey was utterly sincere about this subject, which obsessed him the rest of his life.

Panting for power, seeking a lever to raise himself high in the world, Huey was ill content to remain a lawyer in private practice; he wanted public office. During World War I he claimed exemption from the draft because he was a husband and a notary public—hence, a "state official." Studying the state constitution, Huey discovered there was no minimum age requirement for the post of state railroad commissioner, so he ran and won election. Now, at twenty-five, he had already become an influential state official.

From 1918 until 1928 he served as one of the state's railroad commissioners—a title later changed to public service commissioner. With his genuine feeling for the underdog heightening his passion for personal power, Huey performed effectively. Early in the twentieth century huge claims on the state's resources had been staked out by the Standard Oil Company and by public utility corporations controlled by Northeastern financial interests. Huey took on this oligarchy, battling against entrenched wealth, reducing telephone rates and preventing streetcar fare increases in Shreveport—a city to which he had moved. Posing as a St. George tilting with a dragon, Huey made thrust after thrust at the Standard Oil Company, to the delight of the average voter.

On August 30, 1923, his thirtieth birthday, Huey announced his candidacy for governor of Louisiana. In the Democratic primary he campaigned with characteristic energy, but was defeated—his plurality in the country districts being offset by his weakness in New Orleans, where the upstate country boy was held in contempt. Huey resumed his chores as public service commissioner while practicing law on the side. And despite his venomous attacks on huge corporations, Huey gladly accepted as much money from them as possible.

In his autobiography, *Every Man a King,* Huey wrote: "With the exception of some few big cases, I had generally represented only the poorer class of clients. . . . When the millionaires and corporations of Louisiana fell out with each other, I was able to accept highly remunerative employment from one of the powerful to fight several others which were even more powerful. Then I made some big fees with which I built a modern home in the best residential section of the City of Shreveport at a cost of $40,000."

His brother Julius told a Senate committee that Huey's gubernatorial campaign was financed mainly by a utilities firm. Earl, another brother, said that in 1927 Huey took a $10,000 bribe from a utility executive, but Huey snarled: "That is a God damn lie!"

Now fairly well-to-do, regarded by poor people as their champion in the continuing fight against the rich, smarter than any other politician in Louisiana and aware of it, Huey ran for governor a second time in 1928. He campaigned like a tornado, swirling from one part of the state to another, lashing out repeatedly at the oligarchy dominating Louisiana, posing as the pal of the dispossessed, articulating grievances the common man sensed but was unable to put into words. They gathered, the red-necked farmers and hard-handed field workers, sweat blotching their shirts, lifting their worn faces to the furious young man who promised them paradise long delayed. They listened and cheered and paraded under banners proclaiming EVERY MAN A KING BUT NO ONE WEARS A CROWN. This was a quotation from William Jennings Bryan, who had been considered a radical in his day.

On May 21, 1928, at the age of thirty-five, Huey Pierce Long was sworn in as governor of Louisiana. Although the state ranked thirtieth in area and twenty-second in population, it had the highest illiteracy rate among the forty-eight states then in the Union. Almost half the children of school age were not in school. There were only 30 miles of improved highways in the entire state. No bridges spanned any of the main rivers. There was almost no hospital service for the poor and helpless.

*   *   *

Huey Long was a man of medium height with flesh soon to puff into pudginess. His face was as round and red as a huge tomato, his nose as blunt as the putty noses worn by clowns, and his fat chin was cleft in the middle. His popeyes darted cunningly from side to side, and all his features moved with the elasticity of rubber. His curly red-brown hair ended in front in an unruly forelock. He looked like a crafty country rube, a dissipated cherub or, as John Dos Passos thought, "like an overgrown small boy with very bad habits indeed."

Although he slumped on the end of his spine in a chair and liked to conduct business while lying in bed, his body was in constant motion. He developed into a sensualist fond of wine, women and song—despite his inability to carry a tune. A self-proclaimed hillbilly, he despised high society and good manners, feeling comfortable mostly in the company of farmers and cronies, picking his nose, scratching his bottom. Whenever he ate broiled chicken, he tore it apart with his fingers, and if food was not to his taste, he threw it onto the floor.

Endowed with personal magnetism, a superb actor and mimic, Huey was a natural leader. An exhibitionist and buffoon, he had a fabulous memory and dazzled people by quoting snappily and effectively from Scriptures or the classics. John Gunther described him as "an engaging monster." Forever self-assured, his mind as fast and flashing as lightning, Huey was contemptuous of most people. He was a self-intoxicated man, insensitive to the needs of individuals however much he mirrored the moods of the masses. He was so ruthless he could be flippantly brutal. One night when his chauffeur accidentally hit a bump in the road, Huey screamed for the car to stop, ordered the driver out, took the wheel himself and left the hapless chauffeur stranded on the black and lonely road.

But unlike most tyrants, Huey had a sense of humor and was not afraid to let himself appear ridiculous. Fond of jest, mostly about others but sometimes about himself, he laughed easily when he was not commanding his bodyguards to slug annoying photographers. Scorning dignity, he crowned himself the Kingfish after the Kingfish of the Mystic Knights of the Sea, a smooth-talking schemer on the *Amos 'n' Andy* radio show, so popular in the Thirties. Huey himself used radio to maximum advantage in his leap to power. Never allowing himself to be placed on the defensive, always attacking, Huey candidly said: "I can't make a speech that's worth a damn unless I'm raising hell about what my enemies are doing." He swore all the time—in private and in public. He engaged in primitive politics, declaring: "In a political fight, when you've got nothing in favor of your side, start a row in the opposition."

Curiously, like Boss Tweed of New York before his time, Huey was devoid of religious prejudice. As regards racism, he did tell Negro stories in dialect and called some of his foes "kinkyheads," but he also made a public apology for using the word "nigger" over the air waves. Openly he proclaimed himself a rabble-rouser, perhaps reasoning that his honesty would camouflage his lust for power. Money he wanted, certainly, but more than money he sought power. Dictators need no pockets. Knowingly or unknowingly, Huey practiced a precept articulated during the French Revolution by Danton: "Audacity, more audacity, always audacity."

Soon after becoming governor, Huey fired every state worker under executive control who had failed to support him during his campaign, replacing them with loyal men from the bayous and hills. At the beginning of his term he lacked a majority in the Louisiana legislature but soon won control of both houses by making political concessions for patronage. He used taxation as a club to intimidate or punish foes. He bent men to his will by threatening to publish the names of their relatives who were patients in state mental institutions. Whenever his pet bills came before the legislators, Huey took personal charge of the legislative process on the floor, telling elected officials exactly how to vote. He bragged that he dealt with legislators "like a deck of cards" and claimed to have bought one lawmaker "like a sack of potatoes."

One stubborn man tossed a copy of the Louisiana state constitution at Huey and snorted: "Maybe you've heard of this book!"

Tossing it back, Huey yelled: "I'm the constitution around here now!"

Another time he shrilled: *"I'm* the Democratic party in Louisiana!"

He tightened his grip on the state and its people by means of trickery and bribes, cajolery and beatings, threats and blackmail, cunning and kidnappings. But despite his dirty methods, Huey Long was relatively efficient in administering the state's affairs. He replaced the antiquated Capitol Building with a modern skyscraper. He built seawalls, airports, canals, bridges, levees and hundreds of miles of paved highways. He killed the discriminatory poll tax. He stimulated the rapid growth of Louisiana State University, gave it a school of medicine, founded a home for epileptics, gave schoolchildren free buses and textbooks, did all he could to erase illiteracy.

His wish to provide free textbooks for children in both the public and the parochial schools of Louisiana developed into an issue regarding the separation of church and state. The case of *Cochran vs. Louisiana State Board of Education* wound up before the United States Supreme Court, with Huey arguing the state's position in a personal appearance before this high court in Washington. The justices found in his favor, deciding that the

Louisiana law did not violate the Fourteenth Amendment since the books were given to the children and not to the schools.

This was one of the last cases heard by Chief Justice William Howard Taft, the former President of the United States, who remarked: "Huey P. Long is the most brilliant, competent and intelligent attorney to have appeared before me during my term as the Chief Justice of the Supreme Court."

Governor Long's state improvement program cost money, lots of money, but he knew just where to get it. For every dollar he spent in the glare of daylight he took another dollar under the cover of dark. While exempting small homesteads from public levies, he laid heavy taxes on corporations and public utilities. He imposed a tribute of 2 percent on the salary of every state employee, 10 percent from each of them for elections in which he was interested and ordered every state jobholder to subscribe to his weekly newspaper, the *Louisiana Progress*.

The old oligarchy became frightened when Huey called a special session of the state legislature to slap an occupational tax of 5 cents a barrel on refined oil, with the Standard Oil Company suffering the worst case of jitters. When it was revealed that thirty-five of his relatives were on state payrolls at a total of $75,000 a year, Huey chuckled and said that that wasn't half of them. He was impeached but beat conviction by forming a "round robin" of state senators who declared they would not vote against Huey regardless of what the testimony revealed.

The things that Huey Long did *not* do as governor are as significant as the things he did accomplish. He did not delegate authority to anyone, did not raise teachers' salaries, gave no relief to the unemployed, did not provide pensions for the aged, did not end child labor, did not shorten the working day, failed to support unions, weakened the workmen's compensation system, paid state wages far below the prevailing scale.

He enormously increased Louisiana's public debt, adding thirty-five new taxes, boosting the state budget 74 percent, and made the state debt the second or third highest in the nation. He was a despot who behaved benevolently only when there was something in it for him.

Louisiana's common people were unaware of the dark side of Huey's record or indifferent to it. An upstate farmer said: "At least we got *something*. Before him, we got nothing. That's the difference."

Huey Long sought power, more power, absolute power. Louisiana became too small a stage for his strutting ego, so on July 16, 1930, he announced his candidacy for the United States Senate. "I'm leaving state politics for good," he lied. "I've done all I can for Louisiana. Now I want to help the rest of the country."

The following November 4 Huey was elected to the Senate. He should have taken office in Washington on March 4, 1931, but his four-year term as governor was not due to end until 1932. Huey refused to resign as Louisiana's chief executive because the lieutenant governor, P. N. Cyr, was a political enemy who might try to take control of the state if Huey ventured beyond its boundaries. Therefore, to the amusement of much of the nation, from November 4, 1930, until January 25, 1932, Huey Long was both Senator-elect and governor of Louisiana. As in a kind of burlesque skit, Cyr declared himself governor, whereupon Huey said that Cyr no longer was lieutenant governor, let alone governor; Huey handpicked Oscar K. Allen for his successor as governor and finally felt safe enough at home to leave for the nation's capital.

Riding a special train, wearing gaudy clothes, fawned on by cronies and protected by bodyguards, Huey P. Long arrived in Washington on January 25, 1932.

*   *   *

The United States Senate, which had seen many a spectacle in its day, never saw a one-man circus like Huey Long. Contemptuous of his own state legislators, never having met his intellectual equal, the freshman Senator from Louisiana was unawed by meeting other United States Senators. Most of them looked like old men to him, since he was only thirty-eight. The fact that he was almost a year late in taking his Senate seat did not bother him in the least.

When Huey walked into the Senate wing of the Capitol he was welcomed by Senator Joseph T. Robinson, the sixty-year-old Democratic leader of the Senate—who soon would regret his friendliness. Robinson led Huey to a lounge just outside the Senate chamber to await the moment when he would be sworn into office. As Huey waited, he was approached by fifty-eight-year-old Edwin S. Broussard, who had been a Democratic Senator from Louisiana since 1921. Broussard greeted Huey and explained that it was a Senate custom for the senior Senator from a given state to introduce the junior Senator to the legislators.

In a Washington newspaper Huey had read a remark by Broussard about himself which Huey considered offensive, so he curtly rejected the senior Senator's overture. When Robinson got back to Huey and heard what had happened, he volunteered to introduce him to the other Senators. Following Robinson onto the Senate floor, Huey ignored the rule against smoking, parked his cigar on a clerk's desk, took the oath of office, stuck the stogie back into his mouth and nonchalantly puffed away.

James E. Watson, the sixty-nine-year-old Republican leader of the Senate, did not happen to be on the floor at that moment but took his seat moments later. Suddenly he was dealt a two-handed blow on the chest by a strange man who cried: "Jim, I want to get acquainted with you!"

Wincing from the blow, Watson scowled up and asked: "Well, who in hell are you?"

"*I* am Huey Long!"

At a later date Robert Reynolds walked up to Huey in the Senate cloakroom, stuck out his hand and said: "I'm Senator Reynolds of North Carolina."

"Yeah," drawled Huey, coolly looking him up and down. "I knew you when you ran an ice-skating rink."

From the very start of his term in the Senate, Huey became a terror to most of the other Senators. The only ones he respected were George Norris of Nebraska, Burton K. Wheeler of Montana and William E. Borah of Idaho. Instead of sitting back and listening at first, as is expected of a freshman Senator, Huey delivered his maiden speech just two days after taking office. He danced jigs in the Senate aisles wearing odd outfits such as white flannels, a pink necktie and an orange kerchief. He won publicity by supplementing the Senate's dining room menu with potlikker—the "heavenly remains," as Huey put it, after greens, turnips and salt pork had been boiled together. Within three months of his ascension to the Senate he became one of the capital's greatest tourist attractions.

January, 1932, the month in which Huey took the oath of office, was a troubled month indeed. Now the Depression was worldwide, more men being unemployed than the total of all soldiers mobilized by all nations on all fighting fronts at any one time during World War I. In the United States, according to AFL President Green, the number of the jobless and their dependents came to a total of 20,000,000 people. The Reverend James R. Cox, a Catholic priest from Pittsburgh, led 18,000 workless people to Washington, was received by President Hoover and at least was listened to by Congressmen.

In Detroit, with 4,000 children standing in breadlines daily, the city's suicide rate was 30 percent higher than the previous five-year average. In Cook County, which includes the city of Chicago, all local relief funds were exhausted. New York City borrowed $12,500,000 from bankers for eleven days at 6 percent interest, the highest interest rate the city ever had paid thus far, but its welfare department temporarily lacked enough postage stamps to mail relief checks to the needy.

Novelist Theodore Dreiser was so disgusted he told Earl Browder he wanted to join the Communist Party. The governor of Virginia urged a 10 percent cut in the salaries of all state employees, including schoolteachers. A twelve-year-old pupil scratched himself so vigorously that his teacher examined him and found $1,000 in big bills taped to his chest; the boy said his parents were afraid of banks. Governor Roosevelt said: "The economics of America, and indeed of the whole world, are out of joint."

Huey Long knew little about economics but much about human nature. He understood the genesis of dictatorships, silently agreeing when Roosevelt said: "History proves that dictatorships do not grow out of strong and successful governments but out of weak and helpless ones." Huey also may have agreed with Mussolini, who said: "Men are perhaps weary of liberty." Before long the Louisiana Senator was telling New York reporters: "What this country needs is a dictator." Few people took Huey seriously at first, just as few people had paid much attention when Hitler blueprinted his scheme for taking over Germany.

Congress, those first few months of 1932, wrestled with the problem of taxation. Drastic levies seemed to be needed, for the national budget was nearly a billion dollars off. At the beginning of the session there was a movement for heavy increases in income and inheritance taxes, and this gave Huey Long a chance he had sought.

Late in April he introduced a resolution calling on the Senate finance committee to revise a pending revenue bill so that incomes of more than $1,000,000 a year and inheritances above $5,000,000 would be confiscated. The only answer to Communism, Huey shouted, was to share the wealth. Thumping his desk, he cried: "Rockefeller and Morgan would sleep much safer tonight if they had $100 million each under their pillow case, instead of a billion or two!" While John D. Rockefeller's total assets may have approximated $1 billion, J. P. Morgan never had anywhere near this wealth.

Democratic leader Robinson opposed Huey's resolution, which got only a few votes. Huey then attacked Robinson, reading into the *Congressional Record* a list of the Arkansas Senator's law clients, which included banks and corporations. Huey also resigned all his committee assignments and thereafter went it alone in the Senate. Never was his name attached to any measure of prime importance. Never could he control more than four to seven votes in the Senate. He was so hated and feared by other Senators that one of them said Huey "couldn't get the Lord's Prayer endorsed in this body." Although Huey complained a few times about being an outsider in the Senate, he really did not mind. He agreed with Machiavelli, who said it is safer to be feared than loved.

Although Huey never became a positive power in the Senate, he was a negative nuisance. Democratic Senators were more wary of their Louisiana colleague than they were of Republican Senators. Brash and talkative, Huey treated his peers like stuffed shirts, staged one-man filibusters that delayed the passage of bills—some of which provided relief for the needy. Alben Barkley said that in debate Huey was like a horsefly: "He would light on one part of you, sting you, and then, when you slapped at him, fly away to land elsewhere and sting again." Whenever word went out that Huey Long was to address the Senate, sightseers thronged into the visitor's gallery as they might have flocked the Colosseum to watch Christians being slaughtered.

Off the Senate floor one day some people from Montana asked Huey what he thought of their Senator, Thomas J. Walsh. Huey startled them by replying: "You know, Walsh is like a guinea hen. Do you know the habits of a guinea hen? It's a very peculiar bird. If you take a long-handled rake and rake the eggs out from under the guinea hen's nest, she'll keep on laying eggs. But if you reach your hand in and take the eggs, she'll never lay in that nest again. Now, Walsh is like the guinea hen. He lays the ideas, and Joe Robinson takes a long-handled rake and rakes the ideas out. And so Walsh keeps giving Robinson the ideas."

Senator Wheeler, one of the few Senators who liked Huey, thought he fancied himself as a kind of Robin Hood of the bayous. During a night session Wheeler saw two Republican Senators lead Huey into the cloakroom and ply him with liquor—which took little doing, since at this point in his career Huey was boozing it up. After Huey had made two or three trips inside for a nip, Wheeler took him aside to warn him that the Republicans were trying to get him drunk so he would make a fool of himself on the Senate floor. Wheeler cajoled Huey into drinking coffee and eating doughnuts to absorb the alcohol in his system, and when Huey returned to his Senate seat, he turned to Wheeler, grinned and said: "I'm so sober I'm ashamed of myself."

*   *   *

The day Huey took office as a Senator some reporters asked what he thought about the forthcoming Presidential election. Roosevelt, only a couple of days earlier, had announced his availability as the Democratic candidate. Huey told the press he liked John Garner of Texas and Al Smith of New York but did not think much of Roosevelt as the party's standard-bearer. Wheeler and Norris, aware of Huey's influence in the South, tried to woo him to Roosevelt's side, their task being eased by a Roosevelt speech which Huey liked. Roosevelt said: "The millions who are in want will not stand by silently forever while the things to satisfy their needs are within easy reach. Many of those whose primary solicitude is confined to the welfare of what they call capital have failed to read the lessons of the last few years and have been moved less by calm analysis of the needs of the nation as a whole than by a blind determination to preserve their own special stakes in the economic disorder. We may build more factories, but the fact remains that we have enough now to supply all our domestic needs and more, if they are used. No, our basic trouble was not an insufficiency of capital; it was an insufficient distribution of buying power coupled with an oversufficient speculation in production."

This sounded to Huey as though Roosevelt also wanted to share the wealth. Chancing to meet Clark Howell of the Atlanta *Constitution* on a train, Huey said he was warming up to Roosevelt. Soon he got a letter from Roosevelt saying that Howell had passed along his comment. FDR ended his letter by telling Huey: "You and I are alike for the rights in behalf of the common man of this country."

The Democratic Party's 1932 National Convention was due to begin in Chicago on June 27. At the request of Jim Farley, who was managing Roosevelt's bid for the nomination, Huey arrived a few days before the opening session. With Roosevelt the front-runner, Arkansas and Mississippi planned to enter favorite son candidates in an attempt to weaken Roosevelt's lead, so Huey went to work on leaders from those states, trying to win them over to Roosevelt. Frank Hague, the boss of Jersey City, sneered that Huey had "no other thought but patronage." Patronage Huey wanted, to be sure, but he also hoped to be consulted about party policy if Roosevelt were elected President, and he even dreamed of a Cabinet post.

The night before the convention opened, Edward J. Flynn, the boss of the Bronx and a Roosevelt lieutenant, went to bed in his Chicago hotel room about 2 A.M. only to be awakened by a loud knock on his door.

"Wearily, I asked who it was," Flynn later wrote. "A trumpet-like voice informed me it was Huey Long. I opened the door and there, sure enough, stood the Kingfish, somewhat the worse for wear and completely surrounded by bodyguards. Long and his little army marched into the room and, after the briefest of preliminaries, Huey announced that he thought he would support Roosevelt."

Despite Flynn's annoyance at the intrusion, the news delighted him. After Roosevelt was nominated on the fourth ballot, Flynn declared: "There is no question in my mind but that without Long's work Roosevelt might not have been nominated."

Huey, growing cockier by the day, was certain of this. Approaching Farley, the Democratic national chairman, Huey demanded a special train for himself so he could visit all forty-eight states to campaign for Roosevelt. Farley knew all about Huey's theatrical and oratorical skill and was afraid that the Louisiana Senator might overshadow Roosevelt himself during the campaign. He vetoed the idea of a special train, saying it would cost too much. Huey banged his fist on Farley's desk and snarled: "Jim, you're gonna get licked! . . . I tried to save you, but if you don't want to be saved, it's all right with me!"

Farley compromised. He mapped out a speaking tour that would take Huey into northern Midwestern states which he felt were already lost or so firmly committed to Roosevelt that Huey could do nothing in them to harm the Democratic ticket. Huey accepted this curtailed itinerary, stumped for Roosevelt and was a huge success wherever he appeared. The more national exposure Huey got, the more he wanted. His Senate seat was next to that of Mrs. Hattie Caraway of Arkansas. After the death of her husband, Senator Thaddeus Caraway, she was appointed and then elected to fill out his term, becoming the first woman to sit in the Senate. In November, 1932, she faced a regular election for the full six-year term, and she told Huey she was afraid that she might lose. He promised to send some of his men into her state to find out what kind of chance she had.

Huey's advance men reported that Mrs. Caraway was up against such strong Democratic opposition she could not even take the primary. When he relayed this opinion to her, she burst into tears. Huey thereupon decided to campaign in Arkansas for the "poor little widow woman against six big-bellied bullies," as he described the situation.

Wheeler felt that Huey acted from a sense of chivalry. It is far more likely that he was motivated by gratitude, revenge and ambition. Mrs. Caraway had been one of the few Senators who voted for his resolution to limit incomes. Arkansas was the home state of Senator Robinson, whom

Huey wished to humble. Most of all, however, Huey sought to extend his influence beyond Louisiana's borders.

On August 1, 1932, Huey invaded the neighboring state of Arkansas with a group of political cronies and bodyguards riding in four sound trucks owned by Louisiana. With Mrs. Caraway by his side, he led this caravan over more than 2,000 miles of Arkansas highways and dusty byways, spoke in thirty-nine county seats and attracted to Little Rock the largest crowd ever assembled in the state's history. He sprayed his throat with an atomizer, kept a well-thumbed Bible on the lectern beside him, played popular music over loudspeakers, told his aides to hold babies so their mothers could listen to him, depicted himself as just one of the folks, denounced the rich and distributed pamphlets. One was entitled *Wall Street Versus the People* and another *Why Financiers Oppose Mrs. Caraway*. In little more than one week of whirlwind campaigning, Huey won over enough rural Arkansas to return Mrs. Caraway to the Senate.

Two months later Huey conferred with Roosevelt. To waiting reporters, Huey said: "When I was talking to the governor today, I felt just like the depression was over. That's a fact! I never felt so tickled in my life."

Huey's optimism—real or faked—did not square with the facts of national life. Wages were down, banks were closing, children were suffering, farmers were fighting foreclosures, a stockbroker had just killed himself, hungry people marched in Chicago, cops arrested vagrants for sleeping in a New York subway arcade and Seattle was reeling from the effects of the Depression.

Roosevelt was elected in November, 1932, and the following January Huey called on the President-elect in the Mayflower Hotel in Washington. Huey pounded at the door to Roosevelt's suite, pounded again for photographers, then shouted to reporters: "I'm going to ask him, 'Did you mean it or didn't you?' Goddam it, there ain't but one thing I'm afraid of—and that's the people!"

More Machiavelli: *Be careful not to be hated by the people.*

Half an hour later Huey emerged from the Roosevelt suite with a grin on his face. "I come out of this room happy and satisfied," he told correspondents. "We've got a great President!"

A reporter asked whether Roosevelt planned to crack down on him.

"Crack down on me?" Huey echoed. "He don't want to crack down on me. He told me, 'Huey, you're going to do just as I tell you'—and that is just what I'm agoin' to do!"

This is just what Huey P. Long did not do.

*   *   *

Roosevelt realized he had a wildcat by the tail. It was all very well for the President-elect to preach party unity to his fellow Democrat from Louisiana, but Roosevelt was a realist. The patrician New Yorker must have felt uncomfortable about the fact that this gauche politician from

Louisiana had helped him win both the nomination and the election. This kind of political assistance is usually rewarded, but Roosevelt knew that Huey was a dangerous demagogue. How was Roosevelt to contain the man's obsessive bid for power?

He did not offer Huey a Cabinet seat, did not consult him about party policy, and although he consulted with Huey about patronage for Louisiana, he soon began withholding that patronage in an attempt to sap Huey's strength in his home state. Huey reacted by telling administration officials they could take their federal patronage "slap-dab to hell!"

Hundreds of Louisiana citizens, victims of Huey's wrath or worried idealists, had written complaining letters to the Hoover administration back in 1930. Their gripes and tips were brought to the attention of Elmer Irey, chief of the Treasury Department's intelligence unit. Was Huey the lawbreaker and grafter the letters charged? Irey sent Archie Burford, head of treasury agents in the South, into Louisiana to investigate. Burford soon reported to Irey: "Chief, Louisiana is crawling! Long and his gang are stealing everything in the state . . . and they're not paying taxes on the loot."

Irey dispatched thirty-two agents to Louisiana to probe the situation in depth. They interviewed Huey's enemies and took affidavits—which bothered Huey. He demanded that the Hoover administration call off its watchdogs. Hoover's treasury secretary, Ogden L. Mills, asked Irey whether he had enough evidence to support an indictment. Irey replied that his men hadn't had enough time to nail down all the facts. Mills said: "Very well, then. Suspend your investigation immediately and write a full report of what you have done and what you propose doing and submit it to my successor. After all, the Senator is one of their babies. Let them decide what to do with him."

Mills' successor as treasury secretary was Henry Morgenthau. Three days after Morgenthau took office, he sent for Irey and said: "Get all your agents back on the Louisiana job. Start the investigation of Huey Long and proceed as though you were investigating John Doe." Morgenthau promised to protect the federal agents from political pressures and ordered Irey to report to him about Huey once a week.

Huey's income-tax returns were of especial interest, since he had become prosperous, if not exceedingly wealthy. Almost every contract let out by state officials was graft-ridden. Two of Huey's brothers said they saw corporation agents hand Huey huge rolls of bills—one so bulky he had trouble stuffing it into his hip pocket. Huey and some cronies set up the Win or Lose Corporation, which acquired natural-gas fields, browbeat natural gas firms into buying this property at vast profit by threatening to boost their taxes if they didn't buy; soon the new corporation cleared one-third of a million dollars. And Huey gave the state slot machine concession to Frank Costello, described by newspapers as "the Prime Minister of the Underworld."

Despite Huey's disgust over lack of federal patronage, he did not break immediately with Roosevelt. For his part, FDR told Raymond Moley and Rexford Tugwell to watch Huey closely and try to prevent him from going on a rampage. Moley later said of Huey: "There could be no question about his extraordinary mental—or, if you will—intellectual capacity. I have never known a mind that moved with more clarity, decisiveness and force." Moley soon learned that no one could handle the rambunctious Senator from Louisiana. One day an apple-chewing Huey Long marched to Moley's room in the Mayflower Hotel, kicked open the door and snarled: "I don't like you and your goddam banker friends!" After Huey left, Moley found a Senator hiding in the bathroom.

At one point during the famous Hundred Days of Roosevelt's first administration, Huey told a group in the Senate cloakroom: "Men, it will not be long until there will be a mob assembling here to hang Senators from the rafters of the Senate. I have to determine whether I will stay here and be hung with you, or go out and lead the mob." Almost no one laughed.

Did Huey Long really plan to lead a nationwide revolution?

Well, as Arthur M. Schlesinger, Jr., has said, in Louisiana he had led a revolution of poor whites against a decadent oligarchy. Huey's aging father told a journalist: "There wants to be a revolution, I tell you!" New Orleans Mayor T. S. Walmsley said publicly he thought that Huey sought revolution. One of Huey's admirers was a Montana banker, who wrote President Roosevelt a letter saying that Huey was "the man we thought you were when we voted for you." And Huey himself said something to the effect that if Fascism ever came to the United States, it would come disguised as anti-Fascism.

Moving further away from the Roosevelt administration, Huey charged that it had sold out to Wall Street. He ranted endlessly about the unequal distribution of wealth, saying things such as: "How many men ever went to a barbecue and would let one man take off the table what was intended for nine-tenths of the people to eat? The only way you'll ever be able to feed the balance of the people is to make that man come back and bring back some of the grub he ain't got no business with!"

Huey could speak grammatically, but an Associated Press reporter listened in astonishment as Huey greeted a Louisiana farmer by saying: "Hey, I haven't—I *ain't* seen you in a long time!" Bad grammar gave Huey the flavor of the common man.

Huey completed his break with the New Deal by launching personal attacks on the President, whom he now called Frank-lin De-La-No Roo-Se-Velt, heavily emphasizing every syllable of the name. With cruel wit he compared Roosevelt and Hoover with peddlers of two patent medicines, High Popalorum and Low Popahiram, which were made from the bark of the same tree. "But for one," Huey said, "the peddler peeled the bark off from the top down, and for the other he peeled it off from the bottom up.

And that's the way it is in Washington. Roosevelt and his crowd are skinning us from the ear down, and Hoover and the Republicans are doing the job from the ankle up. But they've both been skinning us and there ain't either side left now."

To the delight of spectators in the Senate gallery, Huey sneered at Jim Farley, Henry Morgenthau, Henry Wallace, Harold Ickes, Hugh Johnson, Carter Glass, Bernard Baruch and other Roosevelt supporters. He bedeviled John Garner whenever the Vice President presided over Senate sessions. One day, after making himself especially obnoxious, Huey jumped up again and asked banteringly: "Mr. President, I rise to make a parliamentary inquiry. How should a Senator, who is half in favor of this bill and half against it, cast his vote?"

Garner glowered at Huey and snapped: "Get a saw and saw yourself in half!"

This was one of the few times Huey was ever squelched. A spoiler and obstructionist, he filibustered, he taunted his colleagues, he sabotaged legislative action, and finally he was held in contempt of a Senate committee. He so enraged Carter Glass that the elderly Senator tried to attack Huey physically, and he so disgusted the other Virginia Senator, Harry Byrd, that Byrd changed his seat so he would not have to look at Huey.

But the blithe Huey gloried in the fact that regardless of what other Senators thought of him, he was winning the admiration of more and more Americans. Disturbed by the Depression, attracted by Huey's simplistic solutions to this problem, they applauded his audacity and his antics. As early as June 17, 1932, he was asked to run for President on the Farmer-Labor ticket—a mere straw in Huey's whirlwind. No one could be sure what harvest he might reap.

In January, 1934, the month in which Dr. Francis E. Townsend announced his own plan, Huey organized the Share-Our-Wealth Society. It may be remembered that as early as 1918 Huey had made his first public pronouncement about the maldistribution of wealth. He also had noted one sentence in Roosevelt's acceptance speech: "Throughout the nation, men and women, forgotten in the political philosophy of the government of the last years, look to us here for guidance and for a more equitable opportunity to share in the distribution of national wealth."

The name of Huey's new society was copyrighted by his secretary, Earle Christenberry. As his national organizer, Huey chose an anti-Semitic preacher, the Reverend Gerald L. K. Smith, chuckling that "next to me, Gerald Smith is the greatest rabble-rouser in the country." At first the society's staff consisted of twenty girls, who mailed out hundreds of thousands of circulars and copies of Huey's speeches. "In this country," Huey proclaimed, "we raise so much food there'd be plenty for all if we never slaughtered another hog or harvested another bushel of grain for the next two years—and yet people are going hungry. We've got enough material for clothes if in the next two years we never tanned another hide or raised another lock of cotton—and yet people are going barefoot and naked. Enough houses in this land are standing empty to put a roof over every head at night—and yet people are wandering the highways for lack of shelter."

No one could dispute these facts. What to do about them was something else, the key question being the precise manner in which wealth should and could be distributed equitably, legally and morally among all Americans. Huey was explicit about objectives but vague about methods. His economic theory was obscure. He discouraged discussion of specifics, saying that this would breed "division and destroy the practical techniques of the political strategy necessary to attain power required for reform."

In general, his plan shaped up as follows:

The federal government would buy all farm surpluses and store them until they were needed. All surplus property, in fact, would be turned over to the government, which would then hand it out to the needy. Every family would be given a house and lot worth $6,000, an annual income of about $2,500, an automobile, a radio and perhaps even an electric refrigerator. Every youth would get a free four-year college education. No one would be permitted to receive an annual income of more than $1,000,000, and private fortunes would be limited to $50,000,000. There would be pensions for the aged and bonuses for veterans. Working hours would be increased or decreased to balance production and consumption.

Where would the government find the money for all of this? The Share-Our-Wealth program ended with the following clause: "The raising of revenue for the support of this program to come from the reduction of swollen fortunes from the top."

While part of Huey's plan may have had some merit, its foundations were shaky. It drew no distinction between physical wealth and monetary wealth. It did not resolve the question of ownership or operation of factories, railroads, shipping lines and the like.

To join Huey's new society was the easiest thing in the world. Gerald Smith, paid $650 a month to plug the program, would ask his audiences whether they were receiving a fair share of the world's goods. In this Depression-stricken land the answer had to be a resounding "No!" Smith would then promise the people that Huey would get them all they needed and wanted if they would just give him a chance. Dues? There were no dues. All one had to do was to accept the card handed to him, sign his name and mail it to Huey. This automatically made him a member of the society and entitled him to wear a Share-Our-Wealth badge. The organization had no state directors and no important officer other than Huey. New members were urged to meet in private homes to organize Share-Our-Wealth clubs, elect a president and secretary—but no treasurer. The movement was financed by "friends in Louisiana," as Huey vaguely described them.

The simplicity of this technique, the gullibility of the people and the evangelical fervor of Gerald Smith began bringing in new members at the rate of 20,000 a day. Even some black people signed up, for Huey said his society recognized no racial barriers. Soon he claimed 2,000,000 converts, and at a later date he announced in an expansive mood that there were 9,000,000 people on the Share-Our-Wealth rolls. According to Smith, at the time of Huey's death there were 100,000 Share-Our-Wealth clubs scattered throughout all forty-eight states.

The movement had its own theme song, "Every Man a King," which Huey sometimes warbled off-key over radio stations. It went this way:

> (Verse)
> Why sleep or slumber, America?
> Land of brave and true;
> With castles, clothing, and food for all,
> All belongs to you.
>
> (Chorus)
> Ev'ry man a king; ev'ry man a king;
> For you can be a millionaire.
> But there's something belonging to others,
> There's enough for all people to share.
> When it's sunny June or December too,
> Or in Winter time or Spring,
> There'll be peace without end,
> Every neighbor a friend,
> With ev'ry man a king.

Huey Long used another song to brand New Dealers as the tools of Wall Street:

> Black sheep, Wall Street, have you any gold?
> Yes, sir; yes, sir; all I can hold.
> Thanks to the New Deal I've made a million more
> And I've stuck it all away in my little chain store.

Who didn't want to be a king and a millionaire, rolled into one? The Share-Our-Wealth movement burst across state lines, mushroomed throughout the South, pushed up through border regions, seeped into the industrial Northeast and finally settled in every state of the nation. Roosevelt and his advisers were alarmed.

One day, strutting around Senator Wheeler's office in Washington, Huey alluded to the President, muttering: "I'm going to beat that son-of-a-bitch at the other end of the avenue!"

Wheeler said Huey was talking through his hat.

Huey snarled: "You've never seen the crowds I get!"

"That's right," Wheeler agreed, "but, Huey—they come out to see you as a curiosity."

Huey nodded. "Sure! But when they get there—I *get*'em!"

He did indeed. His flamboyance, his oratorical powers, his amusing publicity stunts, his harangues in the Senate, his brilliance, his energy, his empathy with the common man's hopes and dreams—these qualities transformed Huey Long into the most influential politician in the nation next to Roosevelt.

Wheeler, who continued to like Huey despite his braggadocio, once told Roosevelt to his face that he was not treating Huey right. The President said he thought Huey was a crook. "Well," Wheeler replied, "I don't think so, but if he is a crook, he's too smart for you to catch him."

* * *

When Huey was sworn in as Senator, he gave up his title of governor but continued to run Louisiana by means of his puppet governor, O. K. Allen. From time to time, as well, Huey went back to his home state and barged onto the floors of both houses of the legislature to oversee passage of the bills he wanted enacted into law. His power was enormous, but not yet absolute, for he ruled Louisiana through an alliance with the old regulars. They broke with Huey soon after he began denouncing Roosevelt and defeated his candidate for mayor of New Orleans. Furious, Huey decided that he would beat the defiant city of New Orleans to its knees once and for all.

He got his chance in the summer of 1934 during another election—this one for Congressional offices. Surrounding himself with rural legislators, sycophants and bodyguards, Huey descended on the city to stage a phony vice investigation. Acting on Huey's orders, Governor Allen declared martial law in New Orleans and called out the National Guard. Wearing helmets, carrying grenades and gas canisters and rifles tipped with bayonets, the militiamen captured the office of the registrar of voters and set up machine guns pointing directly at City Hall. Newspapers across the country talked excitedly of civil war, but on election day not a shot was fired. Huey's Congressional candidates won.

Huey then reorganized the entire structure of state government by holding eight special sessions of the legislature in 1934 and 1935. He ordered the drafting of all bills he wanted passed and made sure they went to a single committee. His measures were not debated but were rammed through both houses at the rate of one every two minutes. Despite the fact that he was a United States Senator without any legal right to take command of the state legislature, Huey was always there on the spot, in personal command of everything, rapping out orders, bullying hesitant lawmakers, shouting down weak opposition.

By the early part of 1935, at the age of forty-one, Huey P. Long had become the dictator of Louisiana.

He totally controlled the executive, legislative and judicial branches of state government. He abolished local government. He ran elections and counted votes. His attorney general could supersede any district attorney in any trial in any part of Louisiana. He controlled the appointment of every cop, every fireman, every teacher in the state. He owned all tax-assessing bodies. He owned the governor, the legislature, the state treasury and all public schools. He held life-and-death power over private business. He could call out the militia whenever he chose. He converted state troopers into his secret police. They did everything he wanted—kidnapped men, held them incommunicado, beat them up, pried into their private lives, tried them on trumped-up charges and found them guilty. All of Louisiana's more than 2,000,000 citizens were completely at his mercy.

Huey's totalitarianism in Louisiana was as absolute as Hitler's in Germany, Mussolini's in Italy and Stalin's in Russia. His brother Julius called him "the greatest political burglar of modern times." Huey Long was America's first dictator *de facto,* the first American demagogue to become a national menace.

Huey knew all about the technique of the big lie. Hitler, writing in *Mein Kampf,* explained it this way: "The greatness of the lie is always a certain factor in being believed; at the bottom of their hearts, the great masses of a people are more likely to be misled than to be consciously and deliberately bad, and in the primitive simplicity of their minds, they are more easily victimized by a large than by a small lie. . . . Some part of even the boldest lie is sure to stick."

As insolent and impudent as Hitler himself, Huey Long denied that he was a dictator. "There is no dictatorship in Louisiana," he said—grinning. "There is perfect democracy there, and when you have a perfect democracy it is pretty hard to tell it from a dictatorship." He described his regime as "the greatest triumph for human uplift and sober government this country has ever witnessed." When a reporter dared to ask Huey whether he was an American Fascist, Huey laughed: "Fine! I'm Mussolini and Hitler rolled into one. Mussolini gave them castor oil. I'll give them Tabasco, and then they'll like Louisiana."

At the end of 1934 Huey declared he had no further political ambitions. Politicians knew better than to accept this remark at face value and were not unduly surprised when Huey subsequently threatened to lead Louisiana out of the union and create an independent nation. Thoughtful men did not laugh off Huey's threat, since there was a precedent for it. In 1861 Fernando Wood, the mayor of New York City, seriously recommended that that city secede from the Union and become a free city. Of course, Huey was so masterful at creating confusion that no one could know whether he was being serious or mischievous.

He declared that Louisiana would never have suffered from the Depression if it had not been a part of the United States. Only because of outside opposition, Huey said, was his state imperfect—forgetting he had called it a perfect democracy. He shrilled: "We've got bureaucrats, autocrats, hobocrats and fifty-seven varieties of 'crats' that are trying not only to run the United States government but sticking their noses into the affairs of individual states. How in hell do you expect Louisiana to progress under present conditions? If I was left alone and Louisiana could get out of the union, instead of the 2,000,000 or 3,000,000 population, we would have maybe 45,000,000 people right here. This state would become the Empire of Utopia."

Remarks such as this were for public consumption. Privately, however, Huey sent three of his men to Washington to ask for federal funds from Harold Ickes, head of the Public Works Program. At a press conference Ickes had said that the trouble with Huey Long was that he had halitosis of the intellect. Now he enjoyed the spectacle of Huey's underlings begging for aid from the administration Huey had attacked. Ickes told them they were committing *lèse-majesté,* since Senator Long had announced that Louisiana needed no assistance from the federal government. When they left Ickes' office they were crestfallen.

Despite Huey's pledge that he had no further political ambitions, he reached out for still more power. With his every word and deed publicized by newspapers and broadcast over the radio, with millions of Americans joining his Share-Our-Wealth clubs, with the intensification of his attacks on Roosevelt and the New Deal, with a change in the name of his personal newspaper from the *Louisiana Progress* to the *American Progress,* Huey became a nationwide menace or messiah—depending on the observer.

Jokingly, he called himself the King of the Ozarks, while others nicknamed him the Pied Piper of Louisiana, the Bonaparte of the Bayous, the Red-necks' Robin Hood, the Karl Marx of the Hillbillies and the Messiah of the Red-necks. Huey cared little what people said about him. When the New Orleans *Item* quit using his name, he sent a delegation to see the editor. "Call me what you will," he is reported to have said, "but use my name." He also snarled, "I'm gonna be President some day," and dictated a book entitled *My First Days in the White House.*

Huey influenced Roosevelt's policies. His radicalism was winning so many millions of Americans to his side that the President told friends he might have to "steal Long's thunder." Roosevelt did this in part, moving to the left politically by promoting an increasing number of liberal measures. Some commentators said the National Youth Administration, to cite one case, was created partly as a result of Huey's pressures. After Huey predicted the demise of both the Democratic and the Republican parties, the Democratic National Committee conducted a secret poll on a national scale and discovered in alarm that he might hold the balance of power in the 1936 election.

On August 13, 1935, Huey announced that he planned to run for the Presidency on the Democratic ticket—or maybe on an independent ticket. Privately he told a crony he had enough cash to finance his campaign. Cocksure of winning, Huey boasted to a reporter that he would be elected President and serve *four* terms; when Americans saw how well he did in the White House, no one would be able to budge him out of it in less than sixteen years.

Other than his plan to share the wealth, Huey had no ideology. "I don't know anything about that kind of thing," he often said. "I haven't any program or philosophy. I just take things as they come." Strange, to say the least, was his concept of democracy: "A leader gets up a program and then he goes out and explains it, patiently and more patiently, until they get it. He asks for a mandate, and if they give it to him, he goes ahead with the program in spite of hell and high water. He don't tolerate no opposition from the old-gang politicians, the legislatures, the courts, the corporations or anybody."

The very month in which he announced for the Presidency he took the Senate floor to declare melodramatically that he had uncovered a plot against his life. Many times previously Senator Wheeler had heard him moan: "They'll kill me, they'll kill me!" No doubt he had been threatened, for Huey had wrecked many a career and family in Louisiana. He drove around Washington with two tough bodyguards carrying shotguns on their laps, toted a gun on his own person, but refused to wear the bulletproof vest designed for him at the request of his secretary. One evening Huey appeared before the "Little Congress," an organization of secretaries to Congressmen, and hardly had begun speaking when a photographer's flashbulb popped; Huey screamed that he had been shot, and the meeting ended in wild confusion that left Lyndon B. Johnson and other secretaries slack-jawed in amazement.

Now, addressing his peers in the Senate, Huey charged that his assassination had been hatched at a secret meeting held in the Hotel De Soto in New Orleans on Sunday, July 21, 1935. He said some of his men had concealed a dictagraph in one of the rooms and recorded comments about "one man, one gun, one bullet." According to Huey, one plotter had said: "Does anyone doubt that President Roosevelt would pardon the man who rid the country of Huey Long?" The Louisiana Senator, standing on the floor of the Senate, went so far as to charge that "Franklin Delano Roosevelt the first, the last, and the littlest" was linked to the plot against his life.

There *had* been a meeting, and the man Huey named *had* been present; but the meeting was not secret, and the men did not plan to kill him. Five Congressmen were among those present. Opposed to Huey Long, they had gathered to select an anti-Long candidate to run for governor of Louisiana. One of the participants was Hodding Carter, a Louisiana newspaper publisher and editor who later won a Pulitzer Prize for distinguished editorial writing. Carter has said: ". . . I was at that meeting. It was a caucus of die-hard oppositionists, dolefully trying to decide what to do for the next state campaign. And the 'plotting' was limited to such hopefully expressed comments as 'Good God, I wish somebody would kill the son-of-a-bitch!' "

One of the few Louisiana legislators who had stood up to Huey as the Senator rammed through his latest election rules was a young man, big-boned and unafraid, by the name of Mason Spencer. Spencer spoke words that still reverberate: "When this ugly thing is boiled down in its own juices, it disfranchises the white people of Louisiana. I am not gifted with second sight, nor did I see a spot of blood on the moon last night, but I can see blood on the polished floor of this capitol. For if you ride this thing through, you will travel with the white horse of death. . . ."

After months of undercover work, Elmer Irey and his treasury agents had found proof that almost every contract let out by the state administration had been shot through with graft and that no income taxes were paid on this boodle. Now the federal government had a chance to get Huey and his associates on charges of income-tax evasion. Dan Moody, a former governor of Texas, was chosen to prosecute them. Meeting in Washington with Irey, Moody told him: "I will go before the grand jury when it meets next month and ask for an indictment against Long."

Moody spoke these words on September 7, 1935.

The next day Huey acted as ringmaster at still another special session of the Louisiana legislature in Baton Rouge. Aware that a Congressional subcommittee planned to enter his state to probe charges about election affairs, Huey prepared a curious law. This made it an offense for anyone to perform, in the name of the United States, a function which the federal Constitution did not specifically authorize.

Huey planned to pass a total of thirty-one bills, which, as he put it, would "put a crimp into Roosevelt's notion that he can run Louisiana."

September 8, 1935, was a Sunday, but Huey and his legislative leaders worked hard all day and into early evening. He circulated about the floor of the House to chat and joke with first one member and then another, sat awhile on the rostrum with House Speaker Allen Ellender, then jumped up and strode out of the chamber. As he left, he shouted his final order of the evening: "Everybody be here in the morning!"

Wearing a silky-looking cream-colored double-breasted suit and black-and-white sports shoes, Huey strode down a corridor to the governor's suite, ducked inside, remained there only a few minutes, walked back out.

As Huey emerged into the marble corridor, a slim young man in a white suit stepped forward, pointed a gun at his right side and fired.

The time was 9:21 P.M.

Huey got a split-second look at the gunman's face and knew he never had seen him before.

A bodyguard named Murphy Roden grabbed the gunman's hand just as the revolver went off. The bullet entered Huey's body just under his right nipple. Roden threw his right arm around the gunman's neck. Roden's leather heels slipped on the marble floor. He fell, pulling the gunman with him. While falling, Roden jerked out his own gun. By the time they hit the floor Roden had fired one shot into the gunman's throat. Roden rolled free. This gave the other bodyguards a clear target. Their .44's and .45's were in their hands. They fired—again and again and again. They poured lead into the prostrate gunman. His body jerked convulsively. Sixty-one bullets ripped into his flesh. He jerked again, gave a massive twitch, slumped dead on the floor. His spectacles had fallen off. He lay facedown.

The moment Huey was hit he grabbed his side with both hands, grunted and cried: "I'm shot!" Then he darted off, all by himself, ran down the corridor to a stairway and reeled down the steps. He spat blood. In the distance he could hear his bodyguards still blasting away at the gunman. Huey was helped into a car and driven to a nearby hospital. During this short trip he muttered: "I wonder why he shot me?"

At Our Lady of the Lake Sanitarium it was discovered that the gunman's bullet had passed through three loops of Huey's intestine, cut away part of his kidney and then emerged from his body. An emergency operation was performed, and for thirty-one hours Huey Long fought for his life. A close friend, aware that Huey would die, asked where he had hidden the cash and documents that Huey intended to use in his Presidential race. Huey whispered: "Later, I'll . . . tell . . . you . . . later." His cache never was found.

The end came a little after 4 A.M. on September 10, 1935. Huey Pierce Long, age forty-two, the first genuine dictator in all American history, was no more.

*   *   *

Huey's assassin had died with his face pressing against the marble floor of the corridor in the State Capitol Building. The chief of the state highway police lifted his head so that the features could be seen. No one recognized the young man. His identity was not established until the coroner came and took the man's wallet out of his pocket. Only then was it learned that he was Dr. Carl A. Weiss, age twenty-nine, a surgeon who lived with his wife and three-month-old son just outside Baton Rouge.

Why did this respectable physician give his life to become Huey's executioner? Over the ensuing months and years several motives were suggested: Weiss was an idealist who mourned the death of democracy in his home state. He had been chosen as the triggerman for a gang of plotters. He felt incensed at Huey's plan to gerrymander his father-in-law out of office as a judge. He was afraid Huey would revive a false rumor that there was Negro blood in the judge's family, and to his Southern mind this would have reflected on his own small son. No one can be absolutely sure why Weiss killed Huey, but perhaps the fear of a racial slur was the strongest motive. Certainly he was not among the "plotters" in the Hotel De Soto; none of the men who attended that meeting had ever heard of him.

On September 9, while Huey hovered between life and death, President Roosevelt issued this short statement: "I deeply regret the attempt made upon the life of Senator Long of Louisiana. The spirit of violence is un-American and has no place in a consideration of public affairs, least of all at a time when calm and dispassionate approach to the difficult problems of the day is so essential."

Dr. Francis E. Townsend wrote in his weekly newspaper: ". . . Newspapers called him a dictator. He met the death of other dictators of the world. But his was a dictatorship of a state by consent of the majority. He was the product of the ballot box, not the bullet. . . ."

The Reverend Charles E. Coughlin called Huey's assassination "the most regrettable thing in modern history."

The day Huey died the New York *Times* put out two extra editions for only the second time in the previous fifty-five years. The United States Senate passed a resolution of sorrow over the death of Senator Long.

The body of Huey P. Long, the self-professed hillbilly, was dressed in a tuxedo and displayed for two days in the main hallway of the skyscraper capitol he had built. From the hills in the northern part of Louisiana and from the swamps to the south, 150,000 men, women and children moved toward Baton Rouge to see their fallen leader, some riding in battered cars and some coming afoot. Scorning the broiling sun, they clogged roads on both sides of the Mississippi River, with automobiles backed up eight miles waiting to cross the waterway on ferries.

Laborers worked around the clock to dig a grave and prepare a vault in a sunken garden in front of the Capitol Building. The day of the funeral the plain people of Louisiana, together with awed and curious sightseers from out of state, massed about the site, some standing on rooftops and some perched in moss-draped oak trees, to watch as Huey Long's body was lowered into the earth. The Reverend Gerald L. K. Smith, organizer of Share-Our-Wealth clubs, preached the funeral sermon, saying in part: "The blood which dropped upon our soil shall seal our hearts. . . . His body shall never rest as long as hungry bodies cry for food, as long as lean human frames stand naked, as long as homeless wretches haunt this land of plenty. . . ." In a mournful minor key, the Louisiana State University band played "Every Man a King."

Huey's widow, Mrs. Rose Long, was appointed and then elected a United States Senator to fill the vacancy left by the death of her husband, serving from January 31, 1936, to January 3, 1937. Their son, Russell B. Long, was elected to the Senate on November 2, 1948. Never before in the annals of this nation had a man, then his widow and later their son served in the United States Senate.

The murder of Huey Long caused concern to Sinclair Lewis, the novelist —a talented mimic who had often given clowning impersonations of the Louisiana dictator. Lewis had just finished writing a timely novel about the advent of Fascism in the United States, calling his book *It Can't Happen Here*. Huey died on September 10. Lewis' novel was due to be published on October 10. From Europe, where he was vacationing, Lewis cabled his publishers, ordering them to change references in his book so they would read "the late Huey Long."

One of the main characters in the Lewis novel was a demagogue named Berzelius "Buzz" Windrip, obviously patterned upon the personality and career of Huey Long. However, in an attempt to avoid a libel suit, Lewis had drawn a red herring across the trail by writing carefully about the real Huey Long and also by describing Buzz Windrip as a grotesque dwarf. In the novel Windrip became the dictator of this nation. *It Can't Happen Here* exploded into a sensational success, total sales running to more than 320,000 copies.

Robert Penn Warren, who once taught English at Louisiana State University, also wrote a novel based on the life of Huey Long. Entitled *All the King's Men,* it depicted the rise and assassination of a politician from the Deep South. In 1947 this book won a Pulitzer Prize, and three years later it was made into a movie. Broderick Crawford, who starred in the film as a thinly disguised Huey Long, won an Academy Award for his performance.

If Huey's life had been spared, would he have run for the Presidency in 1936 or 1940? Could he have been elected President?

Although Huey himself had talked a lot about making the race in 1936, he told friends that "1940 will be my real year." His secretary, Earle Christenberry, agreed that Huey would not have become a candidate until 1940. Three months before Huey's death Supreme Court Justice Louis D. Brandeis had worried privately about Huey's chance of taking over the White House. Norman Thomas, who openly had called Huey a Fascist, had expressed this same fear. Charles Beard, the historian, felt that Huey could have taken part of the so-called solid South away from Roosevelt. Walter Lippmann felt that Huey might have decided the fate of the Roosevelt administration in the 1936 election. Jim Farley told Harold Ickes that he had been worried about Huey's candidacy in 1936. Raymond Gram Swing, a columnist, considered Huey the greatest danger faced by this nation.

Rexford Tugwell said that Dr. Townsend, Father Coughlin and other American demagogues were pygmies compared with Huey Long. Tugwell admitted that Roosevelt had been concerned about Huey. And in a revealing phrase, Tugwell said of Roosevelt: "He must have regarded Huey's removal as something of a providential occurrence. . . ."

*　　　*　　　*

President Roosevelt had first heard about the assassination of Huey Long while lunching at Hyde Park with Joe Kennedy and the Reverend Charles E. Coughlin.

23

Father Coughlin

A FEW DAYS after Roosevelt told Tugwell that Huey Long and Douglas MacArthur were the two most dangerous men in the country, the New York governor got a letter from a friend living in Syracuse. This was in July, 1932. The man from Syracuse reported that the Reverend Charles E. Coughlin was preparing to broadcast some remarks about Mrs. Eleanor Roosevelt and her alleged intention of writing a book on birth control. As a Catholic priest, Coughlin opposed birth control.

Roosevelt replied to his Syracuse friend, saying: "There is, of course, nothing to these stories, but I am taking it up with Father Coughlin, who is a friend of mine." The governor then wrote to the priest: "Dear Father Coughlin: I have received the inclosed [sic] letter, and I am sending it to you with a copy of my reply just for your information. I do hope if you come East you will stop off in Albany to see me. I want to talk with you about many things."

Tugwell may have winced, for he already had become wary of Father Coughlin. But this was at the time when Roosevelt was the Democratic nominee for the Presidency and sought all the help he could get. Coughlin did not belong to Roosevelt's party or any other political party, for that matter. He liked to say: "In politics I am neither Republican, Democrat, nor Socialist. I glory in the fact that I am a simple Catholic priest endeavoring to inject Christianity into the fabric of an economic system woven upon the loom of greed by the cunning fingers of those who manipulate the shuttles of human lives for their own selfish purposes." Coughlin liked lush phrases.

He was far more than "a simple Catholic priest," as Roosevelt very well knew. His regular Sunday broadcasts had made him the most influential figure in the history of the radio. In February, 1932, five months before Roosevelt invited him to Albany, Coughlin had gone on the air to attack

416

President Hoover as "the banker's friend, the Holy Ghost of the rich, the protective angel of Wall Street." This single broadcast brought Coughlin an astounding 1,200,000 letters—most of them favorable. Roosevelt certainly welcomed the support of a man with such an enormous following. But the Democratic candidate, who lived to regret the help he got from Huey Long, did not now foresee that soon he would be on collision course with the powerful priest.

*　　　*　　　*

Charles Edward Coughlin was born on October 25, 1891, in Hamilton, Ontario, the only son of Thomas J. and Amelia Mahoney Coughlin. Both of his parents were descended from Irish immigrants from County Cork. His father was a native of Indiana who did not give up his American citizenship when he moved to Canada, while his Canadian-born mother acquired United States citizenship after her marriage. Thus, although Coughlin himself was born and reared in Canada, he was an American citizen.

The elder Coughlin was a bakery foreman earning $12 a week when his son was born. The boy began his education in St. Mary's, a parochial school in Hamilton, played baseball and football with boys his age, and practiced on the piano. At the age of twelve he was sent to Toronto, 40 miles away, to enroll in St. Michael's College, a part of the University of Toronto. St. Michael's was run by the Basilian order, a congregation of priests who educated young men and prepared them for the priesthood. Mrs. Coughlin wanted Charles to become a priest. The Basilian order traditionally emphasized problems connected with economic justice. Charles developed into an apt student of social philosophy, a skillful debater, and in 1911 he was graduated from St. Michael's with a degree in Honor Philosophy.

After a three-month tour of Europe he went back to Toronto and entered the Basilian novitiate to prepare himself for the priesthood. But when his health began to decline, he interrupted his theological studies for a year and went to sunny Waco, Texas, where he taught philosophy. Finally, in a ceremony held in St. Basil's Church in Toronto in 1916, the twenty-four-year-old Charles E. Coughlin was ordained as a priest in the Roman Catholic Church.

For the next six years he taught philosophy at Assumption College, Sandwich, Ontario, directly opposite Detroit. In 1923 he was brought into the Detroit diocese by Michael J. Gallagher, the Bishop of Detroit. The bishop ordered the young priest to organize a new parish in Royal Oak, a half-developed suburban town 13 miles north of Detroit, starting with the mere thirty-one Catholic families living there. Gallagher gave Coughlin $79,000 to erect a small church at the intersection of Woodward Avenue and the Twelve Mile Road—a site soon to become one of the most important postal addresses in the United States.

The brown frame building was completed in the summer of 1926 at a total cost of $101,000. Because the church was dedicated to St. Thérèse de Lisieux, popularly known as the Little Flower, it took the name of the Shrine of the Little Flower. And two weeks after the shrine opened the Ku Klux Klan burned a fiery cross on its lawn.

Beset by bigots and deep in debt, Coughlin decided to dramatize his problems. A mutual friend introduced him to Leo J. Fitzpatrick, the manager of WJR, a small independent radio station in Detroit. After Coughlin had poured out the story of his woes, Fitzpatrick, also an Irish Catholic, asked whether he would like to make a broadcast. Fitzpatrick said he would give free radio time to the priest if Coughlin would just pay the $58 it would cost to hook up a line the 12 miles between the station and the church. With this kind of technical setup the priest could broadcast directly from his altar. Coughlin ran to Bishop Gallagher, who gave his approval.

One of the most fabulous careers in the history of radio began at 2 P.M., Detroit time, on Sunday, October 17, 1926, when the Reverend Charles E. Coughlin made his first broadcast. He was not quite thirty-five years old. Wearing his vestments, a black biretta on his head, he stood at the altar of the Shrine of the Little Flower and spoke into a microphone suspended near his round face.

Coughlin had a beautiful baritone voice—"one of the greatest speaking voices of the twentieth century," according to a writer named Wallace Stegner. His range was spectacular. He always began in a low rich pitch, speaking slowly, gradually increasing in tempo and vehemence, then soaring into high and passionate tones until veins stood out in his neck and his face reddened as he reached a rhetorical period. His diction was musical, the effect authoritative. His Irish ancestry betrayed itself in the way he trilled his r's, making the word "church" sound like "charrch." He held his e's unduly long—as in "unpreeecedented." Sometimes he mispronounced words. For example, he made "the Treaty of Versailles" sound like "the Treaty of Ver-sales."

Coughlin, like Huey Long, was a man of medium height and stocky build with flesh soon to run to plumpness. The priest had brown hair and beautiful blue eyes behind rimless steel glasses. His moon-fat face was perhaps too smooth, too bland, too pink and genial. Blessed with physical vitality and a magnetic personality, friendly with everyone, a good listener, Coughlin combined priestly piety with brisk worldliness. He paced the floor when talking to guests, chain-smoked cigarettes, played the piano, enjoyed bridge and the theater, wore tailored clothes and sprinkled his conversation with "hells" and "damns." Hugh Walpole, the English novelist, decided after a visit that the priest was "very free in his talk about sex."

Coughlin's first broadcast was an immediate and emphatic success. It was heard not only in Detroit but in several Midwestern states as well, and so many enthusiastic letters poured into station WJR that Fitzpatrick decided to present the priest as a regular Sunday feature. In the early part of his radio career Coughlin spoke only on religious themes, but as his popularity grew and he gained a sense of personal power, he shifted to political topics. Unable to think creatively or even systematically, Coughlin tried to compensate for these deficiencies by indulging in colorful rhetoric. A natural spellbinder and propagandist, he employed all the tricks of their trade. He employed the glittering generality—hoping to lure his listeners into acceptance of an idea without examining the evidence. He stacked the cards—selecting and using facts or falsehoods to present the best or worst possible case for an idea, program, product or person. He posed as just plain folks—describing himself, as we have seen, as "a simple Catholic priest." He stooped to name-calling—carelessly denouncing a wide spectrum of individuals and institutions.

One of his first political targets were Communists. Instead of asking thoughtful questions such as why some Americans were attracted to the Communist philosophy, Coughlin asked pointlessly: "Christian parents, do you want your daughter to be the breeder of some lustful person's desires, and, when the rose of her youth has withered, to be thrown upon the highways of Socialism?" This was as meaningless as the rhetorical question "Do you want your daughter to marry a 'nigger?' " Coughlin continued: ". . . Choose today! It is either Christ or the Red Fog of Communism!" The priest's first book was entitled *Christ or the Red Serpent*. Fog? Serpent? Coughlin seemed to have difficulty in identifying the enemy.

Then the Depression began to engage his attention.

Thomas Huxley once said that Herbert Spencer's idea of tragedy was a theory killed by a fact, and so it was with Father Coughlin. Wildly theorizing, twisting facts to suit his ravaging imagination, the priest started by blaming the Depression on the "international bankers." Not the neighborhood banker, whom people saw daily and with whom they exchanged nods, but the vague and menacing group of high-powered "international bankers." He charged that these "modern Shylocks" were so greedy for profits that they purposely produced an artificial prosperity based on private loans to Europe.

But this was far from the whole story, according to the gospel of Father Coughlin. He linked international bankers with Communists. He declared that "the Jewish bankers, Kuhn, Loeb and Company of New York, were among those who helped to finance the Russian Revolution and Communism." He also warned that "the most dangerous Communist is the wolf in sheep's clothing of conservatism who is bent upon preserving the policies of greed."

Moreover, since bankers dominated capitalism, Coughlin wanted to destroy capitalism as well as the bankers. "I oppose modern capitalism," he said, "because by its very nature it cannot and will not function for the common good. . . . Modern capitalism as we know it is not worth saving." The priest never seemed to realize that in calling for the destruction of capitalism he was echoing the Communists.

Why did so many millions of Americans believe him? A partial answer may be found in a comment made in 1932 by Walter Lippmann: "A demoralized people is one in which the individual has become isolated. He trusts nobody and nothing, not even himself. He believes nothing, except the worst of everybody and everything. He sees only confusion in himself and conspiracies in other men. That is panic. That is disintegration. That is what comes when in some sudden emergency of their lives men find themselves unsupported by clear convictions that transcend their immediate and personal desires."

Like Coughlin, many Americans were disenchanted with capitalism and, consciously or unconsciously, sought scapegoats whom they might blame for their private woes. Because the radio priest's primitive reasoning and guilt-transferring name-calling matched their mood, they listened to him in ever-escalating numbers.

At 7 P.M. on Sunday, October 5, 1930, the Reverend Charles E. Coughlin began making nationwide broadcasts. The Columbia Broadcasting System started airing his talks over a network of seventeen stations, plus an occasional cut-in by other stations, bringing him an audience of 10,000,000 people. As had happened after his first broadcast from a single station in Detroit, the response was overwhelming. Now, seeking to consolidate his expanding power, he organized his listeners into the Radio League of the Little Flower, with himself as president. Anyone could join by mailing him $1. Coughlin called this a charitable organization, although all the charity flowed only to him and his church.

Delighted with his fame, the priest called himself "a religious Walter Winchell." Now he was reaching the largest regular audience of any man in history and receiving 50,000 letters a week. *Fortune* magazine called Coughlin "just about the biggest thing that ever happened to radio."

One of his adoring aides said that "at all times Father Coughlin considered economics as merely a branch of the moral law"—which was an interesting concept. Obsessed with money matters, Coughlin wanted to do away with "the filthy gold standard which from time immemorial has been the breeder of hate, the fashioner of swords, and the destroyer of mankind." His anti-Semitism ever more blatant, Coughlin advanced the curious notion that gold is Jewish currency while silver is Gentile currency. He kept pounding away at the idea that silver is the key to world prosperity. His own prosperity too, apparently, for he ignored his priestly vow of poverty by using one of his secretaries to invest in silver futures.

While Coughlin railed against Wall Street, he was playing the market. In 1929 he used the brokerage firm of Paine, Webber & Company to invest his own funds, and those of his Radio League, in Packard and Kelsey-Hayes stock. In speech after speech he thundered about "saving" America, but he paid no income tax until the year 1931. His explanation for this quaint lapse was that not until then did he have a personal income large enough to tax. He denounced gold but was helped in the preparation of his speeches by a noted gold trader, George LeBlanc, and by a New York cotton broker named Robert M. Harriss.

As Coughlin's broadcasts became ever more intemperate, CBS officials began to worry. Because Treasury Secretary Andrew Mellon opposed the immediate payment of the bonus to the veterans, Coughlin compared him to Judas. He accused three big oil companies of conspiring to restrict the production of American oil. He charged the Federal Council of Churches in America with "abetting the doctrines of Lenin and of advocating the ideals of Bolshevism." At the end of his 1930–31 broadcast season, CBS insisted that Coughlin submit his sermons to their executives in advance of delivery. When he refused, CBS declined to renew his contract. One of the people who sympathized with Coughlin for his troubles with CBS was Franklin D. Roosevelt.

By the fall of 1932, when Roosevelt and Hoover were vying for the Presidency, the priest was back on the air. His friend Leo Fitzpatrick of WJR put together an independent radio chain of twenty-seven stations that reached most of the United States. Coughlin and his Radio League now had to bear the cost, which never fell below $10,000 a week and sometimes rose to $14,000. Now, however, he was heard by more people than had listened to his CBS broadcasts, and eventually he attracted the largest steady radio audience in the entire world.

Free of network censorship, supported by Bishop Gallagher, protected from hecklers by speaking over the radio from inside his church, Coughlin said whatever he chose as he discussed the Presidential campaign. He opposed the reelection of Herbert Hoover. Besides attacking Hoover repeatedly, the priest referred to J. P. Morgan, Andrew Mellon, Ogden Mills and Eugene Meyer as "the Four Horsemen of the Apocalypse." He urged the election of Roosevelt, who was pleased to have his support. And all the while Coughlin repeated his assertion that the solution to the Depression was to switch from the gold standard to the silver standard.

One of Coughlin's worshipful biographers called him "the man most responsible" for Roosevelt's election. The priest himself boasted: "I was instrumental in removing Herbert Hoover from the White House." Like Huey Long, Coughlin expected to be rewarded by Roosevelt, and like Huey, he was disappointed. At the beginning of the Roosevelt administration Coughlin tried to pose as a spokesman for the New Deal, but a politician as crafty and magnetic as FDR did not need this kind of help. William V. Shannon has said that "from 1933 to 1936, the relationship of Coughlin and Roosevelt passed through the classic stages of all uneasy alliances: from cooperation to coexistence to conflict." During the first phase, Coughlin praised Roosevelt time and again, predicting that he would rank with the great American Presidents, describing him as being twenty years ahead of his time, announcing that "the New Deal is Christ's Deal," shouting "it is Roosevelt or ruin!"

Meantime, using $500,000 contributed by his radio audience, Coughlin moved his small frame church down the street in Royal Oak. On its former site he erected another church, this one made of marble and granite and sandstone, this one seating a congregation of 2,500. This handsome new edifice was built in the shape of a cross, enabling every worshiper to get a clear view of Coughlin at the altar. Its most distinctive feature, a blunt Crucifixion Tower, was 100 feet tall, 30 feet square, and girded on each side by enormous crosses. Irreverent people called the tower the silo. Coughlin was so grateful for the continuing approval of his superior, Bishop Gallagher, that he had the bishop's facial features carved into a stone statue of St. Michael. One of the priest's followers called this "a sly but beautiful gesture on Father Coughlin's part." Unimpressed officials of the American Federation of Labor censured Coughlin for building his new Shrine of the Little Flower with nonunion labor, some of it Canadian, and paying wages below the union scale.

After the dedication of his new church Coughlin lived in a bungalow not many yards away, and at 3 A.M. on March 30, 1933, his home was bombed. The glass was broken in every basement window, a steam radiator was torn from the ceiling, and damage was done to canned food kept in the basement for distribution to the poor. Royal Oak police and Detroit detectives never discovered who touched off this bomb.

The Depression had hit the Detroit area faster and harder than any other city in the nation. In the winter of 1929–30 the Red Cross declared that the blackest spot in the entire country was southern Oakland County, in which Coughlin's church was located. In the wake of the Crash few Americans had the money to buy new cars, so there was a decline in the production of automobiles. In 1931 alone 150,000 people moved out of Detroit. Its mayor, Frank Murphy, declared that the city was "in ashes," its people were "dead broke" and the metropolis was "a political ruin." Murphy, who happened to be an Irish Catholic, became friendly with Father Coughlin, praising the priest's "grand voice" and his "spirit and interest in our problems."

Earlier, in the summer of 1930, five Congressmen had arrived in Detroit to hold a two-day hearing in the Federal Building into the activities of Communists in that city. Some witnesses believed there were from 1,500 to 5,000 Reds in Detroit. Father Coughlin, a self-styled expert on Communism, was among those invited to testify. Instead of launching an attack on Communism, as expected, the priest startled everyone by attacking Henry Ford instead. Folding his arms upon the table before him, Coughlin said: "The greatest force in the movement to internationalize labor throughout the world is Henry Ford."

Asked to explain, the priest went on to say: "A year ago, on the eve of the Automobile Show in New York, Mr. Ford issued a statement that was printed on the front page of every daily newspaper in the United States, that he required 30,000 more workers at his plant in Detroit. As a result of that statement, more than 30,000 men who were out of work flocked to Detroit from Alabama, Mississippi, Tennessee, Texas and other Southern states and, while the weather was at zero, stood in front of the Ford plant trying to get those jobs. There were no jobs for them, and the only redress they had was to have a fire hose turned on them to drive them away."

Such an act, Coughlin concluded, embittered workers against all capitalists and incited them to listen to the teachings of Communism.

Hamilton Fish, Jr., the committee chairman, nervously asked: "Getting all those men here in that manner was not done on purpose, was it?"

"No," Coughlin replied. "It was done through ignorance."

*   *   *

Coughlin approved of most of President Roosevelt's financial policies. Among other things, this included the Silver Purchase Act of 1934, which established a hybrid monetary standard of mixed gold and silver. However, the priest felt that the President did not go far enough. Coughlin wanted Roosevelt to nationalize all banks—which would have pleased his enemies the Communists. He also wanted him to abolish the Federal Reserve System; but this system had been independent of the President since its inception, and Roosevelt had no intention of tampering with it. Coughlin demanded "a nationally-owned banking system as sound as our army and as honest as our post office."

Arthur M. Schlesinger, Jr., has said: "Coughlin was, of course, more correct than the orthodox economists of 1932 in his preference for inflation over deflation. His plea for monetary management was defensible. Certainly these were fairly basic issues. But his economics were nonetheless rudimentary, specious, and incoherent. . . ."

Whenever Coughlin was unable to get his way, he reacted like a spoiled child by calling people names. Down through the Thirties he attacked a mixed bag of individuals such as J. P. Morgan and David Dubinsky, Carter Glass and Upton Sinclair, Bernard Baruch and Joseph T. Robinson, John D. Rockefeller and Frances Perkins.

The priest never had much use for Huey Long's Share-Our-Wealth program. The Michigan demagogue and the Louisiana dictator met a few times and, in a figurative sense, circled and sniffed warily at one another. Coughlin was delighted when the United States Supreme Court quashed one of Huey's laws intended to enslave newspapers. Huey, for his part, told Emile Gauvreau: "I think there's a menace in what Father Coughlin is doing. I agree with a lot of his points, which he swiped from me, but there's something dangerous in the political outcries of a priest. If religion ever sinks to the level of politics, God help us!"

J. David Stern, who published a small string of newspapers, dropped into the Mayflower Hotel in Washington to visit Huey and found Coughlin in Huey's suite. In his broadcasts Coughlin had quoted from some of Stern's editorials, while Huey had read many of them into the *Congressional Record*. That morning Stern found Huey wearing purple silk pajamas and sprawled on his bed. Coughlin was pacing up and down the room, head bowed, hands clasped behind his back, muttering again and again: "I fear there will be a revolution! I fear there will be a revolution!" Suddenly Huey leaped from the bed shouting: "Hell, what I'm afraid of is that there *won't* be a revolution!" Stern said he left the room "with the sickening sensation of a man who has just discovered that his friends are out of their minds."

Coughlin established the Social Justice Publishing Company, Inc., to publish his own newspaper called *Social Justice*. According to the Michigan Corporation and Securities Commission, this company was a corporation set up "for pecuniary profit." He also created the Social Justice Poor Society, Inc., "to relieve sick and destitute persons and to perform such charitable acts as may come before the Society." But this second corporation turned out to be just a holding company for *Social Justice* stock.

The women of Coughlin's parish eagerly joined the society to do all they could to alleviate the distress of their neighbors. Men lucky enough to have jobs let their wives take food to the church, and some of these provisions, as we have seen, were stocked in the basement of Coughlin's bungalow. Local firemen and policemen put barrels in grocery stores to solicit the offerings of people able to buy their own food. Among Coughlin's congregation were men who made trips out into the surrounding countryside to buy vegetables or to beg farmers to donate produce to the society. During his broadcasts the priest appealed for help and contributions came from distant places. A carload of beans was shipped from Boston to Royal Oak. Various mills sent truckloads of flour. The society even paid the rent for some impoverished people.

One Sunday Coughlin said over the air: "If those who are walking the streets of Greater Detroit tonight—hungry and cold and penniless—will come tomorrow to the Shrine of the Little Flower, we will feed and we will clothe you." This broadcast was heard, among other places, in Chattanooga, Tennessee, and the Chattanooga *News* remarked: "We thought of Greater Detroit's horde of 100,000 unemployed, and we pictured that horde marching, like an army with terrible banners, on the tiny Shrine of the Little Flower. . . ."

They came, not by the tens of thousands, true, but by the thousands, and Coughlin opened his church to all of them. He and his hardworking parishioners served as many as 600 people at one meal. With this single broadcast Coughlin had overextended himself, strained his resources, the arrival of thousands of outsiders watering down his relief program until it gave substantial help to almost no one. His record of feeding people never matched that of the Negro mystic and conman Father Divine, who had hit on the idea of persuading his followers to give him their wages.

Dr. C. H. Benning, the health officer of Oakland County, told Coughlin that owing to lack of milk, the health of many local schoolchildren was declining. What the county needed, the doctor said, was $15,000 to establish a milk fund. Coughlin offered to help by calling a mass meeting in a civic auditorium to launch a drive to collect the needed sum. "Although my personal means are limited," said the silver-owning priest, "I will give five dollars each week to help out." The meeting was held, and the drive begun; but unemployment was so widespread in Royal Oak that few familes could afford to donate. At a second public rally, Coughlin said his church would give $7,500 if others would raise the balance. His offer was so stimulating to campaign workers that they collected a matching sum, and soon 1,200 needy children began getting daily rations of milk.

* * *

By now Father Coughlin was called the Shepherd of the Air and the Teddy Roosevelt of the American Priesthood. In the early part of 1934 radio commentator Harlan E. Read of radio station WOR in New York City conducted a poll to determine which public figures Americans most revered. Read specifically excluded President Roosevelt. When WOR's popularity contest was over, it was found that Father Coughlin had been voted the nation's most useful citizen in the year of 1933. The runner-up was General Hugh S. Johnson, head of the NRA. Even so, Walter Lippmann doubted whether this was an accurate way of judging Coughlin's influence, since only 22,000 people had voted in the WOR poll.

Despite Lippmann's skepticism, Coughlin by this time had become a powerful national figure. His regular Sunday broadcasts were heard by about 10,000,000 people, and in a normal week he received some 80,000 letters—as many as 500,000 after an especially provocative talk. In another poll, Philadelphia radio station WCAU found that 187,000 of its listeners tuned in to Coughlin's sermons while only 12,000 preferred to listen to the New York Philharmonic.

His loyal followers were the urban lower-middle-class Irish Catholics, the German Catholics of the East and Midwest, small homeowners, debt-ridden farmers and blue-collar workers. They were fanatical in their devotion. For a long time, however, Coughlin did not seem to know precisely what he wanted to do with all this power. Upon becoming convinced that Roosevelt would not kill the Federal Reserve System and nationalize the banks, Coughlin felt like breaking with the administration. Still, he was not sure whether he could do so and maintain his popularity in the face of the President's massive popularity. Roosevelt, sensing Coughlin's indecision, assigned two devout Catholics, Joseph P. Kennedy and Frank Murphy, the chore of trying to keep the priest in line.

Meantime, the Treasury Department had been compiling a list of Americans who were speculating in silver. In the spring of 1934 Secretary Morgenthau began releasing their names. One of those named was Miss

Amy Collins, treasurer of Coughlin's Radio League, who had been speculating in silver with the funds the priest solicited from his radio audience. Coughlin was holding 500,000 ounces of silver in the hope that the price would rise, and this meant that he had more silver than anyone else in Michigan. Cynics quickly nicknamed his church the Shrine of the Silver Dollar. Coughlin attacked Morgenthau and angrily denied that he owned any silver whatsoever.

Throughout the rest of 1934 Coughlin feinted at Roosevelt, backed away, feinted again. At one moment he accused the New Deal of catering to high finance and big business, while at another he declared he would support the New Deal so long as he retained the power of speech. Then, testing public opinion, he began to criticize both major political parties, snarling that they should "relinquish the skeletons of their putrefying carcasses" to a museum. Still unsure of himself, he sensed that each Sunday he had to deliver an ever more sensational sermon in order to keep his vast audience on the increase, and at last he cast away all restraint. Washington, D.C., he smirked, was fast on its way to becoming "Washingtonski."

Hugh Johnson counterattacked, comparing Coughlin to Hitler and calling him a menace to the nation.

In November, 1934, the month in which Huey Long became Louisiana's dictator, the priest announced the formation of his own movement, called the National Union for Social Justice. This was not a third political party, Coughlin declared, but merely a nonpolitical lobby. The union's stated objective was the protection of the masses against "domination of and exploitation by powerful vested interests."

The union was incorporated on December 22, 1934, its headquarters were established in Royal Oak, and Coughlin became its president. More than half the members of the board of trustees had Irish names, and the union's first major rally was addressed by three Irish-American Representatives of Congress—Thomas O'Malley of Wisconsin, William Connery, Jr., of Massachusetts, and Martin L. Sweeney of Ohio. The new organization soon set up units in many states, and before long Coughlin claimed more than 1,000,000 members.

Having created a political base for himself, Coughlin now broke openly with Roosevelt. He ranted that the President was "willing to hand over the reins to the United States Chamber of Commerce and the international bankers." The gentlemen within these categories only wished that this were true. Then, in a bumbling analogy, Coughlin said that Roosevelt's effort to save capitalism was as hopeless as "removing in a sieve the water from the Atlantic ocean to the swimming pool in the New York Athletic Club." According to the priest, private capitalism was a Siamese twin, with Socialism as its brother. He called for "class co-operation"—a guiding doctrine of Nazism and Italian Fascism that was used as an excuse for destroying all other political parties in Germany and Italy. He urged that the United

States be reorganized into a "corporate state"—which was what Italy had become under Mussolini.

Coughlin highly approved of Italy's invasion and conquest of Ethiopia, as did publisher William Randolph Hearst; the priest socialized with Hearst in California and often stayed at the Hearst-owned Hotel Warwick when in New York. Aware of Coughlin's political stance, the Socialist Party in the United States warned farmers and laborers against building a third party with the priest as its leader. Percy L. Gassaway, a Democratic Congressman from Oklahoma, openly denounced Coughlin.

The radio priest attacked Representative John J. O'Connor, a Manhattan Democrat and chairman of the House Rules Committee, for delaying a vote in the House on the new Frazier-Lemke bill. The original Frazier-Lemke Act had been intended to help farmers by granting them five years in which to pay off mortgages but the Supreme Court had held that it was unconstitutional. The authors of the measure had then drafted a new bill limiting the moratorium to three years.

Congressman O'Connor was so enraged by Coughlin's attack that he wired the priest: "I can guarantee to kick you all the way from the Capitol to the White House, with clerical garb and all the silver in your pocket which you got by speculating in Wall Street."

On February 18, 1936, O'Connor arose in the House before a crowded gallery to make an impassioned defense of his career and reputation. He berated Coughlin for abusing his trust as a priest and entering politics. Summarizing Coughlin's attacks on him, the Manhattan Democrat asked: "How much of that can you stand? Just because you are a member of Congress, just because you belong to the same church, do you have to take that?" The House roared its approval of O'Connor. Then the Democratic majority whip, Representative Patrick J. Boland of Pennsylvania, personally congratulated O'Connor, adding: "I, too, have a reputation at stake and I do not propose to allow any gentleman under the garb of religion to attack me without putting up a battle to fight him off!"

Boston, with its concentrated Catholic population, was perhaps the strongest Coughlinite city in the nation. This was true despite the antipathy toward Coughlin voiced by Henry Cardinal O'Connell, the Archbishop of Boston. Regardless of the cardinal's own conservatism, he had spoken out against Coughlin, saying: "You can't begin speaking about the rich or making accusations against banks and bankers, or uttering demagogic stuff to the poor. You can't do it, for the church is for all." The cardinal cautioned his own flock not to be "whisked off their feet by spectacular talk, mostly froth, but with some poison in it. . . . We do not like to hear almost hysterical addresses from ecclesiastics."

Coughlin, a mere parish priest, had the audacity to snap back at the cardinal. He reminded his radio audience that the cardinal held no jurisdiction outside his own archdiocese of Boston; that he could speak only as an individual, not as a prince of the church; and that the cardinal should do

something about promoting the welfare of the people instead of hobnob-
bing with the rich. Coughlin's impudence dismayed some Catholics, but he
got away with it. "It would be egotistical for me," Coughlin said, "to
disclose the confidence which Bishop Gallagher has oftentimes spoken to
me about my broadcasts." Like any other crafty politician, Coughlin made
this disclosure while pretending he was not disclosing it.

Bishop Gallagher, the priest's immediate superior, promptly defended
Coughlin. "Christ was not setting class against class when he rebuked the
abuse of wealth," said Gallagher. To accuse Coughlin of stirring up class
bitterness was to "accuse the popes and to accuse Christ." It was interesting to hear a bishop compare a priest to Christ. Gallagher went on to say
that if Coughlin had lived in Russia before the revolution, "and had he
possessed the radio facilities," there probably would be no Communism in
Russia today.

In a moment of rare candor, Coughlin said of himself: "Do you know
how I would live if I renounced religion and was illogical enough to dis-
believe in a life beyond—in the real life? Why, if I threw away and
denounced my faith, I would surround myself with the most adroit hi-
jackers, learn every trick of the highest banking and stock manipulations,
avail myself of the laws under which to hide my own crimes, create a
smoke screen to throw into the eyes of men and—believe me!—I would
become the world's champion crook!"

A man is the sum of his fantasies.

During the Massachusetts primary of April, 1936, several persons wrote
in the name of the Reverend Charles E. Coughlin as their choice for
President of the United States. But could a man of the cloth really rise to
political power in a nation? It has happened. History contains many
precedents—the corrupt and sensual Popes who dominated Italy, the
shrewd and worldly Jesuits who manipulated French kings, the grim God-
fearing ministers who made a theocracy of early New England. Admittedly,
these were shaky precedents, since they obtained in other centuries and in
vastly different cultures. Could a Catholic priest win control of the pre-
dominantly Protestant United States of America in the 1930's? Who could
tell? Coughlin kept shouting that this nation faced "a contest between
Christ and chaos," and many Americans believed him.

With the appproach of the 1936 Presidential campaign, some people
began to worry about what might happen if Coughlin were to unite his
National Union for Social Justice with the remnants of Huey Long's Share-
Our-Wealth Society and the Townsend movement.

24

Dr. Francis E. Townsend

I SHALL TELL YOU what sold me on old age insurance—old age pensions,"
Franklin D. Roosevelt told a campaign crowd in Detroit on October 2,
1932.

"Not so long ago—about ten years—I received a great shock. I had
been away from my home town of Hyde Park during the winter time and
when I came back I found that a tragedy had occurred. I had had an old
farm neighbor, who had been a splendid old fellow—supervisor of his
town, highway commissioner of his town, one of the best of our citizens.
Before I left, around Christmas time, I had seen the old man, who was
eighty-nine, his old brother, who was eighty-seven, his other brother, who
was eighty-five, and his kid sister, who was eighty-three.

"They were living on a farm. I knew it was mortgaged to the hilt, but I
assumed that everything was all right, for they still had a couple of cows
and a few chickens. But when I came back in the spring, I found that in the
severe winter that followed there had been a heavy fall of snow and one of
the old brothers had fallen down on his way out to the barn to milk the
cow, and had perished in the snow drift.

"The town authorities had come along and had taken the two old men
and had put them into the county poorhouse, and they had taken the old
lady and had sent her down, for want of a better place, to the insane
asylum, although she was not insane but just old.

"That sold me on the idea of trying to keep homes intact for old
people. . . ."

*   *   *

In late autumn of 1933, about a year after Roosevelt made this speech,
an elderly physician was shaving in the bathroom of his home in Long
Beach, California. Happening to glance out a window and down into an

alley, he saw three old women clawing through garbage cans in search of food. The doctor froze, his razor suspended in midair. Then, cold horror turning to fury, he cursed savagely—curses he'd learned in his youth as a cowboy, miner and hobo.

His oaths frightened his wife, who ran into the bathroom crying: "Doctor! Oh, you mustn't shout like that! All the neighbors will hear you!"

"I want all the neighbors to hear me!" the old man raged. "I want God Almighty to hear me! I'm going to shout till the whole country hears me!"

This was the moment that was to transform Dr. Francis Everett Townsend into a figure of national stature. Besides the pity he felt for the old women picking through garbage, he was frightened about his own future. He was sixty-six years old, unemployed, and had less than $100 in savings. His nineteen-year-old son was working on a farm in the Midwest, the doctor and his wife went day after day without a penny coming in, and every time they had to buy anything they knew they were steadily eroding their bank account.

At a later date Dr. Townsend said: "I was an old man. I mean that literally. I was tired and worn out and just about ready to roll over and call it a day."

He felt he was too old to work, but he still had the right to vote—and think. Farmers were plowing under cotton and slaughtering hogs with the blessings of the federal government. Dr. Townsend sat down and began an open letter:

> . . . It is just as necessary to make some disposal of our surplus workers as it is to dispose of our surplus wheat or corn or cotton. But we cannot kill off the surplus workers as we are doing with our hogs. . . . It is estimated that the population of the age of 60 and above in the United States is somewhere between nine and twelve millions. I suggest that the national government retire all who reach that age on a monthly pension of $200 a month or more, on condition that they spend the money as they get it. . . . Where is the money to come from? More taxes? Certainly. . . .

This first rough draft of the famous Townsend Plan was published in the Long Beach *Press-Telegram* on September 30, 1933. The letter evoked considerable interest, which was not surprising since Long Beach had many old, retired Midwesterners whose savings had been wiped out in the Crash. Some wrote the local paper to comment on Townsend's proposal, and he scrupulously replied to each published letter. Within a few weeks the *Press-Telegram* was devoting a full page every day to opinions about the "ridiculous" or "sublime" Townsend Plan. Then a few elderly people began visiting the doctor's home, where he patiently explained his idea, and before long they urged him to launch a campaign.

The following November the doctor opened modest headquarters in a small room in the rear of a real estate office. Digging down into his modest savings, he paid to have a tiny advertisement published in the paper, asking idle old people to distribute some petitions he had had printed at his own expense. The petitions, addressed to local Congressmen, requested them to try to get the Congress to pass two laws which would put the Townsend Plan into effect. Some of the doctor's former patients, penniless and starving, eagerly agreed to help, as did many other old folks with nothing but time on their hands. Picking up the petitions in his office, they started trudging through the city streets.

Pensions were nothing new in American history. The first pension act was passed in 1636 by the Plymouth Pilgrims, who promised that any soldier maimed in the line of duty would be cared for by the colony the rest of his life. In 1776 the Continental Congress enacted a pension measure for the benefit of officers and privates. In 1923 Montana and Nevada became the first states to pass old age pension laws. In 1932, as we have seen, Franklin D. Roosevelt thought about old age pensions before the idea occurred to Dr. Townsend. In 1933 eleven more states enacted this kind of welfare measure. By 1934 a total of twenty-seven states had some sort of pension plan on their statutes.

Townsend was unimpressed. "Before our appearance on the scene," he said, "old-age pensions in America were limited to supreme court justices and their widows; police, firemen, war veterans and other such organized pressure groups also received pensions. The little people were not organized as a pressure group, so they were left out in the cold."

Within two weeks Townsend's volunteer workers got thousands of signatures on his petitions. His movement mushrooming faster than he had expected, the old doctor now turned for help to Robert E. Clements, his former boss and present landlord. Townsend had tried his hand at selling real estate for Clements, who owned the office building in which the doctor rented a tiny room. Born in Texas, now thirty-nine years old, Clements was a hard-boiled real estate promoter. Always chasing a fast buck, his eyes narrowed thoughtfully when he saw the long list of signatures brought in by Townsend's people. Maybe he could help shape Townsend's program into a structured and profitable organization. Yeah, he would help the old boy. But the main thing, he told the doctor, was to keep this enthusiasm "at a high pitch."

On January 24, 1934, Townsend and Clements and Townsend's brother (a porter in a Los Angeles hotel) incorporated a new nonprofit California corporation called Old Age Revolving Pensions, Ltd., with Doc Townsend as president and Clements as national secretary. This was the month in which Huey Long organized his Share-Our-Wealth Society.

*   *   *

Francis E. Townsend, like Huey Long, was born in a log cabin. He entered this world on January 13, 1867, on his father's farm in north-central Illinois three miles east of the village of Fairbury—at that time part of the frontier. He attended rural schools, soaked up books and memorized his favorite passages. His father seldom handled more than $100 a year in cash, and the boy wore patched and faded clothing. As he approached his eighteenth birthday, his father sold the farm and moved to Franklin, Nebraska, where he bought into a hardware store.

Franklin had a Congregational academy which young Townsend attended for two years. Instead of staying until he won a diploma, he left to wander through the West, becoming a farmhand, cowboy, miner and hobo. When this aimless existence failed to satisfy him, he went back to Franklin, reentered the academy and was graduated in 1893 at the age of twenty-six. Restlessness drove him away again, however, but during his second venture into the wide world he ran up against the depression of the 1890's. After digging irrigation ditches, riding the rails, homesteading, teaching school and selling kitchen ranges, he finally decided that he needed a profession.

In 1899, at the age of thirty-one, he enrolled in the Omaha Medical College. One of his professors was an ardent Socialist who encouraged him to think about social issues. Townsend later said his teacher gave him the hope that "in a poverty-free world we might see an end to vice and disease." For a while Townsend thought of himself as a Socialist. In 1903 he was graduated from the medical school in the first class ever produced by the University of Nebraska.

That same year the fledgling physician went to Belle Fourche, South Dakota, a hamlet of 450 inhabitants on the north slope of the Black Hills, to take over the practice of a doctor who wanted to spend a year studying in Germany. The departing doctor left a nurse named Wilhelmina Mollie Bogue, a widow four years younger than Townsend and the mother of a nine-year-old daughter. In 1906 Townsend married "Bogie," as he called her. He had remained a bachelor until he was almost forty.

For sixteen years Townsend struggled along as a frontier doctor, writing squibs for the local paper and acquiring three farms of 160 acres each. At the age of fifty-two his health began to fail, so he moved to Long Beach, California. There he picked up such a meager practice that he supplemented his small income by selling building lots for Clements, managing to survive this way from 1919 until the Crash of 1929. Then he was fortunate enough to be hired as an assistant city health officer, and in this capacity he witnessed the beginnings of the Depression from the inside.

In clinics and in private homes, Dr. Townsend saw "such distress, pain and horror, such sobbing loyalties under the worst possible circumstances." But what deeply touched him was the hopelessness of the old people—their "spiritual panic," as he put it. He experienced his own personal panic in 1933, when a new city administration took office and he lost his municipal job. And it was in the fall of that year that he saw the three desperate old women turned scavengers.

*   *   *

Dr. Townsend was a skinny old man. His face was long and lean, ridged with high cheekbones, seamed with age lines and set in a bony jaw. His hair and tiny mustache were linen-white, but his spectacles were overhung with black eyebrows. He wore a stiff, high old-fashioned collar and dressed conservatively. Most of the time he was mild-mannered and soft-voiced. He called his wife Mother, and she and all their friends addressed him as Doctor. He lived in an ordinary house, played cribbage, and the general opinion was that Dr. Townsend was as plain as an old shoe.

But the pull of power twisted his life into new patterns. After his volunteer workers collected 75,000 signatures in Long Beach alone, after elderly people from coast to coast began writing to him, Dr. Townsend declared that "no such crusade as ours has been seen on this earth in two thousand years." By September, 1934, Townsend and Clements needed a staff of ninety-five just to handle the mail flooding in. Clements, who took the title of co-founder of the movement, organized Townsend's followers into an autocratic body rigidly controlled by Townsend and himself.

They moved their headquarters from Long Beach to Los Angeles, founded a weekly newspaper to promote the Townsend Plan and began organizing Townsend clubs. Membership cost 25 cents a year, and each new member received a copy of an eighteen-page pamphlet describing the plan. The first club was put together on August 7, 1934, in Huntington Park, a small community south of downtown Los Angeles. Each club was supposed to consist of 100 members. Clements, who knew more about organizational work than Townsend, divided the nation into districts, each with its own headquarters.

Neither the districts nor the clubs had any degree of self-government. They obeyed orders handed down from the overall governing board, which bore the grandiloquent title of Citizens Maximi. All the lowly faithful were given speakers' manuals, Townsend buttons, Townsend stickers, Townsend tire covers and Townsend automobile plates. At club meetings they sang songs such as this:

> Onward pension soldiers
> Marching as to war,
> With the plan of Townsend
> Going on before.
> This great pension leader
> Bids depression go.
> Join him in the battle;
> Help to fight the foe.

Such a noble crusade appealed to the 9,000,000 or 10,000,000 Americans who were sixty years of age or older. Convinced that Dr. Townsend would get the monthly pensions of $200, these old folks freely contributed to the cause, some mailing him their contributions in dimes and pennies. A few foolish and fanatical people sold all they owned and gave most of their profits to the movement. By the end of 1934 there were some 1,200 Townsend clubs in existence, most located in Western states.

Since 1927 the fight for more and better old age pensions had been waged in this nation by the American Association for Social Security. Becoming alarmed about the Townsend Plan, which it considered unworkable and dangerous, the association now came out publicly against the zealous doctor. AFL President Green criticized Townsend, while Dan Tobin of the teamsters' union reported that his members were asking whether they should form Share-Our-Wealth clubs. But nothing could lure Townsend's followers from the path of righteousness and riches.

Stanley High, an editor and a liberal Methodist preacher, wrote the White House about the Townsend movement: "The more I see of it the more I am impressed with its power. It is doing for a certain class of people what—a few years ago—was done by the prohibition movement; giving them a sublimation outlet."

Townsend's devotees were mostly lower-middle-class people, Anglo-Saxons, Fundamentalist in religion and either Republicans or without any formal political affiliation. A majority were elderly, of course, but some young people joined the movement in the hope that they would be relieved of the care of their aged parents. Townsend himself said he won over people "who believe in the Bible, believe in God, cheer when the flag passes by—the Bible Belt, solid Americans."

Indeed they were ardently religious and superpatriotic. Club meetings began with the singing of "America," a short prayer and the pledge of allegiance to the flag of the United States. Commonly displayed was a banner saying GOD IS LOVE. When Dr. Townsend was introduced—often as "the world's greatest humanitarian"—he would hold up his bony-fingered hands for silence, look out over the audience and then say simply: "I like you people very much." This, as E. B. White has remarked, "was like a handclasp, a friendly arm placed round the shoulder. Instantly his listeners warmed and smiled, and wriggled with sudden newfound comfort." As a boy the doctor had been fond of old-time hymns, and these became a regular part of every Townsend meeting. Audiences often interrupted him and other speakers with cries of "Amen!" The Michigan district published a bulletin describing Townsend as "the man whom God raised up to do this job." One Townsend leader was a Baptist minister, Dr. Clinton Wunder, who declared that "God is with us, and with God all things are possible."

So it seemed to Townsendites. Many local newspapers, especially those in rural areas, regularly published items about the activities of Townsend club members. Here and there across the land the enraptured believers began exerting pressures, boycotting merchants who refused to put Dr. Townsend's picture in their shopwindows or who declined to circulate their petitions to Congress. Governors, Senators, Representatives and everyone planning to run for high office received letters demanding that they state exactly where they stood in regard to the plan. At public meetings speakers were heckled by Townsendites and some let themselves be bullied into commitment.

One conservative Congressman became alarmed at the volume of petitions flowing from the voters in his district. Upon checking, he found that almost every businessman in his home town had signed up in favor of the Townsend program. He went back home, visited the merchants and asked whether they really liked this Townsend thing. They replied, hell, no! They just signed because so-and-so, who had stuck the petition under their noses, was a regular customer, and they wanted to keep his trade.

In some stores all salesmen vanished whenever an old person entered. Many merchants were boycotted after they refused to give credit to old folks who said they would pay him back when they got their pension checks. San Francisco's immigration office was crowded with elderly aliens demanding naturalization before the Townsend Plan became law. Old folks rushed to railroad stations to get estimates for trips they expected to make when they received their checks. Announcing that they knew they would get their first check the following month, one elderly couple asked a store to send them a stove, refrigerator, kitchen cabinets, twin beds and other furnishings.

In January, 1935, only a year after incorporating his organization, Townsend wrote to co-founder Clements: "You and I have the world by the tail with a downhill pull on this thing, Earl, if we work it right." At about this same time the once-modest physician wrote his autobiography. It contained an interesting parenthesis. Townsend said: "I had become an old dog (spelled backwards) to a lot of people. . . ."

*　　*　　*

In November, 1934, a heavy Townsend vote sent to Congress seventy-two-year-old John S. McGroarty, a lawyer, author and poet laureate of California. "From then on," as Townsend said, "we stayed up to our necks in national politics." On January 3, 1935, McGroarty took his seat in the House as a Democrat from California. Thirteen days later he presented the Seventy-fourth Congress with the first Townsend Plan bill, numbered HR 3977. Considered a revenue measure, it was referred to the House Committee on Ways and Means. On February 1 Dr. Townsend went to Washington and stepped into the national limelight by appearing before this committee to explain his plan.

He began by saying his proposal was only incidentally a pension plan. Its two main objectives were to solve the unemployment problem and to bring back prosperity by restoring purchasing power to the people. Upon reaching the age of sixty, every citizen would get $200 a month from the federal government, provided: (1) that he or she retire from a paying job; (2) have no criminal record; (3) have no income other than this $2,400 a year; (4) spend the entire $200 each and every month. A man and wife over sixty would get a total of $400 a month. Although there were about

10,000,000 Americans sixty years old or older, Townsend thought that only about 8,000,000 would qualify for pensions. The money would come from a 2 percent tax on every commercial transaction. Each month the secretary of the treasury could make out forty-eight checks, one to each state. These big checks would then be broken up by state administrators who would pay the money to qualified pensioners.

Congressman Robert Doughton, chairman of the House Ways and Means Committee, asked whether Townsend was sure the tax he proposed would raise the necessary funds. Townsend replied: "I'm not in the least interested in the cost of the plan."

Others felt differently. If Townsend were correct in his guess that 8,000,000 people would qualify for the pension, and if each received $2,400 a year, the cost of the plan would be enormous. It would run to $19.2 billion, plus the cost of administration, or about $20 billion a year.

"This sum," Walter Lippmann pointed out, "has to be raised by a general sales tax. Retail sales this year have been about thirty billion dollars. So the Townsend plan would have meant that for every dollar any one spent in a store this year, he would have to pay an additional seventy cents tax. Thus, for example, a ten cent loaf of bread would have had to cost seventeen cents, a twenty-cent gallon of gasoline would have had to cost thirty-four cents, a six hundred dollar car would have had to cost over a thousand dollars."

Some experts felt that not just 8,000,000 but 10,000,000 people would qualify for the Townsend Plan. If this were the case, the program would cost not $20 billion a year but $24 billion. This greater sum was twice as much as all existing federal, state and local taxes combined. It was about half the total national income. In other words, the Townsend Plan would give half the national income to the one-eleventh of the population over the age of sixty.

A 2 percent levy on every commercial transaction would tax every servant, every waiter, every beautician, every barber, every telephone call, every radio, every theater ticket, every circus, every book, every lecture, etc. The Townsend tax would have been an extra tax added to every existing federal, state and local tax on these transactions and items. The Townsend tax would pyramid like compound interest. It would ruin most businesses. Since failure to spend the $200 each month would become a punishable offense and since many pensioners might hoard part of their money, the government would have to create an army of informers to make sure that every cent was gone by the end of the month. The final result could be a police state.

Townsend's testimony before the committee did nothing to promote his proposal; the committee refused to order the McGroarty bill out for a vote. The following April 1 McGroarty introduced an amended bill which abandoned the flat $200 promise in favor of pensions as big as the reserve fund would permit, but not to exceed $200 a month. However, even this amended bill was pigeonholed and died in the Ways and Means Committee.

Congressional defeat of his plan enraged Townsend, but only slightly more than its criticism by Labor Secretary Perkins, Interior Secretary Ickes, former President Hoover, Socialist leader Norman Thomas, former New York Governor Al Smith, professional economists, tax experts, university professors, well-informed Senators and others.

"Every time a brain truster says this plan is crazy," Townsend snapped, "a hundred thousand new converts come to our banner. . . . I myself am not an economist, for which fact millions of people have expressed thanks. . . . God deliver us from further guidance by professional economists!"

His Congressional stooge, Representative McGroarty, added: "I refuse to talk to college professors. Give me the names of some practical people."

President Roosevelt, who had sanctioned attacks on the Townsend Plan by his Cabinet members, refrained from making any public comment. He also declined to meet Dr. Townsend. When the doctor sought a White House appointment, he was invited to meet Frances Perkins instead of the President. The *Townsend Weekly* regarded this as "an insult that the masses of the people should resent," a sign that "we have aristocracy in the White House—not democracy."

In January, 1935, Townsend and Clements had founded the *Townsend National Weekly* with an initial press run of 25,000 copies. Eleven months later, having picked up more readers and many patent medicine advertisements, circulation soared to 310,047 copies. Although the paper was created as the official periodical of Old Age Revolving Pensions, Ltd., ownership was not vested in the organization but in Townsend and Clements personally. Each held 50 percent of the stock. Townsend, less greedy than Clements, felt that profits should go to the movement, but Clements had convinced him that the founder and co-founder should split the take.

Despite Townsend's failure to prove the worth of his plan to Congress, only a month after his appearance in Washington it was rumored that he planned to run for election as President of the United States. Next came word that Townsend—like Huey Long and Father Coughlin—hoped to sunder the two major political parties. Townsend issued a public statement denying that his organization would try to upset either the Republicans or Democrats; he said his only interest was to support Congressional candidates who backed his plan. However, only two days later Townsend reversed himself by offering to replace the two-party system. He was already on record with a denial that he hoped to join forces with Coughlin.

The first national convention of Townsendites opened on October 24, 1935, in the Stevens Hotel in Chicago. It was attended by 6,993 delegates representing 4,552 Townsend clubs. Speaker after speaker praised the

Townsend Plan, and everyone present vowed to support all Congressional candidates chosen by Townsend and Clements. President Roosevelt was repeatedly attacked, one Townsendite claiming: "If only he would spend as much time looking after the welfare of the people as he does playing on his yacht, he might be of more help."

Roosevelt was being helpful, regardless of what the Townsend people thought of him. Working long and hard, he persuaded the Congress to pass a Social Security Act that became the law of the land on August 14, 1935—two months before the first national Townsend convention. The assumption of national responsibility for general Social Security, as Henry Steele Commager has said, constituted a notable chapter in the history of federal centralization in the United States. The act enabled the states to make more adequate provisions for the aged, the blind, dependent and crippled children, maternal and child welfare, public health and the like.

Dr. Townsend told his followers at the Chicago convention that the new Social Security program was "wholly unfair, inadequate and unjust." It did leave millions of elderly Americans unprotected, and the Townsend movement fed on this fact.

By the end of 1935 Townsend had at least 10,000,000 supporters. This was more than the 9,000,000 members Huey Long had claimed for his Share-Our-Wealth Society, and now Huey was dead. Presidential adviser Raymond Moley wrote in December: "Townsendism is easily the outstanding political sensation as this year ends." Economist E. E. Witte said: "The battle against the Townsend Plan has been lost, I think, in pretty nearly every state west of the Mississippi and the entire Middle-Western area is likewise badly infected." In another warning to the White House, Stanley High said it would be a mistake to try to laugh off the Townsend movement in the coming election year. And Townsend's associate, Clements, boldly declared the Townsendites would hold the balance of political power in 1936.

The danger erased by the death of Huey Long had been revived in another form by Dr. Townsend.

*   *   *

Columnist Raymond Clapper said that Townsend had Congress scared within an inch of its life. Senators and Representatives were afraid that in the 1936 election they might be defeated by ambitious men riding on Doc Townsend's coattails. A New York *Times* reporter named Nicholas Roosevelt, a fifth cousin of the President, agreed that it would be foolish to underestimate the movement's political power.

A former national publicity director of the organization accused Townsend and Clements of corruption, providing worried politicians with precisely the opportunity they sought. In February, 1936, apparently with the tacit approval of President Roosevelt, a House committee of Democrats and Republicans alike voted to investigate Townsend and Clements.

Both major parties felt threatened by the movement, but neither cared to antagonize voters by accepting sole responsibility for doing it in. Therefore, after the House committee agreed to the probe, Democratic and Republican leaders in the House itself organized a special committee consisting of four Democrats and four Republicans. An eight-man committee was an oddity, since most had an uneven number of members. Furthermore, in the hope of blunting accusations that this committee was trying to frame Dr. Townsend, one Democratic member of the special committee, and one Republican, were open advocates of Townsend.

The eight-man committee chose as its chairman C. Jasper Bell, a Democratic Representative from Missouri who owed his election to Tom Pendergast, the political boss of Kansas City. Raymond Clapper said: "This Congressman was chosen for the risky task of busting Townsend because, being safe in the arms of the Pendergast machine, he did not need to fear being defeated for re-election by outraged Townsendites."

But despite all the pussyfooting and political maneuvering, or perhaps because of it, Clements immediately charged that he and Townsend were being persecuted. McGroarty, the Townsend-owned Congressman, criticized Bell's appointment as committee chairman. Sheridan Downey of California, once a lieutenant of Upton Sinclair and now Townsend's attorney, asked the committee to delay its hearing for two weeks on the grounds that Townsend was ill. Federal agents seized all documents in the national and state headquarters of the Townsend movement and impounded them for use at the hearing.

Clements, who privately and cynically called the Townsend movement "the racket," was subpoenaed to appear before the committee on March 24, 1936. He immediately resigned as second-in-command. Some people believed Townsend demanded his resignation because of differences between them regarding finances. A week later McGroarty also withdrew from the Townsend movement. The good doctor said in a national broadcast that the departure of these two men had strengthened his cause, but many listeners were unable to understand his logic. It was beginning to appear that Townsend strength had never been as potent as some politicians had been scared into believing.

Clements' resignation did not get him off the Congressional hook, however; he was forced to testify before the committee. He counterattacked by accusing Townsend of failure to account for $1,700 in collections. Under oath, though, Clements admitted that the Townsend organization had paid for his—Clements'—own rent, food and servants. At last the committee decided that although Clements had not broken any law during his two and a half years with the organization, he had profited by $79,000.

Then Townsend took the stand.

He testified reluctantly, for he felt that this investigation had become "a national circus" and was "a fake trial." Glaring at the committee members, he declared that the Roosevelt administration was responsible for this modern-day inquisition. When he complained about the committee's tactics, one member asked him to be more specific. "It has appeared to me from the beginning," Townsend replied, "that this committee is more interested in besmirching my character than in learning about the virtues of my movement." He especially resented the fact that he had been told to confine his answers to a mere yes or no.

After two days on the stand Townsend let his attorney know he refused to take any more "bullyragging" and planned to walk out. Sheridan Downey strongly advised him not to do so, but the tough old man was determined. On May 21, 1936, a beautiful spring day in Washington, Townsend sat down at his portable typewriter in the Lafayette Hotel and pecked out a statement he planned to read to the committee. Then he and Downey and two others rode a cab back to the Capitol for the afternoon session.

In the hearing room Congressman Bell asked him to take the stand again. Townsend said that before doing so, he wanted to read a statement. Bell asked to see it. Instead of showing the paper to the chairman, Townsend began reading aloud. Bell interrupted to say that if he wanted to make a statement, he could submit it to the committee in writing. Townsend's prepared speech began with the reminder that he had testified under oath that he never profited personally from his movement, and it went on to say that in point of fact the committee had failed to prove him guilty of any wrongdoing. Now, prevented from reading his statement aloud, Townsend said the committee was unfair and unfriendly, he refused to testify further and was leaving.

"Thank you and good-bye, gentlemen."

The doctor got up and started for the door. Committee members blinked in surprise. For a moment or two there was dead silence in the room. Then some spectators began applauding. A couple of Townsend associates sprang forward to convoy the doctor past the people and out an exit. A big cop planted himself in Townsend's path. Bell shouted: "Stop that man! Hold him, officers! Don't let him out!" A huge hawk-nosed man let out a Rebel yell, leaped to Townsend's side and helped push him past the guards and out into the corridor. This was Huey Long's former organizer of the Share-Our-Wealth Society, the Reverend Gerald L. K. Smith, a self-proclaimed leader searching for another cause. Until that moment Townsend had never seen Smith.

Just outside the Capitol there was a cab. Into it jumped Townsend, his two aides and the uninvited minister. Upset and tired, the doctor did not wish to return to the Lafayette Hotel, where reporters would doubtless descend on him, so he told the cabby to drive them to Baltimore. Upon arriving in that city, they visited H. L. Mencken, the writer and so-called sage of Baltimore, who had described Gerald L. K. Smith as "the gustiest and goriest, the deadliest and damndest orator ever heard on this or any other earth—the champion boob-bumper of all epochs."

*   *   *

After Huey Long's assassination Gerald Smith had tried to take over the Share-Our-Wealth movement but was thwarted by Huey's political heirs. Although the public regarded Smith as Huey's chief disciple, the insiders scorned him as a mere hired hand. Smith tried to magnify his reputation by saying Huey had died in his arms, which was a lie. Huey's lieutenants had become rich on graft and knew they could not fool the people into believing they wanted to maintain a program which might deplete their own fortunes. Huey's secretary, Earle Christenberry, sold the Share-Our-Wealth membership rolls to the Townsend movement, and when Smith heard this news, he realized he had been left out in the cold.

But now that Clements had resigned from the Townsend movement and now that Townsend himself felt persecuted, Smith thought he had found another opportunity. He would latch onto Townsend. The hot-eyed rabble-rouser had made sure he was present in that Congressional hearing room when Townsend walked out of it and into his open arms. Smith later confessed to a reporter that he pursued Townsend "like a bridegroom still trying to catch up with my bride."

The day after he had spurned the committee, Townsend said publicly that he did not intend to amalgamate his movement with any other, but by the end of May he was won over by Smith's persuasiveness. Appearing together at Valley Forge, Pennsylvania, the lean physician and the burly minister announced they were joining forces. Although Townsend had never had any serious Fascist leanings, Smith betrayed his dictatorial yearnings by declaring: "Dr. Townsend and I stood under the historic arch at Valley Forge and vowed to take over the government."

It was at this time, in the early summer of 1936, that Father Coughlin entered the picture. Regarding Townsend as a fool and Smith as a knave, Coughlin had denounced the Townsend Plan as "economic lunacy." Townsend, for his part, felt that Coughlin's National Union for Social Justice lacked any "definite program for achievement." But Townsend did agree with Coughlin's wish to replace the Federal Reserve System with a central bank. Regardless of their differences, Townsend, Coughlin and Smith all had one thing in common: They wanted to make sure that Roosevelt lost the 1936 Presidential race, and they thought the way to ensure this was by banding together into a third party.

Time and again Coughlin had said he was against the formation of a third party. Even so, his representatives began negotiating with Townsend and

Smith, and on June 16 Smith let the cat out of the bag. Always seeking headlines for himself, Smith on that day announced the formation of a Coughlin-Townsend-Smith-Lemke united front with "more than twenty million votes" and unified by common opposition to "the communistic philosophy of Frankfurter, Ickes, Hopkins and Wallace."

25

The Third Party Movement

FRANKLIN D. ROOSEVELT was well aware that he might have to buck a third party when he sought reelection in 1936.

As early as February 16, 1935, the President wrote a letter to Colonel Edward M. House, former adviser to Woodrow Wilson, saying that some Republicans were flirting with Huey Long "and probably financing him." Buoyant as ever, though, Roosevelt added: ". . . but when it comes to Show-down these fellows cannot all lie in the same bed and they will fight among themselves with almost absolute certainty."

The President had a slight acquaintance with the man toward whom Coughlin, Townsend and Smith now turned—William Lemke. In 1936 Bill Lemke was a fifty-eight-year-old Republican Congressman from North Dakota. Born in Minnesota, he had worked his way through the University of North Dakota and the Yale Law School, was admitted to the bar in 1905 and then began practicing law in Fargo, North Dakota.

From 1917 to 1921 Lemke was a member of the national executive committee of the National Nonpartisan League—a curious organization. Founded in 1915 as a kind of protest subparty within the Republican Party, it dominated North Dakota politics for more than two decades. Anyone could join the league if he was a farmer and could pay the $16 membership fee. Because of the many reforms the league advocated, it was almost a precursor of the New Deal.

Lemke believed wholeheartedly in its program. As a lawyer, as the state attorney general and then as Congressman from North Dakota, he did all he could to help the farmers of that state. Two-thirds of its farms were foreclosed between 1929 and 1936. Lemke was passionately devoted to the idea of initiating new bankruptcy and refinance proposals.

It had been in January, 1932, that Lemke's friends first urged him to run for Congress. Because he belonged to the league, he had to campaign as a nominal Republican, although he liked Roosevelt better than Hoover. FDR, seeking all the help he could get to win the Democratic nomination and then the election, agreed to let Lemke visit him. Lemke showed Roosevelt a statement explaining his monetary ideas, and Roosevelt said: "Yes, yes, I am all for that." Lemke left with an even more favorable impression of Roosevelt, and during the 1932 campaign Lemke was regarded by FDR's advisers as "the chief strategist of the Nonpartisan League in his state."

Lemke's financial theories actually differed from Roosevelt's—a fact which became quickly apparent after Lemke was elected to Congress and Roosevelt became President. A mere freshman in the House, Lemke naïvely expected the new President to consult him about major fiscal policies. When Roosevelt failed to include Lemke in his decision-making circle, the North Dakota Congressman reacted with surprise, disappointment and frustration. Lemke was also disappointed with the administration's farm bills emphasizing the control of production. Working with Lynn J. Frazier, a Republican Senator from his home state, Lemke pushed through Congress the Frazier-Lemke Farm Bankruptcy Act, which was approved on June 28, 1934.

Lemke's obsession with monetary policies to aid farmers won him a reputation in Congress as the "madman from the sticks." While it was true that he was eccentric, it was equally true that he was genuinely devoted to the public welfare. He had one glass eye, a long face pitted with smallpox scars, and he went for days without shaving. He neither smoked nor drank, probably because of his Lutheran background. Clad in ill-fitting clothes and a gray cloth cap, Bill Lemke looked like a farmer. In his high-pitched voice, however, he could dazzle his peers with a barrage of statistics. He knew more about economics than most Congressmen but repelled some of them with his messianic air.

When Roosevelt failed to support Lemke's inflationary measures and continued to exclude him from the New Deal's policy-making sessions, the rejected Congressman turned on the President. Father Coughlin knew all about Lemke's disaffection. The priest, who had endorsed Lemke's refinance bill, kept in touch with the North Dakota Congressman through Louis B. Ward, Coughlin's aide in Washington. And about the time that Coughlin joined forces with Townsend and Smith, the priest started thinking of bringing Lemke into their third party movement.

*   *   *

On July 15, 1936, in the midst of a heat wave, 11,000 elderly men and women gathered in Cleveland for the second annual Townsend convention. Most delegates were prim and plain, the women shunning rouge and lipstick and wearing print dresses and flat shoes, the men in shirt sleeves and pants held up by suspenders. Nervously guarding their coin purses, carrying box lunches under their arms, they sat down in an auditorium where Alfred Landon of Kansas had won the Republican Presidential nomination a few weeks earlier.

They began by singing some old-time hymns, and then they listened to a denunciation of the Roosevelt administration by their leader, Dr. Townsend. Two months previously the House of Representatives had voted to cite Townsend and two of his assistants for contempt because of their defiance of the committee investigating the Townsend Plan. He had invited all Presidential candidates to come to his convention to express their views, but the only one who accepted was Norman Thomas. Thomas looked down at the old men and women, slumped in their seats, stunned by the heat, and felt sorry for them. He began his speech by expressing sympathy for all Americans who had arrived at an advanced age with so little economic security. Applause.

The tall spare Socialist then went on to tell the Townsendites why their plan would fail. He said that masses of citizens would be unwilling to pay more to people for not working than to people with jobs. Boooo! Townsend jumped up and requested his followers to listen respectfully. Norman Thomas grinned and suggested that if the audience would let him finish a sentence or paragraph, then they might feel free to boo. After that, he would say a few words; the people booed; he resumed; they booed again. Their hostility climaxed when he told them that the Townsend Plan was like "treating tuberculosis with cough drops."

But when the Reverend Gerald L. K. Smith ambled onto the platform in a blue shirt and coat, this dark mood lifted. Cunningly, he started by saying he had heard of a plot to break up his speech. Now what he wanted to know was this: How many of those present would promise to hang anyone who interfered? Up shot every hand in the hall. A group of old men and women were pledging themselves to violence, to murder.

Swinging into a wild attack on the New Deal, Smith roared that his "real mission" was "to see that the red flag of bloody Russia is not hoisted in place of the Stars and Stripes!" Pounding the lectern with his right fist, brandishing a Bible in his left hand, Smith poured it on, booming out sneers and challenges, pausing now and then to drink from a pitcher of ice water, shedding his coat, sweating until his blue shirt was sopping wet, ending some of his rhetorical periods with the command: "Give that a hand!" And they did—beating their palms together until they hurt. Smith bellowed that old Doc Townsend's enemies had scoffed at all of his followers as the "lunatic fringe," but now this "lunatic fringe" was about to "take over the government!" The frenzied delegates screamed: "Amen! Amen! Amen!"

Among the reporters covering the convention was H. L. Mencken, who had entertained Townsend and Smith in his Baltimore home. A connoisseur of tub-thumping oratory, Mencken described Smith's tirade as "a magnificent amalgam of each and every American species of rabblerousing, with embellishments borrowed from the Algonquin Indians and the Cos-

sacks of the Don. It ran the keyboard from the softest sobs and gurgles to
the most ear-splitting whoops and howls, and when it was over the . . .
delegates simply lay back in their pews and yelled. . . . Never in my life,
in truth, have I ever heard a more effective speech."

But when Smith shut up and sat down, no one could remember exactly
what he had said.

Smith's swift rise to power inside the Townsend movement had been
especially resented by two Townsend leaders, Sheridan Downey of California and Gomer Smith of Oklahoma. Unlike most Townsendites, both
were Democrats. Gomer Smith, a onetime farm boy who had become an
able lawyer, now took the platform to attack Gerald Smith and to defend
the Roosevelt administration. Although Gomer Smith did not tear off his
coat or brandish a Bible, he also indulged in some strong-lunged old-
fashioned revivalism. He maintained that the President was a "church-
going, Bible-reading, God-fearing man," a "golden-hearted patriot who had
saved the country from Communism." The very people who had cheered
Gerald Smith's attack on Roosevelt now cheered Gomer Smith's defense.
This worried Doc Townsend. According to Father Coughlin, Townsend
hurriedly called the priest to come to his rescue.

This man of the cloth, who once vowed, "I will never change my
philosophy that the New Deal is Christ's Deal," was not a man of his
word. Now he swooped down on Cleveland like an avenging angel. These
demagogue-worshiping delegates to the Townsend convention were about
to have their guts twanged to the new tune he was calling.

For the first forty minutes of his speech Coughlin sweet-talked them,
assuring the old folks that their comfort and welfare were very dear to his
heart. Mencken noted that Coughlin had "developed a habit of enforcing
his point by revolving his backside." Then the speaker sashayed his
remarks into criticism of the New Deal, into a denunciation of the man in
the White House, into a no-holds-barred attack on "the great betrayer and
liar, Franklin D. Roosevelt!" Reporters gaped at the spectacle of a Roman
Catholic priest publicly calling the President of the United States a "liar."
But the audience howled its approval. Aping Gerald Smith, the priest shed
his black coat, tore off his clerical collar and spat out a series of insults. He
sneered at "Franklin Double-crossing Roosevelt!" He offered a cynical new
slogan: "Roosevelt *and* Ruin!" His listeners went berserk with delight.
When Coughlin asked how many of those present would follow Dr.
Townsend and himself into the Union Party, they leaped and struggled out
of their seats crying that they would, they would, they would!

Thanks to Coughlin's help, Townsend beat down a revolt within his
movement and won ever more publicity for his campaign against Roosevelt. Townsend club members lacked the technical right to endorse any
Presidential candidate chosen by the National Union for Social Justice, of
course, but the way had been smoothed for the blessing of Bill Lemke. At

the close of the Townsend convention Coughlin, Townsend and Gerald Smith posed as a cozy trio for photographers.

Smith's last contribution to the convention was the dangerous suggestion that 100,000 Townsend youths band together as storm troopers to guard the polls on election day.

* * *

One month prior to his dramatic appearance at the Townsend convention, Coughlin had secretly handpicked Lemke as the Presidential candidate of his National Union for Social Justice. Despite his intemperate oratory, the priest was enough of a political realist to know that Lemke would be unable to defeat either Roosevelt or Landon. What the priest hoped to do was to embarrass Roosevelt, even if he had to embarrass Lemke himself in the process. The North Dakota Congressman was such a baby on the national political scene and so naïve that he let Coughlin dub him "Liberty Bell" Lemke. In other words—cracked. Gerald Smith, for his part, sneered at Lemke as "a colorless, inadequate little fellow." Seldom has any candidate received such dubious support from his backers.

Although this third party movement was supposed to be an alliance of Coughlin's followers, Townsend's followers and Smith's followers, in point of fact all power was kept in the hands of Father Coughlin. It also may be remembered that when Coughlin formed his National Union, he denied that it was a third political party, calling it merely a nonpolitical lobby. On August 14, 1936, members of this so-called lobby met in Cleveland with most of the trappings of a full-blown political convention.

The priest's first appearance upon the platform touched off a stormy demonstration. One woman shrilled, "Two, four, six, eight—whom do we appreciate? *Father Coughlin!*" Then she beat a reporter over the head with her handbag and shrieked curses at other journalists in the press section. Coughlin stoked the fire of this hot belief that he and his followers were the victims of press prejudice.

"So much misinformation has been spread about my beliefs in the Tory bank-controlled press," he told the delegates, "that the time is ripe for me to reveal once and for all just what I believe and do not believe about money. I will talk in short sentences and speak slowly so that the representatives of the press will have no trouble in following me."

Glaring at the reporters, the delegates booed.

If the journalists had had any difficulty understanding Coughlin's theory about money, it was not because they were inept but because he had changed his mind. Instead of scorning "the filthy gold standard" and insisting that silver was the key to world prosperity, Coughlin had now turned his attention to the Federal Reserve System and its power to create money based on the business loans of its member banks. The priest's new line was that Federal Reserve notes were "fictitious money."

With the use of a contraption that might have been designed by Rube

Goldberg, Coughlin's point was dramatized by the Reverend L. A. Tobin, pastor of St. Catherine's Church of Vernon, New York. A huge board was lugged out onto the platform. This board had one big light bulb and six small bulbs. It was explained that the big bulb represented the Federal Reserve System. The six little ones were the businesses that feed the system.

Father Tobin turned on the little bulbs. The big bulb, sapping the current from the small ones, glowed brighter and brighter. The big bulb (the Federal Reserve System) was draining the little bulbs (businesses). This, said the priest, demonstrated the evils of the present banking system. Now here was what Father Coughlin would do to remedy this situation: The priest turned off the big bulb. As a result, all the small bulbs became ever more brilliant until their combined radiance exceeded that of the big bulb when it had been on.

At the end of this profound object lesson all the delegates roared their approval.

As for the real business of the convention, Coughlin managed everything like a puppet master. The delegates were told to adopt a National Union constitution without even seeing it; they were assured they could read its provisions in a forthcoming issue of Coughlin's magazine, *Social Justice*. They voted as ordered.

The new constitution established the union's national headquarters in Royal Oak, empowered Coughlin to appoint members of the board of trustees, gave him the right to pick members of the nominating committee, who then would select candidates for president and vice-president of the organization. But there was only one candidate for president—Coughlin— and in whiz-bang fashion he was nominated and elected. Coughlin despised majority rule, which he spoke of contemptuously as "the magic of numbers." Behaving like a dictator himself, he tried to pin the label of dictator on Roosevelt, who once said: "Majority rule must be preserved as the safeguard of both liberty and civilization."

Coughlin, who acted imperiously and recklessly because of the size of his radio audience, now claimed that 6,000,000 people belonged to his National Union for Social Justice. All that was required to become a member was to mail a postcard to him. Basking in the worship of his mesmerized delegates, the priest forgot his charge of "liar" and his subsequent apology to the President. Now he openly called Roosevelt a Communist and declared that FDR was "anti-God." He also ranted that the choice between Democrats and Republicans was one "between carbolic acid and rat poison."

The only alternative to Roosevelt or Landon, according to Coughlin, was his own candidate for President of the United States—Bill Lemke. Although Lemke's friends worried about the priest's slanderous remark that Roosevelt was "anti-God," the North Dakota Congressman came to the Coughlin convention and made a speech offering himself as a Presidential candidate. The delegates endorsed Lemke by a vote of 8,152 to 1.

The sole dissenting vote was cast by John O'Donnell of Pittsburgh, who took the floor to say that he was all for Father Coughlin and social justice but did not like to see the delegates victimized by "mob psychology." Charles J. Madden, a delegate from Pennsylvania, then apologized to everyone for O'Donnell's dissent.

Drunk on dreams of power, perhaps deluding himself, Coughlin foolishly promised: "I will discontinue radio broadcasting if I do not swing at least nine million votes to Lemke." But in the ensuing campaign the priest did about all he could to contribute to the defeat of his candidate. When he failed to give Lemke all the money he had promised, Lemke had to set up and finance his own national headquarters. Posters advertising Union Party rallies printed Coughlin's name in big type and Lemke's name almost imperceptibly. Coughlin made speech after speech without even mentioning Lemke.

As the election neared, as it became obvious that Lemke would not even run a good third to Roosevelt and Landon, the priest's tirades sharpened. He cried: "As I was instrumental in removing Herbert Hoover from the White House, so help me God I will be instrumental in taking a Communist from the chair once occupied by Washington!" He called Roosevelt "the dumbest man ever to occupy the White House." He accused Frances Perkins, Cordell Hull, Harold Ickes, Henry Morgenthau and Rexford Tugwell of being Communists. He declared that "every international banker has Communist tendencies." He warned that "this is our last election." He said that if he had to choose between Communism or Fascism, he would "take the road of Fascism." Ending one fiery speech with praise of Christian brotherhood, the priest roared: "I challenge every Jew in this nation to tell me that he does or doesn't believe in it!" Then he collapsed.

All this was too much for the Vatican's official newspaper, *L'Osservatore Romano,* which rebuked Coughlin. Even his loyal bishop, Michael J. Gallagher, deplored some of Coughlin's remarks about Roosevelt but praised his general policies. Bishop Gallagher went to Rome, conferred with Pope Pius XI about Coughlin, then denied there was any papal curb on the radio priest. *L'Osservatore Romano* coldly said that the bishop's reported claim that the Holy See approved of Coughlin's activities did not "correspond with the truth" and that the bishop knew "quite well what he was told on the subject." As a result of this, Gallagher hinted that Coughlin would be tamed. Infuriated, the priest exhibited a telegram from his bishop denying any kind of restriction on his activities.

The third party movement failed.

In the 1936 election Roosevelt was reelected when he got more than 27,000,000 votes while his Republican opponent, Alf Landon, won only 16,000,000 votes in the greatest political landslide in all American history. Lemke received a mere 882,479 popular votes and not a single electoral vote. Where were the "more than twenty million votes" which Gerald L. K. Smith had boasted about? Where were the 9,000,000 votes pledged by Coughlin?

For a change, Coughlin was true to his promise by quitting broadcasting —temporarily. Then he came back on the air and developed into an overt anti-Semite.

The *New Republic* commented: "The American Hitler may have died with Huey Long, but the Paul Joseph Goebbels of Royal Oak believes his successor will come."

26

Droughts and Dust Storms, Okies and Vigilantes

H UBERT H. HUMPHREY never forgot the days of drought and dust
storms: "God, it was terrible! . . . So hot, so terribly hot. . . .
The dust, it was everywhere. . . . There was a desolation, a drab-
ness. . . . The sky and horizon—dull and bleak. . . . Hope would leave.
. . . You didn't want to stay, but there was no way to leave. . . . You
felt trapped. . . ."

Humphrey was born in the prairie town of Wallace, South Dakota, in
1911. When he was four, the family moved to Doland, also in South
Dakota, where he grew up. Because of the plight of the farmers, the
Depression hit Doland in 1927, two years before the Crash, and Humphrey's father had to sell the family home. In 1929 young Humphrey went
to Minneapolis to enter the University of Minnesota. His father's drugstore
business became so bad that customers were unable to pay in cash and
bartered farm produce for the medicine they needed. After two years at the
university the son left it to go back home and try to help his father, but the
two of them could not make a go of it, so finally the elder Humphrey gave
up, moved the family to Huron, South Dakota, and opened a new drugstore
there. That was in 1931.

By this time a series of droughts had begun to parch far-flung areas of
this country while dust storms were blowing away the top soil. And each
year conditions got worse. On November 11, 1933, when Hubert Humphrey was twenty-two years old, a gigantic dust storm raged over the
western plains states from the Texas Panhandle up to the Canadian border.
Its effect on the 470-acre Karnstrum farm in Beadle County, South
Dakota, was described by R. D. Lusk in an article in the *Saturday Evening
Post*:

By mid-morning a gale was blowing, cold and black. By noon it was blacker than night, because one can see through night and this was an opaque black. It was a wall of dirt one's eyes could not penetrate, but it could penetrate the eyes and ears and nose. It could penetrate to the lungs until one coughed up black. If a person was outside, he tied his handkerchief around his face, but he still coughed up black; and inside the house the Karnstrums soaked sheets and towels and stuffed them around the window ledges, but these didn't help much.

They were afraid, because they had never seen anything like this before. . . .

When the wind died and the sun shone forth again, it was a different world. There were no fields, only sand drifting into mounds and eddies that swirled in what was now but an autumn breeze. There was no longer a section-line road fifty feet from the front door. It was obliterated. In the farmyard, fences, machinery and trees were gone, buried. The roofs of sheds stuck out through drifts deeper than a man is tall.

The next day this black blizzard darkened the sky over Chicago, and the day after that it shrouded Albany, New York.

At a later date Hubert Humphrey said: "I learned more about economics from one South Dakota dust storm than I did in all my years in college."

In the Huron drugstore the father and son noted that as dust storms became more common, people bought more remedies for stomach ailments and constipation. Hubert understood why. Time and again his own belly churned and ached, his face paled, he felt nauseated, and then he fainted. The family doctor put him in the hospital and ran a series of tests, but after being in and out of the hospital several times, Hubert was told he had nothing physically wrong with him. The young man developed a lifelong habit of vigorously dusting everything within reach.

Sullen, disgusted, feeling trapped, Hubert went about his work mechanically, eager to get back to college, to escape a prairie turning into a desert. Seventy-two dust storms in South Dakota in one year—this was too much. One day, unable to control the ferocity building up inside himself, Hubert smashed a dozen glasses in the sink behind the drugstore counter. His father watched with sad eyes. Hubert adored his father, but even this deep love was not enough to hold him in South Dakota. The elder Humphrey, sympathizing with his brilliant son and wishing to ease his tensions, offered him half ownership in the family business. Hubert replied: "I can't stay. These dust storms—I just can't take them any more! I'm so tense I'm sick all the time. I get these pains, and I know it's because of the worry. But the depression, the dust, the drought—they're wearing me out!"

*　　　*　　　*

The droughts of the 1930's—worldwide in scope—were the worst in the nation's history. Their effects were felt in twenty-two states constituting almost three-fourths of the land area of the United States. Thousands of people died from heat and hundreds from dust pneumonia. The black dirt that once carpeted South Dakota blew away to become new topsoil in Indiana and Illinois. Dust storms originating in the Western states swirled all the way to the Eastern Seaboard, out into the Atlantic, and deposited grit on the decks of ships 200 miles at sea. In a single day 50,000,000 tons of topsoil blew away. Before this prolonged natural disaster ended near the end of the decade, severe damage had been done to more than one-sixth of the once-fertile earth across this country. And the havoc was worst in the plains states.

The grasslands begin in Ohio and extend westward to Illinois, where they develop into the central plains. When the first white man reached the interior, the central plains were a sea of grass, some of it higher than a tall man. Still farther west the grass did not grow so high. The Great Plains themselves start about 400 miles east of the Rocky mountains and sweep more than 1,000 miles north and south, from Canada to Mexico.

The eastern half of the country is humid while the western half is dry, this aridity increasing every few miles as one moves toward the setting sun. The winds blowing eastward over the Rockies have almost all their moisture squeezed out before they reach the Great Plains. Very little moisture from the Gulf of Mexico can reach this rain shadow of the Rockies. The semiarid West is sometimes wet, but any sporadic bounty of moisture is certain to be balanced off by a long period of almost total rainlessness. In that part of the United States weather and water are prime topics of conversation, since they are matters of life and death.

In the Mississippi Valley total precipitation is about 40 inches a year, but in the Great Plains it is a scant 8 to 20 inches. While the 1920's had been years of relatively high moisture in the grasslands, after 1930 the rains stopped coming. No longer did farmers see gully washers, as they called heavy rains. Just about the time the Depression began, so did the drought. By 1931 the Midwest needed a foot of rain.

At first the plainsmen met this developing disaster with humor, one of them drawling: "A raindrop hit a fellow over in the next county yesterday, and they had to throw three buckets of dirt on him to bring him to." The story was told about a rancher who hauled a load of gravel to his house one day and that night threw it on the roof to let his children learn the sound of rainfall.

In the grasslands there were three kinds of agriculture—the grazing of livestock, irrigation and dry farming. Dry farming is the use of methods suitable to the growth of crops in semiarid or dry climates; for example, in one-crop dry farming half the land is allowed to lie fallow each year to accumulate moisture, while furrows must be plowed farther apart than elsewhere. The drought struck at a time when the prairie already was in bad shape for a variety of reasons. The land had been overgrazed by cattle and sheep. By 1930 more than half of all state-controlled irrigation districts had failed. The soil had been eroded by wind and water. It was exhausted after generations of careless cultivation. Too much of the prairie had been plowed up to plant wheat, this sodbusting breaking the skin of soil covering the earth.

Then came the grasshoppers. First appearing in 1931, they scourged Iowa, Nebraska and South Dakota. That year and following years they swarmed by the billions over millions of acres of grasslands with a deafening and almost metallic buzz, chewing up the dry yellow grass, the sick and wilting corn. In his book called *Humphrey: A Candid Biography,* writer Winthrop Griffith tells of a Doland, South Dakota, farmer remembering how his father reacted to the invasion of grasshoppers:

> He walked out of the house and into his field as the last 'hoppers moved away. He looked up at the sky for a minute—it was still filled with dust kicked up by the 'hoppers—then he dropped down on his knees. He stared at the ground for a long time. It was hard; there wasn't a sprout or root left in it. He started pounding his fists against the ground real hard. His hands were tough, but blood came running out of the knuckles. Then he moaned and started screaming: "God damn you, land! . . . God damn you, earth!"
>
> I'll never forget his face—all covered with dust and a look of pain. Mom couldn't move; she just stood on the porch with her hands against her face. I was little and scared. My big brother came out. He was real good, real gentle. He took Dad over to the water pump. Dad just stood there and let my brother wash his face and hands. He didn't say anything, and got a funny smile on his face, and sort of relaxed—as though somebody else finally was taking care of things. The doc came out the next day. A couple of weeks later the sheriff came. Dad just smiled at him and let us guide him into the car. The sheriff drove him away to the state hospital."

                    *   *   *

The prolonged drought puzzled scientists. At a Cabinet meeting President Roosevelt said a Harvard geologist had advanced the idea that we were in a geological cycle of a hundred years in which the western part of the country would become a desert. The President was not sure about this theory, saying at a press conference: "What was the result of this plowing up of land that had never been plowed up before in all history? Dust storms began, and they have been getting steadily worse year by year. The result is that we have in this country an area which is subject to dust storms. This was caused solely by the fact that we have been using land for the wrong purpose. Instead of using it for pasture, we are using it for wheat." Roosevelt's own farm in Georgia suffered from lack of rain.

People began praying for rain. A farmer said: "We went to church and knelt down. It seemed to me we were like fools there, on our knees, Sunday after Sunday, praying for rain, and no rain coming at all." In Georgia a Negro was paid $10 for offering up similar prayers. In New York State the Onondaga Indians revived their rain-prayer dance for the first time in forty years. In Russia, also afflicted by drought, Communists were displeased by the fact that some old people, still clinging to their religion, prayed for rain.

Father Coughlin said that the droughts and dust storms were divine punishment inflicted on the American people by God for the sin of electing Roosevelt as President in 1932. Stricken farmers and ranchers did not accept Coughlin's extreme view, but they did wonder whether they had offended the Lord in some other way. Maybe this was heavenly vengeance for the evil practice of plowing under cotton and killing little pigs. Some Colorado residents blamed the lack of rain on the disturbance of the ether by radio broadcasts, just as some New Yorkers during the wet summer of 1969 felt that this bad weather was due to the fact that we had just landed two men on the moon. Syria, too, was getting drier by the day, and Moslem religious leaders said this was caused by the importation of the new tops called Yo-Yos from the United States.

It did seem that some curse lay on this and other lands. North Dakota had 399 dust storms. Mishek, North Dakota, suffered in 120-degree heat. In South Dakota men with tight grins on their faces handed out cards saying: IF AT FIRST YOU DON'T SUCCEED . . . THE HELL WITH IT! People joked about a farmer who went to a bank to ask the banker to inspect his farm so he could get a loan; the farmer happened to glance out a window and saw his farm blowing past the bank.

In 1935 this nation reaped its smallest harvest in forty years. Small lakes dried up, little streams vanished, there was a lowering of the water level of big rivers, brush fires and forest fires became more common, parched field mice crept into country schools to drink from ink bottles, fish were left gasping in dry beds of creeks, there was an increase in the sale of cowbells to put on cattle wandering far afield in search of pastures, cattle rustling broke out again, city fathers had water hauled into town, cops were told to arrest anyone using water illegally, mines and railroads suffered from the water shortage, the hunting season was shortened, in some towns the drinking water took on a milky appearance, farm prices rose as surpluses fell, and even the moist prickly-pear cactus of the Far West began dying.

The dust blotted out the sun, and streetlights burned at noon. Georgia's watermelon crop shriveled; whining windmills kept turning, but they pumped no water; people winced when they saw their sun-warped wooden churches; nights were pitch black because the stars could not pierce the dust; wells dried up; roads and barns and tractors and homes and automobiles and even telegraph poles were buried under dust. Rexford Tugwell toured the stricken areas and then reported that the soil showed through the grass everywhere, and the wheat was thin "like the stubble on an old man's chin." But the stunned farmers kept on plowing just in case a rain might come, using two horses at first and then hitching up four horses for the hard work of ripping open the hardpan left after the topsoil blew away.

A man could not roll or light a homemade cigarette in the wind that blew, blew, forever blew. Day and night one heard the soft dry clashing of parched corn in the wind. A person walking along a road would lift a thin layer of flourlike dust as high as his waist. Everyone wore a handkerchief over his nose, while some folks put goggles over their bloodshot eyes. At night they laid wet towels over their cracked lips but still felt the grit between their teeth. Housewives tried to seal up every crack in their homes with strips of gummed paper, only to watch helplessly as the choking dust filtered inside and spread in ripples on the floor.

Nathan Asch, a novelist and Hollywood scriptwriter, wandered through the country in what he called "a search for America," then told of his experiences in a book entitled *The Road*. In one passage he says:

> It was in Oklahoma that I went inside the dust storm that for three weeks obscured the sun and made everything, food, water, even the air taken into the lungs, taste gritty. It blew into the eyes, underneath the collar; undressing, there were specks of dust inside the buttonholes; in the morning it had gathered like fine snow along the window ledge; it penetrated even more; it seeped along the wiring of the house; and along the edges of the door button there was a brown stain.
>
> Sometimes it did not blow; it stood between the buildings, dulling them, and dulling the mind, making thoughts oppressive, giving the city a mood of foggy melancholy. As in a disaster one only thought of dust, one saw it, felt it, tasted it and lost his sense of smell. In the country, the road, the ditches, the fields, the grass, the plants, even the sky above, everything was covered by the dust; cattle stood head down, immovable, not tasting the gritty leaves; automobiles went slowly; and when even the road was obscured from the driver's vision and all the world, everything that one could possibly see was just a brownness, one had to stop and wait. . . .

Gene Howe, the publisher of a newspaper in Amarillo, Texas, counted twenty-seven days out of thirty in April, 1935, when the dust was so thick he could not see across the street. The storm of April 14 of that year was perhaps the worst, and Woody Guthrie was in the middle of it. This experience inspired him to write the words and music of a song he called "The Great Dust Storm." A little weather-worn man with wiry hair, Guthrie later said: "This is a true song. It is about the worst dust storm in anybody's history book. I was in what is give up to be the big middle of it. Right in there north of Amarillo, Texas. I'll never forget how my wife and kinfolks looked. That was before it hit. After it got dark, you couldn't see how nobody looked. You could just reach out and get them by the hand and stand there and wonder how it would all come out. It turned wheat lands into deserts. I've seen hills change locations down there."

During one such storm a seven-year-old boy wandered away from home and was suffocated before he could be found. In South Dakota, halfway between Doland and Huron, two children left school one afternoon and were caught in a ferocious dust storm; they wandered all the rest of that afternoon and part of the night, then dropped from exhaustion and died, their bodies discovered half-buried in dust the next day. Woody Guthrie wrote another song called "Dust Can't Kill Me"—but it could.

In Kansas some rural schools were closed when board members decided things were so bad there was no use keeping them open. In Montana the drought was so devastating and the crops so poor that farmers could not afford to buy overalls for their children, so the kids had to stay at home. In Washington, D.C., a United States Senator wept as he told of the misery of his people in the Great Plains. In Texas a farmer drove his tractor around and around a field, muttering: "I just can't stand sitting 'round the house. I just got to do something, even if it's some fool thing like I'm doing now." Here and there people asked one another: "Is this dust th' end of th' world?"

Preachers quoted dour passages from the Bible: ". . . For, behold, the darkness shall cover the earth. . . . Enter into the rock, and hide thee in the dust, for fear of the Lord. . . . The earth mourneth and fadeth away. . . . The mirth of the land is gone. . . . Awake and sing, ye that dwell in the dust. . . . Behold, the Lord maketh the earth empty, and maketh it waste, and turneth it upside down, and scattereth abroad the inhabitants thereof."

And they were scattered, and they were called Okies.

*   *   *

Devastation was worst in the southwestern part of the country where Oklahoma, Texas, Kansas, Colorado and New Mexico meet or almost meet. Some of this region—Kansas, certainly—had been called the Breadbasket of America. In 1934 people began calling it the Dust Bowl. The heart of the Dust Bowl lay within the northwestern corner of the Texas Panhandle north of Amarillo and only a few miles south of the Oklahoma Panhandle, a grasslands region where cattle were grazed seasonally and general farming was practiced.

The empty look of the Dust Bowl was described by Meridel Le Sueur in an article in the September, 1934, issue of *American Mercury* magazine:

> On Decoration day the wind started again, blowing hot as a blast from hell and the young corn withered as if under machine gun fire, the trees in two hours looked as if they had been beaten. The day after Decoration day it was so hot you couldn't sit around looking at the panting cattle and counting their ribs and listening to that low cry that is an awful asking. We got in the car and drove slowly through the sizzling countryside.
> Not a soul was in sight. It was like a funeral. The houses were closed up tight, the blinds drawn, the windows and doors closed. There seemed to be a menace in the air made visible. It was frightening. You could hear the fields crack and dry, and the only movement in the down-driving heat was the dead withering of the dry blighted leaves on the twigs. The young corn about four spears up was falling down like a fountain being slowly turned off.

There was something terrifying about this visible sign of disaster. It went into your nostrils so you couldn't breathe: the smell of hunger. It made you count your own ribs with terror. You don't starve in America. Everything looks good. There is something around the corner. Everyone has a chance. That's all over now. The whole country cracks and rumbles and cries out in its terrible leanness, stripped with exploitation and terror—and as sign and symbol, bones—bones showing naked and spiritless, showing decay and crisis and a terrific warning, bare and lean. . . .

We kept driving very slowly, about as slowly as you go to a funeral, with no one behind us, meeting no one on the road. The corpse was the very earth. We keep looking at the body of the earth, at the bare and mortgaged and unpainted houses like hollow pupas when the life has gone. They looked stripped as if after a raid. As if a terrible army had just gone through. It used to be hard to look at the fat rich-seeming farms and realize that they were mortgaged to the hilt and losing ground every year, but not now. Now it stands a visible sign. You can see the marks of the ravagers. The mark of that fearful exploitation stands on the landscape, visible, known, to be reckoned with.

The cows were the only thin flesh visible. They stood in the poor shade of the stripped and dying trees, breathing heavily, their great ribs showing like the ribs of decaying boats beached and deserted. But you knew that from behind all those drawn blinds hundreds of eyes were watching that afternoon, that no man, woman or child could sit down and read a book or lie down to any dreams. Through all these windows eyes were watching—watching the wheat go, the rye go, the corn, peas, potatoes go. Everywhere in those barricaded houses were eyes drawn back to the burning windows looking out at next winter's food slowly burning in the fields. You look out and see the very food of your next winter's sustenance visibly, physically dying beneath your eyes, projecting into you your future hungers.

The whole countryside that afternoon became terrifying, not only with its present famine but with the foreshadowing of its coming hunger. No vegetables now, and worst of all, no milk. The countryside became monstrous with this double doom. Every house is alike in suffering as in a flood, every cow, every field mounting into hundreds, into thousands, from state to state. You try not to look at the ribs, but pretty soon you are looking only at ribs.

Then an awful thing happened. The sun went down behind the ridge, dropped low, and men and women began to pour out of the houses, the children lean and fleet as rats, the tired lean farm women looking to see what had happened. The men ran into their fields, ran back for water and they began to water their lands with buckets and cups, running, pouring the puny drops of water on the baked earth as if every minute might count now. The children ran behind the cows urging them to eat the harsh dry grass. It looked like an evacuated countryside, with the people running out after the enemy had passed. Not a word was spoken. In intense silence they hurried down the rows with buckets and cups, watering the wilted corn plants, a gargantuan and terrible and hopeless labor. Some came out with horses and ploughs and began stirring up the deadly dust. If the field was a slope, barrels were filled, and a primitive irrigation started. Even the children ran with cups of water, all dogged silent, mad, without a word. A certain madness in it all, like things that are done after unimaginable violence.

We stop and talk to a farmer. His eyes are bloodshot. I can hardly see from the heat and the terrible emotion. . . . How do you think my cows look? he asks. I think they are a little fatter today. I try not to look at his cows with him. Pretty thin, though, he says, pretty thin. I can see the fine jersey pelt beginning to sag and the bones rise out like sticks out of the sea at low tide.

We both know that a farmer across the river shot twenty-two of his cattle yesterday and then shot himself. I look at him and I can see his clavicle and I know that his ribs are rising out of his skin, too. It is visible now, starvation and famine. So they are going to buy the starving cattle and shoot them and feed the rest to the bread lines. A man isn't worth anything —but a cow. . . .

*   *   *

During the 1934 drought a West Texas rancher felt that the Lord would provide if he just did his part. His cattle were dying near the ranch house, and he and his cowboys were so busy they had not found time to see conditions farther out on the range. One day the rancher sent a cowboy to a distant part of his land to look it over and then report to him. The horseman did not return until long after dark. As he sat down to supper in the ranch house, the owner perched at the far end of the bench and asked: "Well, Jim, how does it look where you were today?"

"It looks bad," the cowboy replied. "I never saw enough grass to build a bird's nest. The water's dried up and there's dead cattle everywhere. If it don't rain purty soon, I don't know what we'll do."

The cattleman said: "I guess the Lord will send us rain when we need it bad enough."

Pouring another cup of coffee, the cowboy drawled: "Well, if He don't know we need rain now, He's a darn poor cow man."

*   *   *

With the disappearance of the life-giving topsoil, with the exposed hardpan almost impervious to the plow, with water scarce and no rain to speak of, with livestock and crops dying for want of water and fodder, flat-faced farmers squatted on their hams doodling in the dust and talking in low tones about the future. The future? What future did they have in their own countryside? Hell, a man couldn't raise enough corn to feed a baby. Call it farmin' when a feller gets only a quarter bale of cotton to a quarter section? A future, you call it, with the banks foreclosing on mortgages and sending tractors across their land? Hell, they better face up to the facts. They been tractored out and droughted out, that's what!

Over in Cochran County, Texas, they's nearly three hundred cotton farmers and their families living in sodded dugouts. Home on the range! Some of them big shots in Washington is talkin' about how they got to evacuate thousands of people from the Dust Bowl, but where's folks to go? Relocate them? Okay, but where? How about California? Why California? Well, you seen them handbills they been passin' out here lately. They need pickers in California, that's what. They say California is prosperous, and they got all them vegetables and fruits in them big valleys that need harvestin'. Great climate, good wages, plenty of work for all. From the Dust Bowl to the Peach Bowl, huh? Hey, that's purty good! Why not? I might give it a try. Yuh know, I just might, at that.

*　　　*　　　*

In A.D. 77 Pliny said: "Here it is that we drive away our neighbors and enclose the land thus seized within our fence."

*　　　*　　　*

From Oklahoma and Kansas, from Colorado and Texas and New Mexico, the grim men and women and children set out, by the thousands at first, by the tens of thousands, and finally by the hundreds of thousands, a drought-weary dust-worn people trekking 1,000 miles to the Golden State. Worrying about whether they would have enough money to complete this trip, they fanned out over all major highways leading to the Pacific, riding in battered old jalopies, chugging along at 35 miles an hour, their faces and arms and hands burned brown by the relentless sun, patching each tire as it blew out, anxiously counting out coins for each gallon of gas, camping at night wherever they could, met with distaste or suspicion or hostility by the people who lived along their line of march.

John Steinbeck watched them. He watched them and worked with them and rode with them, and then he wrote a novel as harsh as the sun, a novel called *The Grapes of Wrath*. Harsh, and strangely tender. The book tells the story of the flight of the Joad family from Oklahoma to California. Its principal characters are Tom Joad, a young man just out of prison where he served a sentence for killing a man in self-defense; his parents, merely called Pa and Ma Joad; his sister, Rose of Sharon; and Jim Casy, a labor agitator. The Joads supposedly began their agonizing trip from the vicinity of Sallisaw, a small town in the hilly region of eastern Oklahoma, and Thomas Hart Benton later painted a picture of their departure.

The Joads and others like them sold what few valuables they had left, abandoned all heavy and bulky possessions, then loaded their flivvers with the things they felt they would need for the journey. Photographs taken of that sad parade show auto springs sagging under too much weight, mattresses strapped to the roof of the car, platforms built onto the rear of the vehicle, threadbare tires, an occasional goat or sheep in a slatted cage on a running board, a jug of water lashed to a fender, a pail hung from a rear window, a garbage can filled with ragged clothes roped to the rear, license plates so dusty that their numbers were obscured, dirty bare feet sticking out from blankets piled on the floor of open-ended cars.

Woody Guthrie wrote a song about them, too, and called it "Dust Bowl Refugee." "This is a song," he said, "I made up right after my wife and kids and me got out to California. . . . We was a trying to get away from the dust and bankers." The Dust Bowl refugees were driven by despair and hope—despair of ever being able to exist in their blighted homeland, hope of making a new life amid the lush greenery of a new Promised Land.

Grampa Joad was senile, and had an exaggerated vision of nature's bounty in the Golden State, squealing: "Gonna get me a whole big bunch a grapes off a bush, or whatever, an' I'm gonna squash'em on my face an' let'em run offen my chin." Many Californians believed that most Okies were shiftless and ignorant, opportunists who wanted something for nothing. But this was not the truth. The Okies had been farmers, farmhands or ranchers who had toiled all their lives to wrest a living from the soil, only to see it blow away. They had become the disinherited of the earth, through no fault of their own, and what they now wanted was "nothing else than to earn their own living by their own efforts," according to a report by the federal Great Plains Drought Area Committee.

Soon after the Joads crossed the Arizona state line and entered California, they stopped to camp and to bathe in a river. Gratefully soaking in the cold water, the men in the Joad family began talking to a stranger. Pa Joad politely asked whether the man was going west. He replied: "Nope. We come from there. Goin' back home. We can't make no livin' out there."

Surprised, Tom Joad began asking questions. Then the stranger told them what to expect when they reached the fertile valleys of California: "Gonna be deputy sheriffs, an' they'll push you aroun'. You camp on the roadside, an' they'll move you on. You gonna see in people's faces how they hate you. An'—I'll tell you somepin. They hate you 'cause they're scairt. They know a hungry fella gonna get food even if he got to take it. They know that fallow lan's a sin an' somebody gonna take it. What the hell! You never been called 'Okie' yet."

Tom said: "Okie? What's that?"

"Well, Okie use'ta mean you was from Oklahoma. Now it means you're a dirty son-of-a-bitch. Okie means you're scum."

John Steinbeck did not coin the word "Okie," according to Woody Guthrie, who has said: "Almost everybody is a Okie now days. That means you ain't got no home, or don't know how long you're gonna have the one you are in. Sort of means, too, that you're out of a job. Or owe more than you can rake and scrape. Okies has come to include all of the folks that the rich folks has et up. I could sleep mighty comfortable with just that one name on my tombstone. Some politicians throwed mud at John Steinbeck for coining the word, Okie. I want to put my nickel in. He aint the guy that made up that word.

"That was made up by people a riding in freight cars and walking down the high ways and working in the potatoes, and celery, and beets, and apricots, and peaches, and celery, and all of the crops—they started it. If you was from Texas, they called you Tex. If you was from Missouri, they called you Mizoo. If you was from Alabama they called you Alabam. If you was from Arkansas, you was called Arkie. From Oklahoma, Okie."

A *Fortune* magazine reporter listened as an Okie said: "Mister, you been to college, you learned things there—maybe you can tell me what's to become of us. You see, back in Oklahoma we had a farm. There's me and the three kids and the old lady and my mother. We got along, yea, and then things started to happen. First came the Depression and we couldn't get nothin' for our crops. Make maybe two hundred dollars a year. Course the farm started to go downhill—to dry up—and fust thing I knowed the whole blamed farm had dried up and blown away. Course, it weren't quite as quick as all that. There were a couple of years when we tried mighty hard. Didn't eat much those years.

"Well, come '35 it weren't no use trying any longer so we just packed up and pulled out. Came out here cause we heard you could make fair money harvesting crops. And ya know we did make fair money the fust year. Ya see the kids are twelve, fourteen, and fifteen years old so all of us can work except my maw—when there's work to be got.

"Well, we picked peas in the Imperial and Santa Maria, potatoes at Stockton, and grapes at Napa. We made high as seventeen, eighteen dollars a day. Course it costs a lot to move around and there was a time when we couldn't get no work, but we done purty good. Then last year we made the same places but it weren't no good. They didn't pay so good last year. Cut from thirty-five to twenty-five cents an hour and piece work was lower. We got by, though. But, God, Mister, what's going to happen to us this year? Here it is March and I only worked about two weeks so far. I tried every place and everybody but it weren't no good. People has kept comin' in here so now there's six for every job—and darn few jobs.

"See that sign? Says forty-five cents for picking a hundred pounds o' cotton. Know how long it takes to pick a hundred pounds o' cotton down here? Well, it takes just about a whole day. You know you can't feed a family o' six on forty-five cents a day. It ain't my fault, is it? Jees, I worked hard since I was a kid. I allus done what I thought was right, and I think I know right from wrong. I allus tried to teach my kids right from wrong.

"But I'm beginning to wonder. I don't know what to do. There's nothin' back in Oklahoma for us to go to and now there's nothin' here. Somehow somethin' don't seem right—I want to work and I can't—I want to bring up my kids decent. You been to college, Mister, maybe you can explain it to me."

*   *   *

President Roosevelt was disturbed when he heard, as he put it, "reports that out in the drought area there was a widespread despondency, a lack of hope for the future, and a general atmosphere of gloom." Agriculture Secretary Henry Wallace said he doubted "if even China can equal our record of soil destruction." Until the advent of droughts and dust storms the nation's big agricultural problem had been crop surpluses, but now these surpluses were being reduced, harvests were poor, and people were fleeing from their blighted land. Congressmen shifted uneasily in their chairs as they read letters from frightened voters back home.

In the second week of May, 1934, a gigantic dust storm rose in the west and started blowing east. Dust-laden clouds crossed the country in four days. On May 12 they passed over the Eastern Seaboard and out to sea. That date happened to be the first anniversary of the Agricultural Adjustment Act of 1933. Besides sweeping 300,000,000 tons of rich soil from the Great Plains, this huge storm forced city people to face up to the fact that something was wrong in the farmlands, and in the nation's capital Congressmen themselves tasted dust in their mouths. Soon afterward they approved when the New Deal earmarked $5,000,000 of Public Works Administration money for soil erosion.

That spring of 1934 AAA officials overhauled their program to try to do something to relieve drought-induced conditions. They appeared before Congressional committees to say that pastures and hay crops had been reduced so much that millions of cattle would die uselessly unless they were slaughtered and canned at central abattoirs for relief purposes. Then the government began buying cattle at an average price of about $13.50 and turning them over to the Federal Surplus Relief Corporation, which distributed the meat to needy families. Other cattle were shipped to states where pastures had not been burned brown. In June the Congress passed the Taylor Grazing Act, which provided for the segregation of up to 8,000,000 acres (later raised to 142,000,000) for grazing purposes.

In the year 1873 drought-resistant hard winter wheat had been brought from Russia to the southwest plains of the United States. In 1935 the Agriculture Department sent Nicholas K. Roerich to the Gobi Desert of central Asia to search for drought-resistant grass. Russian-born Roerich was a talented and rather mysterious man—an explorer, painter, archeologist, collector, author and mystic. Henry Wallace was among those who regarded Roerich as their spiritual leader and addressed him as "my dear Guru." But when Wallace heard that Roerich was in China seeking rifles and ammunition for some vague purpose, the secretary fired him, and Roerich never returned to the United States.

On April 2, 1935, a second dust storm blew over Washington, D.C. Hugh H. Bennett, a soil scientist with the Department of Agriculture, was on Capitol Hill that day asking for more money from the Senate Public Lands Committee. This is how he remembered the occasion: "The hearing was dragging a little. I think some of the Senators were sprinkling a few grains of salt on the tail of some of my astronomical figures relating to soil losses by erosion. At any rate, I recall wishing rather intensely, at the time, that the dust storm then reported on its way eastward would arrive. I had followed the progress from its point of origin in northeastern New Mexico, on into the Ohio Valley, and had every reason to believe it would eventually reach Washington.

"It did—in sun-darkening proportions—and at about the right time—

for the benefit of Public 46. When it arrived, while the hearing was still on, we took a little time, off the record, and moved from the great mahogany table of the Senate Office Building for a look. Everything went nicely after that."

Public 46 was an act establishing the Soil Conservation Service as a permanent unit of the Department of Agriculture. It became the law of the land on April 27, 1935, and Bennett was named chief of the new service. This law gave Secretary Wallace $500,000,000 to pay farmers for their voluntary cooperation with the department in the work of soil conservation—especially in shifting 30,000,000 acres from cultivation of soil-depleting crops to soil-conserving crops.

On May 1 of that year Roosevelt issued an executive order creating the Resettlement Administration. This agency was intended to help farm families that had not received much aid from the AAA, to prevent waste caused by the improper use of land and to oversee the relocation of poor people in areas where they might make a new start. The RA was administered by the undersecretary of agriculture, Rexford Tugwell.

The federal government was producing official movies, and that was all right with Tugwell, but he was annoyed by their subject matter and low quality. Most of the films were dull two-reelers about hog breeding, the love life of the honeybee and the manufacture of paving bricks. In June, 1935, Tugwell summoned Pare Lorentz to Washington and gave him the job of making movies that would dramatize the problems of agriculture. The thirty-year-old Lorentz had been movie critic for the New York *Evening Journal* and the magazine *Vanity Fair*. He also wrote a movie column for Hearst's King Features Syndicate. After he devoted one column to praise of Henry Wallace and the New Deal farm program, Hearst fired him in a wire sent from the publisher's California estate, San Simeon.

Now, given carte blanche by Tugwell, the imaginative Lorentz decided to make a movie explaining why and how the American grasslands had become a desert. He would call it *The Plow That Broke the Plains*. This would be a three-reel film, not a mere two-reeler, and it would declare that much of this continent had been ruined by carelessness, selfishness and the lack of a planned program of soil conservation.

Hollywood producers refused to help Lorentz. After preparing a skeleton shooting script, he took three cameramen to the Dust Bowl, where they shot thousands of feet of film of the wasteland and the people fleeing from it. Upon returning to the East, Lorentz settled down to the work of editing all this footage in the cutting room. What he hoped to produce was a starkly realistic movie in which social criticism was implicit, rather than explicit. Some of his colleagues wanted it to be "all about human greed and how lousy our social system was." Lorentz, who violently objected to being called a leftist, shrugged them off. His finished product was narrated by Thomas Chalmers and had a musical score by Virgil Thomson, one of the nation's most important composers.

The Plow That Broke the Plains was released in May, 1936. When commercial distributing firms declined to book it into movie theaters across the country, Lorentz took a can of the film under his arm and went from town to town, staging private showings for movie critics. "If you like it," he begged them, "please say this picture can't be shown in your town." The critics hailed his production as an artistic triumph, generating a demand that it be seen by the public. So this pictorial story about the Dust Bowl ultimately unfolded in independent theaters and in schools and clubs.

To produce this movie had cost a mere $20,000 or so, but government red tape so fouled up the works that Lorentz not only was paid less than his cameramen but often had to meet immediate expenses from his own pocket. At last he got so fed up that he stalked into Tugwell's office, aired his grievances, resigned on the spot and began walking out. Before disappearing, he pointed to a map on a wall and snapped: "There you guys are, missing the biggest story in the world—the Mississippi river!" Tugwell called him back, raised his salary, gave him an appropriation of $50,000, and work began immediately on another documentary entitled *The River*. It, too, was a creative success, James Joyce saying of it: "This is the most beautiful prose I have heard in ten years."

*   *   *

By the spring of 1935 the Soil Erosion Service had thirty-two erosion projects in thirty-one states, and better farming methods were being tried. One technique, called strip-cropping, was the planting of alternate narrow strips of soil-binding crops, such as grain sorghums, between other strips of ordinary field crops, such as wheat. Contour tillage was the plowing of furrows that followed the slope of the land instead of running in a straight line regardless of differences in elevation. Terracing was raising a series of embankments of land one above the other, but this method alone almost always failed. Farmers were urged to plant cover crops such as maize, soybeans and sweet clover, to hold down the earth and get root and fiber back into the soil. And CCC workers, as has been noted, planted millions of trees such as apricot, Chinese elm and Russian olive, a massive shelter belt serving as a shield against the wind.

The solution to the drought problem, according to a crackpot living on the Atlantic coast, lay with him alone. He vowed that when he sat in one position, the rains came, and when he assumed another, the sun was sure to shine.

It was valid news when rain broke the drought on President Roosevelt's farm in Georgia on July 10, 1936. Twelve days later he appointed a six-man Great Plains Drought Area Committee that included Rexford Tugwell and Harry L. Hopkins. The President asked the members to "carry on a study looking toward the most efficient utilization of the natural resources of the Great Plains area." After touring the West, the committee submitted a preliminary report on August 27.

This report declared that "the basic cause of the present Great Plains situation is an attempt to impose upon a region a system of agriculture to which the Plains are not adapted—to bring into a semi-arid region methods which are suitable, on the whole, only for a humid region."

The committee members said they had not yet been able to make an accurate determination of the extent of erosion on the Great Plains. However, they added, it was safe to say that 80 percent of that area was now in some stage of erosion, and as much as 15 percent may have been injured seriously and permanently. They recommended that overcropping and overgrazing be checked, that the federal government acquire land in range areas, that the size of farms be increased, that water resources be developed, that destructive insects be controlled and that resettlement work be intensified.

Resettlement, as Tugwell later observed, was a massive and complex matter. First fertile land had to be found and acquired, farming equipment had to be provided, and demoralized farm families had to be guided and helped for quite some time. Although this program went forward awkwardly and wastefully, by the summer of 1936 two-thirds to three-quarters of all farm families in the drought regions had been given some kind of aid.

Late that summer the President boarded a train to make a long personal inspection tour of the stricken areas. In Des Moines, Iowa, he convened a meeting of the governors of all afflicted states, and there he chatted with Governor Alfred M. Landon of Kansas, by now his Republican rival for the Presidency. FDR seemed to be a lucky man, for almost everywhere he went in the West the rain began pelting down as he arrived, earning him the nickname of Roosevelt the Rainmaker. At Julesburg, Colorado, he spoke from the rear platform of his train, saying in part: ". . . We have three problems before us: The first is the immediate problem of taking care of the feeding of people during the summer. The second is the problem of taking care of people during the next winter until the next spring, when we hope we shall have more rain. The third problem relates to long-range planning, so that we can beat this problem once and for all by the proper use of land."

*　　　　*　　　　*

California, now becoming a mecca for 350,000 victims of drought and dust, had gone through an agricultural revolution. In the past its chief farm products were hay and cattle. By the Thirties, by means of intensive cultivation and extensive irrigation, the state's most profitable crops had become fruits and vegetables. Agricultural production continued to mount during the Depression while farm wages fell. The long north-south valley in the center of the state had developed into the world's most fertile growing region. It really was two valleys: the Sacramento Valley lying north of the state capital and the San Joaquin Valley to the south. These lush and slender strips were trapped between the coastal mountains to the west and the foothills of the Rockies to the east.

Because of the state's wide range of topography, climate and soil, almost every species of temperate zone and subtropical fruit, vegetable and field crop could be grown. From 1909 to 1936 California's farm production rose more than 120 percent. Pears grew on the cool mountain slopes; asparagus, celery, beans, onions and rice in the black soil of the delta area; lettuce in the Salinas Valley, called the Valley of Green Gold; grapes for dry wines in the sunny foothills of Napa and Sonoma counties; and a fabulous yield of cotton in the brown silted loam of the San Joaquin Valley.

In 1925 deflation had wiped out many owners of medium-size farms, while the Depression finished off others of their kind. Now the state's agriculture was split into two extremes—stubborn men owning very small farms and grasping corporations owning very large farms. Whenever bankrupt farmers defaulted on their credits, their land was taken over by bankers and businessmen, who consolidated these tracts into gigantic and profitable units. By the middle Thirties 2 percent of California farms controlled one-fourth of all acreage, nearly one-third of the crop value, and paid more than one-third of the bill for hired labor.

California agriculture had become modernized, mechanized, industrialized—factories in the fields, they were called. At the southern end of the San Joaquin Valley, to cite one example, a single fruit ranch of 6,000 acres shipped more than two dozen carloads of peaches, plums and grapes each day at the peak of the season and employed 2,500 men and women in orchards, vineyards and packing sheds. Every crop, every region and every specialty had its own protective association; they fixed prices paid to labor and received for their products, maintaining lobbies in the state capital and otherwise promoting the vested interests of the growers, packers and shippers. To name just a couple of these groups, there was the California Raisin Growers Association and the Fruit Growers Supply Company.

Mechanization increased with the invention of a pear-peeling machine, a hop-picking machine, a mechanical beet thinner and similar innovations. But despite these machines, the growers still had to rely on great numbers of stoop laborers. The harvesting of crops such as lettuce and cotton required men and women willing to crawl between rows of the ripening plants. Naturally, these field hands were hostile toward the inventions that had begun to meance their livelihood. One of them said: "They're fixin' to free all us fellows—free us for what? Free us like they freed the mules. They're aimin' at keeping fellows such as me right down on our knees— aimin' at making slaves of us. We've got no more chance than a one-legged man in a foot-race."

Another problem was the seasonal nature of the work. Different crops matured at different times, so the growers sought armies of pickers at harvesttime and shunned them after the crop was in. From about 1860 to

1930 most of these migrant workers were foreigners—Chinese and Japanese, Mexicans and Filipinos. Because of poor pay, racial discrimination and indifference to their welfare, some of these foreigners returned to their motherlands, some saved enough money to buy small plots of their own, and some drifted into the cities. By 1933 only about a fourth of the state's migratory laborers were Mexican. Now the growers had to find a new source of supply for stoop laborers, so they distributed leaflets throughout the Dust Bowl appealing for workers.

They hoped to attract more people than they could use because surplus labor equals low wages, but this equation backfired. California's corporate farmers were unprepared for the tidal wave of Okies that swept into their state. At first the growers had an advantage, since the hungry newcomers fought one another for jobs, but with the passage of time thousands of people were left unemployed and homeless, began to starve, turned sullen and threatening, and at last California found itself in the middle of an explosive social crisis.

Down through American history the migrant workers had been left unorganized or, at best, poorly organized. The Industrial Workers of the World had taken an interest in them, but by the thirties the IWW had lost all its influence in the fields of California. The American Federation of Labor paid almost no attention to pleas by the new harvest pickers that they be pulled together into unions and placed within the protection of the AFL. The official California spokesman for the AFL was Paul Scharrenberg, whom the New York *Times* quoted as saying: "Only fanatics are willing to live in shacks or tents and get their heads broken in the interests of migratory labor." One migrant worker said sneeringly of Scharrenberg: "He did a swell job for the bosses. He didn't organize a single local!" Another stoop laborer said: "The hay-balers organized a coupla months ago, got a charter in Stockton, but the big shots in the A.F. of L. told'em not to take in any field workers."

The migrants, ignored by organized labor, vied with one another for jobs, took whatever meager wages they were offered and lived in unbelievable squalor. Their plight was observed at first hand by Louis Adamic, who wrote in his diary:

> May is a rich, exciting month in the San Joaquin Valley of California. Vast hay meadows and lucerne and alfalfa fields wave and ripple high and ripe in the breeze. Asparagus and beets need hoeing. There are onions, peas, potatoes, carrots. And cherries are red and must be picked in a hurry.
>
> Migratory workers come to the valley from all sides, on foot and in battered, sputtering flivvers; and for a month from eight to nine thousand of them, mostly men, toil seven days a week. San Joaquin in May has work for nearly everybody who wants it, but wages are meager, ranging from seventeen to thirty cents an hour. You work hard under the hot bright sun and, lest you faint, you must eat solid food at least once a day; and that costs money. Evenings, unless you are Spartan or very old, you crave, if

not a girl who charges two bits, a glass of beer, and you drink two or three glasses against your better judgment. Thus you spend from day to day everything you earn, just to keep going. Then, with the last day of May, the rush is over, and through most of June only about three thousand temporary workers are needed in the valley; the chances are that you move on, with five thousand others, as poor as you were in April.

San Joaquin has many small farms owned and run by little people, most of whom are nice enough folk as husbands or wives or as parents or neighbors, and probably in other ways, but apt to be hard with migratory workers. The idea of paying the hands as little as possible and working them as hard as possible is in the air. Besides, caught up in competition with the big corporation farms and ranches, the little people are up against it, and some cannot very well pay more than twenty-five cents an hour.

The big farms dominate—indirectly, but firmly—the valley's labor policy. They are owned by the big people in San Francisco and elsewhere, who are also in banking and shipping. Very often the land is leased, sometimes to Japanese; but in many instances the owners manage their farms, even if they happen to be big ones. Most operators, however, whether owners or lessees, turn the important work over to labor contractors or bosses. These contractors are Mexicans and Japanese, sprinkled with Americans and Italian-Americans, who, by and large, work on a shoestring.

Petty would-be capitalists without money, trading in the energy and ability of others, they are bent on making as high a profit as possible. They have no labor camps or money for camps. Every morning between four-thirty and five-thirty they go into Stockton, the valley's principal city, and pick up a truckload of men, jamming as many as sixty or seventy into one truck. The trucks bring the men, ten, twenty, forty miles to the job, where they work an average of nine hours, and then are hauled back to town. They are paid only for actual time at work.

A few owner-operators have camps, but these are usually poor, showerless, unsanitary. Some bunk and board the men and profit in the process. One man with whom I spoke went out on a farm at two bits an hour and had to pay a dollar a day for board. He worked an hour in this field, two hours in that orchard, but received wages only for actual labor time—nothing for going from field to orchard—and on quitting collected $1.40 for three days' work. But his net earning was only forty cents, for he had paid an employment agent a dollar for the job!

In cherries, which is probably the most important business in May, the following system is generally in effect: The owner engages a labor contractor to pick and pack the crop. He furnishes ladders, buckets, and packing-boxes. He pays the contractor from thirty-five to forty-five cents a bucket for picking. The contractor goes to the so-called "Skidway" or "slave market" at Market and Center Streets in Stockton, hires the pickers at from twenty to thirty cents a bucket, and although his sole expense is that of running a truck or bus into town, makes from ten to fifteen cents on each bucket. The packing is a different process but is handled similarly.

At four-forty-five A.M. streets around the Skidway in Stockton are jammed with men—Mexicans, Filipinos, Italians and other immigrants, Americans from Oklahoma and Arkansas and probably every other state in the Union. Last night some of them looked like bums. They drank. Some drank on the curb pints of wine charged with "dynamite." Their life is generally low. Bums. Some slept in fifteen-cent flop houses or in the open, or spent the night in two-bit brothels. "Why not? What else is there to this life?" But now, quarter to five, with the rich California sun well up in the blue sky, none look like bums. They are sober. Workers. Thousands of them waiting to be bought off the curb for the day.

Huge trucks with trailers pull in. They are after men for beets. Two bits an hour. No, no more! Smaller trucks for cherry-pickers. Two bits a bucket. No, no more! One truck offers twenty-seven and a half cents a bucket. There is a rush. Fifty men climb aboard. The contractor needs only twenty. He picks his crew. The others climb down.

Most trucks and buses have no trouble filling up. But here is a guy . . . in checkered overalls, a white man, an American, who calls out coaxingly to the dense crowd on the curb. "Royal Anns," he says. "Good pickin', no kiddin'." He looks around, waiting. "Some guys made four bucks apiece yesterday." "Yeah, them and who else?" retort two or three workers from the crowd. Others laugh. "Christ! I wouldn't horse you," says the boss. "Oh, no!" the men roar. They know the guy. They know several other guys, but this guy especially, and some of the fellows tell him from the curb what they think of him and what he did to a gang of cherry-pickers a week ago. "Make it thirty-five cents and pay in advance!" He whines. He has two trucks to fill, wants sixty packers. A woman in white pants who looks shyly at the men drives the other truck. She and the guy are working together. She is the sex appeal in the racket. Her pants are tight, and her arms are bare, and her blouse is thin and low in front, showing part of her loose breasts. "Come on, boys!" she cries, "pickin' is real good where we're goin' today, near Lodi." But there is something decent in her, and she is genuinely embarrassed before all these men—Mexicans, Negroes, Filipinos, Slavs, Italians, and Americans, young and old—some of whom wince and smile sheepishly before her. She is a dame: what wouldn't a man do for a dame? And so, hungry in more ways than one, a few of them jump on her truck. The guy wants more and gives her a quick, sharp look. "Come on, boys!" she cries again and gives a little jump on the runningboard so her breasts bounce in her blouse. By five-thirty the guy fills both trucks at two bits an hour, and he and the woman drive off with their loads.

A worker still on the curb says, "Christ! We'll never stick!" "The hell we won't!" says another worker. "This is their last trick. They gotta use women to get us." "We gotta organize," says a third man. "Organize, organize—"

*   *   *

On the State Capitol Building in Sacramento there is a scroll that says: "Bring me men to match my mountains." California's ruling class members, themselves earlier migrants from other parts of the nation, did not consider the present newcomers the kind of men they wanted. They called the Okies bums, crop tramps, fruit tramps, shiftless idlers—even sexual degenerates. They growled that the migrants did not know what it felt like to plant a tree and see it grow and touch it with one's hand. Before long a "vagrant" was anybody disliked by a cop or judge. One county judge said, "California agriculture demands that we create and maintain peonage."

Laurence Hewes, director of one California region of the federal Farm Security Administration, listened in disbelief as a businessman ranted: "Go right ahead—coddle and pet these worthless people! We can't stop you.

Just keep away from decent people! Do what you want! Preach socialistic claptrap like that young fool out at your camp. Make those ignorant filthy people think they're as good as the next man! Only for God's sake have the decency to keep them out of this town! If we have to, we'll find ways to protect ourselves."

A story was told about a woman and her small daughter who were strolling in a town in the San Joaquin Valley *during the harvest season.* The girl pointed to the migrant workers and asked: "Mommy, who are those people?" The mother is supposed to have replied: "Child, those are cotton pickers." Same scene *after the harvest:* "Mommy, who are those people?" Answer: "Child, those are bums!"

Eight men were given preposterously heavy sentences for trying to organize a strike of melon pickers in the Imperial Valley in 1931. The commander of an American Legion post told an observer: "The way to kill the Red Plague is to dynamite it out. That's what we did in the Imperial valley. The judge who tried the Communists was a Legionnaire. Fifty percent of the jurors were war veterans. What chance did the Communists have? That's the way we stamped it out of our county."

That same year a young man named Carlos Bulosan, born in the Philippines and brought to this country as a small boy, was *sold* for $5 to an Alaskan fish cannery owner. When he finally got back to California he tried to organize migrant workers into a union, was stripped and whipped and driven out of one town after another, lost the ribs on one side of his body and the use of one lung, but survived to become a distinguished author.

When an official of a farm association was asked what he meant by a Communist, he replied: "Why, he's the guy that wants twenty-five cents an hour when we're paying twenty." At one growers' association meeting a farmer member was accused of being "kind of communistic" because he advocated separate toilets for men and women in a local squatters' camp.

Dust Bowl refugees—the lucky ones, that is—found shelter in federal camps, state camps, houses rented by growers or squatters' camps. The federal camps run by the Farm Security Administration were the cleanest and best. Second-best were the state camps. Large farmers rented houses to workers at $4 to $8 a month; most of these houses had just one room and no running water; all 200 or 300 people occupying a group of these one-room houses had to share one toilet and one bathroom. Small farmers provided no sanitary facilities—except one or two holes dug in the ground. Lowest in the social scale were the squatters' camps. Usually these were on the bank of a river used by the inhabitants for drinking, bathing, washing their clothes and receiving their refuse. Naturally, epidemics often broke out in the squatters' camps. Carey McWilliams, a young California attorney who became head of the California Division of Immigration and Housing, said some camps were the equivalent of concentration camps.

Laurence Hewes flew to Washington to try to get more money to help the migrants. This was at a time when California Republicans were accus-

ing Secretary Henry Wallace of scheming to influence the California vote
by herding workers from Democratic states into the California camps.
Wallace, who knew of Hewes' passionate interest in the welfare of the
displaced Okies, asked him to attend a press conference at which Wallace
would tell his side of the story to the press. Hewes was surprised when
Wallace sidestepped a question and told reporters that the man from California would give them their answers. But Hewes acquitted himself well.

Late that night Hewes was told that Mrs. Franklin D. Roosevelt wanted
him to have lunch in the White House the next day. He arrived at the
appointed time and was ushered into a small room warmed by a blazing
fire in a fireplace. Hewes had seen Eleanor Roosevelt at a distance a couple
of times in the past and had not been impressed with her. Now, at close
range, he was taken at once by her vitality, her charm and, above all, her
sincerity. She showered him with questions about the migrants and finally
said she would like to see conditions for herself. Surprised and pleased,
Hewes said if she would just name the day, he would show her around
himself. But there was one thing he had to know: Did Mrs. Roosevelt plan
to let the press in on her inspection tour?

"Of course I want the press to be there." She smiled. "On the other
hand, I don't want to make a Roman holiday out of other people's misfortunes. Why don't we make a date with the reporters at some designated
place?"

Several weeks later Hewes waited at the Bakersfield airport in California
to welcome the President's wife. She arrived in a small plane. With her
were Melvyn Douglas, the movie actor, and his wife, Helen Gahagan
Douglas, a former actress and opera singer who was now a Democratic
national committeewoman for California. Hewes escorted them into a car
and drove to a migrant slum at Oiltown, near Bakersfield. He stopped the
automobile in a crooked, muddy, noisy alley, and Mrs. Roosevelt stepped
out.

Soon she was chatting with migrant women, asking about their babies,
the work their husbands did and the wages they received. Suddenly one
woman pointed dramatically and cried: "My stars, ain't you Mrs.
Roosevelt?"

Smile lines crinkling the corners of her eyes, the First Lady replied:
"You didn't expect me, did you?"

Hewes felt that her interest in these displaced persons was absolutely
genuine. When she saw a standpipe and water faucet braced against one
corner of a privy, she asked in horror: "Do you get drinking water from
that?"

"Yes'm," the woman answered, "and so do all our neighbors."

Mrs. Roosevelt was appalled: "That's perfectly dreadful! Don't you
realize that water from such a place will make you sick?"

"We only rent here," the woman said, "and we can't do nothin' about it.
We complained to the health people, but they only said this place was

condemned and we should move out. But we can't move—leastways not while there's work."

By now a crowd surrounded Mrs. Roosevelt, and Hewes worried about extricating her, getting her back into the car and then driving away without accidentally hitting anybody. She solved this problem by telling him: "I should like to walk back the way we drove in here." Then, turning to one of the women, she smiled and said: "Perhaps you'll show me the way." The delighted migrants tagged along behind the First Lady as she left their alley. Hewes turned the car around, his famous guest climbed inside, and as he pulled away, she waved to the women.

One of them called out: "Mrs. Roosevelt, tell your husband when you see him we're sure goin' to vote for him!"

After she got back to the White House, what she told her husband was this: "Franklin, I wonder if it strikes you as it does me how remarkable it is that people can keep up their courage and struggle in the face of so many hardships?"

*   *   *

Squatting in the brush near Wasco, California, a former tenant farmer, the father of six children, remembered what it was like back in Cook County, Texas: "People just can't make it back there, with drought, hailstorms, windstorms, duststorms, insects. People exist here and they can't do that there. You can make it here if you sleep lots and eat little, but it's pretty tough, there are so many people. They chase them out of one camp because they say it isn't sanitary—there's no running water—so people live out here in the brush like a den o' dogs or pigs."

*   *   *

The Fresno *Bee* published a letter written by the Reverend E. Alexander Gray, who was moved to impassioned protest when he saw one of these camps:

> Let anyone visit the camps for cotton pickers on the west side of Fresno County if he has any doubts as to the reality of hell. Dante must have had a vision of these camps when he portrayed the Inferno. If you want to know his Satanic Majesty, ask the slave herders to introduce you to the chief executive of the finance corporation.
>
> Is there any reason why individuals farming more than twenty sections of fertile land should subject human beings to treatment unbecoming even a dog? One camp which this fall housed more than 600 men, women and children in squalid tents, had less than half a dozen water outlets, not a bath or wash house, one cold shower under the water tank (now out of order) and only five dirty, stinking outside toilets. Not even the poorest poor want to live in such a hell.
>
> I thought child labor was abolished until I visited the cotton fields; I know better now. I talked with the men—strong, willing and able-bodied men. Four of the best had that day picked a total of 700 pounds of cotton

for which they were paid 40 cents a hundred pounds. Yes, for the day's toil they received 70 cents apiece. The next day it rained and they could live on the soupy mud of the cotton camp. If that wouldn't make a Communist out of one it would make him an anarchist. . . .

*   *   *

Conditions in California were "almost beyond belief," according to a report of a Congressional subcommittee headed by Senator Robert M. La Follette, Jr. After making an on-the-spot investigation, the committee summarized its findings: "Unemployment, underemployment, disorganized and haphazard migrancy, lack of adequate wages or annual income, bad housing, insufficient education, little medical care, the great public burden of relief, the denial of civil liberties, strife, corruption, are all part and parcel of this autocratic system of labor relations that has for decades dominated California's agricultural industry."

To that state the National Labor Board sent a three-man commission of inquiry, led by Dr. J. L. Leonard. Subsequently, the Leonard Commission Report further spelled out the rotten state of affairs. Carey McWilliams, who wrote *Factories in the Fields,* summed up the report: "The Commission found that Constitutional rights had been openly disregarded by the law-enforcement agencies in the [Imperial] valley; that the right of free speech and assembly had been wholly suppressed; that excessive bail had been demanded of arrested strikers; that the State Vagrancy Law had been prostituted; and that a Federal Court injunction had been flouted."

Simon J. Lubin, one of the commissioners, said that growers were "paying less than a starvation wage. I have a tabulation of the pay checks of 204 pea pickers showing an average daily wage of 56 cents. The earnings were somewhat larger at the peak of the harvest, but never were sufficient to satisfy the most primitive needs."

A reporter for the *Illustrated Daily News,* published in Los Angeles, found that families of ten were making $2 a day. The citrus industry, the second richest industry in California, was paying its workers an annual wage of about $300. A survey of wages of farmworkers in Los Angeles County showed they averaged $12 per week. Cotton pickers earned from 75 cents to $1.25 a day. In the Decoto-Hayward section of the state the pea pickers got 12 cents an hour.

Much of this mess was due to the fact that the growers and packers had advertised for more workers than they could use, but by the time they began making reluctant admissions of their fault among themselves the situation had got out of hand, or almost so. Policemen took up positions along the California line at various points of entry, stopped all cars that looked as though they might contain "unemployables" and turned them back. The American Civil Liberties Union brought suit in a federal district court to test the constitutionality of this procedure. A police chief ordered his so-called intelligence squad to work over the plaintiff in whose name the action had been commenced. The man, his wife and child were threatened and browbeaten by officers—one of whom later was convicted in Los Angeles of attempted murder.

Then the California legislature passed a law that made it a misdemeanor to bring or aid in bringing into the state any nonresident known to be indigent. Despite this, a California resident named Fred F. Edwards left his home in Marysville, in the Sacramento Valley, and drove to Spur, Texas, to get his wife's brother, Frank Duncan. Duncan's last job in Texas had been with the Works Progress Administration. He had about $20 when he headed west with his brother-in-law, and by the time they reached Marysville he was broke. For the next ten days Duncan lived with the Edwards family, dependent on their charity, and then he got financial help from the Farm Security Administration.

Edwards was arrested, brought to trial, admitted the facts, was found guilty of violating the new state statute and was sentenced to six months' imprisonment. This verdict was sustained by the Superior Court of the State of California in and for the County of Yuba. Since it was impossible to appeal to a higher court in California, Edwards appealed to the United States Supreme Court, which accepted his case. He contended that the California law barring indigents was unconstitutional.

A majority of justices of the nation's highest court decided to reverse the California Superior Court. At first they differed over whether their opinion should be based on the commerce clause of the Constitution or on the grounds that the right to move freely from one state to another was a right inherent to American citizenship. Newly appointed Associate Justice James F. Byrnes, a former Senator from South Carolina, wrote the court's decision—his first since taking the bench. Basing the reversal on the commerce clause, Byrnes said in part:

> . . . The gravity and perplexity of the social and economic dislocation which this statute reflects is a matter of common knowledge and concern. We are not unmindful of it. We appreciate that the spectacle of large segments of our population constantly on the move has given rise to urgent demands upon the ingenuity of government. Both the brief of the Attorney General of California and that of the Chairman of the Select Committee of the House of Representatives of the United States as *amicus curiae* [friends of the court] have sharpened this appreciation. . . . In the words of Mr. Justice Cardozo: "The Constitution was framed under the dominion of a political philosophy less parochial in range. It was framed upon the theory that the peoples of the several states must sink or swim together, and that in the long run prosperity and salvation are in union and not division. . . ."

*   *   *

But there was no union—of minds or workers. Organized labor had left a vacuum, and into it rushed a handful of Communists. Society abhors a vacuum as much as nature itself, and the Communists were quick to see the chance presented to them. They attached themselves to spontaneous strikes, sought to blow each one into gigantic proportions, rallied the workers and began organizing them into one big union for an all-out counterpunch at the oppressors. These Communist leaders do not seem to have had the full force of the Communist Party of the United States behind them, for its general secretary, Earl Browder, did not even mention this new union in his official history of the party. Browder, apparently, was as indifferent as top AFL officials.

The Cannery and Agricultural Workers' Industrial Union was organized for the benefit of the migrants in 1931. The hungry, miserable pickers did not much care who organized them, just so long as someone cared enough to do the job. They were unafraid of the words "Communist" and "Red." All they knew was that they had been "droughted" and "tractored" off their farms back home, had responded to leaflets promising them work, had arrived in California broke, had found neither the jobs nor the wages they had been led to expect, now had to vie with five or six men for every job opening, had been herded into squalid camps, had run out of food and hope. Where else could they turn for help? They lacked political sophistication. To them a Communist looked like one of themselves, and only the Communists promised them anything.

Still, of the 350,000 Okies who poured into California only about 30,000 of them joined the new Communist-led union—which must say something about Americans and Americanism. A majority of these migrants may have possessed, after all, a degree of native political sophistication. It is possible that tens of thousands more sympathized with the Communists without ever joining the party. As might be expected, the landowners of California began to regard every stubborn migrant as a Red.

The first California farm strike led by Communist agitators occurred in 1931, when fruit pickers at Vacaville protested against low wages. Four hundred workers held out for sixty days against beatings and persecutions. These were described by Orrick Johns in his book called *Time of Our Lives:* "In the first week of December when the strike was a few weeks old, a masked mob of forty men in a score of cars, took six strike leaders out of the Vacaville jail, drove them twenty miles from town, flogged them with tug straps, clipped their heads with sheep clippers, and poured red enamel over them."

The town was in a state of martial excitement by the time a Red delegation arrived to organize a defense program; 180 deputized vigilantes were under arms; scabs were carrying gas pipes and pruning shears. A Presbyterian minister by the name of Fruhling denounced the strikers from the pulpit and urged his congregation to drive them out of the community. When the men in the pews failed to respond, Reverend Fruhling bellowed: "There isn't a red-blooded man in this church! You're all yellow!"

The strike was broken. However, in Vacaville, as elsewhere in California, police brutality and attacks by self-righteous vigilantes drove some wavering migrants straight into the arms of the Communists. One worker told Orrick Johns: "We have to starve working so we decided to starve striking." In some ways the Red leaders were as self-righteous and brutal as the strong-arm men of the vested interests. They sought to provoke widespread indignation, sought to convert a series of small strikes into a general uprising, secretly felt that violence served their means.

John Steinbeck's novel *In Dubious Battle* tells the story of a few Communists who precipitated a strike by apple pickers. One of the characters is a physician, called Doc Burton, a friend of the strikers with a philosophical turn of mind. In talking with Jim Nolan, who has just joined the party, Doc Burton says: ". . . In my little experience the end is never very different in its nature from the means. Damn it, Jim, you can only build a violent thing with violence."

Such wisdom was lost on Communists and owners alike as they locked in battle, but of course, philosophical detachment is difficult in time of war. For the first year or so the Cannery and Agricultural Workers' Industrial Union existed mostly in name, its membership tiny, its results puny. Then, as the hapless workers heaved their collective shoulders to get misery off their backs, one strike after another broke out in the valleys of California, and to their surprise the migrants won many of them. This was prior to the San Francisco general strike led by Harry Bridges and cries about a "Red invasion."

Now the cry arose. Now the owners reacted—overreacted, in fact. Those private armies called vigilantes sprang up everywhere. California was a home of vigilantism, for back in the frontier days, back in a time before constituted government could be created or attain real force, citizens had banded together in vigilante committees to take law and order into their own hands. Now, in the 1930's, the vigilantes rode again. Carey McWilliams has said that the drive toward Fascist control probably was "carried further in California than in any other State in the Union." Steinbeck added: "The large growers' groups have found the law inadequate to their uses; and they have become so powerful that such charges as felonious assault, mayhem and inciting to riot, kidnaping and flogging cannot be brought against them in the controlled courts." They practiced, Steinbeck went on to say, "a system of terrorism that would be unusual in the Fascist nations of the world."

A California state senator named John Phillips visited Germany and attended a Nazi Party rally in Nuremberg. Upon returning to his home state, he published his impressions in a magazine called the *California Cultivator*. Phillips was particularly taken with the new type of German citizenship—the *Reichsbürger*—under which "you simply say that anybody who agrees with you is a citizen of the first class, and anybody who does not agree with you is a non-voting citizen." This elected state official admired Hitler, writing: "I would like to tell you how the personality of Hitler impressed me and how I feel that he has a greater personal appeal, a

greater personal influence on his people than many of the nations realize."
Later, in a speech, Phillips flatly declared: "Hitler has done more for
democracy than any man before him."

Fascism also won the approval of William Randolph Hearst, who owned
land in California. In October, 1935, the publisher editorialized: "Whenever you hear a prominent American called a 'Fascist,' you can usually
make up your mind that the man is simply a LOYAL CITIZEN WHO
STANDS FOR AMERICANISM." (Capitals supplied by Mr. William
Randolph Hearst.) Steinbeck did not use Hearst's name in *The Grapes of
Wrath,* but he had one Okie say: " 'They's a fella, newspaper fella near the
coast, got a million acres—'

"Casy looked up quickly. 'Million acres? What in the worl' can he do
with a million acres?'

" 'I dunno. He jus' got it. Runs a few cattle. Got guards ever'place to keep
folks out. Rides aroun' in a bullet-proof car. I seen pitchers of him. Fat,
sof' fella with little mean eyes an' a mouth like a ass-hole. Scairt he's gonna
die. Got a million acres an' scairt of dyin'.' "

In 1934 in the San Joaquin Valley workers for the Tagus ranch built a
huge moat around an orchard "to protect the properties," armed guards
stood at every entrance, and a machine gun was mounted on a truck. A
United Press dispatch said: "All roads leading to the ranch, with the
exception of the main entrance where guards are stationed, are blocked by
barbed wire and flooded with water by dikes. Fifty old employees report
nightly to the ranch manager regarding the conduct of employees under
suspicion."

Fiery crosses burned at night here and there on the California landscape.
Americans had the right to strike, but some communities passed laws
prohibiting picketing. El Centro's police chief ordered his cops to "arrest
all white girls and Filipinos seen together at or near Main Street." More
and more gun permits were issued. American Legion members held trial
"mobilizations." Radio stations warned that Communist organizers were
descending on this or that valley. Newspapers shrilled about "foreign
agitators," although most of the Red recruiters were native-born Americans. Suspects were arrested "to avert a possible strike among lettuce
workers," as one paper put it.

The connection between this hysteria and the powerful farm associations
was spelled out by a San Jose newspaper when it said:

> Santa Clara County orchardists today were armed with legal weapons to
> combat recurrences this year of Communist agitation, striking and rioting
> in Valley fruit orchards, which were a feature of last year's pear harvest.
>   Two county ordinances, one regulating the holding of parades and pro-
> cessions on any public highway, sidewalk or alley in the unincorporated
> area of the county, and the other regulating the establishment of camps on
> county ranch properties outside the incorporated limits of cities and towns,
> were adopted by the board of supervisors.

The ordinances were prepared with the cooperation of the Santa Clara County Pear Growers Association. . . .

On March 28, 1934, the Associated Farmers of California was organized. It collected all local and regional farm associations within one supergroup having close ties with the state Chamber of Commerce and a strong lobby in the state capital. The stated purpose of this new organization was to fight Communism. Soon, though, an annual report declared its opposition to the "unionization of farm labor on any basis." It was obvious that the Associated Farmers agreed with the judge who said California agriculture needed peonage. As their president they elected Colonel Walter E. Garrison, whom Carey McWilliams characterized as "the Führer of the California farmers."

McWilliams was struck by the efficiency and ruthlessness of the Associated Farmers, saying: "Carefully coordinated from the top, the organizational network functions with clocklike precision, policing entire crop industries, enforcing uniform decisions, holding recalcitrant employers in line. When the need arises, the full weight of this powerful apparatus can be brought to bear upon any threatened sector of the agricultural front with crushing force and effectiveness. Local, county, state, and, on occasion, federal officials jump when the Associated Farmers crack the whip."

Both the state of California and the federal government had employment services in that state, and both were controlled by the big growers and packers. In fact, corporate farmers used these unemployment services as a club to beat relief agencies into line. In Los Angeles County the workers were told their children must help them harvest walnuts—otherwise they would get no relief. Clients were forced off relief rolls and told to report for work in the fields—sometimes in fields far distant from their camps. The growers demanded that relief agencies deliver workers to them. In some instances, relief allowances were cut so low that the recipients had to accept the cheapest kind of wages offered them by the bosses.

One county after another announced the formation of vigilante committees. They used threats and violence to try to keep the workers from organizing, confining their terror tactics to their own counties at first. Then four vigilante committees merged into the Imperial Valley Anti-Communist Association with headquarters at Brawley and an initial membership of 3,000. Local police departments beefed up their forces with so-called Red squads or intelligence squads. Some members of the American Legion drilled with "obsolete" rifles which Congress turned over to them. Small private armies were raised.

The Silver Shirts, for example, was very active in southern California. Its full name was the Silver Shirt Legion of America, its headquarters were in Asheville, North Carolina, and its leader was William Dudley Pelley. This man was so Fascist-minded that he would not let Silver Shirt members vote on their own affairs. The California subleader of this organization was

Captain Eugene R. Case, who published an anti-Communist weekly paper which he proclaimed was 100 percent pro-American. Case may have been unaware of George Bernard Shaw's remark that "anyone who says he is 100 percent anything is usually 90 percent a fool."

In February, 1935, the Associated Farmers sponsored the formation in Sacramento of the California Cavaliers, a paramilitary unit with the announced purpose of "stamping out all un-American activity among farm labor." That same year a man named Colonel Arthur Guy Empey formed the Hollywood Hussars and recruited several movie stars, including Gary Cooper; many of them resigned when the pro-Fascist nature of the Hussars became clear.

The disenchantment felt by some members of the movie colony about the Hussars did not deter one of the biggest stars of them all—Victor McLaglen. An Irishman born in England, McLaglen won an Oscar for his portrayal of a traitor of the Irish rebellion in a great picture called *The Informer*. Spectacularly strong, standing six feet three and weighing 240 pounds, McLaglen always said, "I'm a farmer and my big interest in life is my farm." In 1936, at the height of his fame, he put together a volunteer outfit called McLaglen's Light Horse Troop. The nucleus of his private army consisted of Irish, Scottish and English war veterans. They wore uniforms not unlike those of the Canadian Mounties and performed military maneuvers in public. McLaglen paid all expenses. He is reported to have said: "Sure, we're organized to fight! We consider an enemy anything opposed to the American idea, whether it's an enemy outside or inside these borders." He denied that his troopers were Fascists, but its vigilante overtones aroused bitter comment in Hollywood and elsewhere.

In 1937 the port of San Francisco was closed by another strike. On January 15 the Associated Farmers announced that they had mobilized an army of 10,000 "farmers" to march on that city and open the waterfront. The governor of California promised them police protection. So did the mayor of San Francisco. Carey McWilliams felt that this announced march on San Francisco was planned in all seriousness and might have taken place if the dock strike had not ended when it did. "The threat," McWilliams went on to say, "was highly significant as an indication of the close co-operation that now exists between the Industrial Association of San Francisco and the Associated Farmers, the two groups now functioning as a single unit."

At a convention of the California Sheriffs Association a representative of the Lake Erie Chemical Company of San Francisco made a hard pitch for chemical warfare. "Any time any of you people want any information," he said, "we will be glad to have you call on us." Besides tear gas, he recommended the use of vomiting gas in special situations. "Where you have a Mexican camp and they tell you to keep out, a couple of these vomiting candles just tossed over the fence will start them going and your two or three thousand Mexicans will decide to move, and move very suddenly, and you will never have them back in your county again."

In his book called *Factories in the Fields* Carey McWilliams wrote:

On June 15, 1936, 2,500 Mexican orange pickers struck in Southern California, tying up, for several weeks, a $20,000,000 citrus crop. Vigilantism immediately began to flourish. Workers were evicted from their homes; Orange County was virtually in a state of siege, with highway traffic under police surveillance; 400 special armed guards, under the command of former "football heroes" of the University of California masquerading as amateur storm troopers, were recruited; over 200 workers were arrested at the outset of the strike and herded in a stockade, or bull pen, in which the court proceedings, such as their arraignment, were conducted; bail was fixed at a prohibitive figure; and, when attorneys entered the county to defend the workers, they were arrested on petty traffic charges, followed about by armed thugs, and threatened in open court.

State highway patrolmen moved in and established a portable radio station, KAPA, by means of which armed patrols were directed throughout the region. Guards with rifles and shotguns patrolled the fields and "protected" strikebreakers, and the sheriff instructed these guards, mostly high school and college youngsters, "to shoot to kill," his orders being enthusiastically headlined and warmly italicized in the *Los Angeles Times* and *Examiner*. When arrested strikers were brought into court (I was an eye witness to these proceedings), submachine guns, shotguns, rifles and revolvers were openly displayed in the courtroom. The *Los Angeles Examiner* spoke touchingly of the "quieting effect of the drastic wholesale arrests" while the *Times* gave a graphic account of one raid:

"Suddenly, late in the night, three or four automobiles loaded with grim faced men appeared out of the darkness surrounding the little settlement (a workers' camp). In a few seconds, tear gas bombs hissed into the small building where the *asserted* strikers [Note: Italics by McWilliams] were in conclave, the conferees with smarting eyes broke, and ran out under cover of darkness and the meeting was at an end. Witnesses said they heard the mysterious automobiles and the night-raiders whirring away without leaving a trace of their identity."

On July seventh, in a front-page story, the *Times* joyously announced that "old vigilante days were revived in the orchards of Orange County yesterday as one man lay near death and scores nursed injuries." The *Examiner* proclaimed the fact that the growers had, in addition to state highway patrolmen and special deputies, commissioned "bands of men, armed with tear gas and shotguns," to conduct "open *private* warfare against citrus strikers." [Note: Italics by the author of this book.]

McWilliams went on to say:

No one who has visited a rural county in California under these circumstances will deny the reality of the terror that exists. It is no exaggeration to describe this state of affairs as Fascism in practice. Judges blandly deny Constitutional rights to defendants and hand out vagrancy sentences which approximate the period of the harvest season. It is useless to appeal, for, by the time the appeal is heard, the crop will be harvested. The workers are trapped, beaten, terrorized, yet they still manage to hold out. In the Orange County strike food trucks, sent by strike sympathizers in Los Angeles, were hijacked and dumped on the highways.

The provocation for this vicious assault, which was carefully directed by the local shipper-growers and the Associated Farmers, was a union demand for forty cents an hour, together with payment of transportation to and from work, and the correction of certain minor grievances (the prevailing wage rate at the time was twenty cents an hour). It should be remembered, moreover, as the growers themselves have repeatedly conceded, that orange picking involves a variety of skilled labor.

At the time of this particular strike, the growers had just received a reduction in freight rates which resulted in an annual saving of over $2,000,000 a year.

The mass violence in Orange County was successful in its aim, however, and the strike was broken. At the end of the third week, the strikers began to go back to work, with slight wage increases, in some instances. . . .

It may be noted that many of Carey McWilliams' opinions were supported by the La Follette Committee and the National Labor Board's commission.

* * *

The night of August 21, 1935, vigilante violence broke out in Santa Rosa, California. Lying 50 miles north of San Francisco, a part of Sonoma County, this city is a shipping center for the rich fruit grown in the surrounding region. Toward the end of the summer of 1935, with the approach of harvesttime for hops and grapes and prunes, some local citizens began to fear that union organizers might interfere with the gathering in of the crops. Vigilantes started scheming.

In a book called *You Can't Do That,* George Seldes says that the Santa Rosa vigilantes consisted of "several bankers, a head of the federal re-employment bureau, motorcycle policemen, a member of the state legislature, American Legionnaires, petty politicians, members of the Chamber of Commerce, and, according to a suit filed by a victim in the county court, the mayor himself, who is a banker."

The Santa Rosa *Press-Democrat* published a story that was astonishing, since it was written by a vigilante who took part in the action. In part, this man said:

. . . Never in my life have I seen such a grim, serious minded band of citizens as determined upon their objective as the vigilantes were in seeking to oust radical agitators.

It was just at dusk that we assembled after an emergency call from our leaders. Nearly 300 men responded. . . . We formed in two groups. . . . It was an awe-inspiring sight . . . carrying weapons ranging from rifles to home-made billy clubs and ready to battle against men who ridicule the American flag. . . . Someone has to teach these communists they are not wanted. . . .

Gathering in a hall in downtown Santa Rosa, the vigilantes discussed their strategy. No Communist meeting was being held in the city that night, so the men decided to invade the homes of their intended victims. The night raider who wrote the newspaper story went on to say:

> . . . Soon six men returned dragging a cringing and pitiful looking specimen of a man to the center of the hall. . . .
> "What'll we do with him?" someone shouted.
> And came a multitude of answers. . . .
> "Give him the works!"
> "Run him out!"
> "Get the tar!" . . .

This first victim was Jack Green. The vigilantes decided to use him as a decoy to lure his friends into their clutches. Green was led to a ranch owned by Sol Nitzberg. As ordered, Green knocked on the door. Nitzberg, aware of what was happening, threw open the door, dragged Green inside, then slammed the door in the face of the vigilantes. Next, Nitzberg fired a warning shot.

Writing about Nitzberg, the self-confessed vigilante said:

> . . . He was in plain sight of the viligante gunmen but they wouldn't shoot because of fear they might hit the wife or children. It became a strange siege almost like war days. . . . Two of the gas shells ripped through the window into the house but failed to explode. A third struck on the window sill and burst outside, sending a great wave of painful searing tear gas back upon all of us. It was awful! After gagging and choking a while [sic] our gang, looking all the wilder with tear-stained faces, finally shot a successful shell into house.
> A cry arose as the gas went through every room in the structure. The woman shouted "We'll come out, we'll come out." A cheer went up from the boys outside. . . . In a few minutes out walked Nitzberg—sullen, bitter, refusing to say a word. With him was Green, terror-stricken and gasping at the thought of going back into the hands of the wild mob. Our boys surged down onto the pair, seizing them roughly and dragging them down the road to the cars. . . .
> When we got back to the warehouse, the story of the shooting and Green's attempt to escape spread like wildfire. The pair was dragged into the hall—stupefied from fright and beatings. By that time another man, C. Meyer of Cotati, had also been brought in and a short time later Ed Wolff of Healdsburg was added to the four victims. It was a sight that few who saw it will ever forget. Dimmed lights added to the ghastly scene caused by the milling crowds of vigilantes in varied masks and other disguises.

It had been an all night task, but at last the climax was near and everyone was on edge. Our leader addressed us and radicals caught, declaring, "Sonoma county is not large enough for such men as you who are attempting to overthrow the government under which you live!" . . .

An American flag was produced and the pair asked to drop to the floor on bended knees and kiss it. Both refused sullenly, but not for long. After a count of three, fists swung through the air. Both men dropped to the floor, semi-conscious. They were shaken back to sensibility enough to obey the order and kiss the Stars and Stripes. Wolff pleaded that he was not a Communist. . . . One man pushed his way through the crowd to face Wolff, grasping him around the throat in powerful hands. A hush came over the crowd as the viligante cursed and berated Wolff with Communist activity and finally ended with a dramatic shout: "Ed, my hands are on your throat—and the only thing that keeps me from crushing the life out of your cursed body is that I believe in Almighty God!"

After pleading that he would gladly get out of the country at once and stay out, the crowd agreed to release Wolff. Meyer and Ford were given the same warning and also escaped the tar and feathers. But the impatient mob waited no longer with Green and Nitzberg. Clippers were produced and hair hacked from their heads. Shirts were ripped from their backs. Buckets of tar paint were hurled over them. Pillows were broken and feathers hailed down upon the sticky black substance. From two men they had been transformed into fantastic, ghostlike creatures of some other world.

Communism in Sonoma county was getting its due—and the vigilantes, restrained through most of the night, came near going wild. Kicked, beaten, dragged and shoved, the two staggering tar victims—their eyes glazed with torture and terror—were taken out into the street. Then came a procession that Santa Rosa has never seen the like before. Down Fourth Street they walked, clear past the courthouse and on out of the city limits —while behind them followed the wildly shouting and triumphant vigilantes.

It was a long night, a wild night. But the vigilantes are just as determined that there will be other such nights as long as Communists continue attempts at radical agitation in Sonoma county. The ultimatum has been issued. The vigilantes have proven that they are ready and willing to back it up with violence. It's up to the Communists to get out now, or suffer the consequences.

This pious confession in the Santa Rosa *Press-Democrat,* together with the mob brutality it described, evoked cries of outrage from Americans all across the land. Attorneys for the American Civil Liberties Union filed a suit against Fred Cairns, secretary of the Chamber of Commerce of nearby Healdsburg, that accused him of being the leader of the mob. The ACLU also issued a report declaring that the so-called better citizens of the region, using weapons supplied by local authorities, had overthrown law and order and violated every fundamental right of the mob victims.

But the governor and attorney general refused to institute criminal action against any of the vigilantes. Six were identified, and at last civil suits were brought against them; but of the few who were tried, all were acquitted. None of the mob's victims won any kind of redress.

*   *   *

It has been said by Eric Hoffer, the longshoreman-philosopher, that we are "most self-righteous when irrevocably in the wrong."

*   *   *

At a statewide convention of the American Legion held in California in 1934 the Legionnaires talked about establishing a penal colony in the "practically inaccessible lands west of Point Barrow, Alaska," where undesirable aliens, Reds and agitators might be sent. Nothing came of this lawless idea, but Alaska did become the scene of another kind of experiment.

The Federal Emergency Relief Administration decided to try to transfer some drought victims to Alaska and resettle them in colonies. From relief rolls in Minnesota, Michigan and Wisconsin, the FERA culled the names of candidates and then checked on their hardihood, pioneer background and knowledge of farming. Chosen at last were 208 farmers willing to emigrate from their profitless lands. In May, 1935, together with their wives and children, they were loaded into an Army transport ship and carried up to Alaska.

They were settled in the 20-mile-long Matanuska Valley denting the southern shore near the Pacific, a fertile wooded region hemmed in by the snow-crowned Chugach Mountain range. Each family was given a 40-acre tract from the 8,000 acres of public land in the valley, plus a $3,000 grubstake, houses and farming tools. Furthermore, as they struggled to sink their roots into the strange soil, they received monthly allotments ranging from $40 a month for a family of two to $104 for a family of thirteen; the average was about $8 a head.

Fifty-two families returned to the States, but their places were taken by Alaskans. On the first anniversary of their arrival the settlers proudly displayed the 176 log cabins and bungalows they had built, 123 barns, 188 wells, 82 miles of new roads, a power plant, trading post and community house. Nearing completion were a creamery and cannery, a modern hospital, a workers' dormitory, and a central grade school and high school. And increasing thousands of acres of land were being plowed and planted.

*   *   *

Woody Guthrie was the poet laureate of the Depression, while John Steinbeck was its chronicler. No novelist ever approximated the sensitivity and mastery of Steinbeck in describing the droughts and dust storms, the despoiling of the plains states, the exodus of the Okies, their disenchantment with California, their troubles with elected officials and self-appointed vigilantes.

On February 27, 1902, John Steinbeck was born in Salinas, Monterey

County, California, and by the time of his death the Salinas Valley was known as Steinbeck country, just as the state of Missouri and the Mississippi River were known as Mark Twain country. Steinbeck came of German, Irish and New England extraction. For many years his father was the treasurer of Monterey County, while his mother taught in public schools. John was a blue-eyed boy who grew into a six-footer with the rugged build of an athlete.

He attended Stanford University but left without taking a degree, worked in New York City as a reporter for the New York *American* until he was fired, toiled as a hod carrier during construction of the third Madison Square Garden on Manhattan's upper Eighth Avenue. For two years he lived alone in the High Sierras of California, employed as a caretaker for a private estate. Then he worked in a trout hatchery, as a fruit picker on a ranch, as a surveyor, an apprentice painter and a chemist. This long association with laborers enabled Steinbeck to depict them realistically after he became a writer.

His first novel, *Cup of Gold,* appeared in 1929 and sold only about 1,500 copies. Now married and existing on a $25 monthly allowance from his father, Steinbeck slaved over short stories and novels and perfected his craft. Using a pencil, he wrote tiny cramped words on lined yellow sheets, somewhat careless about punctuation, his hand-scrawled manuscripts being typed by others.

Steinbeck's fourth published novel, *In Dubious Battle,* appeared in 1936. In telling this story of an apple pickers' strike, he attacked both the militant strike leaders and the insensitive growers. His sympathy clearly lay with the "working stiffs," caught in the middle between capitalists and Communists. André Gide called this book the best psychological portrayal he knew of Communism. On the strength of the novel Steinbeck was hired by the San Francisco *News* to write about California's camps for migrant workers. To do the necessary research, get the feel of the background, he went to Oklahoma and then actually traveled with some Okies as they painfully inched their way to the Golden State. Out of this personal experience, out of the moral indignation he felt over the indignities heaped on the victims of the Dust Bowl, came a perceptive series of newspaper articles together with his sixth and best book.

He called it *The Grapes of Wrath,* deriving the title from the "Battle Hymn of the Republic" by Julia Ward Howe. Viking Press published the novel on April 14, 1939, and it took the country by storm, selling 300,000 copies that year and remaining on the best-seller list the following year. A great social document, as well as a great novel, it did for the Okies what Harriet Beecher Stowe's *Uncle Tom's Cabin* had done for slavery and Upton Sinclair's *The Jungle* had done for packinghouse workers. Henry Steele Commager, the noted historian, has said: *"Grapes of Wrath* is more than the story of the flight of the Okies from the dust bowl to golden California. It is an indictment of the economy that drove them into flight, that took the land from those who tilled it and handed it over to the banks, that permitted hunger in the land of plenty and lawlessness in the name of law and made a mockery of the principles of justice and democracy."

Literary critics acclaimed the book. Alexander Wollcott said: "I am not forgetting such books as *Moby Dick* and *Leaves of Grass* and *Life on the Mississippi* and *Death Comes for the Archbishop* when I say it seems to me as great a book as has yet come out of America." Louis Kronenberger wrote: "No novel of our day has been written out of a more genuine humanity. . . . Homeric chronicle of a great migration—breathless, comic, heart-breaking, almost historical . . . a fiery document of protest and compassion . . . a story that has to be told . . . and a book that must be read." At a later date Carl Van Doren said: "Readers who had thought of migrant workers as so many negligible thousands on the road or at work in masses, now suddenly realized that they were not that at all. The Joads might have been any ordinary farm family uprooted and turned out to drift over the continent. This novel did more than any other Depression novel to revise the picture of America as Americans imagined it."

One cannot be sure that Hitler ever read *The Grapes of Wrath,* but it has been reported that he accepted Steinbeck's Okies as typical Americans. The author's "cry to conscience," as the New York *Times* phrased it, failed however to move the hearts of some comfortable Americans. An economist named Ruth Alexander blasted the novel as a "one-sided emotional appeal to class prejudice and unworthy of America." Edmund Wilson sneered at what he called Steinbeck's presentation of life in animal terms.

Although Steinbeck did not mention the Bank of America by name, he criticized banks and land companies for putting small farmers out of business. One of his characters says to another: ". . . Now, do you know who runs the Farmers' Association? I'll tell you. The Bank of the West. That bank owns most of this valley, and it's got paper on everything it don't own."

This jab worried officials of the powerful Bank of America. They denied that the bank owned most of the valley. But their worry began to compound itself when they heard that Treasury Secretary Morgenthau had said that the Bank of America had furnished thousands of dollars to finance the Associated Farmers. Lawrence Mario Giannini, son of A. P. Giannini and now president of the bank, wrote James Roosevelt, the son of the President, to declare that his bank had never contributed "so much as one dollar to Associated Farmers," despite urgent solicitation. Marquis and Bessie James, in their authorized history of the Bank of America, said that Steinbeck and Carey McWilliams, as well, "were careless of some of the facts."

A bank officer named Howard Whipple was given the job of trying to find out whether *The Grapes of Wrath* had done any damage to the institution. Subsequently he reported that although the novel probably had strengthened the notion of "land-grabbing on our part . . . it has not hurt us [as] shown by the extraordinary maintenance of our deposit levels."

When Steinbeck's masterpiece came up for consideration by judges of the Book-of-the-Month Club, indecision was shown by one of them—William Allen White. This Kansas editor, widely regarded as a spokesman for the nation's middle class, sent the club president a wire that said: ". . . Far and away the best novel is *The Grapes of Wrath* but it would be a mistake to buy it. Thousands of our readers would be offended by its necessary but to me quite inoffensive indecency." White may have had in mind the book's last scene in which the Joad girl, who had just given birth to a stillborn child, acquiesces to her mother's urging and offers her breast to a man dying of starvation.

But despite White, the other judges accepted the Steinbeck novel for republication by the Book-of-the-Month Club. It won Steinbeck the Pulitzer Prize in 1940, was made into a movie with music composed by Woody Guthrie, went through twelve editions and had been published in fourteen foreign languages by 1957, eventually sold more than 3,000,000 copies, and helped Steinbeck capture the Nobel Prize for Literature in 1962.

It was the right book at the right time. It touched off a national explosion of protest about the plight of the dispossessed. It was debated less as a novel than as a profound sociological treatise. Down through the years it became required reading in scores of colleges and universities. Of those who read *The Grapes of Wrath,* few could forget its terrible indictments, such as the one in this paragraph:

. . . And the companies, the banks worked at their own doom and they did not know it. The fields were fruitful, and starving men moved on the roads. The granaries were full and the children of the poor grew up rachitic, and the pustules of pellagra swelled on their sides. The great companies did not know that the line between hunger and anger is a thin line. And money that might have gone to wages went for gas, for guns, for agents and spies, for blacklists, for drilling. On the highways the people moved like ants and searched for work, for food. And the anger began to ferment. . . .

27

The Works Progress Administration

H ARRY HOPKINS loped into the federal security building in Washington, D.C., twisting his scrawny neck from side to side and barking orders at the assistants trying to keep up with him.

The previous day, May 22, 1933, President Roosevelt had named him the administrator of the Federal Emergency Relief Administration. His lips taut, his movements jerky, Hopkins scurried down a hall, saw a desk that had not yet been moved into the room that was to become his office, flopped down into the chair behind it. Oblivious to the confusion swirling about him and raising his voice to be heard over the clatter of heels in the corridor, the former social worker began dictating telegrams to the governors of all forty-eight states.

Eleven days earlier Congress had passed the Federal Emergency Relief Act creating this new agency FERA, as it came to be known. The act said the FERA's purpose was "to provide for co-operation by the federal government with the states and territories . . . in relieving hardship and suffering caused by unemployment." It was set up for only two years since it was intended as a stopgap measure.

The FERA began with $500 million taken from RFC funds. Half this sum was to be given to states applying for aid through their governors; then the governors would spend this money for the relief of transients, for educational programs, for self-help and barter and for direct relief in the purchase of surplus food for distribution to needy families. The other half was to be held in reserve for emergency allotments. For every $3 spent for relief by states and cities, the federal government would contribute $1. Under the Hoover administration the federal government had *lent* money to states and their subdivisions; the FERA was ready to *give* it to them.

Little was known in Washington about the efficiency of the various state

489

and local relief organizations across the country. Some states and many counties had no relief agencies at all. Also lacking in the national capital were reliable statistics about relief needs at the local level. However, it was known that states and cities were giving less and less relief to jobless men and their families. In New York City, for example, families got an average of only $2.39 a week in relief money. The ugly mood of the nation was evident in the fact that a second bonus army had entered Washington just two weeks before Harry Hopkins took office.

Roosevelt had told Hopkins he wanted immediate action, and Hopkins was delighted. A man as restless as an atom, he was a chain smoker of cigarettes and a gulper of one cup of coffee after another. New to the Washington scene, inexperienced in national politics, loathing red tape, unimpressed by famous men and fat titles, Hopkins began his job with a twisted smile and the remark "I'm not going to last six months here, so I'll do as I please!"

A month after Roosevelt had been elected President the independent-minded Hopkins had written his brother: "It seems to me that the principal idea of the public administrators for the past several years has been to protect big business, and I have a great deal more confidence in the 'hoi polloi' that are going into office on the fourth of March than I ever had in Andy Mellon and his crowd of highbinders. . . ."

Hopkins' personality was so cross-grained that he could be curt to his friends, but his heart was so soft he always was gentle with poor people. As a boy he had known poverty firsthand. "The poor are not poor because they're bad or lazy," he said. "Anyway, I don't see why, because a man is lazy, his wife and children shouldn't eat. A man drinks, he is a drunkard. Well, what are you going to do with his wife and children? I believe people are poor, in the main, because we don't know how to distribute the wealth properly."

Hopkins wore rumpled clothes and had trouble making both ends meet in his personal life. Although he had earned $15,000 as a social service executive, he had taken this new federal job at an annual salary of less than $8,000. Divorced from his first wife and paying her alimony of $5,000 a year, he was left with a mere $3,000 a year for living expenses. But this never seemed to matter too much to Harry Hopkins, who knew little about the value of money—his or the government's. Nonetheless, he was completely honest and died a poor man.

Two hours after he sat down at his desk in a corridor of the Federal Security Building, he disbursed more than $5,000,000 to Colorado, Illinois, Iowa, Michigan, Mississippi, Ohio and Texas. This alarmed the Washington *Post,* which published a headline saying MONEY FLIES and then went on to declare that the half billion appropriated by Congress for direct relief of the states would not last a month if Hopkins kept up this pace.

Hopkins, a lover of horse racing, was off and running as the world's greatest spender and one of the world's largest employers.

*   *   *

Harry Lloyd Hopkins was born in Sioux City, Iowa, on August 17, 1890, the fourth of David and Anna Hopkins' five children. His father was a harness maker; his mother taught school. After Harry became the most influential man in the United States government, next to Roosevelt himself, he continued to boast about his humble origins—sometimes to the annoyance of his friends. Frances Perkins thought this a sign of insecurity—that he always felt inferior to others despite what she considered to be his superior mind and character.

When Harry was two years old, his family moved to Nebraska. By the time he was eleven the Hopkins had settled in Grinnell, Iowa, a folksy town with a strong Methodist flavor. From his mother, a zealous Methodist, he got his strong sense of righteousness, while from his father he inherited geniality and wit. As a boy Harry scrubbed floors, beat carpets, milked cows and toiled on nearby farms like other underprivileged young people. In 1908 he entered Grinnell College, a small institution with a high reputation for scholarship. He made only average grades, seldom revealing the probing intelligence which later caused Winston Churchill to dub him Lord Root of the Matter. And just for the fun of it, so it seems, he became a hot-shot campus politician. During one summer vacation his mother took him to New York City for a short visit, and the big city excited him so much he knew he just had to live there.

In 1912, after graduation, he headed for the East Coast. One of his professors, who was connected with a Manhattan settlement house named Christodora House, had won his appointment as head of a summer camp for boys across the Hudson River in New Jersey. When camp was over, he began working in Christodora House itself, located on Manhattan's Lower East Side, and there the naïve youth from the Corn Belt met Jewish boys for the first time in his life. He was amazed to see gangsters stroll into settlement dances and street bullies fighting with broken bottles.

Over the next few years Hopkins developed into a social worker and an executive of social agencies, slaving sixteen hours a day, organizing boys' clubs, plodding up tenement stairs, listening to the laments of the underprivileged, making pioneer surveys of unemployment. Humble and sincere, he was able to get along with all kinds of people. With the stench of the slums constantly in his nostrils, he made a slight turn to the political left and seemingly was registered for a while as a Socialist—a matter of some concern after he entered the federal government. And after his divorce he suffered so much personal strain that he had himself psychoanalyzed.

*   *   *

In 1930, with the Depression worsening, Governor Roosevelt of New York wrote a letter expressing what might be called his willow tree theory about averting revolution. Roosevelt said it was "time for the country to become fairly radical for at least one generation. History shows that when this occurs occasionally, nations are saved from revolutions." In a heavy storm, of course, the rigid oak falls while the flexible willow survives.

While Roosevelt held office as governor, he had convinced the New York legislature of the wisdom of creating a Temporary Emergency Relief Administration to give jobs, food, clothing and shelter to needy people who had lived in the state for two years. As chairman of this state agency the governor chose Jesse Straus, chairman of the board of Macy's department store. Harry Hopkins, whom Roosevelt had first met in 1928, was named executive director. Before long Straus resigned because of the pressures of his business career and urged Roosevelt to replace him with Hopkins. That was in 1931. Hopkins headed TERA for two years before the President summoned him to Washington.

Now that Hopkins was the national Santa Claus, ready to hand out goodies, people wondered about his character, appearance and personality. Far from a stereotyped Santa, Harry Hopkins was a sardonic thin man who treated Senators and governors like lackeys. Geoffrey T. Hellman wrote in the *New Yorker* that he looked like "an animated piece of Shredded Wheat." Louis W. Koenig said "he had the bent and gangly shape and thinning hair of an ill-used Raggedy Andy." His face was gaunt and lopsided, his dark eyes slitted and suddenly suspicious, all his facial features brightening and darkening like heat lightning on a summer evening. He never wore garters on his skinny ankles. Onto his head he would slap a shapeless hat. A dynamo of energy despite his frail body and poor health, Hopkins had a zest for life.

He felt that all people could be divided into the talkers and the doers— and he was a doer. His humble origin, his mother's rigid conscience and his contact with slum dwellers had made him into a fanatical social worker. But like all of us, Hopkins was a bundle of contradictions. He was Puritanical and pleasure-loving, an ascetic who drank and danced and played poker and lost on the horses. He could be tactless with the powerful of this nation and tender with its dispossessed. He was extroverted, and he was introverted. Forever restless, never quite finding himself despite analysis, Hopkins kept in perpetual motion and drove himself like a maniac.

Before he became a key figure in the New Deal, he read widely and even wrote poetry, though with little success. A fluent and entertaining conversationalist, he never learned how to write well. He was disliked by many people, but none accused him of being a bore. Studiously lacking in polish, he had an explosive laugh like the bark of a dog, indulged in practical jokes and enjoyed teasing his friends. His sharp mind cut to the core of every problem he faced, and he remembered almost everything he had read or heard.

A wisecracker, fond of bawdy remarks and shady stories, he liked to shock proper people. During meetings with influential men he would slump on the end of his spine, glare with beady eyes over his heavy-rimmed glasses and puncture pomposity by snarling: "Oh, yeah?" One of his favorite phrases was this: "We've got to crack down on the bastards!" But the other side of his personality showed in another of his frequent comments: "There's always a civilized way to do things."

Hugh Johnson, who shared honors with Harold Ickes as the best phrasemaker of all New Dealers, said that Hopkins "has a mind like a razor, a tongue like a skinning knife, a temper like a Tartar and a sufficient vocabulary of parlor profanity—words kosher enough to get by the censor but acid enough to make a mule-skinner jealous. . . . He's just a high-minded Holy Roller in a semi-religious frenzy."

*　　*　　*

"Dole" had become an emotionally charged word ever since the advent of the Depression. Throughout the Thirties people criticized the dole or praised the dole, often in a slipshod way since they did not bother to define the term and applied it to a variety of conditions and plans. Their arguments frequently ended in semantics—a debate over the meaning of meaning.

According to the dictionary, a dole is a gift of money, food or anything else given to a people by a private citizen, a ruler or a government. Far from being a gimmick dreamed up by wild-eyed New Dealers, the dole had an ancient history. In the first century of the Christian Era several Roman emperors distributed doles to the populace in times of famine. In the sixteenth century Queen Elizabeth of England instituted a poor law, which made the dole traditional for a while. Toward the end of the eighteenth century a rich New Yorker by the name of John Leake ordered in his will that loaves of bread be given to the poor every Sunday morning after services in Trinity Church. Immediately after the Armistice of 1918 Great Britain began paying a dole to jobless men.

When the Depression struck England, that nation reinstituted the dole, David Lloyd George saying that it averted revolt but adding that it would be better to use the money to provide work. In 1930 Winston Churchill defended the Bitish dole, declaring that it would not "sap the virility and self-reliance of our race." Spain, Holland, France, Czechoslovakia and Germany were among the other nations which started paying a dole to starving people. Mussolini, however, told James M. Curley of Boston that he preferred a works program to the dole. John J. Davis of Wall Street said that the United States did not need a "ruinous dole." Philadelphia Mayor J. H. Moore was against it. The Packard Motor Car Company and the American Engineering Council opposed it. Herbert Hoover frowned on direct relief, although he had helped railroads with the equivalent of the dole—subsidies.

Again, according to the dictionary, a subsidy is any gift of money or property made by a person or a government by way of financial aid. Most

494   A NATION IN TORMENT

of the time, a subsidy is given for purposes deemed beneficial to the government and the people. Down through the years it had become almost traditional for the American government to help railways and shipping lines by giving them direct subsidies, while indirect subsidies went to businessmen who mailed advertisements and goods at postal rates less than the cost to the federal government of handling such items. While businessmen and industrialists were quick to attack the dole, which helped poor people, they preferred to say nothing about subsidies, which enriched themselves.

When people read in the New York *Times* that the croupiers of Monaco had gone on the dole, they were immensely entertained. It also seemed funny when a man in New York City tried to pay a traffic fine with his relief check. A British actress named Wendy Hiller appeared in a Broadway production of a play entitled *Love on the Dole*. Senator Borah and Fiorello LaGuardia declared that they were not afraid of the word "dole."

A few businessmen favored the dole for "practical" reasons—"practical" being one of their favorite words. The National Industrial Conference Board published figures showing that direct relief cost from two to three times less than work relief. Winthrop W. Aldrich, chairman of the board of the Chase National Bank, came out for direct relief, arguing that England "has refused to go further into debt, has balanced its budget, and is taking care of the unemployment relief by a cash dole, similar to our home relief, derived from taxation." But some of Aldrich's fellow Republicans began joking about "From New Deal to New Dole."

Franklin D. Roosevelt, for his part, tried to balance idealism with practicality. As governor of New York he had said that "to these unfortunate citizens aid must be extended by government, not as a matter of charity, but as a matter of social duty." Nonetheless, while still governor, he had also said: "The dole method of relief for unemployment is not only repugnant to all sound principles of social economics, but is contrary to every principle of American citizenship and of sound government. American labor seeks no charity, but only a chance to work for its living."

Harry Hopkins agreed with Roosevelt. He detested direct relief. Work relief, said Hopkins, "preserves a man's morale. It saves his skill. It gives him a chance to do something socially useful." Both the President and his key relief administrator were keenly aware that the Federal Emergency Relief Administration was a quick thrust at a massive problem calling for greater leverage. On November 27, 1934, Roosevelt wrote to a friend: "What I am seeking is the abolition of relief altogether. I cannot say so out loud yet but I hope to substitute work for relief. . . ."

The FERA was born on May 12, 1933, and died on November 29, 1935. During the thirty-one months of its existence it spent a total of $3.6 billion. Of this huge sum, 71 percent was federal money, while the balance came from states, territories and cities. The FERA hit a peak in February, 1934, when almost 8,000,000 families were getting direct relief.

*   *   *

Secretary of the Interior Harold Ickes regarded public works as a cure-all for the Depression.

It may be remembered that Roosevelt had made Ickes the head of the Public Works Administration, which was created under Title II of the National Recovery Act. The PWA was intended to increase employment and help business by priming the pump—that is, raising purchasing power. Congress gave the PWA an initial appropriation of $3.3 billion. It had become Ickes' job to distribute this money to states, cities and other public bodies for the construction or repair of roads, public buildings and other ambitious projects. The way he went about this work was conditioned in part, of course, by his background and temperament.

Harold Le Claire Ickes was born in Frankstown Township, Blair County, Pennsylvania, on March 15, 1874—which made him one of the oldest of the New Dealers. After graduation from the University of Chicago in 1897, he worked as a Chicago newspaper reporter and then won a law degree, *cum laude,* from his Alma Mater. He entered the practice of law in Chicago and emerged as one of the Republican leaders of a city reform movement, becoming better known as a reformer than as a lawyer. Among the Goliaths he attacked was Samuel Insull.

Branching out into national politics, Ickes played a prominent role in Theodore Roosevelt's Bull Moose movement in 1912. In five successive Presidential campaigns, Ickes backed the losing candidates, switching at last from the Republican to the Democratic Party. By supporting Franklin D. Roosevelt in the 1932 campaign, he finally had a winner. FDR had never met Ickes until he had become the President-elect and was forming his Cabinet, but he liked him on sight and appointed him to the Interior Department.

Upon taking over this post, Ickes worked in his shirt sleeves at one end of a long rectangular room with walls decorated with buffalo heads. Rather short, he had a thick body, square face, heavy nose and gold-rimmed spectacles. He liked to call himself a curmudgeon, and it was true that Ickes was a grouchy and cantankerous man. This may have been due to the fact that in Chicago he had seen so much graft and corruption that he trusted no politician, no one seeking favors. People visiting his office were disconcerted by his habit of shuffling papers as they talked, fidgeting in his chair, glowering at them and interrupting to ask incisive questions. He was also deaf in his left ear.

Although he prided himself on his total honesty, he hated it when newspapers called him Honest Harold. Crusty much of the time, charming whenever he chose to be charming, Ickes had a nature as paradoxical in its own way as Hopkins. He belted down whiskey in an effort to get to sleep, and he was fond of dahlias. Wishing to be loved, he antagonized his superiors and subordinates alike with his testiness. He was unaware of the fact that he was an enormously egotistical fellow. Lonely much of the time, he felt a deep concern for friendless groups such as the Indians. He questioned the motives of everyone except himself.

A conscientious worker and a nit picker, Ickes closely examined every paper that reached his desk, signing at least 5,000 PWA contracts in triplicate, among other things. Every day he was appalled by the mountains of documents piled on his desk for signature. He worked every day of the week, including Sunday, and on every holiday, including Christmas. While Hugh Johnson dashed about the country peddling the glories of the NRA, Ickes huddled in his Washington office analyzing PWA projects. He wrote in his diary: "The principle we worked on was to give out to the country at this time only such projects as could be justified as legitimate public works projects."

Raymond Moley felt that Ickes was motivated by a couple of other considerations as well. Ickes, according to Moley, was less interested in quick recovery than in pursuing his theories of public ownership. Moley also thought that Ickes was so egotistical that he wanted to erect gigantic physical monuments to honor the New Deal. "He was like an Egyptian pharaoh," Moley said, "whose greatest contribution to his country was the building of his tomb."

The cautious Ickes noted in his journal something that happened at a Cabinet meeting. Commerce Secretary Daniel C. Roper told the President that a Chinese emperor back in the eleventh century had tried to end a depression in his own country by using recovery methods similar to those employed by the New Deal.

Laughingly, Roosevelt asked: "What happened to the emperor? Was he beheaded?"

"No," Roper replied with a smile. "He wasn't beheaded. But he was defeated."

Although Ickes made no comment about this exchange, he may have made a silent note not to risk his own head or position.

Granted the radically different personalities of Harold Ickes and Harry Hopkins, it was inevitable that they should develop into antagonists. In the expenditure of public money, Ickes was stingy, Hopkins lavish. Ickes was the tortoise, Hopkins the hare. Ickes spent about 70 percent for materials and 30 percent for wages, while Hopkins spent about 75 percent for wages and 25 percent for materials. Unfortunately for Ickes, the President's personality was more like Hopkins' than his own. Roosevelt became impatient with Ickes' slow progress and began hunting for other ways to get the public works program moving faster.

*   *   *

Hopkins was eager to help find a formula the President could use.

By October, 1933, Hopkins was worrying about the approach of winter, which he knew would intensify hardships across the land. Perhaps he could blunt the coming misery with a huge work program that got help to the people faster than Ickes' PWA. There was one big obstacle, though. Organized labor was opposed to the idea of the government "making" jobs.

That autumn Hopkins went to Chicago to see a football game and confer with public administration experts. From Chicago he traveled to Kansas City, where he discussed relief problems with Harry S. Truman, the presiding judge of the Jackson County Court and also the federal unemployment director for the state of Missouri. While in Kansas City, Hopkins took a long-distance call from an aide who said that a labor expert had dug up a helpful quote from the late Samuel Gompers, the father of organized labor in America. Gompers had urged just the kind of work program Hopkins was formulating in his mind, but for which he needed a precedent if he were to overcome labor's opposition and sell Roosevelt on the idea.

The day after Hopkins got back to Washington he lunched with the President and explained his program. It would substitute small public works projects for huge ones. It would abolish the means test, whereby a man who sought government relief was denied it if a member of his family was already employed. The pay envelope was to be substituted for the dole. The entire program would be run from Washington, rather than by the states and cities, as had happened under the FERA. Roosevelt, who liked the overall concept, asked how many jobs would have to be provided. Hopkins said about 4,000,000.

"Let's see," the President mused. "Four million people—that means roughly four hundred million dollars." He went on to say that perhaps he could take this sum from Ickes and give it to the agency Hopkins had proposed.

On November 8, 1933, Roosevelt issued an executive order creating the Civil Works Administration. He said it would give 4,000,000 people short-term jobs on small public works projects during the winter of 1933–34. The CWA would be financed jointly by the PWA and the FERA—with states, counties, cities and towns meeting their share of the cost. Ickes was ordered to give the CWA $400 million of his PWA funds. This was a hard enough blow to Ickes' ego, but he suffered even more when the President named Hopkins the CWA administrator.

Roosevelt tried to salvage Ickes' pride by saying that the PWA had been unable to "commence a very extensive program of large public works because of the unavoidable time consuming process of planning, designing and reviewing projects, clearing up legal matters, advertising for bids and letting contracts."

It may be noted that since the CWA came into existence on November 8, 1933, and since the FERA did not die until November 29, 1935, these two relief agencies overlapped. And Harry Hopkins headed both of them.

With his characteristic élan, Hopkins led the attack along this new relief front. Roosevelt helped by asking banks to cash the CWA checks soon to be issued, and at the end of the workweek of Friday, November 24, a total of 814,511 new CWA workers got checks amounting to a total of more than $7.5 million.

Despite Roosevelt's fondness for Harry Hopkins and Hugh Johnson, together with his own impulse to act swiftly, he was wise enough to realize that a moderating influence was needed. Four months before the creation of the CWA he had established the National Executive Council to coordinate and supervise the several new governmental agencies. Keeping the leadership of the council for himself, the President made Frank C. Walker its executive secretary. Walker was a good lawyer, a keen businessman and a shrewd judge of human nature. Soon after the CWA came into existence, Walker left the capital to tour the nation and observe its impact on the needy. After visiting his home state of Montana, he wrote: "I saw old friends of mine—men I had been to school with—digging ditches and laying sewer pipe. They were wearing their regular business suits as they worked because they couldn't afford overalls and rubber boots. If I ever thought, 'There, but for the grace of God—' it was right then."

One man pulled some silver coins out of his pocket and showed them to Walker, saying: "Do you know, Frank, this is the first money I've had in my pockets in a year and a half? Up to now, I've had nothing but tickets that you exchange for groceries."

Another said: "I hate to think what would have happened if this work hadn't come along. The last of my savings had run out. I'd sold or hocked everything I could. And my kids were hungry. I stood in front of the window of the bake-shop down the street and I wondered just how long it would be before I got desperate enough to pick up a rock and heave it through that window and grab some bread to take home."

After getting back to the capital Walker told the President: "I'd pay little attention to those who criticize the creation of CWA or its administration. Hopkins and his associates are doing their work well. They've done a magnificent job. It is amazing when you consider that within the short time since CWA was established, four million idle have been put to work. During Christmas week many of them were standing in a payroll line for the first time in eighteen months. You have every reason to be proud of CWA and its administration. It is my considered opinion that this has averted one of the most serious crises in our history. Revolution is an ugly word to use, but I think we were dangerously close at least to the threat of it."

In New York City alone there had been 1,500,000 unemployed men and women—a ticking time bomb. It was defused when the CWA began giving them jobs. Under this new Hopkins program all a person had to do to get work was prove that he was unemployed and physically fit. Within the first few weeks of the CWA, shoe stores all over the country sold out, and shoe factories reopened to meet this new demand—which proved that the pump-priming technique was working. In Chicago CWA workers helped chase rats out of the stockyards and Governor Henry Horner of Illinois praised the CWA program.

Skilled laborers were not permitted to earn more than $60 a month under the CWA. Technical and supervisory workers were paid from $24 to $45 a week. White-collar pay ranged from $15 to $24 weekly.

Among the CWA workers were 3,000 writers and artists—the genesis of the federal arts program under the forthcoming Works Progress Administration. At the request of the President, Ickes visited the Corcoran Galleries in Washington to see some paintings by CWA artists. "I will say," Ickes wrote in his dairy, "that most of the paintings were terrible from my point of view and I left wondering why men who turned out that kind of stuff should be supported as artists." Hopkins, however, rebutted all criticism about artists on relief rolls by snarling: "Hell! They've got to eat just like other people."

Although it may be difficult for a taxpayer to believe that a bureaucrat could behave heroically, this very thing happened. Mayor LaGuardia asked Hopkins to make Travis Harvard Whitney the CWA administrator for New York City. Whitney was fifty-eight years old, a Harvard graduate, a member of the Bankers' Club, a Wall Street lawyer and a Republican—but Hopkins cared nothing about a man's politics. Whitney was appointed on December 2, 1933.

He was gravely ill and may have known he was dying, but he made a convulsive effort to place 200,000 New Yorkers on the CWA rolls as fast as possible that bitterly cold winter. One day he phoned Heywood Broun, president of the American Newspaper Guild, to say that if Broun gave him a list of jobless reporters, he thought he could get some under the CWA.

"When do you want to see us?" Broun asked.

"Come down now."

When Broun walked into Whitney's headquarters, he found the administrator at a plain desk in a big and bustling room. Whitney was a thin and shambling man with a wasted face and sunken eyes gleaming from behind his glasses.

"Now," Whitney demanded, "when do I get that list?"

Broun, who had expected a lot of red tape, was taken aback.

"It will take a little time," said Broun.

"That won't do at all!" Whitney snapped. "You don't understand. This is a rush job. Every day counts!"

And every day did count to Travis Whitney. His assistants saw his face go gray late each afternoon, so unsparingly did he drive himself. Never did he forget that outside his office a cold wind bit the bodies of men and women without work, without hope. In less than one month he indeed managed to give employment to 200,000 people. Then, on January 8,

1934, the first part of his job done, his flesh consumed, he crumpled at his desk and was taken to a hospital, where he died.

Broun was so touched that he wrote a newspaper column in which he said of Travis Harvard Whitney: "They put him on his shield and carried him away, and I hope that on his tomb will be written, 'Killed in action.' "

Ten days after Whitney's death the nationwide CWA program reached its peak with 4,263,644 CWA workers being paid more than $64 million per week. *Time* magazine ran a picture of Hopkins on its cover and published a long article praising him for doing "a thoroughly professional job" as administrator. With the original grant of $400 million nearly gone, Roosevelt planned to ask Congress for another $500 million to continue the CWA until May 1, when, he promised, the program would be terminated. This provoked bitter reaction.

Richard Whitney, the esteemed stock market swindler, sneered at all federal relief as being nothing more or less than a dole. The Republican National Committee denounced Hopkins and CWA for "gross waste" and "downright corruption." George Creel, a Democrat and an author, said of Hopkins: "The trouble with Harry, as with so many others that Franklin D. Roosevelt gathered around him, and even the President himself, was that he had never spent his own money. A social worker throughout his adult life, he had obtained his funds from municipal treasuries or foundations, so that dollars were never associated in his mind with work and thrift. Just figures in a budget."

Standing in the House of Representatives, Democratic Congressman George B. Terrell of Texas declared: "The Constitution is being violated here every day because there isn't a line in the Constitution that authorizes the expenditure of federal money for other than federal purposes. . . . I think [CWA] is going to start civil war and revolution when we do stop it, anyway. . . . The others [in Congress] can go through on these things like dumb driven cattle, if they want to, but . . . I won't sacrifice my independence for any office I ever heard of."

By "office" he meant the midterm Congressional elections soon to fall due in 1934. In a letter to the Speaker of the House the President asked for $350 million instead of the $500 million more he had hoped to get, and after heated debate in the House and Senate more money was appropriated to keep the CWA going awhile longer.

Roosevelt, who always regarded the CWA as a temporary measure, had begun to give in to his economy-minded budget director, Lewis Douglas, who wanted the government to spend less money. The President knew that the CWA cost more than the FERA, since work relief cost more than direct relief. Senator Wagner of New York, for his part, was in favor of continuing relief as long as necessary, since industrial production had risen much faster than payrolls.

On February 15, 1934, the CWA began to taper off as 260,000 people were dropped from its rolls. The American Association of Social Workers protested—in vain. Hopkins said he believed that many dropped from the CWA would be hired by the PWA, and on February 24 he ordered 377,500 more reliefers cut off the rolls. Norman Thomas, crying that ending the CWA was like grabbing a bone from a hungry dog, led 700 men and women in a protest march in the national capital.

On March 31, 1934, after a life of slightly less than five months, the Civil Works Administration went out of existence. It had spent more than $951 million to employ jobless people on 180,000 projects.

Al Smith barked happily: "That's one more pork barrel busted!"

The CWA's unfinished projects, its remaining funds and some of its staff members were regrouped under the title of the Works Division of the FERA. But another and larger relief program was in the making. Harry Hopkins and Harold Ickes eyed each other like fighting cocks, wondering which of them would emerge as the new champion of the new agency.

* * *

The CWA's demise was followed by disorders here and there across the land. On April 6 in Minneapolis 4,000 jobless people, including former CWA workers, battled the police for hours until the city council gave in to some of their demands for work and relief. The next day a riot took place outside the City Hall at Scranton, Pennsylvania. The following month, apparently blind to all this strife, Silas H. Strawn of the United States Chamber of Commerce said Roosevelt should declare "that the emergency is over and that there will be no more requests for emergency legislation."

The emergency was over? That May, 1934, millions of Americans found themselves again without jobs. That May, when the state of Kansas withdrew relief from Crawford County, a few hotheads beat up the county commissioner. That May, in New York City, fifteen people were hurt and thirteen arrested when cops broke up a demonstration outside the welfare department office. The emergency was far from over.

Roosevelt knew it, Hopkins knew it, and the people knew it. In the national Congressional elections in the fall of 1934 the Democrats won by such a big margin that the Republicans became less influential in Congress than they had been at any time since before the Civil War. A couple of weeks after the elections Hopkins and some of his associates were driving to a racetrack near Washington when suddenly he cried: "Boys—this is our hour! We've got to get everything we want—a works program, social security, wages and hours—everything! Now or never! Get your minds to work on developing a complete ticket to provide security for all the folks of this country—up and down and across the board!"

After the races were over, they went to work in Hopkins' new office in the old Walker-Johnson Building in Washington. A few days later he traveled to New York City, took a suite in the Hotel St. Regis, and it was in this Manhattan hotel that final shape was given to the agency that became the Works Progress Administration. On November 28 Hopkins stuffed the

WPA plan in his pocket and headed for Warm Springs, Georgia, to confer with the President.

News of his visit was published in the New York *Times,* which said in part: "The fire-eating administrator of Federal Emergency Relief, Harry L. Hopkins, may be safely credited with spoiling the Thanksgiving Day dinners of many conservatives who had been led to believe that President Roosevelt's recent zig to the right would not be followed by a zag to the left. . . . Not that Mr. Hopkins had any idea that his EPIA (End Poverty in America) plan would leak out unauthorized, but now that it has leaked out it will bear examination. . . ."

Hopkins did not call the new program EPIA; that was the *Times'* little joke.

The heavily Democratic Seventy-fourth Congress opened its first session on January 3, 1935, and one day later the President delivered his annual message. After reporting that more than $2 billion had been spent in direct relief, he went on to say: "The federal government must and shall quit this business of relief. I am not willing that the vitality of our people be further sapped by the giving of cash, of market baskets, of a few hours of weekly work cutting grass, raking leaves or picking up papers in public parks. We must preserve not only the bodies of the unemployed from destitution but also their self-respect, their self-reliance and courage and determination. . . ."

Although Hopkins shared Roosevelt's concept of relief, he nonetheless was hurt by this part of the President's speech; after all, the men raking leaves and mowing grass were engaged in the worthwhile work of landscaping parks and school grounds.

Roosevelt then announced that he intended to establish a new relief system to supersede the FERA and pick up where the CWA had left off. This new program, the President added, would be guided by the following principles:

1. All work to be as useful and permanent as possible.
2. Relief wages to be higher than those paid under the FERA and CWA, but not so high as to discourage men from taking jobs in private industry.
3. More money to be spent on wages than on materials.
4. Projects to be authorized by local sponsors.
5. Projects to be located in areas where relief rolls were highest.
6. Job preference to be given to those on relief.
7. Each project to be finished by the end of the fiscal year.

On April 5, 1935, the Senate and House passed a joint resolution giving the President the relief money he had sought—$4 billion in new funds and $880,000,000 unused from previous appropriations. This $4.8 billion was the largest peacetime appropriation in American history. One day later the bill was signed by the Vice President and the Speaker of the House and put on a plane bound for Jacksonville, Florida. Roosevelt, who had been fishing off the coast, came back to port, boarded a north-bound train and on April 8 signed the measure to the contrapuntal clickety-clack of train wheels.

Now that Congress had granted Roosevelt the money necessary to set up a new relief agency, Hopkins and Ickes fought a distant duel for the privilege of becoming its administrator. Their antagonism distressed Henry Morgenthau, while Rexford Tugwell said they "are so worried about who is to do the job that they can hardly think of the job itself." The President preferred Hopkins, the openhanded jester, to Ickes, the tightfisted curmudgeon.

Despite their widely different backgrounds, Roosevelt and Hopkins were amazingly similar. Both had fought courageously against ill health. Both liked teasing and practical jokes and lighthearted conversation. Both disliked stuffed shirts, long-winded bores, pomp and circumstance. They shared the same political and social philosophy. Hopkins had an intuitive sensitivity to Roosevelt's moods, knowing when to broach a subject, how far to pursue it, when to drop it. Frances Perkins said "there was a temperamental sympathy between the men." Although Hopkins revered Roosevelt, he was not afraid to stand up to him, which delighted the President.

To get ahead of the story, at a White House meeting someone suggested that part of the WPA be turned into a national educational system.

The President turned to Hopkins, who was slumped on the end of his spine, glaring over his glasses. "You know, Harry," Roosevelt cried, "that's a great idea!"

Hopkins slid deeper into his chair and shifted his cold gaze to the President.

"Harry, listen," Roosevelt continued, waving his cigarette holder. "That *would* be a wonderful idea!"

His eyes tinged with disgust, Hopkins snorted: "Well, that's fine, Mr. President! We've been doing that for three years."

When it was announced that Hopkins would be named the head of the relief agency now taking shape, Ickes felt cheated. The interior secretary called on Vice President Garner and found bittersweet satisfaction in Garner's remark that Hopkins had done more to harm the nation than any man in history. Ickes was not wholly excluded from the new program, since he was named chairman of its allotment committee, but in his diary he reflected: "Of course, in the end, Hopkins may appear as the outstanding man in the new organization. . . . Hopkins will fly off on tangents unless he is watched, and I am quite likely to be bulldoggish and want to have my own way."

On May 6, 1935, the President issued an executive order establishing the Works Progress Administration. As of that date no one could foretell that, with one change of name, it would continue in existence until June 30, 1943—eight years and two months.

The WPA was designed as the key agency in the government's entire works program, which came to include a total of forty federal agencies. It withdrew the federal government from the field of direct relief, leaving that responsibility to the various states and cities. Roosevelt flatly said that the principal purpose of the WPA was to provide work.

Hopkins began this new job with his usual demonic energy. At one of the first WPA staff meetings he raised the question of whether women should be paid the same wages as men. Everyone said no. Everyone, that is, except Hopkins' assistant administrator, Aubrey Williams, who said he thought women should be paid equal wages with men.

"Oh, you do?" Hopkins barked. "What makes you think you could get away with it?"

Williams said he did not care whether he could get away with it or not.

"Do you know who disagrees with you?" Hopkins persisted. "The secretary of labor—a woman!"

"Pay 'em the same!" Williams said doggedly.

Hopkins, who was testing his assistant, baited him further until Williams became silent and glum.

Then Hopkins ended the session with the words: "Well, fellows, thank you very much. Aubrey's right about this, and that's what we'll do."

As the others walked out, Hopkins turned to Williams, smiled a lopsided smile and asked: "What's wrong with those other fellows?"

The WPA paid wages slightly higher than the grants for direct relief but lower than wages prevailing in private industry. There were exceptions, however, for the WPA refused to lower its rates to meet the substandard ones prevailing in certain districts, notably in the South. For wage-fixing purposes the country was divided into four regions. Monthly rates of pay in each region varied according to the character of the work and to the population. Unskilled work paid as little as $19 a month while professional and technical jobs paid up to $94 a month—and sometimes slightly higher.

The nerve center of the WPA—and thus of the nation's entire works program—was located in the Walker-Johnson Building in Washington at 1734 New York Avenue, NW, a few blocks from the White House. It was a dirty, shabby old place with a blind newsdealer on its front steps. Upon entering it one smelled antiseptic odors and then rode in an elevator so rickety it was frightening. But Hopkins, who detested elegance, felt this was what a relief office should be like. Ernie Pyle of the Washington *News* wrote a graphic description of the administrator and his office:

> . . . And you, Mr. Hopkins, I liked you because you look like common people. I don't mean any slur by that either, because they don't come any commoner than I am, but you sit there so easy swinging back and forth in your swivel chair, in your blue suit and blue shirt, and your neck is sort of skinny, like poor people's necks, and you act honest, too.

And you answer the reporters' questions as tho [*sic*] you were talking to them personally, instead of being a big official. It tickled me the way you would say, "I can't answer that," in a tone that almost says out loud, "Now you knew damn well when you asked me that I couldn't answer that." . . .

And that old office of yours, Mr. Hopkins, good Lord, it's terrible. It's so little in the first place, and the walls are faded and water pipes run up the walls and your desk doesn't even shine. But I guess you don't care. Maybe it wouldn't look right for you to have a nice office anyway, when you're dealing in misery all the time.

One nice thing about your office being so little, tho, the reporters all have to pack close up around your desk, and they can see and hear you well, and it's sort of like talking to you in your home, except there they'd be sitting down, I hope.

The reporters tell me, Mr. Hopkins, that you're the fastest thinker of any of the big men who hold press conferences. Ickes is pretty fast, too, and so is Farley, they say, but you always come back right now with something pretty good. And you've got a pleasant, clean-cut voice, too, and they say you never try to lie out of anything.

The reporters' fondness for Hopkins was not necessarily shared by their bosses, the publishers. In the month that saw the formation of the WPA, Colonel Robert McCormick of the Chicago *Tribune* made an interesting speech in Boston before members of Sentinels of the Republic. This right-wing organization was financed by radio manufacturer Atwater Kent, the rich man who had chided his wife for not spending enough money, and by the Pew oil millions. The Sentinels urged the repeal of the general welfare clause of the Constitution while their president, Alexander Lincoln of Boston, was an anti-Semite who declared that "the Jewish threat is a real one." McCormick said: ". . . Foreign agitators have repaid us for asylum by both insidious and open agitation against our institutions, until today their policies . . . dominate action in Washington. Men who have been parasites their entire lives, have never produced anything and never intended to produce anything, who have always lived at the expense of others and plot to live better than the others who support them, have evolved a doctrine that we and our forebears have produced everything and all that remains to do is to divide the fruit of our efforts. . . ."

Foreign? McCormick's maternal grandfather was born in a foreign country. Parasites? McCormick himself was born rich.

At about the time that the *Tribune* publisher was speaking and the WPA was taking shape, the National Industrial Conference Board said 9,711,000 people were unemployed. This was 5 percent more than in April, 1934, one month after the death of the CWA.

Some people were so afraid that WPA workers would vote as a bloc to perpetuate relief that there was a temporary move to deprive them of their citizenship. Ickes told Hopkins that the WPA would fail, for as soon as some men left the relief rolls, others would be added. Hugh Johnson criticized the cost of administering relief. Some businessmen felt work relief might partly nullify the effect of dropping the NRA codes. Treasury Secretary Morgenthau was so glum about the cost of the WPA that he thought of resigning.

In the aggregate the WPA did spend a great deal of money, but, as has been indicated, individual wages were hardly lavish. In December, 1935, WPA workers averaged $41.57 a month. Between 60 and 70 percent of those on the rolls were unskilled workers.

But among the skilled workers were accountants, architects, bricklayers, biologists, carpenters, chemists, dentists, draftsmen, dieticians, electricians, engravers, foresters, firemen, geologists, gardeners, hoisting engineers, housekeepers, instrument men, ironworkers, jackhammer operators, janitors, kettlemen, kitchen maids, librarians, linotypers, locksmiths, lumbermen, millwrights, machinists, musicians, nurses, nutritionists, oilers, painters, plasterers, plumbers, patternmakers, photographers, printers, physicians, quarry men, quilters, riveters, roofers, roadmakers, riggers, sculptors, seamstresses, stonemasons, stenographers, statisticians, teamsters, truck drivers, teachers, tabulators, upholsterers, veterinarians, welders, woodchoppers, waiters, watchmen, X-ray technicians—and others.

During its more than eight years of existence the WPA employed 8,500,000 different people in more than 3,000 counties and spent in excess of $11 billion on a total of 1,410,000 projects. It was by far the biggest employer and spender of all the New Deal agencies. WPA workers built 651,087 miles of highways, roads and streets; constructed, repaired or improved 124,031 bridges; erected 125,110 public buildings; created 8,192 public parks; built or improved 853 airports. Besides its immediate importance to the people who worked on this massive program, Americans were using and enjoying some of these facilities one-third of a century later. More than anything else, however, the WPA was an escape hatch from the trap of the Depression.

Early in the program Roosevelt had warned: "It must be recognized that when an enterprise of this character is extended over more than three thousand counties throughout the nation, there may be occasional instances of inefficiency, bad management, or misuse of funds." Cases of this kind did, of course, occur. A few Senators, Congressmen, governors, state WPA directors and small-time politicians tried to enrich themselves and enhance their power by means of the WPA.

Harry Hopkins was incorruptible and, for a man who liked to spend money, strangely economy-minded in some ways. Loathing organizational charts and fossilized bureaucratic procedures, he ran the national organization with the smallest possible staff and the smallest possible overhead. He got help to the people as directly and quickly as possible. "Hunger is not debatable," he liked to say. "People don't eat in the long run—they eat every day."

Robert E. Sherwood has said that "Hopkins commanded a degree of loyalty and devotion in his staff that approached the Jesuitical." Believing that they were waging a holy war against want, his staff members slaved so hard that a sixty-hour week would have seemed to them like a siesta. Almost worshiping their boss, they knew they did not have to "yes" him, for he was a realist who could bear to hear bad news. And since he drove his frail body to the last ounce of its endurance, they forgave him his playboy tendencies, his fondness for racehorses and café society.

The WPA's visible and imposing presence, expressed in dams and bridges, slum clearance and rural rehabilitation, won the admiration of most Americans. Some, however, cocked skeptical eyebrows at projects they considered foolish. Anti-New Deal publishers put reporters on the scent of cockeyed work relief.

On April 2, 1935, an aldermanic committee investigating relief projects in New York City heard Robert Marshall, a handicrafts teacher, testify that one of the subjects he taught was boondoggles. Marshall explained that this was a pioneer word for handmade articles such as leather belts, whose usefulness was unquestioned but whose craftsmanship was of a low order. Newspapers pounced on "boondoggle," which from that day forward became a derisive term. Critics yipped that the WPA was engaged in piddling work. On October 4 the Chicago *Tribune* said of boondoggle: "To the cowboy it meant the making of saddle trappings out of odds and ends of leather, and they boondoggled when there was nothing else to do on the ranch."

The President tried to invest the word with dignity. In the fall of 1936, while touring drought-stricken states, he stopped at North Platte, Nebraska, a few miles from a WPA project, the second largest dirt dam in the nation. Speaking from the rear platform of his train, Roosevelt said: ". . . When I was up in one of the New England states, where they have the somewhat different problem of flood control, I saw another great earth dam which was constructed to hold back the waters of one of the rivers in Vermont which, only a few years ago in one cloudburst, did six million dollars' worth of damage. The total cost of that dam was only about a million and a half dollars. This spring there was another cloudburst there, with just as much rain as they had in 1927—but the dam was enough to hold back all the waters resulting from that cloudburst, and there was not one dollar's worth of damage.

"Our problem here is just the opposite, but I can say to you what I said to the governor of Vermont when he was sitting beside me in the automobile on the top of that dam. I said, 'Governor, it seems to me that this is a pretty good example of co-operative boondoggling between your state and the federal government.' "

New York City reporters found that one local WPA project consisted of a study of ancient safety pins. At Harry Hopkins' next press conference, two days later in Washington, a reporter asked whether he planned to investigate.

"You mean," Hopkins replied, "apropos of this stuff in the paper a day or two ago?"

"Apropos of the project of safety pins."

"Sure, I have something to say about that."

"I asked first," the reporter interrupted, "have you contemplated making an investigation?"

"Why should I?" Hopkins flared. "There is nothing the matter with that. They are damn good projects—excellent projects. That goes for all the projects up there. You know, some people make fun of people who speak a foreign language, and dumb people criticize something they do not understand, and that is what is going on up there. God damn it! Here are a lot of people broke, and we are putting them to work making researches of one kind or another, running big recreational projects where the whole material costs three per cent, and practically all the money goes for relief.

"As soon as you begin doing anything for white collar people, there is a certain group of people who begin to throw bricks. I have no apologies to make. As a matter of fact, we do not have enough. The plain fact of the matter is that there are people writing and talking about these things in New York who know nothing about research projects. They haven't taken the trouble to really look into them.

"I have a pile of letters from businessmen—if that is important—saying that these projects are damn good projects. These fellows can make fun and shoot at white collar people if they want to. I notice somebody says facetiously, 'repair all streets.' That is all they think about—money to repair streets. I think there are things in life besides that. We have projects up there to make Jewish dictionaries. There are rabbis who are broke and on relief rolls.

"One hundred and fifty projects up there deal with pure science. What of it? I think these things are good in life. They are important in life. We are not backing down on any of those projects. They can make fun of these white collar and professional people if they want to. I am not going to do it. They can say, let them use a pick and shovel to repair streets—when the city ought to be doing that. I believe every one of these research projects are good projects. We don't need any apologies!"

Some newspaper reports of this press conference quoted Hopkins as saying that "people are too damned dumb." Actually, he said: ". . . dumb people criticize something they do not understand." For the next ten years Hopkins was flayed in editorials as the man who believed that "the American people are too damned dumb." A lady living in Virginia wrote a poem that was published in the Washington *Post*. It ended with this verse:

Though we still pay up our tax,
Mr. Hopkins!
We are sharpening the ax,
(Mr. Hopkins)

Testing it with cautious thumb—
And we're telling you, by gum,
We are not quite too damned dumb,
Mr. Hopkins!

*   *   *

The New Deal did more to promote culture than any previous administration in the history of this nation.

Critics who cried "Boondoggle!" were unaware that New Dealers were
following and enhancing a precept laid down by George Washington. In his
first address to the First Congress, the father of our country declared that
"there is nothing which can better deserve your patronage than the
promotion of science and literature." More than a century after Washington spoke these words, American civilization had become a business
civilization, with art and letters and even education regarded as a luxury.
Roosevelt and Hopkins, however, understood that creativity deserves as
much government support as manufacturing.

With the advent of the Depression, unemployed men and women found
themselves with unlimited leisure time, so millions of them began reading
as never before in their lives. They haunted libraries, borrowed a dozen or
so books at a time, kept librarians among the busiest of all people during
that trying time. But few people could afford to buy their own books, and
in 1930 book sales began to fall sharply. One big publishing house and
four or five smaller ones went bankrupt; this meant that recognized authors
lost all accrued and future royalties, while unknown writers had trouble
selling their manuscripts. Several magazines suspended publication; those
that managed to survive shrank to half their former size. Surprisingly, the
Book-of-the-Month Club prospered during the Depression.

Robert Frost earned less than $3,000 a year each year of the decade.
Norman Mailer's parents were poor. Jesse Stuart found himself penniless in
1932. With publishers less than ever willing to risk money on first novels
by writers lacking a reputation, young men scribbled away without hope of
being published. At a 1932 meeting of young writers in New York an older
writer asked from the platform: "How do you manage to keep going?"
Laughter bubbled from a corner of the hall where half a dozen poets sat
with their wives. Then one of the youths got up and said: "We marry
schoolteachers." Unlike Chicago, where schoolteachers often went unpaid,
New York City managed to pay full salaries to its teachers in the depths of
the Depression, and as a consequence, these young ladies were regarded as
people of economic consequence. Most struggling writers lived off their
wives or off their parents, as in the case of John Steinbeck, took odd jobs
or brooded in cafeterias.

Unable to find meaningful work, ignored by society, their talents rusting,
having ample time to ponder their plight, artists of all kinds—writers and
painters, sculptors and musicians—began to turn radical. Harry M. Kurtz-

worth, a critic of the Los Angeles *Saturday Night,* questioned the glory of the artist who starves in his walk-up attic for the sake of his art. "Art flourishes only in periods of abundance," he said, "of surplus time, money, energy. Starving people have other interests." John Dos Passos snapped at F. Scott Fitzgerald for dwelling on a subject so trivial as his own nervous breakdown: "Christ, man, how do you find time in the middle of the general conflagration to worry about all that stuff? . . . We're living in one of the damndest tragic moments in history." During the Thirties Ernest Hemingway published only one novel, *To Have and Have Not.* Into the mouth of his dying protagonist, Harry Morgan, he put these words: "No matter how . . . a man ain't got no bloody . . . chance."

By 1935 the nation was facing the possibility of an utter collapse in the art movement. In August of that year the federal government announced that it intended to spend $27 million on a four arts division within the WPA to help musicians, actors, writers, painters, sculptors, architects, etchers, frescoists and photographers. Some businessmen grumbled. Several newspapers, though, praised this new program as humane, idealistic and farseeing.

The germ of this arts program was planted in the CWA. At that earlier time it had evoked rhapsodic response from Gutzon Borglum, the sculptor who carved the heads of four American Presidents in the stone face of Mount Rushmore. In a letter to Aubrey Williams, Borglum had said:

> . . . Mr. Hopkins' department has opened the door, a crack, but opened to this great field of human interest and thought. The world of creative impulse, without which people perish. Frankly, a people have as much right to be saved as the trees, the birds, the whole animal kingdom, and no more, but their civilization must be saved. . . . All there is of God in creation is what man in lonely martyrdom wrung from nowhere and everywhere, and it has been his consciousness of that that makes him master of the world, and not business or money, we must save that, civilization contains all that is precious in what we think we are. Will a basket of bread save that, a full belly and a dry back? . . . Have we in gold—the worship of Aaron's calf—made our final bow in the hall of world fame, to be remembered with Rome for our abuse of wealth?

The WPA's arts division consisted of four separate programs. As overall supervisor of them Harry Hopkins chose Jacob Baker, liberal in his tastes and a believer in experimentation. The music program was headed by Nikolai Sokoloff, conductor of the Cleveland Orchestra and a frequent guest conductor of many other symphony orchestras throughout the nation. The art program was directed by Holger Cahill, an art critic, authority on folk art and an outstanding museum technician. The theater project was headed by Hallie Flanagan. The writers' program was headed by Henry Alsberg, an editorial writer for the New York *Evening Post* and a foreign correspondent for liberal magazines.

Alsberg told Hopkins that the WPA could make a lasting cultural contribution to the nation if the men and women employed by the writers' project were put to work preparing a series of guidebooks about the states, one for each state. He pointed out that the latest issue of Baedeker's guide to America had been issued in 1909—so outdated that it advised Europeans planning to visit this land to bring along matches, buttons and dress gloves. Agreeing, Hopkins gave Alsberg the word to launch the American Guide Series.

This series revolutionized the writing of American history by presenting history in terms of communities, in relation to place. For example, the Illinois guidebook presents such a detailed and graphic study of the town of Galena that one can better understand the life of Galena's most famous hometown boy—Ulysses S. Grant.

Alsberg began hiring unemployed writers and editors, librarians and photographers, until at last he had 7,500 people at work. A director was named for each of the forty-eight states, and they, in turn, received the help of local reporters, historians, genealogists, librarians and businessmen. Each did his part in the massive chore of researching, writing, editing and publishing the state guidebooks, and soon copy was pouring into the Washington headquarters at the rate of 50,000 words a day.

Bernard De Voto spoke slightingly of the writers' program as "a project for research workers" while a New Deal critic said that only 21 percent of the people employed on the New York City project had ever written for a living. While all this may have been true, such criticism meant little because a massive literary effort of this kind required the services of skilled researchers. Besides, as Hopkins might have said, even researchers had to eat. There were also Congressmen who disliked the idea of paying money to men and women who pushed pens, and Charles D. Stewart, vice-president of the Society of Midland Authors, called the writers' project completely foolish.

Actually, it helped save the lives, sanity and talents of some writers already famous, along with others who went on to fame. In 1930 Conrad Aiken had won a Pulitzer Prize for his *Selected Poems,* but a few years later he was so badly in need of money that he joined the writers' project. Among the others on the rolls were John Cheever, Claude McKay, Vardis Fisher, Maxwell Bodenheim, Lyle Saxon, Ben A. Botkin and Edward Dahlberg—to name just a few.

They were paid an average of $90 a month. Since this was not enough to permit them to save any money, and since they were individualists, they talked from time to time about getting "a real job." Occasionally they became so disgusted that they took part in demonstrations, such as sit-ins, but the project also contained fringe benefits like the cottages the FERA built for authors in Florida.

Most of the nation's struggling writers lived in New York City, whose writers' project was set up on a par with state divisions. At its peak the

New York City project employed more than 500 workers—writers, administrators, supervisors, photographers, mapmakers and so on. Among them was Maxwell Bodenheim, a poet and novelist of alcoholic habits and eccentric ways.

He haunted Greenwich Village, which he called "the Coney Island of the soul." One of Bodenheim's novels was *Replenishing Jessica,* the story of the promiscuous daughter of a millionaire, and it became a best seller in 1925. But with the coming of the Depression his books stopped selling. Before the creation of the writers' project, he had staggered to a city relief agency to demand help for poets. Given a $2.50 voucher for groceries, he complained that he had no home, no way to cook the groceries and was unable to eat the voucher itself. Later he was taken on the WPA project, where he did good work, but nothing could halt the death march of this self-condemned man. After the program ended Bodenheim wrote poems on scraps of paper, selling them for $1, then 50 cents, finally for 10-cent beers.

Bodenheim's life and career were not at all typical of the writers who took help from the WPA. Thanks to federal funds, they ate regularly, held up their heads pridefully and polished talents which otherwise might have eroded. Among those benefiting from this program was Richard Wright, among the first of the nation's noted black authors and finally one of its greatest.

Born on a Mississippi plantation, Wright moved to Memphis and decided to become a writer, started selling poems and stories to little magazines, moved to Chicago where he joined the writers' project, pushed on to New York in 1937 and went to work for the project in that city. He wrote the essay on Harlem for the WPA book called *New York Panorama.* In 1939 he won a Guggenheim Fellowship, which enabled him to quit the project and finish his novel *Native Son,* picked by the Book-of-the-Month Club as one of its 1940 selections.

Tennessee Williams failed in his effort to get on the writers' project. When he was about twenty-two, he scraped up enough money to take a train from St. Louis to Chicago, where he tried desperately to join the WPA. Of this experience, he later wrote: "My work lacked 'social content' or 'protest' and I couldn't prove that my family was destitute and I still had, in those days, a touch of refinement in my social behavior which made me seem frivolous . . . to the conscientiously rough-hewn pillars of the Chicago project." He later applied to the theater project but was turned down again, largely because of his family's relative affluence.

One of the greatest accomplishments of the writers' project was its historical records survey, instituted in 1936. Relief workers took inventories of local public records stored in city hall cellars, library lofts and courthouse garrets. They indexed old newspaper files. They made abstracts of court cases containing nuggets of local history. They examined business archives, looked through church records, studied tombstones to verify vital statistics. The perfection of microfilm had made it possible for them to photograph, and thus to preserve, millions of pages crumbling into decay. They measured, sketched, diagrammed and photographed 2,300 historic buildings.

In 1937 the American Guide Series became a reality with publication of the first of the set, a book about Idaho. By the end of its life the project produced 378 books and pamphlets—a volume for each of the forty-eight states, 30 about our major cities, others about historic waterways and highways, such as *The Oregon Trail*. Various commercial and university publishers issued these works, with royalties either paying for everything except labor costs or going into the federal treasury.

In a *New Republic* article Robert Cantwell said of the writers' project: "The least publicized of the art projects, it may emerge as the most influential and valuable of them all." Nearly one-third of a century later the American Guide Series continued to be a prime source of information for every serious writer of American history.

*   *   *

Musicians were suffering even before the beginning of the Depression. The popularity of radio, the advent of talking movies and the death of vaudeville had thrown 50,000 musical performers out of work. After the Crash there were few Americans who could afford music lessons for their children, so music teachers lost their pupils or had to cut their fees for the few who remained. Music publishers, recording companies and manufacturers of musical instruments earned less or suffered heavy losses. To most of these people the federal music project, under Nikolai Sokoloff, came as salvation.

Established in July, 1935, the music program put musicians to work in orchestras and bands, in chamber music and choral and operatic groups throughout the nation. Forty-five cities obtained their own WPA symphony orchestra, while 110 other cities got orchestras with more than thirty-five players. Just before the start of a concert by a WPA orchestra in Florida, a violinist apologized to the audience on behalf of his colleagues and himself for the quality of their concert. He explained that their fingers were stiff because of their previous relief job—working on a road gang.

When the music project was at its peak it supported 15,000 people. They gave a total of 150,000 programs heard by more than 100,000,000 people, many of whom had been unfamiliar with anything but popular songs. Each month more than 500,000 pupils attended free music classes. WPA musical groups relieved the boredom of hospital patients. Project workers dug out and recorded American folk music—the Cajun songs of Louisiana, the Indian-flavored songs of early Oklahoma, the British-born ballads of Kentucky mountaineers, the African-inspired songs of Mississippi bayous.

Although the program was designed to help performers more than composers, since the former outnumbered the latter, it established a composers' forum-laboratory. Before the project was terminated, 1,400 native composers produced 4,915 original compositions—some bad, many mediocre, a few hailed by music critics as "distinguished." One prominent critic, Deems Taylor, wrote in 1935: "It is safe to say that during the past two years the WPA orchestras alone have probably performed more American music than our other symphony orchestras, combined, during the past ten."

Thanks to this project, music became democratized in this country. In about the year 1915 there had been only 17 symphony orchestras in the United States; by 1939 there were more than 270. Europe's leadership in the musical world, together with its snobbish aloofness, had been shattered.

*   *   *

The WPA art project was set up by Holger Cahill on "the principle that it is not the solitary genius but a sound general movement which maintains art as a vital, functioning part of any cultural scheme."

All a person had to do to get on the art project was to obtain proof from local authorities that he needed relief and that he had once had some connection, however tenuous, with the world of art. As a result, of the more than 5,000 people ultimately hired, fewer than half ever painted a picture, sculpted a statue or decorated a building with a mural. This does not mean that the art program was a boondoggle. While creativity flowered among the great artists—Jackson Pollock, Aaron Bohrod, Ben Shahn, Willem de Kooning, Concetta Scaravaglione, Anna Walinska and the like—those with limited talent taught free art classes, photographed historic houses, painted posters and designed stage sets for the federal theater project. Others maintained sixty-six community art centers which attracted a total of 6,000,000 visitors.

In addition to the invaluable and enduring artworks produced by the most gifted relief workers, the art project left all of us a monumental *Index of American Design*. This part of the program was directed by Constance Rourke and gave employment to about 1,000 artists. Wishing to find and preserve specimens of early American arts and crafts, they ransacked New England farmhouses, museums, antique shops, historical societies, Shaker barns and California missions. They photographed or painted every treasure they discovered—embroidered seat covers, oil paintings, watercolors, carved figureheads, antique quilts and samplers, weather vanes and such. Collectively, these artists produced 7,000 illustrations of every variety of native American art.

*   *   *

On May 16, 1935, the phone rang in the Poughkeepsie, New York, home of a small, red-headed middle-aged woman named Hallie Flanagan. When she answered it, she heard Jacob Baker, the head of the WPA's four arts program, saying that he was calling from Washington. "Mr. Hopkins wants you to come to Washington to talk about unemployed actors," Baker said. Miss Flanagan was in charge of Vassar College's Experimental Theatre. She knew Hopkins, for they had grown up together in Grinnell, Iowa, and attended the same college.

Over the wire she said to Baker, probingly: "Mr. Hopkins knows, of course, that my theater here is a non-commercial one—that I'm not connected with the commercial theater?"

"Yes, he knows that. He's conferring with commercial theater people, too. There are dozens of theater people down here. Mr. Hopkins wants to see you. Can you come?"

She went to Washington, rode the shaky elevator in the Walker-Johnson Building, walked into Hopkins' plain office. Grinning at her, he said the government was about to establish a federal theater project and he wanted her to take charge of it.

"This is a tough job we're asking you to do," he added. "I don't know why I still hang onto the idea that unemployed actors get just as hungry as anybody else."

She accepted the job, and a few days later Hopkins posed a curious question: "Can you spend money?"

Miss Flanagan confessed that the inability to spend money was not one of her faults.

But Hopkins was serious. "It's not easy," he told her. "It takes a lot of nerve to put your signature down on a piece of paper, when it means that the government of the United States is going to pay out a million dollars to the unemployed in Chicago. It takes decision—because you'll have to decide whether Chicago needs that money more than New York City or Los Angeles."

Actors, as Miss Flanagan knew, were suffering severe hardships. Like musicians, many had lost their jobs with the death of vaudeville and the birth of the talkies. No one knew for sure just how many performers were out of work. Actors Equity said there were 5,000 unemployed actors in New York City alone, while WPA officials put the nationwide total at 20,000 to 30,000 people. In Harlem black entertainers were kissing the Tree of Hope, a local talisman, for luck.

In 1931 two-thirds of Manhattan's playhouses were shut. During the 1932–33 season eight out of every ten new plays failed. The Shuberts had plunged into receivership. In 1932 no less than 22,000 people registered with Hollywood casting bureaus. *Variety* had reduced its price from 25 to 15 cents. Some film stars still commanded huge salaries but fearfully had taken out kidnap insurance policies with Lloyd's of London. With the rise of Hitler in Germany and Mussolini in Italy, thousands of foreign actors— many of them Jewish—had fled to the United States, where they now sought work. The American Federation of Actors was planning to stage circuses to aid those of its members who were broke and hungry.

On July 27, 1935, Miss Flanagan was sworn in as administrator of the new federal theater project. The ceremony was held in a Washington playhouse called the old Auditorium, a vast hulk of a building now abuzz with rushing people, whirring electric fans, riveting machines and cement-slapping plasterers. She sat down in a new cubicle and conferred with her staff of four about the possibility of getting at least 10,000 theater people back to work within a short time.

Since Broadway was the heart of the American theater, Miss Flanagan wanted an especially able man to direct the New York City unit of her project, and her choice was Elmer Rice. The forty-three-year-old Rice had proved himself as a playwright, stage director and novelist. With the deepening of the Depression, his plays had shifted from realistic reporting to social and political themes. Rice already had sent Hopkins a letter outlining a plan for the establishment of a national theater, but he hesitated about accepting Miss Flanagan's offer because he was about to begin writing another novel.

"What could we do with all the actors?" he asked her. "Even if we had twenty plays in rehearsal at once, with thirty in a cast, that would keep only a fraction of them busy."

Badly wanting Rice, she grabbed at a straw and impulsively said: "We wouldn't use them all in plays. We could do *Living Newspapers*. We could dramatize the news with living actors, light, music, movement."

This idea appealed to Rice, who cried: "Yes! And I can get the Newspaper Guild to back it!"

Before taking the job, though, Rice got a promise from Hopkins that there would be no censorship and that he would have no superior but Miss Flanagan. Then he set up headquarters in an abandoned bank on Eighth Avenue. Everything had to be started from scratch. One day Rice asked an assistant, whom he regarded as "a dreary little civil servant," for pencils, writing tablets and paper clips. This helper said they would have to be requisitioned. Rice curtly told him to go ahead and requisition them. His assistant said: "First we'll have to requisition some requisition blanks."

Elmer Rice was paid $260 a month on the theory that he worked thirteen days at $20 a day, but actually he worked from early morning until late at night every day of the month, including Sundays. It amused him to get nasty letters accusing him of making a fortune on a soft government job. Sometimes he opened press conferences by saying to reporters: "Well, what do you vultures want to swoop down on now?"

At first jobs were limited to entertainers on home relief rolls, but this excluded many who had been too proud to ask for help. Miss Flanagan and Rice managed to get this rule modified. She watched in horror as a man applying for work went mad and beat his head against a wall. A famous clown was taken on the WPA rolls, became so excited at the chance to work again that on the opening night of the show he suffered a stroke from which he never recovered.

Rice issued this statement:

> The Federal Theatre Project has been created for the purpose of pro-
> viding worthwhile employment for professional theatre workers. Please bear
> in mind that you are not being offered relief or charity but WORK. The inter-
> viewers have been instructed to receive you with the same courtesy and
> consideration that would be extended by any professional employment
> agency, our object being to set up so high a standard of professional excel-
> lence in these projects that they will be able to continue on their own
> momentum after the federal program is completed.

Into the project flocked young men and women who later became
celebrated actors—Joseph Cotton, Orson Welles, Arthur Kennedy, Burt
Lancaster, Arlene Francis, Ed Gardner, Rex Ingram, Canada Lee, Howard
da Silva, William Bendix, Bil Baird. Another employed by the WPA, but
not on the theater project, was Robert Ryan, who worked as a paving
supervisor.

At its peak the program gave work to 12,700 theater people in twenty-
nine states. Besides the actors themselves, there were producers, directors,
playwrights, stagehands, electricians, propmen—all the crafts found in
stage work. Hopkins had told Miss Flanagan: "We're for labor—first, last
and all the time. WPA is labor—don't forget that." He insisted that $9 of
every $10 be spent on wages, leaving only about $1 to meet operating
costs. Nine out of every 10 people hired had to come from relief rolls.
Wages averaged $83 a month, although some actors were paid up to
$103.40 a month for performing in New York City. According to the place
and circumstance, admission to WPA shows was free, or cost 10 cents, 25
cents, 50 cents, and in rare instances as much as $1.

The federal theater project presented many different kinds of shows—
Negro drama, dance drama, children's theater, puppet and marionette
shows, a documentary about syphilis, classical drama, modern drama,
foreign language drama, musicals, Living Newspapers, pageants, vaudeville, circus, religious drama, spectacles, opera and radio programs.

WPA theater companies toured CCC camps. In October, 1936, Miss
Flanagan watched the Syracuse unit stage an unorthodox show in a CCC
camp in Virginia. It was a warm night. The small hall was crowded with
boys sitting on benches, on the floor, on tables and windowsills. A car
roared up outside and screeched to a halt. Into the hall strode a man who
displayed a sheriff's badge and drew the CCC commander aside for a
whispered consultation. The boys were perplexed. Then, pounding on a
table, the sheriff said: "Men, I'm sorry to break in on your meeting this
way, but on account of the fact that so many witnesses in this case are
CCC workers, and that the camp is so far from the county courthouse, His
Honor has decided to hold court right here."

The CCC boys watched anxiously as they were joined by a judge, the
district attorney, the defense attorney and the defendant himself—a CCC

youth. He was ordered to sit down. Guards were placed near him. The sheriff consulted a list of names and said: "The jurors will be chosen. When your names are called, answer 'here' and rise." With the jurors picked and witnesses called, there began the trial of a CCC boy for murder. As the spectators slowly realized, this was an audience participation play written by Grace Heyward and called *The CCC Murder Mystery*.

Some dramas were written by project playwrights on their own time. Royalties were paid to professional playwrights for use of their material.

George Bernard Shaw let the WPA stage his plays at $50 a week, writing to Miss Flanagan: "As long as you stick to your fifty-cent maximum for admission . . . you can play anything of mine you like unless you hear from me to the contrary. . . . Any author of serious plays who does not follow my example does not know what is good for him. I am not making a public-spirited sacrifice; I am jumping at an unprecedentedly good offer."

Eugene O'Neill released his own plays on similar terms, telling reporters: "The WPA units can present important plays before audiences that never before have seen an actual stage production. The possibilities in this respect are thrilling. . . . These units are translating into action the fact that the government has an obligation to give a reasonable amount of encouragement and assistance to cultural undertakings."

Sinclair Lewis had been offered a lot of money by commercial theater producers to make a play out of his novel *It Can't Happen Here*. Instead, he offered it to the WPA. The red-headed writer told reporters: "I prefer to give it to the federal theater for two reasons: first, because of my tremendous enthusiasm for its work and, second, because I know I can depend on the federal theater for a non-partisan point of view."

Lewis and his collaborators began their rewrite work in the Essex House on Manhattan's Central Park South—but not at government expense. Much newspaper space was given to the fact that this famous author was working on a play for the WPA. Some editorial writers and readers felt that his study of the rise of an American dictator was Communist-inspired, or the result of Fascism, or a plot to reelect Roosevelt, or a scheme to defeat him. Huey Long had been dead only about a year, so New Orleans officials would not book this show into a city where the late dictator still had many friends. *It Can't Happen Here* became so controversial that before it premiered, the nation's newspapers printed 78,000 lines of pro and con comment about the production.

On October 27, 1936, the play opened simultaneously in twenty-one theaters in seventeen states—the most multiple and extensive first night in the history of the American theater. From Bridgeport and Cleveland, Miami and Birmingham, Detroit and Indianapolis—from each of the several cities came reports that audiences had received the play with wild enthusiasm. In its first few weeks it drew more than a quarter million spectators.

In the New York *Times* Brooks Atkinson wrote: "Mr. Lewis has a story to tell that is calculated to make the blood of a liberal run pretty cold. . . . *It Can't Happen Here* ought to scare the daylights out of the heedless Americans who believe, as this column does, that it can't happen here as long as Mr. Lewis keeps his health."

A smash hit, the play was presented here and there across the country for a total of 260 weeks.

However, not all Americans were fond of the federal theater project. Members of a Negro unit wrote and produced *Turpentine*, a social play that exposed the evils of the Southern labor camp system. A Savannah weekly trade paper called *Turpentine* "a malicious libel on the naval stores industry of the South" and called for "a censor on the Works Progress Administration." The Tulsa *Tribune* lambasted a federal dance group in California for staging "dances depicting American life." This newspaper went on to say: "We feel a sort of sentimental nostalgia for the old days when relief meant nothing more than a square meal." The Indianapolis *News* said nervously that if the federal theater "can produce a play simultaneously in fifteen cities, it can be regarded as one of the nation's most powerful agencies for the dissemination of propaganda."

And there came cries that the Commies were behind the whole thing.

It was true that the Communist Party had tried to take over the theater in America, raising the slogan that "Drama Is a Weapon," peddling the party line by means of "agitprop" troupes appearing before audiences of workers and intellectuals. But the Reds failed to win control of the theater. Then they sought to infiltrate the federal theater project, and certainly some Communists got on relief rolls. Although Miss Flanagan was liberal and perhaps even naïve, she wanted no Communist plays which depicted "the over-simplified collision of workers and bosses," as she put it.

"As I have repeatedly said," she declared, "I will not have the federal theater used politically. I will not have it used to further the ends of the Democratic party, the Republican party or the Communist party."

Congressman Everett M. Dirksen of Illinois, who later became the Republican leader of the Senate, denounced WPA productions as "salacious tripe." During a House of Representatives debate on the theater project, Dirksen entertained his peers by reading aloud the titles of some WPA plays, none of which he had seen: "I have one here—*A New Deal for Mary*, which is a grand title. Then there is *The Mayor and the Manicure*, and *Mother Goose Goes to Town*. Also, *A New Kind of Love*. I wonder what that can be. It smacks somewhat of the Soviet. Then there is *Up in Mabel's Room*. There is an intriguing title for you. . . . Here is another, *Be Sure Your Sex Will Find You Out*. . . . Then there is *Cheating Husbands*. That would be well for the front page of some Washington daily. Next we have *Companionate Maggie*, and this great rhetorical and intriguing question, *Did Adam Sin?* . . ."

Dirksen failed to mention that the WPA also presented the works of celebrated playwrights such as William Shakespeare, Christopher Marlowe, Molière, Sean O'Casey, George Bernard Shaw, Eugene O'Neill, Oliver La Farge, Thornton Wilder, Mary Coyle Chase, Robert Nathan and Theresa Helburn. Dirksen did not quote from a story written by Ed Sullivan after the columnist saw a Los Angeles production of *Run, Little Chillun.*

"One of the outstanding plays brought to the American theatre," said Sullivan. "Distinguished by so many fine individual performances that it is difficult to dwell overlong on any one player. If this had been done by the Moscow Art Theatre or any group of foreign actors and actresses, it would be hailed nationally for its dramatic intensity and integrity, its brilliant direction and simple staging . . . its sheer stage magic. This was the first Federal Theatre Project play I'd seen, and it justifies all the money that has been used to subsidize the work."

A majority of Representatives and Senators disagreed with Ed Sullivan. The Dies Committee declared that the plays, the performers and even the audiences were Communistic. This took in a lot of territory, since millions of Americans saw WPA performances. Miss Flanagan replied to this charge with a brief in which she said that "I am not and never have been a Communist; that I am a registered Democrat; that I have never been engaged in any Communistic activities, or belonged to any Communistic organization. . . ."

Called on to testify, she told the committee that "we have never done a play which was propaganda for Communism, but we have done plays which were propaganda for democracy, for better housing." She said the enthusiasm of the federal actors had "a certain Marlowesque madness."

Democratic Congressman Joe Starnes of Alabama said: "You are quoting from this Marlowe. Is he a Communist?"

The hearing room rocked with laughter, but Miss Flanagan did not laugh. Thousands of jobs were at stake.

"I was quoting from Christopher Marlowe," she said quietly.

"Tell us who Marlowe is," demanded the Alabama lawmaker, "so we can get the proper references—because that is all we want to do."

"Put in the record," said Miss Flanagan, "that he was the greatest dramatist in the period of Shakespeare—immediately preceding Shakespeare."

The federal theater project was sponsored and patronized by unions and schools, colleges and universities, Catholics and Jews, Protestants and civic groups, industrial and philanthropic organizations. It brought the living theater to youths who never before had seen flesh-and-blood actors. In the *Federal Theater Magazine* a writer described this huge audience in these words: "We're a hundred thousand kids who never saw a play before. We're students in colleges, housewives in the Bronx, lumberjacks in Oregon, sharecroppers in Georgia. We're rich and poor, old and young, sick and well. We're America and this is our theatre."

But as the project's fate hung in the balance, Brooks Atkinson wrote in the New York *Times:* "Being the most conspicuous of the WPA arts projects, it is the one Congress enjoys worrying the most. Art seems like boondoggling to a congressman who is looking for a club with which to belabor the administration, and there is always something in the Federal Theatre that can be blown up into a scandal. . . ."

Joe Martin, a Republican Representative from Massachusetts, told in his memoirs what happened when there was a WPA request for funds for its dance program: "I got in touch with Representative Dewey Short, a Republican from Missouri, and said, 'Dewey, when this WPA appropriation comes up, why don't you give the boys a little vaudeville show?' He got the idea all right. When the debate began, he jigged down to the well of the House and put on a version of a WPA dance recital that had Democrats as well as Republicans screaming with laughter."

The cultural sensitivities of these lawmakers was not shared by a Republican newspaper, the New York *Herald Tribune.* Foremost among the directors of the WPA dance program was the talented Helen Tamiris, whose temper, as Miss Flanagan said, "is as electric as her hair and her dancing." In reviewing *How Long Brethren,* a dance depicting seven episodes of Negro life, the *Tribune* said that "Tamiris has accomplished the finest composition of her career . . . the most thrilling episode, *Let's Go to De Buryin',* with its frenzied emotional climax heightened by Tamiris' superb dancing, aroused the audience to a state of high excitement."

With the rise of Congressional attacks on the theater project, to its defense came sponsoring bodies, schools and churches, all major units of radio, screen and stage. Perhaps the most colorful among these would-be rescuers was Tallulah Bankhead, currently starring in *The Little Foxes* on the commercial stage. In her autobiography, Miss Bankhead said: "Although I knew there were Communists in the Federal Theatre Project, I raced to Washington to plead with the appropriations committee to extend its life because it was the only source of employment for hundreds of the stage's needy."

The exotic actress knew her way around Washington better than most of her colleagues since her father, William B. Bankhead, was Speaker of the House, while her uncle, John H. Bankhead, was the senior Senator from Alabama. Surrounded by cameramen, she hugged her uncle and cried throatily: "Of course you'll vote to do something for the unemployed actors?"

"No," replied the Senator, "I don't think I will. These city folks in Congress never vote to do anything for the farmers."

Pulling off her blue felt hat and tossing it aside, her rich chestnut hair falling in waves upon her shoulders, Miss Bankhead perched on a table and began reading a statement.

Her father sat nearby. He whispered: "Go slower."

But she raced on with her arguments—that the project should be helped because it yielded a 10 percent federal tax on admissions, because there was no other work available for theater people, because their talents were social assets, because they brought cheer to millions of Americans.

Her voice began to break as she finished. "Actors are people, aren't they?" she pleaded. "They're people!" And she burst into tears.

Her uncle later sent her a telegram saying: I TRIED TO FIND A WEAK PLACE IN YOUR MASTERLY ARGUMENT. CHECK ME OFF AS VOTING FOR THE PROJECT.

But even Miss Bankhead's influential uncle was unable to save the Federal Theater Project, which was killed on June 30, 1939, when Congress cut off all its appropriations.

Brooks Atkinson commented: ". . . For socially useful achievement, it would be hard among the relief projects to beat the Federal Theatre, which has brought art and ideas within the range of millions of people all over the country and proved that the potential theatre audience is inexhaustible. . . . Although the Federal Theatre is far from perfect, it has kept an average of 10,000 people employed on work that has helped to lift the dead weight from the lives of millions of Americans."

*   *   *

Earlier, while the government was setting up the Civilian Conservation Corps, Eleanor Roosevelt lamented that it did nothing for girls. She wanted single, jobless women brought together in urban clubs somewhat similar to CCC camps, but got nowhere. Trying to go it alone, she held a series of meetings in her Manhattan home with a group of about thirty underprivileged young people.

Ensnared in the Depression, few young men and women could afford to attend college, while at the same time they found it increasingly difficult to get jobs. Between 1920 and 1930 college attendance had more than doubled, but from 1932 to 1934 college enrollment fell by 10 percent. High schools, colleges and universities slashed their budgets and cut the salaries of teachers, many of whom went for months without getting a paycheck. By the spring of 1935 a total of 3,000,000 people between the ages of sixteen and twenty-five were on relief—an average of 1 in 7. Even more distressing was the fact that many youths became transients; on a single day in May, 1935, the WPA's transient service counted 54,000 of them registered at its camps and shelters.

Besides the intrinsic misery of this situation, it was also politically dangerous. One confused young man said: "If someone came along with a line of stuff in which I could really believe, I'd follow him pretty nearly anywhere." In Germany and Italy millions of youths had harkened to the evil music of those corrupt pipers, Hitler and Mussolini.

Here in America the President's wife felt it would be wise to create a kind of junior CCC or WPA to help young people and give them a sense of direction. Perhaps such a program could be set up as a subdivision of the

WPA. She explained her plan to Harry Hopkins and his assistant, Aubrey Williams, who liked it so much that they expanded on it and outlined what became the National Youth Administration. However, they hesitated about presenting the idea to the President. Hopkins told Mrs. Roosevelt: "There may be many people against the establishment of such an agency in the government, and there may be bad political repercussions. We do not know that the country will accept it. We do not even like to ask the President, because we do not think he should be put in a position where he has to say officially 'yes' or 'no' now."

One night Eleanor Roosevelt entered her husband's bedroom as he was about to go to sleep. When he saw the expression on her face, he smiled and said: "Well, well—what new program is hanging fire?"

She described the idea for the National Youth Administration, frankly adding that Hopkins was unsure of the wisdom of pushing it.

The President asked: "Do you think it is right to do this?"

"It will be a great help to the young people, Franklin. But I don't want you to forget that Harry Hopkins thinks it may be unwise politically. Some people might say it's like the way Hitler is regimenting German youths."

This, as Mrs. Roosevelt may have intended, was a challenge to the President.

"If it is the right thing to do for the young people," he said, looking up at her, "then it should be done. I guess we can stand the criticism, and I doubt if our youth can be regimented in this way or in any other way."

On June 26, 1935, President Roosevelt issued an executive order creating the National Youth Administration. Its purpose was to administer a relief and employment program for young women between the ages of sixteen and twenty-five, for young men of this age who were physically unsuited for CCC labor, for the children of rural families, for those no longer attending school regularly and for needy students who wanted to finish their educations but lacked the means. The NYA was set up as a part of the WPA. As executive director of this new agency the President appointed Aubrey Williams.

In this year of 1935 Aubrey Williams was forty-four years old, gaunt, wavy-haired, hollow-eyed and something of a zealot. He had been born in Alabama in 1890 and as a small boy he went to work on a laundry wagon at $1 a week. Later he earned $3 a week as a stock boy in a Birmingham department store, painted signs, worked in a coal mine while attending night school. During World War I he went to Paris as a YMCA representative, received a degree from the University of Bordeaux in 1919 and returned to the United States, where he became a social worker. His first New Deal job was as a field representative of the FERA; his second, as assistant administrator of the FERA and CWA; his third, as assistant administrator of the WPA.

Now he faced an enormous task. The first fiscal year Williams had $41.2 million to spend, and in 1936 he got $68 million more. Because the

President wanted the NYA to be as decentralized as possible, separate administrations were set up in each of the forty-eight states and a special one in New York City, owing to its size. These forty-nine administrations were supplemented by district and local directors, together with advisory committees throughout the nation.

Just about the time of the creation of the NYA, a twenty-six-year-old Texan by the name of Lyndon B. Johnson suffered a shock. For nearly three years he had worked in Washington as secretary to Representative Richard M. Kleberg of Texas. Johnson, an aggressive young man, pretty much dominated his boss, and when Mrs. Kleberg told her husband that the boy was planning to run against him in the next election, the enraged Congressman fired his secretary. Johnson scurried to Representative Maury Maverick of Texas with the sad news that he was just out of a job. Maverick, who liked Johnson, knew that President Roosevelt was about to name forty-eight state NYA directors.

On easy terms with Roosevelt, Maverick went to him to say he knew just the man to direct the Texas NYA—Lyndon Johnson. The President was agreeable until he learned that Johnson was only twenty-six years old. He scoffed that he would not give such an important position to a child, but the Texas Congressman persisted. "After all," said Maverick, "you need someone who's honestly interested in helping his own generation work their way through high school and college and improve themselves, rather than sit around unemployed." In July, 1935, President Roosevelt named Lyndon Baines Johnson the head of the NYA in Texas.

Johnson, who hero-worshiped Roosevelt then and thereafter, flew from Washington to Texas and opened state headquarters of the NYA on the sixth floor of the shabby Littlefield Building in Austin. Then he flew back to the national capital to attend the first nationwide meeting of state NYA directors, called into session by Aubrey Williams on August 20, 1935. Johnson was not shy about telling reporters that he was the youngest of all the state directors and was delighted when this news item was published in newspapers from coast to coast. Also making a good impression on Williams, he obtained more funds for Texas than had originally been allocated to it.

Tall and lanky, working sixteen hours a day, ardently favoring education, this graduate of Southwest Texas State College kept nagging his staff: "Put'em to work! Get'em in school!" One day he agreed to an interview by Charles E. Green, who wrote a column for the Austin *American-States-man.* Propping his feet on his desk, Johnson grinned broadly and drawled: "I guess I know a little bit about the youth's hard lot in life. . . . I received my early education in a country school in the hill country. After schoolin', I got a job as a day laborer on the highways. I chopped weeds, earned a dollar here and a dollar there, always with an idea in my mind of finishin' a college education."

During the twenty months that Lyndon B. Johnson served as state director of the NYA in Texas, he helped 18,000 students by giving them money to go to school and by arranging part-time work in colleges at 35 cents an hour. He also aided 12,000 out-of-school youngsters, seeing that they learned trades and did useful work on public projects. Since Texas was the biggest state in the union, Johnson spent much of his time traveling, and the contacts he made were of use to him in furthering his political career.

In the spring of 1937 he decided to run for Congress. When the news reached Aubrey Williams in the national capital, Williams called the White House and spoke on the phone with Presidential aide Tommy Corcoran.

"Tommy," said Williams, "you've got to get the President to make this guy Johnson lay off running for the Congressional seat down in Austin. He's my whole youth program in Texas, and if he quits, I have no program down there."

Corcoran spoke to Roosevelt, who gave him orders to make sure that Johnson stuck to his NYA job and forget about running for Congress. But before Corcoran could locate Johnson to relay this word from on high, LBJ had quit his NYA post and filed for Congress.

*   *   *

Richard M. Nixon, who succeeded Johnson as President in 1969, also benefited from the New Deal. In September, 1934, Nixon arrived in Durham, North Carolina, to enter Duke University's new law school. Having been graduated second in his class from Whittier College in California, the twenty-one-year-old student had been given a $200 tuition grant; to keep it he had to maintain a B average at Duke. Because of the Depression, his family was able to send him only $35 a month. To supplement this grant and allowance, Nixon accepted aid from the National Youth Administration, earning thirty-five cents an hour for doing research in the law library.

"I couldn't afford the dormitory," Nixon later said, "so at first I stayed at a downtown boardinghouse with fourteen preachers. But I had to move because of the noise."

With three other students he rented a room in a ramshackle farmhouse a mile from the campus and set in the midst of tall pines. They shared two double beds in a big bare room heated by an old iron potbellied stove. Their quarters lacked any lights, so Nixon studied in the law library. It was also without water, so he showered in the university gym. He used his trunk for a closet, could afford only secondhand books and paid twenty-five cents a meal in a boardinghouse.

Helen Gahagan Douglas, with whom Nixon later feuded politically, was a member of the California state committee of the NYA. Eric F. Goldman, who developed into a noted historian and educator, got through Johns Hopkins University at Baltimore with NYA help. Raymond Clapper was another who had reason to be grateful to the NYA. After Clapper became a famous columnist, he wrote that "some of our leading citizens who are so violently opposed to institutions like the National Youth Administration are not so opposed to subsidizing college students for football teams."

Arthur Miller, who subsequently won renown as a dramatist, got NYA aid while attending the University of Michigan. Of those days he later wrote:

> I loved the idea of being separated from the nation, because the spirit of the nation, like its soil, was being blown by crazy winds. Friends of mine in New York, one of them a *cum laude* from Columbia, were aspiring to the city firemen's exam; but in Ann Arbor I saw that if it came to the worst a man could live on nothing for a long time.
>
> I earned $15 a month for feeding a building full of mice—the National Youth Administration footing the bill—and out of it I paid $1.75 a week for my room and squeezed the rest for my Granger tobacco (two packs for thirteen cents), my books, laundry and movies. For my meals I washed dishes in the co-op cafeteria. My eyeglasses were supplied by the Health Service, and my teeth were fixed for the cost of materials. The girls paid for themselves, including the one I married.

While still in college, Miller wrote several plays. In the spring of 1938 he was graduated, and two months later he was on relief. Then he returned to his hometown, New York City, where he joined the federal theater project. Before the project could present his first play, though, its activities were ended.

A sampling of 150 NYA work projects for out-of-school youths showed that the young men and women employed on them engaged in 169 types of work. Among other things, they installed floodlights in airports, built athletic courts, beautified parks, made brooms, canned vegetables and fruits, took care of infants, cleaned bricks for reuse, cleaned lagoons, cleared land, clipped newspapers in libraries, cooked for lunchrooms, excavated for artifacts, made furniture, worked as nurses, laid pipes, planted grass and so on.

In Fort Morgan, Colorado, fifty-two NYA boys converted a dump into a public recreation ground with 40 acres of grass, shrubs, trees and a new 5-acre swimming pool. At Gloucester, Massachusetts, rubber-booted NYA youths took eggs from lobsters to restock a federal fish hatchery. On the Onondaga Indian reservation in New York State some Indian boys working for the NYA chopped down trees, shaped logs and built a summer camp for children. At the Fort Valley Normal and Industrial School in Georgia a group of Negro boys and girls, few of whom had finished grade school, were paid by the NYA as they were trained in farming, homemaking and various trades. In the Flint-Goodridge Hospital in New Orleans black NYA girls helped regular staff members in every department of the hospital.

Under NYA rules the youths were to work no more than eight hours a day, forty hours a week or seventy hours a month. They earned from $10 to $25 a month, depending on prevailing local wage standards. What did they do with these meager earnings? First they helped their families. Then they bought themselves new clothes, since they had worn nothing but hand-me-down clothing for years. Telling what the NYA meant to him, one boy said: "Maybe you don't know what it's like to come home and have everyone looking at you, and you know they're thinking, even if they don't say it, 'He didn't find a job.' It gets terrible. You just don't want to come home. . . . But a guy's gotta eat some place and you gotta sleep some place. . . . I tell you, the first time I walked in the front door with my paycheck, I was somebody!"

If it had not been for the NYA and other New Deal agencies, an entire generation of American youths might have lost all hope in themselves and in America. The temper of the times was expressed by one graduating class, which chose as its motto: "Here we come, WPA!"

*   *   *

However, to some Americans who ate three square meals a day without the help of the government, the overall program of the Works Progress Administration seemed less than noble. One of the popular pastimes was telling WPA jokes like the following:

"A farmer asked a druggist for 'some of that WPA poison. It won't kill squirrels, but it will make them so lazy I can just stomp them to death.' "

"A WPA worker sued the government because he hurt himself when the shovel he was leaning on broke."

"Why is a WPA worker like King Solomon? . . . Because he takes his pick and goes to bed."

"I hear Harry Hopkins is planning to equip all of his WPA workers with rubber-handled shovels."

"Don't shoot our still life—it may be a WPA worker at work."

"There's a new cure for cancer, but they can't get any of it. It's sweat from a WPA worker."

Some of these jokes were thought up by professional comedians, but at last the American Federation of Actors ordered all its members to stop poking fun at the WPA.

Newspaper readers chuckled when they read that a cow had halted work on a WPA fish hatchery in Florida by eating the blueprints. There was further merriment when a Massachusetts woman held up construction of a WPA-built wall by planting her foot in the way of the workers and refusing to remove it.

Harry Hopkins got his lumps as criticism fell like hail on his head. It was embarrassing to learn that the WPA was employing a cousin of Nazi leader Hermann Göring. Harold Ickes wrote in his diary: "Hitler sees that everyone in Germany has a job. He has a public works and a WPA program that exceeds ours." Congressman Vito Marcantonio of New York declared that "the WPA is doing more to destroy the American standard of living than any group of reactionary industrialists."

On July 25, 1935, Hopkins had appointed Hugh Johnson, former head of the NRA, to the post of WPA administrator for New York City. In a wire to the New York State WPA director in Albany, Hopkins made it clear that Johnson would report directly to Washington, not to the state WPA headquarters. Because of its size, New York City had been made a forty-ninth "state" under the national WPA setup. In fact, one-seventh of all federal relief money went to the metropolis on the Hudson.

General Johnson established his headquarters in the Port Authority Building at 111 Eighth Avenue, which had been used as a relief center since the days of the CWA. Because of his military background, he chose as assistants a great many Army Engineer officers. With $100 million to spend at the start, Johnson soon had 97,000 New Yorkers employed on WPA projects in the city. Even so, this left such a reservoir of jobless people that 20,000 of them stormed relief offices begging for work. In the next three days the WPA hired 13,000 more men and women, and thereafter it accepted people as fast as jobs could be found for them.

Johnson soon found himself locked in combat with Robert Moses, the brilliant and trigger-tempered city parks commissioner. Moses, planning the most massive rehabilitation of the parks in the city's history, needed more relief workers than any other local WPA project. "We aim," said Moses, "to rebuild New York, saving what is durable, what is salvageable, and what is genuinely historical, and substituting progress for obsolescence."

The strong-minded parks commissioner insisted on complete control of the WPA workers assigned to him. Before long he snarled that he was getting a lot of "bums" from the WPA, when what he needed was more skilled workers and efficient foremen. The day after this outburst Moses called the WPA stupid, inefficient and arrogant. Johnson counterattacked, charging Moses with "obstructionism." Moses then sent Mayor LaGuardia a letter saying: "There is an immense amount of loafing on park jobs due primarily to the fact that in the last few weeks almost 11,000 new men have been assigned to us by General Johnson without supervision. The total number of new supervisors provided for these men is twelve. On any reasonable theory some 700 supervisors would be required."

Another time Moses wired Johnson: GOD HELP THE FEDERAL WORKS PROGRAM IF YOU AND YOUR COLONELS ARE GOING TO RUN IT. The day Johnson took office as head of the city WPA program he had said he would serve only temporarily. After losing battle after battle to the prickly parks commissioner, the general quit his job on October 15, 1935. In a farewell address broadcast by radio, Johnson made his usual emotional speech, and this time he pointed his closing words at Moses: "Good-bye, little bright eyes!"

Robert Moses was not a hardhearted man despite his passion for efficiency. After a fishing trip off Long Island he cleaned 500 flounders and gave them to the poor. But the city's parks had been deteriorating for more than a decade, and Moses meant to save and beautify them.

In the Central Park Zoo the lions' cages were so flimsy that animal keepers toted shotguns to protect children if the beasts escaped. The park itself teemed with so many rats that in a single week Moses' exterminators killed more than 200,000 of them. In two years Moses increased the city's recreational facilities by about 35 percent. With parks and playgrounds multiplying at incredible speed, Moses snapped at the city sanitation commissioner for piling garbage cans along a certain park. That bewildered official asked plaintively how in the world were his men to know when they set down garbage cans that a new park would be beside them the next day?

*   *   *

As has been said, the WPA employed 8,500,000 people on 1,410,000 projects in more than 3,000 counties at a cost of more than $11 billion. Naturally, in a program of such magnitude there were bound to be inequities and injustice, scandals and corruption. Campaigning by WPA staff members in Pennsylvania, Kentucky and Tennessee in the 1938 Congressional elections led to adverse comment and passage of the Hatch Act of July, 1939, curbing "pernicious political activities" by federal appointees. President Roosevelt discharged at least one state WPA director and began keeping a closer eye on the others.

Harry Hopkins was loved and hated by relief workers and politicians according to how well the WPA treated them. While he certainly had personal preferences in which he indulged, he was totally honest and therefore beyond the reach of provable scandal. Except for betting on the horses and lifting a glass of champagne with rich friends, he maintained his modest way of life. None of that $11 billion ever found its way into his pockets. But he was criticized in proportion to the increase in his political power.

Besides these mounting attacks, Hopkins had personal problems. His second wife died, and he learned that he had cancer. He entered the Mayo Clinic, where a large part of his stomach was removed in December, 1937. He recuperated at the Florida estate of Joseph P. Kennedy. After a long absence from the job, he returned to Washington, where the President took over the supervision of his health. Despite Hopkins' ills, Roosevelt seemingly wanted him to run for the Presidency in 1940, and to enhance Harry's career, the President nominated him for the post of secretary of commerce.

In the fall of 1938 the Baltimore *Sun* published a column by Frank R. Kent, who said that in a conversation with friends critical of the New Deal's spending policy, Hopkins had retorted: "We will spend and spend, tax and tax, elect and elect!"

This alleged remark was repeated by Joseph Alsop and Robert Kintner in their syndicated column, with the comment that it was "probably apocryphal." The next journalist to enter the picture was Arthur Krock, head of the Washington bureau of the New York *Times*. Although Krock was a Democrat, he had turned against the New Deal after Roosevelt's reelection in 1936. On one occasion he said that FDR was guilty of "more ruthlessness, intelligence, and subtlety in trying to suppress legitimate unfavorable comment than any other figure I have known."

Despite this barb, the President gave a private interview to Krock, who won a Pulitzer Prize for it.

When Krock read Kent's column containing the alleged quotation from Hopkins, he asked Kent for his news source, and Kent confidentially named the man from whom he said he had heard the story. In his *Times* column of November 12, 1938, Krock repeated the charge that Hopkins had said: "We will spend and spend, tax and tax, elect and elect!" At a private dinner, a few days later, Harold Ickes gleefully said to Krock: "I see you have Harry by the short hairs."

Publication by the powerful *Times* of an alleged remark so nefarious and cynical was damaging to the President in his pursuit of New Deal measures. It also endangered Senate confirmation of Hopkins as the new secretary of commerce. Hopkins wrote the *Times* a letter flatly denying that he had said what he was accused of having said. This caused concern to Frank Kent.

"I called up the friend who had told me," Kent later wrote, "and asked if he would let his name be used to substantiate the truth. Somewhat alarmed at the prospect of a controversy, he was much adverse to this. He gave several personal reasons why it would only embarrass him and he asked me not to use his name. I told him that if that was the way he felt, of course I would protect him—and I have."

Kent, Alsop and Krock were called before the Senate committee considering the Hopkins nomination. Kent declined to appear to testify, sending the committee a letter saying he had to protect his news source. Alsop and Krock were sworn in as witnesses, but they too said they had given their word not to reveal any identities. From the witness stand, Krock said the phrase in question "seemed to me a concentrated gem of Mr. Hopkins' philosophy." Krock then added: "I made what seemed to me serious efforts to discover whether it was a chance remark—in which event I would not have printed it. It was a most logical statement, it seemed to me, of what Mr. Hopkins might have said."

By this time Hopkins had appeared before the committee and repeated his denial. In the light of this, Democratic Senator Bennett C. Clark of Missouri asked Krock: "Do you not think the balance of credibility would be very strongly on the side of a prominent, responsible officer of the government, when he comes into a hearing of this sort and makes an explicit, categorical denial, as against an anonymous, clandestine, and mysterious witness, who has not the manhood to come forward with a confirmation of the statement which it has been said he made, and which has been printed by you and Mr. Kent?"

"Senator," Krock said, "I think that is a tenable position for you to take."

Many years later Krock defended Dwight D. Eisenhower, who was being victimized by another canard. Krock said that the discussion in which Eisenhower made the alleged remarks was "of the private and informal character that important public men should be able to engage in without distortion through 'leaks.' "

Here is what really happened in the Hopkins affair:

One August afternoon in 1938 Hopkins went to a racetrack in Yonkers, New York. There he met and chatted with Max Gordon, a New York theatrical producer; Heywood Broun, the columnist; and Daniel Arnstein, a transportation expert. Broun and Arnstein later said they did not hear Hopkins use the phrase "spend and spend." Gordon admitted that Hopkins did not employ these precise words, but insisted "that's what he meant."

Because a Broadway showman pretended to know what was in Hopkins' mind, Hopkins suffered for many years afterward. The lie was dignified and perpetuated by H. L. Mencken in his *New Dictionary of Quotations,* under a section devoted to "electioneering." Mencken wrote: " 'We will spend and spend, tax and tax, and elect and elect,' Ascribed to Harry L. Hopkins: To Max Gordon at the Empire racetrack, Yonkers, N.Y., Aug., 1938."

But despite all this, Hopkins was confirmed as the new secretary of commerce and then went on to serve Roosevelt well as his personal emissary to our Allies during World War II.

In 1939 the Works Progress Administration had its named changed to the Works Projects Administration, and it continued in existence until June 30, 1943.

This vast, long-lived agency created enduring public works, helped the United States prepare for the approaching war, increased purchasing power and left grateful memories among millions of Americans who, without it, might have lost their lives, their hope of salvation, their faith in their country.

28

Toward the Promised Land

PRESIDENT ROOSEVELT was asleep in the White House when the phone rang beside his narrow bed. Switching on a light, he saw that the time was 2:50 A.M. The date was Saturday, September 2, 1939. The President picked up the telephone. William C. Bullitt, the United States ambassador to France, was calling on a transatlantic line from Paris. FDR and Bullitt had known each other since the days of World War I, when they occupied adjoining offices in the old State Department Building.

The ambassador told the President that Hitler had attacked Poland. Although the Führer had issued no formal declaration of war, Nazi ground troops had smashed across the German-Polish border and Luftwaffe planes were bombing scores of cities, including Warsaw, Lwow and Cracow.

World War II had begun.

Instantly wide-awake, Roosevelt had a strange feeling, a feeling of familiarity, the feeling that he had been through all this before. In this historic moment he scribbled a note to himself before calling his secretaries of war, navy and state and ordering them to place this nation in a defensive posture. Then, as lights started flicking on in federal buildings throughout Washington, the President wrote a few more lines, saying: ". . . Unless some miracle beyond our present grasp changes the hearts of men, the days ahead will be crowded days—crowded with the same problems, the same anxieties that filled to the brim those September days of 1914. For history does in fact repeat."

*　　　*　　　*

Although the United States did not become a combatant in the war until December 8, 1941, the day after the Japanese bombed Pearl Harbor, it soon developed into the arsenal of democracy. Many factories expanded operations, new plants opened, men and women were hired and industrial production soared.

War restored American prosperity—something the New Deal had been unable to do. As has been said, the core of every depression is unemployment, and Roosevelt failed to solve the unemployment problem. He did alleviate it by giving jobs to about half of all those who had been without work, but when war erupted in Europe in 1939, there still were between 8,000,000 and 9,000,000 unemployed Americans. It was not until 1943, two years after this nation took up arms, that the last of the jobless finally disappeared.

What had happened to the United States during the Depression decade? How close did we come to total economic collapse? Were we near revolution? Did either the Communists or Fascists win their tug-of-war for the nation's soul? What did the New Deal accomplish? How effective a President was Franklin D. Roosevelt?

What happened was that the fabric of our society was strained and torn worse than at any time since the Civil War. For a few frightening weeks there was real danger that our economic structure might disintegrate. For a few chilling moments, as angry bonus marchers teemed outside the Capitol Building in Washington, there was the possibility that the government might be overthrown. The Communists failed in their efforts to trigger a nationwide revolution. The Fascists also failed to seize power. Roosevelt thwarted the menace from both the far left and the far right by moving slightly left of center, by making a revolutionary response to a revolutionary crisis.

A successful revolution is one in which power shifts from one group to another. The New Deal brought about a social revolution, for power shifted from Wall Street to Washington, from capitalists to other classes of Americans. But for the most part, it was a peaceful and bloodless revolution. President Hoover used the Army to drive the bonus army from the center of Washington, several governors called out the National Guard to deal with disorders in their home states, but President Roosevelt never employed military might against Americans. And never did Roosevelt become a dictator; often he sat with his back to a window, something no dictator would think of doing.

The New Deal changed, but never destroyed, the basic structure of our economic and political systems. Roosevelt saved capitalism despite capitalists. Although the federal government became an entrepreneur, as in the Tennessee Valley Authority, it did not socialize the nation as some capitalists had begged that it do when things were at their worst. Of course, the New Deal did tighten governmental control of business. It put banks and stock exchanges under closer federal supervision, making improvements which these institutions, left to themselves, had failed to make.

Despite alarms from those who hated and feared Roosevelt, he did not kill off the two-party system. National elections continued to be held every four years. But Roosevelt did mobilize massive political power against the power of corporations. He cracked the monolithic control of our economy by the white Anglo-Saxon Protestant property-holding class. He broadened the base of the power structure by giving greater representation to laborers and farmers, intellectuals and minority ethnic groups. He changed the role of the state from that of an umpire to an active participant in society's welfare. He brought about better balance among the various branches of the economy.

Although Roosevelt may have weakened the privileged class, he did not destroy it—nor did he seek to destroy it. He preserved most property rights. He always meant it whenever he said he wanted to save capitalism. He did save capitalism by purging it of gross abuses and forcing an accommodation to the larger public interest. He made the industrial system more humane and protected workers from exploitation. He truly believed that government should govern in behalf of all citizens.

The New Deal instituted the most sweeping changes in economics and politics, in governmental procedures and social institutions, since the adoption of the Constitution. More progress was made in relief and public welfare during a single decade than in the entire previous history of this nation. The rugged individualism of the nineteenth century, which had allowed robber barons to flourish, gave way to collective action and social security and the rights of individuals.

When no sound solutions to the Depression were advanced by capitalists, when state and local governments proved unable to meet the crisis, the federal government expanded enormously. Inheriting a vacuum, Roosevelt probed and pierced its shrinking walls. He met the emergency with emergency measures. He gave some wrong answers but asked many of the right questions. Self-assured, he was willing to experiment, to improvise. Tough-minded, he ignored shrill cries that it was blasphemous to interfere with the "laws" of economics. For the first time in American history, economic and social planning by the government became a way of life.

In the early days of the New Deal it seemed that Roosevelt was a poor administrator, but in the end he proved to be a superb one. Generally willing to listen to advice, while reserving the right to make final decisions, he often played off one group of advisers against another and somehow brought out the best in most of them. Welcoming intellectuals who had been spurned by capitalists, he attracted thousands of brilliant and devoted men to Washington. Despite some infighting among New Dealers, the majority of them looked to Roosevelt for inspiration.

The New Deal saved lives. It relieved distress. It gave jobs to some of the jobless. It bestowed hope on the hopeless. It restored self-respect to millions of Americans. A conservative as much as an innovator, Roosevelt did much to end the waste of natural resources. He added to the nation's physical assets. He broadened cultural opportunities. By renewing faith in self-government, Roosevelt and the New Deal preserved the glories of democracy. Once and for all, they proved that ultimately it is the government which is responsible for the welfare of all the people. They demonstrated that curbs can and should be placed on capitalism whenever it runs amok, that a mixed economy is perhaps the best economy.

In the days of the New Deal many Americans realized, for the first time in their lives, that the federal government was responsive to their needs, was an intimate part of themselves—not some strange and shapeless something on the banks of the Potomac. They sensed that in Roosevelt they had a President who was genuinely concerned about their happiness.

Using the radio to touch the hearts of the people, using his strong personality as a lever, using his high office as both a pulpit and a lectern, Roosevelt re-created the Presidency and greatly expanded its legislative functions. He was not power-mad, as some people still believe. Upon taking office he was begged by the people, by legislators, by capitalists to save them. Something had to be done—so he did what he could. Someone had to act—and he acted. Someone had to continue to believe in the future of America—and he kept the faith.

Assuming a legislative role like that of a prime minister, Roosevelt invested the Presidency with more power than it had known during the administrations of his predecessors, Calvin Coolidge and Herbert Hoover. And in doing so, he somewhat upset the traditional balance of power among the three branches of the federal government—the executive, the judicial and the legislative.

The Supreme Court balked awhile, invalidating one New Deal measure after another, but after this flexing of muscles, after proving that it was not about to wither away, it then approved many of the things Roosevelt did. The Congress also balked from time to time, some Senators and Representatives denouncing the President, but it too remained intact if slightly less influential, well aware that Roosevelt was supported by most citizens. And, in the end, this expansion of the Presidency gave new vigor to the whole political system. The two major parties split into liberal and conservative wings or coalitions, while the voters became more active in politics than ever before.

Roosevelt entered the White House without any master plan for ending the Depression. However, he knew the general direction in which he hoped to move, and once he explained his shifting policies this way: "It is a little bit like a football team that has a general plan of game against the other side. Now, the captain and the quarterback of that team know pretty well what the next play is going to be, and they know the general strategy of the team; but they cannot tell you what the play after the next play is going to be until the next play is run off. If the play makes ten yards, the succeeding play will be different from what it would have been if they had been thrown for a loss. I think that is the easiest way to explain it."

*　　　*　　　*

In 1962, in an article published in the *New York Times Sunday Magazine,* seventy-five historians evaluated the American Presidents in terms of their contributions to the nation while they held office. All but two of these scholars were American, the others British. They did not judge two Presidents who served very short terms: William Henry Harrison died within a month of his inauguration, and James A. Garfield served little more than a half year. The rest of the Presidents were rated in five categories—great, near great, average, below average and failure.

In the nearly unanimous opinion of these historians we have had five great Presidents, in the following order: (1) Abraham Lincoln; (2) George Washington; (3) Franklin D. Roosevelt; (4) Woodrow Wilson; (5) Thomas Jefferson.

According to these historians, Herbert Hoover was an average President who ranked nineteenth. Calvin Coolidge was below average, ranking as our twenty-seventh best President.

*   *   *

In telling the story of the Depression it would be wrong to leave the impression that this nation was in torment every moment. The honest historian must confess his inability to catch every note of the past; he must be concerned with change, change makes more noise than serenity, and the kettledrums of strife often drown out the flutelike sound of peace. The quiet and kind people of this earth are heard less clearly than the loud and the cruel, although there are pleasant exceptions such as St. Francis of Assisi and Mahatma Gandhi.

The 1930's were troubled, true, but there also was a rhythm running through the cacophony of change. The earth swung about the sun to make day and to make night. The coming and going of the tides were a counterpoint to the pulsations of blood in the veins. Spring quickened the hearts of men, summer poured into the laps of idling women, autumn spilled multicolored wines upon leaves, and winter stabbed the lungs with air like icicles.

Children laughed. Birds sang. Stars glittered. In troubled times the common people are kind to one another, and so it was during the Depression. Smiles were exchanged, and housewives gossiped across friendly fences. There were flagpole sitters to watch and marathon dancers to ogle and miniature golf to be played. The morning's first cup of coffee shocked one awake while night hid the eternal mystery of procreation, and always and always lovers' kisses fused souls. Good people lived and loved and endured.

They sang popular songs such as "Brother, Can You Spare a Dime?" "Ten Cents a Dance," "Smoke Gets in Your Eyes," "Deep Purple," and "I'm in the Mood for Love." Leaning close to radios they listened and laughed at Fanny Brice as Baby Snooks, Edgar Bergen with Charlie

McCarthy on his knee, Jim and Marion Jordan as Fibber McGee and Molly, Bing Crosby and Bob Burns on the *Kraft Music Hall* program. Alone in their rooms they read *Gone with the Wind* by Margaret Mitchell, *Anthony Adverse* by Hervey Allen, *The Good Earth* by Pearl Buck, *How to Win Friends and Influence People* by Dale Carnegie—and, of course, *The Grapes of Wrath* by John Steinbeck.

In this decade there also was plenty amid poverty, frivolity in the face of want. Some people who had been rich before the Crash remained rich, if a little less rich, and behaved as though nothing had happened.

A few men had incomes of more than $1 million a year, cruised aboard their yachts, sat down to sumptuous banquets in mansions and posh hotels. Doris Duke, Barbara Hutton and other debutantes made formal bows to society, their hired orchestras muting the moans of the poor and the hungry. Sportsmen raced horses and played polo, gambling flourished in Reno, and Harold Ickes was dazzled by the luxury of the Boca Raton Club in Florida. William Randolph Hearst spent $6,000 a day to maintain his San Simeon estate in California, paid $10,000 for a single fireworks display and once chartered a plane just to fetch him shrimp from Louisiana.

Gourmet magazine began publication, and Duncan Hines started rating restaurants. The New York *Sun* advertised a British manor house for sale, while Doris Duke built herself a $1 million mansion in Hawaii. Actress Constance Bennett earned $30,000 in one week endorsing a variety of products, and Maurice Chevalier was paid a weekly salary of $12,000 for appearing at the Chicago Theater in Chicago. Helena Rubinstein opened a new beauty salon while John Robert Powers prospered with his model agency. Football pools ran to $1.5 million per week, Samuel Goldwyn paid film writer Ben Hecht $260,000 a year, and two rich movie stars were convicted of smuggling gems into the United States.

J. P. Morgan launched his fourth yacht and sold six paintings for $1.5 million. Joe Louis got $215,000 for beating Max Baer in the prizefight ring. Fairs were held in Chicago, Dallas, Cleveland, San Diego, New York City, Fort Worth and Philadelphia. Jimmy Walker raised his own salary as mayor of New York, Walter Winchell was paid $3,500 a week to go on the stage of the Palace Theater in Manhattan, and Edsel Ford shelled out $400,000 for a powerboat. The Hialeah racetrack was rebuilt, the Miami *Herald* sold for $2 million, and a woman divorced from her rich husband insisted that her small daughter could not live on less than $3,000 a month.

*   *   *

It was early in the Depression, on October 1, 1931, that the new Waldorf-Astoria opened. It opened on Park Avenue, fifteen blocks north of the site of the old hotel, a site that for the previous five months had been occupied by the newly completed Empire State Building.

The imposing new Waldorf with its bronze portals, its twin chrome-capped towers rising forty-seven stories, its rare marbles, matched woods and selected stones, its murals and its paintings, had 2,200 rooms and cost more than $40 million. Over the main entrance was a figure representing the Spirit of Achievement.

President Hoover, sitting in the Cabinet Room of the White House, saluted the Waldorf on a worldwide NBC radio broadcast, saying in part: "The opening of the new Waldorf-Astoria is an event in the advancement of hotels, even in New York City. It carries on a great tradition in national hospitality . . . marks the measure of the nation's growth in power, in comfort and in artistry . . . an exhibition of courage and confidence to the whole nation."

To the whole nation? Not to a Negro poet named Langston Hughes. This was not the way he evaluated the premiere of a luxurious new hotel. The month in which the new Waldorf opened was also a month in which the *Saturday Evening Post* published an article called "Our Vanishing Economic Freedom," in which 522 banks failed, in which Americans begged for jobs from the Russian firm called Amtorg, in which a rancher killed the 3,000 sheep he could not feed, in which President Hoover held a secret and worried meeting with thirty leading financiers.

Langston Hughes wrote a poem about the irony of opening the new Waldorf at a time when millions of Americans were homeless and hungry. He had been subsidized in part by a wealthy New York patroness. His poem disturbed her. She spoke to him in anger. In turn, the poet became so angry that he fell ill.

       *   *   *

Franklin D. Roosevelt expressed his social philosophy while he still was governor of New York State. On August 28, 1931, only about a month before the opening of the new Waldorf, he asked the legislature to set up a state relief administration.

"What is the State?" Roosevelt asked. "It is the duly constituted representative of an organized society of human beings, created by them for their mutual protection and well-being. 'The State' or 'The Government' is but the machinery through which such mutual aid and protection are achieved.

"The cave man fought for existence unaided or even opposed by his fellow man, but today the humblest citizen of our State stands protected by all the power and strength of his Government. Our Government is not the master but the creature of the people. The duty of the State toward its citizens is the duty of the servant to its master. The people have created it; the people, by common consent, permit its continual existence.

"One of these duties of the State is that of caring for those of its citizens who find themselves the victims of such adverse circumstance as makes them unable to obtain even the necessities for mere existence without the aid of others. That responsibility is recognized by every civilized Nation.

". . . I assert that modern society, acting through its Government, owes the definite obligation to prevent the starvation or the dire want of any of its fellow men and women who try to maintain themselves but cannot. . . ."

*   *   *

His speech was noble, idealistic. But what of reality? How well did Franklin D. Roosevelt live up to his lofty vision? In reality, the New Deal solved many problems, failed to solve others and even created some new ones. The administration of Franklin D. Roosevelt was a warmhearted administration, and the immortal Dante has said that divine justice weighs the sins of the cold-blooded and the sins of the warmhearted in different scales. Henry Wallace made a balanced judgment of the New Deal when he said: "We are children of the transition—we have left Egypt but we have not yet arrived at the Promised Land."

Selected Bibliography

ADAMIC, LOUIS, *My America*. New York, Harper, 1938.

ADAMS, FRANKLIN P., *The Diary of Our Own Samuel Pepys, 1911–1934*. New York, Simon and Schuster, 1935. 2 vols.

ADAMS, JAMES TRUSLOW, *Our Business Civilization*. New York, Albert & Charles Boni, 1929.

———, ed., *Dictionary of American History*. New York, Scribner's, 1940. 7 vols.

ADAMS, SAMUEL HOPKINS, *A. Woollcott: His Life and His World*. New York, Reynal & Hitchcock, 1945.

ALBERTSON, DEAN, *Roosevelt's Farmer: Claude R. Wickard in the New Deal*. New York, Columbia University Press, 1961.

ALINSKY, SAUL, *John L. Lewis: An Unauthorized Biography*. New York, Putnam's, 1949.

ALLEN, FREDERICK LEWIS, *Only Yesterday: An Informal History of the Nineteen-Twenties*. New York, Harper, 1931.

———, *The Lords of Creation*. New York, Harper, 1935.

———, *Since Yesterday: The Nineteen-Thirties in America*. New York, Harper, 1939.

American Heritage, various issues.
Americana Annual. New York, Americana Corp., 1924–1941.
AMORY, CLEVELAND, *The Last Resorts.* New York, Harper, 1948.
————, *Who Killed Society?* New York, Harper, 1960.
————, ed. in chief, *International Celebrity Register.* New York, Celebrity Register, 1959.
Annals of America, Vol. 15, *The Great Depression.* Chicago, Encyclopaedia Britannica, Inc., 1968.
Army Almanac. Harrisburg, Pa., Stackpole, 1959.
ARNOLD, THURMAN W., *The Folklore of Capitalism.* New Haven, Yale University Press, 1937.

BARKLEY, ALBEN W., *That Reminds Me.* Garden City, Doubleday, 1954.
BARNARD, HARRY, *Independent Man: The Life of Senator James Couzens.* New York, Scribner's, 1958.
BARNHART, CLARENCE L., and HALSEY, WILLIAM D., eds., *The New Century Cyclopedia of Names.* New York, Appleton-Century-Crofts, 1954. 3 vols.
BARUCH, BERNARD M., *The Public Years.* New York, Holt, Rinehart and Winston, 1960.
BATES, ERNEST SUTHERLAND, *The Story of Congress, 1789–1935.* New York, Harper, 1936.
BATES, ERNEST SUTHERLAND, and WILLIAMS, ALAN, *American Hurly-Burly.* New York, McBride, 1937.
BEARD, CHARLES A., and MARY R., *America in Midpassage.* New York, Macmillan, 1939.
BEARD, CHARLES A., and SMITH, GEORGE H. E., *The Future Comes: A Study of the New Deal.* New York, Macmillan, 1933.
BEEBE, LUCIUS, *The Big Spenders.* Garden City, Doubleday, 1966.
BELLUSH, BERNARD, *Franklin D. Roosevelt as Governor of New York.* New York, Columbia University Press, 1955.
BENDINER, ROBERT, *Just Around the Corner: A Highly Selective History of the Thirties.* New York, Harper, 1967.
BERGER, MEYER, *The Story of the New York Times, 1851–1951.* New York, Simon and Schuster, 1951.
BERNSTEIN, IRVING, *The Lean Years: A History of the American Worker, 1920–1933.* Baltimore, Penguin Books, 1966.
BINGHAM, ALFRED M., and RODMAN, SELDEN, eds., *Challenge to the New Deal.* New York, Falcon Press, 1934.
BINING, ARTHUR CECIL, and KLEIN, PHILIP SHRIVER, *A History of the United States,* Vol. 2. New York, Scribner's, 1951.
BINKLEY, WILFRED E., and MOOS, MALCOLM C., *A Grammar of American Politics.* New York, Knopf, 1949.
Biographical Directory of the American Congress, 1774–1949. Washington, United States Printing Office, 1950.
BIRD, CAROLINE, *The Invisible Scar.* New York, David McKay, 1966.
BLACK, RUBY, *Eleanor Roosevelt: A Biography.* New York, Duell, Sloan and Pearce, 1940.
BLACKORBY, EDWARD C., *Prairie Rebel: The Public Life of William Lemke.* Lincoln, University of Nebraska Press, 1963.
BLUM, JOHN MORTON, *From the Morgenthau Diaries, Years of Crisis, 1928–1938.* Boston, Houghton Mifflin, 1959.

BOTKIN, B. A., ed., *Sidewalks of America*. New York, Bobbs-Merrill, 1954.
BOWEN, CATHERINE DRINKER, *Yankee from Olympus: Justice Holmes and His Family*. Boston, Little, Brown, 1944.
BOYER, RICHARD O., and MORAIS, HERBERT M., *Labor's Untold Story*. New York, Cameron Associates, 1955.
BRADFORD, FREDERICK A., *Banking*. New York, Longmans, Green, 1932.
BRIDGWATER, WILLIAM, and SHERWOOD, ELIZABETH J., eds., *Columbia Encyclopedia*. New York, Columbia University Press, 1952.
Britannica Book of the Year, 1938–1941. Chicago, Encyclopaedia Britannica.
BROUN, HEYWOOD HALE, *Collected Edition of Heywood Broun*. New York, Harcourt, Brace, 1941.
BURNS, JAMES McGREGOR, *Roosevelt: The Lion and the Fox*. New York, Harcourt, Brace, 1956.
BUSCH, FRANCIS X., *Guilty or Not Guilty?* Indianapolis, Bobbs-Merrill, 1952.
BUSCH, NOEL F., *What Manner of Man?* New York, Harper, 1944.
BYRNES, JAMES F., *Speaking Frankly*. New York, Harper, 1947.
———, *All in One Lifetime*. New York, Harper, 1958.

CAMPBELL, CHRISTIANA McFADYEN, *The Farm Bureau and the New Deal*. Urbana, University of Illinois Press, 1962.
CARLSON, OLIVER, *Brisbane: A Candid Biography*. New York, Stackpole, 1937.
CARLSON, OLIVER, and BATES, ERNEST SUTHERLAND, *Hearst: Lord of San Simeon*. New York, Viking, 1936.
CARMAN, HARRY J., and SYRETT, HAROLD C., *A History of the American People Since 1865*. New York, Knopf, 1952.
CHASE, STUART, *A New Deal*. New York, Macmillan, 1932.
———, *Rich Land, Poor Land*. New York, McGraw-Hill, 1936.
CHURCHILL, ALLEN, *The Improper Bohemians: Greenwich Village in Its Heyday*. New York, Dutton, 1959.
———, *The Year the World Went Mad*. New York, Crowell, 1960.
———, *The Roosevelts: American Aristocrats*. New York, Harper & Row, 1965.
CLAPPER, RAYMOND, *Watching the World*. New York, McGraw-Hill, 1944.
COIT, MARGARET L., *Mr. Baruch*. Cambridge, Mass., Houghton Mifflin, 1957.
Collier's Encyclopedia. New York, Crowell Collier and Macmillan, 1966. 24 vols.
COMMAGER, HENRY STEELE, ed., *Documents of American History*. New York, Appleton-Century-Crofts, 1963.
CONGER, DON, ed., *The Thirties: A Time to Remember*. New York, Simon and Schuster, 1962.
CONKLIN, GROFF, ed., *The New Republic Anthology: 1915–1935*. New York, Dodge, 1936.
CRANE, MILTON, ed., *The Roosevelt Era*. New York, Boni and Gaer, 1947.
CREEL, GEORGE, *Rebel at Large*. New York, Putnam's, 1947.
CRICHTON, KYLE, *The Marx Brothers*. Garden City, Doubleday, 1950.
Crowell's Dictionary of Business and Finance. New York, Thomas Y. Crowell Co., 1923.
CUNEO, ERNEST, *Life with Fiorello*. New York, Macmillan, 1955.
CURLEY, JAMES MICHAEL, *I'd Do It Again*. Englewood Cliffs, N.J., Prentice-Hall, 1957.
Current Biography, 1940–1968. New York, Wilson.

DAN GOLENPAUL ASSOCIATES, *Information Please Almanac.* New York, Simon and Schuster, various years.

DAVIS, KENNETH S., *Soldier of Democracy: A Biography of Dwight Eisenhower.* Garden City, Doubleday, Doran, 1945.

DAY, DONALD, ed., *The Autobiography of Will Rogers.* Boston, Houghton, Mifflin, 1949.

——, ed., *Franklin D. Roosevelt's Own Story.* Boston, Little, Brown, 1951.

DELANEY, JOHN J., and TOBIN, JAMES EDWARD, eds., *Dictionary of Catholic Biography.* Garden City, Doubleday, 1961.

DEUTSCH, HERMANN B., *The Huey Long Murder Case.* Garden City, Doubleday, 1963.

DICE, CHARLES AMOS, and EITMAN, WILFORD JOHN, *The Stock Market.* New York, McGraw-Hill, 1952.

Dictionary of American Biography, Allen Johnson, ed. New York, Scribner's, 1964. 12 vols.

Directory of Directors in the City of New York. New York, Directory of Directors Co., various years.

DRAPER, THEODORE, *The Roots of American Communism.* New York, Viking, 1957.

DULLES, FOSTER RHEA, *The United States Since 1865.* Ann Arbor, University of Michigan Press, 1959.

EINAUDI, MARIO, *The Roosevelt Revolution.* New York, Harcourt, Brace, 1959.

EISENHOWER, DWIGHT D., *At Ease: Stories I Tell to Friends.* Garden City, Doubleday, 1967.

ELLIS, EDWARD ROBB, *The Epic of New York City.* New York, Coward-McCann, 1966.

——, "Briefly I Tarry," an unpublished journal.

ELSON, ROBERT T., *Time, Inc.: The Intimate History of a Publishing Enterprise, 1923–1941.* New York, Atheneum, 1968.

EMERSON, EDWIN, *Hoover and His Times.* Garden City, Garden City Publishing Co., 1932.

Encyclopaedia Britannica. Chicago, University of Chicago, 1945. 24 vols.

Encyclopedia Americana. New York, Americana Corp., 1952. 30 vols.

FARLEY, JAMES A., *Behind the Ballots.* New York, Harcourt, Brace, 1938.

——, *Jim Farley's Story: The Roosevelt Years.* New York, McGraw-Hill, 1948.

Federal Reserve System, Purposes and Functions. Washington, Board of Governors of the Federal Reserve System, 1963.

FEDERAL WRITERS' PROJECT OF THE WORKS PROGRESS ADMINISTRATION. Various states, various publishers, various years. 36 vols.

FIELD, CARTER, *Bernard Baruch: Park Bench Statesman.* New York, McGraw-Hill, 1944.

FILLER, LOUIS, ed., *The Anxious Years: America in the Nineteen Thirties.* New York, Capricorn, 1963.

FITE, GILBERT C., *George N. Peek and the Fight for Farm Parity.* Norman, University of Oklahoma Press, 1954.

FLANAGAN, HALLIE, *Arena: The History of the Federal Theatre.* New York, Benjamin Blom, 1940.

FLEISCHMAN, HARRY, *Norman Thomas: A Biography.* New York, Norton, 1964.

FLYNN, EDWARD J., *You're the Boss.* New York, Viking, 1947.

FLYNN, JOHN T., *Country Squire in the White House*. New York, Doubleday, Doran, 1940.

———, *The Roosevelt Myth*. New York, Devin-Adair, 1948.

FRANKLIN, JAY, *The New Dealers*, by Unofficial Observer. New York, Literary Guild, 1934.

FREDERICK, J. GEORGE, ed., *For and Against Technocracy: A Symposium*. New York, Business Bourse, 1933.

FREEDMAN, MAX, ed., *Roosevelt and Frankfurter: Their Correspondence, 1928–1945*. Boston, Little, Brown, 1967.

FREIDEL, FRANK, *Franklin D. Roosevelt: The Apprenticeship*. Boston, Little, Brown, 1952.

———, *Franklin D. Roosevelt: The Ordeal*. Boston, Little, Brown, 1954.

———, ed., *The New Deal and the American People*. Englewood Cliffs, N.J., Prentice-Hall, 1964.

FRIEDMAN, MILTON, and SCHWARTZ, ANNA JACOBSON, *The Great Contraction: 1929–1933*. Princeton, Princeton University Press, 1963.

FUSFELD, DANIEL R., *The Economic Thought of Franklin D. Roosevelt and the Origins of the New Deal*. New York, Columbia University Press, 1956.

GALBRAITH, JOHN KENNETH, *The Great Crash, 1929*. Boston, Houghton Mifflin, 1955.

GARRETT, CHARLES, *The LaGuardia Years*. New Brunswick, Rutgers University Press, 1961.

GAUVREAU, EMILE, *My Last Million Readers*. New York, Dutton, 1951.

GERHART, EUGENE C., *America's Advocate: Robert H. Jackson*. Indianapolis, Bobbs-Merrill, 1958.

GIBBS, WOLCOTT, *More in Sorrow*. New York, Henry Holt, 1958.

GOSNELL, HAROLD F., *Champion Campaigner: Franklin D. Roosevelt*. New York, Macmillan, 1952.

GRAFF, ROBERT; GINNA, ROBERT EMMETT; and BUTTERFIELD, ROGER, *F.D.R.* New York, Harper, 1962.

GRAHAM, FRANK, *Al Smith, American*. New York, Putnam's, 1945.

GRAMLING, OLIVER, *AP: The Story of News*. New York, Farrar and Rinehart, 1940.

GREEN, ABEL, and LAURIE, JOE, JR., *Show Biz from Vaude to Video*. New York, Holt, 1951.

GRIFFITH, WINTHROP, *Humphrey: A Candid Biography*. New York, Morrow, 1965.

GUNTHER, JOHN, *Roosevelt in Retrospect: A Profile in History*. New York, Harper, 1950.

———, *Inside U.S.A.*, rev. ed. New York, Harper, 1951.

GUTHRIE, WOODY, *Bound for Glory*. New York, Dutton, 1968.

HALLGREN, MAURITZ A., *The Gay Reformer*. New York, Knopf, 1935.

Harper's magazine.

HARRITY, RICHARD, and MARTIN, RALPH G., *The Human Side of F.D.R.* New York, Duell, Sloan and Pearce, 1960.

HART, ALBERT BUSHNELL, ed., *The American Year Book*. The American Year Book Corp., various years.

HATCH, ALDEN, *Franklin D. Roosevelt: An Informal Biography*. New York, Henry Holt, 1947.

HERZBERG, MAX J., ed., *The Reader's Encyclopedia of American Literature*. New York, Crowell, 1962.

HEWES, LAURENCE, *Boxcar in the Sand*. New York, Knopf, 1957.

HIGH, STANLEY, *Roosevelt—and Then?* New York, Harper, 1937.

HIMELSTEIN, MORGAN Y., *Drama Was a Weapon: The Left-Wing Theatre in New York, 1929–1941*. New Brunswick, Rutgers University Press, 1963.

Historical Statistics of the United States, 1789–1945. Washington, Bureau of the Census, 1949.

HOOVER, HERBERT, *Addresses upon the American Road: 1933–1938*. New York, Scribner's, 1938.

———, *The Memoirs of Herbert Hoover*. New York, Macmillan, 1952. 3 vols.

HOOVER, IRWIN HOOD (IKE), *Forty-Two Years in the White House*. Boston, Houghton Mifflin, 1934.

HORAN, JAMES D., *The Desperate Years: A Pictorial History of the Thirties*. New York, Crown, 1962.

HORTON, BYRNE J.; RIPLEY, JULIEN; and SCHNAPPER, M. B., *Dictionary of Modern Economics*. Washington, Public Affairs Press, 1948.

HOWARD, J. WOODRUFF, JR., *Mr. Justice Murphy: A Political Biography*. Princeton, Princeton University Press, 1968.

HOWE, IRVING, and COSER, LEWIS, *The American Communist Party*. New York, Praeger, 1962.

HOWE, QUINCY, *A World History of Our Own Times*. New York, Simon and Schuster, 1953. 2 vols.

HOYT, EDWIN P., *The Tempering Years*. New York, Scribner's, 1963.

HUEBNER, S. S., *The Stock Market*. New York, Appleton, 1929.

HUNT, FRAZIER, *The Untold Story of Douglas MacArthur*. New York, Devin-Adair, 1954.

HURD, CHARLES, *When the New Deal Was Young and Gay*. New York, Hawthorne, 1965.

HUTHMACHER, J. JOSEPH, *Senator Robert F. Wagner*. New York, Atheneum, 1968.

ICKES, HAROLD L., *The Secret Diary of Harold L. Ickes*. New York, Simon and Schuster, 1953. 3 vols.

IRWIN, WILL, *Herbert Hoover: A Reminiscent Biography*. New York, Grosset & Dunlap, 1928.

JAMES, MARQUIS, and JAMES, BESSIE ROWLAND, *Biography of a Bank: The Story of the Bank of America*. New York, Harper, 1954.

JOHNSON, HUGH S., *The Blue Eagle from Egg to Earth*. Garden City, Doubleday, Doran, 1935.

JONES, JESSE H., with EDWARD ANGLY, *Fifty Billion Dollars: My Thirteen Years with the RFC*. New York, Macmillan, 1951.

JONES, RICHARD SEELYE, *A History of the American Legion*. Indianapolis, Bobbs-Merrill, 1946.

JOSEPHSON, MATTHEW, *Sidney Hillman: Statesman of American Labor*. Garden City, Doubleday, 1952.

KAHN, ALBERT E., *High Treason: The Plot Against the People*. New York, Lear Publishers, 1950.

KANE, HARNETT T., *Louisiana Hayride: The American Rehearsal for Dictatorship: 1928–1940*. New York, Morrow, 1941.

KANE, JOSEPH NATHAN, *Facts About the President*. New York, Wilson, 1959.

———, *Famous First Facts*. New York, Wilson, 1964.

KEARNEY, JAMES R., *Anna Eleanor Roosevelt: The Evolution of a Reformer*. Boston, Houghton Mifflin, 1968.

KEMPTON, MURRAY, *Part of Our Time: Some Ruins and Monuments of the Thirties*. New York, Simon and Schuster, 1955.

KENNEDY, JOSEPH P., *I'm for Roosevelt*. New York, Reynal & Hitchcock, 1936.

KINGDON, FRANK, *As F.D.R. Said: A Treasury of His Speeches, Conversations and Writings*. New York, Duell, Sloan and Pearce, 1950.

KIPLINGER, W. M., *Washington Is Like That*. New York, Harper, 1942.

KOENIG, LOUIS W., *The Invisible Presidency*. New York, Rinehart, 1960.

KRAMER, DALE, *Heywood Broun: A Biographical Portrait*. New York, Current Books, 1949.

KROCK, ARTHUR, *Memoirs: Sixty Years on the Firing Line*. New York, Funk & Wagnalls, 1968.

LANGE, DOROTHEA, and TAYLOR, PAUL SCHUSTER, *An American Exodus*. New York, Reynal & Hitchcock, 1939.

LANGER, WILLIAM L., *An Encyclopedia of World History*. Boston, Houghton Mifflin, 1968.

LASH, JOSEPH P., *Eleanor Roosevelt: A Friend's Memoir*. Garden City, Doubleday, 1964.

LAVINE, EMANUEL H., *Gimme: Or, How Politicians Get Rich*. New York, Vanguard, 1931.

LEE, ALFRED MCCLUNG, and LEE, ELIZABETH BRIANT, eds., *The Fine Art of Propaganda*. New York, Harcourt, Brace, 1939.

LEE, CLARK, and HENSCHEL, RICHARD, *Douglas MacArthur*. New York, Henry Holt, 1952.

LEIGHTON, ISABEL, ed., *The Aspirin Age: 1919–1941*. New York, Simon and Schuster, 1949.

LENT, HENRY B., *The Waldorf-Astoria*. New York, Hotel Waldorf-Astoria Corp., 1934.

LERNER, MAX, ed., *The Portable Veblen*. New York, Viking, 1950.

LEUCHTENBERG, WILLIAM E., *Franklin D. Roosevelt and the New Deal*. New York, Harper, 1963.

LEVINSON, LEONARD LOUIS, *Wall Street: A Pictorial History*. New York, Ziff-Davis, 1961.

LEWIS, SINCLAIR, *It Can't Happen Here*. Garden City, Doubleday, Doran, 1935.

Life magazine.

Lincoln Library of Essential Information. Buffalo, Frontier Press, 1955.

LINDLEY, BETTY and ERNEST K., *A New Deal for Youth: The Story of the National Youth Administration*. New York, Viking, 1938.

LIPPMANN, WALTER, *Interpretations: 1933–1935*. New York, Macmillan, 1936.

Literary Digest magazine.

LOHBECK, DON, *Patrick J. Hurley*. Chicago, Henry Regnery Co., 1956.

LOMAX, ALAN, ed., *Hard Hitting Songs for Hard-Hit People*. New York, Oak Publications, 1967.

LONG, HUEY P., *Every Man a King: The Autobiography of Huey P. Long*. Chicago, Quadrangle Books, 1964.

LORANT, STEFAN, *F.D.R.: A Pictorial Biography*. New York, Simon and Schuster, 1950.

LORD, RUSSELL, *Henry A. Wallace: Democracy Reborn.* Reynal & Hitchcock, 1944.

———, *The Wallaces of Iowa.* Boston, Houghton Mifflin, 1947.

LOVETT, ROBERT MORSS, *All Our Years: An Autobiography.* New York, Viking, 1948.

LUDWIG, EMIL, *Roosevelt: A Study in Fortune and Power.* New York, Viking, 1937.

LUNDBERG, FERDINAND, *Imperial Hearst: A Social Biography.* New York, Modern Library, 1936.

———, *America's 60 Families.* New York, Vanguard, 1937.

———, *The Rich and the Super-Rich.* New York, Lyle Stuart, 1968.

LUTHIN, REINHARD H., *American Demagogues: Twentieth Century.* Boston, Beacon, 1954.

LYONS, EUGENE, *The Red Decade.* New York, Bobbs-Merrill, 1941.

———, *Our Unknown Ex-President: A Portrait of Herbert Hoover.* Garden City, Doubleday, 1949.

MACDONALD, WILLIAM, *The Menace of Recovery: What the New Deal Means.* New York, Macmillan, 1934.

MACKENZIE, COMPTON, *Mr. Roosevelt.* New York, Dutton, 1944.

MALONE, DUMAS, and RAUCH, BASIL, *Empire for Liberty.* New York, Appleton-Century-Crofts, 1960. 2 vols.

MANN, ARTHUR, *LaGuardia: A Fighter Against His Times, 1882–1933.* Philadelphia, Lippincott, 1959.

———, *LaGuardia Comes to Power: 1933.* Philadelphia, Lippincott, 1965.

MARTIN, JOE, as told to ROBERT J. DONOVAN, *My First Fifty Years in Politics.* New York, McGraw-Hill, 1960.

MARX, HARPO, *Harpo Speaks!* New York, Geis, 1961.

MASON, ALPHEUS THOMAS, *Harlan Fiske Stone: Pillar of the Law.* New York, Viking, 1956.

———, *Brandeis: A Free Man's Life.* New York, Viking, 1956.

MATHEWS, MITFORD M., ed., *A Dictionary of Americanisms.* Chicago, University of Chicago Press, 1951.

MATTHEWS, J. B., and SHALLICROSS, R. E., *Partners in Plunder: The Cost of Business Dictatorship.* New York, Grosset & Dunlap, 1935.

MATZ, MARY JANE, *The Many Lives of Otto Kahn.* New York, Macmillan, 1963.

MAXWELL, GILBERT, *Tennessee Williams and Friends.* Cleveland, World Publishing Co., 1965.

MAYER, MARTIN, *Wall Street: Men and Money.* New York, Harper, 1955.

MCCOY, DONALD R., *Calvin Coolidge: The Quiet President.* New York, Macmillan, 1967.

MCDONALD, FORREST, *Insull.* Chicago, University of Chicago Press, 1962.

McGraw-Hill Encyclopedia of Russia and the Soviet Union. New York, McGraw-Hill, 1961.

MCINTIRE, VICE-ADMIRAL ROSS T., in collaboration with GEORGE CREEL, *White House Physician.* New York, Putnam's, 1946.

MCLEAN, EVALYN WALSH, *Father Struck It Rich.* Boston, Little, Brown, 1936.

MCWILLIAMS, CAREY, *Factories in the Field: The Story of Migratory Farm Labor in California.* Boston, Little, Brown, 1939.

MEHLING, HAROLD, *The Scandalous Scamps.* New York, Henry Holt, 1956.

MICHAEL, GEORGE, *Handout.* New York, Putnam's, 1935.

MILLETT, JOHN D., *The Works Progress Administration in New York City.* Chicago, Public Service Administration, 1938.

MINTON, BRUCE, and STUART, JOHN, *Men Who Lead Labor.* New York, Modern Age Books, 1937.

The Mirrors of 1932. New York, Brewer, Warren & Putnam, 1931.

The Mirrors of Washington. New York, Putnam's, 1933.

MITCHELL, BROADUS, *Depression Decade, 1929–1941.* New York, Rinehart, 1947.

MOLEY, RAYMOND, *After Seven Years.* New York, Harper, 1939.

———, *27 Masters of Politics.* New York, Funk & Wagnalls, 1949.

———, *The First New Deal.* New York, Harcourt, Brace & World, 1966.

MONTGOMERY, ROBERT H., *Financial Handbook.* New York, Ronald Press, 1925.

MORISON, SAMUEL ELIOT, *The Oxford History of the American People.* New York, Oxford University Press, 1965.

MORRIS, JOE ALEX, *What a Year!—The Colorful Story of 1929.* New York, Harper, 1956.

———, *Deadline Every Minute: The Story of the United Press.* New York, Doubleday, 1957.

MORRIS, RICHARD B., *Encyclopedia of American History.* New York, Harper, 1953.

MOTT, FRANK LUTHER, *News Stories of 1933.* Iowa City, Clio Press, 1934.

MUGGLEBEE, RUTH, *Father Coughlin.* Garden City Publishing Co., 1933.

MYERS, GUSTAVUS, *The Ending of Hereditary American Fortunes.* New York, Julian Messner, 1939.

———, *History of Bigotry in the United States.* New York, Random House, 1943.

MYERS, WILLIAM STARR, and NEWTON, WALTER H., *The Hoover Administration.* New York, Scribner's, 1936.

Nation magazine.

NESBITT, HENRIETTA, *White House Diary: F.D.R.'s Housekeeper.* Garden City, Doubleday, 1948.

NEVINS, ALLAN, *Herbert H. Lehman and His Era.* New York, Scribner's, 1963.

NEVINS, ALLAN, and HILL, FRANK ERNEST, *Ford: Expansion and Challenge, 1915–1933.* New York, Scribner's, 1957.

———, *Ford: Decline and Rebirth, 1933–1962.* New York, Scribner's, 1962.

New Dictionary of American History. New York, Philosophical Library, Gelber, 1952.

New Republic magazine.

Newsweek magazine.

New York City Guide, The Guilds' Committee for Federal Writers' Publications, Inc. New York, Random House, 1939.

New York *Herald Tribune.*

New York *Times.*

New York *Times Index:* 1924–1941.

New York *World-Telegram.*

NICOLSON, HAROLD, *Dwight Morrow.* New York, Harcourt, Brace, 1935.

NORRIS, GEORGE W., *Fighting Liberal: An Autobiography.* New York, Macmillan, 1945.

OPOTOWSKY, STAN, *The Longs of Louisiana*. New York, Dutton, 1960.
Oxford Companion to American History. New York, Oxford University Press, 1966.

PAGE, KIRBY, *Individualism and Socialism*. New York, Farrar & Rinehart, 1933.
PARKER, JOHN LLOYD, *Unmasking Wall Street*. Boston, Stratford Co., 1932.
PARKS, E. TAYLOR, and PARKS, LOIS F., *Memorable Quotations of Franklin D. Roosevelt*. New York, Crowell, 1965.
PAYNE, ROBERT, *The Marshall Story: A Biography of General George C. Marshall*. New York, Prentice-Hall, 1951.
PEARSON, DREW, and ALLEN, ROBERT, *Washington Merry-Go-Round*. New York, Liveright, 1931.
——, *More Merry-Go-Round*. New York, Liveright, 1932.
——, *The Nine Old Men*. Garden City, Doubleday, Doran, 1937.
PECORA, FERDINAND, *Wall Street Under Oath*. New York, Simon and Schuster, 1939.
PERKINS, FRANCES, *The Roosevelt I Knew*. New York, Viking, 1946.
PLANO, JACK C., and GREENBERG, MILTON, *The American Political Dictionary*. New York, Holt, Rinehart, 1962.
POGUE, FORREST C., *George C. Marshall: Education of a General: 1880–1939*. New York, Viking, 1963.
PORTER, KIRK H., and JOHNSON, DONALD BRUCE, *National Party Platforms: 1840–1964*. Urbana, University of Illinois Press, 1966.
PROTHRO, JAMES WARREN, *The Dollar Decade: Business Ideas in the 1920's*. Baton Rouge, Louisiana State University Press, 1954.
PUSEY, MERLO J., *Charles Evans Hughes*. New York, Macmillan, 1951. 2 vols.

RAMSAY, M. L., *Pyramids of Power: The Story of Roosevelt, Insull and the Utility Wars*. Indianapolis, Bobbs-Merrill, 1937.
Recent Social Trends in the United States: Report of the President's Research Committee on Social Trends. New York, McGraw-Hill, 1933.
The Recovery Problem in the United States. Washington, The Brookings Institution, 1936.
RICE, ELMER, *Minority Report: An Autobiography*. New York, Simon and Schuster, 1963.
ROBINSON, EDGAR EUGENE, *The Roosevelt Leadership*. Philadelphia, Lippincott, 1955.
RODGERS, CLEVELAND, *Robert Moses: Builder for Democracy*. New York, Holt, 1952.
ROE, WELLINGTON, *Juggernaut: American Labor in Action*. New York, Lippincott, 1948.
ROLLINS, ALFRED B., *Roosevelt and Howe*. New York, Knopf, 1962.
ROOSEVELT, ELEANOR, *This Is My Story*. New York, Garden City Publishing Co., 1939.
——, *This I Remember*. New York, Harper, 1949.
ROOSEVELT, ELLIOTT, ed., *F.D.R.: His Personal Letters, 1928–1945*. New York, Duell, Sloan and Pearce, 1950. 2 vols.
ROOSEVELT, FRANKLIN D., *On Our Way*. New York, John Day, 1934.
——, *The Public Papers and Addresses of Franklin D. Roosevelt*. New York, Random House, 1938. 5 vols.

ROOSEVELT, JAMES, and SHALETT, SIDNEY, *Affectionately, F.D.R.* London, Harrap, 1960.

ROOSEVELT, NICHOLAS, *The Townsend Plan.* New York, Doubleday, Doran, 1936.

ROSENAU, JAMES N., ed., *The Roosevelt Treasury.* Garden City, Doubleday, 1951.

ROSENMAN, SAMUEL I., *Working With Roosevelt.* New York, Harper, 1952.

ROSS, ISHBEL, *Ladies of the Press.* New York, Harper, 1936.

RUSSELL, FRANCIS, *The Shadow of Blooming Grove: Warren G. Harding in His Times.* New York, McGraw-Hill, 1968.

SALZMAN, JACK, ed., *Years of Protest: A Collection of American Writings of the 1930's.* New York, Pegasus, 1967.

SANN, PAUL, ed., *The Lawless Decade.* New York, Crown, 1957.

Saturday Evening Post.

SCHLESINGER, ARTHUR M., JR., *The Crisis of the Old Order, 1919–1933.* Boston, Houghton Mifflin, 1957.

———, *The Coming of the New Deal.* Boston, Houghton Mifflin, 1958.

———, *The Politics of Upheaval.* Boston, Houghton Mifflin, 1960.

SCHWARTZ, ROBERT J., ed., *Dictionary of Business and Industry.* New York, B. C. Forbes and Sons, 1954.

SEARS, PAUL B., *Deserts on the March.* Norman, University of Oklahoma Press, 1935.

SELDES, GEORGE, *You Can't Do That.* New York, Modern Age Books, 1938.

———, *Lords of the Press.* New York, Blue Ribbon Books, 1941.

SELDES, GILBERT, *The Years of the Locust: America, 1929–32.* Boston, Little, Brown, 1933.

SETTEL, IRVING, *A Pictorial History of Radio.* New York, Bonanza Books, 1960.

SHANNON, DAVID A., *The Socialist Party of America.* New York, Macmillan, 1955.

———, *The Decline of American Communism.* New York, Harcourt, Brace, 1959.

———, ed., *The Great Depression.* Englewood Cliffs, N.J., Prentice-Hall, 1960.

SHANNON, WILLIAM V., *The American Irish.* New York, Macmillan, 1963.

SHERWOOD, ROBERT E., *Roosevelt and Hopkins,* rev. ed. New York, Harper, 1950.

SILLS, DAVID L., *International Encyclopedia of the Social Sciences.* New York, Macmillan, 1968. 17 vols.

SIMON, RITA JAMES, ed., *As We Saw the Thirties.* Urbana, University of Illinois Press, 1967.

SMITH, MERRIMAN, *Thank You, Mr. President.* New York, Harper, 1946.

SNYDER, LOUIS L., and MORRIS, RICHARD B., eds., *A Treasury of Great Reporting.* New York, Simon and Schuster, 1949.

SOBEL, ROBERT, *The Big Board: A History of the New York Stock Market.* New York, Free Press, 1965.

———, *Panic on Wall Street: A History of America's Financial Disasters.* New York, Macmillan, 1968.

SOULE, GEORGE, *Prosperity Decade, 1917–1929.* New York, Rinehart, 1947.

SPARLING, EARL, *Mystery Men of Wall Street.* New York, Greenberg, 1930.

SPIVAK, JOHN L., *A Man in His Time.* New York, Horizon Press, 1967.

SPOLANSKY, JACOB, *The Communist Trail in America.* New York, Macmillan, 1951,

STARLING, COLONEL EDMUND W., as told to THOMAS SUGRUE, *Starling of the White House*. New York, Simon and Schuster, 1946.

STEEHOLM, CLARA and HARDY, *The House at Hyde Park*. New York, Viking, 1950.

STEINBECK, JOHN, *In Dubious Battle*. New York, Modern Library, 1936.

———, *The Grapes of Wrath*. New York, Viking, 1939.

STEINBERG, ALFRED, *Mrs. R.: The Life of Eleanor Roosevelt*. New York, Putnam's, 1958.

———, *Sam Johnson's Boy*. New York, Macmillan, 1968.

STERN, J. DAVID, *Memoirs of a Maverick Publisher*. New York, Simon and Schuster, 1962.

STERNSHER, BERNARD, *Rexford Tugwell and the New Deal*. New Brunswick, Rutgers University Press, 1964.

STOCKHAMMER, MORRIS, *Karl Marx Dictionary*. New York, Philosophical Library, 1965.

STOKES, ANSON PHELPS, *Church and State in the United States*. New York, Harper, 1950. 3 vols.

STUDENSKI, PAUL, and KROOSS, HERMAN E., *Financial History of the United States*. New York, McGraw-Hill, 1952.

SWANBERG, W. A., *Citizen Hearst*. New York, Scribner's, 1961.

———, *Dreiser*. New York, Scribner's, 1965.

SWARD, KEITH, *The Legend of Henry Ford*. New York, Rinehart, 1948.

TEBBEL, JOHN, *An American Dynasty: The Story of the McCormicks, Medills and Pattersons*. Garden City, Doubleday, 1947.

———, *The Life and Good Times of William Randolph Hearst*. New York, Dutton, 1952.

Time magazine.

Time Capsule: 1933. New York, Time, Inc., 1967.

TIMMONS, BASCOM N., *Garner of Texas: A Personal History*. New York, Harper, 1948.

———, *Jesse H. Jones: The Man and the Statesman*. New York, Henry Holt, 1956.

TOWNSEND, DR. FRANCIS E., *New Horizons*. Chicago, J. L. Stewart Publishing Co., 1943.

TUGWELL, REXFORD G., *The Democratic Roosevelt*. Garden City, Doubleday, 1957.

———, *The Brains Trust*. New York, Viking, 1968.

TULLY, ANDREW, *Era of Elegance*. New York, Funk & Wagnalls, 1947.

TULLY, GRACE, *F.D.R.: My Boss*. New York, Scribner's, 1949.

UTECHIN, S. V., *Everyman's Concise Encyclopedia of Russia*. New York, Dutton, 1961.

VANDERBILT, CORNELIUS, JR., *Man of the World: My Life on Five Continents*. New York, Crown, 1959.

VORSE, MARY HEATON, *Labor's New Millions*. New York, Modern Age Books, 1938.

WALDROP, FRANK C., *McCormick of Chicago*. Englewood Cliffs, N.J., Prentice-Hall, 1966.

WARD, LOUIS B., *Father Charles E. Coughlin: An Authorized Biography*. Detroit, Tower Publications, 1933.

WARREN, HARRIS GAYLORD, *Herbert Hoover and the Great Depression*. New York, Norton, 1959.

WARSHOW, ROBERT IRVING, *The Story of Wall Street*. New York, Greenberg, 1929.

Washington, D.C.: A Guide to the Nation's Capital, Work Projects Administration. Washington, George Washington University, 1942.

We Saw It Happen: The News Behind the News That's Fit to Print. New York, Simon and Schuster, 1938.

WECTER, DIXON, *The Age of the Great Depression: 1929–1941*. New York, Macmillan, 1948.

WHALEN, RICHARD J., *The Founding Father: The Story of Joseph P. Kennedy*. New York, New American Library, 1964.

WHEELER, BURTON K., *Yankee from the West*. Garden City, Doubleday, 1962.

WHITE, WILLIAM ALLEN, *A Puritan in Babylon: The Story of Calvin Coolidge*. New York, Macmillan, 1938.

———, *Selected Letters*, Walter Johnson, ed. New York, Henry Holt, 1947.

Who's Who in America. Chicago, Marquis, various years.

Who Was Who in America, 1897–1942. Chicago, Marquis, 1943.

WILBUR, RAY LYMAN, and HYDE, ARTHUR MASTICK, *The Hoover Policies*. New York, Scribner's, 1937.

WILSON, EDMUND, *The Shores of Light: A Literary Chronicle of the Twenties and Thirties*. New York, Random House, 1952.

———, *The American Earthquake: A Documentary of the Twenties and Thirties*. New York, Doubleday, 1958.

WOLFE, HAROLD, *Herbert Hoover: Public Servant and Leader of the Loyal Opposition*. New York, Exposition Press, 1956.

WOLFE, THOMAS, *You Can't Go Home Again*. Garden City, Sun Dial Press, 1942.

World Almanac. New York, Newspaper Enterprise Assn., various years.

WRIGHT, CHESTER WHITNEY, *Economic History of the United States*. New York, McGraw-Hill, 1949.

WYCKOFF, PETER, *Dictionary of Stock Market Terms*. Englewood Cliffs, N.J., Prentice-Hall, 1964.

ZEVIN, B. D., ed., *Nothing to Fear: The Selected Addresses of Franklin Delano Roosevelt, 1932–1945*. Boston, Houghton Mifflin, 1946.

ZINN, HOWARD, ed., *New Deal Thought*. Indianapolis, Bobbs-Merrill, 1966.

Index

KODANSHA GLOBE

International in scope, this series offers distinguished books that explore the lives, customs, and mindsets of peoples and cultures around the world.

To order, contact your local bookseller or call 1-800-788-6262 (mention code G1). For a complete listing of titles, please contact the Kodansha Editorial Department at Kodansha America, Inc., 114 Fifth Avenue, New York, NY 10011.